Nepal
a travel survival kit

Tony Wheeler
Richard Everist

Nepal – a travel survival kit

2nd edition

Published by
Lonely Planet Publications
Head Office: PO Box 617, Hawthorn, Vic 3122, Australia
Branches: 155 Filbert St, Suite 251, Oakland, CA 94607, USA
                10 Barley Mow Passage, Chiswick, London W4 4PH, UK
                71 bis rue du Cardinal Lemoine, 75005 Paris, France

Printed by
Colorcraft Ltd, Hong Kong

Photographs by

David Allardice (DA)	Stan Armington (SA)	Glenn Beanland (GB)
Sonia Berto (SB)	Richard Everist (RE)	Catherine Griffiths (CG)
Richard I' Anson (RI'A)	Peter Kennedy (PK)	James Lyon (JL)
Simon Rowe (SR)	Paul Steel (PS)	Jann Subiaco (JS)
Rob van Driesum (RvD)	Tony Wheeler (TW)	Jeff Williams (JW)

Front cover: Stupa, Namche Bazaar (PS)
Back cover: Lodge at Ghandrung (SB)

First Published
1990

This Edition
August 1993

Although the authors and publisher have tried to make the information as accurate as possible, they accept no responsibility for any loss, injury or inconvenience sustained by any person using this book.

National Library of Australia Cataloguing in Publication Data

Wheeler, Tony
    Nepal : a travel survival kit.

    2nd ed.
    Includes index.
    ISBN 0 86442 189 3.

    1. Nepal – Guidebooks. I. Everist, Richard. II. Title.
    (Series : Lonely Planet travel survival kit).

915.49604

text & maps © Lonely Planet 1993
photos © photographers as indicated 1993

Tony Wheeler

Tony Wheeler was born in England but spent most of his youth overseas. He returned to England to do a university degree in engineering, worked as an automotive engineer, returned to university to complete an MBA then dropped out on the overland trail with his wife Maureen. They've been travelling, writing and publishing guidebooks ever since, having set up Lonely Planet Publications in the mid-70s. Travel for the Wheelers is now considerably enlivened by their daughter Tashi and their son Kieran.

Richard Everist

Richard Everist grew up in Geelong, Australia, has travelled a bit and had a wide variety of jobs. He worked full time in Lonely Planet's Melbourne office before jumping the fence to become a freelance writer. He has co-written LP's travel survival kits to *Nepal* and *South Africa*, as well as updating *Papua New Guinea*, and contributing to the shoestring guides for *West Asia, Africa, Western Europe* and *Mediterranean Europe*.

From Richard

Thanks to Stan Armington, the author of Lonely Planet's *Trekking in the Nepal Himalaya* and managing director of Malla Treks. Sushil Upadhyay, also of Malla Treks, once again answered the hard questions, contributed logistical support and supplied several cold beers. Badri Adhikari, of Lucky Traveller Service, also provided memorable hospitality and invaluable help, particularly on the long trip from Kakarbhitta to Mahendranagar.

Numerous other people also gave generously of their time, expertise, information and hospitality. Many thanks to Brian White (Himalayan Hilltreks & River Tours); Wendy Brewer Lama (KEEP); Vijaya 'BJ' Kumar Aryal (Raging River Runner); Lisa Choegyal (Tiger Mountain); Narendra Gurung (West Himalayan Outdoor); Indra Yonzon (Greenhill Tours); Gerry Moffat, Guy Robbins and Jeremy Brooke (Equator Expeditions); Peter 'Slime' Knowles (co-author *White Water Nepal)*; Jo Chittenden (KEEP); James Giambrone (Himalayan Mountain Bikes); Claire Burkert (Janakpur Women's Art Project); Bridget Crampton (Kumbeshwar Technical School); Nancy Russel; Devendra Gunung (Lamjung Treks & Expeditions); Steve Power; Dr David Shlim (CIWEC Clinic); Ugen Tsering and Dawa Gyaltsen (Utse Hotel); Lesley Craig (UK Embassy); Les & Una Douglas (Australian Embassy); Mahesh Thappa (Himalayan River Exploration); and Suzanne Sziranyi, David Trimble and Steven van den Neucker (for information on Mahendranagar).

Many travellers also wrote letters and postcards that played an invaluable role in the updating process. Without the contribution of these first-hand experiences, this edition would be a 'mere shadow' of its final form. Thanks and keep them coming. See page 428 for a full list of those who wrote in with corrections, suggestions, ecstatic raves and furious abuse.

This Edition

The first five editions of Lonely Planet's guide to Nepal were the work of Nepalese writer Prakash A Raj. In 1989, however, Tony Wheeler and Richard Everist completely rewrote the book to bring it into line with other Lonely Planet travel survival kits.

In 1992 Richard Everist returned to research the 2nd edition, revisiting the towns and temples of the Kathmandu Valley, trekking in the Himalaya, driving the length of the Terai, rafting the Sun Kosi, riding everything from mountain bikes to elephants, and sampling all his favourite restaurants from Freak St to Thamel.

A number of other people also made major new contributions. Bishnu Shrestha, of Dialad Graphics, who was responsible for the temple illustrations used in the 1st edition, contributed additional beautiful drawings.

Lewis Underwood wrote the geography, flora, fauna and ecology sections in the Facts about the Country chapter. Woody first visited Nepal as a Peace Corps worker in the '70s and is currently a trek leader for Mountain Travel and Malla Treks.

John Prosser contributed the Mountain Biking chapter. In 1992 he started Equator Mountain Bikes, which operates tours around Nepal, and he also promotes Nepalese rafting, trekking and biking tours in Hong Kong.

David Allardice wrote the bulk of the Rafting & Kayaking chapter. He is the co-author (with Peter Knowles) of *White Water Nepal*, a specialist guidebook, and operations manager for Ultimate Descents, which organises rafting and kayaking tours throughout Nepal.

From the Publisher

This 2nd edition of *Nepal – a travel survival kit* was edited at Lonely Planet's Melbourne office by Miriam Cannell. Thanks to Sue Mitra and Sharan Kaur for proofreading.

Paul Clifton was responsible for the mapping and layout. The cover was designed by Margaret Jung and Paul. Bishnu Shrestha drew many of the illustrations; additional illustrations were completed by Christopher Orr, Paul and Margaret.

Warning & Request

Things change – prices go up, schedules change, good places go bad and bad places go bankrupt – nothing stays the same. So if you find things better or worse, recently opened or long-since closed, please write and tell us and help make the next edition better. In particular, new roads are constantly opening up new opportunities in Nepal and we'd love to hear just how lost you managed to get!

We greatly appreciate all the letters that are sent to us. They are used to help update the next edition and, where possible, important changes will also be included as Stop Press sections in reprints of this edition. The best contributions are rewarded with a free copy of the next edition, or another Lonely Planet guide if you prefer. We give away lots of books, but not every letter or postcard receives one.

Contents

Map Legend

BOUNDARIES

—·—·—·	International Boundary
—··—··—	Internal Boundary
++++++++	National Park or Reserve
----------	The Equator
············	The Tropics

SYMBOLS

◉	NATIONAL	National Capital
●	PROVINCIAL	Provincial or State Capital
●	Major	Major Town
●	Minor	Minor Town
■		Places to Stay
▼		Places to Eat
⊠		Post Office
✈		Airport
i		Tourist Information
⊖		Bus Station or Terminal
66		Highway Route Number
⚲✝⊞⚱		Mosque, Church, Cathedral
⚊ ⚖		Temple, Stupa
∴		Archaeological Site or Ruin
✚		Hospital
✳		Lookout
⚑		Camping Area
⊼		Picnic Area
⌂		Hut or Chalet
▲		Mountain or Hill
+—■—+		Railway Station
═══		Road Bridge
++++++		Railway Bridge
⇒ ⇐		Road Tunnel
+⇢) (⇠+		Railway Tunnel
⌢⌢⌢		Escarpment or Cliff
⌣		Pass
⊓⊓⊓⊓		Ancient or Historic Wall

ROUTES

———	Major Road or Highway
----------	Unsealed Major Road
———	Sealed Road
- - - - -	Unsealed Road or Track
═══	City Street
++++++++	Railway
●━━●━━●	Subway
- - - - -	Walking Track
············	Walking Tour

HYDROGRAPHIC FEATURES

	River or Creek
	Intermittent Stream
	Lake, Intermittent Lake
	Coast Line
	Spring
	Waterfall
	Rapids
	Swamp
	Salt Lake or Reef
	Glacier

OTHER FEATURES

	Park, Garden or National Park
	Built Up Area
	Market or Pedestrian Mall
	Plaza or Town Square
	Cemetery

Note: not all symbols displayed above appear in this book

Introduction

Draped along the greatest heights of the Himalaya, the kingdom of Nepal is a land of eternal fascination, a place where one visit is rarely enough. It's a land of ancient history, colourful cultures and people, superb scenery and some of the best walking on earth.

Nepal's history is closely related to its geographical location – separating the fertile plains of India from the desert-like plateau of Tibet. Its position between India and China meant the country was able at times to play the role of intermediary, a canny trader between two great powers, while at other times it faced the threat of invasion. Internally the history was just as dynamic with city-states in the hills vying with each other for power until one powerful king, Prithvi Narayan Shah, overran them all. That history is very visible today where the three great towns of the Kathmandu Valley – Kathmandu, Patan and Bhaktapur – still bear witness to their days as fiercely competitive mediaeval mini-kingdoms. Indeed in Nepal it's often possible to suspend belief and mentally roll the clock right back to the mediaeval era.

Behind the time-worn temples and palaces of the Kathmandu Valley, above and beyond the hills that ring the valley, another 'kingdom' rises skyward. The 'abode of snows', which is what *Himalaya* means in Sanskrit, is a natural 'kingdom' and a magnet to mountaineers from all over the world. Fortunately you don't have to be a Sherpa and your surname doesn't have to be

Messner or Hillary in order for you to get in amongst these great mountains. With a dash of enterprise and a modicum of fitness most travellers can walk the trails that lead into the roadless heights of the Himalaya. One trek is rarely enough, and many visitors soon find themselves planning to return.

Fascinating old towns, magnificent temples and great walking are not all Nepal has to offer.

Many visitors come to Nepal expecting to find these things but also discover how outstandingly friendly the Nepalese people are.

Nor is trekking the only activity which draws visitors – Nepal also has some superb white-water rafting opportunities, mountain biking is becoming more and more popular, and down in the jungle lowland in the south of the country, safaris on elephant-back into the Royal Chitwan National Park are another not-to-be-missed part of the Nepal experience.

Warning about Figures, Dates & Names

There doesn't seem to be any 100% correct reference for anything in Nepal. As an example we've seen half a dozen different figures for the number of square km that Nepal occupies. And we lost track of how many times sources A, B and C said Temple 1 is to the right, Temple 2 is to the left while sources X, Y and Z said the opposite. It's open to contention which of the three Taleju temples in Patan's Durbar Square is which. When temples were built also appears to be a matter of speculation: some sources will give a date of construction for a certain temple then on the same page give the period of reign for the king who built it and the two will not agree.

Many temples in Nepal have alternative names. For example, the Vishnu Temple in Patan's Durbar Square is referred to as the Jagannarayan or Charnarayan Temple; the great Shiva Temple in Kathmandu's Durbar Square is sometimes called the Maju Deval, at others simply the Shiva Temple. Where possible, alternative names that are commonly used have been given.

Mandir simply means 'temple' and generally we have used the English word except in cases where mandir is always used, as with the Krishna Mandir in Patan.

Further confusion can be caused by different systems of transliteration from Sanskrit – the letter 'h' appears in some systems, but doesn't appear in others so you may see Manjushri and Manjusri, Machhendranath and Machendranath. The letters 'b' and 'v' are also used interchangeably in different systems – Shiva's fearsome manifestation can be Bhairab or Bhairav, Vishnu is often written as Bishnu and the Nepali word for the Tibetan thunderbolt symbol can be a *bajra* or a *vajra*.

Some confusion is also caused by different places having the same name; so for example, in the Annapurna region there are two villages called Phedi.

Finally, texts differ in their use of the words Nepali and Nepalese. In this book we have used Nepali for the language and Nepalese for anything else relating to the country and its people.

Facts about the Country

HISTORY

Historically, culturally and linguistically Nepal has been the meeting point between the Mongoloid peoples of Asia (with Tibeto-Burmese languages) and the Caucasoid people of the Indian plains (with Indo-European languages). In earlier times, Nepal exploited its position as an intermediary in the trade between India and China. Today the country continues to take advantage of its strategic position between these uneasy giants.

Over the centuries, the boundaries of Nepal have extended to include huge tracts of neighbouring India, or contracted to little more than the Kathmandu Valley and a handful of surrounding city-states.

Legends recount that the Kathmandu Valley was once a great lake and that Manjushri broached the valley wall with a magical sword, draining the water and creating the Kathmandu Valley we know. Or perhaps it wasn't Manjushri; he was, after all, a Buddhist from China. Hindus claim it was Krishna who performed the mighty deed, hurling a thunderbolt to create the Chobar Gorge. Choose whichever legend you prefer, but scientists agree that the valley was submerged at one time and the rivers of the valley do indeed flow southward through the narrow Chobar Gorge.

The Kiratis

Recorded history begins with the Kiratis, Mongoloid people, who arrived in Nepal from the east around the 7th or 8th century BCE. Although they are the first known rulers of the Kathmandu Valley and Yalambar, the first of their kings, is mentioned in the Hindu epic the *Mahabharata*, very little more is known about them.

It was during the Kirati period that Buddhism first arrived in the country; indeed it is claimed that during the reign of the seventh of the 28 Kirati kings, Buddha, together with his disciple Ananda, visited the valley and stayed for a time in Patan.

Other accounts of the Kirati period include a 4th century BCE description of their sheep breeding and agricultural activities. Around the 2nd century BCE the great Buddhist Indian emperor Ashoka visited Nepal and erected a pillar at the Buddha's birthplace at Lumbini, south of Pokhara near the present-day Indian border. Ashoka also visited the Kathmandu Valley and evidence of four stupas he erected around Patan can still be clearly seen. Ashoka may have also enlarged the stupas at Bodhnath and Swayambhunath. His daughter Charumati was said to have founded Chabahil, a village on the road between Kathmandu and Bodhnath, which has now been swallowed up by the capital. There is a stupa, a smaller version of Bodhnath, and a monastery here that are claimed to date back to her time in Nepal.

Kirati domination ended around 300 CE but the Rai and Limbu people of eastern Nepal are said to be modern descendants.

The Licchavis

Buddhism faded and Hinduism reasserted itself with the Licchavis, Indo-Aryan people who invaded from northern India about 300 CE and overthrew the last Kirati king. They brought with them the caste divisions which continue in Nepal to this day but also ushered in a golden age of Nepalese art and architecture.

Manadeva I established the Licchavis' political and military might and a valley inscription dated to 476 CE tells of his prowess; it can be seen at the beautiful Changu Narayan Temple in the eastern part of the Kathmandu Valley. His successor, Manadeva II, left numerous stone inscriptions around his kingdom, most of them commenting on what a wonderful mother he had and how he wouldn't have got anywhere without her!

Nepal

0   50   100 km

Heights in metres

The Thakuris

Amsuvarman, the first Thakuri king, came to power in 602 CE, succeeding his Licchavi father-in-law. Amsuvarman consolidated his power with strategic family connections to the north and south. His daughter Bhrikuti married a Tibetan prince and collected the Buddha's begging bowl in her wedding dowry. She was said to be a reincarnation of Tibetan Buddhism's Green Tara, seen on many *thangkas* (Tibetan paintings on cotton). Meanwhile in Nepal, Amsuvarman constructed a marvellous seven-storey palace at Deopatan near Pashupatinath and contemporary accounts speak with wonder of his luxurious life.

Amsuvarman's was the first of three Thakuri dynasties and although the centuries that followed were a time of confusion, invasion and turmoil, the Kathmandu Valley's strategic location ensured the kingdom's survival and growth even through this Nepalese dark age. It is believed that the city of Kantipur, today's Kathmandu, was founded around the 10th century by Gunakamadeva. His Kasthamandap (House of Wood) gave the city its name and can be seen in Kathmandu's Durbar Square today.

The Golden Age of the Mallas

In 1200, so another legend goes, King Arideva was wrestling when news came of the birth of his son. He instantly awarded his son the title *malla* or 'wrestler' and thus founded the illustrious Malla dynasty. This golden age saw great wealth flow to the valley and the kingdom's architects constructed many of the wonderful buildings we see in Nepal today, but the early Malla years actually saw a series of terrible disasters. A huge earthquake shook the valley and killed thousands, an invasion from the north-west followed and the town of Patan was destroyed in 1311.

The Hindu Mallas were followers of Shiva but considered to be incarnations of the god Vishnu and their tolerance of Buddhism allowed the Himalayan Tantric form of the religion to continue to flourish. An aristocracy grew up under the Malla rulers and the Hindu caste rules were strengthened and

became more rigid. Hari Singh, who arrived in the valley sometime between 1325 and 1330, was one of the best known early Malla rulers and through him Taleju Bhawani became the royal goddess of Nepal. Hari Singh's southern Indian followers may be the Newaris whose name the people of the Kathmandu Valley take to this day.

During this period Nepal began to divide into numerous independent city-states with frequently feuding kings and princes. The hill country began to be more densely settled as agricultural techniques improved, but a Muslim invasion from Bengal swept through the valley damaging Hindu and Buddhist shrines. The wave of Muslim destruction soon passed Nepal, but in India the damage was more widespread and many Hindus were driven from the plains, establishing more small Rajput principalities in the hills and mountains of Nepal. The country we know today was divided at that time into 46 separate small states. These kingdoms minted their own coins and maintained standing armies.

In the Kathmandu Valley the three great towns which remain to this day – Kathmandu, Patan and Bhaktapur – were independent kingdoms with powerful kings who encouraged the construction of many temples and the creation of many enduring works of art. Each city centred around the king's palace with the nobility and high castes concentrated close to the centre. High walls were built to fend off the city's neighbours.

In 1372, however, Jayasthiti Malla founded the third Malla dynasty and took first Patan and then, 10 years later, Bhaktapur to unify the whole valley. In the 15th century Malla art and culture reached its peak and during the reign of Yaksha Malla (1428-1482) the kingdom extended south to the Ganges River, north to the edge of Tibet, west to the Kali Gandaki River and east to Sikkim. With his death, however, the kingdom again split into small warring states and another two centuries of conflict were to follow. Trade was booming, agriculture continued to improve and the valley towns enjoyed an orgy of temple and palace construction, but the constant squabbling of the Malla kingdoms opened the door to a new dynasty.

The Shah Dynasty Unifies Nepal

From the tiny kingdom of Gorkha, halfway between Kathmandu and Pokhara, the Shah kings gradually strengthened and extended their power and dreamed of conquering the rich Kathmandu Valley. In 1768 Prithvi Narayan Shah, ninth of the Shah kings, conquered the valley and moved his capital to Kathmandu. The Shah dynasty, which continues to this day, was established.

From this new base the kingdom's power continued to expand until a clash with the Chinese in Tibet led to an ignominious defeat. The Nepalese had first fought the Chinese in 1790, but by 1792 the Chinese army had struck back and in the ensuing treaty the Nepalese had to stop their attacks on Tibet and pay tribute to the Chinese emperor in Beijing; the payments continued until 1912.

British power on the subcontinent was growing at this time and a British envoy arrived in Kathmandu in 1792, too late to aid the Nepalese against the Chinese invasion. Despite treaties with the British the expanding Nepalese boundaries, stretching all the way from Kashmir to Sikkim by the early 19th century, were bound to cause problems with the Raj, and disputes over the Terai (the lowlands south of the Himalayan foothills) led to a war with the British. In 1810 Nepal was approximately twice its current size but the 1816 Sugauli Treaty with the British ended the growth. Britain took Sikkim and most of the Terai, and Nepal's present-day eastern and western borders were established. Some of the land was restored to Nepal in 1858 as a reward for Nepalese support for the British during the Indian Mutiny (or War of Independence as it is referred to in modern India).

The treaty opened the door for Indian business influence in Nepal and when, a century later, new direct trade routes were established between India and Tibet the Nepalese also began to lose their influence as an intermediary in trade between the two countries. A British resident was sent to Kathmandu to keep an eye on things. The Nepalese, less than entranced with the British, allotted him a piece of land which they considered to be disease-prone and a haven for evil spirits but the British stiff upper lip prevailed. In fact the defeat so rankled with the Nepalese that they decided to shut off all foreign contact and from 1816 right through until 1951 the country's borders were firmly closed to outsiders. The British residents in Kathmandu were the only Westerners to set eyes on Nepal for over 100 years.

Many Nepalese eyes were, however, viewing the outside world. The British were so impressed by the fighting qualities of the Nepalese that they brought mercenaries, known as 'Gurkhas', into the British army. Gurkha mercenaries have fought in the British army ever since, even spreading fear amongst the Argentinians during the Falklands War in 1982. Gurkha earnings are an important element in Nepal's income today and although the importance of Gurkha troops to Britain is diminishing, various other nations are only too happy to pay for their soldiering abilities. The Sultan of Brunei, for example, has a contingent of Gurkha troops.

The Ranas

Although the Shah dynasty continued in power a curious palace revolt occurred in 1846 when Jung Bahadur Rana engineered the Kot Massacre.

Jung Bahadur was an ambitious and ruthless young Chhetri noble from western Nepal. Taking advantage of the complex, often bloody, power struggles within the ruling family, he developed his own power base. On 15 September 1846, he initiated a decisive coup. His soldiers massacred several hundred of the most important men in the kingdom – noblemen, soldiers and courtiers – while they were assembled in the Kot courtyard adjoining Kathmandu's Durbar Square. Jung Bahadur took the title of prime minister and changed his family name to the more prestigious Rana. Later, he extended his title to maharajah and then made the title hereditary. The Ranas became a second 'royal family' within the kingdom and held the real power, keeping the Shah kings as pampered figureheads.

For over a century, the hereditary family of Rana prime ministers held power and although development in Nepal stagnated, the country did manage to preserve its independence during the period when European colonial powers were snatching up virtually every country unable to defend itself. Nepal was never ruled by a colonial power, but it was almost completely isolated from the outside world right through the Rana period. Only on rare occasions were visitors allowed into Nepal and even then they were only allowed to visit a very limited part of the country.

Jung Bahadur Rana travelled to Europe in 1850 and brought back a taste for neoclassical architecture (examples of it can be seen in Kathmandu today). To the Ranas' credit *suttee* (the Hindu practice of casting widows on their husband's funeral pyre) was abolished, forced labour was ended and a school and a college were established in Kathmandu, but overall, Nepal stagnated during the century of Rana power. While the Ranas and their relations lived luxurious lives in huge Kathmandu palaces the peasants in the hills were locked in a mediaeval existence.

Elsewhere in the region dramatic changes were taking place. After WW II India gained its independence and a revolution took place in China. Tibetan refugees fled into Nepal when the new People's Republic of China annexed Tibet and Nepal became a buffer zone between the two Asian giants. The turmoil naturally spread over Nepal's closed borders and while one Rana made moves towards liberalising the country's moribund political system another attempted to move towards stronger central control. Under the charismatic BP Koirala the Nepali Congress party, supported by the ruling Indian Congress party, was established by many Nepalese and even by some Rana family

members. At the same time King Tribhuvan, forgotten in his palace, was being primed to overthrow the Ranas.

The Shah's Restoration

In late 1950 the king escaped from his palace to the Indian Embassy and from there to India. Meanwhile BP Koirala's forces managed to take most of the Terai from the Ranas and establish a provisional government which ruled from the border town of Birganj. Nepal was in turmoil, but there was no clear victor. India finally exerted its influence and negotiated a solution. King Tribhuvan returned to Nepal in 1951 and set up a new government comprised of Ranas and commoners from BP Koirala's Nepali Congress.

Although Nepal gradually reopened its long-closed doors and established relations with many other nations, dreams of a new democratic system were not permanently realised. King Tribhuvan died in 1955 and was followed by his son Mahendra. A new constitution provided for a parliamentary system of government and in 1959 Nepal held its first general election. The Nepali Congress won a clear victory, somewhat to the king's surprise, and BP Koirala became the new prime minister. In late 1960, however, the king decided the government wasn't working to his taste and had the cabinet arrested. Political parties were banned and the king swapped his ceremonial role for real control.

In 1962 King Mahendra decided that a partyless, indirect *panchayat* system of government was more appropriate to Nepal. Local panchayats (councils) chose representatives to district panchayats which in turn were represented in the National Panchayat. The real power, however, remained with the king who retained executive power, directly chose 16 members of the 35-member National Panchayat, and appointed the prime minister and his cabinet. Political parties were banned.

In 1972 Mahendra died and was followed by his son Birendra, who was educated at Eton and Harvard. Birendra's view that Nepal now had the correct and appropriate political system was not supported by everybody, however. Popular discontent with slow development, corrupt officials and rising costs simmered in the '70s. Finally, in 1979 the smouldering anger exploded into violent riots in Kathmandu, and King Birendra announced that a referendum would be held to choose between the current system and one that would permit political parties to operate.

BP Koirala, who had been in jail or in self-imposed exile since 1960, was allowed to campaign but the 1980 referendum result was 55 to 45 in favour of the partyless system.

Nevertheless, the king had already declared that whichever way the vote went, the people would elect the country's legislature on a five-year term and in turn it would elect the prime minister. The king, however, would continue to directly appoint 20% of the legislature, and all candidates would have to be members of one of six government-approved organisations and stand under their own name, not as a representative of any party. The first elections under this system were held in 1981.

On the surface, the panchayat system, which allowed a secret vote and universal suffrage, did not appear to be dictatorial: the

constitution theoretically guaranteed freedom of speech and peaceful assembly, and the right to form unions and associations (so long as they were not motivated by party politics).

The reality was somewhat different. Nepal's military/police apparatus was one of the least publicly accountable in the world and there was strict censorship. Mass arrests, torture and beatings of suspected activists are well documented, and the leaders of the main opposition, the Nepali Congress, spent the years between 1960 and 1990 in and out of prison. (BP Koirala died in 1983.)

Until early 1990, the king wielded considerable power. It is difficult to know quite how much – the inner workings of the palace and the king's relationships with members of the cabinet were not made public – but the constitution guaranteed his supremacy and the National Panchayat basically acted as a rubber stamp.

The aristocracy, in general, managed to retain its influence and wealth (the king and his brothers are all married to Ranas) and the panchayat system did not seem to cramp their style. Firm figures are impossible to find, but it is generally accepted that a huge portion of foreign aid (perhaps up to 50%) was routinely creamed off into royal and ministerial accounts.

People Power

In 1989 the opposition parties formed a coalition to fight for a multiparty democracy with the king as constitutional head; the upsurge of protest was called the Jana Andolan or People's Movement. Popular support was motivated in part by the economic problems caused by an Indian government blockade, and by widespread discontent with blatant corruption.

In February 1990 the government responded to nonviolent protest meetings with bullets, tear gas, thousands of arrests and torture. However, after several months of intermittent rioting, curfews, a successful strike, and pressure from various foreign aid donors the government was forced to back down. The people's victory did not come cheaply. Estimates of the number who died range up to more than 300.

On 9 April the king announced on national radio that he was lifting the ban on political parties and on 16 April he asked the opposition to lead an interim government. He also announced his readiness to accept a role as a constitutional monarch.

Democracy

In May 1991 20 parties contested a general election for a 205-seat parliament. The Nepali Congress and a communist party where the two major players, and their symbols – a tree for the Congress, and a sun for the communists – can still be seen painted on every available surface.

The Nepali Congress won power with 37.75% of the vote, which secured it 110 seats. It is theoretically committed to socialism, but most of its policy positions are middle-of-the-road. Power and influence in the party is divided between three of its leaders: Ganesh Man Singh, the party supremo; Krishna Prasad Bhattarai, the president of the party, and Girija Prasad (GP) Koirala, the prime minister. This has lead to considerable conflict.

Ganesh Man Singh has been involved with the party's struggle for many years and is credited as the leader who initiated the Jana Andolan that brought down the panchayat system. He acts as a feisty elder statesman, although his position as Party Supremo, is not recognised by the party's constitution. KP Bhattarai acted as prime minister of the interim government prior to the May elections and is often cast as the moderator between Singh and Koirala. GP Koirala, the prime minister, is regarded as an able administrator and believes the cabinet and prime minister should be able to act independently of party control (to the dismay of Singh).

The Communist Party of Nepal-Unified Marxist-Leninist (CPN-UML) won 27.98% of the vote, giving it 69 seats. The next largest party, the United People's Front, received only 4.83% of the vote. Although the CPN-UML party presents itself as the champion of the downtrodden masses, its position on the following questions is unclear: how does a communist party justify its participation in a multiparty democratic system, and what policy implications flow from the collapse of communism elsewhere in the world? The inconclusive answers tend to be towards the pragmatic end of the spectrum. The party president is Man Mohan Adhikary.

After nearly three years of democratic government, assessments are divided. For those on the right of the political spectrum, the king's popularity never waned. Many ordinary people, however, had unrealistically high expectations and they have been unsettled by political infighting, hurt by price rises, and already look back nostalgically on the good, old panchayat days. Economic pressures are intense and in April 1992 a general strike degenerated into street violence between protesters and police, and resulted in a number of deaths. Unfortunately, though not surprisingly, corruption continues to flourish, although many say to a reduced degree.

On the positive side, democracy has brought a renewed sense of national pride and optimism to many, especially the educated middle classes. Many cite examples showing a new flexibility and responsiveness on the part of Kathmandu's bloated and stifling government bureaucracy. In November '92 the government showed some steel by sacking 8000 civil servants. A degree of economic liberalisation and improved relations with India have helped boost several infant industries, including the carpet and clothing sectors.

Establishing a workable democratic system at a national level, where one has never existed before, is an enormously difficult task. In Nepal this is further complicated by a fragile economy, extreme poverty, illiteracy, and an ethnically and religiously fragmented population that is continuing to grow at a frightening rate.

CLIMATE

Nepal has a typical monsoonal two-season year. There's the dry season from October to May and there's the wet season, the monsoon, from June to September.

In the summer (May and the early part of June, before the monsoon, are the hottest), Kathmandu can get very hot with temperatures often in the 30s. Even in the winter the bright sunny days often reach 20°C although with nightfall the mercury may plummet to near freezing. It never actually snows in the

Kathmandu Valley and higher up the coldest weather is also the driest weather so snow is unusual. Due to its lower altitude Pokhara is warmer and more pleasant than Kathmandu in the winter, but hotter when the temperature builds up and wetter during the monsoon.

Surprisingly Kathmandu is actually further south than New Delhi, on about the same latitude as Cairo, Miami or Taipei. Nepal is about 1500 km closer to the equator than the Alps in Europe so the snow line is much higher.

See Climate under the Causes of Species Diversity section later in this chapter for more details about Nepal's monsoonal climate. Also, the When to Go section in the Facts for the Visitor chapter has information about the importance of climatic factors in planning a visit to Nepal.

GEOGRAPHY

This section, along with the following Flora, Fauna and Ecology sections, was written by Lewis Underwood, an avid naturalist who first visited Nepal in the '70s and continues to work there as a trek leader for Mountain Travel and Malla Treks.

In two of the three dimensions, length and breadth, Nepal is just another small country. In the third, height, it's number one in the world. Nepal stretches from north-west to south-east about 800 km and varies in width from around 90 km to 230 km. This gives it a total area of just 147,181 sq km according to the official figures.

Within that small area, however, is the greatest range of altitude to be seen on this earth – starting with the Terai, only 100 metres or so above sea level, and finishing at the top of 8848-metre Mt Everest, the highest point on earth.

Often a visitor's overriding goal is to see the mountains, especially Everest and

Annapurna. However, to exclude the people, flowers, birds and wildlife from the experience is to miss the essence of the country.

Geologic Origins

Imagine the space Nepal occupies as an open expanse of water, once part of the Mediterranean Sea, and the Tibetan Plateau, or 'roof of the world', as a beachfront property. This was the prehistoric setting until 60 million years ago, prior to the Indo-Australian plate's collision with the Eurasian continent. As the former was pushed under Eurasia, the earth's crust buckled and folded and mountain-building began.

The upheaval of mountains caused the temporary obstruction of rivers that once flowed unimpeded from Eurasia to the sea. However, on the southern slopes of the young mountains, new rivers formed as trapped, moist winds off the tropical sea rose and precipitated. As the mountains continued to rise and the gradient became steeper, these rivers cut deeply into the terrain.

The continual crunching of the two plates, augmented by phases of crustal uplifting, created yet new mountain ranges and once again the rivers' courses were interrupted. If the forces of erosion eventually prevailed, long east-west valleys were formed. If not, lakes resulted.

The colossal outcome was the formation of four major mountain systems running north-west by south-east incised by the north-south gorges of, not only new rivers, but the original ones with watersheds in Tibet that are older than the mountains themselves. In conjunction with the innumerable rogue ridges that jut out from the main ranges, the terrain can be likened to a complex maze of ceilingless rooms.

The mountain-building process continues today, not only displacing material laterally, but sending the ranges yet higher and resulting in natural erosion, landslides, silt-laden rivers, rock faults and earthquakes.

Physiographic Regions

Nepal consists of several physiographic regions, or natural zones: the plains in the south, four mountain ranges, and the valleys lying between them. The lowlands with their fertile soils, and the southern slopes of the mountains with sunny exposures allow for cultivation and are the main inhabited regions.

The Terai & Bhabar Seen from the air, the Gangetic plain is a flat monotonous expanse that comes to a sudden halt as it turns into mountainous relief. The last of this landscape, about 100 metres above sea level, encroaches up to 40 km into Nepal and is known as the Terai. This region is a montage of paddy fields, interspersed with oases of mango groves, bamboo stands and villages beneath scattered palms.

There is an intermediate strip between the Terai and the first range of foothills, referred to as the Bhabar, that is stony with shallow soils. Due to the porosity of the soil it is virtually useless for agriculture.

Country Cross Section

Continental Plates

Ocean

Indian Plate

Eurasian Plate

Convection currents rose from deep within the earth and
drew the Indian and Eurasian continental plates together.

Rain & Wind

Tibetan Mountains

Ganges Sea

Convection Currents

Convection currents pushed the Indian plate
under the Eurasian plate. Pressure caused the
Eurasian plate to buckle and form mountains.

Rain & Wind

Tibetan Mountains

Khumbu Mountains

Himalaya

Indian Plate

Eurasian Plate

As convection currents continue to push
the Indian plate under the Eurasian plate,
the Himalaya start to rise faster than
the Tibetan mountains

The Himalaya now trap
the rain and wind

Mt Everest

The Tibetan mountains have
eroded to form the Tibetan Plateau

Indian Plate

Eurasian Plate

More of the Eurasian plate is forced upwards
and the Himalaya become higher than Tibet.
The high mountains now trap rain and wind
coming from the south.

Chure Hills The Chure Hills, known as the Siwalik Hills in India, are the first of the four mountain ranges and run the length of the country. They have an average height of 900 metres, but are as high as 1350 metres in places. This range separates the Terai from the Inner Terai and harbours the fossilised remains of many mammals no longer typical of Eurasia. Evidence of a large mountain ape (Gigantolopithecus) roaming the region up to half a million years ago has fuelled hope for the existence of the legendary yeti. Like the Bhabar, the region's immature soils are unsuitable for agriculture and therefore large tracts of undisturbed tropical forest remain.

Inner Terai (Duns) Between the Chures and the next range of foothills are longitudinal basins about 150 metres above sea level, formed by east-west flowing rivers, called the Inner Terai. Before the introduction of DDT in the 1950s, the Terai was inhabited only by the Tharus, who demonstrated a partial resistance to malaria. Otherwise, cultivation was undertaken by people who worked low-lying fields during daylight and returned to homes above 1200 metres before sundown. The Rana prime ministers (1846 to 1951) deliberately preserved portions of the tropical jungles to use the malarial zone as a safeguard against possible invasion from the south by the British.

After the eradication of malaria, a large resettlement by hill people looking for fertile land occurred. Over a period of less than a decade, more than 50% of the natural forest was cleared to make way for cultivated land. The establishment of the Royal Chitwan National Park in 1973 helped abate this trend and preserved prime habitat for indigenous wildlife, such as the royal Bengal tiger and the one-horned rhinoceros.

Mahabharat Range Still northwards, the next range of foothills, often referred to as the Middle Hills, is the Mahabharat Range.

These vary between 1500 and 2700 metres, and though quite steep, are characterised by water-retentive soils allowing for cultivation and extensive terracing. On the lower slopes, remnants of subtropical forests can be found, whereas on the upper reaches, above cultivation, temperate elements begin. These mountains are severed by three major river systems: the Karnali, Narayani and Kosi.

Pahar Zone Between the Mahabharat Range and the Himalaya lies a broad belt referred to as the midlands, or Pahar zone. This includes fertile valleys (previously large lakes) such as Kathmandu, Banepa and Pokhara. This area, which has been inhabited for centuries, supports nearly half of Nepal's population. As a result, the central and eastern parts of this zone have been extensively cultivated. Ranging mostly between 1000 and 2000 metres, subtropical and lower temperate forests are found here, but have been disrupted by fuel and fodder gathering.

The Pokhara area is unique, not only because of its magnificent setting at the foot of the Annapurna massif, but also because there is no formidable barrier directly to the south to obstruct the spring and monsoon rainclouds. Consequently, it is subjected to abnormally high rainfall, which limits cultivation to under 2000 metres. Red laterite soils are typical of such areas, where most

---

Vegetation Zones
In western Nepal, forests usually extend to higher elevations than elsewhere in the country due to drier conditions and a more northerly latitude. Above the temperate cultivation zone and below the tree line, the forests are less disrupted, although they do come under pressure from summer herders and wood-gatherers.

Tropical Zone (up to 300 metres) Sal, a broad-leafed, semideciduous hardwood, dominates here. The leaves are used for 'disposable' plates, and the wood is used for construction. It varies little from east to west and is a fire-climax species.

There is also a deciduous moist forest in this zone, of acacia and rosewood, as well as open areas of tall elephant grass. The grass areas are burned off in winter, which helps preserve them – otherwise they would be succeeded by a moist forest. These two habitats are known as seral communities, because if they are left undisturbed, they would both be replaced by the sal climax forest.

The silky cotton tree *(ceiba pentandra)* with its thorny trunks when young, and smooth-buttressed trunk bases when older, has leafless limbs that burst into bright red flowers in early spring. It is also a part of the moist forest. The cotton or 'kapok' from these trees is used for stuffing cushions and mattresses.

These forest types are typical of the Chure and Inner Terai, though sal and silky cotton are also found in the subtropical zone.

Subtropical Zone (1000 to 2000 metres) The dominant species east of the Kali Gandaki are the true chestnuts and a member of the tea family, schima. The spiky flower clusters of the chestnuts appear in the fall, while the fragrant white flowers of the schima bloom in late spring. Due to chestnut wood's popularity as a source of fuel, it is often depleted.

In the west, the chir pine is found on all aspects. The species has long needles in bundles of three and is also found in the east, but confined to drier southern slopes.

Lower Temperate Zone (1700 to 2700 metres) Evergreen oaks are indigenous to this zone. In the east, the oaks of the wet forests are festooned with moss and epiphytes and have dense understoreys. In the west, another oak preferring dry conditions is present, as well as on the sunny slopes of the east.

A common wet forest that occurs mostly on north and west faces in western Nepal is comprised of horse chestnut, maple and walnut. Alder and birch are prevalent along water courses.

minerals are leached out of the soil except for iron and aluminium oxide.

Conversely, the Humla-Jumla area in the west is protected to the south by ranges over 4000 metres in height that prevent much of the monsoon moisture from reaching this region. As a result wide, uneroded valleys, snowless peaks and drier vegetation are found here.

The Himalaya About one third of the total length of the great Himalaya is contained within Nepal's borders, including 10 of the world's 14 peaks that exceed 8000 metres in height. These mountains are terraced and cultivated up to about 2700 metres, or to the level of cloud and mist that precludes growing crops. As a result, the high temperate forest above this to the tree line is fairly well preserved.

Inner Valleys The inner valleys are those cradled within the Himalayan ranges. These broad glacier-worn valleys, which are found in the Everest, Langtang and upper Kali Gandaki areas, are not affected by strong winds that desiccate the valley floors, but not the surrounding sides. The partial rain screen of these high valleys create still different ecologies.

Trans-Himalaya North of the Himalaya is the high desert region, similar to the Tibetan

Homogeneous blue-pine forests occur extensively in the west, mostly on south faces, and range to the tree line. This species is hardy and fire resistant, thriving well in habitats modified by man. It is also found throughout the east, but to a lesser extent. The blue pine is distinguished from the only other pine in Nepal, the chir pine, by its shorter needles in bundles of five, and long, pendulous cones. Both species are used for carpentry and roofing, while the resin is converted to turpentine.

Upper Temperate Zone (2400 to 4000 metres) Another evergreen oak that is widespread throughout the dry forests of the west exhibits two types of leaves, the young ones spiny, while the older have leaf margins. In the east, this species is confined to southern slopes, but is heavily cut for fodder and fuel.

The spectacular wet rhododendron forests are interspersed with hemlock and fir. Rhododendron arboreum, the national flower, reaches heights of 18 metres and ranges in colour from red to white. There are over 30 species of rhododendron in Nepal, but these are found more extensively in the east than the west. Unfortunately, this tree is felled for fuel or turned into charcoal.

There is also a high conifer forest where blue pine is again found, occurring in the west with fir and spruce, both of which also form pure stands. In the east, firs, hemlocks and yews associate with blue pine. Firewood and roofing shingles are the common usages for these species. A mixed broad-leafed forest of maple and laurel is also typical of this zone.

Subalpine Zone (3000 to 4000 metres) Silver fir mixed with oak and birch extend to the tree line in the west. East of the Kali Gandaki, only birch is found to the tree line, though under wetter conditions, dwarf bamboo and shrub rhododendron replace it. In dry areas, juniper species occur to the tree line.

Alpine Zone (4000 metres to snow line) In this realm above the tree line, vegetation must cope with extremes in ground temperatures, and moisture gradients that range from nothing in winter to profuse in summer. Only the most tenacious of wild flowers thrive here, generally by being hirsute or having thick underground stems (rhizomes). A successful example is stellara, common above 5500 metres.

In the trans-Himalaya, the vegetation is restricted to the arid-adapted species of the Tibetan Plateau. ∎

Plateau. This area encompasses the arid valleys of Mustang, Manang and Dolpo, as well as the Tibetan marginals (the fourth range of mountains that sweep from central to north-western Nepal, averaging below 6000 metres in height). The trans-Himalaya is in the rain-shadow area and receives significantly less precipitation than the southern slopes. Uneroded crags, spires, and formations like crumbling fortresses are typical of this stark landscape.

FLORA

There are 6500 known species of trees, shrubs and wild flowers in Nepal. In the temperate areas the flowers emerge as winter recedes and the rivers swell with snow melt, while in the subtropics, the bloom is triggered by warmer temperatures and spring showers. Americans and Europeans will recognise many of the species in the temperate areas, and residents of South-East Asia will recognise many of the subtropical species.

The height of floral glory can be witnessed in March and April when rhododendrons burst into colour. The huge magnolias of the east with their showy white flowers borne on bare branches are also spectacular, as are the orchids (there are over 300 in Nepal). Not far behind is the blossoming of a variety of shrubs, while on the ground, blue irises and lavender primulas appear. The succession of flowers continues higher up closer to the advent of the monsoon.

Unless one is content and able to identify wild flowers by their leaves or dried seed capsules it is necessary to visit the temperate and alpine areas during the monsoon season. In order to do this, one must be prepared to sacrifice comfort and views. However, this is the time to see the true colours of the Himalaya. The southern slopes and the inner valleys are particularly lush at this time. Mints, scrophs, buttercups, cinquefoils, polygonums and composites abound in these areas, while in the alpine areas, dwarf rhododendrons, junipers, ephedras, cotoneasters, saxifrages, and primulas paint the bleak landscape.

Western Nepal, particularly the Dolpo area, is reminiscent of Kashmir in its rich variety of flora. Being in the rain-shadow area, monsoon conditions are more amenable for visitors – the region is dry and free of leeches. In order to witness the full regalia, the time to visit is July and August. From Jumla east one may recognise ground orchids, edelweiss, corydalis, campanulas, anemones, forget-me-nots, impatiens, and roses. Higher up in the alpine areas, the larkspurs, geraniums, poppies, sedums, and saxifrages proliferate.

In the trans-Himalaya, common vegetation is primarily from the legume family, such as the spiny caragana and astragalus, as well as lonicera from the honeysuckle family.

In the post-monsoon season, when most people choose to visit, the flowers of summer are all but gone, save for some straggler blooms and those not palatable to grazing animals. However, in the subtropical and lower temperate areas, some wild flowers are fortunate and survive environmental degradation, such as the pink luculia, mauve osbeckia and yellow St John's wort. The flowering cherry trees also add colour to the autumn village scenes, and in the temperate areas, the blue gentians. Otherwise, one can enjoy the autumn yellows of withering maples and ginger, and the reds of barberry shrubs. When the dark temperate forests are back lit, the moss appears luminescent, and

Gentians

the epiphytic ferns and orchids shine like tiny paper lanterns.

In the Kathmandu Valley, Australians will find familiar silky oak with its spring golden inflorescence, and bottlebrush and eucalyptus. Though fast-growing timber species in their native country, in the valley these trees are planted as ornamentals along with cherry, poplar and jacaranda. The latter, with its lavender blossoms, is from South America, as is bougainvillaea and the giant pointsettias. Historically, the Nepalese have been avid gardeners of such exotics as hibiscus, camellia, cosmos, salvia, and marigold.

FAUNA
Birds

More than 800 species are known in Nepal, more birds than in Canada and the USA combined, or nearly 10% of the world's species! Resident bird numbers are augmented by migratory species, as well as winter and summer visitors.

Eight species of stork, some as high as 150 cm, have been identified along the water courses of the Terai. Similar in appearance are the cranes, but not as well represented, save for the demoiselle cranes that fly down the Kali Gandaki and Dudh Kosi for the winter, before returning in spring to their Tibetan nesting grounds. Herons and egrets are quite common in the tropics and subtropics, and distinguished in flight by their curved-neck posture, as opposed to the outstretched necks of storks and cranes.

Most of the waterfowl are migratory. Many can be seen at the Kosi Barrage in the eastern Terai and in the Chitwan and Bardia areas. The swift flying bar-headed goose has been observed flying at altitudes near 8000 metres.

Raptors or birds of prey are found in all sizes in the Himalaya, and are especially prevalent with the onset of winter. One of the first raptors to leave is the small Eurasian kestrel that must flap its wings at regular intervals, or rapidly when hovering, as compared to the Himalayan griffon, a heavy bird that must wait for thermal updrafts to allow its soaring, gliding flight. The griffon, as well as the lammergeier, with a wingspan of nearly three metres, are carrion eaters, though often mistaken for eagles. There are, however, true eagles present, including the resident golden eagle common in the Khumbu, as well as other species that are known to migrate in large numbers in the Kali Gandaki region. Many medium-sized raptors have highly variable plumages and are difficult to identify in the sky.

There are six species of pheasant in Nepal, including the national bird, the impeyan pheasant, the male of which has a plumage of iridescent colours. These birds are known as downhill fliers, as they do not fly, per se, and must walk uphill! When flushed they will cant and swerve downhill to evade enemies such as the golden eagle. The cheer and koklas pheasants are only found west of the Kali Gandaki, while the kalij pheasant is common throughout, but with different colour phases.

Nepal hosts 17 species of cuckoo which are characterised by their distinctive calls. Arriving in March, they herald the coming of spring. The Indian cuckoo has a recognisable *kaphal pakyo* call, Nepali for announcing that the fruit of the box myrtle is ripe. The common hawk cuckoo has a repetitious call that sounds like 'brain fever', which rises in a crescendo – aptly described by British sahibs as they lay sweating with malarial fevers. Most cuckoos are social parasites, meaning they lay their eggs in the nests of other species.

One of the most colourful, varied and vocal families is the timalids, or babblers and laughing thrushes, common from the tropical Terai to the upper temperate forest. They are from eight to 33 cm in size and live in both terrestrial and arboreal habitats. They are found individually or in large, foraging parties, and can often be identified by their raucous calls. The black-capped sibia with its constant prattle and ringing song is an integral part of the wet temperate forests. The spiny babbler is Nepal's only endemic species.

There are three pairs of species amongst the crow family; their appearance and behaviour are virtually identical, but each species occupies a different altitudinal range. The red-billed blue magpies are residents of the subtropical zone, while the yellow-billed species are found in the temperates. The Indian tree pie prefers the tropics while the Himalayan species lives in the subtropics and temperates. Above the tree line, two species of chough, congregating in large flocks in winter, are prevalent. Though they often overlap in range, the yellow-billed chough is found higher and is known to enter mountaineers' tents high on Everest. Another of the crow family, also bold and conspicuous in the trans-Himalayan region, is the large raven.

Besides such diagnostic families as kingfishers, bee-eaters, drongos, minivets, parakeets and sunbirds, there are a host of other passerines, or perching birds, present throughout Nepal. These include 30 species of flycatchers and nearly 60 species of thrushes and warblers. Many smaller species congregate in heterogeneous flocks, not only for feeding purposes, but also for protection.

In the Kathmandu Valley, the sparrows and pigeons demonstrate adaptability to urban centres by their sheer numbers. Dark Kites, hawk-like birds with forked tails, are common over the city. At sunset, loose groups of crows, mynas, egrets and kites fly to their respective roosts. After dark, the noisy ruckus of the spotted owlets substitutes for the cacophony of car horns. The robin dayal, with its cocked tail, is the common songster of early mornings. Pulchowki, Nagarjun and Shivapuri are excellent areas for finding birds of subtropical and temperate habitats, while the Gokarna Safari Park offers a cross section of species typical of the valley floor.

In the Pokhara region, the Indian roller is conspicuous when it takes flight and flashes the iridescent turquoise on its wings. Otherwise, while perched it appears as a plain brown bird. Local superstition has it that if someone about to embark on a journey sees a roller going their way it is a good omen. If they see a crow, however, it is a bad omen and the trip is aborted. Many trips must be destined for delay thanks to the presence of the common crow!

Mammals

As one might expect, due to habitat degeneration from both natural and human causes, opportunities for seeing wildlife are usually restricted to national parks, reserves and western Nepal, where population is sparse. Wildlife numbers have also been thinned due to poaching for pelts or other parts that are considered to be delicacies or medicinally valuable. Animals are also hunted because of the damage they inflict on crops and domestic animals.

At the top of the food chain is the royal Bengal tiger, the most magnificent cat, which is solitary and territorial. Males have territorial ranges that encompass those of two or three females and may span as much as 100 sq km. The Chitwan National Park of the Inner Terai and the Royal Bardia National Park in the western Terai protect sufficient habitat to sustain viable breeding populations.

The spotted leopard is an avid tree climber and in general more elusive than the tiger. These nocturnal creatures, like tigers, have been known to prefer human flesh when they have grown old or been maimed. Humans are not only easy prey, but once the taste is acquired, human flesh eaters lose interest in their natural prey. Local people have likened them to evil spirits because their success at evading hunters suggests they can read minds.

The snow leopard is often protected from hunters, not only by national parks, but also by inhabiting inhospitable domains above the tree line and sensitive border regions. Its territory depends upon the ranges of ungulate herds, its prey species, as well as breeding females. Packs of wolves compete directly and when territories overlap, the solitary snow leopard will be displaced.

The one-horned rhinoceros is the largest of three Asian species and is a totally different genus from the two-horned African varieties. It has poor eyesight and though weighing up to two tonnes, is amazingly

Causes of Species Diversity

Not only does Nepal's phenomenal topography range from near sea level to 8848 metres, but it is contained within a country approximately the size of the state of Iowa, or that of England and Wales together. The distance between the tropical lowlands and the realm under ice and snow is, in some places, less than 100 km apart. In most parts of the world these zones are separated by thousands of km! How many places in the world can one see myna birds chattering on banana fronds at 2700 metres before a snowy mountain backdrop seemingly close enough to reach out and touch?

Geographical Location The 28° latitude line runs just north of Mt Everest, as well as through Morocco and central Florida. This southerly latitude is the reason the permanent snow line is above 5000 metres. Longitudinally, Nepal straddles two of the world's zoogeographical zones: the Holarctic to the north and the Oriental to the south. This means that one finds life forms from Europe and northern Asia, typical of the former realm, and species of India and tropical South-East Asia, from the latter.

Climate Nepal is subject to a monsoon-type climate where wet summers and dry winters are characteristic. Without this weather pattern, the country would be a desert with much less extensive speciation.

Every summer between June and July, the sun moves northwards and heats up the mountains creating a massive convection cell. The subsequent rising air produces a vacuum that draws the moisture-laden air off the Bay of Bengal. This air runs into the Himalayan barriers, cools as it rises and condenses in the form of rain. Thus begins the monsoon season, three to four months of high humidity, overcast skies and gentle rain. Deluges that occur during this time are due to tropical storms or squalls in the Indian Ocean.

The eastern Himalaya receives the brunt of the monsoon which loses its impetus as it moves west along the mountains. Consequently there is a distinct moisture gradient from east to west. Biogeographically, there are life forms east of the Kali Gandaki Valley associated with wet forests (typically more prolific in species diversity), while west of this line are dissimilar ones preferring drier habitats.

In winter, western Nepal experiences a reverse monsoon caused by a shift in the jet stream. This phenomenon, which drags weather patterns from the west off the Arabian Sea, brings moisture to the region in the form of snow and is essential for agriculture. The oscillation of the jet stream lasts between November and March and is not only responsible for Everest's snow plume and black appearance, but also renders mountaineering difficult.

Altitude & Aspect Altitude and aspect (the direction that a slope faces) play equal roles in determining climate and vegetation. Temperature decreases with elevation, which affects flora as well as fauna. Conversely, rainfall increases with altitude, up to about 2700 metres. At this level, the clouds have spent their moisture and form a ceiling. This not only establishes the limit for crops, but affects natural vegetation distribution as well.

Aspect, or exposure, is also important in terms of moisture content, fire resistance and defining the height of the tree line. South and east-facing slopes receive more sun and therefore are drier. The shadier northern and western faces are more moist, less prone to fire and thus richer in species. ■

Himalayan griffon

quick. Anyone who encounters a mother with its calf is likely to witness a charge, which is disconcertingly swift, even if you are on an elephant. The rhino is a denizen of the grasslands of the Inner Terai, specifically the Chitwan Valley, although it has also been reintroduced to the Royal Bardia National Park.

The Indian elephant, like the one-horned rhino, is starkly different to its African relative, belonging to a separate genus. The only wild elephants known to exist in Nepal are in the western part of the Terai and Chure Hills, though individuals often range across the border from India. Elephants are known to maintain matriarchal societies, and females up to 60 years of age bear calves. Though able to reach 80 years of age, elephants' life spans are determined by dentition. Molars are replaced as they wear down, but only up to six times. When the final set is worn, the individual dies of starvation.

Periodically, male and occasionally female elephants, enter a 'musth' condition that makes them excitable and highly aggressive. While in this agitated state they have been known to trample villages. When a herd goes on the rampage, outsiders, or non-Hindus, are often summoned as the elephant is considered a holy animal because of the much-loved Ganesh, the elephant-headed god of the Hindu pantheon.

There are several species of deer, but most of them are confined to the lowlands. The spotted deer is probably the most beautiful, while the sambar is the largest. The *muntjac*, or barking deer, which usually makes its presence known by its sharp, one-note alarm call, is found up to 2400 metres, while the unusual musk deer, with antelope-like features and only 50 cm high at the shoulder, ranges even higher.

There are two primates: the rhesus macaque and the common langur. The rhesus are earth-coloured with short tails and travel on the ground in large, structured troops, unafraid of humans. The langur are arboreal, with black faces, grey fur, long limbs and tails. Because of Hanuman, the monkey god

in the Hindu epic the *Ramayana*, both species are considered holy and are well protected. The rhesus ranges from the Terai up to 2400 metres, while the langur goes higher, up to 3600 metres.

Common langur

In the Kathmandu Valley, rhesus macaques at the Swayambhunath and Pashupatinath temples take advantage of their holy status and relieve worshippers of their picnic lunches and consecrated food.

Two even-toed hoofed mammals are found in the alpine regions. They are the Himalayan tahr, a near-true goat, and the blue sheep, which is genetically stranded somewhere between goats and sheep. The male tahr pose majestically in their flowing manes on the grassy slopes of inner valleys, while the blue sheep turn a bluish-grey in winter and are found in the trans-Himalayan biotope.

The Himalayan black bear is omnivorous and a bane to corn crops in the temperate forests. Though it rarely attacks humans, its poor eyesight may lead it to interpret a standing person as making a threatening gesture and to attack. If so, the best defence is not to run, but to lie face down on the ground – particularly effective when one is wearing a backpack. Nepal's bears are known to roam in winter instead of hibernating.

There are some prominent canines, though behaviourally they are fairly shy. The jackal, with its eerie howling that sets village dogs barking at night, ranges from the Terai to alpine regions. It is both a hunter and scavenger, and will take chickens and raid crops.

The pika, or mouse-hare, is the common guinea pig-like mammal of the inner valleys, often seen scurrying nervously between rocks. The marmot of western Nepal is a large rodent, but with a mustelid-like appearance; it commonly dwells in the trans-Himalayan zone. The marmot is also found in Sikkim and Bhutan, but not eastern Nepal – such gaps in speciation are not uncommon across the Himalaya.

Noisy colonies of flying foxes or fruit bats have chosen the trees near the old Royal Palace in Kathmandu and the chir pines at the entrance to Bhaktapur as their haunts. They are known to fly great distances at night to raid orchards, before returning at dawn. They have adequate eyesight for their feeding habits and do not require the sonar system of insectivorous bats.

Pulchowki, Nagarjun and Shivapuri are good areas for possible sightings of small mammals. The Gokarna Safari Park contains introduced deer species.

Reptiles

There are two indigenous species of crocodile: the Gharial and marsh mugger. The Gharial inhabits rivers and is a prehistoric-looking fish-eating creature with bulging eyes and a long, narrow snout. The marsh mugger prefers stagnant water and is omnivorous, feeding on anything within reach. Due to the value of its hide and eggs, the Gharial was hunted to the brink of extinction, but has increased in numbers since the establishment of a hatchery and rearing centre in Chitwan. Both crocodiles inhabit the Terai.

Though venomous snakes such as cobras, vipers and kraits are present, the chance of encountering one is small, not only because of their usual evasive tactics, but also because they are indiscriminantly slaughtered. The majority of species are found on the Terai, though the mountain pit viper is known higher up, along with a few other nonvenomous species.

ECOLOGY

Much of the land between the Himalaya and the Terai has been vigorously modified by human activities and represents the lifeblood of Nepal. This land has been worked and sculpted over the centuries to provide space for crops, animals and houses. Because of this, forests lying within the inhabited zone, especially on the southern slopes, have been lopped, cut and cleared.

Plant Use

The Terai is considered the rice bowl of Nepal, though rice is usually grown up to 2000 metres, or higher in the west. It is usually planted before the advent of the monsoon, transplanted soon after and harvested in the autumn. The rich vibrant greens during the monsoon contrast with the subtle, diffused tones as it ripens.

If possible, wheat is planted in the cleared rice fields and harvested in spring. Fields of yellow-flowering mustard are planted for making cooking oil. Corn is planted in spring, especially on the hillsides, while millet is grown above the rice zone. Barley is sowed in the higher altitudes, as well as buckwheat with its pink and white flower cluster. The Sherpas grow potatoes up to 4000 metres, and have been doing so since the crop was introduced, probably from Darjeeling in the middle of the last century. Besides providing an important food staple, the prosperity attained from trading potatoes allowed Sherpas to begin building their *gompas* (monasteries) and for their culture to flourish.

Amongst the crops, on the berms dividing the plots, various other food crops are grown, including soya beans, lentils, sesame, and chilli peppers. The bright red and yellow plants with clustered seed heads seen amidst the shades of greens are amaranthus, once an important food and medicinal grain for the Aztecs and Incas.

To keep animals out of crops, the Nepalese use assorted spiny or unpalatable exotics as natural barriers. Besides prickly pear cactus and agave, there are several euphorbias used, such as the red-flowering crown of thorns, spurge and physic nut.

There are numerous trees planted around villages and fields, all for some kind of purpose, whether for shade, fruit, fodder or medicine. Bananas, mangoes, papaya, citrus fruits, peaches and apples have all brought new income to the remote hill areas.

Fodder such as rice stalks and corn sheaves are often dried and stored in trees, while seed corn is stored under the eaves of houses. A variety of fig trees provide shade for pilgrims and travellers. The magnificent mushrooming canopies of banyan and pipal tress are unmistakable, usually found together atop a stone dais (platform) designed for accommodating porters' loads. The banyan has hanging aerial roots and leathery elliptical leaves, while the pipal has a heart-shaped leaf with a long spur. The Buddha is believed to have received enlightenment under a pipal tree, and Hindus revere the banyan as an embodiment of Lakshmi, the goddess of wealth, and the pipal as an embodiment of Narayan (Vishnu).

Bamboo grows under a variety of conditions and is found throughout Nepal. Giant bamboo is common in the tropics and dwarf bamboo in the temperates. This grass species is used for basketry, and where forests are depleted, particularly in the east, for building. The Rais work bamboo into everything from water vessels to entire houses.

Kitchen gardens are also common features in villages comprised of greens, beans, turnips, radishes, pumpkins, cucumbers, taro and squash. Bauhinia, with its distinctive camel-hoof leaves and orchid-like flowers, is grown near houses, the former for fodder and the latter cooked or pickled. In the west, tobacco is a commonly seen plot in villages, as well as fields of cannabis grown for hemp. In addition, stinging nettles are picked with thongs, anaesthetised by boiling and eaten as greens. Eupatorium is a red-stemmed daisy with heart-shaped leaves called *ban mara* ('death of forest') by the Nepalese. A native of Latin America introduced into the Himalaya during the last century, it invades subtropical and temperate zones, and is widespread. Covering deforested hillsides, it is unpalatable, even for sheep and goats, and is a prime indicator of environmental degradation.

Animal Husbandry

Bovines play an important role in rural and urban Nepal. Cows are sacred and are not slaughtered, nor used as beasts of burden – they bear calves, and provide milk and, of course, multipurpose dung. The beasts of burden on the lowlands are usually castrated bulls, or oxen. In the Kathmandu Valley, the cows wandering and sleeping in the streets have been let loose by pious Hindus. Because the bull is Shiva's steed, and Pashupatinath is a major Shaivite temple, bulls are also considered holy and generally are not used to pull ploughs in the valley.

Water buffaloes belong to a different genus, but are still lumped with the bovines. These animals lose their body hair as they mature and must wallow to dissipate heat, and for sun protection. The males are used as beasts of burden and are butchered. The females produce a creamy milk, which is also converted into yoghurt. These animals tend to be skittish, a trait probably inherited from their wild ancestors, and those at the Koshi Tappu Reserve in the eastern Terai are considered aggressive and dangerous.

The long-haired yaks, no longer found in the wilds of Nepal, are also very temperamental, and are mostly used for stud service. What one generally sees are hybrids, which have confusing names. First of all, the female yak is called a *nak*. The nak or yak can be crossbred with cattle, which produces a more docile creature suitable for carrying loads. Locally, the male is called a *zopkiok* or *dzopkyo* and the female a *zhum* or *dzum*. The zhum lactates well and produces a better quality milk than the nak. The second generation of these hybrids is sterile.

In the Kali Gandaki and more recently on the southern approaches to the Everest region, donkeys and mules are being used as pack animals. These beasts are often adorned with headgear of dyed plumes and mirrors, and collars of bells. Also, in autumn, during

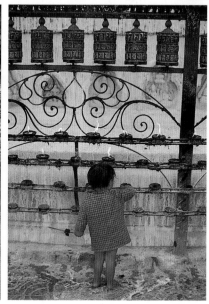

Top: Bodhnath Stupa, Kathmandu Valley (TW)
Left: Changu Narayan, Kathmandu Valley (RI'A)
Right: Girl praying, Swayambhunath (RE)

Top: Market stalls in Asan Tole, Kathmandu (RE)
Middle: Market scene, Kathmandu (TW)
Bottom: Vegetable stalls, Kathmandu (CG)

the prime festival season, herds of goats and sheep are driven down from Tibet to be sold for ritual slaughter and the subsequent feasts.

Conservation

As long as the Nepalese marry early, feel uncertain about infant survival and desire sons to look after them in their old age and to perform funeral rites, the population of Nepal will continue to burgeon. With population tension, the forests will continue to be depleted, erosion caused by humans will compound that which is natural, water supplies will dry up and floods will inundate the lowlands.

The visitor should not, however, adopt the role of the vociferous critic. Nepal is making positive changes, but traditional societies require long lead times for change. Amongst others, there are various alternative energy schemes underway, probably the most successful being the hydroelectric project of Solu and the soon-to-be-augmented unit above Namche Bazaar. The Annapurna Conservation Area Project (ACAP) is also an innovative approach, incorporating not only other alternative-energy developments, forest conservation and environmental education, but an effective strategy of getting the Nepalese people directly involved in determining their own destiny.

Conservation is typically a concept of affluent countries with land and resources to spare, a luxury unknown in the Third World. With dwindling space and forests, it is difficult for a farmer to grasp why land should be set aside for tigers and rhino, especially when they ravage crops, take domestic animals, and generally make a hard life even harder.

Visitors should ensure that they minimise their impact on the environment. Trekking groups or individuals staying in lodges should insist that kerosene, as opposed to firewood, is used for cooking meals and heating water. One should also minimise the use of non-biodegradable products (especially plastic and batteries) as there are no facilities for their disposal. One potential nightmare is the trend to sell water in plastic bottles – which are expensive and completely unnecessary if you carry your own water bottle and iodine. See the Trekking chapter for more information on minimising your impact on the environment.

Also, see the Books section in the Facts for the Visitor chapter for a list of supplementary reading on flora, fauna and national parks.

NATIONAL PARKS & CONSERVATION AREAS

Nepal has nine national parks and four wildlife reserves that protect every significant ecological system in the country – from the tropical plains of the Terai, to the fertile midland valleys, to the highest mountains in the world.

Altogether, over 12,000 sq km are protected, or over 8% of the country's area, and you can add another 2600 sq km if you include the Annapurna Conservation Area. Considering the strength of the demand for land, there has been a particularly impressive commitment to conservation.

Travellers are almost certain to visit a protected area – the Sagarmatha National Park includes Mt Everest, the Annapurna Conservation Area includes many of the most popular treks around the Annapurna Himal, and the Royal Chitwan National Park is famous for its elephant-back safaris in search of royal Bengal tigers and one-horned rhinoceroses.

All visitors are charged Rs 650 (or around US$14) for entering a park or reserve, except for the Annapurna Conservation Area where the entry fee is Rs 200 (US$5). Home movie enthusiasts beware: a US$200 permit is officially required if you take video into a national park, while a permit for a movie camera (from the Ministry of Communications) costs a whopping US$1000. The Department of National Parks & Wildlife Conservation (☎ 01-220912) has a number of brochures on individual parks and can be contacted through PO Box 860, Babar Mahal, Kathmandu. Babar Mahal is a well-known government office complex on the main road to the airport.

National Parks & Conservation Areas

National Park (NP)

Wildlife Reserve (WR)

Conservation Area

Hunting Reserve

The problems that Nepal has faced in setting aside areas for conservation are more acute than those faced in most industrially developed countries, but the Nepalese are responding by developing new management concepts – it is not possible or desirable to set aside areas of land that are totally untouched by humans.

Firstly, very little of Nepal can be accurately described as wilderness. Most of the country is, in some way, used by humans. Virtually every possible inch of arable land is used for farming; the remaining forests are utilised for firewood and hunting; the high country is used for hunting and grazing; and the whole country is crisscrossed with trade routes. The only exceptions are several royal hunting reserves, some of the Terai (large parts of which were virtually untouched until the 1950s), and mountain peaks at high altitude.

Secondly, developing national parks and conservation areas by following the Western model would have meant totally blocking local people's access to a resource that might literally mean the difference between life and death. In most cases, therefore, the Nepalese have attempted to marry the competing interests between conservation (and tourist attractions?) on the one hand and farming (and food?) on the other.

For instance, the Sagarmatha National Park is the traditional home to several thousand Sherpas whose ancestors settled the area 500 years ago. Banishing them from their homeland would have been unthinkable, so the park management has been responsible for encouraging sustainable economic development, as well as controlling the impact of a growing number of tourists. In another example, although thousands of recent settlers were actually moved outside the park's boundary when it was declared, the Royal Chitwan National Park is still used by them as an important source for thatching grass, which is harvested every year.

Despite these essential compromises, there have been some notable successes. The magnificent royal Bengal tiger was saved in Chitwan and there have been impressive achievements in the Sagarmatha National Park and the Annapurna Conservation Area – in forestry, agriculture, health and education, as well as in protecting the most spectacular scenery in the world. See those sections later.

Koshi Tappu Wildlife Reserve

The Koshi Tappu Wildlife Reserve is a small (175 sq km) reserve that lies on the beautiful flood plain of the Sapt Kosi (one of the three largest tributaries to the Ganges) in eastern Nepal. It runs north from the massive Kosi Barrage and the Indian border.

The reserve is often flooded during the monsoon, although mostly to shallow depths only. It is, nonetheless, home to the last surviving group of wild buffalo and several species of deer. The vegetation is mainly grassland with some mixed riverine forest. A total of 280 different species of birds – including many migratory birds – have been recorded. Local villages harvest grasses for thatching, as well as fishing and collecting edible fruits and ferns.

The Mahendra Highway skirts the reserve, but there is no nearby accommodation. See the Terai chapter for more details.

Sagarmatha National Park

North-east of Kathmandu and alongside the Tibetan border the Sagarmatha National Park covers 1148 sq km, all above 3000 metres in altitude. Mt Everest (Sagarmatha to the Nepalese) is the single main attraction, but there are a number of other well-known peaks, including Lhotse and Ama Dablam. The mountains are broken by deep gorges, glacial valleys and lakes.

Tree species include pine, fir, juniper and birch, and there are numerous species of rhododendron. Amongst the animals, there are musk deer, Himalayan tahr, black bears, wolves, and fascinating bird life. The most famous would be the beautiful impeyan pheasant, the national bird of Nepal, but there are choughs, snow pigeons and Himalayan griffons among 130 others.

Over 3500 Sherpas use the park for cropping and grazing (their villages are not included in the park proper) and their unique culture provides yet another reason to visit. There are several important monasteries. For detailed information on this park try to find a copy of *Mt Everest National Park: Sagarmatha, Mother of the Universe* by Margaret Jefferies, an excellent book that gives fascinating background information, as well as some magnificent photos.

This is one of the most popular trekking regions in the country, but it's only accessible by foot, with the nearest airstrip at Lukla and the roadhead at Lamosangu. Many trekkers visit, lured by the highest and most spectacular mountain scenery in the world and Sherpa culture. See the Trekking chapter for general information on trekking, and treks in this region in particular.

Makalu-Barun National Park & Conservation Area

The Makalu-Barun National Park & Conservation Area, just to the east of Mt Everest, was inaugurated in November 1992. It will cover 2330 sq km and its boundaries are marked by the Sagarmatha National Park to the north-west and the Arun River to the east. Its northern boundary is the newly established 35,000 sq km Qomolangma (Mt Everest) Nature Preserve in Tibet. Together these three parks will protect a vast area around the Everest massif.

The park includes Makalu, at 8463 metres the fifth-highest mountain in the world, and a small number of trekkers walk in to the base camp. Elevations range from 435 metres on the Arun River to the 8000-metre summits of the Himal (a *himal* is a range or massif with permanent snow). Nearly all ecological zones, from subtropical forest to the arctic snows of the Himalaya are found in the area. Some of the valleys contain some of the last remaining tracts of pristine mountain landscapes in Nepal that are not yet permanently inhabited.

The wilderness area will have the status of a national park, but the surrounding regions, which are home to more than 32,000 people, will be managed according to the model pioneered by the Annapurna Conservation Area Project (see following section). The majority of people are Rai, followed by Sherpa and Tibetan-speaking groups.

There are plans to build a visitors' centre at Khandbari, which will have road access thanks to the proposed construction of the 402-megawatt Arun III hydroelectric project (via Dhankuta). There is an airstrip at Tumlingtar about 10 km south of Khandbari.

Royal Chitwan National Park

South-west of Kathmandu, near the Indian border on the tropical Terai, the Royal Chitwan National Park and contiguous Parsa Wildlife Reserve cover just over 1431 sq km. The park includes a section of the Chure Hills and the Rapti, Narayani and Reu valleys.

Sal forest covers 70% of the park, with the remainder consisting of grasslands and riverine forests. This is home to the only significant number of one-horned rhinoceroses surviving in Nepal, and other endangered species like the royal Bengal tiger, Gangetic dolphin and Gharial crocodile. Altogether, there are over 50 species of large mammals and over 400 species of birds. There are no human communities actually in the park, but the surrounding countryside is intensively cultivated.

For detailed information on this park try to find a copy of *Royal Chitwan National Park: Wildlife Heritage of Nepal* by Hemanta R Mishra & Margaret Jefferies; some of the photos are magnificent.

The park is easily accessible by road, and accommodation ranges from five-star and expensive, to zero-star and cheap. Many people visit for two or three days (especially if they are going to or from India) to take advantage of elephant safaris through the forest. See the Terai chapter for more details.

Annapurna Conservation Area

North of Pokhara and extending to the Tibetan border, the Annapurna Conservation Area covers 2600 sq km. It includes the Annapurna peaks, the famous Annapurna Sanctuary and a significant section of the Kali Gandaki Valley.

The conservation area is run by a nongovernmental, nonprofit organisation (the Annapurna Conservation Area Project, or ACAP) which is funded by various trusts. Its primary objectives are to improve local standards of living, to protect the environment and develop more sensitive forms of tourism.

Himalayan tahr

This is the most popular trekking region in Nepal, especially for individual trekkers, and this influx of visitors has added to the pre-existing problems in the mountains. The trekkers' demands for heating and hot water have led to increased deforestation, there are litter and sanitation problems, and wildlife has been driven away from many parts.

In response, ACAP has started work on a number of projects, like forestry nurseries, introducing wood-saving technologies (eg efficient stoves), banning fires altogether in certain areas, and building rubbish tips and latrines. Many problems still remain, and it is vital that trekkers cooperate with these and other initiatives. If you would like more information on ACAP activities, contact the King Mahendra Trust (☎ 01-223229), PO Box 3712, Babar Mahal, Kathmandu.

The treks around the Annapurna Himal are undoubtedly some of the best in the world –

not only for the grandeur of the mountains, but also for the variety of fascinating cultures that you can visit (Bhotiya, Tibetan, Tamang, Magar, Gurung, Thakali and others). The area is easily accessible from Pokhara and there is an airstrip at Jomsom. See the Trekking chapter for more information on trekking in general and this region in particular.

Langtang National Park

This is the nearest national park to Kathmandu, extending from 32 km north of Kathmandu to the Tibetan border, and covering 1710 sq km. The park encloses the catchments for two major rivers – the Trisuli and the Sun Kosi – and several 7000-metre mountains.

The complex topography and geology of the area together with the varied climatic patterns means there is a wide variety of vegetation types and animals. There are small areas of subtropical forest below 1000 metres, then temperate oak and pine forests, subalpine juniper, larch and birch, and finally alpine scrub, rocks and snow. The fauna includes pandas, muntjac, musk deer, black bear, ghoral, serows (antelope) and monkeys.

About 45 villages lie within the park boundaries (although they do not come under park jurisdiction). In total, around 18,000 people depend on the park's resources, mainly for wood and pasture land. There are several ethnic groups, but the majority are Tamangs (settlers from Tibet and followers of the pre-Buddhist Bon religion).

There are a number of popular treks in the park, ranging in length and difficulty. There is road access to Dhunche (near the park headquarters) from Kathmandu, or you can walk in from Sundarijal, Panchkhal, or from Chautara or Tatopani on the Kodari road. See the Trekking chapter for more details.

Dhorpatan Hunting Reserve

The Dhorpatan Hunting Reserve lies in the Dhaulagiri Himal in western Nepal. It is characterised by a dry climate in the north and well-developed mixed hardwood forests at lower elevations.

The 1325-sq-km reserve is one of the prime habitats for the blue sheep, a highly prized trophy animal. Other 'game' animals include ghoral, serow, Himalayan tahr, Himalayan black bear, pheasants and partridges. I imagine trekkers would also make good sport.

The only access, unless you have a helicopter, is by foot from Jelbang.

Shey Phoksundo National Park

The Shey Phoksundo National Park is the largest park in Nepal at 3555 sq km. It encompasses the Kanjiroba Himal in western Nepal and runs north to the Tibetan border.

The park stretches across all possible vegetation zones – from the luxuriant forests of the lower Himalaya to the near desert of the Tibetan Plateau. Typical animals include the Tibetan hare, Himalayan weasel and the beautiful snow leopard. Lake Phoksundo and the Shey monastery are the two main attractions in the park, but the entire region has been little touched by the 20th century.

Very few people visit this region, partly because access has, in the past, been officially restricted and requires a dangerous 14-day trek from Pokhara. Permits can now be arranged through trekking companies. See *Trekking in Hidden Land of Dolpa-Tarap & Shey Poksumdo* by Paolo Gondini (Tiwari's Pilgrims Book House, Kathmandu) for more detailed information. According to information from the department, it takes two days to walk to the entrance gate for Sumduwa from Dunai, the district headquarters for Dolpo.

Rara National Park

In little-visited western Nepal, the 106-sq-km Rara National Park was established to preserve the catchment and surrounds of the beautiful Rara Lake – a clear high-altitude lake ringed with pine, spruce and juniper forests and snow-capped peaks. The lake is the largest in Nepal and is an important water-bird habitat.

The only way to get to Rara Lake is a strenuous four-day walk from the airstrip at Jumla, or from the roadhead at Surkhet. Trekking in this area is much more difficult than in east or central Nepal: some areas are still closed and there are frequent food shortages. See Lonely Planet's *Trekking in the Nepal Himalaya* by Stan Armington for more details.

Royal Bardia National Park

In the western Terai, bordering the Karnali River, this 968-sq-km reserve is reminiscent in many ways of the Royal Chitwan National Park. The relative difficulty of access, however, means it is much less popular. And there is a higher likelihood of seeing a royal Bengal tiger.

The reserve is bordered to the north by the Chure Hills, but is predominantly flat and dominated by sal forests and grasslands. Apart from tigers there is a small herd of introduced rhinoceroses, blue bull, a variety of deer and at least one wild elephant. If you're lucky you might also see Gangetic dolphin in the river.

The park is 2½ hours by road from Nepalganj and there is comfortable (though expensive) accommodation available. See the Terai chapter for more details.

Khaptad National Park

Another rarely visited park, Khaptad covers 225 sq km in far western Nepal. Lying at around 3000 metres it is largely a rolling plateau with grasslands, and oak and coniferous forests.

Royal Sukla Phanta Wildlife Reserve

This 155-sq-km reserve lies in the far southwestern corner of Nepal on the Indian border. It covers a riverine flood plain, dominated by sal forest, but like both the Chitwan and Bardia national parks, there are also grasslands which make it ideal for wildlife observation.

Sukla Phanta is one of the last strongholds for the endangered swamp deer, but there are also tigers and possibly a wild elephant or two.

Access to the park is by road from Mahendranagar and it is possible to stay in comfortable tents. See the Terai chapter for more details.

GOVERNMENT

The Jana Andolan People's Movement of April 1990 forced King Birendra to abandon the panchayat system that had been established by his father. (See the earlier History sections for more information.) Under this system the peak legislative body, or National Panchayat, was effectively a rubber stamp and the king enjoyed virtually absolute power.

A new constitution was adopted in November 1990. Basically it provided for a constitutional monarchy, universal adult franchise and a multiparty parliamentary system.

Members of the 205-seat House of Representatives (Pratinidhi Sabha) are elected every five years according to the first-past-the-post system. In the May 1991 elections, the Nepali Congress won 110 seats, giving it a simple majority, and formed the government with Girija Prasad Koirala as prime minister.

Members of the 60-seat National Assembly (Rastriya Sabha) have a six-year tenure; one-third retire every two years. Thirty-five members are elected by proportional representation, 15 members are elected by local government representatives and 10 members are nominated by the king.

ECONOMY

Judged by Western standards, Nepal is one of the poorest countries in the world with an estimated annual Gross Domestic Product (GDP) of only US$170 per person. To a certain extent, this suggests an overly bleak picture because more than 90% of the population is basically, and will almost certainly remain, subsistence farmers operating outside the cash economy.

Agriculture

At present, most farmers succeed in meeting their basic needs and producing a small surplus for cash sales. Indeed, aid workers on the Terai have been known to bemoan the fact that they can't convince peasant farmers to work harder and produce additional cash crops. The problem is that the rewards are not believed to be worth the effort. After all, if a family has food, a house, and perhaps access to a radio and bicycle, what more could they want – or realistically aspire to?

In the late '70s Nepal actually exported large quantities of rice. The development of the Terai opened up new land, temporarily relieving some of the population pressure in the hills, and the so-called green revolution (utilising improved seeds, artificial fertilisers and pesticides) led to increased productivity. The population, however, has again begun to grow more rapidly than production and Nepal will soon be forced to import rice to meet its needs. It is already a net importer of food.

The average size of land holdings has continued to drop; it now stands at around half a hectare in the hills and a little over 1½ hectares in the Terai. In a good year, half a hectare in the hills around Kathmandu might produce around 1000 kg of rice and about 500 kg of mixed vegetables, but if the farmer does not own the land up to 50% of this production will go to the owner as rent. Although there are theoretical limits on the amount of land an individual may own, tenant farmers are still common and many are in debt to moneylenders.

Where possible, crops are supplemented with livestock (especially in the mountain areas), but the animals are often of poor quality, partly because there is a serious shortage of fodder, especially in winter. One of the important uses for Nepal's remaining forests is as a source for animal fodder; unfortunately this can also lead to unsustainable damage. See the earlier Ecology section for more information on plant use and animal husbandry in Nepal.

Manufacturing & Services

Obviously, for many people there's not much food to spare, especially if the rains fail. Although outright starvation is rare, undernourishment is very common, particularly in the undeveloped west of the country. A growing number of people are forced to seek seasonal work, or rely on money that is repatriated by other family members, to supplement what they can produce from their land.

Unfortunately, Nepal's embryonic manufacturing industries (mainly on the Terai) and service sector are unable to meet the demand for work, so there is significant underemployment.

Perhaps the most extraordinary success story of the last few decades, however, has been that of Tibetan carpets. Although weaving is an indigenous craft, in 1960 the Nepal International Tibetan Refugee Relief Committee, with the particular support of the Swiss government, began encouraging Tibetan refugees in Jawlakhel, Patan, to make and sell carpets. Today, Nepal exports more than 1½ million sq metres of rugs, valued at over US$100 million. The industry now earns more than half the country's foreign exchange, and is the largest single employer with nearly 300,000 workers.

For many people, however, the only accessible source of income is the tourist trade – either as a market for handcrafts and other small-scale businesses (lodges, shops, travel agencies etc) or as an employee (hotel staff, porters etc). Others work as day labourers for wealthy peasants, or try to pick up menial work in Kathmandu.

Foreign Exchange & Trade

Tourism accounts for 15.5% of foreign-exchange earnings, although there is some controversy over how much of this leaks out of the country again in paying for the goods and services that Westerners require. Remittances, primarily from Gurkha soldiers in the Indian, British and Sultan of Brunei's armies, account for another 6.5%.

Some cynics claim that the two mainstays of the Nepalese economy are really smuggling and foreign aid – there are no official figures for the smuggling, but foreign aid accounts for 30% of hard-currency receipts!

Almost half the government's revenue depends on foreign aid and borrowing.

The country has always been an intermediary between India and China. More recently, it has become a transit point for goods from Japan, Singapore and Hong Kong. One recent rumour alleged that in one year Nepal imported seven million zips – where are they now? Many other goods, it is claimed, travel in a circuit from India to Nepal and back to India. For instance, it's said that much of the subsidised salt which India supplies to Nepal eventually ends up back in India, after a profit has been skimmed off in Nepal.

Nepal's trade is dominated by India and many activities within the country are Indian-owned or controlled. In the 1990-91 financial year India had a trade surplus with Nepal that amounted to over Rs 6000 million.

Development

It is hard to be optimistic when looking at the prospects for Nepal, despite the ingenuity and decency of the Nepalese people. The growing population threatens to overwhelm the developments that have already taken place – and future developments will always be hampered by the impossible terrain.

Whether the country can continue to carry the population it already has – given that soils and forests are already being exploited at unsustainable levels – might even be questioned. For a very large number of peasant families, existence appears set to become increasingly perilous. This is likely to lead to increased migration to the Kathmandu Valley (where resources are already strained), to the Terai and to India.

In Kathmandu, the gulf between the rich and the poor is extreme. The aristocracy still wields considerable power and influence and many of its members lead lives that are extraordinarily pampered and unrealistic. These feudal survivors have been joined by a new business elite, whose strikingly ugly houses now dot the outskirts of Kathmandu. Corruption is endemic at every level of government.

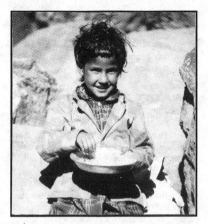

The challenges facing Nepal are clearly immense. A large and growing proportion of the population lives in poverty and nearly 75% is illiterate. Health services, especially outside the Kathmandu Valley, are minimal – the ratio of doctors to people was 1 to 15,000 in 1991, and there were only 4700 hospital beds. The average life expectancy is only 52 years.

Family planning is of primary importance, but the population is currently growing at 2.08% per year. Most people continue to regard children as a blessing. A child is seen as a vital and fulfilling part of the parents' lives, an extra worker and someone to care for them in old age, not just an extra stomach.

Since most people are dependent on agriculture, this is the most important area for development. Much can be done to increase and sustain productivity, but here as elsewhere, the topography means there is an amazing diversity of problems, not least of which is reaching the isolated valleys and ridges where so many of the people live.

On the positive side, education is spreading into distant valleys, and trekkers are likely to come across thriving primary schools in the most remote areas. Also highly visible are the improvements in Nepal's communications network. The telephone system links all major towns, and roads continue to extend further and further into distant parts of the country. Often, however, new roads bring undesirable social changes (thanks to an influx of outsiders and trade goods) and some question whether the huge sums of money involved in road construction and maintenance might not be better allocated to expanding and improving the existing network of walking tracks and bridges.

Nepal's physical resources are extremely limited. There are few accessible minerals, and there is little unexploited arable land. There are, however, great hydroelectric power resources although the market for them is likely to be found in India and the capital and ecological costs involved in construction are huge. Perhaps one of the most optimistic trade delegations in recent times was one from Bangladesh that suggested a number of ways trade could be expanded between the two countries. Amongst other things, they were interested in importing Nepalese boulders!

Foreign Aid

Foreign aid sounds as if it should be a wonderful industry – on the surface, totally nonpolluting and ecologically sound. Nepal has lots of it and the end result is a highly questionable one. If you're interested in the impact of foreign aid on a country like Nepal the magazine *Himal* regularly has articles which will provide food for thought. Two recent books, ostensibly accounts of travels in Nepal, will also prove enlightening.

Peter Somerville-Large's *To the Navel of the World* (Hamish Hamilton, London, 1987) contrasts the successful, heavily touristed and heavily aided Solu Khumbu region of the Sherpas in eastern Nepal with the neglected regions of the far north-west. While critics debate the damage caused by tourism it seems hardly likely that the people living in the areas where trekkers are plentiful and aid projects abound would willingly switch to the areas of Nepal which are still 'off limits'.

Charlie Pye-Smith's *Travels in Nepal* (Aurum Press, London, 1988) was essentially a trek from one aid project to another and what he saw was not always a pretty sight. Too often the projects were pointless, imposed without consulting the people they were aimed at, or without adequately understanding the local physical and cultural environment. Often the only people who benefited were the foreign companies who supplied equipment and expertise and the affluent Nepalese who skimmed off a profit as the project passed by them.

The author contends that most aid donors look for big projects (they like to have something visible to show off) and that government officials like the big ones too (there's more likely to be something in it for them). The projects that actually work, however, are much closer to ground level. He describes disastrous Japanese irrigation projects, ill-planned Austrian hydroelectric power projects and well-meaning but inept US ecological projects, but also tells of a British agricultural project near Dhankuta in the east which really seemed to work and an Australian forestry project which operated on a shoestring and seemed to work much better because of that.

He concludes, however, by questioning the whole basis of foreign aid in Nepal, and in other countries like Nepal. Along the way he turns up numerous interesting thoughts. Hydroelectric power, for example, is touted as an enormous energy saver but its main use is for electric lighting. Lighting with hydroelectric power generated electricity is much cheaper than with kerosene and a great deal of expensive kerosene can be saved. But with cheap lighting people stay up later and when they stay up they burn firewood. The end result of providing hydroelectric power can actually be an increase in the consumption of scarce timber!

One of the aid project disasters he observed was a tree-planting exercise where the trees were not only badly planted but also planted in an area where the first monsoon deluge washed them away. This totally wasted plantation was fenced in by cutting down healthy trees! Even the whole horror story of Himalayan deforestation is brought

into question. 'The only number which has any scientific validity at all in the Himalaya is sixty-seven', he writes. This is the factor by which estimates of per capita firewood consumption vary.

POPULATION
According to the 1991 census, Nepal's population was nearly 18.5 million. The largest city was Kathmandu, the capital, with more than 668,000 people. The rate of population growth is terrifying. Every year the population increases by nearly 400,000.

In the mountains the rate of increase is lower than in the Terai, but this is because many people are migrating in search of land and work. Despite (or because of) extremely high rates of infant mortality and a life expectancy that is a horrifying 52 years, the overall annual rate of population increase is 2.08%. The rapidly growing human population is putting enormous pressures on Nepal's fragile ecology.

The most recent census figures that give any indication of the ethnic breakdown of the population were collected in 1981. The government has shown no enthusiasm for collecting solid data on ethnicity and caste partly, one suspects, because they would help paint a bleak picture of exploitation and inequality. The following figures actually show population by first language, but there is a high correlation between ethnicity and language, with the probable exception of Nepali.

Language	% of Total Population
Nepali	58.4
Maithili	11.1
Bhojpuri	7.6
Tharu	3.6
Tamang	3.5
Newari	3.0
Abadhi	1.5
Rai	1.5
Magar	1.4
Gurung	1.2
Limbu	0.9
Other	6.3

PEOPLE

Like the geography, the population of the country is extremely diverse and highly complex. Simplistically, Nepal is the meeting point for the Indo-Aryan people of India with the Tibeto-Burman of the Himalaya, but this gives little hint of the dynamic ethnic mosaic that has developed and continues to change to this day.

In a south-north direction, as you move from the plains to the mountains, the ethnic map can be roughly divided into layers: the Terai, the midlands or Pahar zone, and the Himalaya. Each zone is dominated by characteristic ethnic groups whose agriculture and lifestyles are adapted to suit the physical constraints of their environment. (See earlier in this section for more detail about the physiographic features of each area.) These zones can be further subdivided from east to west, with different groups in the east, central and western regions of each zone.

Zone	Western	Central	Eastern
Himalaya	Khas, Bhotiya	Bhotiya	Bhotiya
Midlands	Khas	Magar, Gurung, Newari	Rai, Limbu
Terai	Tharu, Abadhi	Tharu Danuwar Bhojpuri	Danuwar, Mithila

Himalayan Zone

In the Himalayan zone, the people are mongoloids of Tibetan descent. They are known in Nepali as Bhotiya or Bhote, terms that are now often considered derogatory because the Shah and Rana regimes categorised Bhotiya as untouchables who could legally be enslaved.

Most Bhotiya identify with a particular region, and attach the suffix *pa* (people) to the name. These include the Sherpa, of the

Two-Legged Transport
Most ethnic groups are increasingly influenced by Indian and Western fashions, so it is difficult to pick someone's ethnicity by their clothing. The method someone uses to carry a load often provides an interesting clue, however. Mountain people carry goods in woven baskets *(doko)* on their backs, but suspended from a jute headband *(namlo)* worn around the top of the head.

The people from the valleys of the Middle Hills, especially the Newaris, often carry loads slung on bamboo poles balanced across their shoulders. People of the plains, more particularly women, balance goods on their heads. And Westerners carry possessions in bags suspended from their shoulders! ■

Everest region, the Manangpa of the Manang region north of the Annapurna Himal, and the Lopa, of the Mustang region. This group also includes Thakalis, the well-known innkeepers from the Thak Khola (Kali Gandaki) on the Jomsom Trek, and Tamangs, around the Kathmandu Valley and the Langtang region.

With a few exceptions in the far west, all these people are Buddhist (or Lamaist as Tibetan Buddhists are sometimes known) and have a similar culture to Tibetans.

Midlands Zone

In the east of the midlands zone, one finds the Kirati (also known as Kiranti) people, which are divided into the Rai and Limbu groups. These groups are also mongoloid peoples who speak Tibeto-Burman languages. Their religion is shamanistic – neither Buddhist or Hindu – although Hinduism is becoming increasingly influential. They entered Nepal from the north and east and founded a kingdom in the Kathmandu Valley around the 7th century BCE that continued for 1000 years. Independent Kirati kingdoms survived in the east until the end of the 18th century.

In the central midlands zone around the Kathmandu Valley live the Newaris. Some believe the Newaris are Kirati, others believe that they are survivors from a still older group. They have absorbed successive waves of immigrants and created a religious environment that is in many ways a synthesis of Hinduism and Buddhism.

In the central midlands around the Kali Gandaki, the two main groups are the Magar and Gurung. Both groups are mongoloid and speak Tibeto-Burman languages, which indicates they came from Tibet, although no-one knows when. The Gurungs tend to occupy middle elevations to the southern flanks of the Annapurna massif, while the Magars occupy lower elevations.

The Gurung's shamanistic religion is under pressure from Hinduism in the south and Buddhism in the north. The Magars have long been Hindu, and have developed close ties with the Indo-Aryan Khas, further to the west. In many cases they have taken the

high-status Chhetri (Kshatriya) caste. Until the 18th century Magar kingdoms dominated the region. The most famous was Palpa, with its capital at Tansen, which fought alongside Gurkha at the beginning of Prithvi Narayan Shah's expansionist wars. (See the earlier History section for more details.)

In the western midlands, the situation becomes confusing, partly because there are few written historical records and ethnicity becomes confused with caste. The area is dominated by Khas, an Indo-Aryan people whose language has evolved into present day Nepali. The numbers of Khas have been continually supplemented by the arrival of Parbatiyas (Hindus of varying caste and ethnicity) from the Indian plains. In the 12th century the Khas, who controlled a large empire, were joined by Bahun (Brahman) and Chhetri refugees from the Muslim invasion of India. Although the Khas were technically low caste, many were given the high Chhetri caste by the Bahun, and the children of Bahun men and Khas women were also made Chhetris.

The unusual fluidity of caste allowed ambitious families to adopt higher castes – the most powerful Chhetris from among the Khas and Magar became Thakuris. The Khas empire fragmented into many small kingdoms ruled by powerful families who further embellished their pedigrees by claiming royal antecedents in India. After Prithvi Narayan Shah's triumph, many Bahuns and Chhetris were rewarded with grants of land in central and eastern Nepal, and since then they have spread throughout the country. In the west, however, they are numerically dominant.

Terai Zone

Until the eradication of malaria in the 1950s the only people to live in the valleys of the Inner Terai, and along much of the length of the Terai proper, were Tharus and a few small, associated groups. Most Tharus, though not all, have a mongoloid appearance. There is considerable speculation, but no hard facts about where they originated.

Their religion is animist, with increasingly important Hindu overtones.

Along the Terai proper, a number of numerically significant groups straddle the border between India and Nepal. In the eastern Terai, Mithila people dominate; in the central Terai, Bhojpuri-speaking people dominate, and in the western Terai, Abadhi-speaking people are significant. All these are essentially cultures of the Gangetic plain, and Hindu caste structure is strictly upheld. In various parts, notably around Nepalganj and Lumbini, there are also large numbers of Muslims.

Since the Terai has been opened for development, it has also been settled by large numbers of people from the midlands – every group is represented.

Sherpas

Living high in the mountains of eastern and central Nepal, in particular in the Solu Khumbu region at the foot of Mt Everest, the Sherpas are probably the best known Nepalese ethnic group. Originally from Tibet, they settled in the area about 500 years ago, and were probably nomadic herders until the introduction of the potato in the middle of the 19th century. The relative increase in wealth that this new crop created allowed them to settle in permanent villages and to create a number of monasteries known as gompas.

The Sherpas are Buddhists, and this century their name has become synonymous with mountaineering and trekking. Not all sherpas – the small 's' word describes a trek guide or mountaineer – are Sherpas but many of them are and they've won worldwide fame for their skill, hardiness and loyalty.

Thakalis

Originating along the Kali Gandaki Valley in central Nepal, the Thakalis are a Tibeto-Burman people who have become the entrepreneurs of Nepal. They honed these skills from the days when they played an important part in the salt trade between the subcontinent and Tibet but now they are found in many areas of modern commercial life. Originally Buddhist, many pragmatic Thakalis have now adopted Hinduism.

Sherpa woman weaving

Most Thakalis are small farmers, but travellers will regularly meet them in their adopted roles as hoteliers. Many small hotels in Nepal are run by Thakalis; the Pokhara to Jomsom trek along the Kali Gandaki Valley is the best 'village inn' trek in Nepal, because of the numerous Thakali lodges along this route through their homeland. The actual number of Thakalis is very small.

Tamangs

Tamangs are the largest Tibeto-Burman ethnic group in Nepal, but unlike many smaller groups, little is known of their history. *Tamang* means 'horse trader' in Tibetan and gives one clue to their past, although most are now sedentary farmers and labourers. Their appearance, language and Lamaist Buddhist beliefs all bear testimony to their origins. Indeed, many of the 'Tibetan' souvenirs for sale in Kathmandu are actually made by Tamangs.

Tamang people

Around half the Himalayan zone of Nepal is inhabited by Tamangs, and it is likely they have been there longer than any other group. Tamangs dominate the high hills surrounding the Kathmandu Valley and the central Himalayan zone, especially in the Langtang region. Unlike the Newaris, their homesteads are often solitary. Houses may be constructed out of brick or stone, but they are often modest in size with a porch and courtyard, a mud finish and a thatched roof.

Many Tamangs have been influenced in their dress by both Western and Newari styles. Traditionally, women wear a colourful wraparound skirt, a blouse, jacket and scarf. On important occasions they wear chunky gold or brass ear and nose rings set with semiprecious stones. Men wear loincloths or the traditional Newari pants, short-sleeved jackets and topis. Both men and women wear several metres of cloth wrapped around the waist.

Their religion is closely associated with Tibetan Lamaism (see the Religion section later in this chapter). Some Tamang follow Bon, the pre-Buddhist religion of Tibet, but the differences are not great. In Tamang areas you are certain to come across *chortens*

(Buddhist shrines with a square base, topped with an onion-shaped dome), and *mani* (prayer stones engraved with mantras).

Tamangs are one of the largest groups in Nepal, but they have been seriously exploited, especially since the unification of Nepal under the Shahs. In the 19th century their legally defined status was the lowest of any hill people, and much of their land was distributed to Bahuns and Chhetris.

Tamangs were relegated to bonded labour, and were dependent on menial work, particularly as porters. They were prevented from joining the government or the military (unlike many other hill groups). They remain, in general, extremely poor and continue to work as porters, *thela gada* (cart pushers), rickshaw pullers and autorickshaw drivers. They produce more than 90% of the thangka paintings sold in Kathmandu, and 70% of Tibetan carpets. Many women have been forced into prostitution, both in Nepal and India.

Tibetans

Mongoloid people from Tibet have settled in Nepal for thousands of years – but the most recent arrivals have been refugees. In 1950 the communist People's Republic of China overpowered the Tibetan army. For the next eight years the Chinese made a heavy-handed attempt to bring the Tibetans into the communist fold, including the imposition of inappropriate agricultural policies that led to mass famine. In March 1959 a Tibetan uprising was brutally crushed, and the Dalai Lama, Tibet's spiritual and political leader fled to India. Thousands of Tibetans followed him across the Himalaya.

There are currently around 120,000 Tibetans in exile, and about 12,000 of them are in Nepal, mostly in Kathmandu and Pokhara. Although their numbers are only small, they have a high profile, partly because of the important role they play in tourism. Many hotels and restaurants in Kathmandu are owned or operated by Tibetans. They have also been responsible for the extraordinary success story of the Tibetan carpet industry, which has grown in 30 years from nothing to the largest single employer in the country. (See the earlier Economy section.)

Tibetans are devout Buddhists and their arrival in the valley has rejuvenated a number of important religious sites, most notably the stupas at Swayambhunath and Bodhnath. A number of large new monasteries have been established.

Rai & Limbu

These two large groups are known as Kirati people, the descendants of the Kiratis who formed the first recorded kingdom in the Kathmandu Valley. They now inhabit the eastern midlands, and many have migrated to the eastern Terai. Large numbers find employment with Gurkha regiments.

They are Tibeto-Burman people, but their traditional religion is distinct from either Buddhism or Hinduism, although Hinduism is exerting a growing influence. The traditional religion is entirely oral and is based on the periodic appeasement of ancestor divinities and nature spirits; there are priests, elders and shamans. Rais and Limbus both bury their dead. The Limbus use a common burial site and erect a whitewashed rectangu-

lar grave marker with three tiers for a female, four for men.

The Rais and Limbus cultivate wet and dry fields, and slash and burn shifting agriculture is still important in places. In the hills, most villages are scattered and the houses are small one- storey edifices built of stone. Along the Arun River and in the Terai, the houses are often timber and bamboo, built on high wooden piles. In the Terai, these houses can be large, and are often surrounded by a verandah.

Newaris

The Newaris of the Kathmandu Valley are a good example of the result of this Himalayan melting pot. They number about 600,000 and speak Newari, a language distinct from Tibetan, Nepali or Hindi, and they follow a version of Hinduism with many Buddhist overtones. See the Kathmandu, Patan & Bhaktapur chapter for more details.

Gurungs

The Gurungs tend to live in higher country and generally further to the east than the Magars, but otherwise are similar to them in many respects. Their homeland is the central midlands, ranging from Gorkha and Baglung to quite high on the southern slopes of the Annapurnas. They are a Tibeto-Burman people with a unique shamanistic religion that is gradually giving way to Hinduism and Buddhism.

They are farmers, raising rice, wheat, maize and millet. Sheep husbandry is also important, with village families contributing a handful of sheep to a larger village flock. During the summer months they move their sheep to higher pastures, then with the end of the monsoon they bring them down to the villages. Like the Magars, the Gurungs also often work as Gurkha soldiers.

Magars

A numerically large group, the Magars are a Tibeto-Burman people who are found in many parts of the midlands zone of western and central Nepal. Until the 18th century they had their own kingdoms, but they also had close contact with the Hindu Indo-Aryans in the west. This led to a gradual increase in Hindu influence and cultural assimilation. Nowadays in terms of religion, farming practices, housing and dress, they are hard to distinguish from Chhetris.

The Magars fought with Prithvi Narayan Shah, and their kingdom of Palpa (based at Tansen) was one of the last to be incorporated into the new unified Nepal. Their martial qualities have been further recognised by the British and Indian armies, since Magars are the single largest group in the Gurkha regiments. Gurkha earnings play an enormously important role, both in improving living standards in the villages, and in the Nepalese economy as a whole.

The Magars generally live in two-storey rectangular or square thatched houses washed in red clay. Historically, these houses were often round or oval in shape. They are farmers, and renowned soldiers. A large number have been recruited to overseas Gurkha forces. The Magars also include Thakalis, the well-known innkeepers from the Kali Gandaki Valley (known locally as the Thak Khola) on the Jomsom Trek, and the Tamangs, from around the Kathmandu Valley and the Langtang region.

Bahuns & Chhetris

In Hindu theory there is no relationship between caste and ethnicity, so Bahuns and Chhetris are simply the two highest castes (respectively the Brahman priests and Kshatriya warriors). In Nepal, however, most are from the Khas kingdoms that flourished in western Nepal for at least a millennia before the unification of Nepal.

The Khas are Indo-Aryans who migrated to Nepal over the centuries; in the Middle Ages their numbers, and their consciousness of caste, were supplemented by refugees from the Muslim invasions of India. The progeny of Bahun men and hill women were considered Chhetri, and a number of high-status families from other hill groups have also adopted Chhetri status, so some do have mongoloid tribal ancestry.

Bahuns and Chhetris played an important role in the court and armies of Prithvi Narayan Shah, and after unification they were rewarded with lands throughout the country. The Khas' language Khas Kura, became the national language Nepali, and the position of Bahuns and Chhetris at the top of the heap was religiously, culturally and legally enforced. Ever since, they have dominated the processes of government in Kathmandu – 57% of the new democratic parliament are Bahun and Chhetri.

Outside the valley, the majority of Bahuns and Chhetris, however, are simple peasant farmers, indistinguishable in most respects from their neighbours. Sometimes their wealth is reflected by relatively large houses (compared to those of neighbouring tribal groups). Most live in two-storey stone, or mud-brick, thatched houses that are washed with lime or red ochre. Many had roles as tax collectors under the Shah and Rana regimes, and to this day many are moneylenders with a great deal of power.

All Bahuns and Chhetris are Hindu, but the Bahuns tend to be more caste-conscious and orthodox than other Nepalese Hindus and this sometimes creates difficulties in their relationship with 'untouchable' Westerners. Many are vegetarians and do not drink alcohol; marriages are arranged within the caste.

There is no particular dress by which they can be recognised but men in both castes wear a sacred thread – the *janai* (see Janai Purnima under Cultural Events in the Facts for the Visitor chapter).

Tharus

Tharus are one of the largest ethnic groups in Nepal. The original inhabitants of the Terai, they are now often heavily exploited by newly arrived hill people, or *zamindars* (moneylenders). Many have been forced by debt into a form of bonded labour (the *kamaiya* system) little different to slavery. They are generally mongoloid in appearance, and have an animist religion that is increasingly influenced by Hinduism. See the Terai chapter for more information.

CULTURE & CUSTOMS

Nepal has always been a dividing line between civilisations and cultures, and a crossroads for the flow of commerce and culture between them. Here the plains of the subcontinent climb up to the high plateau of Tibet, the languages and people of India give way to those of China, and the Hindu religion blends into Buddhism. Nepal, the land at the margin, is often a complex blend of the two influences and this variation is further complicated by the diversity of ethnic groups within the country.

Avoiding Offence

The challenge for you as a visitor to Nepal is to respect the rights and beliefs of the local people, and to minimise your impact – culturally and environmentally. Remember Nepal is not an adventure park or museum established for your convenience, but home to a vital, changing culture. Life for many is extremely hard, but despite the scarcity of material possessions, there are many qualities that shame the so-called 'developed' world.

Your very presence in Nepal will have an effect – an increasing number of people say a negative one. In a totally different culture it is also inevitable that the visitor will make some gaffe at some point. Most Nepalese make allowances, but they do appreciate it when a genuine effort is made to observe local customs. Following is a miscellaneous collection of simple suggestions that will help avoid offence.

Dress

• Always remove your shoes before entering a Nepalese home.
• Dress appropriately – shorts or revealing clothes are never suitable for women. Shorts are acceptable for men when trekking but going without a shirt is not. Nudity is not acceptable anywhere.

Behaviour

• Public displays of affection are frowned upon. Nepalese men often walk around hand in hand, but this does not have the same implications as it does in San Francisco!
• Raising your voice or shouting shows extreme bad manners and will not solve your problem, whatever it might be. Always try to remain cool, calm and collected.
• Bodily contact is rarely made, even for shaking hands, although amongst Nepalese men with frequent Western connections it is becoming more accepted. Never touch anything or point at anything with your feet, the 'lowest' part of the body. In contrast the head is spiritually the 'highest' part of the body, so don't pat children on the head.
• Don't inquire about a person's caste.
• The Nepalese do not like to give negative answers or no answer at all: if you are given a wrong direction or told a place is much nearer than it turns out to be, it may be through fear of disappointing you!
• Don't encourage begging children. The 'give me one rupee, school pen, bonbons' requests become very tedious in some places and acceding to them will only make them worse. If you want to help there are lots of excellent aid organisations which will make good use of your contribution. (See the Begging section in this chapter.) Local schools will be only too happy with a gift of ballpoint pens.

Visiting a Temple

• Always walk clockwise around Buddhist stupas, chortens or mani walls. Always remove your shoes before entering a Buddhist or Hindu temple or sanctuary. You may also have to remove any items made from leather such as belts and bags. Many Hindu temples do not permit Westerners to enter.
• It's the custom to give a white scarf or *khata* to a Buddhist abbot or *rimpoche* when you are introduced. The scarves can easily be found at Tibetan shops.

Visiting a Nepalese Home

• Fire is sacred so do not throw rubbish into it. This particularly applies to a kitchen fire in a Nepalese home and theoretically should apply to a camping site fire when trekking as well. In practice, burning the garbage before leaving camp is accepted, but it's probably best to wait until just before leaving camp before doing it, certainly not before cooking. In a Nepalese home the kitchen is off limits to strangers.

• Avoid 'polluting' food by inadvertently touching it or bringing it into contact with a used plate or utensil. Using your own fork or spoon to serve out more food will do this. Putting your used plate on a buffet table risks making the food still on the table *jutho* or polluted. Notice how the Nepalese drink from a cup or water vessel without letting it touch their lips.

Photography

• Do not intrude with a camera, unless it is clearly OK with the people you are photographing. Ask before entering a temple compound whether it is permissible to enter and take photographs. Do not exchange addresses or offer copies of photos unless you definitely intend to follow it up later.

ARTS

The whole Kathmandu Valley is really one enormous art gallery and museum, but the arts and architecture in Nepal are inextricably intermingled. The finest woodcarving

Begging

Begging of various kinds is relatively common in Nepal, partly because both Hinduism and Buddhism encourage the giving of alms. This presents many visitors with a heart-rending moral dilemma. Should you give? Sometimes, especially if you've just spent Rs 500 (US$10) on drinks, it seems grotesque to ignore someone who is genuinely in need. It is often worth checking to see how the local Nepalese react; if they give, it's a reasonably safe assumption that the beneficiary is genuine.

Around the main religious shrines, especially Pashupatinath, there are long lines of beggars. Pilgrims customarily give a coin to everyone in the line (there are special moneychangers nearby who will change notes for small-denomination coins). This is a culturally sanctioned and traditional form, but most Westerners find it difficult to deal with, and are not really expected to give. Sadhus are another special case, and are usually completely dependent on alms. There are plenty of con men amongst their ranks, but equally, plenty of genuine holy men.

The main tourist centres, especially Thamel and Durbar Marg, have also attracted numbers of beggars. Here, Westerners are expected to give, although whether they should is another matter.

Thamel attracts many of Kathmandu's estimated 1000 street kids. Giving to them, however, is, at best, a double-edged sword. Firstly, the lure of easy money actually attracts kids onto the streets in the first place, and then gives them a powerful incentive to remain. Secondly, it's a dog-eat-dog world, and if a child is seen receiving money, he may well be beaten up and have it stolen.

If you do want to give in this case, it is immensely preferable to give a donation to Child Workers in Nepal, an excellent organisation known as CWIN. This is a nongovernmental organisation that was established by graduates from Tribhuvan University in 1987. Apart from actively campaigning for children's rights, it has established a common room where street children are given a locker (essential if they are going to accumulate any possessions or money), counselling, medical care, literacy classes, a midday meal, and entertainment facilities. CWIN runs a programme called Friends of CWIN (☎ 01-271658, 270336), which encourages various forms of voluntary participation. The common room is off Tripureshwar Marg, and can be contacted through PO Box 4374, Kaumati, Kathmandu.

Also highly visible are women, usually clutching one or two children. Rumours suggest that these women are often part of organised begging rings, and that the money they receive is passed on to a Fagan figure. By giving to them, you are encouraging a further influx of people into Kathmandu where very few facilities exist for them. In this case, your money could be profitably used by a number of craft shops that specialise in marketing handcrafts produced by low-income women. These are nonprofit development organisations, so the money actually goes to the craftspeople in the form of fair wages (as opposed to charity), and also in training, product development, and rehabilitation programmes.

One of the best of these organisations is Mahaguthi (☎ 01-521493) PO Box 396, Kathmandu, which was established with the help of Oxfam. It now has three shops and sells a wide range of crafts produced by thousands of people. Among other things it runs a programme to rehabilitate destitute women and children. Dhankuta Sisters is an outlet for women from the eastern hills, and Dhukuti also works with low-income women. All three have shops on the way to Patan, in Kopundol, just beyond the bridge over the Bagmati River.

Actually in Patan, near the well-known Kumbeshwar Temple, the Kumbeshwar Technical School (☎ 01- 522271) PO Box 2181, Kathmandu, was established to help provide the untouchable community of Patan with skills. They now produce excellent carpets, jumpers and woodwork. See the Kathmandu and Patan Things to Buy sections for more information.

Although the blind and lepers are probably genuinely dependent on begging for their survival, long-term solutions are offered by the Nepal Eye Programme – Australia (☎ 01-474685) PO Box 561, Kathmandu; and the Leprosy Hospital (☎ 01-290545) PO Box 151, Anandban, Kathmandu.

The Nepal Eye Programme – Australia (NEPA) is an innovative and effective programme well known to most Australians because of the involvement of the late Professor Fred Hollows. Many forms of blindness are dealt with in rural clinics; often, relatively simple treatments and surgical techniques can restore people's sight. NEPA is planning to open a factory to manufacture the plastic lenses used in cataract operations. Excess production will be exported to India and China and any profits will be ploughed back into the programme, hopefully making it self-sustaining. In the meantime, NEPA can do with donations.

In the countryside, visitors will quickly be discovered by small children who chant a mantra that sounds something like: 'bonbonpenonerupeeee?'. Someone, somewhere started giving children sweets (bonbons), pens and money, and it sometimes seems that every child in Nepal now tries their luck. Do not encourage this behaviour. Most Nepalese find it offensive and demeaning (as do most visitors), and it encourages a whole range of unhealthy attitudes.

See the Kathmandu Information section for a list of nongovernmental organisations to which you can make donations. ■

and the best sculpture are often part of a building – a temple is simply not a temple without its finely carved roof struts. The crafts also reflect the uniquely Nepalese melting pot where Hindu art has Tantric Buddhist overtones and the dividing line between one religion and another is hard to discern.

Lydia Aran's *The Art of Nepal* (Sahayogi Prakashan, Kathmandu, 1978) is a handy and interesting introduction to Nepalese art and its religious background. There are detailed descriptions of the many Hindu, Buddhist and Hindu-Buddhist deities and their associated religious terminology. This book is particularly interesting because it concentrates on the art actually in Nepal, as opposed to objects in overseas museums and private collections.

Architecture & Sculpture

The earliest architecture in the valley has faded with history. The four Ashoka stupas of Patan are simply grassy mounds today and the great stupas of Swayambhunath and Bodhnath have undoubtedly changed many times over the centuries. Nevertheless these simple hemispherical Buddhist structures are essentially unchanged from their earliest appearance – they're simply a solid mound rising from the ground and topped with a spire. You can find similar Buddhist stupas in Sri Lanka, Myanmar (Burma) and Thailand.

The Licchavi period from the 4th to 9th centuries CE was a golden age for Nepal and while the temples may have disappeared the superb stone sculptures can still be found. Many temples around the valley have beautiful pieces of Licchavi craftwork in their courtyards, the temple of Changu Narayan at the eastern end of the valley in particular. The great reclining Vishnu image at Budhanilkantha is another wonderful example of Licchavi stonework.

The Licchavis undoubtedly worked in wood as well but wood is a perishable substance and no wooden buildings or carvings survive from that era. It was in the Malla period that the Nepalese artistry with wood really came into its own. The earliest wood-carving in the valley dates from the 12th and 13th centuries and includes the roof struts of the great Basantapur Tower in the old Royal Palace in Kathmandu's Durbar Square, and the Kasthamandap building, also in the square, from which the town takes its name. The Uku Bahal monastery in Patan also dates from this period but you have to go out of the valley to Panauti, near Banepa, to find one of the oldest and finest survivors in the shape of the Indreshwar Mahadev Temple.

The artistic skills of the Newari people of the valley flourished under the Mallas and not only woodcarving but metalwork, terra-cotta, brickwork, stone sculptures and other crafts all enjoyed a long golden age. The finest metalwork includes the images of the two Tara goddesses at Swayambhunath and the river goddesses Ganga and Jamuna, standing guard in the palace of Patan.

The spread of the multiroofed Nepalese pagoda design to China and eastern Asia is credited to the architect Arniko, who with 24 assistants visited Tibet in the late 13th century and later also worked for the Ming emperor. The road to the Tibetan border is named the Arniko Highway in his honour. The contact with Tibet also began to make its way back to Nepal and the vivid Tibetan colours and fantastic Tibetan creatures also started to appear in Nepalese art and archi-tecture.

The last centuries of the Malla period saw temple after temple rise over the Kathmandu Valley skyline. The squabbling city-states of Kathmandu, Patan and Bhaktapur vied with each other to raise yet more glorious temples and palaces. Much of the construction was still in the traditional multiroofed Nepalese pagoda style but there was also a great deal of Indian influence – such as the stone Krishna Mandir of Patan's Durbar Square or the spires of the Mahabouddha Temple in Patan and the two temples at the top of the stairway to Swayambhunath.

With the invasion of the valley by King Prithvi Narayan Shah from Gorkha the great age of Nepalese architecture came to a dra-matic end. The great woodcarved temples and palaces you marvel at in the valley today mainly date from that brilliant period prior to 1767. Although the skills used to build them have lain dormant in the centuries since then, there is no doubt that these skills are still present. When the Hanuman Dhoka palace in Kathmandu and the Tachupal Tole buildings in Bhaktapur were restored in the 1970s the work was performed by purely traditional means and with craftwork every bit as good as in the past. More recently the

Temple architecture, Changu Narayan

Chyasilin Mandapa in Bhaktapur, completely destroyed in the great earthquake of 1934, was totally rebuilt in 1989-90, again using traditional skills.

Painting

Nepal has a long history of painting and some high-quality traditional work is still being done today. The earliest Newari paintings were illuminated manuscripts dating from the 11th century and these were followed by miniature paintings, influenced by the miniature styles of northern India, and then by scrolls and murals. By this time the Tibetan influence was starting to make itself felt on Newari painting, although from the 14th to 16th centuries the Newaris also had a great influence on Tibetan art.

Today some of the best examples of old Newari painting are hung in temples where they are rarely seen but the art gallery in Bhaktapur has a fine collection and is an excellent introduction to the development of art in Nepal. Newari artists have their own special caste of Chitrakar. For more information on painting in Nepal today see the Things to Buy section in the Facts for the Visitor chapter.

Music & Dance

Despite the pervasiveness of Western music, Nepalese music hangs constantly in the air, whether it is the plaintive notes of a flute or the gentle twang of the four-stringed *saringhi*. Although the *gaines*, traditional professional musicians, are a dying breed they can still be heard. The folk music of rural Nepal still has a strong following and the gaines are often as much storytellers as musicians.

The *damais* are modern professional musicians, all drawn from the tailor caste, who form the backbone of wedding bands. This music can definitely be hard on Western ears, falling uncomfortably close to the painful standards of Indian video bus music. The blaring wail of long Tibetan horns at Buddhist religious sites probably also qualifies for the unlistenable category.

Dance also has a long and strong history in Nepal both in cheerfully performed folk dances and in the more formal classical dances. The Newaris of the Kathmandu Valley are the chief exponents of classical dancing, but there are also masked dances with a Tantric background, and the colourful masked dances of Bhaktapur which are performed during the Indra Jatra festival each year.

RELIGION

In Nepal, Hinduism and Buddhism are mingled into a complex blend which is often impossible to separate. The Buddha was actually born in Nepal but the Buddhist religion first arrived in the country around 250 BCE, introduced, so it is said, by the great Indian Buddhist emperor Ashoka himself. Later, Buddhism gave way to Hinduism but from around the 8th century CE the Tantric form of Buddhism practised in Tibet also began to make its way across the Himalaya into Nepal. Today Buddhism is mainly practised by the people of the high Himalaya, like the Sherpas and Tamangs, and by the Tibetan refugees who have settled in Nepal.

Officially Nepal is a Hindu country but in practice the religion is a strange blend of Hindu and Buddhist beliefs with a pantheon of Tantric deities tagged onto the list of Hindu gods or, in many cases, inextricably blended with them. Thus Avalokitesvara, the prime Bodhisattva of this Buddhist era, becomes Lokesvara, a manifestation of the Hindu god Shiva, and then appears as Machhendranath, one of the most popular gods of the Kathmandu Valley. Is he Hindu or Buddhist? Nobody can tell.

Although the vast majority of the population is Hindu or Buddhist there are also small groups of Muslims and Christians. The Muslims are mainly found close to the border with India and in a handful of isolated villages.

Hinduism

India, the Indonesian island of Bali, the Indian Ocean island of Mauritius and possibly Fiji are the only places apart from Nepal where Hindus predominate, but it is the largest religion in Asia in terms of the number of adherents. Hinduism is one of the oldest extant religions with firm roots extending back to beyond 1000 BCE.

The Indus Valley civilisation developed a religion which shows a close relationship to Hinduism in many ways. Later, it further developed on the subcontinent through the combined religious practices of the Dravidians and the Aryan invaders who arrived in northern India around 1500 BCE. Around 1000 BCE, the Vedic scriptures were introduced and gave the first loose framework to the religion.

Hinduism today has a number of holy books, the most important being the four *Vedas*, or 'Divine Knowledge', which are the foundation of Hindu philosophy. The *Upanishads* are contained within the *Vedas* and delve into the metaphysical nature of the universe and soul. The *Mahabharata* is an epic poem describing in over 220,000 lines the battles between the Kauravas and Pandavas. It contains the story of Rama, and it is probable that the most famous Hindu epic, the *Ramayana*, was based on this. The *Bhagavad Gita* is a famous episode of the *Mahabharata* where Krishna relates his philosophies to Arjuna.

Hinduism postulates that we will all go through a series of rebirths or reincarnations that eventually lead to *moksha*, the spiritual salvation which frees one from the cycle of rebirths. With each rebirth you can move closer to or further from eventual moksha; the deciding factor is your *karma*, which is literally a law of cause and effect. Bad actions during your life result in bad karma, which ends in a lower reincarnation. Conversely, if your deeds and actions have been good you will reincarnate on a higher level and be a step closer to eventual freedom from rebirth.

Dharma is the natural law which defines the total social, ethical and spiritual harmony of your life. There are three categories of dharma, the first being the eternal harmony which involves the whole universe. The second category is the dharma that controls castes and the relations between castes. The third dharma is the moral code which an individual should follow.

The Hindu religion has three basic practices. They are *puja* or worship, the cremation of the dead, and the rules and regulations of the caste system. There are four main castes: the Brahman, or priest caste; the Kshatriya, or soldiers and governors; the Vaisyas, or tradespeople and farmers; and the Sudras or menial workers and craftspeople. These castes are then subdivided, although this is not taken to the same extreme in Nepal as in India. Beneath all the castes are the Harijans, or untouchables, the lowest, casteless class for whom all the most menial and degrading tasks are reserved.

Westerners have trouble understanding Hinduism principally because of its vast pantheon of gods. In fact you can look upon all these different gods simply as pictorial representations of the many attributes of a god. The one omnipresent god usually has three physical representations: Brahma is the creator, Vishnu is the preserver and Shiva is the destroyer and reproducer. All three gods are usually shown with four arms, but Brahma has the added advantage of four heads.

Each god has an associated animal known as the 'vehicle' on which they ride, as well as a consort with certain attributes and abilities. Generally each god also holds symbols. You can often pick out which god is represented by identifying either the vehicle or the symbols.

Most temples are dedicated to one or other of the gods, but most Hindus profess to be either Vaishnavites (followers of Vishnu) or Shaivites (followers of Shiva). A variety of lesser gods and goddesses also crowd the scene. The cow is, of course, the holy animal of Hinduism.

Hinduism is not a proselytising religion since you cannot be converted. You're either born a Hindu or you are not; you can never become one. Similarly, once you are a Hindu you cannot change your caste – you're born into it and are stuck with it for the rest of that lifetime. Nevertheless Hinduism has a great

Sadhus

Sadhus are often people who have decided that their business and family life have reached their natural conclusions and that it is time to throw everything aside and go out on a spiritual search. They may have been anything from the village postal worker, to a wealthy business person. Many sadhus are, of course, simply beggars and con men following a more sophisticated approach to gathering in the *paisa* (money), but others are completely genuine in their search.

Sadhus perform various feats of self-mortification and wander all over the subcontinent, occasionally coming together in pilgrimages and other religious gatherings *(melas)*. Most sadhus follow Shiva and are known as Shaivas, but there are also those who follow Vishnu and are known as Vaishnavas.

The sadhus you see around Pashupatinath are Shaivas, and can be further recognised by Shiva's symbol, the trident, which they carry. Shaivas apply lines *(tilaka)* to their foreheads in horizontal stripes. Vaishnavas are numerous at Janakpur. They don't carry a symbol but the tilaka on their forehead consists of vertical lines – sometimes three vertical lines that look confusingly like a trident. ∎

attraction for many Westerners and India's 'export gurus' are numerous and successful.

A guru is not so much a teacher as a spiritual guide, somebody who by example or simply by their presence indicates what path you should follow. In a spiritual search one always needs a guru. A sadhu is an individual on a spiritual search. They're an easily recognised group, usually wandering around half-naked, smeared in dust with their hair and beard matted.

Buddhism

Strictly speaking, Buddhism is not a religion, since it is not centred on a god, but a system of philosophy and a code of morality. Buddhism was founded in northern India about 500 BCE when Siddhartha Gautama, born a prince, achieved enlightenment. According to some, Gautama Buddha was not the first Buddha but the fourth, and neither is he expected to be the last 'enlightened one'. Buddhists believe that the achievement of enlightenment is the goal of every being so eventually we will all reach Budddhahood.

The Buddha never wrote down his dharma or teachings, and a schism later developed so that today there are two major Buddhist schools. The Theravada ('doctrine of the elders') or Hinayana ('lesser vehicle') holds that the path to nirvana, the eventual aim of all Buddhists, is an individual pursuit. In contrast, the Mahayana ('great vehicle') school holds that the combined belief of its

followers will eventually be great enough to encompass all of humanity and bear it to salvation. To some, the less austere and ascetic Mahayana school is a 'soft option'. Today it is chiefly practised in Vietnam, Japan and China, while the Hinayana school is followed in Sri Lanka, Myanmar (Burma) and Thailand. There are still other, sometimes more esoteric, divisions of Buddhism including the Hindu-Tantric Buddhism of Tibet which is the version found in Nepal.

The Buddha renounced his material life to search for enlightenment but, unlike other prophets, found that starvation did not lead to discovery. Therefore he developed his rule of the 'middle way', meaning moderation in all things. The Buddha taught that all life is suffering, but that suffering comes from our sensual desires and the illusion that they are important. By following the 'eightfold path' these desires will be extinguished and a state of nirvana, where they are extinct and we are free from their delusions, will be reached. Following this process requires going through a series of rebirths until the goal is eventually reached and no more rebirths into the world of suffering are necessary. The path that takes you through this cycle of births is karma, but this is not simply fate. Karma is a law of cause and effect; your actions in one life determine the role you will play and what you will have to go through in your next life.

In India Buddhism developed rapidly

when it was embraced by the great emperor Ashoka. As his empire extended over much of the subcontinent, so Buddhism was carried forth. Later, however, Buddhism began to contract in India because it had never really taken a hold on the great mass of people. As Hinduism revived, Buddhism in India was gradually reabsorbed into the older religion.

The Gods of Nepal

There are so many gods, and related auspicious beings, in Nepal that being able to identify some of them makes understanding and enjoying Nepalese culture much easier. The definitions that follow include the most interesting and most frequently encountered 'big names' plus associated creatures, consorts, vehicles and religious terminology.

Incarnations, Manifestations & Aspects

There's a subtle difference between these three possibilities, something not easily grasped by the Western mind! Vishnu has incarnations, 10 of them in all. They include Narsingha, the man-lion, Krishna the cowherd and Buddha the teacher. Shiva, on the other hand, may be the god of 1000 names but these are manifestations – what he shows himself as – not incarnations. He is a god of many manifestations but few incarnations. When you start to look at the Buddhist 'gods' their various appearances are aspects rather than incarnations or manifestations.

Shiva Shiva is probably the most important god in Nepal – as creator and destroyer – so it's important to keep on his good side! Shiva is often represented by the phallic lingam, symbolic of his creative role. His vehicle is the bull Nandi and you'll often see this figure outside Shiva temples; there's a huge Nandi guarding the entrance to Pashupatinath. The symbol most often seen in Shiva's hand is the trident or *trisul*. Sadhus, the wandering pilgrims who are often followers of Shiva, frequently carry a trident.

Shiva is also known as Nataraja, the cosmic dancer whose dance shook the cosmos and created the world. Shiva's home

is Mt Kailash in the Himalaya, but across the border in Tibet, and he's also supposed to be keen on smoking hashish. He takes various forms including peaceful Pashupati and destructive Bhairab. Usually his fearsome side is handled by his *shakti* or consort (see the later Shakti section); sacrifices are usually made not to the male but to the female and must be of male animals.

Shiva

Bhairab In Nepal Shiva appears as Bhairab when he is in his fearful or 'terrific' form. Bhairab can appear in 64 different ways but none of them is pretty. Typically he has multiple arms, each clutching a weapon, he dances on a body and wears a headress of skulls. More skulls dangle from his belt, and his staring eyes and bared fangs complete the

Brahma

through Lokesvara, the lord of the world. Machhendranath is then a manifestation of Lokesvara.

Brahma Brahma, despite his supreme position, appears much less often than Shiva or Vishnu. Like those gods he has four arms but Brahma also has four heads, to represent his all-seeing presence. The four *Vedas* are supposed to have emanated from his mouths.

Ganesh With his elephant head Ganesh is probably the most easily recognised of the gods and also the most popular. Ganesh is the god of prosperity and wisdom and there are many Ganesh shrines and temples in Nepal. Ganesh's parents are Shiva and Parvati and he obtained his elephant head due to his father's notorious temper. Coming back from a long trip, Shiva discovered Parvati in bed with a young man. Not pausing to think that their son might have grown up a little during his absence, Shiva lopped his head off! He was then forced by Parvati to bring his son back to life but could only do so by giving him the head of the first living thing he saw – which happened to be an elephant.

Shiva and Parvati's other son is Kumar, the god of war. He is also known as Kartikkaya.

picture. Bhairab is usually black, carries a cup made from a human skull and is attended by a dog. The gruesome figure of Bhairab near the Hanuman Dhoka palace entrance in Kathmandu is a good example of this fearsome god at his worst.

Pashupati In the Kathmandu Valley Shiva is most popularly worshipped as Pashupati, the lord of the beasts. As the keeper of all living things Pashupati is Shiva in a good mood and the temple of Pashupatinath is the most important Hindu temple in the country.

Machhendranath Machhendranath is a strictly Nepalese Hindu god who has power over the rains and the monsoon. It's typical of the intermingling of Hindu and Buddhist beliefs in Nepal that, in the Kathmandu Valley at least, Machhendranath has come to be thought of as an incarnation of Avalokitesvara, the Bodhisattva of our era. In actual fact the connection from Avalokitesvara to Machhendranath is not quite so direct. Purely Buddhist Avalokitesvara is linked with Shiva

Ganesh

Hanuman & Medicine

Hanuman the monkey god has an important medicinal connection in Nepal and other Hindu countries. The *Ramayana* recounts how Rama desperately needed a rare herb grown only in the Himalaya and sent Hanuman to procure it for him. Unfortunately by the time he arrived in the mountains Hanuman had forgotten specifically which herb he had been requested to bring back, but got around the problem by simply grabbing a whole mountain, confident that somewhere on the mountain would be the required plant.

On the walls of the Bir Hospital in Kathmandu you can see a large illustration of Hanuman flying through the air, tightly clasping a whole mountain. It's said that he paused for a rest on the banks of the Hanumante River in Bhaktapur and another picture of this event can be seen there. ∎

Hanuman

Hanuman Hanuman is the monkey god, the important character from the *Ramayana* who came to the aid of Rama and helped to defeat the evil Rawana and release Sita from his grasp. Hanuman's trustworthy and alert nature is commemorated by the many statues of Hanuman seen guarding palace entrances. The best known in Nepal is the image of Hanuman which stands beside the old Royal Palace entrance in Kathmandu, and indeed gives the old palace its name of Hanuman Dhoka.

Vishnu Vishnu is the preserver, although in Nepal, where he often appears as Narayan, he also plays a role in the original creation of the universe. Narayan is the reclining Vishnu, sleeping on the cosmic ocean, and from his navel appears Brahma, who creates the universe.

Vishnu has four arms and can often be identified by the symbols he holds – the conch shell or *sankha*, the disc-like weapon known as a *chakra*, the stick-like weapon known as a *gada* and a lotus flower or *padma*. Vishnu's vehicle is the man-bird Garuda and the figure of a Garuda will often be seen kneeling reverently in front of a Vishnu temple. Vishnu's shakti is Lakshmi, the goddess of wealth and prosperity.

Vishnu has 10 incarnations starting with Matsya, the fish. Then he appeared as Kurma, the tortoise on which the universe is built. Number three was his boar incarnation as Varaha, who destroyed a demon who would have drowned the world. Vishnu was again in a demon-destroying mood in incarnation four as Narsingha (or Narsimha), half man and half lion. See the Changu Narayan section in the Around the Kathmandu Valley chapter for the legend behind this appearance. Narsingha statues often show a man with a lion's head and four arms holding the traditional Vishnu symbols. On the man-lion's lap will be the demon which Narsingha is about to disembowel.

Still facing difficulties from demons, Vishnu's next incarnation was Vamana, the dwarf who reclaimed the world from the demon-king Bali. The dwarf politely asked

Vishnu

and still managed to remain devoted to his wife Radha. The Bhakti cult follow this passionate and happy incarnation.

For number nine Vishnu appeared as the teacher, the Buddha. Of course the Buddhists don't accept that Buddha was just an incarnation of some other religion's god but perhaps it was just a ploy to bring Hindu converts back into the fold? Incarnation 10? Well we haven't seen that one yet but it will be as Kalki the destroyer, when Vishnu wields the sword which will destroy the world at the end of the Kaliyuga, the age which we are currently in.

Krishna

the demon for a patch of ground upon which to meditate, saying that the patch need only be big enough that he, the dwarf, could walk across it in three paces. The demon agreed, only to see the dwarf swell into a giant who strode across the universe in three gigantic steps. Vishnu as the 'long strider' is often seen with his left leg raised, just about to take a mighty step.

In his sixth incarnation Vishnu appeared as Parasurama, a warlike Brahman who proceeded to put the warrior caste Chhetris in their place. The noble Rajputs of India's state of Rajasthan claim they are descended from the survivors of this clash with a god.

Incarnation seven was as Rama, the hero of the *Ramayana* who, with help from Hanuman the monkey god, rescued his beautiful wife Sita from the clutches of Rawana, evil king of Lanka. See the Janakpur section for more information on the *Ramayana* – Sita is believed to have been born in Janakpur, and this is also where she and Rama married.

Incarnation eight was a gentle and much-loved one when Vishnu appeared as Krishna, the fun-loving cowherd, who dallied with the *gopis* or milkmaids, danced, played his flute

Garuda The Garuda is the faithful man-bird vehicle of Vishnu and a winged Garuda statue will often be found kneeling reverentially in front of a Vishnu temple. Garuda has an intense hatred of snakes and is often seen destroying them.

Garuda

Shakti A Hindu god's consort is also known as his shakti as she is far more than just a companion. A shakti often symbolises certain parts of a god's personality, so while Shiva is the god of both creation and destruction it is often his shakti Parvati as Kali or Durga who handles the destructive business and demands the blood sacrifices. She is also the energetic and dominant partner in their sexual relationship, and shakti has come to mean any goddess in her energetic and dynamic mode.

The Kathmandu Valley has numerous shrines and temples dedicated to the great goddesses including four shrines dedicated to the Joginis, the mystical goddesses who are the female counterpart to the Bhairabs. These shrines are found near Sankhu at the eastern end of the valley, at Guhyeshwari near Pashupatinath, at Pharping and at Vijeshwari. Another group of four temples are known as *varahis* and are dedicated to shaktis as she-boars. Other shrines to goddesses are dedicated to the Ashta Matrikas, mother goddesses.

Parvati Shiva's shakti is Parvati the beautiful and she is the dynamic element in their relationship. Just as Shiva is also known as Mahadev, the Great God, so she is Mahadevi, the Great Goddess. Just as Shiva is often symbolised by the phallic lingam so his shakti's symbol is the yoni, representing the female sex organ. Their relationship is a sexual one and it is often Parvati who is the energetic and dominant partner.

Parvati

Shiva's shakti has as many forms as the Great God himself. She may be peaceful Parvati but she may also be fearsome Kali, the black goddess, or Durga, the terrible. In these terrific forms she holds a variety of weapons in her 10 hands, struggles with

Kali

demons and rides a lion. As Kali, the fiercest of the gods and goddesses, she demands sacrifices and wears a garland of skulls. The festival of Dasain, celebrated in her honour, is characterised by the sacrifice of animals.

Saraswati The goddess of learning and consort of Brahma. She rides upon a white swan and holds the stringed musical instrument known as a *veena*.

Tara Another deity who appears in both the Hindu and Buddhist pantheons are the Tara goddesses. There are actually 108 different Taras, but the best known are Green Tara and White Tara. They are sometimes believed to be the two wives of King Songtsen Gompo who was the first royal patron of Buddhism in Tibet. The Taras are two of the female consorts to the Dhyani Buddhas. See the Swayambhunath section of the Around the Kathmandu Valley chapter for details of the Dhyani Buddhas and their shaktis.

Vehicles Each of the gods is associated with a particular animal which can either be simply an attendant or a vehicle on which the god may ride. These creatures are a clue to

identifying a god. Vishnu's vehicle, for example, is the man-bird Garuda and the winged kneeling figure of Garuda in front of a temple usually indicates that it is a Vishnu temple. Similarly elephant-headed Ganesh's creature is the rat or shrew and a statue of a rat will indicate that you are in a Ganesh shrine.

Other vehicles include the great bull known as Nandi which is the vehicle of Shiva. Indra, the king of the Vedic gods, has an elephant. Agni, the Vedic god of fire, has a chariot drawn by parrots while Vasudhara, the wife of Jambhala the god of wealth, has a chariot drawn by a pig! Fearsome Bhairab is accompanied by a dog, Yama the god of death by a crow. Ganesh's brother Kartikkaya, the god of war, has a cock. Brahma's consort Saraswati has a swan.

Snakes Snakes make many appearances in Hindu and Buddhist mythology in Nepal. Vishnu images usually have a snake somewhere in the picture and the sleeping Vishnu reclines upon a bed made from the coils of a snake. Vishnu's consort Lakshmi often carries a snake but Garuda, Vishnu's man-bird attendant, has a passionate hatred of snakes and often kills them. Snakes are thought to have power over water so they're important for ensuring a good monsoon. They also appear guarding doorways to prevent evil entering, but if you get bitten by one you can turn to Janguli, the goddess who cures snake bites. Amoghasiddhi, the Dhyani Buddha of the north, sits under a canopy of seven hooded snakes and Vishnu's snake bed also has seven heads which form a canopy for him. The eight snake deities are known as the *nagas* and Anantnag is their king.

LANGUAGE
It's quite easy to get by with English in Nepal; most of the people the average visitor will have to deal with in the Kathmandu Valley and in Pokhara will speak some English. Along the main trekking trails, particularly the Annapurna Circuit, English is widely understood.

However, it's interesting to learn at least a little Nepali and it's quite an easy language to pick up. Nepali is closely related to Hindi and, like Hindi, is a member of the Indo-European group of languages. If you want to know a bit more Nepali than the phrases and vocabulary that follow, the Lonely Planet *Nepali Phrasebook* is a handy introduction to the language.

Although Nepali is the national language of Nepal and is the linking language between all the country's ethnic groups there are many other languages spoken. The Newaris of the Kathmandu Valley, for example, speak Newari and there are other languages spoken by the Tamangs, Sherpas, Rais, Limbus, Magars, Gurungs and other groups. In the Terai, bordering India, Hindi and Maithili, another Indian language of this region, are often spoken.

Even if you learn no other Nepali, there is one word every visitor soon picks up – *namaste*. Strictly translated it means 'I salute the god in you', but it is used as an everyday greeting encompassing everything from 'hello' to 'how are you?' and even 'see you again soon'. Properly used it should be accompanied with the hands held in a prayer-like position, the Nepalese gesture which is the equivalent of Westerners shaking hands.

Studying Nepali

It is not too difficult to learn basic Nepali and with a few exceptions the pronunciation is straightforward. Peace Corps and other aid workers pick up a working knowledge of the language very quickly and there are language courses available which will enable you to get by with just four to eight weeks of intensive study.

You will often see signs and notices around Kathmandu advertising language courses, many of them conducted by ex-Peace Corps workers. Embassies should be able to recommend somewhere that they themselves use. Most schools offer courses (often around two weeks long) or individual tuition. Places to try include the Speed Language Institute (☎ 01-220999) in Bagh Bazaar; Insight Nepal (☎ 01-418963); Global Language Institute (☎ 01-416116); or the School of International Languages (☎ 01-211713) at the university. Expect to pay around Rs 2500 (US$50) for a two-week course, around Rs 150 (US$3) for private hourly tuition.

Pronunciation

Vowels These are pronounced according to the following guide:

a	as the 'u' in 'hut'
aa	as the 'a' in 'garden'
e	as the 'e' in 'best' (only longer)
i	as the 'i' in 'sister'(only longer)
o	as the 'o' in 'more'
u	as the 'u' in 'put'
ai	as the 'i' in 'mine'
au	as the 'ow' in 'cow'

Consonants Most of the consonants are quite similar to their English equivalents. The exceptions are the so-called retroflex consonants and the aspirated consonants. Retroflex sounds are made by touching the back of the roof of the mouth with your tongue as you make the consonant; they are indicated by doubling the consonant:

tt	*Katthmanddu*

Aspirated consonants are sounded more forcefully than they would be in English and are made with a short puff of air; they are indicated by the consonant followed by an 'h':

bh *bahtmaas*

Both retroflex and aspirated consonants are best learned by having a Nepalese demonstrate them for you. You could start with the word *Katthmanddu*, which contains both retroflex and aspirated consonants.

Greetings & Civilities
hello, goodbye
  namaste
How are you?
  Tapaailai kasto chha?
excuse me
  hajur
please (give me)
  dinuhos
please (you have)
  khaanuhos
thank you
  dhanyabad

People are not thanked as often as in the West. A thank you is rarely necessary in a simple commercial transaction and saying *dhanyabad* too often will sound distinctly odd.

I only speak a little Nepali.
  Ma ali Nepaali bolchhu.
I don't understand.
  Maile bujhina.
Please say it again.
  Pheri bhannuhos.
Please speak more slowly.
  Tapai bistaarai bolnuhos.
I do not need it.
  Malai chahinna.
I do not have it.
  Ma sanga chhaina.
Wait a minute.
  Ek chhin parkhanos.

Some Useful Words
I	*ma*
where?	*kata?*
here	*yaha*

there	*tyaha*
OK	*theek*
yes (I have)	*chaa*
no (I don't have)	*chhaina*
good, pretty	*ramro*
stamp	*tikat*
envelope	*kham*
post office	*post afis*
tourist office	*turist afis*
bank	*baink*

Emergencies
medicine	*ausadhi*
pharmacy	*ausadhi pasal*

Where is the nearest hospital?
  Yahaa aspataal kahaa chha?
Please call a doctor for me.
  Daktar bolaidinus.
I do not feel well.
  Malai sancho chhaina.
I have diarrhoea.
  Dishaa laagyo.
I have altitude sickness.
  Lekh laagyo.
I have a fever.
  Joro aayo.

Accommodation
room	*kothaa*
cheap	*sasto*
expensive	*mahango*
clean	*safaa*
dirty	*mailo*
fan	*pankhaa*
breakfast	*bihaanako khaana*

Can I get a place to stay here?
  Yahaa baas paunchha?
May I take a look at the room?
  Kothaa herna sakchhu?

Food & Drink
food/meal	*khaana*
bread	*pauroti*
rice	*chamal*
rice (cooked)	*bhat*
meat	*masu*
chicken	*kukhura*
boiled	*umaleko*

green, leafy vegetable	*saag*
vegetable (cooked)	*tarkari*
lentils	*dahl*
egg	*phool*
fruit	*phala*
sugar	*chini*
spicy	*peero*
salt	*noon*
pepper	*marich*
curd	*dhai*
milk	*doodh*
tea	*chiya*
water	*pani*

Getting Around

bus	*bus*
taxi	*taxi*
boat	*naau*
ticket	*tikat*

Where does this bus go to?
  Yo bus kahaa jaanchha?
How much does it cost to go to...?
  ...jaana kati parchha?
Does your taxi have a meter?
  Tapaai ko taxi maa meter chha?

Trekking

way, trail	*bato*
bridge	*pool*
descent	*oralo*
ascent	*ukao*
left	*baya*
right	*daya*
cold	*jado*

Please give me ...
  Malai ... dinuhos.
Which is the way to...?
  ...jaane bato kata parchha?
Is there a village nearby?
  Najikai gaun parchha?
Where is the porter?
  Bhariya kata gayo?
Please give me water.
  Malai pani dinuhos.
I want to sleep.
  Malai sutna man lagyo.
I feel cold.
  Malai jado lagyo.

The food is cold.
  Khaana cheeso chha.

Shopping

money	*paisa*
cheap	*sasto*
expensive	*mahango*
less	*kam*
more	*badhi*
little bit	*alikati*

That's enough.
  Pugyo.
How much?
  Kati?
I like this.
  Malai yo ramro lagyo.
I do not like this.
  Malai yo ramro lagena.
Where is the market?
  Bazar kata parchha?

Times & Dates

minute	*minet*
hour	*ghantaa*
day	*din*
today	*aaja*
yesterday	*hijo*
tomorrow	*bholi*
now	*aile*
week	*haptaa*
month	*mahinaa*

What time is it?
  Kati bajyo?
It's one o'clock.
  Ek bajyo.
What day is it today?
  Aaja ke baar?
Today is Thursday.
  Aaja bihibaar ho.

Top: Bodhnath, Kathmandu Valley (TW)
Middle: Erotic art: female image, Jal Binayak, Chobar (TW); couple,
 Jal Binayak, Chobar (TW); Shiva image, Hanuman Ghat, Bhaktapur (TW)
Bottom: Nyatapola Temple, Bhaktapur (GB)

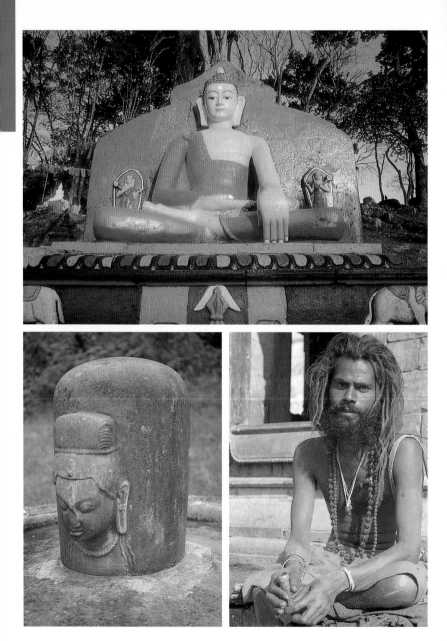

Top: Swayambhunath, Kathmandu Valley (PS)
Left: Shiva lingam (TW)
Right: Sadhu, Pashupatinath (PK)

Numbers

1	*ek*		40		*chaalis*
2	*dui*		50		*pachas*
3	*teen*		60		*saathi*
4	*char*		70		*sattari*
5	*panch*		80		*assi*
6	*chha*		90		*nabbe*
7	*saat*		100		*saya*
8	*aath*		200		*dui saya*
9	*nau*		500		*panch saya*
10	*das*		1000		*hazar*
20	*bees*		100,000		*lakh*
30	*tees*		1,000,000		*das lakh*
			10,000,000		*crore*

Nepalese numerals

Facts for the Visitor

VISAS & EMBASSIES

Visas are required by most nationalities (Indians are an exception) and they are available from embassies and consulates abroad, at the border with India or on arrival at Kathmandu's Tribhuvan Airport.

Initial single-entry tourist visas are issued for up to 30 days, and the fee is US$40 (or approximately the local equivalent if you get it outside the country). Double-entry visa fees are US$60, and multiple-entry visas are US$100; both must be used within the 30-day visa period.

At the airport and at least some border crossings officials insist on payment in US cash dollars. One passport photo is also required. It is possible to get US dollars at the airport currency exchange counter, but US$ in cash will almost certainly be unavailable at the land borders (bring your own!).

Tourist visas can be extended for a total of 90 days, although another 30 days can be granted 'on reasonable grounds'. Over the course of one calendar year (1 January to 31 December) a tourist may not stay longer than 120 days. The fee levied for any extension beyond 30 days and up to 90 days is US$2 per day; beyond 90 days and up to 120 days the fee is US$3 per day. One passport photo is also required, but it is no longer necessary to show proof of changing US$20 per day.

There are inevitably queues at the immigration counter at Tribhuvan Airport, and there can be hassles at the land crossings, so it is preferable to get your visa before arrival. Outside your home country, they are most conveniently obtained in Bangkok (Thailand), Calcutta and Delhi (India). You must, however, use your visa within three months of the date it is issued.

The Department of Immigration's Kathmandu office (☎ 01-412337, 418573) is only a short stroll from Thamel, on Tridevi Marg directly across from the modern shopping centre and the South Asian Association for Regional Cooperation (SAARC). See the Government Offices section in the Kath-

mandu, Patan & Bhaktapur chapter for details of opening hours. In Pokhara the office is near the lake. Apart from extending visas the immigration offices also issue trekking permits. The Pokhara office can only extend visas for a maximum of six weeks (within the 90-day tourist visa period), and issue trekking permits to the Annapurna region. Police stations cannot extend visas or trekking permits.

Nepalese Diplomatic Offices Overseas

Australia
48 Mitchell St, McMahons Point, Sydney, NSW 2060 (☎ 02-956 8815; fax 02-956 8767)
Suite 23, 18-20 Bank Place, Melbourne, Vic 3000 (☎ 03-602 1271; fax 03-670 6480)
Suite 2, 16 Robinson St, Nedlands, WA 6009 (☎ 09-386 2102; fax 09-386 3087)
Bangladesh
United Nations Rd, Road R 2, Baridhara Diplomatic Enclave, Dhaka (☎ 601890)
Belgium
149 Lamorinierstraat, B-2018, Antwerp, Belgium (☎ 03-230 8800)
Burma (Myanmar)
16 Natmauk Yeiktha (Park Ave), PO Box 84, Rangoon
Canada
310 Duport St, Toronto, Canada M5R 1V9 (☎ 416-968 7252)
China
No 1, Sanlitun Xiliujie, Beijing (☎ 532 1795)
Norbulingka Rd 13, Lhasa, Tibet Autonomous Region
Denmark
2 Teglgaardstraede, 1452 Copenhagen K, (☎ 33 13 31 65)
Finland
Erottaja 11 A 14, 00130 Helsinki, (☎ 680 2225)
France
45, bis Rue des Acacias, Paris 75017 (☎ 46224867)
Germany
Flinschstrasse 63, Frankfurt am Main 6000 (☎ 069-40871)
India
1 Barakhamba Rd, New Delhi 110001 (☎ 332 9969)
19 Woodlands, Sterndale Rd, Alipore, Calcutta 700027 (☎ 711224)
Italy
Piazzale Medaglie d'Oro 20, Rome 00136 (☎ 348 176)

Japan
16-23 Highashi-Gotanda, 3-chome, Shinagawa-ku, Tokyo 141
Myanmar (Burma)
16 Natmauk Yeiktha (Park Ave), Yangon (☎ 50633)
Netherlands
Prinsengracht 687, Gelderland Bldg, 1017 JV Amsterdam (☎ 020 25 0388)
Norway
Haakor, Vlls gt-5, 0116 Oslo (☎ 22-41 47 43)
Pakistan
4th Floor, Qamar House, 419 MA Jinnah Rd, Karachi-2 (☎ 200979)
Philippines
1136-38 United Nations Ave, Paco 2803, Manila (☎ 589393)
Spain
Mallorca 194 Pral 2A, 08036 Barcelona (☎ 03-323 1323)
Sweden
Eriksbergsgatan 1A, S-114 30 Stockholm (☎ 08-679 8039)
Switzerland
Asylstrasse 81, 8030 Zurich (☎ 01-475993)
Thailand
189 Sukhumvit 71 Rd, Bangkok (☎ 391 7240)
Tibet
Norbulingka Rd 13, Lhasa
UK
12A Kensington Palace Gardens, London W8 4QU (☎ 071-229 6231)
USA
1500 Lake Shore Drive, Chicago, Illinois 60610 (☎ 312-787 9199)
Heideberg College, Tiffin, Ohio 44883 (☎ 419-448 2202)
Suite 400, 909 Montgomery St, San Francisco, California 94133 (☎ 415-434 1111)
16250 Dallas Parkway, Suite 110, Dallas, Texas 75248 (☎ 214-931 1212)
212 15th St NE, Atlanta, GA 30309 (☎ 404-892 8152)
2131 Leroy Place NW, Washington, DC 20008 (☎ 202-667 4550)

Foreign Embassies in Nepal

Travellers continuing beyond Nepal are likely to require visas for Bangladesh, China, India, Myanmar/Myanma/Burma (or whatever else they're calling it this week), or Thailand.

For those planning to continue on to Tibet/China or Thailand, note that in 1992 permission to enter Tibet from Nepal was only granted to organised groups, and that

visas can be issued on the spot at Bangkok Airport for stays of 14 days or less.

Australia
Bansbari, Kathmandu, just beyond the Ring Rd on Maharajganj (☎ 01-411578, 417566; fax 417533)
open Monday to Thursday from 8 am to 1 pm and 1.30 to 5 pm, and Friday from 8.30 am to 2.15 pm
visa enquiries Monday to Thursday from 10 am to 12.30 pm
Bangladesh
Naxal, Bhagwati Bahal, Kathmandu (☎ 01-414943)
open Sunday to Thursday from 9 am to 1 pm and 1.30 to 5 pm
visa applications Sunday to Thursday from 9 am to 11 pm – no charge, two photos, 24 hours.
China
Baluwatar, Kathmandu (☎ 01-411740, 415383)
open Monday to Friday from 9 am to noon and 2 to 5 pm
visas applications Monday, Tuesday and Friday from 10 to 11 am – passports returned the next working day
France
Lazimpat, Kathmandu (☎ 01-412332, 413839)
open Monday to Friday from 9 am to 1 pm and 2.30 to 5.30 pm
Germany
Gyaneshwor, Kathmandu (☎ 01-412786; fax 416899)
open Monday to Friday from 8 am to 4.30 pm
India
Lainchaur, Kathmandu (☎ 01-410900, 414990; fax 413132)
open Monday to Friday from 9 am to 1 pm and 1.30 to 5.30 pm
visa applications Monday to Friday from 9.30 am to 12.30 pm, collect from 4.45 to 5.30 pm – Rs 300 ($6) application fee for tourist visa, allow at least seven days for processing; one-month (multiple entry possible) tourist visa costs Rs 250 ($5), six months costs Rs 1100 ($22).
Israel
Bishramalaya House, Lazimpat, Kathmandu (☎ 01-411911; fax 413920)
open Monday to Thursday from 8.15 am to 3.45 pm and Friday from 8.15 am to 1.45 pm
Italy
Baluwatar (Lalita Niwas Rd), Kathmandu (☎ 01-412743)
open Monday to Friday from 10 am to 5 pm
Japan
Panipokhari, Kathmandu (☎ 01 414083, 410397)
open Monday to Friday from 9 am to 1 pm and 2.30 to 5 pm

visa applications Tuesday to Friday from 9.30 to
11.30 am

Myanmar (formerly Burma)
Chakupat, Patan City Gate, Patan (☎ 01-521788)
open Monday to Friday from 9.30 am to 12.30
pm and 2 to 4.30 pm
visa applications Monday to Friday from 9.30 am
to 12.30 pm – 14-day visas available, Rs 550
($11), three photos, 24 hours

Pakistan
Panipokhari, Kathmandu (☎ 01- 411421)
open Sunday to Thursday from 9 am to 1 pm and
2 to 5 pm

Thailand
Jyoti Kendra, Thapathali, Kathmandu (☎ 01-
21391/2; fax 226599)
open Monday to Friday from 8.30 am to 12.30
pm and 1.30 to 4.30 pm
visa applications Monday to Friday from 9.30 am
to 12.30 pm – Rs 515 (about $10.50), two photos,
24 hours

UK
Lainchaur, Kathmandu (☎ 01-410583, 411281;
fax 411789)
open Monday to Thursday from 8.30 am to 12.30
pm and 1.30 to 5 pm, and Friday from 8.30 am to
12.30 pm and 1.30 to 3 pm

USA
Panipokhari, Kathmandu (☎ 01-411179,
412718; fax 419963)
open Monday to Friday from 8 am to 5 pm

DOCUMENTS
Trekking Permits
A Nepalese visa is valid for the Kathmandu
and Pokhara valleys and all drivable roads
throughout the country. If you intend to
strike out for more than a days' walk from
the main roads, you must first apply for a
trekking permit.

Trekking permits are only issued in
Kathmandu and Pokhara, and can only be
extended on those cities.

Trekking permits are issued in
Kathmandu by the immigration office. The
office is open for applications from 10.30 am
to 2 pm Sunday to Thursday and 10.30 am
to noon on Fridays, although you have to go
back later to retrieve your passport. It's wise
to start the process early as it can be time-
consuming.

Trekking fees vary depending on the area
you intend to explore. If you plan to trek in
two different areas, two trekking permits are

needed. Two passport photos are required
with each application:

Area	Fee
• Annapurna, Everest, Langtang, Gorkha, Jumla (& others)	first four weeks – $5; after four weeks – $10 per week
• Kanchenjunga & Dolpo	first four weeks – $10 per week; after four weeks – $20 per week
• Mustang	$700 for 10 days
• Manaslu	$75 per week

There are regular trekking permit inspection
points along most trails and you won't get far
out of Kathmandu or Pokhara before being
stopped and turned back if you don't have a
permit. Attempts to trek in the restricted
areas, which still encompass parts of northern and western Nepal, without a permit
could result in deportation. Peter Somerville-Large's amusing *To the Navel of the
World* recounts his adventures of arriving in
western Nepal from Tibet without a permit.
He got away with it.

Work Permits
For a Western visitor, working in Nepal is
very difficult although it is not impossible.
The easiest work to find is teaching English
as there are many private schools and a great
demand for English-language lessons. At
less than $100 a month the pay is very low.
Other possibilities include work with airline
offices, travel and trekking agencies, consul-
tants or aid groups but the prospects are
remote.

Officially you need a work permit if you
intend to find employment in Nepal and you
are supposed to have this before you arrive
in the country. Changing from a tourist visa
once you are in the country is rarely permissible. The work permit has to be applied for
by your employer and you are supposed to
leave the country while the paperwork is
negotiated. The process can take months.

Other Documents

If it is possible you might drive a car or ride a motorbike while in Nepal then it is worth having an international driving permit. An International Student Identity Card (ISIC) can be very useful if you're travelling on a tight budget. There's only one youth hostel in Nepal and it's neither conveniently located or good value, but there are many other hostels in Asia so a Youth Hostel Association (YHA) card may be worth having.

When travelling in Asia it's a good idea to keep a number of passport photos with your passport so they are immediately handy for trekking permits, visa applications and other official documents. Passport photos are easily and cheaply obtained in Kathmandu these days – around Rs 100 ($2) for four in B&W or Rs 150 ($3) for four in colour.

CUSTOMS

You may be searched very thoroughly when you depart. In addition to drugs, customs is concerned with the illegal export of antiques. Visitors are permitted to import the following articles for their personal use (and we quote):

Cigarettes, 200 sticks; cigars, 50 sticks; alcoholic liquor, one bottle not exceeding 1.15 litre; beer, 12 cans; one binoculars; one movie camera with 12 rolls of film or one video camera; one ordinary camera with 15 rolls of film; one tape recorder with 15 tape reels or cassettes; one perambulator; one tricycle; one sleeping bag; and one stick.

Antiques

Customs' main concern is preventing the export of antique works of art – with good reason since Nepal has a great many treasures, many kept under conditions of very light security. It would be a great shame if international art thieves and 'collectors' forced more of it to be kept under lock and key. Unfortunately a lucrative international market has led to the theft of a staggering amount of irreplaceable art.

It is very unlikely that souvenirs sold to travellers will be antique (despite the claims of the vendors), but if there is any doubt, they should be cleared and a certificate obtained

from the Department of Archaeology (☎ 01-215358) in the National Archives building on Ram Shah Path. These controls also apply to the export of precious and semiprecious stones.

Animal Furs & Trophies

Unfortunately, there is still a thriving trade in animal furs and trophies, despite the fact that this is also officially prohibited. Many seriously endangered species, including the beautiful snow leopard, are still being hunted for valuable parts of their corpses.

While there is a market this will no doubt continue – the argument that because the animal is already dead there is no further harm caused by having its skin made into a coat is entirely spurious. If there is any cosmic justice, those that encourage the trade will be reincarnated as rabbits on fur farms in Siberia!

MONEY

The Nepalese rupee (Rs) is divided into 100 paisa (p). Major international currencies including the US dollar and pounds sterling, are readily accepted, and in Nepal the Indian rupee is also like a hard currency. Official exchange rates are:

A$1	=	Rs 33
US$1	=	Rs 47
UK£1	=	Rs 73
DM1	=	Rs 30
I Rs 100	=	Rs 150

There are coins for five, 10, 25 and 50 paisa, and for one rupee. Not all that long ago, once you were outside the Kathmandu Valley, it was rare to see any paper money. Mountaineering books from the '50s often comment on the porters whose sole duty was to carry the expedition's money – in cold, hard, cash! Nowadays it's quite possible a tourist won't see a single coin – prices for Westerners are nearly always rounded up to the nearest rupee and rupee coins are rare.

Bank notes are for one, two, five, 10, 20, 50, 100, 500 and 1000 rupees. Away from major centres changing a Rs 500 or Rs 1000 note can be very difficult, so it is always wise to have at least some of your money in small-denomination notes. Outside the Kathmandu Valley, changing even a Rs 100 note can be difficult. Even in Kathmandu, many small businesses, especially rickshaw and taxi drivers, simply don't have sufficient spare money to allow them the luxury of carrying a wad of change.

Note that all dollar prices quoted in this book are US dollars.

Currency Exchange

There are effectively three exchange rates in operation within Nepal: the rate set by the government's Nepal Rastra Bank, the slightly more generous (but still legal) rate set by the private banks, and the even more generous black-market rate set by carpet shops and travel agencies. The daily *Rising Nepal* newspaper lists the Nepal Rastra Bank's rate, providing a useful reference point.

There are exchange counters at the international terminal at Kathmandu's airport and moneychangers at the various border-crossing points. Pokhara and the major border towns also have official money-changing facilities, but changing travellers' cheques can be difficult elsewhere in the country, even in some quite large towns. If you're trekking take enough small denomination cash with you to last the whole trek.

The usual banking hours are from 10 am to 2 pm from Sunday to Thursday and from 10 am till noon on Friday.

Legal Exchange When you change money officially, you are required to show your passport, and you are issued with a Foreign Exchange Encashment Receipt showing your identity and the amount of hard currency you have changed. Hang onto the receipts as they have a number of potential uses.

Many up-market hotels and businesses are obliged by the government to demand payment in hard currency; they will also accept rupees, but only if you can show a

Foreign Exchange Encashment Receipt that covers the amount you owe them. The amount you pay is then subtracted from the total showing on the receipt and the receipt can be re-used until its full value has been debited; it is then marked 'Used'.

Airlines are also required to charge tourists in hard currency, but most seem unwilling to accept anything other than cash, travellers' cheques, or credit cards. Budget hotels, bus companies and most small businesses are only too happy to get rupees and do not muck around with encashment receipts.

Foreign Exchange Encashment Receipts used to be required in order to extend your visa – you had to prove you had changed $20 per day – but this regulation was abolished in October 1993.

If you leave Nepal via Kathmandu's airport the downstairs exchange counter will re-exchange up to 15% of the amount shown on 'unused' receipts. The receipts that are used for re-exchange are kept by the bank, so make sure you have photocopies if you need them for other purposes. Unfortunately, in 1992 re-exchange was not possible at any of the bank branches at the border crossing points. Even if this is officially possible, the chance of them having a stock of hard currency on hand is very slim.

Exchange rates and commissions can vary quite significantly between banks, so it's worth shopping around. The rate set by the government-controlled Nepal Rastra Bank can be as much as 5% lower than the rates offered by private banks, so it should only be used as a last resort.

The best private banks are the Nepal Bank Ltd, Nepal Grindlays Bank, Rastriya Banijya Bank, and the Nepal Indo-Suez Bank. Some hotels and resorts are also licensed to change money, and while their rates are usually OK it's best to check first.

In 1993 the Nepal Bank (with a large branch at the end of New Road, Kathmandu) had the cheapest commission for changing travellers' cheques at .5% with a minimum charge of Rs 35. The Rastriya Banijya Bank (with a branch in the immigration office,

Thamel, Kathmandu) was next with 1% commission and a minimum charge of only Rs 25. Nepal Grindlays Bank (with a branch in the Namche Bazaar complex in the middle of Thamel, Kathmandu) bought cheques for 1%, with a minimum charge of Rs 125, but their exchange rates were usually the most generous on offer. They also made advances against Visa and Access/MasterCards, charging 2% for advancing cash and travellers' cheques.

Black-Market Exchange Nepal has an active and remarkably open black market although it's principally found around Kathmandu and to a lesser extent in Pokhara. It is by definition illegal, but rip-offs are rare and legal harassment even rarer. Keep your wits about you, however. Don't do a deal in the street, and don't hand over your money until you have counted and checked the rupees and actually have them in your hand.

The black market is principally interested in cash US dollars, but US dollar travellers' cheques are nearly as good. The $50 note was the most popular cash, apparently because of a proliferation of forged $100 notes. You can change European currencies on the black market, but rates are often little different to those offered by private banks.

In 1992 when the official rate for $1 was Rs 47, you could sell a big-denomination bill at Rs 52 and a small bill at Rs 51 – approximately 10% better than the official rate. Large-denomination travellers' cheques got Rs 51, small cheques got Rs 50 – approximately 8% better than the official rate. To buy dollars back, you needed to add around Rs 1.50, so a large-denomination dollar bill cost Rs 53.50.

The young hustlers on the street usually lead you to a shop – often a travel agency or carpet shop – where the transaction is actually completed. Once you know which shop to go to you don't have to deal with the people in the street, and you will also get a slightly better rate if you cut out the intermediary. You're almost certain to be offered below the going rate the first time, so shop around.

Black-market dollars are used in a number of ways, sometimes completely unsavoury ways. A huge demand comes from the carpet industry because the government has set a legally enforced floor price for export carpets. The real price is currently lower, so the carpet buyers pay the official floor price with a bank transfer, but are reimbursed by the seller, under the table, with cash. Smugglers also need hard currency, whether they trade in drugs, or something less destructive. One popular scam is to sell drugs to Westerners for rupees; change the rupees to dollars; smuggle the dollars to Hong Kong and buy gold; smuggle the gold back to Nepal; and finally, smuggle the gold to India. Using the black-market facilitates and encourages these practices.

Money Transfers from Overseas
If you do not follow the right steps money transfers from overseas can be very time-consuming. Make any transfer by telex as transfers by mail can take forever. Pin down every possible detail, ensure that you know which bank the money is going to, make sure they have your name exactly right and if possible ensure that you are notified at the same time as the bank. It's important to choose the right bank as well – check that your bank has links with a bank in Nepal and does not have to operate through an intermediary.

International banks operating in Kathmandu include: Nepal Grindlays Bank (☎ 01-225181; Box 3990) which is owned by Australia's ANZ and has its head office in Kantipath, Thamel; Nepal Citibank (☎ 01-428884; Box 3729) with offices in the Yak & Yeti Park Royal Hotel; Nepal Indo-Suez (☎ 01-411228; Box 3412); and Nepal Standard Chartered (☎ 01-220129).

Nepal Grindlays in Thamel (open standard bank hours) will make cash advances against Visa and MasterCard in Nepalese rupees, and will also sell travellers' cheques against the cards. The bank charges a 2% commission.

American Express has an office off the forecourt of the Hotel Mayalu on Jamal Tol just around the corner from Durbar Marg.

They will accept personal cheques (you can use a standard form so long as you know your account details) and advance travellers' cheques to cardholders. There's a standard 1% commission. The office is open from 10 am to 1 pm and 2 to 5 pm.

You cannot pay your credit card bills in Nepal, so it is essential you make arrangements before you leave home. There are a number of alternatives, including automatic payment by your bank.

Costs

If you stayed in rock-bottom accommodation and survived on a predominantly Nepalese diet you could live in Nepal for less than $5 a day. On an independent 'village inn' trek your living costs are likely to be around that level.

On the other hand if you stayed in comfortable middle-range hotels (say $10 to $20 a double), ate in popular tourist-oriented restaurants, rented bicycles and took taxis from time to time your living costs could be around $20 to $30 a day.

At the top end it is possible to spend $100 a night for a five-star double room in Kathmandu; a meal for two in one of Nepal's very best restaurants can cost $30 to $40; and a deluxe trek booked from overseas can cost $100 a day.

Residents should bear in mind that most of the major up-market tour and trekking operators offer significant discounts, so make your status clear when you ask for prices and make bookings.

Tipping

Tipping is becoming more prevalent in Kathmandu. In expensive establishments you should tip up to 10% whereas in smaller places the loose change or Rs 10 will be appreciated. Don't worry about it in the really cheap restaurants. Taxi drivers don't expect to be tipped.

Bargaining

Before bargaining, try to establish a fair price by talking to locals and other travellers. Paying too much feeds inflation, while paying too little denies the locals a reasonable return for their efforts and investments. Not everything is subject to bargaining: respect standard food, accommodation and entry charges, and follow the going rate for services.

Bargaining should never be treated as a matter of life and death importance – it's usually regarded as an integral part of a transaction and is, ideally, an enjoyable social exchange. Nepalese do not ever appreciate aggressive behaviour. A good deal is when both parties are happy. Try to remember that Rs 10, might make quite a difference to the seller, but in US hard currency it amounts to 20 cents.

WHEN TO GO

Climatic factors are very important in deciding on a visit to Nepal. October-November, the start of the dry season, is in many ways the best time of year in Nepal. With the monsoon only recently finished the countryside is green and lush and Nepal is at its most beautiful. Rice is harvested and there are some important and colourful festivals to enjoy. Bear in mind, however, that these festivals can be disruptive; see the Cultural Events section later in this chapter for more details. At this time of year the air is sparkling clean, visibility is unexcelled and the Himalayan views are as near perfect as you can ask. Furthermore the weather is still balmy, neither too hot (as it can be towards the end of the dry season or during the monsoon) nor too cold (as it can be at the height of winter).

In December-January the climate and visibility are still good, though it can get very cold. Trekkers need to be well prepared, as snow can be encountered on high-altitude treks. Heading for the Everest Base Camp at this time of year can be a real feat of endurance and the Annapurna Circuit trek is often closed by snow on the Thorong La pass. Down in Kathmandu the cheaper hotels, where heating is nonexistent, are often chilly and gloomy in the evenings. There's sometimes a brief 'winter monsoon', lasting just a day or two in January.

February-March-April, the tail end of the dry season, is a good second-best time. The weather gets warmer so high-altitude treks are no longer as arduous, although by the end of the dry season, before the monsoon breaks, it starts to get too hot for comfort. Visibility is not as good as earlier in the dry season since the country is now very dry, and dust in the air reduces that crystal Himalayan clarity. In compensation, Nepal's wonderful rhododendrons and many other flowers are in bloom so there's plenty of colour to be seen along the trekking trails.

May and the early part of June are not the best months as it is extremely hot and dusty and the coming monsoon hangs over you like a threat. Mid-June to September, when the monsoon finally arrives, is the least popular time to visit Nepal. The rains wash the dust out of the air, but the clouds obscure the mountains so you're unlikely to enjoy more than a rare glimpse of the Himalaya. Although it doesn't rain all day it usually does rain every day and the trails (and the roads in most Nepalese towns) will be muddy and plagued by leeches.

Despite leeches and slippery trails it is possible to trek during the monsoon, although high rivers may further complicate matters and it's certainly not as pleasant as other times of year. Landslides sometimes block roads during the monsoon but many visitors still come to Nepal from India as the weather is even less pleasant down on the plains. The latter part of the monsoon, the months of August-September, are a time of festivals which will certainly enliven a visit to Kathmandu.

How Long to Visit

If you are visiting during the monsoon, and your stay is restricted to the Kathmandu Valley, a week is probably quite enough. During the dry season you really need more like a month to enjoy the country: a week or two for Kathmandu and the surrounding area, a week for a short trek, and a week for Pokhara and a visit to the Royal Chitwan National Park. If you want to walk some of the longer trekking routes then you had better extend your visit – it takes three weeks to walk the Annapurna Circuit.

WHAT TO BRING

Nepal's climatic variations due to altitude mean that at certain times of year you'll have to come prepared for almost anything. If you're in Nepal during the winter you'll find it's T-shirt weather if you're tracking wildlife in the Terai, but up at the Everest Base Camp you'll want the best thermal or duck-down gear money can buy!

In the Kathmandu Valley the daytime weather is pleasant year-round, but in winter the temperature drops as soon as the sun sets, or even goes behind a cloud. It never reaches freezing in the valley, however, so it's sweater or warm-jacket weather, nothing worse. Climb higher to the valley edge at Nagarkot and you can find it much colder. If you plan to ride a bike, or have a respiratory problem, Kathmandu's air pollution is sufficiently bad to justify a mask.

During the monsoon you'll need an umbrella or raincoat, particularly in Pokhara where the rainfall is much heavier than in Kathmandu. In the first month after the monsoon it can be pleasantly warm, even on treks so long as you're sticking to lower altitudes. Sunglasses, a hat and covering for unprotected skin are all necessary on high-altitude treks or for prolonged exposure in the Terai. (See the Trekking chapter for more details on clothing recommendations for trekking.)

Most clothing is easily and cheaply available in Nepal so if there's a question about a particular item, leave it behind – you can always get one if you need it.

These days most toiletries are readily available, including toilet paper. Women should, however, bring tampons if needed. Ear plugs can be more than a luxury if you sleep lightly – cheap hotels and lodges are often very noisy. If you're staying in cheap hotels a padlock can be useful as hotels in this category often lock the doors with a latch and padlock. If you're visiting the Royal Chitwan National Park or other places in the

Terai a good insect repellent is a near necessity. Bring a torch (flashlight) for trekking and for power cuts.

TOURIST OFFICE

There is a counter at the airport but the main tourist office (☎ 01-211203) is near the corner of Basantapur Square, on Ganga Path close to Freak St in Kathmandu. It has a limited range of brochures and maps.

The Department of Tourism is behind the National Stadium in Kathmandu. If you're writing from overseas the address is Department of Tourism, Tripureshwar, Kathmandu, Nepal.

BUSINESS HOURS & HOLIDAYS

Most government offices in Kathmandu are open from 10 am to 5 pm from Sunday to Thursday during summer and from 9 am to 4 pm during the three winter months (roughly mid-November to mid-February since the winter starting date for the change of hours varies with the Nepalese calendar).

KEEP Nepal Green

Ecotourism, low-impact trekking, adventure travel and cultural tours are the tourist buzzwords of the '90s. Unfortunately, their meaning has been quickly debased. Package tourists consider any exposure to nature to be adventurous, and independent travellers think that because they are living on a shoestring budget they are ecologically and culturally sound.

The ugly side effects of tourism in Nepal have been widely publicised, but little has been said about what can be done to address the problems. The solution is not to cancel your visit – Nepal's fragile economy needs every dollar it can get – but it is important to be well informed, and to act accordingly. Responsible tourism doesn't take a great deal of effort, but the pay-offs are enormous.

Tens of thousands of trekkers visit the Nepal Himalaya each year, so the potential for damage is enormous. In 1991 for example, 35,000 camping trekkers (mostly with organised tours) and 35,000 independent trekkers (who stay in local lodges) visited.

The average trekker consumes as much fuel wood in a day as an entire Nepalese household uses in a week, but for around $2 to $3 a day, camping trekkers and support staff (including porters) can eat food cooked on kerosene stoves.

Independent trekkers can stay in lodges that use kerosene or fuel-efficient stoves, only take hot showers when the water is heated with solar energy, hydroelectricity or back-burner stoves, and choose their meal times to coincide with other trekkers to minimise the amount of cooking time.

An estimated 50,000 kg of garbage is left behind in the mountains by camping trekkers, but just eight cents a day per person covers the cost of having the rubbish carried out of the hills.

Independent trekkers should support lodges and trekking agencies that practice an environmentally sound approach – creating a financial incentive for others to adopt similar methods. They should also carry out non-biodegradable rubbish – especially plastics and batteries.

On the cultural side, dressing in a way that is consistent with the Nepalese norm will not only ease the communication gap, but help regain respect for women, now sadly eroded by the number of female tourists who sport skimpy and skin-tight clothes.

Offices close at 3 pm on Fridays. Saturday is the weekly holiday and most shops and all offices and banks will be closed but Sunday is a regular working day.

Many holidays and festivals (see the following Cultural Events section) affect the working hours of government offices and banks. These will be closed for, amongst others, Shivaratri, the Nepalese New Year, Teej, Indra Jatra, Dasain, Tihar, the queen's birthday on 7 November and the king's birthday on 29 December.

CULTURAL EVENTS

Nepal's colourful holidays and festivals occur virtually year round and a visit to Nepal is almost certain to coincide with at least one, particularly in the Kathmandu Valley. Certain times of year, particularly August and September towards the end of the monsoon, are packed with festivals. They go a long way towards compensating for the less-than-ideal weather at that time of the year.

Dasain is the most important of all Nepalese celebrations, in terms of impact, perhaps

---

If you want to find out more, or just want to talk to someone about where and how to trek, visit the Kathmandu Environmental Education Project (KEEP). Working in partnership with the well-established HRA, Himalayan Rescue Association, KEEP operates a Trekkers' Information Centre in Kathmandu. Located on the edge of Thamel, about 100 metres west of the Department of Immigration, the Trekkers' Information Centre is open from 10 am to 5 pm daily except Saturdays and Nepalese public holidays.

Visitors can get information on how to minimise their negative impact and maximise their positive impact. Displays and hand-outs illustrate practical do's and don'ts, but there are also professional Nepalese staff and Western volunteers to deal with specific questions. During trekking seasons a slide show on conservation practices and a talk on prevention of acute mountain sickness is given every afternoon.

Green-Keeper's coffee shop sells freshly brewed cappuccinos, home-made cakes and cookies, KEEP T-shirts, biodegradable soaps, sun screen, lip balm, and other items useful for ecologically sound trekking. Guidebooks, periodicals and maps are available in the library. A journal records trekkers' comments on treks, and an outside notice board carries notices from people looking for trekking partners, selling gear, looking for friends...

Although KEEP/HRA information is particularly useful for individual trekkers, it is also helpful for group trekkers, mountaineers, and city sightseers – everyone is welcome. Eventually, KEEP hopes to become a clearing house for information on the environment and conservation for the entire Himalayan region.

Visitor contributions are much appreciated. An annual fee of $20 for individuals, $50 for businesses/institutions, $160 for life, and $200 to $500 for 'Friends of Keep' entitles members to the biannual newsletter and a KEEP T-shirt. KEEP has nonprofit, charitable status.

For more information, contact KEEP (☎ 01-418755; fax 227628), PO Box 4944, Kathmandu.

Wendy Brewer Lama

most closely approximated by Christmas and New Year in the West. Tens of thousands of Nepalese hit the road to return home to celebrate with their families. This means the villages are full of life if you are trekking, but it also means that all the buses are fully booked and overflowing, that porters may be hard to find (or more expensive than usual), and that cars are hard to hire. Doing business in Kathmandu, outside of Thamel, becomes almost impossible.

The most important days, when everything comes to a total halt, are the ninth day when thousands of animals are sacrificed, and the tenth day when blessings are received from elder relatives and superiors. Banks and government offices are generally closed from the eighth day to the twelfth. The final day of Dasain is on the full moon in September or October.

For interesting accounts of many of the festivals and the legends behind them read Mary M Anderson's *The Festivals of Nepal* (Rupa & Co, Calcutta, 1988; first published by Unwin Hyman, London, 1971).

Nepalese holidays and festivals are principally dated by the lunar calendar, falling on days relating to new or full moons. The Nepalese new year starts on 13 April and is 57 years ahead of the Gregorian calendar used in the West. The year 1993 in the West is 2050 in Nepal. The Newaris, on the other hand, start their new year from the day after Deepavali, which falls on the night of the new moon in late October or early November. Their calendar is 880 years behind the Gregorian calendar so 1993 in the West is 1113 to the Newaris of the Kathmandu Valley.

Predicting the exact dates for Nepalese holidays and festivals is not always easy. In Nepal the lunar calendar is divided into bright and dark fortnights. The bright fortnight is the two weeks of the waxing moon, as it grows to become the full moon (*purnima*). The dark fortnight is the two weeks of the waning moon, as the full moon shrinks to become the new moon (*aunsi*). Therefore a festival might fall 'on the 11th day of the bright fortnight of Falgun'.

What sometimes seems like a cavalier attitude towards numbering days actually has a logical explanation. The sun rises every 24 hours but the period between successive moonrises can vary from 22 to 27 hours. Thus several times each year there can be a 'moon day' (the period from one moonrise to the next) which has no sunrise within it, and several others that have two sunrises. Thus the lunar calendar will sometimes jump a day, and on other occasions it will hiccup and repeat a day. Predicting a date far in advance is additionally complicated by the periodic adjustments which have to be made to bring the shorter lunar year back into line with the solar year which the Gregorian calendar follows.

The Nepalese months are:

October-November	Kartik
November-December	Mangsir
December-January	Pus
January-February	Magh
February-March	Falgun
March-April	Chaitra
April-May	Baisakh
May-June	Jeth
June-July	Asaar
July-August	Saaun
August-September	Bhadra
September-October	Ashwin

The festival calendar covers dates through to mid-January 1996, hopefully with reasonable accuracy. Check the dates when you're in Kathmandu.

October-November

Dasain The pleasant post-monsoon period when the sky is clearest, the air is cleanest and the rice is ready for harvesting is also the time for Nepal's biggest annual festival. Dasain lasts for 15 days, finishing on the full-moon day of late September or early October, and there are a number of important days right through the festival. Although much of Dasain is a quiet family affair there are colourful events for visitors to see both in Kathmandu and in the country. Dasain is also known as Durga Puja since the festival

Festival Calendar

Name of Festival	Place	1993-94	1994-95	1995-96
Dasain				
Fulpati	all over Nepal	22 Oct '93	11 Oct '94	30 Sep '95
Vijaya Dashami	all over Nepal	25 Oct '93	14 Oct '94	3 Oct'95
Kartika Purnima	all over Nepal	28 Oct '93	17 Oct '94	6 Oct '95
Tihar				
Deepavali	all over Nepal	13 Nov '93	3 Nov '94	22 Oct '95
Bhai Tika	all over Nepal	15 Nov '93	5 Nov '94	24 Oct '95
Haribodhini Ekadashi	Pashupatinath	24 Nov	13 Nov	3 Nov
Bala Chaturdashi	Pashupatinath	13 Dec	3 Dec	23 Nov
Mani Rimdu	Solu Khumbu	Nov	Nov	Nov
Magh Sankranti	Narayanghat	mid-Jan '95	mid-Jan '96	mid-Jan '96
Basant Panchami	Swayambhunath	15 Feb	4 Feb	25 Jan
Shivaratri	Pashupatinath	12 Mar	1 Mar	late Feb
Holi	all over Nepal	27 Mar	17 Mar	mid-Mar
Chaitra Dasain	all over Nepal	29 Apr	18 Apr	mid-Apr
Bisket Jatra	Bhaktapur	13 Apr	13 Apr	13 Apr
Buddha Jayanti	Kathmandu	25 May	15 May	May
Gai Jatra	Kathmandu	22 Aug	12 Aug	Aug
Krishna Jayanti	Patan	28 Aug	16 Sept	Aug-Sept
Teej	Pashupatinath	8 Sept	28 Aug	Aug-Sept
Indra Jatra	Kathmandu	18 Sept	6 Oct	Sept-Oct

celebrates the victory of the goddess Durga over the forces of evil in the guise of the buffalo demon Mahisasura. Since Durga is a bloodthirsty goddess, the festival is marked by wholesale bloodletting and features the biggest animal sacrifice of the year.

Even before Dasain commences the Nepalese spring-clean their houses, while in the country, swings and primitive hand-powered Ferris wheels are erected at the entrance to villages or in their main square. For trekkers, Dasain is very much 'the festival of swings'! On the first day of the festival, a sacred jar of water is prepared in each house and barley seeds are planted in carefully prepared soil. Getting the seeds to sprout a few cm during Dasain ensures a good harvest.

Fulpati is the first really important day of Dasain and is called 'the seventh day' although it may not actually fall on the seventh day. Fulpati means 'day of flowers'

and a jar containing flowers is carried from Gorkha to Kathmandu and presented to the king at the Tundikhel parade ground. The flowers symbolise Taleju, the goddess of the royal family, whose most important image is in the Gorkha palace. From the parade ground the flowers are transported on a palanquin to the old Royal Palace on Durbar Square where they are inspected again by the king and his entourage.

Maha Astami or the 'great eighth day', and Kala Ratri the 'black night' follow Fulpati and this is the start of the sacrifices and offerings to Durga. The hundreds of goats you may see contentedly grazing in the Tundikhel parkland on the days prior to Maha Astami are destined to die for the goddess. At midnight, in a temple courtyard near Durbar Square, eight buffaloes and 108 goats are beheaded and their executioners must perform the deed with a single stroke of the sword or knife.

The next day is Navami and the Kot Square near Durbar Square, scene of the great massacre of noblemen which led to the Rana period of Nepalese history, is the scene for another great massacre. Visitors can witness the bloodshed but you need to arrive early to secure a place on the foreigners' balcony. Sacrifices continue through the day and blood is sprinkled on the wheels of cars and other vehicles to ensure a safe year on the road. At the airport each Royal Nepal Airlines aircraft will have a goat sacrificed to it! The average Nepalese does not eat much meat, but on this day almost everybody in the country will find that goat is on the menu for dinner.

The 10th day of the festival, Vijaya Dashami, is again a family affair as cards and greetings are exchanged, family visits are made and parents place a red *tika* mark on their children's foreheads. In the evening, the conclusion of Dasain is marked by processions and masked dances in the towns of the Kathmandu Valley. The Kharga Jatra or sword processions feature priests dressed up as the various gods and carrying wooden swords, symbolic of the weapon with which Durga slew the buffalo demon. This day also celebrates the victory of Lord Rama over the evil King Rawana in the *Ramayana*. The barley sprouts which were planted on the first day are picked and worn as small bouquets in the hair.

Kartika Purnima, the full-moon day which marks the end of the festival, is celebrated with gambling in many households and you will see even small children avidly putting a few coins down on various local games of chance. Women fast and many of them make a pilgrimage to Pashupatinath near Kathmandu. Although Dasain is principally a Hindu festival it has also been adopted by Buddhists, and special activities also take place at Buddhist shrines in Patan and Bhaktapur. In the country the swings and Ferris wheels will be busier than ever, before finally being dismantled for another year.

Tihar With its colourful Festival of Lights (Deepavali), Tihar is the most important Hindu festival in India, and in Nepal it ranks second only to Dasain. The five days of activities take place in late October or early November.

The festival honours certain animals on successive days, starting with offerings of rice to the crows which are sent by Yama, the god of death, as his 'messengers of death'. On the second day, dogs are honoured with garlands of flowers and tikas. This must be a considerable surprise to most Nepalese dogs, who are usually honoured with no more than the occasional kick, but the fact that, in the afterworld, it is dogs who guide departed souls across the river of the dead must not be forgotten. Bhairab's vehicle also happens to be a dog. On the third day it is cows who are remembered and on this day you will often see cows with one horn painted silver, one gold. On the fourth day bullocks are honoured.

The third day, Deepavali, is the most important day of the festival when Lakshmi (Vishnu's consort and the goddess of wealth)

The Ages of Brahma

Each universe has a Brahma who lives for 100 years, Brahma years, that is, which are much longer than our earth years. Each day in a Brahma year is a Kalpa, and each Kalpa or Brahma day is in turn divided into 1000 Mahayugas or Great Ages.

In a single Great Age there are four Yugas which follow a prescribed pattern. In the first Yuga everything is fine, but in the second Yuga evil makes its appearance and the eternal struggle between good and evil commences. In the third Yuga good is in serious trouble and in the fourth Yuga, the Kaliyuga, evil comes out on top and it's time for Vishnu to take on his 10th incarnation as Kalki the destroyer and bring the whole mess to a quick end. And where are we currently in this cycle of existence? About halfway through the fourth Yuga. ∎

comes to visit every home which has been suitably lit for her presence. Since one can hardly turn down a surprise visit from the goddess of wealth, homes throughout the country will be brightly lit with candles and lamps for the Festival of Lights. The effect is highlighted because Deepavali falls on the new-moon day.

The fourth day is also the start of the new year for the Newari people of the Kathmandu Valley. The fifth day is known as Bhai Tika and on this day brothers and sisters are supposed to meet and place tikas on each others' foreheads. Sisters offers small gifts of fruit and sweets to their brothers while the brothers give their sisters money in return. The markets and bazaars of Kathmandu will be busy supplying the appropriate gifts.

Haribodhini Ekadashi Ekadashi falls twice in each lunar month, on the 11th day after each new and full moon. Each Ekadashi is celebrated with ceremonies and activities but the Haribodhini Ekadashi, falling in late October or early November on the 11th day after the new moon, is the most important of them. On this day Vishnu awakens from his four-month monsoonal slumbers and the best place to see the associated festivities is at Budhanilkantha, the temple of the sleeping Vishnu. Activities also take place at other Vishnu temples and many Vishnu devotees make a circuit of the important ones from Ichangu Narayan to Changu Narayan, Bishanku Narayan and Sekh Narayan.

Mahalakshmi Puja Lakshmi is the goddess of wealth, but to farmers wealth is rice so this harvest festival, following immediately after Haribodhini Ekadashi, honours the goddess with sacrifices and colourful dances.

November-December
Bala Chaturdashi Like Ekadashi there are two Chaturdashis each month and Bala Chaturdashi falls on the new-moon day in late November or early December. Pilgrims flock to Pashupatinath for this festival, burning oil lamps at night and bathing in the holy river on the following morning. A

pilgrimage is then made along a traditional route through the woods overlooking Pashupatinath, and as they walk the devotees scatter sweets and seeds for their deceased relatives to enjoy in the afterlife. The festival is at its most colourful during the first evening and is best observed from the other side of the Bagmati River, looking down towards the temple with its singing, dancing, lamplit pilgrims.

Bala, incidentally, once worked at Pashupatinath where he cremated corpses until an unfortunate incident transformed him into a demon. He then haunted the area around the temple until a means was found to dispose of him. Various legends relate how the demon was killed by one of poor Bala's former friends and the festival of Bala Chaturdashi was then instituted.

Sita Bibaha Panchami On the fifth day of the bright fortnight in late November or early December, pilgrims from all over Nepal and India flock to Janakpur to celebrate the marriage of Sita to Rama. It was in Janakpur that Sita was born and she and Rama both have temples in the town. The wedding is re-enacted with a procession carrying Rama's image to Sita's temple by elephant. Rama's birthday is celebrated in March in Janakpur and Kathmandu.

Mani Rimdu The Sherpa festival of Mani Rimdu takes place at the monastery of Thyangboche in the Solu Khumbu region. The three-day festival features masked dances and dramas performed by the monastery's monks and celebrates the victory of Buddhism over the older Bon religion. Another Mani Rimdu takes place six months later in May-June at the Thami monastery a day's walk west of Namche Bazaar.

January-February
Magh Sankranti The end of the coldest winter months is marked by this festival with ritual bathing, despite the cold, during the Nepalese month of Magh. The festival is dated by the movement north of the winter sun and is one of the few festivals not timed

by the lunar calendar. Soon after, on the new-moon day, the Tribeni Mela (a *mela* is a fair) is held at various places including Deoghat, on the banks of the Narayani River near the town of Narayanghat in the Terai.

Basant Panchami The beginning of spring is celebrated by honouring Saraswati and since she is the goddess of learning this festival has special importance for students and scholars. The shrine to Saraswati, just below the platform at the top of Swayambhunath, is the most popular locale for the festivities. This is also a particularly auspicious occasion for weddings.

February

Tibetan New Year The new year in Tibet commences with the new moon in February and is welcomed with particular fervour at the great Bodhnath Stupa. The colourfully dressed lamas parade around the stupa carrying banners and portraits of the Dalai Lama. Ceremonies are also performed at Swayambhunath and in the Tibetan community at Jawlakhel near Patan. Crowds of Tibetans, dressed in their most traditional costumes and furiously twirling their prayer wheels, watch the proceedings.

February-March

Maha Shivaratri Shiva's birthday falls on the new-moon day of the month of Falgun. Festivities take place at all Shiva temples but most particularly at the great Pashupatinath Temple, and devotees flock there not only from all over Nepal but also from all over India.

Many sadhus make the long trek to Nepal for this festival and the King of Nepal will also appear late in the day since Shiva, as Lord Pashupati, is asked to protect Nepal at the conclusion of any official message. The crowds bathing in the Bagmati's holy waters at this time are a colourful and wonderful sight. The sadhus, meanwhile, will be up to all their usual fun and games whether it's rolling in the ashes, performing impossible feats of yoga or sticking thorns through their

tongues. Overall, however, Maha Shivaratri is a serene and peaceful festival, reflecting the deep devotion which Hindus hold for their religion.

Holi/Fagu This exciting festival is closely related to the water festivals of Thailand and Myanmar (Burma) and takes place on the full-moon day in the month of Falgun. By this time, late in the dry season, it is beginning to get rather hot and the water which is sprayed around so liberally during the festival is a reminder of the cooling monsoon days to come. Holi is also known as the Festival of Colours and as well as spraying water on everything and everyone, coloured powder (particularly red) and coloured water is also dispensed. Foreigners get special attention, so if you venture out on Holi leave your camera behind (or keep it well protected) and wear old clothes which you don't mind getting colour-stained.

At one time Holi used to take place on the eight days leading up to the full moon; these days (perhaps fortunately) the full onslaught of activities is usually restricted to one day.

The festival is said to be inspired by the exploits of Krishna, particularly an incident when he caught his favourite milkmaids sporting in the Jamuna River. A pole supporting a three-tiered umbrella is set up in front of the Basantapur Tower in the centre of Kathmandu and on the final day the umbrella is taken down and burnt.

Other activities also take place during Holi. Guru Mapa, the demon of the Yitum Bahal in Kathmandu (see Walking Tour 2 in the Kathmandu section), has his annual feed on Holi night. The inhabitants of Yitum Bahal sacrifice a buffalo on the banks of the Vishnumati River, cook it in the afternoon in their great courtyard and in the middle of the night carry it in huge cauldrons to the Tundikhel where the demon is said to live to this day.

More peacefully, singing and dancing continues until late at night during another cheerful festival in the village of Tarke Gyang on the Helambu trek.

March-April

Chaitra Dasain Also known as Small Dasain, in contrast with the Big Dasain in the month of Kartik, this one takes place exactly six months prior to the more important festival. Like the other Dasain it's dedicated to Durga and once again it's a bad day for goats and buffaloes who do their unwilling bit for the goddess early in the morning in Kot Square.

Sweta Machhendranath The Chaitra Dasain sacrifices also signal the start of the Sweta (White) Machhendranath festival, a month prior to the much larger and more important Rato (Red) Machhendranath festival in Patan. The festival starts with the removal of the image of Sweta Machhendranath from the temple at Kel Tole and placing it on a towering and creaky wooden temple chariot or *rath*. For the next four evenings the chariot proceeds from one historic location to another eventually arriving at Lagankhel in the south of Kathmandu. There the image is taken down from the chariot and carried back to its starting point in a palanquin while the chariot is disassembled and put away until next year.

April

Bisket Jatra The Nepalese new year starts in mid-April, at the beginning of the month of Baisakh, and the Bisket festival in Bhaktapur is the most spectacular welcome for the new year and one of the most exciting annual events in the valley. Magh Sankranti is the only other important religious festival set by the solar rather than the lunar calendar.

Bisket is Bhaktapur's great chariot festival but whereas in Kathmandu and Patan it is Machhendranath who gets taken for a ride, here it is Bhairab, accompanied by Betal and, in a second chariot, the goddess Bhadrakali. The ponderous chariots of the gods always appear shaky and unsafe and moving them requires enormous amounts of energy.

From Taumadhi Tole, outside Bhairab's temple, the huge temple chariot proceeds around the town, pausing for a huge tug of war between the eastern and western sides of

town. The winning side is charged with looking after the images of the gods during their week-long riverside sojourn. After the battle the chariots slither down the steep road leading to the river. Here a huge 25-metre-high lingam is erected and in the evening of the following day, new year's day, the pole is pulled down, again in an often violent tug of war. As the pole crashes to the ground the new year officially commences.

As is usual in Nepal, legend is piled upon legend, and far in the past there's a tale of a beautiful princess and a valiant prince behind the Bisket festival:

The king of Bhaktapur had an insatiable daughter who not only required a new lover each night but left them dead each morning! Finally a brave prince showed up and despite an exhausting session with the princess forced himself to stay awake afterwards. Late that night two thread-like whisps emerged from the beautiful princess's nostrils, and grew into venomous snakes in the night air. Before they could strike and consign the prince to the scrapheap of discarded lovers he drew his sword and killed them both. Of course the prince and princess married and lived happily ever after and from the top of the towering Bisket lingam stream two banners, symbolic of those two deadly snakes.

Other festivals and events also take place around Bhaktapur for a week preceding the new year and for some days thereafter. Members of the potters' caste put up and haul down their own lingam, and processions also carry images of Ganesh, Lakshmi and Mahakali around the town. The new year is also an important time in the valley for ritual bathing, and crowds of hill people come down to visit the Buddhist stupas of Swayambhunath and Bodhnath.

Balkumari Jatra Thimi, the smaller town near Bhaktapur, also welcomes the new year with an exciting festival. This event was also instituted by King Jagat Jyoti Malla in the early 1600s but here it is Balkumari, another of Bhairab's consorts, who is honoured.

All through new year's day devotees crowd around her temple in Thimi and as dusk falls hundreds of the ceremonial oil lamps *(chirags)* are lit. Some devotees lie motionless around the temple all night with burning oil lamps balanced on their legs, arms, chests and foreheads.

The next morning men come from the various *toles* or quarters of Thimi and from surrounding villages, each team carrying a palanquin known as a *khat* with images of different gods. As the 32 khats whirl around the temple red powder is hurled at them and the ceremony reaches fever pitch as the khat bearing Ganesh arrives from the village of Nagadish. The crowds parade up and down the main street until late in the morning when Ganesh, borne by hundreds of men, makes a break for home, pursued by the other khats. If they can catch Ganesh the activities are prolonged but eventually Ganesh departs and the festival moves on to the Taleju Temple.

Sacrifices are now made to Balkumari and in the small village of Bode another khat festival, with just seven of them rather than 32, now takes place. Here a volunteer spends the whole day with an iron spike piercing his tongue. Successful completion of this painful rite brings merit to the whole village as well as the devotee.

April-May
Rato Machhendranath Although Sweta and Rato Machhendranath may well be the same deity, the Rato or Red Machhendranath festival of Patan is a much more important occasion than the Kathmandu event. Machhendranath is considered to have great powers over rain and, since the monsoon is approaching at this time, this festival is a plea for good rain.

As in Kathmandu the festival consists of a day-by-day temple chariot procession through the streets of the town, but here it takes a full month to move from the Pulchowk area, where the image is installed in the chariot, to Jawlakhel where the chariot is dismantled.

Along the way the main chariot is accompanied for most of its journey by a second smaller chariot containing the image of Rato Machhendranath's Bodhisattva companion from the Minanath Temple, near the Rato Machhendranath Temple south of Patan's Durbar Square.

From Jawlakhel Rato Machhendranath does not return to his Patan temple, however. He has a second home in the village of Bungamati and he spends six months of each year at this temple, to where he is now conveyed on a khat. Every 12 years, however, the Rato Machhendranath festival becomes an even more important and time-consuming event when the chariot continues all the way to Bungamati. The next enactment of the complete Patan to Bungamati procession will be in 2003.

The temple chariots (raths) used in these processions are immense wooden affairs with wheels metres in diameter and a towering but often rather ramshackle edifice constructed on top. It takes hundreds of devotees to tow the main chariot and the Nepalese army is often called in to help in the Patan Rato Machhendranath festival, despite the intense local enthusiasm to take part in pulling the chariot. The long procession is often halted to await an auspicious occasion for the next leg, or to make important roadside repairs to the chariot.

Similar temple chariot processions take place in India including the largest of them all, the great Jagannath procession in the state of Orissa.

Buddha Jayanti (Buddha's Birthday) Siddhartha Gautama (Buddha) was born at Lumbini, so it is fitting that his birthday should be celebrated in Nepal. Swayambhunath is the centre for the celebrations although events also take place at Bodhnath and in Patan.

A constant procession of pilgrims makes its way around the stupa at Swayambhunath. The stupa's collection of rare thangkas and mandalas are shown on the southern wall of the stupa courtyard on this single day each year. The stupa's lamas dress in colourful silk robes and dance around the stupa with accompaniment provided by musicians.

Mata Tirtha Puja The last day of the dark fortnight of Baisakh is Mata Tirtha Puja. It's the Nepalese equivalent of Mother's Day and every Nepalese should go to 'look upon their mother's face'. Those whose mothers have died in the past year are supposed to bathe at the Mata Tirtha pond, about 10 km southwest of Kathmandu near the Thankot road.

May-June

Kumar Sasthi The birthday of Kumar or Kartikkaya, the god of war and brother of Ganesh, is also known as Sithinakha. The festival also marks the start of the rice-planting season and an annual occasion for cleaning wells. Once upon a time the god of war's birthday was commemorated by stone-throwing contests. Since these often turned into strictly local, but often decidedly real, 'wars' they're now mainly confined to young boys.

July-August

Naga Panchami On the fifth day after the new moon in the month of Saaun, snakes (nagas) are honoured in this festival. Numerous legends are told about snakes and they are said to have all sorts of magical powers including special powers over the monsoon rains. Pictures of the nagas are hung over the doorways of houses and this not only propitiates the snakes but also keeps harm from the household. Various foods are put out for the snakes and there are interesting legends behind the offerings of milk and boiled rice:

A farmer inadvertently killed three baby snakes with his plough and the enraged mother snake chased the farmer back to his house and killed the farmer, his wife and his two sons. The daughter was about to get the same treatment when she offered the serpent a bowl of milk. The snake was so taken by this act of kindness that it spared the daughter and offered her any wish. 'Bring my parents and brothers back to life', replied the daughter and the snake duly did so. Ever since then snakes are offered a bowl of milk on Naga Panchami.

The bowl of rice is offered because of an incident at the Siddha Pokhari pond just outside Bhaktapur which, the legend relates, was once inhabited by an evil naga. A holy man determined to kill the naga himself by taking the form of a snake, and told his companion to be ready with a bowl of magic rice. If,

after he entered the pond, the water turned white then the naga had won and it was all over. If, on the other hand, the water turned red then he had defeated the naga and although he would emerge from the pond in the form of a snake, the magical rice would restore his original form.

Sure enough the water turned red but when the holy man in the form of a hideous serpent emerged from the water his horrified companion simply turned tail and ran, taking the rice with him. The holy man tried to catch him but failed and eventually decided to return to the pond and remain there. To this day the inhabitants of Bhaktapur keep well clear of the Siddha Pokhari pond and on the day of Naga Panchami a bowl of rice is put out – just in case the holy man/snake turns up.

Janai Purnima On the day prior to and on the day of the full moon in the month of Saaun all high-caste men (Chhetri and Brahman) must change the janai (sacred thread) which they wear looped over their left shoulder and tied under their right arm. The three cords of the sacred thread symbolise body, speech and mind, and young men first put on the thread in an important ritual that officially welcomes them into their religion. From that date they wear the sacred thread for the rest of their lives, changing it on this one occasion each year as well as anytime it has been damaged or defiled. One way of defiling the sacred thread is to come into contact with a woman while she is menstruating.

Although only men wear the thread, anybody, including curious foreigners, can wear a yellow thread or *raksha bandhan* around their wrist – right for men, left for women. Wearing this thread on your wrist is said to bring good fortune and on this day priests tie the threads on all comers. You are supposed to wear it for at least a week, but preferably for three months until the Festival of Lights in October-November.

Janai Purnima also brings crowds of pilgrims to the sacred Gosainkund Lake, across the mountains to the north of Kathmandu. There they garland a statue of Shiva and throw coins at the sacred lingam which rises up from the lake. A direct channel is said to lead from the lake to the pond in the Kumbeshwar Temple in Patan and a silver lingam is installed in the pond for the occasion. The rituals at the temple attract *jhankris*, faith healers who perform in a trance while beating drums.

Gai Jatra The Gai Jatra (Cow Festival) takes place immediately after Janai Purnima on the day after the Saaun full moon, and is dedicated to those who died during the preceding year. Hindus believe that after death cows will guide them to Yama, the god of the underworld, and finding your way on this important journey will be much easier if by chance you should be holding on to a cow's tail at the moment of death! Therefore on this day cows are lead through the streets of the valley's towns or, if a cow is not available, small boys dress up as cows.

The festival also celebrates an event during the reign of King Pratap Malla (1641-1674). The king's youngest son died and the queen was utterly grief-stricken. Nothing could cheer her up and eventually the king offered rewards to anybody who could bring a smile to her face. The next day crowds of people appeared before the royal palace and danced and clowned, dressed in outlandish costumes. The queen could not help laughing at this mass outbreak of merry madness and the king proclaimed that henceforward Gai Jatra would be a day for costumes and games. So it is that many other peculiar outfits appear on the streets, apart from boys dressed up as cows, and the festival is celebrated with maximum energy on the streets of Bhaktapur.

Ghanta Karna Ghanta Karna ('night of the devil'), falls on the 14th day of the dark fortnight of Saaun. Ghanta Karna, which means 'bell ears', was a horrible demon who was so named because he wore bell earrings to drown out the name of Vishnu, his sworn enemy. The festival celebrates his destruction when a god, disguised as a frog, lured him into a deep well where the people stoned and clubbed him to death. Ghanta Karna is burnt in effigy on this night and evil is cleansed from the land for another year.

August-September

Krishna Jayanti (Krishna's Birthday) The seventh day after the full moon in the month of Bhadra is celebrated as Krishna's birthday, sometimes known as Krishnasthami. Krishna is an incarnation of Vishnu and his daring exploits, good nature and general love of a good time endear him to many people. The Krishna Mandir in Patan is the centre for the celebrations and an all-night vigil is kept at the temple on the night before his birthday. Oil lamps light the temple and singing continues through the night.

Teej The Festival of Women lasts for three days, from the second to the fifth day following the new moon in the month of Bhadra. It is centred on Pashupatinath and women celebrate the festival in honour of their husbands and in hope of a long and happy married life.

The festival starts with a sumptuous meal and the women gather together and spend the rest of the day feasting and talking, right through until midnight when they must commence 24 hours of fasting. During the day of the fast women from all over the valley converge on Pashupatinath, traditionally dressed in red and gold saris, usually the ones in which they were married. In Nepal red is the colour of happiness and weddings, white is the colour of death and funerals. At Pashupatinath the women take ritual dips in the river and call on the gods to protect their husbands.

The following morning the women must offer their husbands small items of food which had previously been offered to the gods. The day-long fast can then be broken although in some years the festival continues for an extra day in which case this is a day of partial fasting. Another ritual bathing ceremony takes place on this day, preferably at a river confluence, such as where the Bagmati and Vishnumati rivers meet, just south of Kathmandu. Completion of these ceremonies washes away all female sin, including the sin of a woman touching her husband during her period!

Gunla The 15 days before and after the full moon in August or early September is celebrated as a full month of Buddhist ceremonies, penance and fasting. Activities are centred on Swayambhunath. Pancha Dan, the Festival of Five Offerings, is held in Patan during Gunla but there are various other festivals and ceremonies during the month.

Gokarna Aunsi The Nepalese equivalent of Father's Day is celebrated at Gokarna by visiting living fathers at their homes and honouring deceased fathers.

September

Indra Jatra This important festival runs from the end of the month of Bhadra into the beginning of Ashwin. Indra Jatra is a colourful and exciting festival which manages to combine homage to Indra with an important annual appearance by Kumari (the living goddess), respects to Bhairab and commemoration of the conquest of the valley by Prithvi Narayan Shah. The festival also marks the end of the monsoon and the start of the fine months which follow.

Indra is the ancient Aryan god of rain and he once paid a visit to the Kathmandu Valley to pick a certain flower which his mother Dagini needed for the festival of Teej. Unfortunately for Indra he was captured in the act of stealing the flowers and imprisoned until his mother came down to rescue him. When she revealed whom they had imprisoned, his captors gladly released him but the festival continues to celebrate this remarkable achievement – villagers don't capture a real god every day of the week! In return for his release Dagini promised to spread morning moisture and dew over the crops for the coming months and to take back with her to heaven all those who had died in the past year.

The festival therefore honours the recently deceased and pays homage to Indra and Dagini for the coming harvests. It starts with the erection of a huge pole outside the Hanuman Dhoka palace. The carefully selected pole has first been brought to the Tundikhel and then carried to the square. The pole is set up while images and representations of Indra, usually as a captive, are

displayed and sacrifices of goats and roosters are made. At the same time the screened doors obscuring the horrific face of White Bhairab are opened and for the next three days his gruesome visage will stare out at the proceedings.

The day before all this activity, three golden temple chariots have been assembled in Basantapur Square, outside the home of the Kumari, the living goddess. In the afternoon, with the Durbar Square packed with colourful and cheerful crowds, two boys emerge from the Kumari's house. They play the roles of Ganesh and Bhairab and will each ride in a chariot as an attendant to the goddess. Finally, the Kumari herself appears either walking on a rolled-out carpet or carried by attendants so that her feet do not touch the ground.

The chariots move off and the Kumari is greeted from the balcony of the old palace by the king. The procession then continues out of Durbar Square towards Hanuman Dhoka where it stops in front of the huge White Bhairab mask. The Kumari greets the image of Bhairab and then, with loud musical accompaniment, beer starts to pour from Bhairab's mouth! Grabbing a sip of this beer is guaranteed to bring good fortune, but one lucky individual will also get the small fish which has been put to swim in the beer – this brings especially good luck!

The procession moves off again and for the remaining days of the festival, it moves from place to place around the town, to the accompaniment of ceremonies, dances and other activities. Numerous other processions also take place around the town until the final day when the great pole is lowered and carried down to the river. It was during the Indra Jatra festival back in 1768 that Prithvi Narayan Shah conquered the valley and unified Nepal so this important event is also commemorated in this most spectacular of Kathmandu occasions.

Ganesh Chata On Ganesh Chata, the fourth day of the bright fortnight in September, offerings are made to Ganesh. The festival celebrates a bitter dispute between Ganesh and the moon goddess, and the Nepalese try to stay indoors on this night and shut out all signs of moonlight.

September-October
Pachali Bhairab Jatra The fearsome form of Bhairab, as Pachali Bhairab, is honoured on the fourth day of the bright fortnight in September or early October. The festivities are in line with Bhairab's bloodthirsty nature as there are numerous sacrifices.

Other Festivals & Ceremonies
Ekadashi Ekadashi falls twice in each lunar month, 11 days after the full moon and the new moon. The annual Haribodhini Ekadashi is a major festival but the other Ekadashis are also celebrated, often with music and singing.

Marriage Ceremonies It is important that weddings take place on an auspicious date and some months of the year (Pus in particular) are extremely ill-starred for marriages. Only five months of the year – Magh, Falgun, Baisakh, Jeth and Mangsir – are ideal, although if pressed, a talented astrologer can find an auspicious date at even the most inconvenient time. Spring is the favourite time of year and on ideal days in Baisakh there will be numerous wedding bands marching around town at the same time.

A traditional Newari wedding is a complicated affair lasting up to a week. The various stages of the ceremony move back and forth between the bride and groom's homes and include a procession led by a band. The religious ceremony, where a fire 'witnesses' the marriage, is held at the bride's house and the festivities conclude with a wedding banquet. Although more couples are making their own choice of partners many marriages are still arranged.

Very different forms of marriage take place in the hills and in parts of the Sherpa country polyandry, where a women takes more than one husband, is still practised.

In Nepal, as in a number of other Asian countries, the bride never wears white. White is the colour of death and funerals, red is a much happier and more auspicious colour. Married women wear vermilion in the parting of their hair.

POST & TELECOMMUNICATIONS
The postal service to and from Nepal is, at best erratic, and can be extremely slow. Most articles do finally arrive, but they can take weeks. Poste restante services are reasonably well organised, but as with any other Asian country you should ask people writing to you to print your family name clearly and underline it. Misfiled mail often results from confusion between family names and given names.

In Kathmandu, the poste restante section is in the main post office and consists of a room with boxes arranged alphabetically lined up on a long table. You sit down at the table and sort through the letters yourself; you are required to show a passport before you take anything away. The section opens daily at 10.15 am throughout the year, and from Sunday to Thursday it closes at 4 pm in summer (3 pm in winter), while on Fridays it closes at 2 pm year-round. For information on mailing large items from Nepal, see the Things to Buy section later in this chapter.

The Pokhara post office is inconveniently far from the lakeside area where most visitors stay.

Postal Rates
In Kathmandu, stamps are sold from 8 am to 7 pm from Sunday to Friday, and from 11 am to 3 pm on Saturday. Most bookshops in Thamel, including Pilgrims, also sell stamps and deliver postcards to the post office, which is much easier than making a special trip to the post office yourself. Postal rates from Nepal are:

	Africa Europe	Australia UK & USA
Aerogrammes	Rs 9	Rs 10
Postcards	Rs 9	Rs 10
Letters (to 20 gm)	Rs 11	Rs 13

Telephone

Although internal phone communications can still be difficult it's easy to make international calls from Nepal. So-called 'communications centres' (complete with fax machines) have mushroomed around Kathmandu, and although rates do vary, they're pretty competitive. With the private operators, expect to pay around Rs 150 ($3) per minute to Australia, France, the UK and USA, and around Rs 175 ($3.50) for New Zealand and Germany. Many of the hotels also have direct-dial facilities, but always check their charges before you phone. See the Kathmandu Information section in the Kathmandu, Patan & Bhaktapur chapter for more information.

TIME

Nepal is five hours 45 minutes ahead of GMT; this curious time differential is intended to make it very clear that Nepal is a separate place to India, where the time is five hours 30 minutes ahead of GMT! When it's noon in Nepal it's 1.15 pm in Bangkok, 6.15 am in London, 1.15 am in New York, 10.15 pm the previous day in Los Angeles or San Francisco, and 4.15 pm in Sydney or Melbourne, not allowing for daylight-saving time or other variations.

ELECTRICITY

Electricity is only found in major towns and some odd outposts like Namche Bazaar in the Solu Khumbu. When available it is 220 volts/50 cycles and 120-volt appliances from the USA need a transformer. Sockets usually take three round pin plugs, sometimes the small variety, sometimes the large. Some sockets take plugs with two round pins.

Blackouts are a fact of life and can be random, or regular. In winter, power shortages are endemic, especially if there has been low rainfall in the previous monsoon (which means water flow is reduced and the hydro-electric resources have to be rationed). In late '92 there was a scheduled nationwide blackout every second day between 5 and 7 pm and 5 and 7 am.

Power surges are also likely. If you are are using expensive equipment (computers, TVs, fridges etc) it is worth buying a volt guard with spike suppressor (meaning an automatic cut-off switch). These are available from most electronic shops for around Rs 1000 ($20). Beltronix (☎ 01-224984) on Kantipath is one reliable supplier.

BOOKS

There is no shortage of books about Nepal – the Himalaya and heroic mountaineers, the colourful religions and exotic temples, the reclusive history and brave Gurkhas, have all inspired writers and photographers and the results are piled high in numerous bookshops in Nepal. Nepal has a surprisingly good selection of bookshops, mostly in Kathmandu, although there are a number in Pokhara. The books that follow are only some of the more interesting titles and include books that are long out of print and others which may only be available in Nepal.

General

Although Toni Hagen's *Nepal – the Kingdom in the Himalaya* (Kummerley & Frey, Berne, 1980) is now rather out of date, it is still one of the most complete studies of

Nepal's people, geography and geology. Toni Hagen travelled extensively through Nepal in the '50s and the book reflects his intimate knowledge of the country and also has fine colour plates.

Another now rather dated account of Nepal is Jeremy Bernstein's *The Wildest Dreams of Kew* (Simon & Schuster, New York, 1970) which covers the country's history in a very readable style and includes an interesting trek to the Everest Base Camp.

Michel Peissel takes a trip to the fabled region of Mustang, close to the border with Tibet and to the north of Jomsom, in *Mustang – A Lost Tibetan Kingdom* (Collins & Harvill Press, London, 1968).

A more recent saunter around Nepal and Tibet is recounted in the amusingly written *To the Navel of the World* (Hamish Hamilton, London, 1987; paperback by Sceptre, London, 1988) by Peter Somerville-Large. The author also does some deep-winter trekking, using yaks, in the Solu Khumbu and up to the Everest Base Camp. His encounters with tourism in remote locations are very funny.

Although Pico Iyer's recent best seller *Video Night in Kathmandu* (Vintage Books, New York, 1989) gallivants all around Asia, the chapter on Nepal has some astute and amusing observations on the collision between Nepalese tradition and Western culture, particularly video culture.

The Waiting Land: A Spell in Nepal (John Murray, London, 1967; paperback by Century Hutchinson), by Dervla Murphy, is an interesting account of a visit to Nepal at a time when great changes were at hand.

In *Mister Raja's Neighbourhood* (John Daniel, Santa Barbara, California, 1986) and *Shopping for Buddhas* (Harper & Row, San Francisco, 1990), Jeff Greenwald gives amusing accounts of his travels in Nepal. *Shopping for Buddhas* describes, amongst other things, the author's obsessive pursuit of a perfect Buddha statue. It's an acute and funny book.

Helping a captured yeti *Escape from Kathmandu* is only one adventure in Kim Stanley Robinson's off-the-wall romp

around Nepal. There's also an illegal ascent of Everest with a reincarnate lama, an attempt to kidnap King Birendra, a visit to Shambhala, a very logical explanation for why Prince Charles is the way he is, and the best ever description of what they do to Kathmandu while you're away trekking.

Han Suyin's *The Mountain is Young* (Jonathan Cape, London, 1971; also in paperback) is an overly romantic novel set in Nepal in the mid-50s. It is surprising more novelists haven't used Nepal's colourful background for their writing.

History & Economics

Although browsing through a good Kathmandu bookshop will reveal plenty of histories of Nepal there is no definitive book which tells it all in a readable fashion. In particular there has been little accounting of recent events in Nepal, especially the push for greater democracy and the underlying political unrest.

Fatalism & Development – Nepal's Struggle for Modernization (Orient Longman, Hyderabad, 1991), by Dor Bahadur Bista, is an often controversial analysis of Nepalese society and the dynamics that operate within it. There is a very good historical introduction, and the author looks especially critically at the role of the caste system.

The Political History of Nepal (Institute of International Studies, University of California, Berkeley, 1960), by Margaret W Fisher, is now 30 years old and even *Nepal in Crisis* by Blaikie, Cameron & Seddon (Oxford University Press, Oxford, 1978) is rather dated.

Charlie Pye-Smith's *Travels in Nepal* (Aurum Press, London, 1988) is a travel account on one level, but the author's travels around the country are highly directed: he was there to study the impacts and benefits of foreign aid to Nepal and his conclusions are incisive and interesting. In between the aid projects he chain-smokes his way around quite a few interesting places and appears to finish up as much in love with the country as many less single-minded visitors! See the Foreign Aid section in the Facts about the Country chapter for more about this book.

Culture, People & Festivals

Festivals of Nepal (Unwin Hyman, London, 1971; Rupa & Co, Calcutta, 1988), by Mary Anderson, is an excellent rundown on Nepal's many festivals and includes interesting accounts of many of the legends and tales behind them. There is also a great deal of background information about the Hindu religion. Mary Rubel's *The Gods of Nepal* (Bhim Ratna Harsha Ratna, Kathmandu, 1968) is a detailed description of the Hindu and Buddhist deities of Nepal.

People of Nepal (Ratna Pustak Bhandar, Kathmandu, 1974), by the Nepalese anthropologist Dor Bahadur Bista, describes the many and diverse ethnic groupings found in the country. The recently published *Ethnic Groups of Nepal* (Himalayan Booksellers, Kathmandu, 1987), by D B Shrestha & C B Singh, is a readily available account of the many peoples of Nepal.

Sherpas of Nepal (John Murray, London 1964), by C Von Furer Haimen-dorf, describes the Sherpas of the Everest region in a rather dry and academic manner. From the same author *Himalayan Traders* (John Murray, London, 1975) is a rather more read-

able follow-up, concentrating on the changes in trading patterns and cultures among the Himalayan people of Nepal.

Michel Peissel's *Tiger for Breakfast* (Hodder & Stoughton, London, 1966; paperback by Allied Publishers) is a biography of the colourful gentleman who was probably the best known resident expatriate in the kingdom – Boris Lissanevitch of the Royal Hotel and Yak & Yeti Restaurant.

Natural History

The Royal Chitwan National Park's wildlife is detailed in K K Gurung's *The Heart of the Jungle* (Andre Deutsch, London, 1983). *Indian Wildlife* (APA Productions, Singapore, 1987) covers all the national parks of the subcontinent including Chitwan and Bardia in Nepal with this publisher's usual high standards of photography.

Birds of Nepal (Nature Himalaya, Kathmandu, 1984), by Robert Fleming Sr, Robert Fleming Jr & Lain Singh Bangdel, is a field guide to Nepal's many hundreds of birds. *Himalayan Flowers & Trees* (Sahayogi Press, Kathmandu, 1978), by Dorothy Mierow & Tirtha Bahadur Shrestha, is the best available field guide to the plants of Nepal.

Other titles recommended by Lewis Underwood (the author of the Geography, Geology, Flora, Fauna and Ecology sections in the Facts about the Country chapter) are:

A Popular Guide to the Birds & Mammals of the Annapurna Conservation Area (Annapurna Conservation Area Project, Kathmandu, 1989) by Carol Inskipp

Birdwatchers' Guide to Nepal (Prion, London, 1988) by Carol Inskipp

Flowers of the Himalaya (Oxford University Press, Delhi, 1984) by Oleg Polunin & Adam Stainton

Forests of Nepal (John Murray, London 1972) by Adam Stainton

Mount Everest National Park: Sagarmatha, Mother of the Universe (The Mountaineers, Seattle, 1986) by Margaret Jefferies

Nepal's Forest Birds: Their Status and Conservation (International Council for Bird Preservation, Cambridge, 1989) by Carol Inskipp

Royal Chitwan National Park: Wildlife Heritage of Nepal (The Mountaineers, Seattle, 1991) by Hemanta R Mishra & Margaret Jefferies

The Book of Indian Animals (Oxford University Press, Bombay, 1971) by SH Prater
Trees & Shrubs of Nepal & the Himalaya (Pilgrims Book House, Kathmandu, 1990) by Adrian & Jimmie Storrs.

Art & Architecture

Lydia Aran's *The Art of Nepal* (Sahayogi Prakashan, Kathmandu, 1978) is readily available in Nepal and concentrates on the art that can actually be seen in the country, not in overseas museums. See the Arts & Crafts section of the Facts about the Country chapter for more on this book.

The Austrian publisher Anton Schroll published two exhaustive studies of the architecture of the Kathmandu Valley. *Kathmandu Valley I* (Vienna, 1975) covers the most important temples and buildings in great detail while *Kathmandu Valley II* has individual plans of a great many temples and buildings. This is strictly for the academics but it's amusing to see how many other guidebooks have used these titles in their research. Often they've even copied the mistakes!

The Traditional Architecture of Kathmandu Valley (Ratna Pustak Bhandar, Kathmandu, 1989), by Wolfgang Korn, has some superb line drawings showing the most important architectural forms, and an interesting text describing their historical development.

Mary Shepherd Sluiser's *Nepal Mandala – A Cultural Study of the Kathmandu Valley* (Princeton University Press, Princeton, 1982) is another two-volume academic study of the valley.

Nepal – Art Treasures from the Himalaya (Oxford & IBH, London, 1969), by Waldschmidt, describes and illustrates many Nepalese works of art. The art of the whole Himalayan region is covered in Madanjeet Singh's *Himalayan Art* (Macmillan, London, 1968), again with excellent photographs.

In *Kathmandu Valley Towns* (Weatherhill, New York, 1974) Fran Hosken writes about the temples, people, history and festivals of the towns of the Kathmandu Valley. The book is illustrated with a great many colour photographs and halftones.

Erotic Themes of Nepal (S Devi, Kirtipur, Kathmandu, 1981), by Trilok Chandra Majupuria & Indra Majupuria, is an interesting locally produced book on the erotic art seen on some temples, although it has to work hard to make a book-length study of the subject!

If you develop an interest in Tibetan rugs Hallvard Kåre Kuloøy's *Tibetan Rugs* (White Orchid Books, Bangkok, 1982) is a fascinating and well-illustrated introduction to the subject. If you enjoy the Tibetan rugs made in Nepal you may be disappointed to find that the author summarily dismisses modern rugs as doing 'very little justice to a very splendid tradition'.

Travel Guides

Other guidebooks to Nepal include *Insight Nepal* (APA Publications one of the Insight series of photographic coffee-table guides. APA also publish a useful pocket guide, *Nepal*, by Lisa Choegyal, which gives some good day-trip itineraries and plenty of tips. *Nepal Namaste* (Sahayogi Press, Kathmandu, 1987), by Robert Rieffel, is an excellent locally produced book with all sorts of odd titbits of information.

The Himalaya Experience (Simon & Schuster Australia, Gladesville, 1989), by Jonathan Chester, is an interesting, colourful appetite-whetter for the entire Himalayan region. It has a great deal of interesting information about trekking and climbing and some wonderful photographs.

An Introduction to the Hanuman Dhoka (Institute of Nepal & Asian Studies, Kirtipur, 1975) is no longer readily available, but it gives a good short description of the buildings around the Durbar Square area of Kathmandu.

Trekking, Biking & Rafting Guides

Lonely Planet's *Trekking in the Nepal Himalaya* by Stan Armington covers everything you need to know before setting out on a trek in Nepal, plus day-by-day coverage of all the main trekking routes. Stan's book has an excellent medical section covering the problems likely to be encountered in the mountains. *A Guide to Trekking in Nepal* (The Mountaineers, Seattle, 1981), by Stephen Bezruchka, also covers all the main trekking routes with detailed descriptions.

If you're interested in treks close to Kathmandu, *Treks on the Kathmandu Valley Rim* (Sahayogi Press, Kathmandu, 1987), by Alton C Byers III, details a number of one-day and overnight treks near Kathmandu.

A more up-to-date alternative is James Giambrone's *Kathmandu: Bikes & Hikes* (APA Publications, 1993) which gives details on 10 hikes and 11 mountain-bike rides around the valley; it also has a decent foldout map.

Anyone who is seriously interested in rafting and kayaking, and especially anyone contemplating a private expedition, should get hold of Peter Knowles & David Allardice's *White Water Nepal* (Rivers Publishing UK, Menasha Ridge Press USA). It should be possible to get copies of the book in Kathmandu. It has incredibly detailed information on river trips, 60 maps, river profiles and hydrographs, plus advice on equipment and health – in short all the information a prospective river runner could want.

Trekking Accounts
John Morris' *A Winter in Nepal* (Rupert Hart-Davis, London, 1964) recounts in a very readable fashion a trek from Kathmandu to Pokhara. Like other accounts of the time it's interesting to compare it with the situation today – there was no Kathmandu to Pokhara road in those days. Morris was a retired British army Gurkha officer and his ability to speak Nepali gave him an excellent insight into Nepalese life.

Peter Matthiessen's *The Snow Leopard* (Chatto & Windus, London, 1979; also in paperback) is, on one level, an account of a trek from Pokhara up to Dolpo in the west of Nepal, keeping an eye open for snow leopards on the way. On other levels, however, it's clear the author is searching for much more than rare wildlife and this widely acclaimed book doggedly pursues the big questions with the Himalaya as a background.

George Schaller, Matthiessen's companion on this trek, includes this same journey in *Stones of Silence* (Viking, New York, 1979), an account of various journeys in the Himalaya.

Mountains & Mountaineering
There can be few activities that so inspire people to write about them as that of mountaineering. Every first ascent of a Himalayan peak seems to have resulted in a book about it, together with the numerous other books about the mountains written simply because it seemed a good idea. *The Ascent of Rum Doodle* (Dark Peak, Sheffield, 1979), by W E Bowman, is a classic spoof of these often all-too-serious tomes.

Some mountaineering books are excellent reads. If you can find H W Tilman's *Nepal Himalaya* (Cambridge University Press, London, 1952) in a library it gives an often amusing account of some early trekking expeditions together with the odd mountain assault which had, by today's standards, an amazing lack of advance planning. Although Tilman was a Himalayan mountaineering pioneer he probably contributed even more to the current popularity of trekking. His book has recently been republished together with other Tilman classics in *The Seven*

Mountain-Travel Books (The Mountaineers, Seattle). Tilman's dry wit is quite delightful.

Maurice Herzog's *Annapurna* (Jonathan Cape, London, 1952) is a mountaineering classic. Herzog led the first group to reach the top of an 8000-metre peak, but the descent turned into a frostbitten nightmare taking them to the very outer edges of human endurance.

Naturally there have been numerous books about climbing Everest, including *Forerunners to Everest* (Harper & Row, New York, 1954) by Rene Dittert, Gabriel Chevalley & Raymond Lambert. It describes the two Swiss expeditions to Everest in 1952 and includes a good description of the old expedition route march. Sir John Hunt's *The Conquest of Everest* (Hodder & Stoughton, London, 1953) is the official account of the first successful climb of the world's highest mountain. *Everest* (Allen Lane, London, 1981), by Walt Unsworth, is probably the best history of Everest mountaineering.

In the 1970s unconquered peaks were few and far between so mountaineers' attention turned to climbing by more difficult or spectacular routes. This was technical climbing of a high order and Englishman Chris Bonnington's various expeditions were the best known examples of the craft. His book *Annapurna South Face* (Cassell, London, 1971) describes in detail the planning that goes into making a major expedition, the complicated logistics of the actual climb, and makes an authoritative account of a highly technical assault on a difficult face.

Bonnington also wrote *Everest the Hard Way* (Hodder & Stoughton, London, 1976; also in paperback) describing his expedition's first ascent of the south-western face in 1975. This climb was a perfectly planned and executed race to the top, and the book is illustrated with superb mountain photography. Despite his record of leading some of the most acclaimed mountaineering expeditions of the time, Bonnington did not reach the top of Everest until 1985, when he set a record as the oldest Everest summiteer. He was 50 years old at the time but just nine

days later his record fell to 55-year-old American climber Dick Bass.

Galen Rowell, the renowned mountain photographer, has written *Many people come, looking, looking* (The Mountaineers, Seattle, 1981). It is a thought-provoking study of the impact of trekking and mountaineering on the Himalayan region. There's a good description of the Annapurna Circuit trek and a quick sidetrip to knock off a little 6000-metre peak!

Other mountaineering books include *Annapurna to Dhaulagiri* (Department of Information, HMG, Kathmandu) by Harka Gurung, which covers the period between 1950 and 1960 when most of Nepal's major peaks 'fell' to mountaineering expeditions. Herbert Tichy's *Himalaya* (Robert Hale, London, 1970) describes the author's journeys in the region from the 1930s including his ascent of Cho Oyu, the third-highest peak climbed at that time.

Finally, for keen do-it-yourself mountaineers Bill O'Connor's *The Trekking Peaks of Nepal* (Crowood Press, Marlborough, UK, 1989) is a complete description of the climbing routes up Nepal's 18 'trekking peaks'.

MAPS

An interesting account of the history of mapping in Nepal is found in Harka Gurung's *Maps of Nepal* (White Orchid Books, Bangkok, 1983) which covers historic maps right up to the trekking maps of the early '80s.

The Research Scheme Nepal Himalaya maps are better known as Schneider Maps, after their cartographer. These are the best trekking maps available although their price is as high as their quality. The series covers the routes into the Everest region in six separate maps.

There are many locally produced maps available in Nepal which are much cheaper and for most trekkers prove quite adequate. Most of these are produced by Mandala Trekking Maps, and although they are generally only in blueprint form they have recently produced coloured versions of the

Round Annapurna and *Helambu & Langtang* maps.

The problem with all the detailed maps of Nepal is that villages often have widely diverse names and their actual position is often equally open to question. Reality, when you're there on foot, is often very different from what the map says. Even the Schneider Maps often have highly original versions of common place names.

MEDIA
Newspapers & Magazines

Nepal's English-language daily paper, the *Rising Nepal*, is often very hard to find, but it only costs Rs 3. If you want a copy get one early in the day. The paper covers most important international news while events in Nepal are reported in a very individual style! This is basically a government mouthpiece; you're going to have to read papers from abroad if you want to find both sides of the story in Nepal.

The *International Herald Tribune* is widely available in Kathmandu; it's usually much easier to find than the *Rising Nepal*. *Time* and *Newsweek* are readily available and Indian dailies like the *Statesman* or the *Times of India* can also be found.

Nepal Traveller is a useful free monthly tourist magazine distributed at many hotels including the Kathmandu Guest House. It often has very interesting articles about sightseeing, festivals, trekking and other activities in Nepal.

Himal is a bimonthly magazine published in Nepal and devoted to development and environment issues throughout the Himalaya. It's an excellent publication with top-class contributors.

Radio & TV

Radio Nepal has news bulletins in English at 8 am and 8 pm daily. Local television arrived in Nepal in the mid-80s, but the most revolutionary change has been the arrival of satellite TV. Most up-market hotels have dishes, and you can watch everything from the BBC world service, to MTV, and American wrestling.

FILM & PHOTOGRAPHY

A few years ago running out of film in Nepal could be a real problem but now there are numerous camera and film shops and good-quality film is readily available. Do check, however, that the packaging has not been tampered with, and that the expiry date has not been exceeded. There have been cases where people have bought exposed film that has been wound back on the spool. If in doubt, open the cardboard packaging and check, but you are extremely unlikely to be ripped off in the larger shops.

Colour-print film can now be processed, rapidly, competently and economically in Kathmandu and there are numerous places offering a same day service for print film. The developing charge is typically Rs 30 plus around Rs 4.50 for each print. Colour slides can now be developed in Kathmandu (although some have complained of scratched negatives). Pre-paid Kodachrome and Fujichrome has to go overseas.

Typically, Fujicolor 100 colour-print film costs about Rs 200 ($4), Fujichrome 36-exposure slide film about Rs 400 and Kodachrome 64 36-exposure slide film about Rs 625 ($12.50) including processing. A six-volt camera battery costs Rs 325 ($6.50).

Nepal is an exceptionally photogenic country so bring plenty of film. It can also provide you with some challenging opportunities. For great shots you need a variety of lenses, from a wide-angle lens if you're shooting inside compact temple compounds to long telephoto lenses if you're after perfect mountain shots or close-ups of wildlife. A polarising filter is useful to increase contrast and bring out the blue of the sky.

Remember to allow for the exceptional intensity of mountain light when setting exposures at high altitude. At the other extreme it's surprising how often in Nepal you find the light is insufficient. Early in the morning, in dense jungle in the Royal Chitwan National Park, or in gloomy temples and narrow streets you may often find yourself wishing you had high-speed film. A flash is often necessary for shots inside temples or to fill in shots of sculptures and reliefs.

Most Nepalese are content to have their photograph taken but you should always get permission first. Sherpa people are an exception and can be very camera shy. Bear in mind that if someone poses for you (especially those saintly sadhus), they may insist on being given some baksheesh for doing so.

Respect people's privacy and bear in mind that most Nepalese are extremely modest. Although people carry out many activities in public (they have no choice), it does not follow that passers-by have the right to watch or take photographs. Riverbanks and village wells, for example, are often used as bathrooms, but the users expect as much consideration and privacy as you would in your own house.

Religious ceremonies are also often private affairs, so first ask yourself whether it would be acceptable for a tourist to intrude and to take photographs at a corresponding ceremony in your home country, and then get explicit permission from the senior participants. The behaviour of many would-be National Geographic photographers at places like Pashupatinath (the most holy cremation site in Nepal) is horrendous. Imagine the outrage a busload of scantily clad, camera toting tourists would create if they invaded a family funeral in the West.

HEALTH

Travel health depends on your predeparture preparations, your day-to-day health care while travelling and how you handle any medical problem or emergency that does develop. While the list of potential dangers can seem quite frightening, with a little luck, some basic precautions and adequate information, few travellers experience more than upset stomachs.

Travel Health Guides

There are a number of books on travel health:

Staying Healthy in Asia, Africa & Latin America (Moon Publications, Chico, California, 1988) is probably the best all-round guide to carry as it's compact but very detailed and well organised.

Travellers' Health (Oxford University Press, 1986), by Dr Richard Dawood, is easy to read, comprehensive, authoritative and highly recommended although it's rather large to lug around.

Where There is No Doctor (Hesperian Foundation, Palo Alto, California, 1977), by David Werner, is a very detailed guide intended for someone going to work in an undeveloped country (eg a Peace Corps worker), rather than for the average traveller.

Travel with Children (Lonely Planet Publications, Hawthorn, 1990), by Maureen Wheeler, includes basic advice on travel health for younger children.

Predeparture Preparations

Health Insurance A travel insurance policy which covers theft, loss and medical problems is a wise idea. There is a wide variety of policies and your travel agency will have recommendations. The international student travel policies handled by STA or other student travel organisations are usually good value. Some policies offer lower and higher medical expenses options but the higher one is mainly for countries like the USA where medical costs are extremely expensive. Bear in mind, if you get seriously ill in Nepal you will almost certainly have to be evacuated, at least as far as Bangkok. Check the small print:

- Some policies specifically exclude 'dangerous activities' which can even include trekking. You probably don't want that sort of policy.
- You may prefer a policy which pays doctors or hospitals direct rather than you having to pay now and claim later. If you have to claim later make sure you keep all documentation. Some policies ask you to call back (reverse charges) to a centre in your home country where an immediate assessment of your problem is made.
- Check if the policy covers ambulances or an emergency flight home. If you have to stretch out you will need two seats and somebody has to pay for it! If you take out trekking insurance make sure it covers a helicopter rescue service as well. Being flown out by helicopter costs $1500 to $2000 and the companies operate on a pay-first, fly-afterwards basis.

Medical Kit It's wise to carry a small, straightforward medical kit. In many countries if a medicine is available at all it will generally be available over the counter. Medicine is generally cheaper in Nepal than in the West. A possible medical kit includes:

• Aspirin or panadol – for pain or fever.
• Antihistamine (such as Benadryl) – useful as a decongestant for colds, allergies, to ease the itch from insect bites or stings or to help prevent motion sickness.
• Antibiotics – useful if you're travelling well off the beaten track but they must be prescribed and you should carry the prescription with you; see note *.
• Kaolin preparation (Pepto-Bismol), Imodium or Lomotil – for stomach upsets.
• Rehydration mixture – for treatment of severe diarrhoea, this is particularly important if travelling with children.
• Antiseptic, mercurochrome and antibiotic powder or similar 'dry' spray – for cuts and grazes.
• Calamine lotion – to ease irritation from bites or stings.
• Bandages and Band-aids – for minor injuries.
• Scissors, tweezers and a thermometer (note that mercury thermometers are prohibited by airlines).
• Insect repellent, sun block, suntan lotion, Chapstick and water-purification tablets.

* Ideally antibiotics should be administered only under medical supervision and should never be taken indiscriminately. Overuse of antibiotics can weaken your body's ability to deal with infections naturally and can reduce the drug's efficacy on a future occasion. Take only the recommended dose at the prescribed intervals and continue using the antibiotic for the prescribed period, even if the illness seems to be cured earlier. Antibiotics are quite specific to the infections they can treat – stop immediately if there are any serious reactions and don't use an antibiotic at all if you are unsure whether you have the correct one or not.

Health Preparations Make sure you're healthy before you start travelling and that your teeth are OK – a visit to a Kathmandu dentist probably would not be your idea of fun. If you wear glasses bring a spare pair and your prescription, though new spectacles can be made quickly, cheaply and competently.

If you require a particular medication take an adequate supply as it may not be available locally. Take the prescription, with the generic rather than the brand name, as it will make getting replacements easier. It's a good idea to have the prescription with you to

show that you legally use the medication. It's surprising how often over-the-counter drugs from one place are illegal without a prescription or even banned in another.

When buying drugs always check the expiry date and if possible buy from places where correct storage conditions have been followed. In many Third World countries drugs may be dispensed which are no longer recommended, or have even been banned in the West. Nepalese pharmacies stock a reasonable range of Western pharmaceuticals including aspirin (useful for high-altitude headaches when trekking) and cough syrup (often necessary in the cold, dry winter air).

Vital Signs
A normal body temperature is 37°C or 98.6°F; more than 2°C higher is a 'high' fever. A normal adult pulse rate is 60 to 80 per minute (children 80 to 100, babies 100 to 140). You should know how to take a temperature and a pulse rate. As a general rule the pulse increases about 20 beats per minute for each °C rise in fever.

Respiration rate (breathing) is also an indicator of illness. Count the number of breaths per minute: between 12 and 20 is normal for adults and older children (up to 30 for younger children, 40 for babies). People with a high fever or serious respiratory illness (like pneumonia) breathe more quickly than normal. More than 40 shallow breaths a minute usually means pneumonia. ∎

Immunisations Vaccinations are able to provide protection against diseases you might be unfortunate enough to come into contact with. No specific immunisations are required for Nepal, but a number are certainly advisable, particularly if you plan to visit other Asian countries before or after Nepal. The further off the beaten track you go the more necessary it is to take precautions. All vaccinations should be recorded on an International Health Certificate which is available from your physician or health department.

Plan ahead for getting your vaccinations since some of them require an initial shot followed by a booster while some vaccinations should not be given together. Most travellers from Western countries will have been immunised against various diseases during childhood but your doctor may still recommend booster shots against measles or polio, diseases still prevalent in many developing countries. The period of protection offered by vaccinations differs widely and some are contraindicated if you are pregnant.

In some countries immunisations are available from airport or government health centres. Travel agents or airline offices will tell you where. In Kathmandu, the two best places to go are the CIWEC and Nepal International clinics (see under Medical Facilities in Kathmandu later in this section). A list of possible vaccinations includes:

Cholera Cholera vaccination may be required if you are coming from an infected area but protection is not very effective, only lasts 6 months and is contraindicated for pregnancy. Most doctors no longer feel this vaccination is worthwhile.

Meningitis Immunisation is important as there have been recent outbreaks in Nepal. The vaccination offers good protection for more than a year.

Tetanus & Diptheria Boosters are necessary every 10 years and protection is highly recommended.

Typhoid Protection lasts for three years and is useful if you are travelling in rural, tropical areas. You may have some side effects such as pain at the injection site, fever, headache and a general unwell feeling.

Infectious Hepatitis Gamma globulin is not a vaccination but a ready-made antibody which has proven very successful in reducing the chances of hepatitis infection. Because it may interfere with the development of immunity, gamma globulin should not be given until at least 10 days after administration of the last vaccine needed and as close as possible to departure because of its relatively short-lived protection period of six months.

Smallpox Smallpox has now been wiped out worldwide so immunisation is no longer necessary.

Basic Rules

Care in what you eat and drink is the most important health rule; stomach upsets are the most likely travel health problem but the majority of these upsets will be relatively minor. Don't become paranoid: trying the local food is part of the experience of travel after all. (See the Food section later in this chapter for more details.)

Many health problems can be avoided by taking care of yourself. Wash your hands frequently, as it's quite easy to contaminate your own food. You should clean your teeth with purified water rather than straight from the tap. Avoid climatic extremes: keep out of the sun when it's hot, dress warmly when it's cold. Avoid potential diseases by dressing sensibly. You can get worm infections through bare feet. Try to avoid insect bites by covering bare skin when insects are around, screening windows or beds or using insect repellents.

The number one rule is *don't* consume the water and that includes ice. If you don't know for certain that the water is safe always assume the worst. Reputable brands of bottled water or soft drinks are generally fine although in some places refilled bottles are not unknown. Take care with fruit juice, particularly if water may have been added.

Milk should be treated with suspicion as it is often unpasteurised. Boiled milk is fine if it is kept hygienically, and yoghurt is usually good. Tea or coffee should also be OK since the water will have been boiled.

Salads and fruit should be washed with purified water or peeled where possible. Ice cream is usually OK if it is a reputable brand name, but beware of ice cream that has melted and been refrozen. Thoroughly cooked food is the safest but not if it has been left to cool or if it has been reheated (watch out for items like lasagne). Avoid undercooked meat and eggs. In general, places that are packed with travellers or locals will be fine; empty restaurants are questionable.

Nutrition Make sure your diet is well balanced. Eggs, tofu, beans, lentils (dhal) and nuts are all safe ways to obtain protein. Fruit you can peel (bananas, oranges or mandarins for example) is always safe and a good

Top: Women of Sibaghat (RI'A)
Middle: Young boy (DA); children from Landrung (MC);
        smiling woman (DA)
Bottom: Patan men (SB)

Top: Washing clothes (TW)
Left: Woman in field, Tharu village (RE)
Right: Tamang woman weaving, Dhunche (RvD)

source of vitamins. Try to eat plenty of grains (rice) and bread. Remember that although food is generally safer if it is cooked well, overcooked food loses much of its nutritional value. If the food is insufficient in terms of nutrition it's a good idea to take vitamin and iron pills.

When the weather is hot make sure you drink enough; don't rely on feeling thirsty to indicate when you should have a drink. Not needing to urinate or very dark yellow urine is a danger sign. On long trips always carry a water bottle with you. Excessive sweating can lead to loss of salt and therefore muscle cramps. Salt tablets are not a good idea as a preventative but in places where not much salt is used, adding additional salt to food can help.

Water Purification The simplest way of purifying water is to boil it. It used to be thought that a minimum boiling period of 10 minutes was required, but doctors now say that just bringing water to the boil is sufficient. Remember that at high altitude water boils at a lower temperature so germs are less likely to be killed.

Simple filtering will not remove all dangerous organisms so if you cannot boil water it should be treated chemically. Chlorine tablets (Puritabs, Steritabs or other brands) will kill many but not all pathogens. Iodine is very effective in purifying water and is available in tablet form (such as Potable Aqua), but follow the directions carefully and remember that too much iodine can be harmful.

If you can't find tablets, tincture of iodine (2%) or iodine crystals can be used. Two drops of tincture of iodine per litre or quart of clear water is the recommended dosage; the treated water should then be left to stand for 30 minutes. Iodine crystals can also be used to purify water but this is a more complicated process as you have to first prepare a saturated iodine solution. Iodine loses its effectiveness if it is exposed to air or damp so keep it in a tightly sealed container. Flavoured powder will disguise the taste of treated water and is a good idea if you are travelling with children.

Medical Facilities in Kathmandu

Medical facilities in Nepal are distinctly limited. The entire country of around 19 million has a meagre 4600 hospital beds, and in most cases you wouldn't want to seen dead in them. Anyone requiring serious surgery or critical care – and who has the necessary insurance or money – flies out to Bangkok or the West.

The centrally located, government-operated Bir Hospital (☎ 01-221119) cannot be recommended. The best bet in the Kathmandu Valley is the Patan Hospital (☎ 01-521034, 522266), which is partially staffed by Western missionaries and is in the Lagankhel district of Patan, close to the last stop of the Lagankhel bus. Bear in mind that they have to give reasonable care to as many people as possible. The Teaching Hospital (☎ 01-412303) is reasonably well equipped (they have a ventilator, for instance), and is also OK.

The CIWEC clinic (☎ 01-410983) in Baluwatar is used by many foreign residents of Kathmandu. It has operated since 1982 and has developed an international reputation for research into travellers' medical problems. It's open from 9 am to 1 pm and 2 to 4 pm and is staffed by Westerners. With a single visit costing $28, it is hardly surprising the clientele is almost exclusively Western as well.

The Nepal International Clinic (☎ 01-412842) is near the Jaya Nepal cinema, close to Thamel. It also has an excellent reputation and is a bit cheaper than the CIWEC clinic. It's open from 9.30 am to 1 pm and 2 to 5 pm; a consultation costs $23.

If you need an optometrist, Mr Kaiser Malla (☎ 01-222504) in Bagh Bazaar next to the French Cultural Centre, has been recommended. For dental work, Dr Shambhu Singh (☎ 01-220452) has a dental clinic in New Rd, opposite Gem Palace, which is open from 3 to 7 pm. Dr KK Pradhan (☎ 221142) also has a dental clinic in New Baneshwar with a good reputation.

Sunburn

At high altitude you can get sunburnt surprisingly quickly even through cloud. You should use a sun block, and wearing a hat provides added protection. Use zinc cream or some other barrier cream for your nose and lips. Calamine lotion is good relief for mild sunburn.

Hypothermia

Too much cold is just as dangerous as too much heat, particularly if it leads to hypothermia. If you are trekking you should always be prepared for cold, wet or windy conditions.

Hypothermia occurs when the body loses heat faster than it can produce it and the core temperature of the body falls. It is surprisingly easy to progress from very cold to dangerously cold due to a combination of wind, wet clothing, fatigue and hunger, even if the air temperature is above freezing point. It is best to dress in layers: silk, wool and some of the new synthetic fibres are all good insulating materials. A hat is important as a lot of heat is lost through the head. A strong, waterproof outer layer is essential to help you keep dry. Carry basic supplies including high-energy food which contains simple sugars to generate heat quickly, and lots of fluid to drink.

Symptoms of hypothermia are exhaustion, numb skin (particularly toes and fingers), shivering, slurred speech, irrational or violent behaviour, lethargy, stumbling, dizzy spells, muscle cramps and violent bursts of energy. Irrationality may take the form of sufferers claiming they are warm and trying to take off their clothes.

To treat hypothermia first get out of the wind and/or rain, remove wet clothing and replace with dry, warm clothing. Drink hot liquids, not alcohol, and eat high-calorie, easily digestible food. This should be enough for the early stages of hypothermia, but if it has gone further it may be necessary to place the victim in a warm sleeping bag and get in with them. Do not rub the patient, place them near a fire or remove wet clothes in the wind.

If possible place them in a warm (not hot) bath.

Altitude Sickness

Called Acute Mountain Sickness (AMS) this occurs at high altitude and can be fatal. The lack of oxygen at high altitudes affects most people to some extent. It's important to allow for acclimatisation: take it easy at first, increase your intake of liquid and eat well. However, even with acclimatisation you may still have trouble adjusting – headaches, nausea, dizziness, a dry cough, insomnia, breathlessness, loss of appetite are all signs to heed. If you reach a high altitude by trekking, acclimatisation takes place gradually and you are less likely to be affected than if you fly straight there.

Mild altitude problems will generally abate after a day or so but if the symptoms persist or become worse the only treatment is to descend – even a few hundred metres can help. Breathlessness, a dry, irritative cough – which may progress to the production of pink, frothy sputum – severe headache, loss of appetite, nausea and sometimes vomiting are all danger signs. Increasing tiredness, confusion and lack of coordination and balance are real danger signs. Any of these symptoms individually, even just a persistent headache, can be a warning.

There is no hard and fast rule as to how high is too high: AMS has been fatal at altitudes of 3000 metres, although 3500 to 4500 metres is the usual range. It is wise to always sleep at a lower altitude than the greatest height reached during the day and remember those three basic rules for the treatment of AMS – descend, descend, descend.

The voluntary Himalayan Rescue Association publishes a pamphlet on AMS which is available from the immigration office and from all trekking agencies. They have an office in the Kathmandu Guest House compound in Thamel.

Motion Sickness

Eating lightly before and during a trip will reduce the chances of motion sickness. If you are prone to motion sickness try to find a place that minimises disturbance – near the wing on aircraft, near the centre on buses. Fresh air usually helps, reading or cigarette smoke doesn't. There are commercial preparations to prevent motion sickness, but they may cause drowsiness. Preparations have to be taken before the trip commences: when you're feeling sick it's too late. Ginger is a natural preventative and is available in capsule form.

Diarrhoea

A change of water, food or climate can all cause the runs, but more serious is diarrhoea due to contaminated food or water. Despite all your precautions you may still have a bout of mild travellers' diarrhoea but a few rushed toilet trips with no other symptoms is not indicative of a serious problem. Moderate diarrhoea, involving half a dozen loose movements in a day, is more of a nuisance. Dehydration is the main danger with any diarrhoea, particularly for children, so fluid replenishment is the number one treatment. Weak black tea with a little sugar, soft drinks left to go flat and diluted with water or soda water are all good. With severe diarrhoea a rehydrating solution is necessary to replace minerals and salts. You should stick to a bland diet as you recover.

Lomotil or Imodium can be used to bring relief from the symptoms although they do not actually cure it. Only use these drugs if absolutely necessary – if you *must* travel for example. For children, Imodium is preferred. Do not use these drugs if the sufferer has a high fever or if he/she is severely dehydrated. Antibiotics can be very useful in treating severe diarrhoea especially if the illness is accompanied by nausea, vomiting, stomach cramps or mild fever.

Giardia

This intestinal parasite is present in contaminated water and the symptoms are stomach cramps, nausea, bloated stomach, watery foul-smelling diarrhoea and frequent gas. Giardia can appear several weeks after exposure to the parasite, and the symptoms may disappear for a few days and then return; this might go on for a number of weeks. The recommended drug is metronidazole (known as Flagyl) but should only be taken under medical supervision; antibiotics are no use.

Dysentery

This serious illness is caused by contaminated food or water and is characterised by severe diarrhoea, often with blood or mucus in the stool. There are two kinds of dysentery. The first, bacillary dysentery, is characterised by a high fever and rapid development; headache, vomiting and stomach pains are also symptoms. It generally does not last longer than a week, but is highly contagious.

The second type, amoebic dysentery, is more gradual in developing, causes no fever or vomiting but is a more serious illness. It's not a disease that is self-limiting: it will persist until treated and can recur and cause long-term damage.

A stool test is necessary with dysentery but if no medical care is available tetracycline is the prescribed treatment for bacillary dysentery, metronidazole for amoebic dysentery.

Cholera

The cholera vaccination is not very effective. Cholera outbreaks are generally widely reported so you can avoid these areas. The disease is characterised by a sudden onset of acute diarrhoea with 'rice water' stools, vomiting, muscular cramps, and extreme weakness. Medical help is required, but you should treat for dehydration which can be extreme. If there is an appreciable delay in reaching a hospital begin taking tetracycline. This drug should not be given to young children or pregnant women and it should not be used past its expiry date.

Viral Gastroenteritis

Viral gastroenteritis is not caused by bacteria but, as the name suggests, by a virus and is characterised by stomach cramps, diarrhoea, sometimes vomiting, and sometimes a slight fever. All you can do is rest and drink lots of fluids.

Hepatitis

Hepatitis A is the most common form of this disease and is spread by contaminated food or water. The symptoms are fever, chills, headache, fatigue, feelings of weakness and aches and pains. This is followed by loss of appetite, nausea, vomiting, abdominal pain, dark urine, light coloured faeces and jaundiced skin. The whites of the eyes may turn yellow. In some case there may just be a feeling of being unwell, tired, no appetite, aches and pains and the jaundiced effect. You should seek medical advice, but in general there is not much you can do apart from resting, drinking lots of fluids, eating lightly and avoiding fatty foods. People who have had hepatitis must forego alcohol for six months after the illness as hepatitis attacks the liver and it needs that amount of time to recover.

Hepatitis B, which used to be called serum hepatitis, is spread through sexual contact and through skin penetration (for example via dirty needles and blood transfusions). Avoid having your ears pierced, tattoos done or injections where you have doubts about the sanitary conditions. The symptoms and treatment of type B are much the same as type A but gamma globulin as a prophylaxis is only effective against type A.

Typhoid

Typhoid fever is another intestinal infection that travels the faecal-oral route, ie contaminated water and food are responsible. Vaccination against typhoid is not totally effective and it is one of the most dangerous infections so medical help must be sought.

The early symptoms are like so many others: you may feel like you have a bad cold or flu on the way, headache, sore throat and a fever which rises a little each day until it is around 40°C or more. The pulse is often slow for the amount of fever present and gets slower as the fever rises, unlike a normal fever where the pulse increases. There may also be vomiting, diarrhoea or constipation.

In the second week the high fever and slow pulse continue and a few pink spots may appear on the body along with trembling, delirium, weakness, weight loss and dehydration. If there are no further complications, the fever and symptoms will slowly go during the third week. However, you must get medical help before this as common complications are pneumonia (acute infection of the lungs) or peritonitis (burst appendix). Typhoid is very infectious.

The victim's fever should be treated by keeping them cool and watching that they don't become dehydrated. Chloramphenicol is the recommended antibiotic but there are fewer side affects with ampicillin.

Worms

These parasites are most common in rural, tropical areas and a stool test when you return home is not a bad idea. They can be present on unwashed vegetables or in undercooked meat and you can pick them up through your skin by walking in bare feet. Infestations may not show up for some time, and although they are generally not serious, if left untreated they can cause severe health problems. A stool test is necessary to pinpoint the problem and medication is often available over the counter.

Tetanus

This potentially fatal disease is found in undeveloped tropical areas and is difficult to treat but is preventable with immunisation. Tetanus occurs when a wound becomes infected by a germ which lives in the faeces of animals or people, so clean all cuts, punctures or animal bites. Tetanus is known as lockjaw and the first symptom may be discomfort in swallowing, followed by stiffening of the jaw and neck, and then painful convulsions of the jaw and whole body.

Rabies

Rabies is found in many countries and is caused by a bite or scratch from an infected animal. Dogs are a noted carrier. Any bite, scratch or even lick from a mammal should be cleaned immediately and thoroughly. Scrub with soap and running water then clean with an alcohol solution. If there is any possibility that the animal is infected medical help should be sought immediately. Even if the animal is not rabid, all bites should be treated seriously as they can become infected or can result in tetanus. A rabies vaccination is now available and should be considered if you are in a high-risk category, eg people working with animals.

Meningococcal Meningitis

There have been outbreaks of meningitis in Nepal. An epidemic occurred in the Kathmandu Valley in 1983 and in the ensuing two years, six foreigners contracted meningococcal meningitis and two died. In 1985 the US Centres for Disease Control advised travellers to be vaccinated against the disease, and since then there have still been sporadic cases in travellers. Vaccination is still sound advice, especially for trekkers. The disease is spread by close contact with people who are carrying it in their throats and noses, and it is spread by coughing and sneezing. These people may not be aware that they are carriers. Lodges in the hills where travellers spend the night are prime spots for the spread of infection.

This very serious disease attacks the brain and can be fatal. The first symptoms are a scattered blotchy rash, fever, severe headache, sensitivity to light and neck stiffness which prevents forward bending of the head.

Death can occur within a few hours so it is important to get immediate treatment.

The treatment is large doses of penicillin given intravenously, or, if that is not possible, intramuscularly, ie in the buttocks.

Tuberculosis

Although this disease is widespread in many undeveloped countries it is not a serious risk to travellers. Young children are more susceptible than adults and vaccination is a sensible precaution for children under 12 travelling in endemic areas. TB is commonly spread by coughing or by unpasteurised dairy products from infected cows. Milk that has been boiled is safe to drink and the souring of milk to make yoghurt or cheese kills the bacilli.

Diptheria

Diptheria can be a skin infection or a more dangerous throat infection. It is spread by contaminated dust contacting the skin or by the inhalation of infected cough or sneeze droplets. Frequent washing and keeping the skin dry will help prevent skin infection. A vaccination is available to prevent the throat infection.

Sexually Transmitted Diseases

The most common of these diseases are gonorrhoea and syphilis. Note that HIV/AIDS can be spread through infected blood transfusions or by dirty needles – vaccinations, acupuncture and tattooing can potentially be

---

AIDS in Nepal

Prostitution does exist in Nepal, particularly in the border towns and along the main truck routes, but it is virtually invisible to Western visitors. In addition, it is believed that over 100,000 Nepalese women work in Indian brothels, often in conditions little different to slavery, and over 30,000 of these are estimated to be HIV positive. When obvious AIDS symptoms force these women to retire, some do manage to return to Nepal. Sadly, they are shunned by their families and there is virtually no assistance available to them or their children.

Up to half a million Nepalese men seek seasonal work in Indian cities, and in common with migrant workers elsewhere it is likely that many patronise brothels while they are away. Finally, there are estimated to be 10,000 intravenous drug users in Nepal who are at risk. No official figures are available, but it is clear that AIDS has the potential to become a major problem. ■

as dangerous as intravenous drug use if the equipment is not clean.

Malaria

This serious disease is spread by mosquito bites. Symptoms include headaches, fever, chills and sweating which may subside and recur. Without treatment malaria can develop more serious, potentially fatal effects. Malaria has been virtually eradicated from the Terai but malarial phrophylactics are still advisable, especially if you are travelling during the wet season. If your visit to Nepal is restricted to the high country – Kathmandu, Pokhara and the trekking routes – malaria protection is not necessary.

Antimalarial drugs do not actually prevent the disease but suppress its symptoms. Chloroquine is the usual malarial prophylactic and treatment consists of a tablet taken once a week for two weeks prior to arrival in the infected area until six weeks after you depart. Chloroquine-resistant malaria is not a problem in Nepal.

Chloroquine is quite safe for general use, the side effects are minimal and it can be taken by pregnant women. Maloprim, generally recommended for areas where chloroquine resistance has been reported, can have rare but serious side effects. Fansidar, once used as a chloroquine alternative, is no longer recommended because of dangerous side effects but it may still be recommended as a treatment for malaria. Chloroquine is also used for malaria treatment but in larger doses than normal prophylaxis.

Mosquitoes appear after dusk and making an effort to avoid being bitten by covering bare skin and using an insect repellent will further reduce the risk. Insect screens on windows and mosquito nets on beds offer protection, as does burning a mosquito coil. Mosquitoes may be attracted by perfume, aftershave or certain colours.

Dengue Fever

There is no prophylactic available for this mosquito-spread disease and the main preventative measure is to avoid mosquito bites.

A sudden onset of fever, headaches and severe joint and muscle pains are the first signs before a rash starts on the trunk and spreads to the limbs and face. After a few more days, the fever subsides and recovery will begin. Serious complications are not common.

Cuts & Scratches

Skin punctures can easily become infected in hot climates and may be difficult to heal. Treat any cut with an antiseptic solution and mercurochrome. Where possible avoid bandages and Band-aids which can keep wounds wet.

Snake Bite

The chances of being bitten by a snake in Nepal are remote. Snake bites do not cause instantaneous death and antivenins are usually available. Keep the victim calm and still, wrap the bitten limb tightly, as you would for a sprained ankle, and attach a splint to immobilise it. Then seek medical help, if possible with the dead snake for identification. Don't attempt to catch the snake if there is any remote possibility of being bitten again. Tourniquets and sucking out the poison are now comprehensively discredited.

Insect & Spider Bites

Bee and wasp stings are usually painful rather than dangerous. Calamine lotion will give relief or ice packs will reduce the pain and swelling. There are some spiders with dangerous bites but antivenins are usually available.

Bedbugs & Lice

Bedbugs live in various places, particularly dirty mattresses and bedding. Spots of blood on bedclothes or on the wall around the bed can be read as a suggestion to find another hotel. Bedbugs leave itchy bites in neat rows. Calamine lotion may help.

All lice cause itching and discomfort and make themselves at home in your hair (head lice), your clothing (body lice) or in your pubic hair (crabs). They get to you by direct contact with infected people or sharing combs, clothing and the like. Powder or shampoo treatment will kill the lice and infected clothing should be washed in very hot water.

Leeches

Leeches (*jukha*) are common along trekking trails or in the Royal Chitwan National Park during the monsoon. They attach themselves to your skin to suck your blood. For some time after the monsoon finishes they can still be found in damp areas. Walkers often get them on their legs or in their boots. Salt or a lighted cigarette end will make them fall off. Do not pull them off as the bite is then more likely to become infected. An insect repellent may keep them away so if they're a real nuisance it's worth soaking your socks in repellent.

Women's Health

Gynaecological Problems Poor diet, lowered resistance due to the use of antibiotics for stomach upsets and even contraceptive pills can lead to vaginal infections when travelling in hot climates. Keeping the genital area clean, wearing cotton underwear and skirts or loose-fitting trousers will help to prevent infections.

Yeast infections, characterised by a rash, itch and discharge can be treated with a vinegar or even lemon juice douche or with yoghurt. Nystatin suppositories are the usual medical prescription. Trichomoniasis is a more serious infection with a discharge and a burning sensation when urinating. Male sexual partners must also be treated and if a vinegar-water douche is not effective medical attention should be sought. Flagyl (metronidazole) is the prescribed drug.

If you are depending on the pill for contraception, bear in mind that stomach problems can reduce the degree to which you absorb the ingredients, and therefore the pill's effectiveness.

Pregnancy Most miscarriages occur during the first three months of pregnancy so this is the most risky time to travel. The last three months should also be spent within reasonable distance of good medical care as quite serious problems can develop at this time. Pregnant women should avoid all unnecessary medication, but vaccinations and malarial prophylactics should still be taken where possible. Additional care should be taken to prevent illness and particular attention should be paid to diet and nutrition.

WOMEN TRAVELLERS

Nepal is perhaps among the safest countries in the world for women travellers; theft is rare and prostitution is nonexistent from a Westerner's point of view. However, as is the case in most countries, women should still be cautious, especially when trekking. Never trek alone, and only trek with companies that have been recommended by trustworthy friends. Also, bear in mind that some Nepalese men have peculiar ideas about the morality of Western women, given exposure to Western films, 'immodest' clothing, and interracial holiday flings. Dress modestly, and avoid situations where you cannot call for help should a situation get out of hand.

DANGERS & ANNOYANCES
Trekking

Surrounded by Western comforts in Kathmandu, it is easy to forget that Nepal is, in terms of many physical resources, an undeveloped country. This means that people are extremely poor, hygiene is often bad, transport (particularly of the road variety) is dangerous, rescue facilities are limited, and medical facilities are often primitive or nonexistent.

Fired up by the gung-ho stories of adventurous travellers, it is also easy to forget that mountainous terrain is always potentially dangerous. Nepal, of course, is a continuous series of the most spectacular mountains in the world. And the risks are correspondingly real.

Only a tiny minority of people do finally end up in trouble, but the tragedy is that accidents and their consequences can often be avoided or minimised – if people have a realistic understanding of where they are and what they are doing, and they observe commonsense rules and take a few basic precautions. See the Trekking chapter for more details.

The combined Kathmandu Environment Education Project (KEEP) and Himalayan Rescue Association (HRA) Trekkers' Information Centre in the Hotel Tilicho, near the immigration office on Tridevi Marg, Kathmandu can give up-to-date information on trekking conditions and health risks. A visit is strongly recommended. Several embassies and consulates have registration forms at the centre; if they don't, you can register at the actual embassy/consulate. The forms record your name, rough itinerary, insurance details and next of kin, and can obviously speed up a search, or a medical evacuation.

Theft

Things do get stolen in Nepal, just like anywhere else in the world, but theft is still extremely rare. There are pickpockets in crowded areas of old Kathmandu; backpacks can disappear from bus roofs and from hotel storage rooms; possessions get stolen from camp sites; and on rare occasions lone trekkers have even been mugged and robbed.

There's little chance of ever retrieving your gear if it is stolen, and even getting a police report, a necessity for an insurance claim, can be difficult. Try the local police station, but if you aren't getting anywhere, go straight to Interpol (☎ 01-411210/705/ 059, 410088) at the Police Headquarters in Laxal, Kathmandu; the postal address is PO Box 407. There is a local Interpol office just off Durbar Square but it will only handle your case if the theft actually took place in Kathmandu. The documentation requires a passport photograph, and photocopies of your passport and visa; the process takes two days.

ACCOMMODATION

In Kathmandu there is a very wide variety of accommodation from rock-bottom flea pits to five-star international hotels. The intense competition between the many cheaper places keeps prices down and standards up – Kathmandu has many fine places with pleasant gardens and rooms for less than $10 a night including private bathroom and hot water. At peak times, on the other hand, rooms in the four and five-star places can be in short supply.

Pokhara also has a variety of accommodation although the choice is concentrated more at the bottom end of the market. There's only one real luxury hotel in Pokhara. Elsewhere in the country the choice of hotels can be very limited but there are now places to stay along most of the major trekking trails. These days it's quite possible to trek from lodge to lodge rather than camping site to camping site. On some trails the standards may be spartan – the accommodation may be dormitory-style or simply an open room to unroll your sleeping bag. Smoke can be a real problem in places where the chimney has yet to make an appearance. At the other extreme some trails, like the popular Pokhara to Jomsom route, have excellent lodges and guest houses at every stopping place.

FOOD & DRINK

Real Nepalese food is distinctly dull. Most of the time it consists of a dish called *dhal bhat tarkari* which is made up of lentil soup, rice and curried vegetables. The occasional dhal bhat tarkari, prepared to tourist tastes in Kathmandu restaurants, can be just fine. Strictly local versions, eaten day in and day out while trekking, can get very boring indeed. Of course Indian cuisine has had a major influence on Nepal and many Tibetan dishes have come over the border, along with Nepal's many Tibetan refugees. Other popular local food and drink includes:

beer – the locally produced beer is quite good, especially after a hard day's walking or bicycling around the valley. Beer is sometimes found in the hills as well, carried there by porters especially for thirsty trekkers, but is unlikely to be very cold. There are a number of locally produced brands that theoretically replicate the original recipes – Tuborg (Danish), Star (German), Iceberg (Indian), San Miguel (Philipino). Star and Iceberg are generally less expensive.

buff – water buffalo, casually abbreviated to buff, is the usual substitute for beef since cows are sacred and (officially at least) cannot be eaten. You may come across anything from buff burgers to buff steaks. Increasingly, beef steaks are imported from India.

chang – the home brew of the Himalaya, a mildly alcoholic concoction made from barley

curd – yoghurt is known throughout the sub-continent as curd and the buffalo milk curd of Nepal can be very good.

gundruk – dried vegetables are used in this traditional Nepalese soup

gurr – potatoes are the staple food of the Sherpas and although they are a relatively recent introduction, potatoes have come to assume the same importance in the Solu Khumbu as they do in Ireland. Gurr is made from raw potatoes ground and mixed with spices and then grilled like a large pancake and eaten with cheese.

lassi – refreshing drink of curd mixed with water; make sure the water is safe

momo or *kothe* – typical Tibetan dish made by steaming or frying meat or vegetables wrapped in dough; very much like dim sum or ravioli.

sikarni – a sweet curd dessert that may include nuts and dried fruit

tama – traditional Nepalese soup made from dried bamboo shoots

thupka – traditional Tibetan meat soup

tsampa – ground grain mixed with tea, water or milk and eaten dry either instead of rice or mixed with it; the staple dish in the hill country

Although the real local food is often limited in its scope and heavily influenced by Indian cuisine, Kathmandu's restaurants offer an amazing variety of dishes. In the days of 'Asia overlanding', when many travellers arrived in Kathmandu having made a long and often wearisome trip through Asia from Europe, Kathmandu's restaurants had a near mythical appeal. Ecstatic reports filtered back along the trail of superb restaurants and fine cuisine.

These days, when most travellers jet straight in from abroad, the food doesn't seem quite so amazing, but Kathmandu's many restaurants still do give international cuisine a damn good try and they will attempt almost anything. There's a special appeal to being high in the Himalaya and being able to choose between not just European and Asian dishes but also almost anything else from Mexican tacos to Japanese sukiyaki. Of course Nepalese interpretations of foreign dishes often arrive a little off target but Nepal is a great place to try Tibetan dishes and the Indian food can also be very good.

Such a variety of restaurants is particularly amazing when you consider that in 1955 Kathmandu had just one restaurant. Leave Kathmandu behind, however, and apart from a few places in Pokhara and other scattered centres you're soon back to dhal bhat tarkari.

Many of the 'international' restaurants use large quantities of imported food. Cows, for instance, are theoretically not killed in Hindu Nepal, so beef is imported frozen from Calcutta. By ordering with a little care, and especially avoiding beef steaks, it is possible to eat local ingredients and prevent the vital foreign currency you are contributing to the economy heading straight out of the country to pay for your luxuries.

Eating & Drinking Customs

There are a number of 'rules' and customs relating to eating and drinking in Nepal and a number of ways in which you can make life much easier for yourself. For a start the Nepalese eating schedule is quite different from that in the West. The morning usually begins with little more than a cup of tea. Not until late morning is a substantial 'brunch' taken. In areas where Western visitors are not often seen and even more rarely catered for, finding food will be much simpler if you go along with this schedule.

You can also save yourself a lot of time and frustration if you pay attention to what you order as well as when you order it. In small local restaurants the cooking equipment and facilities are often very primitive. Places with some experience of catering to Western tastes will often offer amazingly varied menus, but just because they offer 20 different dishes doesn't mean they can fix two of them at the same time. If you and your five friends turn up at some small and remote cafe and order six different dishes you can expect to be waiting for dinner when breakfast time rolls around next day. In that situation it makes a lot of sense to order the

same dish six times! Not only will you save time, but you will also save firewood.

There are a number of religious restrictions you should observe. The kitchen of a home is a holy of holies where few, and certainly no non-Hindus, may venture. Touching somebody else's food is a major faux pas – in Nepal you do not taste the soup from the pot! Notice how the Nepalese, when drinking from a jug or bottle, do so by pouring the liquid into their mouth without ever touching the container with their mouth.

Caste rules also play a part in Nepalese eating habits. A high-caste Brahman simply cannot eat food prepared by a lower caste individual, which effectively bans practising Brahmans from restaurants since they cannot know what is going on behind the kitchen door. If you are invited out to a meal at a Nepalese home you may find the women of the household remain totally in the background and do not eat with the men or with guests. As in India even at quite Westernised homes socialising goes on before the meal

---

Chang Recipe

If you develop a taste for chang and would like to brew some at home here's the recipe. Get a 25 or 50-litre fermenting vessel from a brewery supply shop. For the smaller vessel boil about two kg of millet for several hours. Millet swells considerably so make sure there is plenty of water and it doesn't stick. When it cools add water to liquefy it; you can also pass it through a blender to smooth it out. Then add burgundy yeast and the juice of a lemon and leave to ferment. This can take several weeks or a couple of months depending on taste. If you like a little extra kick to your chang add sugar, several kg, to the fermenting brew – this is really cheating since in Nepal sugar would be too expensive to be used in this way.

The final product will have to be strained through a cloth and racked to remove the yeasty taste. This should not be taken as the only way to produce chang – experiment with it; in Bhutan for example they drink a chang made from half millet and half rice.

Karel Tiller, Australia

rather than afterwards. As the last mouthful is consumed the guests head out the door – nobody hangs around for conversation over the coffee!

Of course some foods are strictly taboo in Nepal. High-caste Hindus and all Brahmans are, ostensibly at least, vegetarian, but carnivore or not, beef is strictly banned from the menu since the cow is a holy animal. The number one eating rule in Nepal, as in much of Asia, is always use your right hand. The left hand, used for washing yourself after defecating, is never used to eat food and certainly should not be used to pass food to someone else.

Care in Eating & Drinking

Don't drink the water is the prime health rule on the subcontinent and it certainly applies to Nepal. Diarrhoea, dysentery or even hepatitis can all result from indulging in contaminated drinking water. It is much easier nowadays to keep clear of unhealthy water as bottled mineral water is readily available.

In actual fact the relative safety of the water varies with the season. Drinking tap water is never a good idea, but during the dry season from around November to April you would probably get away with it, in Kathmandu at least. During the monsoon, however, when the heavy rains wash all sorts of stuff into the water supply, don't even consider it. Drinking boiled and filtered water is a better idea at any time of year and absolutely imperative in the wet season.

Most good restaurants do boil and filter their water, and although there's no way of telling if it has been boiled or not, tea will be safe, because boiling water is essential for its preparation. Plastic bottles of mineral water are becoming increasingly popular. Although these seem to be safe (mostly anyway), the empty bottles are creating a major litter problem. The best alternative is to have your own water bottle and to treat the water with iodine. This is 100% safe and has the added benefit of not requiring a fire. See the Health section earlier in this chapter for information on iodine treatment.

At higher altitudes the water is generally safer than lower down and in more densely populated areas. Nevertheless, trekkers should never drink water from springs or streams unless they are absolutely positive they are at a higher level than any villages or cattle. In Nepal that is a very hard thing to guarantee and it is always wiser to prepare your drinking water carefully. Chang, the popular Tibetan beer, is generally safe and is found along many trekking routes.

Food stalls on the street should be approached with extreme caution and ice cream from street vendors should be completely avoided. In good restaurants the ice cream is usually fine. Meat is more likely to be unhealthy than vegetable or egg dishes; a glance at most Nepalese butchers will soon show you why! If you're in doubt about the quality of meat dishes stick to vegetarian dishes.

Beware of salads except in places you know take special care with their food preparation. Salads rinsed in untreated water are notorious for causing stomach problems. Sandwiches can also be risky.

Many travellers do develop some sort of stomach upset while in Nepal although fortunately it's usually just travellers' diarrhoea. In that case a little fasting, hot tea and fighting it off naturally is the best cure. That way you develop some resistance against further attacks. See the Health section for more details.

THINGS TO BUY

Nepal is a shopper's paradise whether you are looking for a cheap souvenir or a real work of art. Although you can find almost anything in the tourist areas of Kathmandu there are specific specialities in different parts of the valley. Wherever you shop remember to bargain, although with the increasing number of totally tourist-oriented shops more fixed-price establishments are beginning to appear.

One place you could start is the Amrita Craft Collection, south of the Kathmandu Guest House in Thamel. They have quite a broad collection of crafts and clothing, all priced. (Subtract 20% and you get a good bench mark for what you should pay on the street if you are an excellent bargainer.)

Antiquities cannot be taken out of the country, and baggage is inspected by Nepalese customs with greater thoroughness on departure than on arrival. If you've bought something which is possibly antique, you should get a receipt and a description of the object from the shop where you bought it. Art theft is a real problem in Nepal and it would be a great shame if some of the superb museum pieces which currently stand in the open, where they may have been for over 1000 years, have to be moved into protected museums.

A permit is required from the Department of Archaeology (☎ 01-215358) in order to take any object which looks as if it could be more than 100 years old out of the country. The office is in the National Archives building on Ram Shah Path and if you visit between 10 am and 1 pm you should be able to pick up a permit by 5 pm the same day. The customs office (☎ 01-215525) at Tripureshwar can also provide information.

Thangkas
Thangkas are the traditional Tibetan paintings of religious and ceremonial subjects. They illustrate gods, associated deities, mandalas, the wheel of life and other such subjects. The figures may be of the various Buddhas, Bodhisattvas or Taras although often they are of the fierce and angry Tantric gods. Thangkas are usually colourful and packed with detail to every corner of the painting.

Although there are genuine antique thangkas to be found it's highly unlikely that anything offered to the average visitor will date from much beyond last week. Judicious use of a smoky fire can add the odd century in no time at all. Thangkas do vary considerably in quality but buy one because you like it, not as a valuable investment.

Thangkas are available in many locations including the Tibetan shops around Bodhnath. There are some good thangka shops in Thamel in Kathmandu and in the Durbar Square shops in Bhaktapur. There is also an outlet near the Pujari Math monastery. Thangkas can cost anything from Rs 200 ($4) to Rs 2000 ($40) and beyond, and like many other crafts the more you see the more you will appreciate the difference between those of average and those of superior quality. Size also plays a part in the final price of course. Traditionally thangkas are framed in silk brocade.

Block Prints
Locally produced rice paper is used for the block prints of Nepalese, Tibetan and Chinese deities. They are sold as pictures or for calendars, cards, lanterns and many other uses. A print would typically cost from Rs 50 to Rs 100 ($2). In Thamel near the Kathmandu Guest House there is a particularly good selection in The Print Shop.

Other Paintings
Patan has some very interesting small shops selling paintings just north of Durbar Square. The two interesting specialities here are paintings of Nepalese birds and a naive art style clearly influenced by the Sherpa paintings of the Solu Khumbu region. See the Things to Buy section of Patan for more details.

Tibetan Carpets
Carpet-weaving is a major trade in Nepal, brought from Tibet by the refugees who now carry on the craft with great success in their new homes. There are carpet-weavers around the Kathmandu Valley and also in Pokhara. Some of their output is now exported to Tibet, where the Chinese have unfortunately managed to totally stamp out the archaic craft. A genuine Tibetan carpet purchased in Tibet is probably indeed made by genuine Tibetans, but in Nepal the Tamang people also make carpets.

Jawlakhel, on the southern outskirts of Patan, is the carpet-weaving centre in the valley and there are numerous carpet shops as you enter the area. You can see carpets being woven here but also in other places around the valley, including around the

> **Antiques**
>
> Treat the word 'antique' with great caution in Nepal. Maureen and I were sitting on the top platform of the Shiva Temple in Kathmandu's Durbar Square watching life pass by one afternoon when one of Kathmandu's numerous young wheelers and dealers came by to practise his English with us. We talked about this and that, and then noticed another young man several steps below us busily working away on something with a variety of tools and a small blowtorch.
>
> 'Do you know what he's making?' said our companion.
>
> 'No,' we replied, 'what is he making?'
>
> 'He's making it very old,' was the reply.
>
> **Tony Wheeler**

Bodhnath Stupa. There are larger and smaller sizes available, but the traditional size for a Tibetan carpet is 1.8 metres by 90 cm. They're sturdily woven with colourful designs featuring Tibetan Buddhist symbols and dragons. These days it is more difficult to find the brilliant reds and blues produced by chemical dyes: more often carpets will be in the pale pastel shades which come from vegetable dyes. Small square carpets are often used to make seat cushions.

Clothing & Embroidery

Tibetan and Nepalese clothes have always been a popular buy but recently Western fashions made strictly for the tourist market have also become an important industry. You can buy handmade shirts at outlets in Thamel and there are also shops in Kathmandu (see the Kathmandu Things to Buy section) selling superb handpainted silk dresses at a fraction of what they would cost in the West.

Despite the growing market for Western fashions there is still a demand for traditional styles such as the Tibetan wool jackets which are popularly known as *yakets*. Nepalese coats, crossing over at the front, closed with four ties and traditionally made in purple velvet material, are a popular buy.

Embroidery has always been popular in Nepal and there are lots of little tailor shops around Kathmandu where the sewing machines rattle on until late at night adding colourful dragons and Tibetan symbols to customers jackets and jeans. Mountaineering expeditions like to return from Nepal with jackets carrying the message that this was the Country X, Year Y expedition to Peak Z. You can take your own clothes to be embroidered or buy T-shirts and other items already embroidered. Badges embroidered with suitable messages are another good buy – you can add a badge to your backpack saying that you walked to the Everest Base Camp or completed the Annapurna Circuit.

A Nepalese cap or *topi* is part of Nepalese formal wear for a man and they are traditionally made in Bhaktapur. There's a cap shop right beside the Bhairabnath Temple in Bhaktapur as well as a group of cap specialists between Indra Chowk and Asan Tole in the old part of Kathmandu. Caps typically cost from Rs 50 to Rs 300 ($6).

Pottery

Terracotta pottery is made in a number of sites but particularly in Thimi and Bhaktapur. The Potters' Square, just south of Durbar Square in Bhaktapur, is a wonderful sight. Thousands of pots are neatly lined up across the square while in the shelters around the sides of the square, potters busily turn out more and more. In Thimi they specialise in making attractive little flowerpots, often in the shape of dragons, elephants or mythical beasts. You can buy them in Thimi or from stalls near Indra Chowk in Kathmandu or Taumadhi Tole in Bhaktapur.

Jewellery

Kathmandu's many small jewellery manufacturers turn out a wide variety of designs with an equally wide range of standards. You can buy jewellery ready-made; ask them to create a design for you or bring in something you would like copied. There are several good shops around Thamel, particularly down towards Chhetrapati.

These outlets mainly cater to Western tastes but there are also many shops for the local market as Nepalese women, like Indian women, traditionally wear their wealth in jewellery. Cheap ornaments can also be fun; you can buy an armful of plastic bangles for a few rupees or colourful beads by the handful.

Masks & Puppets

Papier-mâché masks and colourful puppets are sold at shops in Kathmandu, Patan and Bhaktapur. Thimi is the centre for manufacturing the masks which are used in the traditional masked dances in September and it's interesting to see them being made and painted there. Ganesh, Bhairab and the Kumari are the most popular subjects for the mask and they make good wall decorations. Prices typically range from around Rs 50 to Rs 200 ($4).

Puppets make good buys as gifts for children and are made in Bhaktapur as well as other centres. They're often of multiarmed deities, clutching little wooden weapons in each hand. The puppet heads may be made of easily broken clay or more durable papier-

Prayer wheel

mâché. Smaller puppets cost from around Rs 100 ($2) to Rs 300 ($6) but you can also pay Rs 500 ($10) to Rs 700 ($14) for a larger figure. As usual, quality does vary and the more puppets you inspect the more you will begin to appreciate the differences.

Metalwork

Patan is the valley centre for bronze casting and the best variety of metalwork will be found in the shops around Patan's Durbar Square. See the Patan Things to Buy section for more details. Often beautifully made figures featuring the full range of Tantric Buddhist deities can be bought at costs ranging from Rs 2000 ($40) to Rs 5000 ($100) for good-quality smaller figures. Of course cheaper and simpler work can be found much more cheaply. The metal game boards and pieces for the traditional Nepalese game *bagh chal* make a good buy.

Other Nepalese Crafts

A khukuri, the traditional knife of the Gurkhas, can cost from Rs 300 ($6) to Rs 1000 ($20). Bhaktapur is the centre for woodcarving and you can find good objects in and around Tachupal Tole. Cassettes of Nepalese, Indian and general Himalayan music are a fine souvenir of a visit to Nepal. There are lots of music shops in Kathmandu selling local music as well as bootlegged Western tapes. For all sorts of small souvenirs the huge market area in Basantapur Square in Kathmandu is a good place to browse. Wandering the crowded and bustling market street from Indra Chowk to Asan Tole is always likely to turn up some interesting bargain.

Other Tibetan Crafts

Tibetan crafts include a variety of religious items including the dorje symbols and the popular Tibetan prayer wheels. Tibetans are keen traders and prices at Bodhnath and Swayambhunath are often very high.

Tea

Tea is grown in the east of Nepal, close to the border with India near Darjeeling where the finest Indian tea is grown. Ilam and Mai Valley are the best Nepalese brands.

Sending Purchases Home

By far the best way of getting something back home is to take it with you. Shipping or mailing objects is fraught with dangers and hidden expenses. For a start there's no guarantee that it will be sent at all. If you leave your purchase for a shop to mail to you and it never turns up what can you prove? They will say they mailed it and the post office has lost it somewhere along the line, and you have no idea whether they have or not.

If an object is shipped to you it's easy to find that customs charges, clearance and collection charges at your end can add up to more than the initial cost of sending it. Often it would have been worth paying extra to bring it with you in the first place.

If you absolutely cannot carry your purchase with you it could be mailed from the Foreign Post Office. The object must be inspected by officials before it is wrapped so do not take it to the post office already wrapped up. There are packers at the post office who will package it for a small fee.

Unless you are very sure about the reliability of the shop, do not ask the shop where you made the purchase to send it for you. There are a number of packing companies in Kathmandu but some of them are no more reliable than a shop might be. Sharmasons Packers & Movers (☎ 01-411474), Dolha Continental Exports (☎ 01-414997), opposite the Hotel Mandap in Thamel, and Atlas Packers & Movers (☎ 01-221402) have been recommended. The international courier company DHL has an office on Durbar Marg and in Thamel.

Air freight costs around $4.30 per kg to Europe, $8 to the USA, and $5.40 to Australasia. Rates drop if you have more than 45 kg. Sea freight is only marginally cheaper than air, and is much slower and less reliable – packages are sent overland to Calcutta or Bombay, and then wait until a full container has been consolidated.

Getting There & Away

AIR

Kathmandu is the site for Nepal's only international airport, Tribhuvan Airport. Flying from Europe, North America or Australia usually requires a change of aircraft and/or airline en route. Lufthansa and Condor have a Frankfurt to Kathmandu service, and Royal Nepal Airlines Corporation (RNAC) has a London, Frankfurt, Kathmandu service – the only airlines with direct flights to Nepal.

Travellers arriving from Europe or from the east coast of North America transfer to RNAC or Indian Airlines in New Delhi for the final short flight from New Delhi to Kathmandu. Both airlines give a 25% discount to those under 30 years of age on flights between Kathmandu and India; no student card is needed. RNAC also gives a 25% discount for students travelling to other destinations who are under 26 and have valid identification.

From the west coast of North America or from Australasia, Bangkok is the usual transfer point although there are also flights to Kathmandu from Hong Kong and Singapore. Thai International and RNAC share the Bangkok to Kathmandu route. The schedules are so designed that it is likely you will have to spend at least one night in Bangkok to make your connection. Fourteen-day visas to Thailand are issued at Bangkok Airport.

Where to Sit

If you want to see the mountains as you fly into Kathmandu you must sit on the correct side. Flying from the east – Bangkok, Calcutta, Hong Kong, Yangon (Rangoon), or Singapore – you want the right side. Flying from the west – New Delhi or Varanasi – you want the left side.

Arriving in Nepal

The international terminal is a new building and everything operates reasonably smoothly. The most gruelling part is the thorough baggage search. Touts are excluded from the building, so everything is fairly calm until you hit the outside world.

When you arrive, there's a branch of the Nabil Bank prior to clearing immigration on the 1st floor. The Nabil Bank charges 2% or Rs 100 for cashing cheques (whichever is higher). This is relatively expensive, so you are best to only change a small cheque, or wait until you get into town. There's another branch on the ground floor of the departure section; both are open for flights, which normally means up to 8 pm.

There's a duty-free shop with a limited range of liquor and cigarettes available for sale in US dollars to arriving and departing passengers. You are allowed to import 200 cigarettes and one bottle of alcohol (up to 1.15 litres), as well as 'one perambulator, one tricycle and one stick'. (See the Customs section in the Facts for the Visitor chapter for more details.)

When leaving you can cash up to 15% of the rupees for which you have unused Foreign Exchange Encashment Receipts. If you are leaving for India, you can get between Indian Rs 500 and Rs 2000 on presentation of your ticket.

After checking in, you can proceed to a pleasant restaurant on the top (2nd) floor, which is open to all, or go through immigration on the 1st floor, where there is a restaurant, open to passengers only. There's a small duty-free shop, and on the ground floor is a post office.

See the Getting Around section in the Kathmandu, Patan & Bhaktapur chapter for information on transport to/from the airport.

To/From the UK & Europe

Check the travel page ads in the dailies, the weekly London 'what's on' magazines like *Time Out* or the London giveaway papers. Reliable specialists for cheap tickets in London include Trailfinders at 46 Earls Court Rd, London W8, and STA (Student Travel Australia) at 74 Old Brompton Rd, London SW7, or 117 Euston Rd, London, NW1. Count on around UK£500 to UK£600 for a London to Kathmandu return ticket.

Kathmandu to Frankfurt on Lufthansa's direct flight is US$816 return, US$514 one way. Aeroflot have Kathmandu-Moscow flights for US$400 (one way). Pakistan International Airlines (PIA) have connections to Kathmandu via Karachi; Kathmandu to Karachi one way is US$200.

Delhi now has a new international airport so transits are fine. You won't save money by flying via Delhi, but seat availability is usually better than on the direct flights. The Delhi-Kathmandu flight is US$142.

To/From North America

Fares to Kathmandu will often be about the same from the east or west coast – it's about as far away as you can get in either direction! Typical return fares are from around US$1200 to US$1400. Check the Sunday travel sections of papers like the *New York Times, San Francisco Chronicle-Examiner* or *Los Angeles Times* for cheap fares. Good budget travel agencies include student travel chains such as STA and the Council on International Educational Exchange (CIEE).

Fares from Canada are similar to the USA, westbound from Vancouver or eastbound from Toronto or Montreal.

To/From Australia & New Zealand

Fares from Australia depend on the season and typically cost around A$1500 return. Bangkok is still the most popular transit point although you can also fly via Singapore or Hong Kong.

Since Kathmandu flights depart from Bangkok early in the morning you will probably have to overnight there. Dedicated shoestringers may decide to sit it out in the reasonably comfortable terminal and save paying for accommodation and the $8 departure tax. Travel into Bangkok from the airport can be time-consuming and exhausting, so some sort of package deal including transport and accommodation is recommended. Those less concerned about watching every penny can stay in the conveniently located *Airport Hotel*, right across the highway and railway line from the terminal and connected by a covered walkway. This hotel has a swimming pool, an excellent restaurant and a very good bookshop. Doubles cost around US$150 and short-stay rooms are US$25 for three hours. The terminal is so close you can conveniently check in for the flight and return to the hotel for breakfast. Also directly across the highway is the small town of Don Muang, with a variety of restaurants and other facilities.

To/From India

Royal Nepal Airlines Corporation (RNAC) and Indian Airlines share routes between India and Kathmandu. Both airlines give a 25% discount to those under 30 years of age on flights between Kathmandu and India; no student card is needed.

New Delhi is the main departure point for flights between India and Kathmandu. The daily one-hour New Delhi to Kathmandu flight costs US$142.

Other cities in India with direct air connections with Kathmandu are Bombay (US$257), Calcutta (US$96) and Varanasi (US$71). The flight from Varanasi is the last leg of the popular New Delhi, Agra, Khajuraho, Varanasi, Kathmandu tourist flight.

To/From Elsewhere in Asia

Other departure points for Kathmandu and approximate one-way fares include:

Bangkok, Thailand	US$220
Dhaka, Bangladesh	US$100
Dubai, UAE	US$325
Hong Kong	US$320
Karachi, Pakistan	US$200
Lhasa, Tibet	US$190
Singapore	US$350

In most cases there are return advance-purchase excursion (APEX) fares available. There are also some interesting through fares; one to consider is Bangladesh Biman's Kathmandu, Dhaka, Yangon (Rangoon), Bangkok ticket which sells for US$385.

Leaving Nepal

The departure tax for international flights is Rs 600 (US$12), payable at the check-in counters; the tax is only Rs 500 (US$10) if you are flying to a SAARC member-country (ie India, Bangladesh, Bhutan, Maldives, Pakistan or Sri Lanka).

Check in at least two hours early; for some airlines in high season (those that have a reputation for overbooking) it is worth getting there even earlier. Also, don't forget to confirm and reconfirm your flight at least 72 hours before your departure. On departure at the airport, it is possible to re-exchange up to 15% of the Nepalese rupees you have officially changed, but you must be able to show unused Foreign Exchange Encashment Receipts.

Make sure you have clearance for anything that might be construed as an antique – metal statues show up on the baggage x-ray and are often checked. The x-ray machines that screen cargo baggage are definitely not film safe. Those that screen hand luggage are meant to be film safe, but on my last trip, my film was either fogged in Nepal or Bangkok.

Insist that the security officers physically inspect your precious film.

The airport duty-free shop has a limited range of liquor and cigarettes available for purchase with US dollars. Shoestring travellers often take their duty-free allowances with the intention of selling them at their next halt. Myanmar (Burma) is a particularly popular country for selling duty-free items.

LAND

Political and weather conditions permitting there are four main entry points into Nepal by land: three from India, one from Tibet.

The most popular crossing points with India are Sunauli/Bhairawa (south of Pokhara), Raxaul Bazaar/Birganj (south of Kathmandu) and Kakarbhitta (near Siliguri and Darjeeling). There are other less popular, but still viable, options.

If you are travelling to or from New Delhi or elsewhere in western India the route through Sunauli/Bhairawa is the most convenient. This entry point is now much more popular than the crossing at Birganj – it's closer to Varanasi, and marginally quicker to Kathmandu and Pokhara. Delhi to Varanasi takes about 13 hours, Varanasi to Sunauli say 11 hours, Sunauli to Kathmandu, nine hours. Both the Delhi to Varanasi and Sunauli to Kathmandu sectors could be done at night. During the monsoon, the Siddhartha Highway (Bhairawa to Pokhara) may be closed for a few days by landslides.

Travelling to/from Calcutta or Patna in the east of India the Raxaul Bazaar/Birganj entry point is still the most convenient option. Since the completion of the Narayanghat to Mugling road, all buses travel via Mugling rather than the slower, though more scenic, Tribhuvan Highway via Daman. This does mean however, that all buses go through Tadi Bazaar, the jumping off point for Sauraha and the Royal Chitwan National Park. Calcutta to Patna takes about 10 hours, Patna to Birganj, say five hours, Birganj to Kathmandu, 11 hours.

From Darjeeling, Kakarbhitta is the obvious entry point, but the Mahendra Highway can be blocked by floods during the monsoon, in which case it would be necessary to travel by train from Siliguri to Patna before entering Nepal at Birganj. Normally however, Darjeeling to Kakarbhitta would take around six hours, Kakarbhitta to Kathmandu, around 18 hours.

From India, people usually take an overnight Indian bus to the border, then take a Nepalese bus from the border to Kathmandu or Pokhara. Raxaul Bazaar/Birganj and Bhairawa/Sunauli can be reached on the Indian side by train or bus, but the trains in question travel on the narrow-metre gauge rather than the much faster broad gauge, and tend to be tediously slow. It is faster and more convenient to take a bus from Patna, Muzaffarpur, Varanasi, or Gorakhpur (which are also on broad-gauge rail).

Travel agencies can handle all these bookings in advance, but it's easy, cheaper, and more reliable, to do it yourself as you go. Many travellers have complained about scams involving ticket packages to India. The package usually involves coordination between at least three different companies so the potential for an honest cock-up is at least as high as the potential for a deliberate rip-off. (See the Ticket Scams to India section later in this chapter.)

Two longstanding and reliable Nepalese companies handling through tickets are Student Travels & Tours (☎ 220234) in Thamel, Kathmandu; and Yeti Travels (☎ 221234) in Durbar Marg, Kathmandu. Bear in mind, however, that everyone has to change buses at the border whether they book a through ticket or not, and that despite claims to the contrary, there are no 'tourist' buses on either side of the border. Buses through to Varanasi cost from Rs 500 ($10), and to Darjeeling Rs 700 ($14). Bus/train packages to Agra cost Rs 1850 ($37) including an air-con sleeper on the train, or Rs 850 ($17) in 2nd class. Bus/train to Delhi costs Rs 1950 ($39) with air-con, Rs 1000 ($20) in 2nd class.

It is worth considering making advance bookings if you are in a major hurry, or plan to use the Indian railway system. Some trains, and especially sleeping compartments, can be heavily booked (this is apparently the case for Gorakhpur to Delhi trains). A Nepalese agent will need a week to organise a booking. Beware – there's always a chance that what you pay for and what you get will be two different things. Make sure you get a receipt clearly specifying what you think you have paid for, and hang onto it.

It is also possible for tourists to cross the border at Nepalganj, Dhangadhi, and in the

---

Ticket Scams to India

Many people have written complaining about scams involving through tickets to India, especially out of Pokhara. Mind you, there's always plenty of scope for disaster when travelling on the subcontinent. That's why it's such good fun! The following extract is a classic example:

I paid Rs 2000 ($40) for a bus to the Indian border, a bus from there to Gorakhpur and an air-con sleeper on a train to Delhi. The bus to the border ran out of fuel three times and was four hours late. The bus to Gorakhpur broke down five km into the 100-km trip, was abandoned, forcing me to catch a taxi for the remainder of the journey.

Once in Gorakhpur, I was to take a receipt to a travel agency to have my air-con sleeper ticket to Delhi issued. The receipt was issued by the travel agent in Pokhara, but the travel agent in Gorakhpur denied any knowledge of air-con on this particular train and refused to issue me with anything other than a 2nd-class ticket. I spoke to the stationmaster about my problem and he was extremely unhelpful, arousing my suspicion that he may have been in with the travel agent.

While I was in the middle of a heated argument with the Gorakhpur travel agent, two English guys stormed into the shop screaming 'Liar, I'll kill you.' The three of us bombarded the agent with facts, asking for our money back, but he just laughed, closed up his shop for the night and walked off. ■

far west, Mahendranagar. The entry at Mahendranagar is the most interesting possibility. It may take a while for things to start operating smoothly, but when they do, this will present an interesting alternative route to Delhi, plus access to some of the hill stations in northern Uttar Pradesh. When the Mahendra Highway is finally completed (theoretically in mid-1993, but don't count on it) the route will be open all year, but until then it is a dry season-only proposition, and strictly for the hardy. Allow at least 13 hours from Delhi to Mahendranagar, nine hours from Mahendranagar to Nepalganj, and 16 hours for the Kathmandu to Nepalganj section.

A steady trickle of people drive their own motorbikes or vehicles overland from Europe – there are some interesting, though difficult, new routes to the subcontinent through Eastern Europe and the republics that were once a part of the USSR. An international carnet is required. If you want to abandon your transport in Nepal, you must either pay a prohibitive import duty or surrender it to customs. It is not possible to import cars more than five years old.

The route to Tibet from Nepal (via Kodari) was closed to individual travellers in late 1992, but independent travellers were entering Tibet through China and continuing on, without problems, to Nepal. There were rumours that the border would soon open for east-bound travellers (but there are always rumours). Organised groups are allowed to cross from Nepal, but this option is expensive.

On the face of it, it doesn't make much sense to allow individuals into Tibet from China, but not from Nepal. However, the package business is so lucrative and Nepal is so full of seditious Tibetans, the Chinese must see little incentive to change. Bear in mind the road is of poor quality and is regularly closed by landslides during the monsoon.

Routes to Kathmandu & Pokhara

Varanasi to Sunauli/Bhairawa

Buses are the quickest and easiest way of getting from Varanasi to the Nepalese border. The Varanasi bus station is next to the main railway station. There are direct deluxe buses between Varanasi and Sunauli for around Indian Rs 100, or much cheaper local buses for around Indian Rs 60, if you can stand the pain. Alternatively, buses leave almost hourly to Gorakhpur, five hours away. From Gorakhpur there are regular departures (between 5 am and 7 pm) from the bus stand near the railway station. Buses cost Indian Rs 17 and take three hours.

Some private companies make bookings all the way through to Kathmandu and Pokhara for Indian Rs 200, including spartan accommodation at Sunauli. However, if you organise things yourself as you go, it will be cheaper, plus you will have more flexibility, including a choice of bus within Nepal and also of accommodation in Sunauli. Catch a bus to Sunauli, stay overnight on the Nepal-

ese side of the border (there are several reasonable hotels in Sunauli and Bhairawa), then catch a Nepalese bus the next morning. There are plenty of day and night buses to Kathmandu and Pokhara.

Sunauli/Bhairawa to Kathmandu (Mahendra Highway)

Day buses to Kathmandu from Sunauli cost around Rs 86 and take nine hours – they are quicker and cheaper than the night buses. The blue, government-owned Sajha Yatayat buses are faster and less crowded than most of the privately run buses.

From Bhairawa, a few km north of Sunauli, the buses travel north along the Siddhartha Highway until Butwal, where they turn east. After 45 km you cross the low Someshwar Hills and enter the Inner Terai, an area that has developed very rapidly since the late 1950s when malaria was eradicated. It's then another 70 flat, hot km until you get to Narayanghat on the Narayani

River. Narayanghat is the main town and administrative centre for the Inner Terai; another modern, fast-growing city with little charm. You then turn north, following the river through the hills until you get to Mugling. See the Pokhara chapter for more information on the Kathmandu-Pokhara (Prithvi) Highway.

Sunauli/Bhairawa to Pokhara (Siddhartha Highway)

Buses to Pokhara travel north along the beautiful Siddhartha Highway and then north to Mugling before joining the Kathmandu-Pokhara (Prithvi) Highway. The trip takes nine hours and costs Rs 66. The Siddhartha Highway takes you through a cross-section of classic Nepalese landscapes.

From Bhairawa it's 24 km across the Terai until you reach the unattractive city of Butwal, which marks a sudden transition from the plains to the hills. One minute you're surrounded by dust and people, the next you're in a narrow mountain gorge. For the next 30 km you drive through lush subtropical forest with some great views over the Tinau River. The road is subject to avalanches and is not in particularly good condition.

The turn-off to Tansen is 35 km from Butwal. Tansen, an interesting, little-visited town, lies four km off the main road and is a good possibility if you want to break the journey. Ten km further on, at Ramdi, you cross the distinctive Kali Gandaki River, that drains the Dhaulagiri and Annapurna massifs.

From the Kali Gandaki you climb a ridge and then descend into the subtropical valley of the Andhi River. The valley is densely populated and there are small bazaar towns and villages along the road at regular intervals. As you wind closer to Pokhara there are superb views of the Annapurna Range, and particularly of Machhapuchhare, the famous 'fish-tail' mountain with its distinctive twin peaks.

Patna to Raxaul Bazaar/Birganj

It makes little sense to take a train to the Nepal border – the buses are much faster. The main bus station in Patna (for buses to Muzaffarpur and Raxaul Bazaar just south of the Nepalese border) is at Harding Park. Buses cost Indian Rs 38 for the five-hour trip to Raxaul Bazaar. From there, it costs about Indian Rs 12 for a rickshaw across the border to Birganj.

Raxaul Bazaar is virtually a twin town with Birganj in Nepal. Both towns are dirty, unattractive transit points strung along the highway and are full of heavy traffic. The border is open from 7 am to 7 pm every day, and it takes about 30 minutes and Rs 10 to get from the border itself to the bus station in Birganj by bicycle rickshaw.

The best cheap place to stay in Patna is the *Hotel Shyama* which has singles/doubles/ triples for Indian Rs 40/60/85. The conveniently situated *Hotel Mayur* is a mid-range hotel where singles/doubles with private bath cost Indian Rs 116/147. Alternatively you can cross the border and stay in Birganj.

Birganj to Kathmandu or Pokhara

See the Terai chapter for details on the Nepalese towns that are mentioned in this section. All direct buses go via the Mahendra Highway because the road is easier, but it is still possible, with a little trouble, to go via the beautiful Tribhuvan Highway.

Mahendra Highway All direct buses between Birganj and Kathmandu or Pokhara turn west at Hetauda, then at Narayanghat turn north to Mugling which is on the Kathmandu-Pokhara (Prithvi) Highway. Although it is not as spectacular as the Tribhuvan Highway, this is nonetheless an interesting route with some beautiful views.

Between Birganj and Kathmandu direct buses take around 11 hours and cost Rs 102; between Birganj and Pokhara they cost Rs 97 and are marginally quicker. There are numerous night and day buses. It is worth catching a day bus, even though they no longer take you over the Tribhuvan Highway, since there is a lot of interesting country to see and some great views even if you go via Narayanghat. The best buses are the blue, government-owned Sajha Yatayat buses which are faster and less crowded than most of the privately run buses. Sajha Yatayat has a booking office at the new Birganj bus station.

From Birganj you travel past a depressing line-up of Dickensian factories until you climb into the Chure Hills. Here the country becomes more attractive – and the road falls apart. Sixty bone-jarring km from the border, Hetauda lies at the north-western edge of a wide valley known as the Inner Terai. It's not a particularly interesting town, although it is the starting point for a cableway that carries bulk goods from the Terai to Kathmandu.

From Hetauda, the road runs along the edge of the Mahabharat Range and the Rapti River. There are some rich, cultivated fields, but a great deal of forest remains. On the other side of the Rapti lies the Royal Chitwan National Park, famous for its tigers and rhinoceroses.

After Belva, the valley begins to broaden and the reason it is called the Inner Terai becomes clear – it's flat, fertile and heavily populated. There are some Tharu villages as well as many Gurung and other hill peoples. Seventy-seven km after Hetauda, you come to the small roadside town of Tadi Bazaar, the departure point for the Royal Chitwan National Park. Buses to this point from Birganj cost around Rs 50 and take three hours. From Tadi Bazaar it takes around six hours to reach Pokhara or Kathmandu; costs can vary from Rs 55 to Rs 200 ($4) depending on whether you catch a Sajha bus or a tourist minibus.

The road from Tadi to Narayanghat is not particularly interesting; there's a lot of development and Narayanghat and Bharatpur run together and sprawl a long way to the east. All buses travel west to Narayanghat then turn north, following the Narayani River through the hills to Mugling. See the Pokhara chapter for more information on the Kathmandu-Pokhara (Prithvi) Highway.

Tribhuvan Highway The Tribhuvan Highway (or Rajpath) was the first road to link the Kathmandu Valley with the outside world; it was built by the Indian government and was not completed until 1956. If you have time and feel energetic, consider catching a bus to Hetauda (where direct buses turn west to Narayanghat), then a Sajha Yatayat bus over the mountains to Kathmandu. There are numerous buses between Birganj and Hetauda for Rs 17, but only one a day (in each direction) between Hetauda and Kathmandu via Daman; they leave at 7 am, cost Rs 48 and take eight hours. It's easier to undertake this route coming from Kathmandu, as you'll have no problem finding a bus from Hetauda to Birganj, whatever time you arrive.

If you are travelling in a group or have the funds, consider hiring a car. It won't be cheap, partly because you'll have to pay for the driver's return trip whether you go along or not. Think in terms of $150. Alternatively, if you're fit and have a mountain bike, this is regarded as one of the most spectacular cycling routes in the country; see the Mountain Biking chapter.

You begin to climb into the Mahabharat Range the moment you leave Hetauda. The road is in good condition, but it's very narrow, so it's a case of drivers leaning almost constantly on their horns and hoping they won't meet an out-of-control Tata truck around the next blind corner.

The change from the Terai is remarkably sudden; you're soon amongst forested hills and it is almost impossible to believe the plains are so close. As you gain altitude you enter magnificent rhododendron forests. The highest point on the road is 2400 metres, just before you reach Daman. Daman is famous for being a viewpoint with one of the most complete panoramas of the Himalaya that you can find. The view – from Dhaulagiri to Everest – is simply awe-inspiring.

After Daman you travel through the intensely cultivated Palung Valley. From here to Kathmandu, every possible inch of the hills is farmed. There are more good views of the Himalaya before you reach Naubise on the Kathmandu-Pokhara (Prithvi) Highway. Daman is about three hours from Kathmandu and Hetauda by car, four hours by bus.

Darjeeling to Kathmandu (Mahendra Highway)

There are a number of companies that handle bookings between Darjeeling and Kathmandu – although with all of them you have to change buses at the border and Siliguri.

In Darjeeling the main ones are Assam Valley Tours & Travels, opposite the post office, and Mahendra Tours on Laden La Rd above the main block of budget restaurants. In Kathmandu try Student Travels & Tours in Thamel.

It's almost as easy to get from Darjeeling to Kathmandu on your own though it involves four changes – a bus from Darjeeling to Siliguri (Indian Rs 41), then a minibus from Siliguri to Raniganj at the border (Indian Rs 5), a rickshaw across the border to Kakarbhitta (Indian Rs 3) and a bus from Kakarbhitta to Kathmandu (Rs 232 or $4.50). This is cheaper than the package deal, you have a choice of buses from the border, plus you have the option of travelling during the day and overnighting along the way.

Buses to Kathmandu travel west along the Mahendra Highway to the Tribhuvan Highway between Birganj and Hetauda, then head briefly north to Hetauda. They then travel west again until Narayanghat where they turn north to Mugling, on the Kathmandu-Pokhara (Prithvi) Highway. During the monsoon, floods can sometimes close the road between Hetauda and Kakarbhitta.

It's more than 600 km between Kakarbhitta and Kathmandu, which means direct buses can take an exhausting 17 hours to complete the trip. The direct buses all travel at night; from Kakarbhitta they leave between 3 and 5 pm, from Kathmandu between 4 and 5.30 pm. From Kathmandu, it's worth booking in advance.

If you have time it is worth considering breaking your journey at Janakpur, which is roughly halfway, and an interesting place in its own right. This will enable you to travel during the day and get a feel for the Terai; the flood plain of the Sapt Kosi is particularly interesting. There are day buses from Kakarbhitta that go to a number of towns on the Terai including Janakpur (Rs 107), and night buses direct to Pokhara (Rs 223, or $4.50).

Fifteen minutes from Kakarbhitta, past several tea plantations, is the town of Birtamod. A dirt road from here goes to Ilam, a starting point for treks in the Kanchenjunga region. The road is very poor, although it was being improved in 1992. Buses cost Rs 70 and take seven hours.

The first town of real consequence that you come to is Itahari, 100 km from Kakarbhitta. There's nothing much to be said for it, however, apart from the fact that it is at the intersection of the road that runs south to Biratnagar, Nepal's second-largest city, and north to Hile and Basantpur, starting points for Kanchenjunga, Makalu and Arun Valley treks.

After Itahari the road enters the flood plain of the Sapt Kosi, one of the largest tributaries to the Ganges. This mighty river is now partially controlled by the impressive Kosi Barrage and its surrounding earthworks. Even so, this low-lying region seems at times to be more water than land. Metres of silt have obviously made the fields extremely fertile and there is a high population density.

Mud and thatch villages are built on small areas of high ground, and the people are closely related to their Indian neighbours. Emerald green paddies stretch to the horizon and the villages are surrounded by water lilies and hyacinths. Often, the houses are overgrown with pumpkin plants, which are trained onto the roofs. Fish are a vital part of the local diet, and wherever you look you'll see children and women fishing for the tiny fish that live in the canals and ponds. The bird life is prolific, with Brahmani kites, greater and lesser egrets, and cranes and ducks of every description.

On either side of the barrage the road is built on a raised levy, but parts are in extremely poor condition. By the time you get to Mohanpur, you'll be lucky to have your teeth fillings still in place. After Mohanpur you begin a long stretch of the Terai proper, skirting the Chure Hills, which seem to jump from the plains.

Since the eradication of malaria in the 1950s, much of this land has been settled. Many of the settlers have come from the hills, but have swiftly adapted to their new environment and many have prospered. Frequently, houses have been built on stilts to cope with the annual floods. Some of the Rai and Limbu towns look as if they could have been transplanted from northern New South Wales, Australia – stilts, verandahs and corrugated iron roofs contribute to the illusion.

Nearly 110 km past the Kosi Barrage you reach Lalbiti, the turn-off to Janakpur (25 km from the highway), one of the most attractive cities in Nepal. The countryside is intensively cultivated and densely populated. As you travel further east, however, there are fewer people, fewer of the bright Indian saris and more trees. Between Dalkebar and Amlekhganj (on the Tribhuvan Highway) there is an almost unbroken stretch of magnificent sal forest.

At Amlekhganj the Mahendra Highway briefly joins the Tribhuvan Highway to Hetauda. See the earlier Birganj to Kathmandu or Pokhara section in this chapter for the rest of the route.

Banbassa to Mahendranagar

In 1992, a trickle of intrepid travellers entered Nepal at the far western border post of Mahendranagar. There are daily buses from New Delhi to Banbassa, the nearest Indian village to the border (11 hours, Indian Rs 56). Banbassa is also connected by rail to Bareilly, and by bus with the hill station Almora in India. From Banbassa, a rickshaw to the border and across to Mahendranagar takes 20 minutes.

Mahendranagar to Kathmandu or Pokhara

There are direct night buses from Mahendranagar to Kathmandu, but they take a gruesome 25 hours and cost Rs 260 ($5). The countryside is beautiful and fascinating, so

it's much better to travel during the day and to break the journey at Nepalganj. In 1992 there was only one direct bus from Mahendranagar to Nepalganj; it left at 4 am, took around nine hours and cost Rs 140 ($3). Alternatively, buses run to Ataria (at the junction for Dhangadhi) and from Ataria to Nepalganj. There are plenty of night and day buses from Nepalganj to Kathmandu (16 hours, Rs 162 or $3) and night buses to Pokhara (15 hours, Rs 172 or $3.50).

The far west is the least developed and most traditional part of the Terai. It's inhabited by Tharus, Bajis (Abadhi speakers from India), Muslims, and more recent migrants from the hills. In late 1992 there were three small unbridged rivers between Ataria and Chisopani (on the western bank of the Karnali River) and a diabolical stretch of track for the last 10 km into Chisopani. The major remaining engineering problem, however, is the bridge over the Karnali River.

The Karnali is one of the largest rivers in Nepal, draining the western third of the country. Thanks to the World Bank an enormous single-span suspension bridge is being built at Chisopani, at the point where the river flows through its last gorge and spills out onto the plains. Officials hope the bridge will be completed by June 1993, but nothing can be guaranteed. The World Bank also plans to build the world's largest hydroelectric dam, a km further up the gorge; fortunately these plans are currently on hold.

Until the bridge is completed, the only means of crossing the river is by two wire-pulled pontoons, that provide an erratic service at best. In theory the pontoons operate from September to May and from 10 am to 5 pm. There is no formal accommodation at Chisopani, but travellers have stayed with families and at chai shops (around Rs 15).

After the Karnali River you run through the sal forest of the Royal Bardia National Park; keep your eyes peeled for monkeys, deer, and peacocks. After you leave the forest you enter an agricultural zone inhabited by Tharus and a growing number of migrants from the hills. As you approach Kohalpur, 71 km from Chisopani and the turn-off for Nepalganj, there are increasing numbers of Muslims – the white spires of mosques can be seen in the villages.

Nepalganj is 16 km south of Kohalpur, and lies on the flat, hot Gangetic plain at the western end of the Rapti Valley. The Rapti Valley, like the Chitwan Valley, is described as the Inner Terai, and lies along the Rapti River between the Duduwa Hills to the south and the Chure Hills and Mahabharat Range to the north.

The Rapti Valley is attractive and intensively cultivated and seems to become more fertile the further east you travel. There are

Pontoons Over the Karnali

We arrived at the east bank of the Karnali River about 9 am to find a completely anarchic queue. Tata trucks and buses were backed up for miles, completely jamming the track that ran down to the river. Drivers and passengers sat disconsolately in a cold and gritty wind wondering why there wasn't a chai shop.

Finally, at 10.30 am one of the winch engines on the west (Chisopani) side sputtered into action. Apparently the second winch is temperamental and only works on some days; not this day. Chaos ensued on the eastern bank as trucks and buses jockeyed to get to the front of the queue by doing some sneaky cross-country driving through the bush.

One truck was loaded and the pontoon went slowly across. Another truck was loaded on the far side and slowly the pontoon returned. There was more chaos as the queue was reshuffled to allow the eastbound truck through. The barrage of Tata air horns indicated drivers were getting tense.

Suddenly we realised that our bus had managed to work its way to the front of the queue. Our spirits lifted. Then the winch stopped. Was it also broken? 'Ke garne' – what to do? We would get across, or we wouldn't get across. it would take one hour, or maybe three. It was clearly beyond our mortal power to influence events.

At around 11.30 am the winch restarted and 15 minutes later we were in the thriving shanty village of Chisopani where, of course, we were obliged to stop for dhal bhat. This is when we discovered that the winch driver had downed tools so that he could eat his dhal bhat (it being around 11 am). We finally set out for Mahendranagar at about 12.30 pm.

Returning from Mahendranagar we arrived at Chisopani about noon. Strangely, there was no queue on the west side and both pontoons were operating. We were loaded immediately – onto the unreliable pontoon that had not been functioning when we first crossed.

Everything went smoothly. The engine sputtered once or twice, but we made good progress. When we reached the east side (with a resounding crash) one of the crew leapt ashore to secure the pontoon with a wire rope. The force of the impact however, spun the pontoon and the rope was not made fast quickly enough, so we drifted upstream in an eddy, tangled the two overhead wires, and wedged on a rock. The crew thought this was very funny.

After much waving of arms we were dragged off the rock and back into midstream. An unsuccessful attempt was made to try and untangle the wires, and after much waving of arms we started towards the east bank again.' We went a metre or two, then the winch engine stalled.

After five minutes or so the engine was resuscitated and we were moving again. We met the bank with another crash and once again spun back into the river, further tangling the overhead wires. The crew did not think this was very funny. What to do? Swimming in a deep, fast-flowing Karnali River with or without a backpack did not seem appealing. Neither did staying indefinitely on the pontoon.

After much waving of arms the crew made a third attempt. In general Nepalese don't like water, so the bus passengers' equanimity was quickly fraying. Some seemed to be praying, others shouted conflicting advice to the crew. A man in a suit told the crew they were incompetent and that he would 'report them to the minister'.

Our karma was good, because somehow everything came together, despite the tangle of wire ropes. And it was only 1.30 pm. Not only had we survived, we were on the right side of the river and the odds seemed good that we'd make it to Nepalganj in time for dinner.

Richard Everist

endless fields of mustard, interspersed with small Tharu settlements and the much grander Newari-style houses of their landlords (zamindars). There are a number of grubby and depressing roadside villages with the usual chai shops – the largest being Kusum (71 km from Nepalganj) and Lamahi (52 km from Kusum).

Twenty-five km from Lamahi, the road crosses the Rapti River, and climbs over the foothills before dropping down to the Terai proper. Butwal, where buses turn north to Pokhara, is the next major town, 97 km from the bridge over the Rapti, and 245 km from Nepalganj. See the earlier section on the Siddhartha Highway (Sunauli/Bhairawa to Pokhara).

The road from Butwal to Narayanghat (93 km) is not particularly interesting. There are a couple of places where there are quite steep climbs over ridges of the Chure Hills, but most of the countryside is flat and monotonous sal forest. The soil is too sandy to be farmed. There are some unattractive strips of roadside development, mainly with relatively recent migrants from the hills. From Narayanghat there is a link to Mugling on the Kathmandu-Pokhara (Prithvi) Highway; see that section.

Lhasa to Kathmandu

Travel between Kathmandu and Lhasa in Tibet can be complicated by natural and political considerations. The natural problem is that the road is frequently cut by earthquakes, floods, landslides and other disasters.

Political disasters are even more likely than natural ones. Tibet is a volatile region with regular violent protests against Chinese rule and these upheavals are often followed by restrictions on visitors to the region. Usually these restrictions are applied more stringently to independent visitors than to people on organised tours. The baseline is that if you intend to enter or leave Nepal via Tibet you should come prepared with alternative plans in case travel along this route proves impossible.

Organised Tours Organised tours (with a minimum of three people) were only briefly interrupted in 1989 (after the Tiananmen Square Massacre) but they are expensive. A number of agencies in Kathmandu organise fully inclusive round trips to Lhasa, with prices around US$100 per day for eight to 12-day trips.

Most tours from Kathmandu take eight days and involve a flight to Lhasa and an overland return trip (or vice versa). The flights stop from the end of November to the end of March because of the weather. China International Travel Service (CITS), the state travel agency, operate the tours within China.

Travel agencies in Nepal specialising in trips to Tibet include:

Kathmandu Travels & Tours
    PO Box 459, Ganga Path, Kathmandu (☎ 01-224536)
Marco Polo Travels
    PO Box 2769, Kamal Pokhari, Kathmandu (☎ 01-414192; fax 418479)
Natraj Tours & Travels
    PO Box 495, Durbar Marg, Kathmandu (☎ 01-222014)
Nepal Travel Agency
    PO Box 1501, Ram Shah Path (☎ 01-413188; fax 227782)
Tibet Travels & Tours
    PO Box 1397, Tridevi Marg, Thamel, Kathmandu (☎ 01-410303; fax 415126)
Yeti Travels
    PO Box 76, Durbar Marg, Kathmandu (☎ 01-221234)

Independent Travel If independent travel into Tibet is permitted you must first get a Chinese visa (see the Embassy section in the Around the Kathmandu Valley chapter for more details).

From Khasa (Zhangmu), the Tibetan town just over the border, there are just two buses a week to Lhasa, so you must plan carefully or you may be stranded for several days. Take food and drink on this trip, as there's not much available along the way. It's also possible to get rides on trucks to Shigatse, but the 15-hour trip in the back of a truck is strictly for the hardy. From Shigatse there are local buses to Gyantse and from there to Lhasa.

This is not an easy trip by any means. Altitude sickness is a real danger as the maximum altitude along the road is 5140 metres and there have been reports of deaths.

Regardless of the situation with the border, the Arniko Highway to Kodari, the small town on the Nepalese side of the border, is an interesting trip from Kathmandu – as long as you don't have to do it in a bus. There are some interesting towns on the highway and there are several points where you can get access to the Sun Kosi. If you have the use of a car it would be an enjoyable expedition; it's nearly four hours to Kodari from Kathmandu. Alternatively, this also makes an interesting, though exhausting, mountain-biking route.

It is not possible to catch a bus direct to Kodari, but eight buses a day do run to Barabise for Rs 30. They take around five agonising hours. From Barabise there are buses for Rs 34 that take two hours to get to Kodari. Since there's nothing much to see from Kodari, travelling out here by bus is a little pointless unless you are actually going on to Tibet. See the Around the Kathmandu Valley chapter for more information on the Arniko Highway.

WARNING

This chapter is particularly vulnerable to change. Prices for international travel are volatile, routes are introduced and cancelled, schedules change, rules are amended and special deals come and go.

Airlines and governments seem to take a perverse pleasure in making price structures and regulations as complicated as possible and you should check directly with the airline or a travel agent to make sure you understand how a fare (and ticket you may buy) works.

The upshot of this is that you should get opinions, quotes and advice from as many airlines and travel agencies as possible before you part with your hard-earned cash. The details given in this chapter should be regarded as pointers and are not a substitute for your own careful, up-to-the-minute research.

Getting Around

Getting around Nepal can be a challenging and frustrating business. The impossible terrain and extreme weather conditions, plus a combination of incompetence and disorganisation, mean that trips rarely go exactly according to plan. On the other hand, Nepalese ingenuity will usually get you to your destination in the end. Although travel can be frustrating, it also creates memorable moments by the score. Good humour and patience are essential prerequisites. Losing your cool will get you nowhere fast.

The whole gamut of transport options is available in Nepal, with the possible exception of submarines and monorails. Most of the others can be found together on the average road, simultaneously competing with ducks, dogs, chickens, pigs, children and adults, and none of them have the vaguest traffic sense.

Walking is still the most important, and the most reliable method of getting from A to B and for moving cargo, both for the Nepalese and tourists. More is carried by people and porters than by every other form of transport combined.

Bike-riding is quickly gaining popularity with visitors – local buses are so slow and uncomfortable that bikes are often almost as quick, even over long distances, and have the added advantage of allowing you to travel at your own speed and to stop whenever you like. There are a number of other human-powered contraptions ranging from barrows to bicycle rickshaws, canoes, kayaks and rafts.

There are numerous forms of animal transport. Bullocks, oxen, buffaloes and ponies are all attached to carts. Elephants, donkeys, and yaks are all ridden or used to carry loads.

The 'infernal' combustion engine is making an increasingly obnoxious impact on the environment. There are two-stroke autorickshaws, three-wheeled *tempos* and motorbikes, petrol-driven cars and motor-bikes, and smoke-belching diesel buses and trucks. The buses range from lumbering dinosaurs held together by bits of wire and the combined hopes of the passengers, to brand new Tatas from India, the kings of the road.

Then there are jets, planes (of ranging sizes) and helicopters. There's even a steam train at Janakpur, and a cableway (a kind of ski lift that carries cargo) at Hetauda.

AIR

There are now a number of private companies operating alongside the long-running, government-owned Royal Nepal Airlines Corporation (RNAC). The new companies are Everest Air, Necon Air, Nepal Airways, and Himalayan Helicopters. The prices are the same, and many feel the private companies offer better service, and are more reliable. Everest Air has been highly recommended.

RNAC still operates the most comprehensive range of scheduled flights around the country. The aircraft used are Hawker Siddeley 748s on the major routes and short take-off and landing (STOL) Twin Otters and Pilatus Porters to the smaller places. RNAC has flights to Baglung, Baitadi, Bajhang, Bajura, Bhairawa, Bharatpur, Bhojpur, Biratnagar, Chaurjhari, Dang, Darchula, Dhangadhi, Dolpa, Janakpur, Jomsom, Jumla, Kathmandu, Lamdanda, Lukla, Mahendranagar, Manang, Meghauli, Nepalganj, Phaplu, Pokhara, Ramechhap, Rumjatar, Sanfebagar, Silgadhidoti, Simara, Simikot, Surkhet, Taplejung, Tikapur and Tumlingtar.

Everest Air flies two German Dornier 228 planes, with air-con cabins, comfortable seats, and good-sized windows. It has scheduled flights to Pokhara, Jomsom, Bharatpur, Biratnagar, Lukla, Jumla and Nepalganj.

Nepal Airways has three Y12s, Chinese made Twin Otter-type aircraft, and flies to Biratnagar, Nepalganj, Lukla and Pokhara.

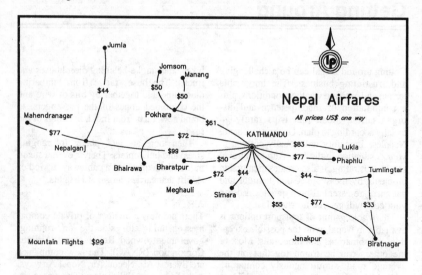

Nepal Airfares

All prices US$ one way

Mountain Flights $99

Necon Air has an old Avro aircraft and flies to Pokhara, Bharatpur, Biratnagar and Nepalganj. Himalayan Helicopters is basically a charter operation and has two Bell helicopters.

Some flights, such as the Kathmandu to Lukla services, are used mainly by trekkers. These trekking flights are frequent during the trekking season but the schedules can be extremely variable. Kathmandu to Jomsom flights, for example, are plagued by bad weather at both ends. Early-morning departures from Kathmandu are often delayed by fog but if they don't arrive in Jomsom by around 11 am landing may be impossible due to high winds! The end result is regular cancellations. Flights out of Lukla are equally unreliable – the airport can easily be closed for a week by bad weather – and there are often enormous backlogs of frustrated trekkers waiting for flights, both in Kathmandu and Lukla.

It is advisable to book domestic flights a week in advance and, just as for flights out of Nepal, the most important rule is to reconfirm and reconfirm again. Names can easily 'fall off' the passenger list, particularly where there is pressure for seats.

Airlines

Everest Air
   Durbar Marg, opposite Rani Pokhari, Kathmandu (☎ 01-228392/2290; fax 226795)
Himalayan Helicopters
   (☎ 01-524664; fax 524944)
Necon Air
   Kamal Pokhari, Lal Durbar, Kathmandu (☎ 01-418608/809; fax 416754)
Nepal Airways
   Kamaladi, Kathmandu (☎ 01-415191/8494; fax 416754)
Royal Nepal Airlines Corporation (RNAC)
   corner Kantipath and New Rd, Kathmandu (☎ 01-226574/0757)

Airfares Chart

Residents and Nepalese citizens pay approximately 75% of the tourist price for domestic airfares. Airlines will only accept payment in hard currency from visitors. The following is a list of tourist airfares (in US$) from Kathmandu.

Bhairawa	$72
Bharatpur	$50
Biratnagar	$77
Janakpur	$55
Jomsom	$111
Jumla	$143

Lukla	$83
Mahendranagar (direct)	$160
Manang	$111
Meghauli	$72
Nepalganj	$99
Pokhara	$61

All the airlines also have daily mountain flights which costs $95. See the Himalaya & Mountaineering chapter for details.

Domestic Airport
The domestic terminal is the old Kathmandu airport, and its age shows. It can be a nasty and chaotic spot, particularly when flights are cancelled and crowds of stressed tourists generate an atmosphere of fear and loathing. You can escape the worst of the crush in the restaurant on the 1st floor; it's allegedly run by the Hotel de l'Annapurna, so you are unlikely to be poisoned although it is very shabby.

Check in an hour early for domestic flights; there is no airport tax. Once through security, the waiting lounge is reasonably comfortable and you can also get drinks. Remember not to carry pocket knives in your carry-on luggage, and do not feel obliged to pay the security guards baksheesh. It can be difficult finding a taxi into Kathmandu if you arrive late. If the worst comes to the worst, it's a 15-minute walk to the international terminal, where you are certain to find something.

See Kathmandu's Getting Around section in the Kathmandu, Patan & Bhaktapur chapter for information on transport to/from the airport.

BUS
Buses are the main form of public transport in Nepal, and in relative terms they're incredibly cheap. Very often, they're also incredibly uncomfortable. It's always best to

---

Bus Ride – a traveller's account
Ah! The Kathmandu to Kakarbhitta bus trip. I remember it as if it were yesterday. It was. I'm sitting in Darjeeling eating buffalo curd and reflecting on how nice it is to be alive.

As we climbed out of the Kathmandu Valley at 4.30 pm we were 'shaking down' – trying to contort ourselves into the tight spaces we had rented and attempting to find some semblance of comfort. Then we reached the rim of the valley and began hurtling down that *awesome* series of hairpin bends and switchbacks. As we thundered suicidally down this impossible road I mused whimsically on the average life expectancy of Nepalese bus drivers, that is until the rather obvious realisation dawned that, given my present position, a much more pertinent question might be the life expectancy of the average passenger!

I gave up such dark thoughts to think about the love of my life, far off in England, but the moment was rudely interrupted as, lurching into yet another precipice-edged corner the driver breaked violently to avoid another bus lying on its side diagonally across the road. Not a sight calculated to inspire confidence, but one has to look on the bright side. Firstly, it had toppled *onto* the road rather than *off* into the chasm. Secondly, it wasn't my bus.

The road steadily deteriorated, as roads are want to do in Nepal. A little over an hour later I found my face pressed against the window, a gravel embankment flying towards me, inches from ruining my complexion. Looking on the bright side seemed rather more difficult. I am convinced it was only my slender 54-kg frame catapulting across the lap of my Nepalese travelling companion that tipped the balance – literally – in favour of the bus returning to the point at which any good bus should be: extremely horizontal.

Things returned to normal – or as normal as they can be on that highway. Several hellish hours later, the road surface suddenly changed from obscene to impeccable. But the cruel hoax was soon revealed when the road quickly reverted to type. This stretch on the Terai is the worst road I've ever travelled, worse even than one memorable track into the Australian outback.

All in all it was a great trip, but don't forget to pack your stoicism and humour, and get some extra fat on your bum in Kathmandu to absorb the bumps!

Lloyd Donaldson, New Zealand

book a couple of days in advance. Keep an eye on the festival calendar; buses are packed out for days either side of an important festival, as everyone wants to go home and party.

There are numerous services with buses and smaller minibuses around the Kathmandu Valley, out from Kathmandu towards the Tibetan border, down to the Indian border or to Pokhara. Buses also run from Pokhara down to the Indian border as well as along the length of the country from near Darjeeling in the east. This road runs through the Inner Terai, parallel to the Indian border. As well as the regular public buses between Kathmandu and Pokhara there are also a number of services aimed particularly at the Western tourist market.

Many people – locals and Westerners – prefer to ride on bus roofs. The arguments in favour are that you get an exhilarating ride with great views, the opportunity to watch your bags and, sometimes, room to stretch your legs. Some people argue it is also safer, because you can jump off before the bus goes over the side into a gorge! This latter point is debatable. If you are on top, make sure you're well wedged in, so you don't catapult off when the bus swerves, brakes, or lurches (see the Bus Ride story in this section). It's also best to sit facing forwards – that way you can see low-hanging wires and branches before you get swatted. Make sure you've got sunscreen and appropriate clothing too.

TAXI

Larger towns like Kathmandu and Pokhara have taxis which, between a group of people, can be a good way to explore the Kathmandu Valley. Metered taxis have black licence plates while private cars, which often operate as taxis particularly on long-distance routes or for extended periods, have red plates.

Fuel prices and therefore taxi rates often rise faster than meters can be recalibrated, so frequently there is a surcharge on top of the meter reading. Tourists will, in any case, be hard pushed to convince drivers to use their meters (with or without a surcharge) and will almost certainly have to negotiate their fare in advance.

CAR & MOTORBIKE

There are no drive-yourself rental cars available in Nepal but you can easily hire cars with drivers. Expect to pay around $50 a day, plus fuel, which in 1993 cost Rs 28.40 ($0.60) per litre.

It is quite popular to hire cars for round trips to both Pokhara and the Royal Chitwan National Park. A car from Kathmandu to Pokhara should cost around $40 one way, although this can rise to $60 at peak times, maybe even $80. A car to Chitwan should cost around around $70, but could rise to $90 at peak times.

Motorbikes can be rented in Kathmandu. See Kathmandu's Getting Around section in the Kathmandu, Patan & Bhaktapur chapter for more details about car and motorbike rental.

BICYCLE

In Kathmandu and Pokhara there are many bicycle-rental outlets and this is a cheap and convenient way of getting around. Virtually the entire valley is accessible by bike, though if you are venturing far outside the Kathmandu and Patan area, a mountain bike is definitely worthwhile. A regular bicycle only costs from Rs 20 to Rs 30 per day, and a mountain bike costs from Rs 80 to Rs 100 ($2). Children's bicycles can also be hired. See the Mountain Biking chapter for more information on cycling in Nepal.

RICKSHAW

Autorickshaws, those curious and noxious three-wheeled motorcycle-engined devices, are also found in Kathmandu. Bicycle rickshaws are common in the old part of Kathmandu and can be a good way of making short trips through the crowded and narrow streets.

Note that autorickshaws and bicycle rickshaws operate much like taxis, and that the three-wheeled tempos are more like minibuses; leaving when full and having fixed fares.

Top Left: Bhupatindra Malla's Column, Kathmandu (TW)
Top Right: Vishnu figure, Changu Narayan (RE)
Bottom Left: Nepalese masks, Kathmandu (PS)
Bottom Right: Temple strut, Patan (RE)

Top: Splashes of colour, Holi festival, Kathmandu (RI'A)
Middle: Man and child near Pokhara (RE); monk at Swayambhunath,
Kathmandu Valley (PS); Tibetan boy near Langtang (RvD)
Bottom: Pilgrims queue at Pashupatinath (PK)

TOURS

Travel agencies in Kathmandu run organised tours (public and private) by car or bus to places of interest around the valley and further afield. If your stay in Nepal is too short to permit exploration on your own, then it is best to join a conducted or private tour. For more information, see Tours in the Kathmandu section of the Kathmandu, Patan & Bhaktapur chapter.

Kathmandu, Patan & Bhaktapur

For most visitors to Nepal, the Kathmandu Valley is their arrival point and the focus of their visit. This small mountain-sheltered valley is the historical centre of Nepal, the place where kingdoms rose and fell, palaces and temples were built and rebuilt, and Nepalese art and culture were developed and refined.

The three major towns – Kathmandu, Patan and Bhaktapur – each have an artistic and architectural tradition that rivals anything you'll find in the great cities of Europe. Kathmandu is the capital and the largest city in the country; it also has the international airport and is where most visitors stay. Patan, the second largest, is separated from Kathmandu by a river but in other respects the two cities are virtually continuous. Bhaktapur, the third largest, is towards the eastern end of the valley and its relative isolation is reflected in its slower pace and more distinctly mediaeval atmosphere.

Beyond the cities lie hundreds of temples and shrines, traditional villages and agricultural scenes of timeless beauty (see the Around the Kathmandu Valley chapter for more details). A great deal is easily accessible by foot, bicycle, bus or taxi, but the more time you have the better. You will be hard-pressed to do any justice to the place in less than a week.

HISTORY

The Newaris are regarded as the original inhabitants of the valley, but their origins are shrouded in mystery. They speak a Tibeto-Burmese language, which indicates they originated in the east, but their physical features range from distinctively Mongoloid, again suggesting the east, to Indo-Aryan, which of course points to India.

In balance, it seems most likely that the Kathmandu Valley has long been a cultural and racial melting pot with people coming from both east and west. This fusion has resulted in the unique Newari culture that is responsible for the valley's superb art and architecture.

The Newari golden age peaked in the 17th century when the valley consisted of small city-states, and Nepal was a vitally important trading link between Tibet and the north Indian plains. The valley's visible history is inextricably entangled with the Malla kings. It was during their reign, particularly in the 1600s and 1700s, that many of the valley's finest temples and palaces were built. Competition between the cities was intense and an architectural innovation in one place, such as the erection of a column bearing a statue of the ruling king, would inevitably be copied in the other cities.

Sorting out who built what and when is considerably complicated by the fact that at any one time there was not just one Malla king. Each of the three city-states in the valley – Kathmandu, Patan and Bhaktapur – had its own. Some of the most important Malla kings are listed in the introduction to the relevant cities.

The unification of Nepal in 1768 by Gorkha's King Prithvi Narayan Shah signalled the end of the Kathmandu Valley's fragmentation. Nepali, an Indo-European language spoken by the Khas of western Nepal, replaced Newari as the country's language of administration.

GEOGRAPHY

The bowl-like valley is about 25 km from east to west, perhaps 20 km from north to south. Kathmandu lies at a height of around 1300 metres, which gives it a temperate climate, while the surrounding hills range from 1500 metres to 2800 metres in height. If you fly in, you clearly see how isolated and unusual the valley is – embedded like a jewel amongst endless rugged mountains.

A large and growing human population is posing numerous problems. Thanks to the surrounding mountains, Kathmandu is particularly vulnerable to air and water pollution, and both of these problems are already serious. The mountains also make transport extremely difficult: the valley has only three fragile overland lifelines. There's one two-lane road and a cableway to India, and another road to Tibet that washes away every year.

The valley is phenomenally fertile, capable of growing grain (rice, corn, wheat) and a wide range of fruit (from bananas to oranges) and vegetables. However, urban development is rapidly encroaching on valuable agricultural land, so the valley is increasingly dependent on imported food and fossil fuels.

A number of rivers drain towards the centre of the valley and join the holy Bagmati River, which then flows south through the Chobar Gorge to finally reach the Ganges River. Geologists have confirmed ancient myths that claim the valley once lay under water.

CLIMATE

The Kathmandu Valley has a temperate climate that is pleasant most of the year. Snow is almost unheard of, although there are frosts, and the monsoons are nowhere near as debilitating as they are on the plains.

Between October and March it can get quite cold at night (0°C) and the days become short, although it's sunny and warm between mid-morning and mid-afternoon (say 20°C). Visibility is particularly good from October to early February.

By April things start to heat up and there are often storms in the afternoon. The real heat and humidity coincide with the monsoon proper, which usually commences in mid-June. Expect daytime temperatures around the low to mid-30°Cs, and night-time temperatures between 15°C and 20°C. Fortunately, much of the rain falls during the night or on the surrounding hills.

FLORA & FAUNA

Most of the valley has been converted to highly productive farmland, but several pockets of uncleared land remain: Gokarna, just past Bodhnath, Nagarjun, just past Balaju, and others on several of the surrounding hills, notably Pulchowki.

The native forests consisted of oak and other broad-leafed trees, pines and magnificent rhododendrons (*laliguras*) that grow over 15 metres high. Pulchowki, the highest point overlooking the valley, has a magnificent rhododendron forest and shouldn't be missed if you're in the valley in spring (February to April). Australians will recognise the eucalyptus, grevillea and bottlebrush that line many of the valley's roads.

Once upon a time the valley probably had populations of leopards, jungle cats, wolves, black bears, sloth bears, otters and jackals. These are long gone. If you visit Gokarna you will definitely see wild spotted deer (*chital*) and hog deer (*laghuna*), and you might see squirrels, porcupines or langur monkeys (with grey hair and black faces). There are also a number of domesticated Asian elephants.

No visitor to Swayambhunath will avoid the rhesus macaque monkeys that infest the hillside. Nor, if you stay near the old Royal Palace in Kathmandu, will you miss the colonies of fruit bats that spend their days chattering in the trees before they take to the sky every evening.

ECONOMY

Today the valley is the most developed part of Nepal with a network of roads and electricity linking most of the villages. Despite rapid development, however, much of the valley is still devoted to small-scale farming. The availability of improved seeds, fertilisers and extensive irrigation has increased productivity and made it possible to grow wheat as well as the traditional rice.

Nepal's small industrial base is mainly concentrated in the lowland towns of the Terai, although the factories in the valley (including cement, brick, light engineering, food and beverage) contribute nearly 20% of the country's industrial output.

The Kathmandu Valley is the centre for many traditional crafts. Newari craftspeople have long exported pottery, brassware and bronze religious artefacts. The tradition continues, only these days the buyer is often a tourist. The 'Tibetan' carpet industry is now the valley's largest private employer, and carpets are the country's major export earner.

Kathmandu is the administrative and educational centre for the kingdom. Many of the Rana's grand palaces are now home to bureaucracies that are, arguably, of greater benefit to the general populace. Kathmandu is also the main focus for visiting tourists, so there has been a large investment in the necessary infrastructure and many people are dependent on the tourist dollar.

PEOPLE

Today the Newaris still form the largest single group in the valley and there are some smaller towns and villages, such as Thimi, Chapagaon or Sankhu, which remain Newari strongholds. Many of the people living on the surrounding hills are Tamangs, Bahuns and Chhetris, who can generally be distinguished from the Newaris by their solitary households.

In recent years, however, many immigrants from throughout the country have come to the valley in search of jobs and education. There are, therefore, significant minorities of almost every Nepalese ethnic group. Since the Chinese invasion of Tibet, thousands of Tibetan refugees have settled in the valley; there is also a large community of Indian traders and business people and significant communities of other foreigners.

The 1991 census found that Kathmandu had a population of 419,000 (up from 235,000 in 1981), Patan had 117,000 (up from 110,000), and Bhaktapur had 61,000 (up from 60,000). The combined population of the valley was 1,099,000 (up from 617,000 in 1981) meaning that the valley is home to nearly 6% of Nepal's people and that the population density is about 1800 per sq km.

Newaris

It is not surprising that the Newari people were influenced by Tibet and India. What is surprising is their creative response to this stimulus, which actually led to a genuine exchange with their giant neighbours. Mediaeval Newari society has left a religious, architectural and artistic legacy that is unique and spectacular by any standard.

Although most Newaris have Mongoloid physical characteristics, some don't, so their origins are shrouded in mystery. It is now generally accepted that they are a mixture of many different peoples who were attracted to the valley, possibly originating with the Kiratis, or an even earlier group. (See History in the Facts about the Country chapter.)

Perhaps the Newaris' most striking characteristic is their love of communal life. Newari houses were invariably clustered together, usually around sites of religious significance. Although their economy was centred around agriculture and trade, they created sophisticated urban communities which catered to a breadth of human needs in an integrated way that has rarely been matched.

Today, there are around 600,000 Newaris, largely centred in the Kathmandu Valley. Always traders and merchants, the Newaris continue to fill this role throughout the kingdom. Their proximity to the centre of power has also led to them having a disproportionate influence in the bureaucracies of Kathmandu. Many now live in heartbreakingly ugly bungalows on the outskirts of the city proper, and many of their traditions are on the wane.

Architecture The most important social unit was the family and the family house was the starting point for urban planning. Rich Newaris built handsomely proportioned brick houses with tiled roofs that were up to five storeys high. In the country, the ground floor was often used for stabling animals, while in the city it was used for commerce.

A community developed when a series of houses was built in a rectangle around a courtyard/square or *chowk*. The *chowk*, often with running water and a temple or shrine, would be the centre of day-to-day life, and still is today. The markets buzz, children play, women work (weaving, washing, drying grain...) and chat, old people doze in the sun, men talk over the community's business and religious ceremonies take place.

The cities and towns of the valley were made up of a compact network of these interlocking squares, courtyards, twisting alleyways, ponds and temples, often centred around a main square. Fortunately, much of this tradition remains. Decorated with carved windows and doorways, statues and shrines, and humming with gregarious people, a Nepalese town is a remarkable synthesis of art and life.

Religion The vast majority of Newaris are Hindu and fall under a caste system, although there is still a significant minority of Buddhists. This simplistic description, however, masks an incredibly diverse and complex system of beliefs.

Since the 5th century, kings and aristocrats have been Hindu and their influence gradually led to Buddhists adopting castes and a hereditary priesthood (the Banrhas). There are many collapsing *bahals* (monasteries) that testify to a long-gone Buddhist golden age.

The end result is that a purist from either religion would not recognise many of the Newari gods or the practices that go into their worship. For not only have aspects of both religions combined, they have been added to by a Tantric tradition, Lamaism and even older local deities and beliefs.

This has led to a confusing proliferation of gods who are often hybrids unashamedly shuffled from one pantheon to another. There are literally hundreds of these divinities, and over 150 days of festivals a year to celebrate them. From a functional point of view, most people are free to follow whatever gods and goddesses particularly appeal to them, so theological consistency (including the distinction between Hinduism and Buddhism) is irrelevant, certainly to the people themselves. See the Religion section in the Facts about the Country chapter for more details.

Customs The Newaris are divided into castes, whether they nominally consider themselves Hindu or Buddhist, and these include untouchables (tinkers, butchers and some others). Caste rules are not quite as rigid as in some parts of India, but intermarriage is still rare and untouchables are still grossly disadvantaged.

The usual dress for a Newari woman is a sari and blouse, often with a shawl. The men wear trousers with a baggy seat that are tighter around the calves (like jodhpurs), a long untucked double-breasted shirt, a vest (waistcoat) or coat and the traditional Nepalese cap (topi). The most distinctive caste is the Jyapu (farmers), and many of them still lead highly traditional lives. Jyapu women wear black saris with a red border, while the men often wear the traditional trousers and shirt with a long piece of cotton wrapped around the waist. They prefer to carry goods and vegetables on a shoulder pole.

Newari children are welcomed into their community and caste at the age of seven when boys' heads are shaved leaving only a topknot, and girls are symbolically married to the soul of their future husband. Most Newaris have arranged marriages and on auspicious dates wedding processions are a common sight. The procession starts at nightfall and is led by a band, often in ragtag uniforms making a cacophony with clarinets, trumpets and drums.

Traditionally, men were members of a unique cooperative institution known as a *guthi*. This is a religious and social group that may be based on family and other local links. Guthis may own land and are often responsible for the upkeep of particular temples and financing particular rites, as well as the welfare of their members.

Tamangs

The Tamangs are closely related to Tibetans. Their name apparently means 'horse trader', although most are now sedentary farmers, or labourers. Their appearance, language and Lamaist Buddhist beliefs all bear testimony to their origins. Indeed, many of the 'Tibetan' souvenirs for sale in Kathmandu are actually made by Tamangs. Tamangs can be found throughout the central Himalaya, and especially around the Kathmandu Valley. See the People section in the Facts about the Country chapter for more information.

Bahuns (Brahmans) & Chhetris (Kshatriyas)

In Hindu theory Bahuns and Chhetris are the two highest castes (respectively the priests and warriors). In Nepal, however, most are descended from the Khas kingdoms that flourished in western Nepal and were home to Indo-Aryans who migrated to Nepal over the centuries. They played an important role in the court and armies of Prithvi Narayan Shah, and after unification many were rewarded with lands in and around the Kathmandu Valley.

They have dominated the processes of government in Kathmandu, and continue to do so – 57% of the new democratic parliament are Bahun and Chhetri. See under People in the Facts about the Country chapter for more information.

Kathmandu

Kathmandu is the capital of Nepal, the largest city in the country and the main centre for hotels and restaurants. This amazing city can seem, in places, to be a huge intricate sculpture unchanged since the Middle Ages. At other times it can be just another Third World capital rushing carelessly into the 20th century.

For many people, arriving in Kathmandu is as shocking as stepping out of a time machine – the sights, sounds and smells can lead to sensory overload. There are narrow streets and lanes with carved wooden balconies leaning over tiny shops, squares packed with extraordinary temples and monuments, markets bright with fruit and vegetables and a constant throng of humanity. Then there's choking dust and fumes, stinking gutters,

concrete monstrosities, touts, Coca-Cola billboards and maimed beggars.

The gap between rich and poor is a chasm, but despite the pressures of extreme overcrowding and poverty, people retain a good-humoured self respect and integrity. It is probably safer to walk the streets here than it is in your home town – and certainly much more interesting.

Like Patan and Bhaktapur, the other major towns of the valley, Kathmandu's historic centre is concentrated around the Durbar Square *(durbar* is Nepali for palace). There's a distinct difference between the tightly packed old city area and the more spacious newer parts of town.

When to Go

Although the best time to visit Nepal is during October and March (see the When to Go section in the Facts for the Visitor chapter) a visit to the Kathmandu Valley during the monsoon is still feasible because most of the rain falls during the night or on the surrounding hills. Other good reasons for visiting at this time are that several important festivals are celebrated, there are fewer tourists, and prices are lower.

Malla Kings

Malla kings of particular importance in Kathmandu included:

Ratna Malla	1482-1528
Mahendra Malla	1560-1574
Sadasiva Malla	1574-1583
Shiva Singh Malla	1578-1620
Pratap Malla	1641-1674
Prithvibendra Malla	1680-1687
Bhaskara Malla	1687-1714
Jagat Jaya Malla	1722-1736
Jaya Prakash Malla	1736-1768

ORIENTATION

Most of the interesting things to see in Kathmandu are clustered in the old part of town from Kantipath west towards the Vishnumati River. New Rd, constructed after the great earthquake of 1934, starts from the ornamental entranceway by Kantipath and goes straight into the heart of old Kathmandu, changing its name to Ganga Path before it comes to Durbar Square.

The international office of Royal Nepal Airlines (RNAC) is at the Kantipath end of New Rd and along the road are banks, shops and the modern shopping centre where Indian visitors come to buy consumer goods not readily available back home. Continue further along New Rd to Ganga Path and you reach the large Basantapur Square, then Durbar Square where the old Royal Palace is located. Freak St, Kathmandu's famous street from the hippie/overland era, runs off Basantapur Square.

Running north-east from Durbar Square is the thoroughfare that was once the main trading artery of the city and is still the busiest street in old Kathmandu. This narrow road, usually thronged with people, cuts through the heart of old Kathmandu from Indra Chowk through Kel Tole to Asan Tole.

Kantipath forms the north-south boundary between the older and newer parts of the city. Just south of the New Rd junction is the main post office, easily located by the nearby Bhimsen Tower (also known as Sundhara). This is a major bus station area and is known as Khichapokhari, the 'pond of the dogs'. On the eastern side of Kantipath is the large open field known as Tundikhel.

Continuing north along Kantipath from New Rd takes you past the government-run Bir Hospital on the left – look for Hanuman on the wall carrying a Himalayan mountain complete with medicinal herbs. On the right is Ratna Park and then Rani Pokhari. Kantipath crosses Tridevi Marg at the corner of the new Royal Palace compound and continues into Maharajganj, the embassy sector.

Running parallel to Kantipath is Durbar Marg, a wide street flanked by travel agencies, airline offices and a number of restaurants and expensive hotels. It ends at the main entrance to the new Royal Palace. Turn left from Durbar Marg in front of the palace, cross Kantipath, and Tridevi Marg will take you past the South Asian Association for Regional Cooperation (SAARC) and after a couple of blocks will bring you into

the Thamel area, the popular cheap-accommodation centre of the city. Thamel is 15 to 20 minutes' walk north from the centre of Kathmandu.

Addresses

In old Kathmandu streets were not given names, and although some of the major thoroughfares now do, most still don't. Smaller streets and laneways never do. Kathmandu grew up as a series of interlocking squares that gradually swallowed neighbouring villages. The names of these squares, villages, and other landmarks (perhaps a monastery or temple) came to be used as addresses of sorts.

For example, the address of everyone living within a 100-metre radius of Thahiti Tole is Thahiti Tole and if you want to find them you go to Thahiti Tole and ask around – simple if you can speak Nepali and can find your way around the warren of laneways and courtyards. Thamel is now used to describe a sprawling area with at least a dozen roads and several hundred hotels and restaurants. They all have the same one word address – Thamel.

Given this anarchic approach it is amazing that any mail gets delivered – it does, but slowly. Most businesses have post office box numbers. If you're trying to find a particular house, shop or business, make sure you get detailed directions (unless, of course, you have a foolproof Lonely Planet map!).

INFORMATION

There are a number of good notice boards in Thamel that are worth consulting if you are looking for information on such diverse things as apartments, travel and trekking partners, Yoga and Buddhist courses, language courses and cultural events. The Kathmandu Guest House has a good board (to the left of the entrance), as does the Pumpernickel Bakery.

There's another particularly useful board outside the Trekkers' Information Centre (run by KEEP and HRA) in the Tilicho Hotel, just to the west of the immigration office. The people in the information centre are happy to answer general queries, and

Kathmandu

To Bhaktapur, Airport & Arniko Hwy

Singh Durbar

Ram Shah Path

Prithvi Path

Tukuca Khola

Bhrikutimandap Marg

Exhibition Ground

THAPATHALI

Tundikhel

Tripureshwar Marg

Freak St

See Freak Street Map

Walking Tour 2

Walking Tour 3

TEKU

Bagmati River

Footbridge

Vishnumati River

To National Museum & Art Gallery

To Oberoi Hotel & Pokhara

To Kirtipur

To Kirtipur

To Patan

● BUS STOPS
T1 Paknajol (Sorakhutte) –
   for Kakani, Trisuli Bazaar & Dunche
T2 Tridevi Marg –
   for Sundarijal
T3 Rani Pokhari (Jamal) –
   for Budhanilkantha
T4 Ratna Park –
   for Gokarna, Patan & Kirtipur
T5 Bagh Bazaar –
   for Bhaktapur

T6 Central Bus Station –
   for Banepa, Dhulikel, Panauti & Jiri
T7 Tukuchapel –
   for Sundarijal
T8 Bhimsen Tower (Sundhara) –
   for ?
T9 Martyrs' Gate (Shahid Gate) –
   for Sankhu, Pharping & Dakshinkali
T10 Bhaktapur Trolley Bus
T11 Kantipath –
   for Tourist buses to Pokhara

■ PLACES TO STAY

4   Hotel Vajra
5   International Guest House
6   Holy Lodge
7   Kathmandu Guest House
10 Hotel Malla
21 Yak & Yeti Park Royal Hotel
22 Hotel de l'Annapurna
23 Hotel Sherpa & Cafe de la Paix
26 Yellow Pagoda Hotel
27 Hotel Nook
29 Tibet Guest House
30 Sita Guest House
31 Shambala Guest House
49 Kathmandu Lodge
52 Crystal Hotel
58 Ajima Guest House
62 Eden Hotel
70 Hotel Valley View
90 Blue Star Hotel

▼ PLACES TO EAT

8   KC's Restaurant
9   Utse Restaurant
20 Kushi Fuji Restaurant
24 Mike's Breakfast
28 Narayan's Restaurant
40 Bhanchha Ghar Restaurant

OTHER

1   Shobabaghwati Temple
2   Bijeshwari Temple
3   Indrani Temple
11 Kaiser Library
12 Immigration Office
13 Three Goddesses Temples
14 SAARC Secretariat
15 Royal Palace
16 Chinese Embassy
17 Nepal International Clinic
18 Indian Airlines
19 British Council
25 American Express
32 Kathesimbhu Stupa
33 Nateshwar Temple
34 Chusya Bahal

35 National Theatre
36 Ikha Narayan Temple
37 Annapurna Temple
38 Clocktower
39 Himalayan Book Sellers
41 Nara Devi Temple
42 Narsingha Temple
43 Yatkha Bahal
44 Yitum Bahal
45 Jana Bahal Temple
46 Sweta Machhendranath Temple
47 Shiva Temple
48 Akash Bhairab Temple
50 Hanuman Dhoka (Old Royal Palace)
51 Tourist Office
53 Nepal Bank
54 US Library & Information Service
55 RNAC (International)
56 Bir Hospital
57 Mahakala Temple
59 Bhimsen Temple
60 Hari Shankar Temple
61 Adko Narayan Temple
63 Vegetable Market
64 Bhimsen Tower (Sundhara)
65 Main Post Office
66 Ram Chandra Temple
67 Jaisi Deval Temple
68 Takan Bahal
69 Machhendranath Temple
71 Martyrs' Memorial Gate
72 Bhadrakali Temple
73 Duty-Free Centre
74 Supreme Court
75 National Archives
76 Army Headquarters
77 Cableway Station
78 Pachali Bhairab Temple
79 Tindeval Temple
80 Raj Ghat
81 Nepal Traveller Office
82 Central Telegraph Office
83 National Stadium
84 Swimming Pool
85 Ministry of Tourism
86 RNAC (Domestic)
87 Nepal Rastra Bank
88 Tripureshwar Mahadev Temple
89 Kalmochan Temple
91 Bluebird Supermarket

there are some useful notebooks with up-to-date information from other trekkers.

Most travel agents are happy to answer queries, but most swing into a pretty hard sell. The people in the office of Greenhill Tours & West Himalayan Outdoor (in the Tukche Peak Guest House compound) are tuned into independent budget travellers' needs, and won't sell you something you don't want.

Nepal Traveller is a good-quality, free magazine that covers a broad range of interesting topics and has a good section of practical information, with addresses and phone numbers. If you can't find a copy or are interested in back copies, visit their office on the south side of Tripureshwar Marg about 400 metres from the roundabout at its intersection with Kantipath.

Emergency

Red Cross Ambulance	☎ 01-228094
Police, Durbar Square	☎ 01-211162
Fire Brigade	☎ 01-221177

Tourist Office

The government tourist office (☎ 01-220818) is on Ganga Path diagonally opposite Basantapur Square, and it may or may not have some brochures and maps. If it doesn't (and it should have a useful visitors' guide) try the Ministry of Tourism (☎ 01-214519, Tripureshwar, Kathmandu) behind the National Stadium. There is also a tourist office at the airport.

Money

See the Facts for the Visitor chapter for a discussion on the differing exchange rates and commissions. In brief, it is worth checking the rate banks offer and the commission they charge – both vary.

The most convenient bank for travellers staying in the Thamel region, is the small branch of the Nepal Grindlays Bank in the Namche Bazaar building. There's also a branch of the Rastriya Banijya Bank inside the immigration office building; this can be convenient if you're doing battle with the bureaucrats, but after your first visit to this building you're unlikely to want to return.

The main Nepal Bank in New Rd is handy if you're staying in Freak St and has the important advantage of being open from 7.30 am to 7.30 pm seven days a week. There are several banks on Durbar Marg; the Nepal Indo-Suez Bank is convenient and efficient.

Kathmandu also has a Nepal Grindlays Bank (with superb murals by Mithila women from Janakpur) at the Thamel end of Kantipath; Citibank (☎ 01-228843), GPO Box 2865, with an office in the Yak & Yeti Park Royal Hotel; Standard Chartered (☎ 01-220129), GPO Box 1526, Durbar Marg; and the Nepal Arab Bank (☎ 01-211785), GPO Box 3729, Kantipath.

American Express has an office off the forecourt of the Hotel Mayalu on Jamal Tol, just around the corner from Durbar Marg. It will make cash advances between 10 am and 1 pm. Grindlays will make advances on Visa and MasterCard in Nepalese rupees and travellers' cheques. Note that you cannot make credit-card payments to these offices – arrangements should be made before you leave home.

Kathmandu also has a great number of 'change money' men and although this black market is officially illegal it is so widely accepted that letters are regularly written to the *Rising Nepal* complaining about the constant importuning by moneychangers. A popular T-shirt worn by many visitors announces that they don't want to change money!

Post

The main Kathmandu post office is on the corner of Kantipath and Khichapokhari, close to Bhimsen Tower. The stamp counter is theoretically open from 8 am to 7 pm, Sunday to Thursday, and from 11 am to 3 pm on Saturdays, but it can provide a classic dose of queuing and frustration. Unless you have a *lot* of mail, you are best off to take advantage of the hotels, bookshops (including Pilgrims) and communications centres who will tackle the bureaucracy for you for a nominal charge. See the Facts for the Visitor chapter for postal charges.

The poste restante section at the main post office is quite efficient: the staff sorts letters into alphabetically arranged boxes and you simply sit down and go through them yourself. You are required to show your passport before you take anything away. Make sure your correspondents print and underline your surname; if in doubt check under your first name as well. The section is open from 10.15 am to 4 pm Sunday to Thursday (closing one hour earlier from mid-November to mid-February), and from 10.15 am to 2 pm on Fridays; it's closed on Saturdays.

Parcels may be sent from the separate Foreign Post Office just north of the main post office. It's open from 10 am to 5 pm Sunday to Thursday and from 10 am to noon on Fridays. Parcels have to be examined and sealed by a customs officer and then packed in an approved manner. It's something of a procedure, so if you're short of time you're best off using one of the many cargo agencies. Dolha Continental Exports (☎/fax 01-414997), opposite the Hotel Mandap in Thamel, and Sharmasons Movers (☎ 01-222709; fax 222026) are two that have been recommended.

American Express has a clients' mail service at its offices off the forecourt of the Hotel Mayalu in Jamal Tol. Address letters to American Express, Yeti Travels Pty Ltd, Hotel Mayalu, Jamal Tol, PO Box 76, Durbar Marg, Kathmandu.

Telephone

Nepal is linked to the rest of the world by satellite and there is international direct dialling (IDD). Unfortunately, reverse-charge (collect) calls can only be made to Canada, Japan and the UK.

International phone calls can be made and faxes can be sent from the Central Telegraph Office about 500 metres south of the post office, opposite the National Stadium. The service is open 24 hours and there are numerous signs to guide the novice, including the important admonition, 'For your confusion please see tariff.'

As I understood it, there is a minimum charge for the first three minutes (whether you use all the time or not) then a per-minute rate. For Australia, Canada, France, New Zealand, the UK and the USA, the first three minutes is approximately $7 and additional minutes are $2.40. For the Netherlands the first three minutes cost $8, followed by $2.70 per minute. For southern Africa, Denmark, Israel and Italy, the first three minutes cost $9, followed by $3 per minute.

Over the last couple of years, a number of communication centres have sprung up in Thamel offering fax, telephone and mailing services. They range in expense, but seem to be reliable.

Faxes can be a very useful means of instant communication, but since you are charged by the minute the costs can vary widely depending on the efficiency of the sending and receiving equipment. The Central Telegraph Office charges a three-minute minimum for one A4 page, but in most cases an A4 page should take no more than a minute to send. The Galaxy Communication Centre, on the 1st floor opposite Pilgrims Bookshop in Thamel is recommended.

For telephone calls with the private operators, expect to pay around $3 per minute to Australia, France, the UK and USA, and around $3.50 for Germany and New Zealand. If a phone call is short, the convenience of the private operators outweighs the comparative expense, but if you talk for any length of time you're better off to catch a taxi or tempo to the Central Telegraph Office (around Rs 30).

Many of hotels now have IDD facilities, but always check their charges before you phone; they usually charge by the minute and add a service charge.

For international call information phone ☎ 186, for domestic information ☎ 197, and for domestic trunk calls ☎ 180.

Government Offices

Most government offices in Kathmandu are open from 10 am to 5 pm from Sunday to Thursday and from 10 am to 4 pm during the three winter months (mid-November to mid-February). Offices close at 3 pm on Fridays.

The immigration office, where trekking permits are also issued, is on Tridevi Marg, close to Thamel. It's open from 10.30 am to 2 pm Sunday to Thursday and 10.30 am to noon on Fridays for applications, although you have to go back later to retrieve your passport. It's wise to start the process early as renewing a visa or obtaining a trekking permit can be very time-consuming. (See Visas in the Facts for the Visitor chapter for more details.)

Aid Organisations

Kathmandu has a number of nongovernmental aid organisations pursuing small-scale, community-based programmes. These are either run by Nepalese, or in close association with Nepalese, and are recommended. All would gratefully accept donations. (See Begging in the Facts about the Country chapter for background information.) Alternatively, give to reputable organisations in your home country.

Adventist Development & Relief Agency (ADRA)
 PO Box 4481, Kathmandu (☎ 01-417013)
Child Workers in Nepal (CWIN)
 PO Box 4374, Kaumati, Kathmandu (☎ 01-271658)
Creative Development Centre
 PO Box 5484, Naxal, Kathmandu (☎ 01-416093)
Kumbeshwar Technical School
 PO Box 2181, Patan, Kathmandu (☎ 01-522271)
Nepal Eye Programme – Australia (NEPA)
 PO Box 561, Kathmandu (☎ 01-474685)
Sreet Children's Assistance Programme (SCAP)
 PO Box 1018, Kathmandu
The Leprosy Hospital
 PO Box 151, Anandban, Kathmandu (☎ 01-290545)

Travel Agencies

Kathmandu has a great number of travel agencies, particularly along Durbar Marg, Kantipath and in Thamel. See the Trekking chapter for information on trekking agencies.

Libraries

There are a number of libraries and cultural centres in Kathmandu. The British Council Library (☎ 01-221305) on Kantipath has a good selection of books on Nepal as well as British newspapers and magazines. It's open from 11 am to 6 pm, Sunday to Friday.

Unfortunately only Nepalese and foreign residents in Nepal are allowed to use the US Library & Information Service (☎ 01-221250) on New Rd. If you qualify, it's open from 11 am to 7 pm, Monday to Friday.

The French Cultural Centre (☎ 01-224326) is in Bagh Bazaar opposite the Bhaktapur bus stand (Bus Stop 4) and has French publications and organises French film nights for which there is a small admission charge. The German Goethe Institute (☎ 01-220528) in Ganabahal, near Bhimsen Tower, has film nights and occasional exhibitions as well as library facilities.

Rastriya Pustakalaya, the Nepal National Library, is at Pulchowk in Patan and has books in English and Indian. The Tribhuvan University Library of Kirtipur has a good collection and is open Sunday to Friday from 9 am to 6 pm.

The Kaiser or Kesar Library is worth a visit just to see the building. It's on Kantipath opposite the new Royal Palace and has an incredible collection of books on Buddhism, Tibet and Nepal. Kaiser Shamsher Jung Bahadur Rana was a Rana aristocrat, scholar, scientist and gourmet. He built up a superb collection of books all of which, it is said, he read in their original language. Most of his palace is now used for government offices, but his library is kept as he left it and can be visited.

Bookshops

Kathmandu has a large number of very good bookshops. Many have particularly interesting selections of books on Nepal including books that are not usually available outside the country. Prices for British and US books are surprisingly competitive with their home-market prices.

As well as shops with new books there are many shops with second-hand books for sale and trade. Most dealers will buy back books for 50% of what you paid for them.

Tiwari's Pilgrims Book House is a couple of doors north of the Kathmandu Guest House and has an extensive collection of books on Nepal and other Himalayan regions. It also has books on Buddhism, Hinduism, Tantrism, yoga, mountain-climbing and trekking plus general books, maps, games, envelopes and a superb postcard selection. There's another even better shop owned by the same company, on the road from Durbar Marg to the Hotel Yak & Yeti Park Royal Hotel. Known as the Kailash Bookshop, it also has an antiquarian section.

There are many other good bookshops around Thamel, including Bookland on Tridevi Marg opposite the immigration office. Mandala Book Point on Kantipath has an excellent selection of books, with a good range in French and German.

Himalayan Book Sellers at Ghantaghar by the clocktower is a long-term survivor in the Kathmandu book business with an excellent selection of books on Nepal and the Himalaya. Everest Book Service and Asia Book House are good bookshops just round the corner from Durbar Marg towards the National Theatre.

Ratna Book Distributors at Bagh Bazaar near the French Cultural Centre, Educational Enterprises beside the Mahakala Temple on Kantipath near the New Rd gate, and the Himalaya Book Store at Bagh Bazaar near Bus Stop 5, are all worth visiting.

COURSES
Yoga & Buddhism
Check the bulletin boards in Thamel for up-to-date information and shop around before you commit yourself. A number of courses are regularly advertised.

The Hotel Asia (☎ 01-220441) in the centre of Thamel is home to the Kathmandu Western Buddhist Centre and there are regular one and two-day courses, as well as talks. These have been highly recommended. The leaders are good and give a broad introduction to meditation and Buddhism. Live-in courses are held at the Pulchowk monastery in Patan, which overlooks the valley. It has been renovated to a high stan-

dard; there are comfortable double rooms and the food is good.

Arogya Ashram (☎ 01-470776) near the Pashupatinath Temple teaches yoga. Arogya also has a branch in Kathmandu.

The Himalayan Yogic Institute & Buddhist Meditation Centre (☎ 01-413094), PO Box 817, Kathmandu, has talks, retreats and courses. To find the centre, head away from Thamel on Lazimpat until you get to the Hotel Kathmandu; turn right after the hotel and the centre is on the right after about 200 metres.

This centre is affiliated with the monastery at Kopan (☎ 01-226717), north of Bodhnath, which offers very reasonably priced courses which run from seven to 28 days. (See the Around the Kathmandu Valley chapter for details.) For more information on Kopan write to the Nepal Mahayana Centre, PO Box 817, Kathmandu, Nepal.

Yoga House has been highly recommended for lessons in Hatha Yoga, and is open to anyone from beginners upwards on a drop-in basis from 10.30 am to noon and 5.30 to 7.30 pm. Yoga House (☎/fax 01-417900), PO Box 5098, Kathmandu, is at Tangal Pokhari, a 10-minute bicycle ride east of the palace. You can recognise it by the Buddhist prayer flags festooned across the roof.

ACTIVITIES
Swimming Pools & Sauna
Generally, pools in the major hotels can be used by friends of hotel guests or, at some hotels, by outsiders for a $2 to $3 charge. The biggest hotel pool is at the Hotel de l'Annapurna but, reflecting its popularity, it charges a ridiculous Rs 345 ($7) for one-day membership. Longer membership charges are a bit more reasonable.

There are public pools at Balaju and at the National Stadium although they close during the October to February winter months. The National Stadium pool in the south of Kathmandu costs Rs 15 and is open from 10 am to 5 pm; Monday is reserved for women. The Balaju pool costs Rs 10 but it can get very crowded.

The Kathmandu Physical Fitness Centre (☎ 01-412473) in Lazimpat, has weight-training equipment, a jacuzzi and a sauna. Membership for one week is Rs 300 ($6), for one month Rs 800 ($16), and for three months Rs 1700 ($34). A sauna or jacuzzi for a nonmember costs Rs 150 ($3).

There's also an excellent sauna, open to visitors, at the Vajra Hotel on the way to Swayambhunath.

DURBAR SQUARE

Durbar in Nepali means 'palace' and in Patan and Bhaktapur, as well as Kathmandu, there are durbar squares in front of their old palaces. The king no longer lives in the old Royal Palace in Kathmandu: the palace was moved north to Narayanhiti about a century ago. At that time it was on the edge of the city, now it's close to the popular tourist area of Thamel.

Clustered around the central Durbar Square are the old Royal Palace (Hanuman Dhoka), numerous interesting temples, the Kumari Chowk or Kumari Bahal (House of the Living Goddess) and the Kasthamandap (House of Wood).

It's easy to spend hours wandering around Durbar Square and the adjoining Basantapur Square. This is very much the centre of old Kathmandu and watching the world go by from the terraced platforms of the towering Maju Deval is a wonderful way to get a feeling for the city. Although many of the buildings around the square are very old, a great deal of damage was caused by the great earthquake of 1934 and many buildings were subsequently rebuilt, not always in their original form.

The Durbar Square area is actually made up of three loosely linked squares. To the east is the open Basantapur Square area, off which runs Freak St. The main Durbar Square area, with its popular watch-the-world-go-by temples, is to the west. Running north-east is a second part of Durbar Square which contains the entrance to the old Royal Palace and an assortment of temples. From this open area Makhan Tole, at one time the main road in Kathmandu and still the most interesting street to walk down, continues north-east.

A good place to start an exploration of the square is with what may well be the oldest building in the valley, the unprepossessing Kasthamandap. Note: the numbers in the following sections correspond to item numbers on the key for the Durbar Square (Kathmandu) map.

Kasthamandap (35)

In the south-western corner of the square the Kasthamandap or House of Wood is the building which gave Kathmandu its name. Although its history is uncertain, it is possible that it was originally constructed around the 12th century. A legend relates that the whole building was made with the wood from a single sal tree. At first it was a community centre where visitors gathered before major ceremonies, but later it was converted to a temple to Gorakhnath.

A small wooden enclosure in the centre of the building houses the image of the god. Images of Ganesh can be found at each corner of the building and there are also shrines to a number of other gods. Bronze lions guard the entrance, and Hindu epics are illustrated around the 1st-floor cornices of the three-storey building.

The squat, mediaeval-looking building is busy in the early-morning hours when

Kasthamandap

Durbar Square
(Kathmandu)

porters sit here, waiting for customers who need to have loads carried.

Ashok Binayak (33)

On the northern side of the Kasthamandap, at the top of Maru Tole, the laneway down to the river, stands the tiny Ashok Binayak or Maru Ganesh Shrine. The small size of this shrine belies its importance, as this is one of the four most important Ganesh shrines in the valley. Ganesh is a much-loved god and there is a constant stream of visitors here. A visit to this shrine is highly recommended by Hindus to ensure safety on a forthcoming journey. It's uncertain how old the temple is although its gilded roof was added in the 19th century.

Shiva Temple (32)

The Shiva Temple near the Kasthamandap and the Ashok Binayak is used by barbers who can generally be seen squatting on the temple platform, administering 'short back and sides'.

Maru Tole

Maru Tole leads down to the Vishnumati River where a footbridge meets the pathway to Swayambhunath on the other side. This was a busy street in the days of hippies and flower power, but today there's little sign of why it should have been called either Pie or Pig Alley – not only are the pie shops gone it's also much cleaner. One thing Maru Tole does have is Maru Hiti, one of the finest sunken water conduits in the city.

Maju Deval (31)

A pleasant hour can easily be spent sitting on the platform steps of the Shiva temple known as the Maju Deval. From here you can watch the constant activity of fruit and vegetable

■ PLACES TO STAY		21	Narsingha Statue
		22	Audience Chamber
7	Kathmandu Lodge	23	Panch Mukhi Hanuman Temple
36	Kumari Guest House	24	Dancing Shiva Statue
43	Hotel Sugat	25	Narayan Temple
50	Crystal Hotel	26	Shiva-Parvati Temple
		27	Bhagwati Temple
	OTHER	28	Sweta (White) Bhairab
		29	Degutaleju Temple
1	Mahendreshwar Temple	30	Tribhuvan Museum
2	Mahavishnu Temple	31	Maju Deval
3	Kotilingeshwar Mahadev Temple	32	Shiva Temple
4	Kakeshwar Temple	33	Ashok Binayak (Maru Ganesh
5	Taleju Temple		Shrine)
6	Tana Deval Temple	34	Lakshmi Narayan Temple
8	Great Drums	35	Kasthamandap (House of Wood)
9	Krishna Temple	37	Garuda Statue
10	Saraswati Temple	38	Trailokya Mohan Narayan Temple
11	Stone Vishnu Temple	39	Gaddi Baithak
12	Great Bell	40	Singh Sattal
13	King Pratap Malla's Column	41	Kabindrapur Temple
14	Kala (Black) Bhairab	42	Kumari Bahal
15	Jagannath Temple	44	Basantapur Tower
16	Indrapur Temple	45	Coronation Platform
17	Vishnu Temple	46	Kirtipur Tower
18	Stone Inscription	47	Bhaktapur Tower (Lakshmi Bilas)
19	Mohan Tower	48	Patan Tower (Lalitpur Tower)
20	Hanuman Statue	49	Tourist Office

hawkers, the comings and goings of taxis and rickshaws and the flute and other souvenir sellers importuning tourists. The nine-stage platform of the Maju Deval is probably the most popular meeting place in the city. The large, triple-roofed temple has erotic carvings on its roof struts and offers great views over the square and across the roofs of the town.

Maju Deval

The temple dates from 1690 and was built by the mother of Bhaktapur's King Bhupatindra Malla. Although the temple has a well-known Shiva lingam inside, the roof is topped by a pinnacle shaped like a Buddhist stupa. At the bottom of the temple stairway is a small temple to Kam Dev, a 'companion' of Shiva. It was built in the Indian *shikhara* style, with a tall corncob-like spire.

Trailokya Mohan Narayan Temple (38)

The other temple standing out in the open area of the square is the smaller five-tiered, three-roofed Trailokya Mohan Narayan. The temple was built by Prithvibendra Malla in 1680 and is easily identified as a temple to Narayan or Vishnu by the fine Garuda kneeling before it. The Garuda figure was a later addition, erected by the king's widow soon after his death. Look for the Vaishnavite images on the carved roof struts and the window screens with their decoratively carved medallions.

Trailokya Mohan Narayan Temple

Shiva-Parvati Temple (26)

From the steps of the Maju Deval you can look across the square to the Shiva-Parvati Temple, where images of Shiva and his consort look out from the upstairs window on the comings and goings below them. The

---

Visiting Hindu Temples
Non-Hindus are barred from entering a number of temples in Nepal although Nathalie Nellens, a Belgian visitor, commented that 'non-Hindu is rather meaningless when it is much more your colour than your religious beliefs that count'. She's probably right: an Indian Christian or Indian Muslim would probably find it easy to gain entrance! ■

The big gate beside the Kumari Bahal conceals the huge chariot which takes the Kumari around the city of Kathmandu once a year, a festival begun during the rule of Jaya Prakash Malla.

Shiva-Parvati Temple

Kumari Bahal

temple was built in the late 1700s by Bahadur Shah, son of Prithvi Narayan Shah. Although the temple is not very old by Kathmandu standards, it stands on a two-stage platform which may have been an open dancing stage hundreds of years earlier. A Vishnu temple stands to one side of it.

Kumari Bahal (42)
At the junction of Durbar and Basantapur squares is a white three-storey building with intricately carved windows. The House of the Living Goddess (Kumari Bahal) faces Durbar Square, its door guarded by stone lions. The building, in the style of the courtyarded Buddhist *viharas* of the valley, was built in 1757 by Jaya Prakash Malla. Inside lives the young girl who is selected to be the town's living goddess, until she reaches puberty and reverts to being a normal mortal!

Inside the building the three-storey court-yard, or Kumari Chowk, is enclosed by magnificently carved wooden balconies and windows. A little baksheesh to a waiting attendant may well prompt a brief appear-ance – he calls out 'Hey goddess' in Newari! Photographing the goddess is forbidden, but you are quite free to photograph the court-yard when she is not present. Westerners are not allowed to go beyond this area. The courtyard contains a miniature stupa carry-ing the symbols of Saraswati, the goddess of learning.

Gaddi Baithak (39)
The eastern side of Durbar Square is closed off by this white neoclassical building. The Gaddi Baithak with its imported European style was built as a part of the palace during the Rana period and makes a strange contrast to the traditional Nepalese architecture that dominates the square.

Bhagwati Temple (27)
Next to the Gaddi Baithak, this triple-storey, triple-roofed temple is easily missed since it surmounts the building below it. The best view of the temple with its golden roofs is probably from the Maju Deval across the square. The temple was built by Jagat Jaya Malla and originally had an image of Narayan. This image was stolen in 1766, so when Prithvi Narayan Shah conquered the valley only two years later he simply substi-tuted it with an image of the goddess Bhagwati, which he just happened to be toting around with him. In April each year

Kumari Devi

Not only does Nepal have countless gods, goddesses, deities, Bodhisattvas, *avatars* (incarnations of deities living on earth) and manifestations, which are worshipped and revered as statues, images, paintings and symbols, the country also has a real living goddess. The Kumari Devi is a young girl who lives in the building known as the Kumari Bahal, right beside Kathmandu's Durbar Square.

The practice of having a living goddess probably came about during the reign of Jaya Prakash Malla, the last of the Malla kings of Kathmandu whose reign abruptly ended with the conquest of the valley by Prithvi Narayan Shah in 1768. As usual in Nepal, where there is never one simple answer to any question, there are a number of legends about the Kumari.

One is that the Malla king had intercourse with a pre-pubescent girl, that she died as a result and that he started the practice of venerating a young girl as a living goddess in penance. Another tells of a Malla king who regularly played dice with the goddess Taleju, the protective deity of the valley. When he made an unseemly advance she threatened to withdraw her protection but relented and promised to return in the form of a young girl. Still another tells of a young girl possessed by the goddess Durga and banished from the kingdom. When the furious queen heard of this she ordered her husband to bring the young girl back and keep her as a real goddess.

Whatever the background, the reality is that there are a number of living goddesses around the Kathmandu Valley but it is the Kumari Devi or Royal Kumari who is the most important. The Kumari is selected from a particular caste of Newari gold and silversmiths. She is customarily somewhere between the ages of four and five and puberty and must meet 32 strict physical requirements ranging from the colour of her eyes and the shape of her teeth to the sound of her voice. Her horoscope must also be appropriate of course.

Once suitable candidates have been found they are gathered together in a darkened room where terrifying noises are made, men dance by in horrific masks and gruesome buffalo heads are on display. Naturally these goings-on are unlikely to frighten a real goddess, particularly one who is an incarnation of Durga, so the young girl who remains calm and collected through this ordeal is clearly the new Kumari. In a process similar to the selection of the Dalai Lama the Kumari then chooses items of clothing and decoration worn by her predecessor as a final test.

Once chosen as the Kumari the young girl moves in to the Kumari Bahal with her family and lives there apart from a half-dozen ceremonial forays into the outside world each year. The most spectacular of these occasions is the August-September Indra Jatra festival, when she travels through the city on a huge temple chariot over a three-day period. During this festival the Kumari customarily blesses the king of Nepal and it is curious that Prithvi Narayan Shah's defeat of the Malla kingdoms took place at this time, just as if the goddess Taleju had indeed withdrawn her protection over the valley. The new king was blessed by the Kumari and the custom continued without skipping a beat!

The Kumari's reign ends with her first period, or any serious accidental loss of blood. Once this first sign of puberty is reached she reverts to being a normal mortal, and the search must start for a new Kumari. During her time as a goddess the Kumari is supported by the temple income and on retirement she is paid a handsome dowry. It is said that marrying an ex-Kumari is unlucky, but it's more likely a natural belief that taking on a spoilt ex-goddess is likely to be hard work! ■

Bhagwati Temple

Vishnu Temple (11)
Next to the bell is a small stone Vishnu temple about which very little is known. It was badly damaged by the earthquake of 1934 and has only recently been restored.

Saraswati Temple (10)
Next is the Saraswati Temple which also suffered badly from the great earthquake. Prior to the quake it was over 14 metres high, now it is only half that height. Like the adjoining Vishnu temple little is known about its history.

Saraswati

the image of the goddess is conveyed to the village of Nuwakot, 65 km to the north, then returned a few days later.

A succession of interesting buildings and statues stand to the north-east of the Bhagwati Temple.

Great Bell (12)
On your left as you leave the main square along Makhan Tole is the Great Bell erected by Rana Bahadur Shah (son of Prithvi Narayan Shah) in 1797. During the Malla era a novel addition to one of the valley town's Durbar squares would almost immediately be imitated in another's. Curiously, Patan and Bhaktapur got their bells in 1736, while the Kathmandu version did not follow until long after the fall of the Mallas. The bell's ring will drive off evil spirits, but it is only rung during puja (worship) at the Degutaleju Temple.

Krishna Temple (9)
The history of the octagonal Krishna Temple is well documented. It was built in 1648 by Pratap Malla, perhaps as a reply to Siddhi-narsingh's magnificent Krishna Mandir in Patan. Inside there are images of Krishna and two goddesses which, according to a Sanskrit inscription, are modelled from the king and his two wives! The temple also has a Newari inscription but this neglects to

Krishna Temple

prayer room on the 3rd floor of the Degutaleju Temple (29). The column was erected in 1670 by Pratap Malla and preceded the similar columns in Patan and Bhaktapur.

Sweta Bhairab (28)

Sweta (White) Bhairab's horrible face is hidden away behind a grille opposite the Pratap Malla column. The huge mask dates from 1794 during the reign of Rana Bahadur Shah, the third Shah dynasty king. Each September during the Indra Jatra festival the gates are swung back to reveal the mask for a few days. At that time the face is covered in flowers and rice and at the start of the festivities beer is poured through the horrific mouth. Crowds of men fight to get a drink of this blessed beer! At other times of year you can peek through the lattice to see the mask which is used as the symbol of Royal Nepal Airlines.

Jagannath Temple (15)

This temple, noted for the erotic carvings on its roof struts, is the oldest structure in this part of the square. Pratap Malla claimed to have constructed the temple during his reign but it may actually be much older, dating back to 1563 during the rule of Mahendra

mention the king's little act of vanity. The triple-roofed temple has lower roofs of tile topped by a copper roof.

Just beyond the temple are the **Great Drums** (8) to which a goat and a buffalo must be sacrificed twice a year. Then there is the police headquarters building beyond which is Kot Square. It was here where Jung Bahadur Rana perpetrated the famous 1846 massacre which led to 100 years of Rana rule. *Kot* means 'armoury' or 'fort'. During the Durga Puja festival each year, blood again flows in Kot Square as hundreds of buffaloes and goats are sacrificed. Young soldiers are supposed to lop each head off with a single blow.

King Pratap Malla's Column (13)

Across the road from the Krishna Temple there are a host of smaller temples and other structures, all standing on a huge raised platform in front of the old Royal Palace and the towering Taleju Temple (5). The square, stone pillar known as the Pratap Dhvaja is topped by a statue of the famous King Pratap Malla, seated with folded hands and surrounded by his two wives, his four sons and his infant son. He looks towards his private

Jagannath Temple

Malla. The temple has a three-tiered platform and two storeys. There are three doors on each side of the temple but only the centre door opens.

Kala Bhairab (14)

Behind the Jagannath Temple is the large figure of Kala (Black) Bhairab. Bhairab is Shiva in his most fearsome aspect and this huge stone image of the terrifying Kala Bhairab has six arms, wears a garland of skulls and tramples a corpse, symbolic of mankind's ignorance. The figure was said to have been brought here by Pratap Malla, having been found in a field to the north of the city. The image was originally cut from a single stone although the upper right-hand side has been repaired with another stone and the sun and moon to the left and the lions at the top are later additions. It is said that telling a lie while standing before Kala Bhairab will bring instant death and it was once used as a form of trial by ordeal!

Indrapur Temple (16)

Immediately to the east of horrific Bhairab stands the mysterious Indrapur Temple. This curious temple may be of great antiquity but little is known of its history. Even the god to

which it is dedicated is controversial – inside there is a lingam indicating that it is a Shiva temple. But half-buried on the southern side of the temple is a Garuda image, indicating that the temple is to Vishnu. And to compound the puzzle the temple's name clearly indicates it is dedicated to Indra! The temple's simple design and plain roof struts together with the lack of an identifying *torana* (the space above temple doors indicating the deity to which the temple is dedicated) give no further clues.

Vishnu Temple (17)

Little is known about the adjoining Vishnu Temple either. The triple-roofed temple stands on a four-level base. The roof strut

Vishnu Temple

carvings and the golden image of Vishnu inside show that it is a Vishnu temple, but it is not known how old the temple is, although it was in existence during Pratap Malla's reign.

Kakeshwar Temple (4)

North of the Vishnu Temple, this temple was originally built in 1681 but rebuilt after it was badly damaged in the 1934 earthquake. It

Indrapur Temple

may have been considerably altered at that time as the temple is a strange combination of styles, starting with a two-level base from which rises a lower floor in typical Nepalese style. Above the 1st floor, however, the temple is in Indian shikhara style, topped by a spire shaped like a water vase or *kalasa*, indicative of a female deity.

Kotilingeshwar Mahadev Temple

Kakeshwar Temple

Stone Inscription (18)
On the outside of the palace wall, opposite the Vishnu Temple (17) is a stone inscription to the goddess Kalika written in 15 languages, including English and French. King Pratap Malla, renowned for his scholastic abilities, set up this inscription in 1664 and a Nepalese legend relates that milk will flow from the spout in the middle if somebody is able to read all the languages!

Kotilingeshwar Mahadev Temple (3)
This early Malla temple dates from the reign of Mahendra Malla in the 1500s. The three-stage plinth is topped by a temple in the *gumbhaj* style, which basically means a square structure topped by a dome. The bull facing the temple indicates that it is a Shiva temple.

Mahavishnu Temple (2)
Built by Jagat Jaya Malla, this double-roofed temple on a four-level plinth was badly damaged in the 1934 earthquake and was not restored to its former magnificence. Only the golden spire on the roof, topped by a golden umbrella, hints at its appearance prior to the tremblor.

Mahendreshwar Temple (1)
At the extreme northern end of the square this temple dates from 1561, during Mahendra Malla's reign. The temple was restored in 1963 and is dedicated to Shiva. Inside there is a lingam, a small image of Shiva's bull Nandi fronts the temple and at the north-eastern corner of the temple there is an image of Kam Dev. The temple has a wide, two-level plinth and a spire topped by a golden umbrella.

Taleju Temple (5)
The square's most magnificent temple stands at the north-eastern extremity of the square but is not open to the public. Even the Nepalese can only visit the temple during the annual Dasain festival. You will have to be content with the view of the beautiful three-storey golden temple from the outside.

The Taleju Temple was built in 1564 by Mahendra Malla. Taleju Bhawani was originally a goddess from the south of India, but she became the titular deity or royal goddess of the Malla kings in the 14th century. Taleju temples were erected in her honour in Patan and Bhaktapur as well as in Kathmandu.

Taleju Temple

The temple stands on a 12-stage plinth and reaches over 35 metres high, dominating the Durbar Square area. The eighth stage of the plinth has a wall around the temple, in front of which are 12 miniature temples, four more miniature temples stand inside the wall which has four wide and beautifully carved gates. If entry to the temple were permitted it could be reached from within the palace or from the Singh Dhoka (Lion Gate) from the square.

HANUMAN DHOKA (OLD ROYAL PALACE)

Hanuman's brave assistance to noble Rama during the exciting events of the *Ramayana* has led to the monkey god's appearance guarding many important entrances. Here,

cloaked in red and sheltered by an umbrella, **Hanuman's statue** (20) marks the entrance, or *dhoka*, to Kathmandu's old Royal Palace and has even given the palace its name. The statue dates from 1672, but the face has disappeared under a coating of red paste applied by faithful visitors.

Standards bearing Nepal's double-triangle flag flank the statue while on each side of the palace gate are stone lions, one ridden by Shiva, the other by his wife Parvati. Above the gate a brightly painted niche is illustrated with a figure of a ferocious Tantric version of Krishna in the centre. On one side is the gentler Hindu Krishna in his traditional blue colour accompanied by two of his comely gopis (milkmaids). On the other side is King Pratap Malla and his queen. Entrance to the palace costs Rs 10 and it is open from 10.30 am to 4 pm daily.

The palace was originally founded during the Licchavi period, but as it stands today most of it was constructed by King Pratap Malla in the 17th century. The palace was renovated many times in later years and the

Hanuman's statue

Shah kings continued to live here until the end of the 19th century. The oldest parts are the smaller Sundari Chowk and Mohan Chowk at the northern part of the palace. From here construction moved south and in all there are 10 courtyards, or *chowks*, in the palace. The largest is the Nasal Chowk, immediately inside the palace entrance.

Nasal Chowk

Inside the palace there are many *chowks* and from the entrance gate you immediately enter the most famous one. *Nasal* means 'dancing one' and the courtyard takes its name from a small figure of the Dancing Shiva (24) on the eastern side of the square. Although the courtyard was constructed in the Malla period many of the buildings around the square were Rana constructions. During that time the Nasal Chowk became the square used for coronations, a practice which continues to this day. King Birendra was crowned in the 1975 ceremony on the platform (45) in the centre of the courtyard.

The rectangular courtyard is aligned north-south and the entrance is at the north-eastern corner. The nine-storey Basantapur Tower (44) looms over the southern end of the courtyard. Near the entrance there is a surprisingly small but beautifully carved doorway which once led to the Malla kings' private quarters. The panels have images of four gods.

Beyond the door is a large **statue of Nar-singha** (21), Vishnu in his man-lion incarnation in the act of killing a demon. The stone image was erected by Pratap Malla in 1673 and the inscription on the pedestal explains that he placed it here in fear that he had offended Vishnu by dancing in a Nar-singha costume! The **Kabindrapur Temple** (41) in the main square was built for the same reason.

Next there is the Audience Chamber (22) of the Malla kings. The open verandah houses the Malla throne and portraits of the Shah kings. The small dancing **Shiva figure** (24) which gave the courtyard its name is on the eastern wall; the Malla kings probably used the courtyard for dance performances.

A golden image of Mahavishnu is set into an open verandah on the eastern wall. This image was originally in the **Mahavishnu Temple** (2) in the square, but was moved here after the 1934 earthquake.

Panch Mukhi Hanuman Temple (23)

At the north-eastern corner of the Nasal Chowk stands the Panch Mukhi Hanuman with its five circular roofs. Each of the valley towns has one five-storey temple although it is the great Nyatapola Temple of Bhaktapur which is by far the best known. Hanuman is worshipped in the temple in Kathmandu but only the priests of the temple may enter it.

Basantapur Tower (44)

King Prithvi Narayan Shah, who unified Nepal, was involved in the construction of the four red-coloured towers around the Lohan Chowk. The towers represent the four ancient cities of the valley: the Kathmandu or Basantapur Tower (44), the Kirtipur Tower (46), the Bhaktapur Tower (47) and the Patan or Lalitpur Tower (48).

The dominant nine-storey Basantapur Tower was extensively restored prior to King Birendra's coronation in 1975. A series of steep stairways climbs to the top from where there are superb views over the palace and the city. The struts along the facade of the Basantapur Tower, particularly those facing out to Basantapur Square, are decorated with erotic carvings.

Mul Chowk

This courtyard was completely dedicated to religious functions within the palace and is configured like a vihara (a dwelling place for Buddhist monks) with a two-storey building surrounding the courtyard. Mul Chowk is dedicated to Taleju Bhawani, the royal goddess of the Mallas, and sacrifices are made to her in the centre of the courtyard during the Dasain festivals. A smaller Taleju temple stands in the southern wing of the square and the image of the goddess is moved here from the main Taleju Temple during the Dasain festival. Images of the river goddesses Ganga and Jamuna guard the

Erotic Art

The most interesting woodcarving on Nepalese temples is on the roof struts, and on many temples these carvings include erotic scenes. The erotic scenes are rarely the central carving on the strut, usually they're the smaller carving at the bottom of the strut, like a footnote to the larger image. Nor are they the sensuous, finely sculptured erotic figures like those at Khajuraho and Konarak in India. In Nepal the figures are often smaller, cruder, even quite cartoon-like.

The themes have a Tantric element, a clear connection to the intermingling of Tibetan Buddhist and Hindu beliefs in Nepal since both have Tantric elements, but their real purpose is unclear. Are they simply a celebration of an important part of the cycle of life? A more explicit reference to Shiva's creative role than the enigmatic lingams and yonis scattered around so many temples? Or are they supposed to play some sort of protective role for the temple? It's popularly rumoured that the goddess of lightning is a shy virgin who wouldn't dream of striking a temple with such goings-on, although that's probably more a tourist-guide tale than anything else.

Whatever the reason for their existence the Tantric elements can be found on temples in all three of the major towns of the valley. On some temples it may just be the odd depiction here and there while on others something will be happening on every roof strut. The activities range from straightforward exhibitionism to the *mithuna* scenes of couples engaged in often quite athletic acts of intercourse. More exotic carvings include ménages à trois scenes of oral or anal intercourse or couplings with demons or animals. Temples with some of the more interesting erotic carvings include:

Kathmandu In Durbar Square there are carvings on many of the roof struts of the Jagannath Temple just outside the Hanuman Dhoka palace entrance. The lofty Basantapur Tower of the old palace, overlooking Basantapur Square, has some of the finest erotic carvings on its roof struts. The large Shiva Temple in the middle of the square, also known as the Mahadev Temple or the Maju Deval Temple, is a popular place to watch the activity in the square and also has some erotic struts.

North of the centre, near the restaurant and guest house centre of Thamel, the Three Goddesses Temples dedicated to Dakshinkali, Mankamna and Jawalamai have a number of interesting roof struts. The Indrani Temple, on the east bank of the Vishnumati River where you cross it going from Thamel to Swayambhunath, is another temple with interesting scenes. South of Durbar Square the small Ram Chandra Mandir has some tiny carvings on each of its roof struts.

Patan In Patan's Durbar Square the Jagannarayan or Charnarayan Temple is the most interesting temple in the town for erotic carvings.

Bhaktapur Several temples in Bhaktapur have erotic scenes including the Pashupatinath Temple in Durbar Square. There are also some carvings in the Cafe Nyatapola in Taumadhi Tole where the soaring five-storey Nyatapola Temple is located. The Dattatraya Temple near the Pujari Math monastery in the eastern part of town also has low-relief figures around its base.

Elsewhere in the Valley There are many other temples with erotic artwork around the valley. The Jar Binayak Temple dedicated to Ganesh at Chobar Gorge, just south of Patan, has many interesting roof struts as does the Mahadev Temple at Gokarna, east of Bodhnath. Other temples worth inspecting include the small Ajima or Shitla Devi Temple in the Balaju park, near the sleeping Vishnu figure, and the Bagh Bhairab Temple in Kirtipur.

Several temples in and around Pashupatinath have erotic scenes but non-Hindus aren't permitted to enter the temple courtyards to see them. En route to Pashupatinath, however, you can visit the Mahadev Gyaneshwar in Deopatan, the village by Pashupatinath. ■

golden temple doorway which is topped by a golden torana. Unfortunately, from the Bhaktapur Tower or Lakshmi Bilas (47), where visitors normally observe the courtyard, the view is less than inspiring and the temple itself cannot be seen at all.

Degutaleju Temple (29)

Degutaleju is another manifestation of the Malla's personal goddess Taleju and this temple was built by Shiva Singh Malla and is integrated into the palace structure itself, like the Bhagwati Temple (27) just round the corner. The triple-roofed temple actually starts from above the common buildings it surmounts.

Mohan Chowk

North of the Nasal Chowk is the residential courtyard of the Malla kings. It dates from 1649 and at one time a Malla king had to be born here to be eligible to wear the crown. The last Malla king, Jaya Prakash Malla, had great difficulties during his reign even though he was the legitimate heir because he was born elsewhere. The golden waterspout,

known as Sun Dhara, in the centre of the courtyard delivers water from Budhanil-kantha in the north of the valley. The richly sculptured spout is actually several metres below the courtyard level. The Malla kings would ritually bathe here each morning.

The courtyard is surrounded by towers at its four corners and north of the Mohan Chowk is the small Sundari Chowk.

Rana Additions & Tribhuvan Museum (30)

The part of the palace west of Nasal Chowk, overlooking the main Durbar Square area, was principally constructed by the Ranas in the mid to late part of the last century. Ironically, it is now home to an interesting museum that celebrates King Tribhuvan's successful revolt against their regime. If you are interested in Nepal's modern history a visit is a must; it costs Rs 10. There are some fascinating recreations of the king's bedroom and study with genuine personal effects that give quite an eerie insight into his life. There are also lots of photos and newspaper clippings that catch the drama of his

Marijuana

In Kathmandu's flower-power era in the '60s and early '70s, the easy availability of marijuana and hashish was undoubtedly a major attraction. In its hippie heyday Kathmandu had hash shops and hash calendars, and hash cookies appeared on every hip restaurant menu. Many of the 'freaks' who congregated in Nepal in those days were high in other places than the Himalaya!

The drug had always been easily available, but its users were mainly sadhus for whom it has religious importance. Then, in the run-up to King Birendra's coronation, hashish was banned and, possibly in protest, the huge Singh Durbar building, a palace from the Rana period, burnt down the next night!

Hashish is still banned but illegal or not it's readily available in Nepal, although potential smokers should keep the less than five- star condition of Nepalese jails firmly in mind. Don't try taking any out of the country either – travellers have been arrested at the airport on departure. ∎

escape and triumphant return. And there are several magnificent thrones, some superb stone carvings and, oddly, a coin collection.

FREAK ST

Kathmandu's most famous street from the old hippie overland days of the late '60s and early '70s runs south from Basantapur Square. Its real name is still Jochne but since the early '70s it has been far better known as Freak St. In its hippie prime this was the place for cheap hotels, colourful restaurants, hashish shops, moneychangers and, of course, the weird and wonderful 'freaks' who gave the street its name. In those days Freak St was one of the great gathering places on the road east.

Times change and Freak St today is a pale shadow of its former colourful self and, while there are still cheap hotels and restaurants, it's now the Thamel area in the north of the town which is the main gathering place. Shoestring travellers still stay here, and as Thamel becomes an increasingly hectic tourist ghetto, it is starting to regain popularity. Its recent historical connections are interesting and you are right in the heart of old Kathmandu where real life continues.

WALKING TOURS

A stroll around Kathmandu will lead the casual wanderer to many intriguing sights, especially in the crowded maze of streets, courtyards and alleys in the market area north of Durbar Square. There are temples, shrines and many individual statues and sculptures hidden away in the most unlikely places. You really appreciate Kathmandu's museum-like quality when you stumble upon a 1000-year old statue, something which would be a prize possession in many Western museums, used as a children's plaything or something on which to hang washing. The walks that follow can be made anytime you have an hour or two to spare. Walking Tour 1 and Walking Tour 2 can be used as routes from the accommodation centre of Thamel to the central Durbar Square area.

All the walks take you to a number of markets, temples and *chowks*, which are the centre of Nepalese life. A number of *chowks* are surrounded by bahals or bahils, dwellings for monastic Buddhist communities, although none are used for that purpose today – they have been taken over by families and sometimes schools.

The courtyards may be large and open, dotted with *chaityas* (small stupas) and shrines, or they may be tightly enclosed within a single building. A bahil is distinguished from a bahal because it also includes accommodation for non-monastic visitors, is generally simpler, and the main shrine may not necessarily be in the centre of the courtyard.

The first three walks can be made as individual strolls or linked together into one longer walk. The first walk gives you a taste of the crowded and fascinating shopping streets in the oldest part of Kathmandu and also takes you to some of the city's most important temples. The second walk visits some very old bahals, an important Buddhist stupa, passes by a number of ancient and important stoneworks and introduces you to a toothache god. The third walk takes you to a lesser known section of Kathmandu, without spectacular attractions but where the normal life of the city goes on and tourist intruders are fairly rare. The fourth and last walk runs along the peaceful banks of the Bagmati River past a number of rarely visited temples.

Walking Tour 1 -
North from Durbar Square

The road angling across the town from Durbar Square to the artificial lake of Rani Pokhari is the most interesting street in old Kathmandu. Modern roads like Durbar Marg are no match for this narrow artery's varied and colourful shops, temples and people. The road, which starts from the north-eastern end of Durbar Square as Makhan Tole, was at one time the main street in Kathmandu and the start of the route to Tibet. It was not replaced as Kathmandu's most important street until the construction of New Rd, after the great earthquake of 1934, and it was not paved until the '60s.

1	Garuda Statue	10	Pagoda Temple Platform
2	Tana Deval Temple	11	Yitum Bahal
3	Akash Bhairab Temple	12	Stupa
4	Ganesh Shrine	13	Kichandra Bahal
5	Shiva Temple	14	Chaitya
6	Sweta (White) Machhendranath	15	Nara Devi Temple
	Temple	16	Dance Platform
7	Lunchun Lunbun Ajima	17	Wooden Window
8	Krishna Temple	18	Yatkha Bahal
9	Jana Bahal Temple	19	Kathmandu Lodge

Makhan Tole The crowded street known as Makhan Tole (*makhan* is Nepali for 'butter') starts from the north-eastern corner of Durbar Square, by the Taleju Temple, towards the busy market place of Indra Chowk. Many shops along this stretch of the street sell thangkas, paintings and clothes.

Directly across from the Taleju Temple, at the start of the street, is a kneeling 10th-century **Garuda statue** (1). It probably faced a now long-lost Vishnu temple. To your right, just past the long row of stalls selling thangkas, artefacts and other tourist necessities, is the **Tana Deval Temple** (2) with three carved doorways and struts showing the multiarmed Ashta Matrikas (mother goddesses).

Indra Chowk The busy shopping street of Makhan Tole soon spills into Indra Chowk, the courtyard named after Indra, the ancient Vedic deity. On the left of the square is a building covered in brightly coloured modern ceramic tiles. From the balcony four metal lions rear out over the street. This is the **Akash Bhairab Temple** (3) or Bhairab of the Sky Temple, which is actually upstairs; the ground floor is occupied by shop stalls.

Akash Bhairab Temple

To get to the temple you have to climb a flight of steps at the right-hand end of the building, guarded by two more metal lions. Halfway up a sign announces that non-Hindus may not enter, and in any case there's not much to see. The silver image is visible through the open windows from out in the street, and during important festivals, particularly Indra Jatra, the image is displayed in the square. A large lingam is also erected in the centre of the square at that time.

In a small niche just before the Akash Bhairab Temple is a very small but much visited brass **Ganesh shrine** (4). Indra Chowk is traditionally a centre for the sale of blankets and cloth and there are usually many sellers and buyers on the platforms of the Mahadev Temple. Shawls and woollen rugs are sold from the platform of the **Shiva Temple** (5), which is a smaller and simplified version of Patan's Krishna Mandir.

The many flower-sellers around Indra Chowk add a bright touch to the busy square. From the south of the square Shukra Path leads to New Rd; the shops along this road sell consumer goods imported from Hong Kong and Singapore; many of them end up

in India. The road heading directly north from Indra Chowk leads to Thamel. Before you leave Indra Chowk look for the narrow alley to the right, crowded with stalls selling the glass bangles and beads which are so popular with Nepalese women.

Kel Tole It's only a short stroll from Indra Chowk to the next square, Kel Tole, where you'll find one of the most important and ornate temples in Kathmandu, the **Sweta (White) Machhendranath Temple** (6). The arched entranceway to the temple is guarded by a small Buddha figure on a high stone pillar, facing two metal lions. The temple attracts both Buddhists and Hindus as the Buddhists consider him to be a form of Avalokitesvara while to the Hindus he is an incarnation of Shiva who can bring the rain. Although the temple's age is not known, it was restored during the 17th century.

In the courtyard there are numerous small shrines, chaityas and statues including a mysteriously European-looking figure facing the temple. It may well have been an import from Europe, which has been simply accepted into the pantheon of gods. Facing the other way, just in front of the temple, are two graceful bronze figures of the Taras seated on top of tall pillars.

Inside the temple you can see the white-faced image of the god, sitting rather like a

Sweta Machhendranath Temple

seated Buddha image. The image is taken out of the temple during the Sweta Machhendranath festival in March-April each year and is paraded around the city in a chariot. The procession finally ends at the Machhendranath Temple in the south of the city, visited on Walking Tour 3.

During the day the courtyard is busy with worshippers, playing children and the people whose homes surround it, but at night musicians come here to play in the entrance porch. You're quite welcome to drop by; the traditional music usually starts around 9 pm.

As you leave the temple to the right there are a number of stores which specialise in Nepalese caps. The small triple-roofed **Lunchun Lunbun Ajima** (7) is a Tantric temple, white-tiled around the lower level and with some erotic carvings on the struts at the back. The diagonal street continues to Asan Tole, the busiest of the junctions along the old street, but that is covered on Walking Tour 2. Walk partway towards Asan Tole to see the three, four and five-storey houses, tightly squeezed together on this stretch of the street. On the left, the polygonal **Krishna Temple** (8) is jammed between other buildings with the ground floor occupied by shops. The woodcarvings on this temple are very elaborate.

Return to Kel Tole and turn west. At the next junction the large **Jana Bahal Temple** (9) is on your left. The domed temple is of little interest, it was probably a hastily thrown up construction after an earlier temple was destroyed, perhaps by an earthquake.

A Child-Eating Demon Continue across the junction and on your left you pass the small **Kilgal Tole** beside the road. It's a grubby little square with a couple of decaying temples and, in the middle, a fine chaitya with faces on each side. For some reason there is often a calf or two standing on the pagoda-temple platform (10).

An opening leads into the long, rectangular **Yitum Bahal** courtyard (11). A small white-painted stupa (12) stands in the centre of the courtyard. Opposite it, on the western side of the courtyard, is one of the oldest

bahals in the city, its entrance flanked by the usual stone lions. This is the **Kichandra Bahal** (13), dating from 1381. Until recently there was a superb torana above the entrance – one can only hope it is being restored, and that it has not, like so many masterpieces, been stolen. A chaitya (14) in front of the entrance is completely shattered by a *bodhi* tree which has grown right up through its centre.

Inside the courtyard there is a pagoda-like sanctuary in the centre and to the south is a small chaitya decorated with Bodhisattvas in a standing, rather than the usual sitting, position. On the northern side of the courtyard are four brass plaques mounted on the upper-storey wall. The one on the extreme left shows a demon known as Guru Mapa taking a child from a woman and stuffing it greedily into his mouth. The demon had an appetite for bad children and the two central plaques show two more children, presumably lining up to be consumed! Eventually the demon was bought off with a promise of an annual feast of buffalo meat and the plaque to the right shows him sitting down and dipping into a pot of food. To this day Guru Mapa is said to live in a tree in the Tundikhel field and a buffalo is sacrificed to him every year. With such a clear warning on the end result of juvenile misbehaviour it's probably fitting that the courtyard houses a kindergarten, right under the Guru Mapa plaques!

Nara Devi Temple From Yitum Bahal go back into the large courtyard and exit again at the north and turn left. On your right at the next junction is the Nara Devi Temple (15) which gives the street its name. The temple is dedicated to Kali, Shiva's consort in her destructive incarnation, and is also known as the White Kali (Sweta Kali) Temple.

Although the temple, with its three tiers, glowing golden roof and red and white guardian lions, is quite old, some of the decorations (including the black and white chequerboard paint!) are clearly much later additions. Kali's powers protected the temple from the 1934 earthquake which destroyed so many temples in the valley. A

Top: Kumari Chowk, Kathmandu (TW)
Left: Black Bhairab, Kathmandu (TW)
Right: Street scene, Kathmandu (TW)

Top: Kathmandu from Kirtpur (RI'A)
Middle: Shiva Temple, Durbar Square, Kathmandu (TW)
Bottom: Street scene, Thamel, Kathmandu (TW)

Malla king once stipulated that a dancing ceremony should be held for the goddess every 12 years and dances are still performed on the small platform (16) across the road. Hidden away across the road is a three-roofed **Narsingha temple** to Vishnu as the demon-destroying man-lion. You have to find your way to it through a maze of small courtyards.

Postage Stamp Window At the Nara Devi corner turn left (south) and you soon come to a nondescript modern building on your left with an utterly magnificent wooden window (17). It's been called *deshay madu* in Nepali, which means 'there is not another one like it'. A Rs 0.50 stamp issued in 1978 showed the window. Next to the building is an unimportant triple-roofed pagoda which serves as a locator.

A little further south and on your right is the entrance to the **Yatkha Bahal** (18), a huge open courtyard with an unremarkable stupa in the centre. Directly behind it is an old building which used to have its projecting upper storey supported by four superb carved wooden struts. Dating from the 14th century they were carved in the form of *yakshis*, or nymphs, one of them gracefully balancing a baby on her hip. Unfortunately in late '89 they had been removed, hopefully just for refurbishment and replacement.

Back on the road and heading south you soon pass Kot Square, scene of the great massacre that brought the Ranas to power in 1846. The Kathmandu Lodge (19) is on your right and you soon see Durbar Square ahead.

**Walking Tour 2 –
South of Thamel**
The second walk can be started from the southern end of Thamel or can easily be linked to Walking Tour 1 to make a figure eight either from Thamel or Durbar Square. This walk can be started from Thahiti Tole or, if that's hard to find, from the Hotel Nook on Kantipath. To get to Thahiti Tole walk south from Thamel on the road from the main junction. Soon after La Cimbali Restaurant you enter the square.

Thahiti Tole In the stupa (1) in the centre of the square is a stone inscription indicating it was constructed in the 15th century. Legends relate that it was built over a pond which was plated with gold and the stupa served to keep thieves at bay. Or perhaps the pond was full of dangerous snakes and the stupa kept the snakes in their place, these legends vary!

Nateshwar Temple

The **Nateshwar Temple** (2), on the northern side of the square, is dedicated to Shiva and the metal plates on the doors show creatures busily playing a variety of musical instruments. Above the door are somewhat crudely painted pictures of Shiva's *ganas*, or companions, in this case a skeleton-like creature and what looks remarkably like a yeti!

Two Ancient Bahals Walk to the northeastern corner of the square and take the narrow road running east. You soon come to the entrance of the **Musya Bahal** (3) on your right, guarded by white-painted lions. The road continues east and then takes a right-left bend at the corner of which is a second, and much better preserved, old monastery, the **Chusya Bahal** (4).

This stretch of street is popular with potters and you often see them working in

Chusya Bahal

the road outside the bahals, or see their products piled up inside. Often it's just the simple little disposable cups used by chai sellers.

Beyond the second bahal there's a string of upper-level budget hotels, the New Kabab Corner Restaurant (5) and, right at the

Kantipath intersection, the Hotel Nook (6). Turn south past the Air India office and cross the road to the Rani Pokhari.

Rani Pokhari First cross the road to the large fenced lake called Rani Pokhari (Queen's Pond). It was built by King Pratap Malla in 1667 to console his queen over the death of their son. Unfortunately the gate to the tank is kept locked except on one day each year during the festival of Diwali; you will have to be content with peering through the fence. A causeway leads across the tank to a small and undistinguished **Shiva temple** (7) which was rebuilt after it collapsed in the 1934 earthquake. Various legends and tales are connected with the tank and it's believed that it may actually have been built by Pratap Malla at an earlier date and only renamed for his queen after their son died: according to records the son was trampled by an elephant.

Behind the tank is the **clocktower**, a useful landmark dating from 1895. Across

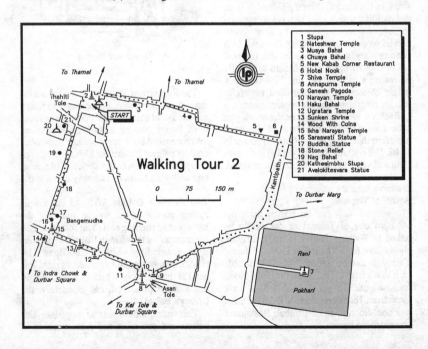

To Thamel
To Thamel

Thahiti Tole

START

1 Stupa
2 Nateshwar Temple
3 Musya Bahal
4 Chusya Bahal
5 New Kabab Corner Restaurant
6 Hotel Nook
7 Shiva Temple
8 Annapurna Temple
9 Ganesh Pagoda
10 Narayan Temple
11 Haku Bahal
12 Ugratara Temple
13 Sunken Shrine
14 Wood With Coins
15 Ikha Narayan Temple
16 Saraswati Statue
17 Buddha Statue
18 Stone Relief
19 Nag Bahal
20 Kathesimbhu Stupa
21 Avalokitesvara Statue

Walking Tour 2

0   75   150 m

Kantipath

To Durbar Marg

Bangemudha

To Indra Chowk &
Durbar Square

Asan Tole

To Kel Tole &
Durbar Square

Rani

Pokhari

Kantipath from the tank is the long building originally known as the Durbar School, which was the first school in Nepal. It has been renamed the **Bhanubhakta School** after the Nepalese poet of that name. Retrace your steps north to the junction at the north-western corner of the Rani Pokhari and cross Kantipath to Bhothahiti then walk south-west past the bicycle hire and repair shops to Asan Tole.

Asan Tole From dawn until late at night, Asan Tole is jammed with buyers, sellers and passers-by. The six roads meeting at this crossroads make it the busiest junction in Kathmandu. Every day fresh fruit and vegetables are carried to this popular marketplace from all over the valley so it is fitting that the three-storey **Annapurna Temple** (8) is dedicated to the goddess of abundance, Annapurna. The smaller two-storey pagoda (9) is dedicated to Ganesh. On the left-hand (western) side of the square are shops which sell dried fruit. Near the centre of the square

Annapurna Temple

is a third temple, a small Narayan or Vishnu temple.

Asan's Fish

A few steps in front of the Annapurna Temple in Asan Tole is a paving stone with a foot-shaped depression which is said to be of a fish. Since the square is almost always crowded with fruit and vegetable sellers there's likely to be a pile of cauliflowers on top of it – but don't worry, it is there, and an interesting little legend relates how this 'fish' fell out of the sky one day.

Once upon a time a famous astrologer named Barami was about to become a father. A bell would be rung to announce the birth of his child so he waited expectantly in his study. At the instant that he heard the sound of the bell across the rooftops, he cast his newborn son's horoscope, and discovered to his horror that he was not the father. In anger and disgust he abandoned his wife and new child and fled from the kingdom. Not until many years later did he return to Kathmandu where he became the pupil of a younger but even more brilliant astrologer named Dak.

As a final test Dak asked Barami to foretell what miraculous event would shortly occur in Asan Tole. Barami correctly predicted that a fish would fall from the heavens, he correctly predicted the exact time this strange event would occur, but he missed by several steps the exact place where it would crash to earth. His teacher suggested that he had forgotten to take account of the wind. Sure enough this was found to be the case.

Barami realised he had forgotten to take account of the wind once before: on the occasion that the sound of a bell carried to his ears the news of his son's birth. Correcting for the wind factor Barami once again cast his son's horoscope. To his delight he discovered that it was indeed his own son, and to his amazement that the boy's name was Dak!

This left Dak and Barami with a peculiar problem: a son must revere his father and a pupil must revere his teacher yet here the son had been teaching the father. Eventually the decision was reached that father and son should jointly erect a monument to the event that had brought them together again. And there it is in Asan Tole, a small memorial to a fish that fell out of the sky. ■

Sore Eyes & Toothache Take the road leading directly west out of Asan Tole and after a short distance, on your left, an anonymous entranceway leads into Haku Bahal (11). Look for the sign advertising 'Meeta's Beauty Parlour'. This tiny bahal has a finely carved wooden window overlooking the courtyard.

A few strides further you come to the triple-roofed **Ugratara Temple** (12), directly across from a small lane which heads off north. Come here if your eyes are sore: a prayer at the shrine is said to work wonders for the eyes. A few steps further along is a small sunken shrine (13) and you then arrive at a crossroads with a large open square to the north. Turn left (south) and on your left you will see a lump of wood (14) into which thousands coins have been nailed. A coin and nail embedded in the wood is supposed to cure toothache, and the deity who looks after this ailment is represented by a tiny image in the ugly lump of wood. The square at the junction here is known as Bangemudha, which means 'twisted wood'.

Ancient Buddha Turn north again to the open square where the small double-roofed **Ikha Narayan Temple** (15) is easily identified by the kneeling Garuda figure in front of it. The temple houses a beautiful 10th or 11th century four-armed Vishnu figure. The square also has a fine image of the goddess Saraswati (16) playing her lute.

The northern side of the square is closed by a modern building with shops shut by grey roller doors on the ground floor. In the middle of this nondescript frontage, directly beneath an upper-storey sign announcing 'Tintin's' is a standing Buddha figure (17), framed by modern blue and white tilework. The image is only about 60 cm high but it dates from the 5th or 6th century. A very similar Buddha figure stands on the riverbank near the temple of Pashupatinath.

If the toothache god hasn't done his duty you now pass a string of dentists' shops, proclaimed by the standard signs showing a smiling mouthful of teeth. On the right there's a small open area surrounded by concrete with a red-coloured Ganesh head and then a small but intricate stone relief (18) dating from the 9th century. It shows Shiva sitting with Parvati on Mt Kailash, her hand resting proprietorially on his knee in the pose known as Uma Maheshwar. Various deities and creatures, including Shiva's bull Nandi, stand around them.

There's a good wooden balcony across the road which is said to have had the first glass windows in Kathmandu! Nearby is a rather worn out, and bricked-in, stone trough. A little further on your left a single broken stone lion (his partner has disappeared) guards a passageway above which hangs a carved wooden torana. Inside is the small enclosed courtyard of the **Nag Bahal** (19) with painted murals above the shrine, which is flanked by banners with double-triangle flags.

Mini Swayambhunath Just a couple of steps beyond the Nag Bahal entranceway is a

Kathesimbhu Stupa

wider entrance to the **Kathesimbhu Stupa** (20), just south of Thahiti Tole. The entrance is flanked by stone lions which have been beheaded, and more-recent metal lions atop tall pillars.

In the courtyard is a copy, dating from around 1650, of the great Swayambhunath complex just outside Kathmandu. If a devotee is unable to make the ascent to Swayambhunath then a circuit of this miniature replica is said to be a good substitute. Just as at Swayambhunath, there is a small pagoda to Harti, the goddess of smallpox, right behind the main stupa.

Various statues and smaller chaityas stand around the temple including, off the northeast of the stupa, a fine standing image of Avalokitesvara (21). He carries a lotus flower in his left hand; the Dhyani Buddha Amitabha can be seen in the centre of his crown and his eyes are downcast.

From Kathesimbhu it's only a short walk north to the starting point of Walking Tour 2 at Thahiti Tole.

Walking Tour 3 -
South from Durbar Square
Starting from beside the Kasthamandap (1) in Durbar Square another circular walk can be made to the older parts in the south of the city. This area is not as packed with historical interest as the walks north of Durbar Square, but the streets are less crowded and you are far less likely to run into other tourists.

Bhimsen Temple Starting from the Kasthamandap in the south-western corner of Durbar Square the road out of the square forks almost immediately around the **Singh Sattal** (2), a squat building with small shop stalls around the ground floor and golden-winged lions guarding each corner of the upper floor. Take the road running to the right of this building and you soon come to a square tank-like *hiti* (3), or water conduit, where people will usually be washing clothes.

Immediately beyond this is the brightly painted Bhimsen Temple (4) which is fronted by a brass lion on a pillar and has white-painted lions guarding the two front corners.

Bhimsen Temple

Bhimsen is supposed to watch over traders and artisans so it's quite appropriate that the ground floor of this well-kept temple should be devoted to shop stalls. Immediately beyond the Bhimsen Temple a road branches off down to the river and across to the National Museum and Swayambhunath.

Jaisi Deval Temple Continue south beyond the Bhimsen Temple then turn sharp left

Jaisi Deval Temple

Walking Tour 3

0   100   200 m

1   Kasthamandap
2   Singh Sattal
3   Hiti (Water Conduit)
4   Bhimsen Temple
5   Diamond Guest House
6   Jaisi Deval Temple
7   Stone Lingam
8   Dance Platform
9   Shattered Chaitya
10 Ram Chandra Mandir
11 Takan Bahal
12 Shikhara Temple
13 Musum Bahal
14 Bahal & Many Chaityas
15 Machhendranath Temple
16 Hari Shankar Temple
17 Vishnu Temple
18 Adko Narayan Temple
19 Golden Bird Lodge &
     Bluebird Restaurant

(uphill) where the road ends. At the top of the hill you'll come out by the tall, triple-roofed, 17th-century Jaisi Deval Temple (6). It stands on a seven-level base, its tiers painted a becoming shade of pink. This is a Shiva temple, as shown by the bull on the first few steps and the mildly erotic carvings on some of the temple struts. Right across the road from the temple is a lingam-shaped rock (7) rising a good two metres from a yoni. This is definitely a god-sized phallic symbol and a prayer here is said to aid fertility.

In its procession around the town during the Indra Jatra festival, the Kumari Devi's

chariot pauses here. During its stop, dances are held on the small platform (8) across the road from the temple.

Ram Chandra Mandir Cross the road from the broken chaitya and enter the courtyard of the Ram Chandra Mandir (10). This small temple is notable for the teensy little erotic scenes on its roof struts. This is straightforward sex and no funny business, it looks as if the carver set out to illustrate 16 different positions, starting with the missionary position, and just about made it before running out of ideas.

Bahals & Machhendranath Temple There are a series of bahals on the next stretch of the walk but most of them are of little interest. Cross the road from the Ram Chandra Mandir and enter the small courtyard of the **Takan Bahal** (11). The 14th-century stupa in the centre is decidedly dilapidated as a tree has grown straight up through the precise centre of the stupa, lifting the crown a good four metres above the stupa top!

The road continues with a few slight bends then turns sharply back at a junction marked by several temples (12) including a taller shikhara-style one. If you take the downhill road leading from this junction you merge on to Tripureshwar Marg, just beyond the Vishnumati River bridge. Across this busy road another road continues down to the river and the starting point of the cableway used to transport goods over the foothills from the Terai. Ignoring this possible diversion the walk continues to the **Musum Bahal** (13) with four ancient Licchavi chaityas and a caged-in well. Turn sharp left (north) at the next junction and look into a large, open bahal (14) packed with numerous chaityas.

The road opens into Lagankhel, an open square with a Machhendranath temple (15) standing about 10 metres high. During the annual Sweta Machhendranath festival the image of the god is transported here from the Sweta Machhendranath Temple in Kel Tole (see Walking Tour 1). The final stage of the procession is to pull the god's chariot three times around the temple, after which the image is taken back to its starting point on a palanquin while the chariot is dismantled here.

Turn left out of Lagankhel and walk back to the tall Jaisi Deval Temple, then turn right (north) back towards Durbar Square.

Shiva & Vishnu Temples At the next crossroads the small, spindly looking **Hari Shankar Temple** (16) stands to the left of the road. The narrow brick-paved laneway beside this combination Shiva and Vishnu temple runs down to the Bhimsen Temple passed earlier on. Continue north past a Vishnu temple (17) to a second Vishnu

Adko Narayan Temple

temple, the **Adko Narayan Temple** (18). Although this may not look impressive, it is said to be one of the four most important Vishnu temples in Kathmandu. A Garuda figure fronts the temple, lions guard each corner, tiny ceramic tiles decorate the ground floor and there are mildly erotic scenes on some of the upper roof struts. It's also the temple of motorbike repairs, and mechanics work away around the back of the building.

Immediately beyond the temple is the long-running Blue Bird Restaurant (19) and then you pass the Singh Sattal building once again and arrive back at the starting point of this walk.

Walking Tour 4 - West from Patan Bridge

The Bagmati River is a tributary of the Ganges River and is doubly holy to some because of its association with Shiva, who is believed to have lived on its banks at Pashupatinath. Not surprisingly, there are many temples along its length.

Apart from the complex at Pashupatinath there is a string of temples west of Patan Bridge to the Bagmati River's junction with the Vishnumati River. This is a quiet and forgotten corner of Kathmandu. There is no traffic and, although it is only a short walk from Durbar Square, there are few visitors.

Nothing much seems to have happened here in the last 30 years and as a consequence you can see some of the best and worst of Kathmandu. Many of the temples are in a state of picturesque decline and the traffic, crowds and noise of the city seem a long way away. Their place is taken by water buffaloes, egrets, sadhus and children.

Unfortunately, the riverbanks are littered with rubbish and the impressive ghats are no longer in serious use. There is also a great deal of poverty, with many families living in squalor in and amongst the decaying buildings, or in shanties in the river bed. It is hard to imagine that this must once have been a thriving, vital part of Kathmandu and difficult not to feel sadness at its decline.

It's possible to walk from Patan Bridge to the confluence of the rivers and back to Tripureshwar Marg in an hour or so, but you may choose to linger. Probably the best way to do it is to catch autorickshaws, or ride a bike to/from the starting and finishing

points. The track is rough in places, too rough to ride, but not so rough that you can't just push a bike along.

Kalmochan Temple (1) On the Kathmandu side of the Bagmati River, 150 metres to the west of the Patan Bridge, you'll see a huge, square, whitewashed block, topped by a mosque-like onion dome with gilt beasts rearing up at each corner. This is the Kalmochan or Satya Narayan Temple. To get to it and start the walk, descend the steps to the riverbank beside the bridge, turn right and walk downstream past a well-kept army building. Enter through a carved doorway.

The Kalmochan Temple may have been commenced as early as 1852, but it was completed in 1873 by Jung Bahadur Rana. It is dedicated to Jagannath and was built to commemorate the Gurkha wars with Tibet and Britain. It is one of the most successful of the buildings in Nepal with Moghul (Muslim north Indian) influences, but the decorations are pure Nepalese. The beasts once stood on a Vishnu temple in the Tundikhel field and there is some very high-quality woodcarving.

1 Kalmochan (Satya Naryan) Temple
2 Tripureshwar Mahadev Temple
3 Tindeval Temple
4 Pachali Bhairab
5 Shiva Temple
6 Raj Ghat
7 Shikhara Temple
8 Shikhara Temple
9 Nava Durga Temple

Walking Tour 4

0   250   500 m

Kalmochan Temple

as the best examples of pagoda architecture. There are some fine gilded figures on columns, including one of Mrs Rana herself sitting under an umbrella.

Tripureshwar Mahadev Temple

The temple's name (*kal* means 'death') indicates that it was built in connection with a person's funeral and it is said that the temple is actually built over the mass grave of the noblemen that Jung Bahadur Rana killed in the Kot Massacre which brought him to power. A statue of Mr Rana faces the temple from the courtyard and, whether or not he built it to appease his conscience, the inscription below his statue extols his many achievements, but totally omits the bloody and decisive mass murder which brought him to power!

Tripureshwar Mahadev Temple (2) After leaving the Kalmochan Temple, continue downstream and cross the grubby little Tukucha Khola stream. Veer right from the river towards the huge three-roofed temple, Tripureshwar Mahadev. The footpath goes through to Tripureshwar Marg, the main road, past the entry to the temple itself.

The temple was built in the 19th century by the wife of Jung Bahadur Rana but, despite its impressive size, attracts few tourists or worshippers. It's monumental but doesn't have the same pleasing proportions

Tindeval Temple (3) Return to the river and continue to the west on a rough path for about a km. After about 10 minutes you'll come to the unusual and beautiful Tindeval Temple. It is easily recognised by its three shikharas (spires reminiscent of a folded umbrella). Enter the *chowk* from the south. The surrounding bahal is now occupied by families and there are bound to be children playing and clothes hanging out to dry.

The shikhara style began to develop under the Guptas in India (during the 5th and 6th centuries) until it became the most distinctive and common temple forms in north India (especially from the 9th to 11th centuries). There are a number of examples around the Kathmandu Valley, and the style was also used in Buddhist countries throughout South Asia.

The intriguing aspect of the Tindeval Temple is the way the shikharas have been successfully integrated with a pagoda-style base and 1st floor. Note the beautiful decorative brickwork forming nagas (snakes) around the base of the shikharas.

Pachali Bhairab (4) Leave the Tindeval Temple by the western door (to the left as you entered) and veer to the right towards the huge *pipal* tree 25 metres away. This ancient tree forms a sanctuary over the image of Pachali, which is surrounded by tridents. Nearby lies what some believe to be the brass body of Baital, another of Shiva's manifestations. Others believe it is Surya, the sun god. Worshippers gather here on Tuesdays and Saturdays.

Raj Ghat Return directly to the river past a very dilapidated Shiva temple on the right (5) that nonetheless has some fine erotic carvings. If you're feeling energetic, cross the river on the old pedestrian footbridge to the Raj Ghat (6), where there is another small group of shrines. There's an attractive view looking back to the city.

Teku Cross back to the northern side of the river and turn left towards the confluence of the Vishnumati and Bagmati rivers which is marked by another shikhara-style temple (7). River junctions are always regarded as significant in Nepal and until recently the riverbank between the bridge and the Vishnumati was a veritable art gallery densely packed with shrines and sculptures. There were lingams representing Shiva, Buddhist chaityas (most with the Dhyani Buddhas), and statues of Vishnu, elephant-headed Ganesh, Saraswati with her lute and many more. Sadly, over the last few years, much has disappeared, probably into the hands of Western collectors.

Nava Durga Temple From the river junction turn inland (north-east) and backtrack along a paved road past another dilapidated and unusual shikhara-style temple (8). In five minutes you come to what looks like a bomb site – in actual fact it is a Roads Department depot – adjoining the Pachali Bhairab. When you intersect with the road that runs through to the pedestrian bridge on your right, turn left and keep heading north-east.

After about five minutes you reach a point where the road forks, about 50 metres before

Tripureshwar Marg. Take the right fork and you pass the Nava Durga Temple (9), a small two-storey pagoda. From Nava Durga you can turn right along Tripureshwar Marg to complete the loop.

OTHER TEMPLES & BUILDINGS
Three Goddesses Temples
Next to the modern shopping centre and across the road from the immigration office, near Thamel, are the temples of the three goddesses. The street here is named Tridevi Marg – *tri* means 'three' and *devi* means 'goddesses'. The goddesses are Dakshinkali, Mankamna and Jawalamai and the temples are chiefly interesting for the roof struts, some with erotic carvings illustrating rather interesting positions.

Mahakala Temple
This temple, on the Tundikhel side of Kantipath just north of New Rd, was very badly damaged in the 1934 earthquake and is of little architectural merit following its reconstruction. If you can see inside the darkened shrine you may be able to make out the 1½-metre-high figure of Mahakala, the Great Black One, a particularly ferocious form of Shiva. Kal means 'death' as well as 'black' in Nepali so it can also be described as the Temple of Great Death. The Tantric god has Buddhist as well as Hindu followers. You can climb to the top of one of the buildings around the courtyard to look over the Tundikhel field.

Bhimsen Tower
This white, minaret-like watchtower, also known as Sundhara, is a useful landmark although it's of no importance. It stands near the main post office and was built by a Rana prime minister and rebuilt after being severely damaged by the 1934 earthquake.

NATIONAL MUSEUM & ART GALLERY
Not far from Swayambhunath, the National Museum is a bit disappointing, but the art gallery (when it is open) has a fine collection of religious art. A visit can easily be combined with a trip to Swayambhunath.

The museum has a rather eccentric collection that includes some moon rock, a number of moth-eaten stuffed animals, a vast number of uniforms and military decorations, swords and guns, and a mind-numbing portrait gallery. The most interesting exhibit is a leather Tibetan cannon.

The gallery displays a number of treasures. There's a superb collection of statues and carvings (stone, wood, bronze, terracotta) – some pieces date to the 1st century BCE. If you have an interest in this area of art a visit is a must.

The museum is closed on Tuesdays and is open from 10.30 am to 2.30 pm on Fridays. The rest of the week it opens from 10.30 am to 4.30 pm in summer and until 3.30 pm in winter. Ticket sales stop an hour earlier than the closing time and the sign announcing the hours enigmatically adds that on Friday the museum opens at 10 am, but tickets won't go on sale until 10.30! The entry fee is Rs 5, or Rs 10 with a camera.

PLACES TO STAY

Kathmandu has an excellent range of places to stay, from expensive international-style hotels to cheap and comfortable lodges.

This section is divided by price into bottom, middle and top end, then by location. A bottom-end hotel or guest house is a place where you can get a double room for less than Rs 500, say $10. There are quite a few where you can get a room for less than Rs 150 ($3) and some where you can pay less than Rs 100 ($2). Middle means from $10 to $40 a night and the top end is from $40 up. A double room in the most expensive hotels in Kathmandu now costs more than $125 a night, getting close to the nation's average annual per capita income! Quite a few hotels bridge the bottom-end and middle categories by having a range of room standards and charging accordingly – these places have been grouped according to their lowest price.

All mid-range and top-end hotels charge a government tax which varies from 10% to 15%, depending on the hotel's star rating. Almost all quote their prices in US dollars, and most only accept payment in foreign currency (see the Money section in the Facts for the Visitor chapter) – which means either cash, travellers' cheques, credit cards, or rupees accompanied by an unused Foreign Exchange Encashment Receipt. Bottom-end places usually quote prices in rupees, rarely bung on a tax, and will let you pay in rupees without fiddling around with exchange receipts.

It is definitely worth looking around if you plan to stay for any length of time. It's difficult to recommend particular hotels, especially in the bottom-end and middle brackets, because particular rooms in each hotel can vary widely. Many of these hotels have additions to additions, and while some rooms may be very gloomy and run-down others might be very pleasant! A friendly crowd of fellow travellers can also make all the difference.

For bottom-end and middle places the Thamel area is the main locale – and it is becoming an increasingly unpleasant tourist ghetto. Its development has been rapid and uncontrolled, with ugly multistorey hotels and signboards taking the place of beautiful Newari houses. This is where the largest number of independent travellers stay, and there are dozens and dozens of lodges, restaurants, travel agencies and shops, and a bustling cosmopolitan atmosphere. It's still a convenient and enjoyable area to stay for a short time, however, especially if you want to meet fellow travellers. It can also be a welcome relief to find Western menus, people who speak English and hot showers at budget prices.

Thamel is now used to describe a sprawling area with at least a dozen roads and several hundred hotels and restaurants. It is so well known and has such cachet that many places now claim Thamel as their address, even though they are in bordering areas that have traditionally had different names. The problem is partly due to the fact that these areas never had strictly defined limits anyway.

Despite what the hotel owners might think, however, many people prefer to be a bit removed from the crowded centre of Thamel. There are a number of places on its periphery that are close enough to be reasonably convenient but aren't absolutely in the centre of the maelstrom!

In a megalomaniacal attempt to establish some order, we have somewhat arbitrarily divided the greater Thamel area (see the Thamel Area map) into Thamel, around the two main intersections; Paknajol, to the north; Bhagwan Bahal, to the north-east; Jyatha, to the south-east; and Chhetrapati, to the south-west.

There is still a scattering of really rock-bottom places along Freak St, close to Durbar Square, but its hippie heyday is long past. There are signs it might be experiencing the beginnings of a revival, however, as people look for alternatives to Thamel. The Freak St location is excellent, and real Newari city life continues in the surrounding side streets. Most of the accommodation possibilities are *very* basic, but they are also among the cheapest in Kathmandu.

Middle-range places are more widely scattered: you'll find the majority in and around Thamel, but there are others. Kathmandu's limited number of international-standard hotels are also widely spread, some of them quite a distance from the city centre.

There is a hotel reservations counter as soon as you get out of customs at the airport. Most of the hotels it represents are reasonably expensive, but it has a few in the Rs 250 ($5) to Rs 500 ($10) bracket, and the staff arrange for free transport. If you don't feel like tackling the touts and taxis outside the main doors, this can be useful, however the staff seem to concentrate on sending people to out-of-the way places, and their advice is not always accurate. You can always change to another hotel the next day after you've had a chance to get your bearings.

Taxi drivers and hotel touts (they are often one and the same) lie in wait outside the airport terminal and around bus stations. If you ask to be taken to one of the hotels recommended in this book, you may well be told that the place in question has closed or become ridiculously expensive. Though this may be possible, it is considerably more likely that they want you to go to the hotel where they get the best commission – often more than 50% of the room price. The best solution is to take a taxi ride to Thamel or Freak St (Rs 100 to Rs 150, or $2 to $3, from the airport) and look for yourself. If you are travelling as a group or couple, leave one person in a restaurant to look after heavy bags while a search is made.

During the peak times (October, November, February, March, April) rooms in the top hotels can be in short supply. Otherwise, there are so many fiercely competitive middle-range and bottom-end places that only the really popular hotels are likely to be full. The prices given here are the high-season prices shown on hotel tariff cards. Outside the high season, prices are highly negotiable; 50% discounts can be offered.

Long-Term Rental

For longer stays you can rent a house for as little as $75 a month. Cheaper places are mainly around Freak St, Swayambhunath or Bodhnath, but there are many other areas where more expensive houses can be found. The Jawlakhel area of Patan is popular with many foreign residents as a number of the aid agencies are based there.

If you're looking for a place to rent, check the notice boards around town or simply inquire in the appropriate areas. If you can take over a house from a departing visitor you will probably save having to find furniture and other essentials. As refrigerators are not readily available try to be near a market.

Real estate agencies which can sometimes find appropriate places include Kantipur Real Estate Services (☎ 01-220566) on Kantipath next to the British Council, or New Kathmandu Real Estate Service (☎ 01-223019) near the clocktower.

Places to Stay – bottom end

Intense competition between Kathmandu's enormous number of low-priced hostelries means that you can find hot showers in even the cheapest places, although the hot water may only be operating at certain hours.

Hotels in this category do not have heating

and Kathmandu in winter is a rather chilly place. In winter you'll appreciate places with a garden as it's always pleasant to sit outside during the cool, but invariably sunny, autumn and winter days. A south-facing room will mean you get some sunlight in your room. In general, the top-floor rooms are the best, as you stand a chance of getting a view and having easy access to the roof (usually a nice place to relax).

The greater Thamel area (including Thamel, Paknajol, Bhagwan Bahal, Jyatha and Chhetrapati) is the main budget-accommodation zone, and is a 20-minute walk from the centre of Kathmandu. From the city centre walk along Kantipath, the road north from the New Rd gate towards the embassy area, and turn left when you come to the corner by the new Royal Palace. Three more blocks will bring you to the centre. When you've been in Kathmandu for a while you'll discover shorter and much more interesting routes through the maze of narrow streets and alleys that wind between Thamel and the Durbar Square area.

Thamel Any mention of Thamel has to start with the *Kathmandu Guest House* (☎ 01-413632) the first hotel to open in the area, and still one of the most popular. It also serves as the central landmark – everything is 'near the Kathmandu Guest House', 'five minutes from the Kathmandu Guest House' or whatever. It's not the best value for money in town, but most people enjoy the atmosphere and it's often booked out.

The position is excellent and you definitely feel you're at the nerve centre with various expeditions coming and going, trekkers looking for partners and a constant hum of activity. There's parking space for cars out front, a very pleasant garden, a popular restaurant, a money-change desk, a storage area for luggage and for valuables, a phone office where you can conveniently and quickly make overseas calls, a travel desk, even an art gallery upstairs – this is budget travel in the deluxe category!

In the newer wing quite pleasant rooms with bath are $17/20 a single/double. Simi-

larly equipped rooms in the old wing are $9/12. Other rooms, with just a washbasin or without private facilities at all, cost from $4 to $8. There's a 12% tax on top of all these prices.

If this is too luxe for your budget you don't have to go far for something cheaper – there are a dozen or more places within a stone's throw. Next door is the *Tukche Peak Guest House* (☎ 01-215739) where rooms with shared bath are Rs 90/120 ($2/2.50), or Rs 150/200 ($3/4) with private facilities. It's another long-term survivor, with a popular adjoining restaurant. The rooms are fairly simple and spartan, but the price is right. Continue north a few doors and you come to the similar *Yeti Cottage* (☎ 01-417089) which also has a garden and restaurant. Singles/doubles here are Rs 150/200 ($3/4), plus 10% tax.

On the other side of the street and down a cul de sac, the *Ned Kelly Guest House* has sunny, good-value rooms for Rs 100/150 ($2/3). Continue a little further and you get to the *Acme Guest House* (☎ 01-414811) which has a great position and sunny, pleasant rooms. Singles/doubles with shared bath

---

The Name Game

Hotel names in Kathmandu can change rapidly, especially if the authorities are sniffing around looking for unpaid taxes. With each incarnation the owners seem to get more desperate to find something that 'says it all'. Copyright and trademark protection doesn't exist, so these restraints do not apply.

Although some of the names are truly awful, you should not allow yourself to be influenced by them – I must admit your cool quotient drops when you say you're staying at My Mom's Place. There's a Hotel Hilton (not a bad place, but don't expect a minibar and colour TV), and a Lonely Planet (also not bad, but don't expect a word processor and free drinks every Friday afternoon). Other inspiring choices include the Ned Kelly Guest House, the Acme Guest House, Aloha Inn, Hotel Nook, Lucky Carpet Guest House, and Hotel Greeting Palace. ■

Greater Thamel

■ PLACES TO STAY

1	Kathmandu Peace Guest House
2	Tibet Peace Guest House
3	The Chalet
5	Kathmandu Peace Guest House
6	Hotel Manang
7	The Lonely Planet
8	Hotel Gauri Shanker
9	Hotel Greeting Palace
10	Hotel Nepal View & Pilgrims Restaurant
11	Thamel Rest House
12	Hotel Malla
13	Hotel Marshyangdi
14	Hotel Buddha & Valentine Guest House
16	Hotel Iceland
17	Hotel Thamel
18	Souvenir Guest House
19	Hotel Shakti
20	Rara Guest House
21	Hotel Hilton
22	Gurans Guest House
23	Holy Lodge
25	Hotel Mandap
27	Mustang Guest House
28	HI:MA Lodge
29	Hotel Karma
30	Hotel Dreamland
31	Hotel Garuda
33	Acme Guest House
34	Ned Kelly Guest House
36	Yeti Cottage & Rainbow Restaurant
39	Bali Guest House
41	Tukche Peak Guest House & Himalayan Country Kitchen
42	Kathmandu Guest House & Ashta Mangala Restaurant
43	International Guest House
48	Siddhartha Guest House & Tibetan Thanka Treasure
53	Hotel Star
54	Cosy Corner Lodge
55	Pheasant Lodge
61	Himal Cottage
62	My Mom's Place
64	Hotel Excelsior
65	Unique Guest House
68	Old Vienna Inn
70	Pema Guest House
71	Hotel Earth House
72	Hotel Madhev Mani
73	Marco Polo Guest House
74	Sherpa Guest House
75	Gorkha Guest House
76	Hotel Horizon

77	Manaslu Guest House
78	Fuji Guest House
79	Thorong Peak Guest House
80	Hotel Tashi Dhelek
81	Hotel Puska
82	Hotel Asia
83	Everest Guest House & Les Yeux Restaurant
86	Imperial Guest House
87	Shangrila Guest House
88	Hotel White Lotus
89	Mustang Holiday Inn
92	Lucky Carpet Guest House
93	Tibet Guest House
94	Trans Himalaya Guest House & Himalayan Kitchen
102	Potala Guest House
104	Yak Lodge & Restaurant
106	Hotel Blue Diamond
107	Tibet Rest House
108	Hotel Utse
109	Lhasa Guest House
110	Siddhartha Guest House
111	Shambala Guest House
112	Thahity Guest House & Cafe de la Cabine
115	Hotel New Gajur

▼ PLACES TO EAT

15	Boris' Restaurant
24	San Francisco Pizza Palace
32	Spam's Place
35	Pizza Hut
40	Helena's Country Kitchen
44	Hem's Bar & Restaurant
45	La Dolce Vita
46	Mona Lisa
47	KC's Restaurant
49	Pumpernickel Bakery
50	Helena's Restaurant
52	Le Bistro
58	Himthai
59	Alice's Restaurant
60	Third Eye Restaurant
63	Skala
66	Two Faces Restaurant
67	Utse Restaurant
84	German Bakery
90	Sidewalker's Restaurant
91	Al Pollo Restaurant
95	Everest Steak House
96	Nepalese Kitchen
97	Pizza Maya
98	Rimini Pizzeria
103	Narayan's Restaurant
105	La Cimbali Restaurant

	OTHER
4	Paknajol (Sorakhutte) Bus Stop
26	Dolha Continental Exports
37	Pilgrims Book House
38	Galaxy Communications Centre
51	Namche Bazaar
56	Tantric Book Shop
57	Wayfarer's Travel Services
69	Bhagwan Bahal
85	Tridevi Marg Bus Stop
99	Craft Collection
100	Nepal Colour Lab
101	Student Travels & Tours
113	Nateshwar Temple
114	Lucky Traveller Service

are $6/10, with private bath $14/18. There are good long-term discounts.

Turn the other way (south) from the Kathmandu Guest House and there's a cluster of hotels starting with the *Hotel Star* (☎ 01-414000), right next door. It has long been a popular alternative to the Kathmandu Guest House, although the rooms are shabby and ordinary. They start at $3, and go to $8 with a bathroom. The basic *Cosy Corner Lodge* is adjacent to the Hotel Star, and has OK singles/doubles at Rs 85/150 ($1.50/3).

The *Pheasant Lodge* (☎ 01-417416) is tucked further around the laneway so it feels quite removed from the Thamel bustle, although it is as central as you can be. There's an atmospheric courtyard and although the rooms are basic, they're good value – which is why it's often full. Singles/doubles are Rs 70/110 ($1.50/2).

Continue south a bit further and you come to *My Mom's House* (☎ 01-417184), which aside from the awful name, is run by very helpful people and has basic but clean singles/doubles from Rs 100/120 ($2/2.50), or Rs 200/250 ($4/5) with private bath. The only drawback is the noise from the surrounding restaurants and bars, although this does stop around 10 pm.

The *Hotel Horizon* (☎ 01-220904; fax 227929) is off the main street, down near the bank of tapestry shops, and has a range of

rooms at reasonable prices. They start at $6 for fairly spartan rooms with bathroom and go to $20 for luxury rooms, which are good if you can deal with the over-the-top decor.

Tucked in behind the Pumpernickel Bakery, the *Unique Guest House* (☎ 01-211683) is one of the last budget hotels in Thamel to be housed in a traditional Newari building. On the positive side, it's atmospheric, clean and cheap; on the negative side, mutant Europeans keep bumping their heads, and have to shower while sitting on the toilet. Singles/doubles are a bargain Rs 60/100.

The main road from the centre of Kathmandu to Thamel runs into the anarchic intersection where taxis and rickshaws wait. Cheapies in this area include the *Hotel Puska*, which is not great; the adjacent *Hotel Asia* (☎ 01-216541), which is OK; and the *Lucky Carpet Guest House*, which is further down the road.

Closer to the centre of Thamel on the traffic-choked extension of Tridevi Marg the *Marco Polo Guest House* (☎ 01-227914) is popular. The rooms at the back are particularly good and there are some surprisingly pleasant rooftop patios. Doubles cost Rs 120 ($2.50); or Rs 180 ($3.50) with bath.

Paknajol This area lies to the north-east of Thamel and can be reached by continuing north from the Kathmandu Guest House, or by approaching on Lekhnath Marg.

There are a number of good-quality hotels along the road on the right at the next T-intersection. Tucked down an inconspicuous laneway, the *Mustang Guest House* (☎ 01-416596) is good value, with pleasant, quiet rooms. Singles/doubles are $5/8 with shared bath, or $9/12 with private bath.

On the main road, the *Hotel Iceland* (☎ 01-416956) is well kept, but characterless – singles/doubles cost $6/8 with shared bath or from $8/12 to $10/16 with private bath, all plus 10%.

Further north and also down a laneway *The Lonely Planet* (☎ 01-412715) is absolutely no relation, and the owners didn't even offer the LP researcher a bribe. The building is new, and the rooms, though spartan, are quite good. Singles/doubles are from $8/10.

Not far from the steep Paknajol intersection (north-west of Thamel) there's a batch of three pleasant guest houses. They're away from traffic, a short walk from Thamel (but it could be a million miles), and they have beautiful views across the valley towards Balaju and Swayambunath. The *Tibet Peace Guest House* (☎ 01-415026) has well-equipped rooms with lockers, bathrooms and telephones; singles/doubles cost from $6/8. At the end of the road the *Kathmandu Peace Guest House* (☎ 01-414623) is the most spartan of the three (but still fine) and offers singles/doubles from $4/5 with shared bath or from $8 with private bath. The *Chalet* (☎ 01-419363) has the nicest garden; prices are similar to the Tibet Peace House, although the rooms are more basic. They hire bikes for Rs 20 per day

Turn left at the T-intersection after the Garuda Hotel and you come to several reasonable cheapies. Neat and clean rooms at the *Holy Lodge* (☎ 01-416265; fax 419317) cost from Rs 175 ($3.50) without bath to Rs 500 ($10) with bath. There's an excellent deluxe room at the top.

Next door, the *Gurans Guest House* (☎ 01-414150) is a very decent bottom-end place. The rooms are quite spartan (needless to say), but those at the front with balconies are especially good value. Singles/doubles with shared bath cost Rs 150/250 ($3/5).

There's a small group of hotels built around a cul de sac off Lekhnath Marg. *Hotel Nepal View & Pilgrims Restaurant* (☎ 01-416910; fax 229983) is undistinguished (especially some of the dark singles), but the place is clean, well managed and provides pretty good value for money. There's also a pleasant outdoor restaurant area. Singles/doubles are $6/10 with shared facilities; $15/20 with en-suite. As always, the prices are negotiable.

Continue across Lekhnath Marg (actually into the area known as Galkopatha) and after a five-minute walk you reach the *Kathmandu Tourist's Bungalow* (☎ 01-419239). The rooms are good, and you're some distance from Thamel. Singles/doubles start at $4/6 and go up to $10/15.

On the road that runs north from the Thamel taxi stand, the *Hotel Dreamland* has definitely seen better days, but the location is good and the people are pleasant, which may or may not make up for the fact that it is very run-down. Doubles with bath cost Rs 150 ($3).

Bhagwan Bahal This area to the north-east of Thamel takes its name from a Buddhist monastery. It is much quieter than Thamel, and has not yet been completely taken over by restaurants, souvenir shops and travel agencies.

The *Hotel Earth House* (☎ 01-418436; fax 418197), just off Tridevi Marg, is a top-class budget hotel, with friendly staff, a nice rooftop garden and a variety of clean and decent rooms. Singles/doubles start at $3/4 but can go as high as $8/12 (although I find this hard to believe). The rooms at the back are best.

The *Souvenir Guest House* (☎ 01-413471) has a good position beyond Earth House on the way north to the Malla Hotel, and a nice garden. The official rate card says singles/doubles are $5/8 with shared bath, or $8/12 with private bath, but these are highly negotiable – go for 50% less. Next door, the *Rara Guest House* is similar, as are the prices. The rooms are a bit dark, but they're OK.

Turn right just before the Rara (as you head south) and you come to the *Hotel Hilton* (☎ 01-414858) – no relation – which is a good place with a garden and sunny rooms. Singles/doubles with shared bath are $6/8, or $8/15 with private facilities.

Jyatha The neighbourhood to the south-east of Thamel has traditionally been known as Jyatha, but increasingly the word is used to describe the main north-south road that runs into the western end of Tridevi Marg.

The *Tibet Rest House* (☎ 01-225319) is run by the same people as the popular Tibet Guest House in Chhetrapati and has singles/doubles at $6/9; $8/11 with bath. The *Lhasa*

Guest House is another cheaper place that is not bad.

The Jyatha area runs into Thahiti Tole, where there is a large stupa. On the square, the *Hotel Paramount* has been recommended as a friendly place. Rooms are around Rs 100 ($2).

Chhetrapati This neighbourhood is named after the important five-way intersection (with a distinctive bandstand) to the southeast of Thamel. The further you are from Thamel, the more traditional the surroundings become.

South of the Kathmandu Guest House and left at the junction (Narayan's Restaurant is a good landmark here) you'll see the very popular *Potala Guest House* (☎ 01-220467) where singles/doubles are from $7/10, plus 10%. There's hot water and a small, quiet garden.

Just to the west of Thahiti Tole, heading towards Chhetrapati, the *Thahity Guest House* above the Cafe de la Cabine Restaurant, is a surprisingly decent place. It's on a pleasant street and although Thamel is close by you're still in an authentic (untouristed) part of the city. All rooms have hot-water baths, and there's a roof garden. Singles/doubles are $5/8.

The *Shambala Guest House* (☎ 01-225986), half a block from Chhetrapati toward Durbar Square, is a friendly well-run place built around a garden courtyard. It's nicely furnished with carpeted rooms, hot showers and outstanding service. Singles/doubles cost from $6/8 to $10/18.

Further west, the *Park Hotel* (☎ 01-211753) in Chhetrapati has a few excellent rooms with views across to Swayambunath; these, however, are often full. Prices are very reasonable with singles/doubles at Rs 200/250 ($4/5) with private bath, or Rs 150 ($3) with shared bath.

The *Sita Guest House* (☎ 01-215927), on the way down to the bridge across to Swayambunath, has some excellent rooms with good views. Singles/doubles cost $3/4 with shared bath, or $5/8 with private bath.

Freak St & Durbar Square Area
In the late '60s and '70s when hippies wandered overland through Asia, Freak St was one of the main stopping points on the trail. Although you can still spot a few skinny, bead-draped long-hairs, Freak St's glory days have passed. Nevertheless, a few determined restaurants and lodges have hung on. Staying here offers two big pluses – you won't find anything cheaper and you're right in the heart of the old city. Thamel is so crowded and hectic that Freak St is making some tentative steps towards a comeback. With the addition of one or two more clean lodges, it will definitely be up and running again.

Freak St's real name is Jochne (although no-one uses it) and it runs south from Basantapur Square, the open square full of souvenir-sellers adjoining Durbar Square. The *Hotel Sugat* (☎ 01-216656) actually overlooks the square and is one of the best options in the area. Rooms tend to be dark, but they're large and decent. Singles/doubles with shared bath start at a rock-bottom Rs 35/120; or Rs 120/180 ($2.50/3.50) with private bath.

Just off Freak St proper is the excellent *Annapurna Guest House & Diyalo Restaurant*. The place is well kept and cheerful, in contrast to some of the Freak St dives. A double is Rs 125 ($2.50) with shared bath, or Rs 175 ($3.50) with private bath.

Century Lodge (☎ 01-215769) is one of Freak St's long-term survivors and remains a popular, atmospheric place offering excellent value for money. A double room costs just Rs 90, or Rs 120 ($2.50) with bath. Century is often full, which is the best testimony any place can have. The *Pagoda Lodge* is reached from the same courtyard in the heart of Freak St.

Right across the road is the *Monumental Lodge* (☎ 01-214864) with singles/doubles for Rs 40/60, or Rs 110/150 ($2/3) with private bath. Conditions are as spartan and straightforward as the price would indicate, but if you're travelling on a very tight budget they offer all you can expect!

Take a few steps further down Freak St

Freak Street

0   40   80 m

Hanuman Dhoka
(Old Royal Palace)

To Kathmandu
Lodge

Basantapur
Square

Ganga Path

To Kumari
Guest House

Freak Street (Jochne)

1   Tourist Office
2   Himalaya's Coffee Bar
3   Hotel Sugat
4   Mona Lisa Restaurant
5   Cosmopolitan Restaurant
6   German Bakery
7   Monumental Lodge
8   Kanchan Lodge
9   Pagoda Lodge, Century Lodge
    & Kumari's Restaurant
10 Meggi Restaurant
11 GC's Lodge
12 Saymi Lodge & The Lunch Box
13 Annapurna Guest House &
    Diyalo Restaurant
14 Paradise Restaurant
15 Oasis Garden Restaurant
16 Buddha Guest House &
    Lost Horizon Restaurant
17 New Mandarin Restaurant
18 Jasmine Restaurant
19 Eden Hotel

The rooms are basic, but clean. Rooms with shared bathroom are a bargain Rs 80/150 ($2/3).

Only a few steps north of Durbar Square, then to your right on Pyaphal Tole, the *Kathmandu Lodge* (☎ 01-214893; fax 01-226820) is obviously doing something right as it's often full. Rooms cost Rs 80/100 for a single/double with shared bath, Rs 160/200 ($3/4) with private bathroom. Triples are also available.

Other Areas A scattering of budget places can be found away from Thamel, Freak St or Bhote Bahal. There are several interesting possibilities at Bodhnath (see that section).

Bagh Bazaar is east of Durbar Marg and there are a couple of places to stay right by the Bhaktapur bus stop. They don't come much cheaper than the *Ajima Guest House* (☎ 01-226716), where singles/doubles are just Rs 40/60.

For those who really want to get away from it all, take the road to Swayambhunath via the National Museum; just after you cross the bridge you come to the *Peace Lodge* where you can still get singles/doubles for as

and turn left (east) to reach the popular *Saymi Lodge* where doubles are Rs 120 ($2.50). Its Lunch Box restaurant is still part of the Freak St 'scene' and is a great place to spend an afternoon. The food is good and cheap and the company is interesting.

Other minimum-price Freak St hostelries include the *Buddha Guest House, Kanchan Lodge* and *GC's Lodge*. GC's is very basic, but very cheap – you can't do better than Rs 40/60 for a single/double.

Overlooking Durbar Square, the *Kumari Guest House* is an old-style building (mind your head) with great views over the square.

little as Rs 30/60. It's basic, friendly and quite OK.

Continue towards the museum and Sway-ambhunath, then turn off (it's signposted) and follow the meandering route back towards the river to find the very quiet *Hotel Catnap* (☎ 01-272392). It's well off the beaten track but if you don't mind the location it's good value at Rs 170/250 ($3.50/5) for doubles, all plus 10%.

Places to Stay – middle

Middle range in Kathmandu means from around $10 to $40 for a double. The borderlines are fuzzy. These days the Kathmandu Guest House is partly a middle-range hotel as many of its rooms are over $10, but it does offer cheaper ones as well. In most cases, where a hotel has cheap and mid-range rooms, it has been included in the bottom-end section.

Thamel The *Hotel Namche* (☎ 01-413503, 414944) is a cut above the usual Thamel offerings, with comfortable rooms and a very pleasant rooftop garden. Singles/doubles are $20/25 which includes an excellent breakfast.

The *Thorong Peak Guest House* (☎ 01-224656; fax 524571) has a good location in the centre of things, but off the main street in a small cul de sac. The hotel has a rather garish Tibetan-moderne decor and some of the rooms are a bit dark and expensive for what you get. On the other hand, the location is good. Singles/doubles are $14/18 with private bath, or $8/12 with shared bath.

Paknajol The *Hotel Garuda* (☎ 01-416340; fax 413614), about 100 metres north of the Kathmandu Guest House, is well run, clean, and excellent value. There's a great view over the Thamel area from the rooftop. Singles/doubles are from $10/14 plus 12% tax.

The *Hotel Mandap* (☎ 01-413321), just around the double bend north of the Kathmandu Guest House, has rooms for $20/25. The *Hotel Buddha* (☎ 01-413366), further on, is another new up-market place.

The rooms, particularly at the back, are large and comfortable with en-suite bathrooms, telephones and wall-to-wall carpeting. Singles/doubles are $17/25, but discounts are possible

The *Hotel Thamel* (☎ 01-417643) is down the first lane on the left as you head due north from the Thamel taxi-stand intersection. It's one of the new breed of comfortable concrete monstrosities, with deluxe air-con rooms from $30, rooms with private balconies looking back to the city for $22, and standard rooms for $20. Prices are very negotiable.

The *Hotel Tilicho* (☎ 01-410132), on Tridevi Marg near the immigration office, is a clean rather characterless place, but offers pretty high standards. Singles/doubles are $13/18, but it's worth negotiating the price and checking a number of rooms before you pick one. Credit cards are accepted.

Follow the double bend north of the Kathmandu Guest House and turn left towards the Holy Lodge, continuing through several more sharp bends, and you'll find the *International Guest House* (☎ 01-410533). It's in an area known as Kaldhara and has singles/doubles for $10/15 with shared bath, or $16/19 with private bath, plus 10% tax. This area is quieter and less of a scene than Thamel but not too far away from the restaurants. It's a pleasant hotel.

Jyatha Turn left (east) only a short distance down the Jyatha road and a couple of twists and turns will bring you to a neat little cluster of newer guest houses, directly behind the modern shopping centre on Tridevi Marg. This is a central, but quiet location. The *Mustang Guest House* (☎ 01-416596; fax 419361), has pleasant rooms and is well run. Singles/doubles are $8/12 with shared bath, or $14/18 with private bath, though these are negotiable, even in the high season. Subtract 30% and you're talking good value.

The *Shangrila Guest House*, *Imperial Guest House*, and *Hotel White Lotus* are in this area. The hotels all seem similar to each other, but the *Imperial* (☎ 01-229339) is pleasant and well equipped with singles/doubles at a negotiable $9/12.

Continuing south along Jyatha road you reach the *Hotel Blue Diamond* (☎ 01-226320) which has rooms at $12/15 or $16/19 with air-con, plus 12%. It's a fairly new place, set well back from the street.

The new *Hotel Utse* (☎ 01-226946, 228952) is a comfortable hotel owned by Ugen Tsering, one of the original Thamel pioneers with his long-running and popular Utse Restaurant. The restaurant is famous for its good value, and the same effort is being put into the hotel. The rooms are spotlessly clean and very comfortable – putting some of the more expensive hotels to shame. Singles/doubles cost from $15/20.

Chhetrapati Two popular middle-range hotels can be found in Chhetrapati. Coming from the Kathmandu Guest House in Thamel turn right at the junction by Narayan's Restaurant and you pass a string of restaurants, bookshops and guest houses on your way to Chhetrapati Square. The *Trans Himalaya Guest House* and the *Tibet Guest House* (☎ 01-214383, 215893) are in adjoining new buildings, both in the lower middle bracket. The Tibet Guest House has rooms with bath from $11.50, and others with shared bath for a few dollars cheaper, all plus 10% tax. There's a restaurant, a pleasant garden and good views from the rooftop of this recommended hotel.

Central Kathmandu There are several older middle-range hotels right in the centre of old Kathmandu. *Hotel Panorama* (☎ 01-221 502) is a larger hotel near New Rd with singles/doubles from $10/15. *Hotel Mt Makalu* (☎ 01-223955, 224616) is also centrally located at 65 Dharmapath and has singles/doubles for $14/16.

Other Areas North of Thamel, in the southern part of the embassy area, the *Hotel Ambassador* (☎ 01-410432; fax 413641) is in Lazimpat and run by the same people as the Kathmandu Guest House. There's a good restaurant and a garden which has shrunk with recent extensions. The hotel is within walking distance of Thamel or Durbar Marg. Rooms cost from $20/22 for a single/double.

Across the river in the Bijeshwari area, on the way from Thamel to Swayambhunath, *Hotel Vajra* (☎ 01-272719; fax 271695) is one of Kathmandu's most interesting hotels in any price category. For all the glories of the old Nepalese temples, the less said about most modern Nepalese architecture the better. The Hotel Vajra *(vajra* means thunderbolt) is a pleasant exception with a distinct style and a superb location looking across the river to Kathmandu.

The Hotel Vajra has an art gallery, its own theatre where classical Nepalese dances are performed as well as its own unusual annual performances, a library with books on Tibet and Buddhism, a rooftop garden and the Explorer's Restaurant. Singles/doubles start at $23/27 and peak at $55/60 plus 12% tax. The one catch to staying at the Hotel Vajra is its location which, though great for the view, is terrible for getting a taxi. If you're staying here it's wise to have a bicycle at the ready.

Finally, there are two other medium-price hotels near Bodhnath, the *Hotel Stupa* (☎ 01-412400) and the *Tara Gaon Resort Hotel* (☎ 01-470409). The Tara Gaon is part of a government-owned mini-chain with hotels in Nagarkot, Kakani and Pokhara. The hotel at Bodhnath is an imaginative design, and the rooms (suites really) include kitchenettes and sitting areas. This would be a good place to stay, but because guests are rare you would feel pretty isolated without a group of people, or at least transport. Singles/doubles cost $19/25.

Increasingly, people are looking to escape the pollution and bustle of central Kathmandu, and one of the nicest alternatives, which is not too far removed, is the *Hotel Sunset View* (☎ 01-229172; fax 220049) at New Baneswar – continue along the Arniko Highway and take the first right past the Everest Hotel. There's a beautiful garden with great views, 12 comfortable rooms and an excellent restaurant that serves some of the best Nepalese cuisine in Kathmandu. Singles/doubles are $32/44, and main meals are around $7.

Places to Stay – top end

Top-end hotels in Kathmandu cost from $40 for a double room; the most expensive hotels are around $125 for a double. Only a handful of these hotels are centrally located although the less conveniently positioned hotels usually offer a free bus service into town. All offer 24-hour room service, 24-hour satellite television and the best available communications.

Whether the really expensive places are worth the prices they charge is, at least in some cases, questionable. Most are large, souless places, and their battle to keep everything in tip-top condition is often only partly successful. Whether it's because of shoddy construction or the climate, things seem to start looking worn very quickly. Some of the mid-range places in Thamel come very close to the same standard, are more convenient, friendlier, and at least half the price.

The rates that follow are the standard individual rates for the high season; they're certainly negotiable for groups and are also likely to be flexible during the monsoon. A government tax is levied on all hotels and reflects the star rating; 15% for a five-star hotel, 14% for a four-star hotel, 13% for a three-star hotel, and so on.

Thamel The *Hotel Manang* (☎ 01-410993; fax 415821) in Paknajol, Thamel, is a new three-star hotel with everything you could possibly need. It exemplifies a new breed of Thamel hotel that will give the more established international hotels a serious run for their money. Many of the rooms have magnificent views, and the quality of the finish is very good. All rooms have TV and air-con, and facilities include an in-house restaurant, 24-hour room service and a parking area. The hotel accepts Amex, Diners, Visa and MasterCard. Standard singles/doubles are $30/45, deluxe rooms are $50/60, and suites $65/75, plus 13% tax.

Next door, the *Hotel Marshyangdi* (☎ 01-414105; fax 410008) has been established longer and offers a similarly high standard. In addition, it has a business centre with secretarial and fax services. Singles/doubles

cost $35/45 in standard rooms, $55/65 in deluxe rooms, plus 13% tax.

Central Kathmandu Entered from Durbar Marg, but set well back from the road, the *Yak & Yeti Park Royal Hotel* (☎ 01-222635, 413999) boasts probably the best known hotel name in Nepal, due to its connections with the legendary Boris Lissanevitch, its original owner. It is also the hotel that, more than any other in Kathmandu, actually achieves five-star standards without abandoning all references to the country it happens to be in.

There are three sections to the hotel. The oldest is part of a Rana palace that now houses the Naachgaar theatre restaurant and a number of spectacular function rooms that retain their overblown, but spectacular Rana-baroque decor. The rooms are in a modern six-storey wing – call it '70s international-hotel style. Fortunately, the interior has been well decorated and the rooms incorporate elements of carved wood and local textiles without becoming kitsch. They're very comfortable and well maintained. The third and newest wing, under construction in 1992, seemed promising.

Singles/doubles start at $125/135 and rise to $170, plus 15% tax. Businesspeople will find a well-equipped business centre with secretarial, translation and interpretation facilities.

The *Hotel de l'Annapurna* (☎ 01-221711; fax 225236) is one of Kathmandu's longest established 'new' hotels, and is architecturally an undistinguished example of a 1960s international hotel. Its central location on Durbar Marg is convenient, and apart from the usual five-star facilities, including bars and restaurants, there's a casino, nightly dance shows (see Entertainment), and the largest hotel swimming pool in Kathmandu (around 25 metres).

The air-con rooms appear a bit worn, although a wing was being renovated in 1992 and will no doubt look good, at least for a while. Singles/doubles are $110/120, plus 15% tax. The hotel's Ghar-e-Kabab restaurant (access from Durbar Marg) serves some of the best Indian food in Kathmandu.

The *Hotel Sherpa* (☎ 01-227000; fax 222026), opposite the Hotel de l'Annapurna on Durbar Marg, is cheaper, and rates four stars. It lacks a swimming pool, or even a nice garden (a garden oasis where you can escape can be a much-appreciated luxury in Kathmandu). The rooms are well equipped and quite pleasant, but suffer from shoddy detailing like poorly laid carpets. Singles/doubles are $90/100.

Just south of the Hotel de l'Annapurna on Durbar Marg, the *Hotel Woodlands* (☎ 01-220123) is a four-star hotel that has decent facilities, including a swimming pool and the Greenlands vegetarian restaurant. It's much better than its unprepossessing exterior suggests, although these days the better Thamel hotels certainly give it tough competition. Rooms are large but worn; standard singles/doubles are $67/80.

The *Hotel Malla* (☎ 01-418385; fax 418382) is on the northern edge of Thamel, near the new Royal Palace – a five-minute walk to all the Thamel restaurants. The rooms are air-con, although the furniture is getting a bit old. There's a restaurant and bar and a superb garden, complete with a mini-stupa topping a mini-hill in the centre. Singles/doubles are $90/107, plus 14% tax.

Other Areas Kathmandu's original luxury hotel, the *Soaltee Oberoi* (☎ 01-272550/1), is on the western edge of town but operates a bus service into town for its guests. It's one of the largest hotels in Nepal and apart from restaurants, bars, swimming pool and other facilities it also has a casino. Singles/doubles at the Soaltee Oberoi are $125/135.

The *Hotel Everest* (☎ 01-220567; fax 226088) is on the eastern edge of town, beside the main road to the airport and Bhaktapur. The modern building is eight stories high, making it one of the tallest buildings in Nepal, and the views, especially on the northern side, are spectacular. The standards are reasonably high and the facilities are good, as well they should be with singles/doubles at $115/125.

North of the city in the Lazimpat embassy area, the *Hotel Shanker* (☎ 01-410151) is an atmospheric place in a converted Rana palace. The exterior of the building is grandly baroque, but the modern decor in the rooms is tacky and second-rate. The main restaurant retains its grandeur and has good food and service. The palace has a fine lawn and gardens. Rates are $80 to $105.

The *Hotel Shangri-La* (☎ 01-412999; fax 414184), north of Thamel on Kantipath, is one of Kathmandu's best hotels. The rooms are attractive and well maintained, the service is swift and professional, and best of all, there's a beautiful garden with an adjoining restaurant, and a swimming pool. Singles/doubles are not cheap at $90/105, but here the price is fair.

Dwarika's Village Hotel (☎ 01-470770; fax 225131), built in traditional style and featuring superb examples of antique woodwork, is an outstanding and unusual hotel.

The owners have rescued thousands of carvings from around the valley (from buildings facing demolition or collapse) and many have been incorporated into the complex, which consists of a small cluster of buildings, separated by pleasant brick-paved courtyards. A large workshop (funded by the hotel) operates in the hotel grounds, and craftspeople patiently repair and restore lattice windows and carvings that would otherwise almost certainly be lost in Kathmandu's rush to survive and modernise. The end result is a beautiful hybrid – a cross between a museum and a boutique hotel.

The complex is near the airport and Pashupatinath, and its only disadvantage is that it's a bit of a distance to the eating places in Thamel or Durbar Marg; taxis are not a problem, however. The hotel has won a Heritage Award from the Pacific Asia Travel Association (PATA), and has just 31 rooms at $64 to $81. The rooms are large, atmospheric and very comfortable, but do not have air-con or TV.

PLACES TO EAT

Kathmandu's restaurants attempt an amazing variety of international cuisines with a reasonable degree of success. There are few places in south Asia where your

Durbar Marg

0   50   100 m

To Thamel

Royal Palace

To Hotel Yak & Yeti

■ PLACES TO STAY

15 Hotel de l'Annapurna
22 Hotel Sherpa
27 Hotel Woodlands &
   Greenlands Restaurant
30 Hotel Mayalu &
   American Express

▼ PLACES TO EAT

5 Kushi Fuji Restaurant
9 Kingsway Chinese Restaurant
12 Koto Restaurant
13 Ghar-e-Kebab Restaurant
14 Annapurna Coffee Shop
18 Nirula's Restaurant
19 Nanglo Chinese Room
20 Nanglo Cafe & Pub
21 Cafe de la Paix
23 Mike's Breakfast
24 Amber Restaurant
25 Moti Mahal
29 Bangalore Coffee House

OTHER

1 Burma Airways &
  Mercantile Tours & Travels
2 Bangladesh Biman Airways
3 Indian Airlines
4 Ritual Art Gallery
6 Singapore Airlines
7 Pakistan International Airlines
8 Dragonair
10 Potala Art Gallery
11 Curio Arts
16 Thai International
17 Lufthansa
26 Dawa Arts
28 Noor Gems

choice of restaurants is so varied. After long months on the road in India or long weeks trekking in Nepal most travellers find Kathmandu a culinary paradise. Recent arrivals from the West may not be quite so impressed, but some places are great value by any standards.

If you are eating in the really rock-bottom restaurants around Kathmandu it is wise to be cautious about hygiene. Few travellers spend long in Nepal without coming across something which disagrees with them even if they're very fastidious about where they eat. Eating 'street food' from stalls and pave-

ment kitchens in Kathmandu is likely to wreak havoc on all but the strongest of stomachs. Health standards have definitely improved in Kathmandu over the years, however, and you're very unlikely to have serious problems if you eat in the popular tourist-oriented restaurants. In these places it's even safe to try a salad, drink a glass of water and eat the ice cream – although some would argue that this is living dangerously.

At the bottom end of the price range Kathmandu has numerous tea stalls and shops. Many may not even have a name but at these stalls dhal bhat tarkari – the lentil soup, rice and vegetable everyday meal of most Nepalese – will be the main dish on offer. By up-country standards these places aren't cheap – dhal bhat tarkari will probably set you back Rs 30.

In Thamel, if you stay away from beer, you can eat until you burst for less than Rs 150 ($3). A bottle of the excellent Iceberg beer can cost anything from Rs 70 to Rs 100 ($2) and nearly double your bill.

As you might expect, the top restaurants have prices to match, but they're still reasonable by Western standards. More expensive restaurants slap a 10% to 15% government tax on top of their bill, but you'll still probably only pay between $10 and $20 per person.

Tipping is becoming more accepted (and appreciated) in Nepal but the loose change or 5% is fine in cheaper places; a bit more will be expected in the expensive restaurants.

This section is divided geographically, with a final section on expensive places.

Thamel

Thamel restaurants spill into Paknajol, Jyatha and Chhetrapati, just like Thamel hotels. The junction just outside the Kathmandu Guest House is the centre of Thamel dining and you can find numerous budget-priced restaurants within a minute's walk in each direction. Many of these restaurants offer a virtually standard try-anything menu with Asian and Western dishes. Italian and Mexican food features on many of these menus and you can try some amazing interpretations of pizza, pasta, tacos and the like.

The central Thamel restaurants include the best known of the lot, *KC's Restaurant*. Kaysee himself may no longer preside, but he hit the magic travellers' restaurant formula spot-on. Although the food is still very good, the restaurant has become a bit expensive by Thamel standards. A delicious breakfast starts at around Rs 45 (which isn't bad), but a vegetarian lasagne is Rs 135

($2.50), and one of KC's famous steaks (Kathmandu's sizzle plate mania started right here) is around Rs 150 ($3).

On this same stretch of Thamel's restaurant centre you can try the *Pumpernickel Bakery* for freshly baked bread. In the morning, overland travellers crowd in here for croissants in the pleasant garden area at the back. There's a useful notice board. The bakery counter up front offers brown bread, rolls, cinnamon rolls and other goodies.

Also across the road from KC's is *Helena's Restaurant* with the standard Kathmandu menu ranging from vegetarian dishes and soups through pastas and burgers to steaks with a great selection of cakes and pies to follow at around Rs 30. Nearby, and upstairs, the *Clay Oven* is a pleasant spot with a good Indian menu.

Alice's Restaurant, in the Namche Bazaar building south of the Kathmandu Guest House, is a decent place, a cut above the cheapies, but still very reasonable. Pizza is Rs 70, vegetable moussaka is Rs 65 and pancakes Rs 30.

The *Third Eye* is a long-running favourite that retains something of the old Kathmandu atmosphere. There's a sit-down section at the front, and a more informal section with low tables and cushions at the back. The speciality is Indian food, but there are also a small number of continental offerings. A half tandoori chicken is Rs 125 ($2.50).

Himthai serves authentic Thai food (vouched for by an extremely fussy Thai). It's not particularly cheap, with starters around Rs 70 and main meals from Rs 90, but the food is good and you can eat in a pleasant garden. Avoid lunches, which are suspiciously like reheated leftovers.

Across the road from the Himthai on the 1st floor, the attractive, *Roadhouse Cafe* is noisy and popular. Soup is Rs 28, steaks Rs 80, pizza Rs 70, beer Rs 75, and there's dhal bhat for Rs 99.

Down the road from My Mom's Place, *Skala* serves good vegetarian food. It has a pleasant garden and is a nice quiet place for breakfast, with newspapers to read and classical music playing in the background. The set breakfast will set you up for the day for Rs 50.

Nearly every Thamel restaurant has a go at some Italian dishes, but *La Dolce Vita Restaurant*, right on the corner, with the movie motifs, makes the best attempt at true Italian cuisine, and, considering the difficulties, it does a very good job. Being on such a busy intersection it's a bit noisy, but the food compensates. Prices are a little higher than the rock-bottom Thamel average, but so is the quality. Minestrone is Rs 50, spaghetti from Rs 75 to Rs 100 ($2), and there are a range of veal (!?) dishes if you're so inclined. Beer is Rs 90.

Just past the Kathmandu Guest House is the compound with the Greenhill Tours & West Himalayan Outdoors office, the Tukche Peak Guest House and, finally, the *Himalayan Country Kitchen*. The restaurant has a standard Thamel menu, but the service is good, and the atmosphere is pleasant. It's a good place for a drink, some food, and perhaps another drink.

Continue a little north and you come to Yeti Cottage where the inexpensive *Rainbow Restaurant* has a nice garden and a good reputation for pizza and pasta dishes (around Rs 55). Avoid their gravy-soaked hamburgers, however. It's a pleasant place for breakfast, although service can be infuriatingly slow.

Tucked in behind the corner is a *Pizza Hut*, which is no relation whatsoever, but does have crisp and tasty pizzas; large ones are around Rs 85, small about Rs 40. Mexican and Italian standard dishes are also available for around Rs 60. One drawback/advantage is the video, which tends to dominate.

Several other popular restaurants cluster close to the landmark Kathmandu Guest House corner. The name may be French, but *Le Bistro Restaurant* has the familiar international menu with lots of pasta dishes. A prime attraction here is the large open courtyard, ideal for pleasant outdoor dining. The good-value breakfasts are particularly popular; two eggs, toast and tea will cost around Rs 50. There are a number of decent vegetarian dishes like pizza and enchiladas for around Rs 60, but steaks jump to Rs 100.

Above Pilgrims Book House is the efficiently run *G's Terrace*. It's a pleasant spot for an evening drink – it has a good music selection – and the food is of a high standard. The menu features a number of authentic German dishes. It's a bit more expensive than some places, but the standards are correspondingly high. Fillet steak is Rs 170 ($3.50), Bavarian potato soup with sausage is Rs 105 ($2), and chicken chilli is Rs 105 ($2).

The Kathmandu Guest House's *Ashta Mangala Restaurant* serves up straightforward, well-prepared food and is another popular breakfast spot. This is a good place to try traditional Tibetan dishes like *momo* (pasta stuffed with meat and/or vegetables, a bit like large ravioli). Directly across the road and upstairs is *Hem's Bar & Restaurant*, a pleasant rooftop spot where you can overlook the Thamel activity below. Hem's used to do very good tandoori and curry dishes, but, unfortunately the only survivor on the menu is chicken tandoori (which is still good for Rs 100). Apart from that, there are all the Thamel specialities ranging from Rs 60 to Rs 100 ($2).

Continue a few steps north of the Kathmandu Guest House entranceway and you'll see the alley to *Helena's Country Kitchen* which, to the despair of many, took over the site once occupied by the infamous Rum Doodle. The new restaurant is one of the most pleasant in Thamel, with attractive surroundings and professional service, and though the continental menu is limited, meals are prepared well. Prices are reasonable, with soup from Rs 36, lasagne, pizza and pasta around Rs 80, and steak for Rs 110 ($2).

The *Rum Doodle Restaurant* was named, of course, after the world's highest mountain, the 40,000½-foot Mt Rum Doodle. The heroic conquest of Rum Doodle was dramatically described in that spoof on heroic mountaineering books *The Ascent of Rum Doodle* (Dark Peak, Sheffield, 1979). Unfortunately the restaurant was in transit in late 1992, but large signs proclaimed it was reopening at a new site, near the Holy Lodge.

The old restaurant specialised in steak and pasta and was a favourite meeting place for mountaineering expeditions, particularly in the upstairs 40,000½ Foot Bar of course. The new incarnation will be worth checking out.

The *Utse Restaurant* (☎ 01-412747), near the Thamel taxi stand, is one of the longest running restaurants in Thamel and turns out Chinese food such as sweet & sour dishes, as well as Tibetan momo and *kothe* (fried pasta stuffed with meat/vegetables). The food is good and excellent value, and the restaurant is one of the most atmospheric in Thamel. It retains some of the style of Kathmandu in the '70s, and a visit is recommended. Soup costs around Rs 20, Tibetan kothe Rs 22, and vegetable fried rice Rs 21. The restaurant also serves traditional Tibetan-style meals – banquets would be a better word – which are highly recommended. Because of the preparation required, you have to order two hours in advance. Kadug dhayshey for four is Rs 560 ($11), gacok for four is Rs 520 ($10.50). *Gacok* (also spelt gyakok) is a meal for two named after the brass tureen which is heated at the table and from which various meats and vegetables are served.

On the same side of the road, across from the Marco Polo, is the *Old Vienna Inn* with excellent service and very good food. If you're after wiener schnitzel, goulash and other middle-European dishes this is the place. Most mains are around Rs 150 ($3). The *Gourmet Delicatessen* in front of the restaurant is also good, with all sorts of unlikely food – from sausages and salami, to apple strudel and ice cream.

Head south from Thamel into Chhetrapati to find more popular travellers' restaurants including *Narayan's Restaurant*, another of the long-term survivors in this area. It's very popular, competent and low priced with a wide range of breakfast dishes (fixed menu Rs 40), pasta and pizza from Rs 60. The vegetarian lasagne and the enchiladas are very good (Rs 65). Narayan's also produces delicious ice cream in half a dozen different flavours, and offers a great selection of pies and cakes.

Turn right towards Chhetrapati and you

find *Pizza Maya* for, that's right, pizza and Mexican food. This is a popular spot with a good range of vegetarian dishes. A pizza will cost from Rs 60 to Rs 80. There are some vegetarian dishes for Rs 35.

Next is the *Nepalese Kitchen*, an interesting venture attempting something rather different from the ubiquitous pseudo-Western food. Traditional Nepalese food is definitely rather unusual in Thamel – unfortunately, in this restaurant it's overpriced and not very good.

Across the road, the *Everest Steak House* is very popular, especially with returned trekkers suffering from protein deficiency. The steaks are excellent and range from Rs 120 ($2.50) to Rs 150 ($3). The enormous chateaubriand (Rs 300, or $6) is best shared between two. There are also some vegetarian alternatives, including pizza and pasta.

In Jyatha on the opposite side of the road near the Hotel Utse, *Sidewalkers Restaurant* is a fairly classic variation on the Thamel theme, but there's a pleasant garden if it's sunny and an atmospheric open-sided pavilion if it's not. The food is good, if not inspired: burgers cost from Rs 45 to Rs 65, steaks around Rs 90, and pizza from Rs 75 to Rs 95. There's also a reasonable range of vegetarian dishes.

Finally, on the northern edge of Thamel, in the courtyard of the Malla Hotel, the *Mountain City Chinese Restaurant* concentrates on the hotter Sichuan and Shanghai dishes rather than the familiar Cantonese ones.

Freak St

Despite its decline in popularity, Freak St still has a number of restaurants where you can find good food at low prices. Even if you're staying in other areas of the city it's nice to know there are some good places for lunch if you're sightseeing around Durbar Square.

Just off Durbar Square beside the Great Bell, with slightly complicated access through a courtyard and upstairs, is the *Big Bell Restaurant*. This is a good place to relax if your feet are giving way and you want a calm, rooftop oasis overlooking the street.

On Freak St itself the *Oasis Garden Restaurant* has a cramped outdoor dining area that is, unfortunately, starting to look very run-down. It has a standard travellers' menu (with prices from Rs 60 to Rs 80) and does a reasonable job. Across the road from the Oasis Garden the *Paradise Restaurant* is also good for vegetarian food.

The long-running *Lunch Box* is just off Freak St and is still very much a 'scene'. Come here for a faint reminder of those hippie overland trail days when Freak St really was the 'flower-power' centre. You can get pizza and pasta for Rs 40 and steaks for Rs 70. The set breakfasts are particularly cheap and good for Rs 25.

Up at the Basantapur Square end of Freak St the *Mona Lisa* is a pleasant place with friendly staff. Right next door and also overlooking the square is the *Cosmopolitan Restaurant*. Both places have newer offshoots in Thamel.

Other consistent Freak St places include *Kumari's Restaurant* in the same courtyard as the Century Lodge. Or there's the *Lost Horizon* near the Lunch Box and the *Bluebird*, just south of the Kasthamandap and Singh Sattal, near Durbar Square.

Central Kathmandu

New Rd restaurants are aimed at the local rather than the tourist market but try *Marwari Sewa Samiti*, near the cinema, or the nearby *Tripti Restaurant* for very economically priced all-you-can-eat south Indian vegetarian thalis.

The restaurants in the glossier Kantipath and Durbar Marg areas are generally more expensive than around Thamel although there are a few lower-priced exceptions. See the concluding Expensive Restaurants section for some of Kathmandu's real night-out possibilities.

You can start the day with one of the best and most popular breakfast places in the city. As the name suggests *Mike's Breakfast* specialises in breakfasts and they do them well. The restaurant is directly behind the Sherpa Hotel. Meals are served in the attractive garden of an old Rana house, and are accompanied by soothing recordings of Baroque string quartets. Mike's is open every day for breakfast and lunch, and does pizza on Monday nights only. It's not cheap, but is certainly a laid-back way to start the day. The breakfast menu includes excellent pancakes at Rs 80 for three, waffles at Rs 90 for two, chocolate brownies for Rs 40; toast, eggs and tea will come to about Rs 80. Lunch is also good, with dishes like quiche and salad costing around Rs 90.

Several places on Durbar Marg have good food from the subcontinent. The *Bangalore Coffee House* serves good south Indian vegetarian dishes like *masala dosa* (curried vegetables wrapped in lentil-flour pastry) for only Rs 10, and is a popular local gathering place.

The *Nanglo Cafe & Pub* has a popular rooftop dining area and an international menu. There's quite a lively atmosphere and the place is a favourite for people in the travel business. A large pizza will cost Rs 52, a steak Rs 95, and a fixed Nepalese lunch with rice, dhal, meat, vegetable curry, pickle and green salad is Rs 65. In the Woodlands Hotel the *Greenlands Restaurant* is an Indian vegetarian restaurant.

Nirula's near the Hotel de l'Annapurna on Durbar Marg, is the closest you'll find to a McDonald's in Nepal. Its menu features burgers (like the Mahaburger) from Rs 40 to Rs 60, pizza from Rs 40 to Rs 80, and 21 flavours of ice cream at Rs 16 to Rs 20 for cones or cups. This is also the place to come if, while trekking, you've developed an uncontrollable urge for a chocolate milk-shake (Rs 32). Despite the fast-food atmosphere and service it still operates the traditional Indian way where you decide what you want, pay the cashier, then take your receipt to the service counter to get your goodies.

Beside the entrance to the Hotel de l'Annapurna the *Annapurna Coffee Shop* offers a standard 'big hotel' style menu with burgers from Rs 80, pizza from Rs 70, and milkshakes or lassi (yoghurt with sugar and fruit) at Rs 40. It's popular but the food is only average. Across the road the Hotel Sherpa's *Cafe de la Paix* has a similar coffee-shop menu.

Other Durbar Marg possibilities include the moderately priced *Koto Restaurant* which many say prepares the best Japanese food in town. A set menu is Rs 225 ($4.50), but there are plenty of dishes around Rs 120 ($2.50).

Still on Durbar Marg the *Amber Restaurant* serves good-quality Indian food (it also has a continental menu) and attracts a lively crowd of affluent young Nepalese, especially when the music is good. The crowd varies depending on who is playing, but this can be a fun night out. Without beer it's possible to eat well for less than Rs 200 ($4).

Nearby, the *Moti Mahal* serves, according to some, the best Indian food in Kathmandu. In some ways it's similar to the Amber. There's live music and most main dishes are around Rs 80.

The *Aroma Restaurant*, on the eastern side of Kantipath, overlooking Rani Pokhara, is a pleasant place to watch the sunset and rest your feet after a day of exploring Kathmandu. There's a pleasant rooftop garden and you can get reasonably priced snacks and drinks.

Expensive Restaurants

Kathmandu's big hotels have some interesting restaurant possibilities and although the prices are sky-high by Nepalese standards, they're remarkably cheap compared to the cost of similar restaurants in the West. One thing you will consistently find in these more expensive places is heating, which is rare in the cheaper places.

One of the most famous possibilities is the Yak & Yeti Park Royal's *Chimney Room* (☎ 01-413999). It retains a tenuous historical link with Russian-born Boris Lissanevitch the founder of the Royal Hotel, Kathmandu's first hotel for Western visitors. The central open fireplace gives it plenty of atmosphere, but unfortunately apart from the borsch, which is still excellent, there are few reminders of Boris' days. Nevertheless, the food is

well prepared, if somewhat bland. The borsch is Rs 90, and chicken stroganoff is Rs 260 ($5). A complete meal for two including drinks will cost about Rs 1200 ($24).

Also in the Yak & Yeti, the *Naachghar Restaurant* (☎ 01-413999) is in a section of the hotel that was once a theatre in a Rana palace. It's a grand, baroque room with high ceilings, gilt mirrors, marble, and ornate plasterwork. Performances of Nepalese music and dance are given, but ring ahead to check what nights they are on. The menu is strong on Indian and Nepalese dishes – those from the tandoor are meant to be good – but there are also some continental options. Prices are marginally cheaper than in the Chimney Room, especially if you stick to vegetarian curries.

The *Ghar-e-Kebab*, on Durbar Marg outside the Hotel de l'Annapurna, has some of the best Indian and tandoori food in the city. Indian miniatures hang on the walls and in the evenings classical Indian music is played and traditional Urdu *ghazals* (songs) are sung. A complete meal for two including drinks will cost about $20. The *Arniko Room* at the Hotel de l'Annapurna has good Chinese food.

At the Royal Palace end of Kantipath, the *Fuji Restaurant* (☎ 01-225272) serves good-quality Japanese food. It's away from the road in an atmospheric pavilion that was built in 1905 in the grounds of the nearby Bahadur Bhawan Palace (now government offices). It is not cheap (unless you convert from Yen). The tempura set menu is Rs 320 ($6.50), and the sukiyaki set menu, Rs 340 ($7). Alternatively, you can choose from the à la carte menu and probably get away with a lower charge – say around Rs 300 ($6) per person, including a beer.

The trek out to the Soaltee Oberoi Hotel, on the western side of town, may be worthwhile to try the excellent Indian and Nepalese dishes at the *Himalchuli Restaurant*. It features woodcarvings from Bhaktapur and traditional Nepalese music plays in the background. Many say the Oberoi's *Al Fresco Italian Restaurant* serves the best Italian food in Nepal; count on about Rs 800 ($16) for two including drinks.

Also out of town, the *Far Pavilions Restaurant* at the Everest Hotel offers great views over Kathmandu from its 7th-floor vantage point and serves a popular chicken tandoori. Closer to the centre, the Hotel Shanker's *Kailash Restaurant* does a variety of Indian, Nepalese and even Russian dishes.

Bhanchha Ghar (literally, 'Nepalese Kitchen') is in a traditional three-storey Newari house just east of Durbar Marg from the turn-off by the clocktower. It's worth eating here just to see the imaginative redevelopment of this beautiful old building. There's an upstairs loft where you can stretch out on handmade carpets and cushions for a drink, then take advantage of an excellent menu of traditional Nepalese dishes and delicacies. Downstairs, musicians stroll between the tables playing traditional Nepalese folk songs. It's not cheap (around Rs 1000, or $20, for two, with drinks), but the food is delicious.

The best place for gourmets to sample Newari cuisine is *Thayabhu* (☎ 01-411570), just off the entrance road to the Hotel Shanker. The service is slick, and all sorts of unusual delicacies are available. Expect to pay around Rs 350 ($7) per person.

ENTERTAINMENT

Nepal is an early-to-bed country and even in Kathmandu you find few people on the streets after 10 pm. Few visitors come for nightlife and Kathmandu's discos and other nightspots have had a remarkably low survival rate. Of course the crowded restaurants and bars are great places to meet and talk with people and the big hotels do offer some traditional nightlife for those who positively cannot live without it. Kathmandu also has cultural shows, cinemas and two of West Asia's very few casinos.

Bars

There are half a dozen bars scattered around Thamel, all within a short walk of each other. They each have quite distinctive atmospheres, so it's worth poking your nose in each one to see which has the crowd and the style that appeals to you.

The most well known was the Rum Doodle, which attracted an interesting crowd of adventurers. It was closed in late '92, but its new incarnation across the road from the Holy Lodge should be worth checking out. At the end of the Kathmandu Guest House street, Spam's Place has a friendly pub-style atmosphere thanks to the inimitable style of the 'guvnar'. It also has the best toilets in Thamel (something to bear in mind).

Tom & Jerry's, upstairs opposite Pilgrims, is a rowdy place with a second-rate sound system. If the rooftop garden is open, it can be fun. The Blue Note is one of the most civilised offerings, with excellent jazz and blues, and some interesting paintings on the wall (thanks to Bishnu Shrestha who did most of the line illustrations for this book). The nearby Pub Maya is rather labyrinthine and poky, but it invariably attracts some hard-core party animals.

Casinos

The government has recently liberalised gambling regulations, and a number of the five-star hotels are likely to introduce casinos. At the time of writing, there were casinos at the Soaltee Oberoi and the Hotel de l'Annapurna.

Until recently, the Soaltee Oberoi Casino was the only casino on the subcontinent. If you turn up within a week of arrival with your onward airline ticket and your passport you can get Rs 100 ($2) of free coupons. You can play in either Indian rupees (almost a hard currency in Nepalese terms) or US dollars, and winnings (in the same currency) can be taken out of the country when you leave. The casino is open 24 hours a day and there are free buses from all the leading hotels of Kathmandu from 8 to 11 pm. They return hourly from 11 pm to 4 am.

The Casino Anna at the Hotel de l'Annapurna is a new addition to the scene, and although it is convenient (just off Durbar Marg) the atmosphere is not very inspiring. If you present your airline ticket at the casino within seven days of arriving in Nepal you receive a free bottle of beer and sandwich.

Music & Dance

There are regular performances of Nepalese music and dancing in Kathmandu, including at the National Theatre, although these are usually in Nepali. All the big hotels have nightly 'cultural shows' usually in their main restaurant around 7 pm.

The Sweta Machhendranath Temple in Kel Tole has traditional Nepalese music around 9.30 pm each evening. 'The warming up of the musicians', reported one visitor, 'is done with a large chillum (clay pipe) and the music begins when the coughing stops.'

Cinemas

Video Night in Kathmandu has certainly had an impact on the city – there are video shops everywhere and cinemas are having a hard time of it. Indian films, usually not subtitled, are the usual cinematic fare in the valley although there are occasional English-language films. Admission charges range from Rs 8 to Rs 15 and catching a Hindi movie is well worthwhile since not understanding the language is not a real obstacle to enjoying these comedy-musical spectaculars. The Indians call them 'masala' movies as they have a little bit of everything in them.

In the small video parlours, popular Western movies appear on pirated videos almost as soon as they hit the cinemas in the West.

THINGS TO BUY

Everything turned out in the various centres around the valley can be found in Kathmandu although you may often find a better choice or more unusual items in the real centres – head for Jawlakhel, south of Patan, for Tibetan carpets for example, to Patan for cast metal statues and other craftwork, to Bhaktapur for the finest woodcarvings and pottery, and to Thimi for more pottery and masks. (See the Patan and Bhaktapur Things to Buy sections later in this chapter for more details.)

Crafts of various kinds are on sale all around Kathmandu, and the money tourists spend on craft items makes an important contribution to Nepal's economy – as has been the case for hundreds of years.

The most important rules when buying anything worth a reasonable amount of money are firstly, to put in some legwork and secondly, buy just before you leave, not just after you arrive. Prices vary hugely and until you have done some research, you'll have no idea whether you're being ripped off (to an acceptable degree) or not. Lastly, all serious shoppers should read Jeff Greenwald's funny and acute book *Shopping for Buddhas* (Harper & Row, San Francisco, 1990), which gives fair warning of the fate that can befall obsessive types.

Bronze Statues

The best place to start is on Durbar Marg, but there are also some shops worth visiting on New Rd. This is one area where research is vitally important, as quality and prices do not necessarily have any direct correlation. Curio Arts on Durbar Marg is a good place to start.

Curios

An endless supply of curios, stuff, knick-knacks, pieces, thingos and plain junk is turned out for tourists. Most do not come from Tibet (but from the local Tamang community) and most are not more than six weeks old, but none of this matters. If you shop around you can find creations that are beautifully made by craftspeople whose time is obviously not worth a lot of money. Basantapur Square is the headquarters for this trade, but before you match wits with these operators, visit the Craft Collection in Thamel. This relatively small shop has a wide collection, all with marked prices that are reasonably fair.

Thangkas

The main centre for thangkas is just off Durbar Square, and this is where you'll find the best salespeople (not necessarily the best thangkas). For modern work in Thamel, visit the Tibetan Thangka Treasure, near KC's, and the Indigo Gallery, near the Tara Guest House.

Top: Krishna Mandir, Patan (TW)
Left: Porters awaiting work, Patan (RI'A)
Right: Kumbeshwar, Patan (TW)

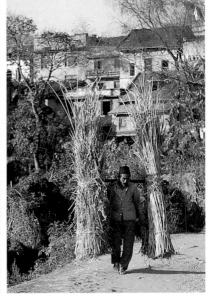

Top: New year celebrations, Kathmandu (RI'A)
Left: Bungamati, Kathmandu Valley (RE)
Right: Rural scene, Kathmandu Valley (TW)

Clothing

Kathmandu is the best place in the valley for clothes and many places now have good-quality ready-to-wear Western fashions, particularly shirts. Amusing embroidered T-shirts are a popular speciality. There are lots of good tailors around Thamel and apart from gembroidered T-shirts they'll also embroider just about anything you want on your own jacket or jeans. Tara Boutique, with shops on Tridevi Marg near Thamel and on Durbar Marg, makes wonderful hand-painted pure silk women's fashions. Dresses are certainly not cheap at $50 to $100 and up, but in the West they would be many times that price.

Kathmandu's clothing manufacturing industry seems to be going from strength to strength. Recent trade liberalisation by the new government has helped to reduce the traditional problem of maintaining stocks of cloth. The cheapest items have a tendency to shrink and to fall apart, but standards both in terms of durability and design are improving. It's worth trying some of the shops in Freak St; prices tend to be better than in Thamel, partly because rents are more reasonable but also because the usual clients are shoestring travellers.

Gems

Buying gems is always a risky business unless you know what you're doing. Be immediately suspicious of anyone who tells you that you will be able to make an enormous profit – if it was possible and legal they would do it themselves. Noor Gems on Durbar Marg is a long-running and reputable place.

Tibetan Antiques

Kathmandu seems to be the world clearing house for a continual stream of antiques being brought out of Tibet. This includes everything from thanks, to carpets, storage chests, carvings, religious objects, saddles, and clothing. Since the Chinese have done their utmost to destroy Tibetan culture, removing some of what remains to safety is perhaps more morally acceptable than some

other 'collecting' that goes on in Nepal. There are a number of good shops on Durbar Marg, but don't go without a very healthy wallet. The Ritual Art Gallery and Potala Art Gallery are all worth a look.

Kashmiri Goods

Since the war in Kashmir killed the tourist trade there, many Kashmiris have migrated to Nepal to sell their traditional crafts – tapestry, woollen shawls and papier-mâché. These guys are excellent salespeople, so buy with caution. Prices are pretty good; they would be cheaper in Kashmir of course, but might well come with a bonus bullet. Cottage Crafts on the ground floor of the Sanchaya Kosh Shopping Complex (across the road from the immigration office) has a good selection and reliable prices.

Indian Goods

With the resurgence of popularity for Gujarat and Rajasthan embroidered clothing and manchester, a number of shops have opened in Kathmandu. Prices are, needless to say, considerably higher than if you buy in India, but considerably less than if you buy in the West.

Trekking Supplies

The Bluebird supermarkets have a wide variety of goods. There's a branch near the Blue Star Hotel near the main bridge across the Bagmati to Patan, and another in Lazimpat on the continuation of Kantipath (on the right-hand side about a km from Thamel). In Thamel, for trekking food like noodles, nuts, dried fruit and cheese, there's a 'supermarket' at the end of Tridevi Marg, at the corner where it narrows and enters Thamel proper.

GETTING THERE & AWAY

See the Getting There & Away chapter for details of getting to Kathmandu by air or land.

Air

Kathmandu is the only international arrival point for flights to Nepal and is also the centre for most domestic flights. Airlines with offices in Kathmandu include:

Aeroflot
    Kamaladi (☎ 01-226161)
Air India
    Kantipath (☎ 01-211730)
Bangladesh Biman
    Durbar Marg (☎ 01-222544)
British Airways
    Durbar Marg (☎ 01-222266)
China Southwest Airlines
    Lal Durbar Camp, Kamaladi (☎ 01-411302)
Cathay Pacific
    Kantipath (☎ 01-226704)
Dragon Air
    Durbar Marg (☎ 01-223162)
Druk Air
    Durbar Marg (☎ 01-225166)
Indian Airlines
    Durbar Marg (☎ 01-223053)
Lufthansa
    Durbar Marg (☎ 01-223052)
Myanmar (Burma) Airways
    Durbar Marg (☎ 01-224893)
Pakistan International Airlines
    Durbar Marg (☎ 01-223102)
Royal Nepal Airlines
    Ramshah Path – domestic (☎ 01-220757)
    Kantipath – international (☎ 01-214491)
Singapore Airlines
    Durbar Marg (☎ 01-223233)
Thai International
    Durbar Marg (☎ 01-224917)

Numerous other airlines are represented in Kathmandu. There are three important rules with flights out of Kathmandu – reconfirm, reconfirm and reconfirm! This particularly applies to Royal Nepal Airlines, but at peak times when flights are heavily booked you should reconfirm when you first arrive in Nepal and reconfirm again towards the end of your stay. Even this may not guarantee you a seat – make sure you get to the airport very early as people at the end of the queue can still be left behind.

Bus

When this book was researched, a new long-distance bus station was under construction, just off the Ring Rd at Balaju. This will be called the Gongbu Bus Park, but will also be referred to as the Kathmandu Bus Terminal.

It is uncertain just what will happen when it opens, except for maximum confusion. Presumably, all long-distance buses will use the new terminal and there will be shuttle buses to central points in the city. Presumably buses departing for destinations within the valley will continue to use the bus stops they currently use, but there is the possibility they will all be moved to the old Central Bus Station.

Before the Kathmandu Bus Terminal opened, your destination or point of origin determined which of 11 bus stops you would use. See the main Kathmandu map and the bus stop key to locate these stops. With the new terminal, it is uncertain which of these will remain and who will use them!

If you used public buses between Kathmandu and the Terai and Indian border, your bus stop was either at the foot of Bhimsen Tower near the main post office (Bus Stop 8) or at the Central Bus Station (Bus Stop 6). From either of these points it's only a short walk to Freak St and Durbar Square or a quick taxi or rickshaw ride to the Thamel area.

Public buses for Pokhara departed from the foot of the Bhimsen Tower (Bus Stop 8) or from the Central Bus Station (Bus Stop 6) and cost around Rs 60. The more expensive tourist buses (around Rs 200, or $4) and minibuses (around Rs 240, or $5) – heavily promoted in Thamel – usually departed from the Thamel end of Kantipath (Bus Stop 11). See the Pokhara chapter for more details.

GETTING AROUND

The best way to see Kathmandu and the valley is to walk or ride a bike. Most of the sights in Kathmandu can easily be covered on foot, and this is by far the best way to appreciate the city. When and if you run out of steam, there are plenty of reasonably priced taxis and autorickshaws. There are also limitless opportunities for short walks around the valley. A number are described in the Around the Kathmandu Valley chapter.

The valley is the perfect size and shape for bicycling. A single-speed bike is fine around the three main cities, but if you want to get into the countryside consider hiring a multi-geared machine. Since the furthest point in the valley is never more than about 20 km from Kathmandu you can ride out (uphill) and return (downhill) easily within a day. Bike speed allows you to appreciate your surroundings and stop whenever you like.

To/From the Airport

Kathmandu's international airport is named Tribhuvan Airport after the late king, though it used to rejoice in the name Gaucher (literally, 'cow pasture'!).

Getting into town is quite straightforward. There is now an organised taxi service on the ground-floor foyer immediately you leave the arrivals baggage collection and customs section. Called Down Town Services, the taxis have a fixed fare of Rs 100 ($2) to Thamel or Durbar Marg, and do not accept dollars.

The touts outside the building will often offer a free taxi if you take them up on their suggested hotel. This can be useful at very busy times, as long as you make it clear how much you want to pay. However, the commission they make on your hotel tariff can be outrageous.

Buses are sometimes available from Royal Nepal Airlines for Rs 15. There are public buses but they're only really usable if you have very little luggage.

Bus

While bus travel is very cheap, it is often unbelievably crowded. The primary disadvantage, apart from severe discomfort, is that you cannot see the views or stop when you want to. Still, if you're short of cash and want to get from point A to B *reasonably* quickly they'll do. Over a short distance – say from Thamel to Bodhnath – you'll probably be just as quick on a bicycle. The smaller minibuses and curious little three-wheeled tempos are generally quicker than the full-sized buses and are a bit more expensive.

With the opening of the new Kathmandu Bus Terminal, however, the bus system described in this section is likely to be thrown into confusion. There are a number of different stops, depending on your destination/starting point, which may or may not be closed and moved to the Central Bus Station (Bus Stop 6). Time will tell.

See the main Kathmandu map and bus stop key to locate the stops that were operating in 1992.

Kakani, Trisuli Bazaar & Dhunche Buses left from the intersection of Lekhnath Marg and the road to Balaju (Bus Stop 1 – Paknajol). Buses to Dhunche (for Langtang treks) left at around 6.30 am (nine hours, Rs 65). Buses to Trisuli left from 6.30 am to 2.30 pm (five hours, Rs 29). Kakani is about three km off the main road, so you had to catch one of the buses going through, and get off at Kaulithana (about Rs 12).

Budhanilkantha Minibuses left regularly from Rani Pokhari (Bus Stop 3) for Rs 4 (1½ hours).

Pashupatinath & Bodhnath Minibuses left regularly (when full) from Rani Pokhari (Bus Stop 3) travelling via Pashupatinath (Rs 2). The stop for Pashupatinath is Gosala.

Gokarna Buses left from Ratna Park (Bus Stop 4) and cost Rs 4.

Sundarijal Buses left from Tukuchapul (Bus Stop 7) for Rs 9 (two hours).

Sankhu Two or three buses a day left from near Martyrs' Memorial Gate (Bus Stop 9), not far from the Bhadrakali Temple (two hours, Rs 9).

Bhaktapur Regular electric trolley buses run along the Arniko Highway and leave from the roundabout at the southern end of Kantipath near the National Stadium (Bus Stop 10). These cost Rs 2 and drop you off a 10-minute walk from the centre of Bhaktapur.

Alternatively, you could catch an ordinary bus (not as comfortable) from Bagh Bazaar (Bus Stop 5) for Rs 3.

Nagarkot Tourist buses for Nagarkot left from Thamel at 1.30 pm (Rs 85 one way, Rs 165 return). Tickets were available from most tour agencies and tourist information centres.

Banepa, Dhulikhel & Panauti Regular buses left from the Central Bus Station (Bus Stop 6), took about two hours and cost around Rs 9.

Jiri Buses for this small town (the starting point for the Everest Trek) left between 5.30 and 6.30 am (Rs 98) from the Central Bus Station (Bus Stop 6). You could also take a bus to Lamosangu and change.

Patan Regular buses and minibuses left for central Patan, Lagankhel and Jawlakhel from Ratna Park (Bus Stop 4), took 30 minutes and cost Rs 2. The Lagankhel bus stop in Patan services those towns to the south of Kathmandu (Godavari, Lele and Chapagaon), while buses to Bungamati leave from Jawlakhel. See the Patan map for the stops to these towns.

Godavari Local minibuses and several Sajha Yatayat buses leave from Lagankhel in Patan (one hour, Rs 3.50).

Chapagaon Local minibuses and a Sajha Yatayat bus leave from Lagankhel in Patan (one to 1½ hours, Rs 5).

Bungamati Buses leave from Jawlakhel in Patan (1½ hours, Rs 5).

Pharping & Dakshinkali Ordinary buses to Dakshinkali leave from Martyrs' Gate (Bus Stop 9) on Tuesday and Saturday only and are very crowded (1½ hours, Rs 7). After you pass the police checkpoint on the Ring Rd you can sit on the roof and enjoy the spectacular views. Minibuses run in the mornings, and there are also express buses (one hour, Rs 20). Buses to Pharping run regularly every day; it's a one-km walk to Dakshinkali from Pharphing.

Kirtipur Buses and minibuses departed from Ratna Park (Bus Stop 4) for Rs 3 (45 minutes).

Taxi

Taxis are quite reasonably priced, but fuel prices often rise faster than meters can be recalibrated, so there is frequently a surcharge on top of the meter reading. Tourists will, in any case, be hard-pushed to convince drivers to use their meters (with or without a surcharge) and will almost certainly have to negotiate their fare in advance. Shorter rides around town should come to less than Rs 50 ($1). Between several people, longer trips around the valley, or even outside it, are also affordable. A half-day sightseeing trip within the valley should cost around Rs 450 ($9 or $10), and a full-day trip, Rs 750 ($15 or $16).

Other approximate taxi fares (from Thamel) include:

Pashupatinath	Rs 50
Bodhnath	Rs 60
Patan	Rs 80
Bhaktapur	Rs 175 ($3.50)
Changu Narayan	Rs 300 ($6)
Dhulikhel/Nagarkot	Rs 500 ($10)

For longer journeys outside the valley count on about $50 per day plus fuel, which in 1993 was Rs 28.40 ($0.60) per litre.

Note that in Nepal, real taxis have black licence plates while private cars (many of which operate as taxis but don't have meters) have red plates. If you need a taxi at night call ☎ 224374.

Rickshaw

Metered autorickshaws have become quite common in Kathmandu and cost as little as half of what you would pay for a cab. They're still a bit of a lottery – most will blankly refuse to use the meter and if this is the case make sure you establish a price. Most rides around town should cost less than Rs 30.

Bicycle rickshaws cost Rs 30 to Rs 50 for most rides around town – they can be more expensive than going by autorickshaw or taxi. The tourist rate from Thamel to Durbar

Square is Rs 30, from Thamel to the Hotel de l'Annapurna Rs 16. You must be certain to agree on a price before you start.

Car

Although you cannot rent cars on a drive-yourself basis they can readily be rented with a driver from a number of operators. Try Gorkha Travels (☎ 01-224896) or American Express (☎ 01-223596) in Kathmandu or just go to the alley by Mike's Breakfast, behind the Sherpa Hotel on Durbar Marg. This is the main hang-out for drivers looking for hire by the day.

The rental cost is fairly high both in terms of the initial hiring charge and fuel. Full-day charges are as high $75 a day, although they can be lower, especially if you are not covering a huge distance. Around the valley expect to pay about $65 plus fuel.

Motorbike

There are a number of motorbike rental operators around Freak St and Thamel. You need an international drivers' license and are required to leave a substantial deposit. For Rs 300 ($6) to Rs 350 ($7) per day you'll get a 100 cc Indian-made Honda road bike, and will basically be restricted to the Kathmandu Valley (but also including Daman, Kakani, Nagarkot and Dhulikhel). Think carefully before you do hire, as you will be encouraging the proliferation of noisy, polluting machines and adding to Nepal's trade imbalance. Most reasonably fit people will find that a mountain bike is a better option, especially as you can get to more places.

Bicycle

Once you get away from the crowded streets of central Kathmandu, bicycle riding is a pleasure and if you're in reasonable shape this is the ideal way to explore the valley. It costs from Rs 20 to Rs 30 a day for a regular single-speed Indian or Chinese-made bicycle. Check the brakes before taking it out and be certain to lock it whenever you leave it.

Multigeared mountain bikes have become the current rage in Kathmandu and a number of places around Thamel – at Chhetrapati

Square and Thahiti Tole for example – rent them out. Count on Rs 120 ($2.50) to Rs 150 ($3) a day, which, if you are planning to really explore the valley, is money well spent. It's a real pleasure to surge up the long hill into Patan, effortlessly sweeping by all the riders of regular bikes who have to get off and push.

Tours

There are numerous tour operators in Kathmandu with bus and car tours to all the established tourist sights. Typical costs for half-day tours are Rs 175 ($3.50) to Rs 250 ($5) and if your time is limited this can be a good way of seeing the valley's scattered attractions.

Grayline (☎ 01-412899, 413188) has a wide variety of tours including Bhaktapur to Bodhnath and Pashupatinath on Monday, Wednesday, Friday and Saturday; Patan to Swayambhunath on Sunday, Tuesday and Thursday; Chobar Gorge to Dakshinkali on Tuesday and Saturday; plus dawn trips to Nagarkot, Dhulikhel and Kakani for the Himalayan sunrise.

Kathmandu Travel (☎ 01-224536), Everest Travel Service (☎ 01-222217) and others also operate tours or will arrange them.

Patan

Patan is separated from Kathmandu only by the Bagmati River and is the second-largest town in the valley. It is sometimes referred to as Lalitpur, which means 'city of beauty'. Patan has a long Buddhist history and the four corners of the city are marked by stupas said to have been erected by the great Buddhist emperor Ashoka around 250 BCE. Later inscriptions refer to palaces in the city in the 5th century CE although Patan's great building boom took place under the Mallas in the 16th, 17th and 18th centuries.

Patan's central Durbar Square is absolutely packed with temples: it's an architectural feast with a far greater concentration of

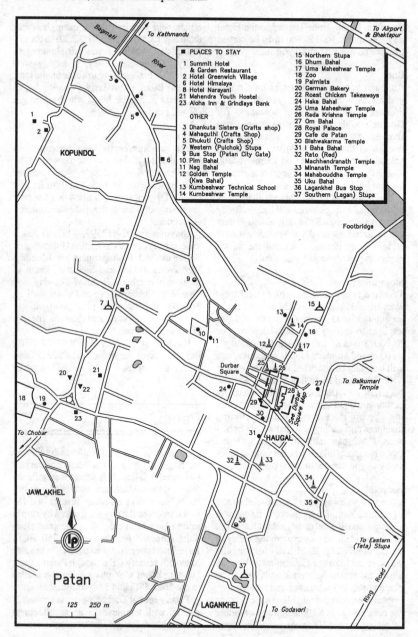

To Kathmandu

Bagmati River

To Airport & Bhaktapur

PLACES TO STAY

1 Summit Hotel & Garden Restaurant
2 Hotel Greenwich Village
6 Hotel Himalaya
8 Hotel Narayani
21 Mahendra Youth Hostel
23 Aloha Inn & Grindlays Bank

OTHER

3 Dhankuta Sisters (Crafts shop)
4 Mahaguthi (Crafts Shop)
5 Dhukuti (Crafts Shop)
7 Western (Pulchok) Stupa
9 Bus Stop (Patan City Gate)
10 Pim Bahal
11 Nag Bahal
12 Golden Temple (Kwa Bahal)
13 Kumbeshwar Technical School
14 Kumbeshwar Temple
15 Northern Stupa
16 Dhum Bahal
17 Uma Maheshwar Temple
18 Zoo
19 Palmists
20 German Bakery
22 Roast Chicken Takeaways
24 Haka Bahal
25 Uma Maheshwar Temple
26 Rada Krishna Temple
27 Om Bahal
28 Royal Palace
29 Cafe de Patan
30 Bishwakarma Temple
31 I Baha Bahal
32 Rato (Red) Machhendranath Temple
33 Minanath Temple
34 Mahabouddha Temple
35 Uku Bahal
36 Lagankhel Bus Stop
37 Southern (Lagan) Stupa

KOPUNDOL

Footbridge

Durbar Square

See Durbar Square Map

To Balkumari Temple

HAUGAL

To Chobar

JAWLAKHEL

Patan

0   125   250 m

LAGANKHEL

To Godavari

To Eastern (Teta) Stupa

Ring Road

temples per sq metre than in Kathmandu or Bhaktapur. Numerous other temples of widely diverse style as well as many bahals (Buddhist monasteries) are scattered around this fascinating town.

Malla Kings
The Malla kings of Patan were responsible for most of the city's great buildings. The Malla kings included:

Jayasthiti Malla	1372-1395
Siddhinarsingh Malla	1620-1661
Srinivasa Malla	1661-1684
Yoganarendra Malla	1684-1705
Vishnu Malla	1729-1745
Rajya Prakash Malla	1745-1758
Visvajita Malla	1758-1760

ORIENTATION & INFORMATION
The Durbar (Palace) Square is the centre of Patan to a greater extent than the equivalent palace squares are to Kathmandu or Bhaktapur. From the square, four main roads lead to the four Ashoka stupas while the city radiates out in concentric circles.

It is possible to stay in Patan, although it's so close to Kathmandu that it scarcely seems worthwhile and the choice of accommodation and restaurants is far more limited than in the capital.

Jawlakhel, to the south of the city, has a major Tibetan population and is the centre for carpet-weaving in the valley.

Buses from Kathmandu drop you at the Patan city gate, about 15 minutes' walk from Durbar Square. There's another, larger bus stop directly south of Durbar Square, near the Lagan (Southern) Stupa. Taxis normally drop you at the square. If you come to Patan by bicycle an interesting route is to take the track down to the river from opposite the big Everest Hotel on the Bhaktapur road. A foot-bridge crosses the river here and you enter Patan by the Northern Stupa near the Kumbeshwar Temple.

DURBAR SQUARE
As in Kathmandu, the ancient Royal Palace of the city faces on to the square, but Patan's Durbar Square is a concentrated mass of temples, undoubtedly the most visually stunning display of Newari architecture to be seen in Nepal. The rectangular square has its longer axis running north-south and the palace forms the eastern side of the square while a continuous row of temples in widely diverse styles face it on the western side.

The square rose to its full glory during the Malla period, and particularly during the reign of King Siddhinarsingh Malla. Patan's major market, the **Mangal Bazaar**, is beside the square.

Bhimsen Temple (3)
At the northern end of Durbar Square the Bhimsen Temple is dedicated to the god of trade and business, which possibly explains its well-kept and prosperous look. Bhimsen, a hero of the *Mahabharata*, was said to be extraordinarily strong. The three-storey temple has had a chequered history.

Bhimsen Temple

Although it is not known when it was first built, an inscription records that it was rebuilt in 1682 after a fire. Restorations also took place in 1934, after the great earthquake which did so much damage throughout the valley, and again in 1967. A lion tops a pillar in front of the temple, while the brick building has an artificial marble facade and a gilded facade on the 1st floor.

Durbar Square
(Patan)

0   15   30 m

Approximate scale

To Bus Stop
To Golden Temple
To Kumbeshwar Temple
Art Galleries
Metalwork Shops
Mani Keshar Chowk
Royal Palace
Mul Chowk
Sundari Chowk
To Cafe de Patan
To Rato Machhendranath Temple
To Mahabouddha Temple

1 Bird Paintings
2 Arjun Art
3 Bhimsen Temple
4 Ganesh Temple
5 Cafe Pagode View
6 Mani Mandap
7 Manga Hiti
8 Vishwanath Temple
9 Garuda Statue on Column
10 Krishna Mandir
11 Third World Crafts & Restaurant
12 Jagannarayan Temple
13 Golden Gate (Sun Dhoka)
14 Vishnu Temple
15 Narsingha Statue
16 King Yoganarendra Malla's Statue
17 Mahaguthi Craft Shop
18 Taleju Temple
19 Hari Shankar Temple
20 Degutaile Temple
21 Bhai Dega Temple
22 Taleju Bell
23 Statue of Ganga
24 Statue of Jamuna
25 Krishna Temple (Chyasim Deval)
26 Narsingha Statue
27 Ganesh Statue
28 Hanuman Statue
29 Taxi Stand

Manga Hiti (7)
Immediately north of the palace is the sunken Manga Hiti, one of the water conduits with which Patan, and even more so Bhaktapur, are so liberally endowed. This one has a lotus-shaped pool and three wonderfully carved stone crocodile-head waterspouts. Next to it is the **Mani Mandap** (6), a pavilion built in 1700 and used for royal crownings.

Vishwanath Temple (10)
Next to the Bhimsen Temple stands the Vishwanath (Shiva) Temple. The elaborately decorated two-storey temple was built in 1627 and has two large stone elephants guarding the front entrance. Shiva's vehicle, the bull, is on the other side of the temple while inside is a large lingam. As yet further proof of Shiva's influence, the roof struts are decorated with erotic themes. The temple has been recently restored.

Krishna Mandir

Vishwanath Temple

Krishna Mandir (11)
Continuing into the square, the third temple you reach is the Krishna Mandir which is dedicated to Krishna and was built by King Siddhinarsingh Malla. Records indicate that the temple was completed with the installation of the image on the 1st floor in 1637. With its strong Moghul influences, this stone temple is clearly of Indian design, unlike the nearby brick and timber, multiroofed Nepalese temples. The 1st and 2nd floors are made up of a line of pavilions from the top of which rises a corncob-like shikhara. Musicians can often be heard playing upstairs.

Krishna is an incarnation of Vishnu so the god's vehicle, the man-bird Garuda, kneels with folded arms on top of a column (9) facing the temple. The stone carvings along the beam above the 1st-floor pillars recount events of the *Mahabharata* while on the 2nd floor there are scenes from the *Ramayana*. These fine friezes are accompanied by explanations of the narrative scenes in Newari.

A major festival is held here in August-September on the occasion of Krishna's birthday, Krishnasthami.

Jagannarayan Temple (12)
The two-storey brick Jagannarayan or Charnarayan Temple is dedicated to Narayan, one of Vishnu's incarnations. It is reputed to be the oldest temple in the square, dating from 1565, although an alternative date in the late 1600s has also been suggested. The temple stands on a brick plinth with large stone lions, above which are two guardian figures. The roof struts are carved with erotic figures.

Jagannarayan Temple

Hari Shankar Temple

King Yoganarendra Malla's Statue (16)
Immediately north of the Jagannarayan Temple, between it and the Krishna Temple, is a tall column topped by a figure of King Yoganarendra Malla. The golden figure of the kneeling king has been facing towards his palace, protected by the hood of a cobra, since the year 1700. On top of the cobra's head is the figure of a bird: legends say that as long as the bird remains there the king may still return to his palace. Accordingly a door and window of the palace is always kept open and a hookah (a water pipe used for smoking) is kept ready for the king should he return. A rider to the legend adds that when the bird flies off, the elephants in front of the Vishwanath Temple will stroll over to the Manga Hiti for a drink!

Other Vishnu Temples
Behind the statue of the king are three smaller Vishnu temples. The small plastered shikhara-style temple was built in 1590 and is dedicated to Narsingha, Vishnu's man-lion incarnation. To one side is a small Narayan temple and behind it another Vishnu temple.

Hari Shankar Temple (19)
This three-storey temple to Hari Shankar, the half Vishnu, half Shiva deity, has roof struts carved with scenes of the tortures of the damned, a strange change from the erotic scenes on the Jagannarayan. It was built in

1704-05 by the daughter of King Yogana-rendra Malla.

Taleju Bell (23)
Diagonally opposite the Taleju Temple (18) in the palace complex, the large bell, hung between two stout pillars, was erected by King Vishnu Malla in 1736. An earlier bell, erected in 1703, was moved to the Rato Machhendranath Temple at that time. Petitioners could ring the bell to alert the king to their grievances. Shop stalls are in the building under the bell platform, and behind it is a lotus-shaped pool with a bridge over it.

Krishna Temple (25)
This attractive octagonal stone temple, also known as the Chyasim Deval, completes the 'front line' of temples in the square. The stairway to the temple, which faces the palace's Sundari Chowk, is guarded by two stone lions. The temple was built by King Vishnu Malla in 1723 and, like the square's Krishna Mandir mentioned earlier, makes a clear contrast with the usual Nepalese pagoda temple designs.

Bhai Dega Temple (21)
Behind the Krishna Temple stands the squat Bhai Dega, or Biseshvar, dedicated to Shiva. It's a singularly unattractive temple although it is said to contain an impressive lingam. A

Krishna Temple

few steps back from the square is another stone shikhara-style temple, clearly owing inspiration to the important Krishna Mandir of the square. This same design pops up in several other temples around Patan. The popular Cafe de Patan is just behind this temple.

ROYAL PALACE

Forming the whole eastern side of the Durbar Square is the Royal Palace of Patan. Parts of the palace were built in the 14th century, but the main period of construction was during the 17th and 18th centuries by Siddhinarsingh Malla, Srinivasa Malla and Vishnu Malla. The Patan palace predates the palaces of Kathmandu and Bhaktapur. It was severely damaged during the conquest of the valley by Prithvi Narayan Shah in 1768 and also by the great earthquake of 1934, but it remains one of the architectural highlights of the valley with a series of connecting courtyards and three temples dedicated to the valley's main deity, the goddess Taleju.

Mul Chowk & the Taleju Temples

The central courtyard is the largest and oldest of the palace's three main *chowks*. Two stone lions guard the entrance to the courtyard which was built by Siddhinarsingh Malla, destroyed in a fire in 1662 and rebuilt by Srinivasa Malla in 1665-66. At the centre of the courtyard stands the small gilded **Bidya Temple**.

The palace's three Taleju temples stand around the courtyard. The doorway to the Shrine of Taleju or **Taleju Bhawani**, on the southern side of the courtyard, is flanked by the river goddesses Ganga on a tortoise and Jamuna on a mythical crocodile or *makara*.

Bhai Dega Temple

Taleju Bhawani

The five-storey **Degutalle Temple**, topped by its circular triple-roofed tower, is on the north-eastern corner. The larger, square, triple-roofed **Taleju Temple** is directly north, looking out over Durbar Square. It was built by Siddhinarsingh Malla in 1640, rebuilt after a fire and totally rebuilt after the earthquake of 1934 which completely demolished it. The goddess Taleju was the personal deity of the Malla kings from the 14th century, and Tantric rites were performed to her in this temple.

Sundari Chowk & Tusha Hiti

South of the larger Mul Chowk is the Sundari Chowk with its sunken tank known as the Tusha Hiti. The superbly carved stonework in the tank depicts the eight Ashta Matrikas, the eight Bhairabs and the eight Nagas. The tank was originally built in about 1670 and restored in 1960. A toy-size replica of the Krishna Mandir in the main square sits above the tank.

The courtyard is surrounded by a three-storey building with finely carved struts and windows. The entrance to the courtyard from the main square is guarded by stone statues of Hanuman (28), Ganesh (27), and Vishnu as Narsingha, the man-lion (26). The gilded metal window over the entrance from the square is flanked by windows of carved ivory. Behind the Sundari Chowk, but unfortunately not open to the public, is the Royal Garden with a water tank known as the Kamal Pokhari.

Mani Keshar Chowk

The northern courtyard is entered from the square by the Golden Gate, or Sun Dhoka. This is the newest part of the palace, its construction was completed in 1734. The courtyard is entered through a magnificent gilded door topped by a golden torana showing Shiva, Parvati, Ganesh and Kumar. Directly above the golden door is a golden window, at which the king would make public appearances.

There is another courtyard reached by a passage between the Mani Keshar Chowk and the Taleju Temple but this is not open to the public. It was used for dance and drama performances during the Malla period and one wall is decorated with erotic figures.

GOLDEN TEMPLE

Also known as the the Kwa Bahal, Hiranya Varna Mahavihar, or the Suwarna Mahavihara (Golden Temple), this unique Buddhist monastery is only a few minutes' walk north of Durbar Square. Legends relate that the monastery was founded in the 12th century although the earliest record of its existence is 1409. From the street a sign points to the monastery which is entered through a doorway flanked by painted guardian lion figures. The simple entrance gives no hint of the magnificent structure in the courtyard within.

The large rectangular building has three roofs and a copper-gilded facade. Inside the shrine are images of the Buddha and Avalokitesvara and a stairway leads to the 1st floor where monks will show you the various Buddha images and frescoes which illustrate the walls. The life of the Buddha is illustrated in a frieze in front of the main shrine.

The inner courtyard has a railed walkway around three sides. Leather shoes and other leather articles must be removed if you leave the walkway and enter the actual inner courtyard. In the centre of the courtyard is a small but very richly decorated three-storey temple crowned by a golden roof with an extremely ornate *gajur* (a bell-shaped top). Look for the sacred tortoises who potter around in the courtyard, they are temple guardians. The monastery was dedicated by a Patan merchant, grown rich from the important trade with Tibet.

KUMBESHWAR TEMPLE

Directly north of Durbar Square is one of the valley's three five-storey temples. The others are the towering Nyatapola Temple of Bhaktapur and the smaller Panch Mukhi Hanuman of the old Royal Palace in Kathmandu.

The Kumbeshwar Temple dominates the streets around it and is said to date from 1392, when it was completed by Jayasthiti

Malla, making it the oldest extant temple in Patan. The temple is noted for its fine proportions and elegant woodcarvings and there are numerous statues and sculptures around the courtyard dating from a number of Nepalese dynasties from the Licchavis to the Mallas. They include a particularly fine Ganesh figure and others of Ganesh and other Hindu deities. The temple is, however, dedicated to Shiva, as the large Nandi, or bull, facing the temple inside the main entrance indicates.

Kumbeshwar Temple

The temple platform has two ponds whose water is said to come straight from the holy lake at Gosainkund, a long trek north of the valley (see the Trekking chapter). An annual ritual bath in the Kumbeshwar Temple's tank is claimed to be as meritorious as making the arduous walk to Gosainkund.

South of the courtyard is an important **Bhairab temple** with a life-size wooden image of the god. Also on the southern side of the Kumbeshwar Temple is the single-storey **Baglamukhi Temple** where the goddess is represented by the small temple's gilded archway with its canopy of snakes. On the western side of the Kumbeshwar Temple courtyard is the large **Konti Hiti tank**, a popular gathering place for local women.

Also on the western side, the Kumbeshwar Technical School, which was established to give training to local untouchables, sells very good value carpets and woollen jumpers. They do not have a formal outlet, but there is a small display area on the ground floor of the school.

Thousands of pilgrims visit the temple during the Janai Purnima festival in July and August each year to worship the silver and gold lingam which is set up in the tank. It's a colourful occasion with bathers immersing themselves in the tank while members of the Brahman and Chhetri castes replace the sacred thread they wear looped across their left shoulder. Jhankris (sorcerers) beating drums and wearing colourful headdresses and skirts dance around the temple to complete the dramatic scene.

UMA MAHESHWAR TEMPLE

There are a number of other interesting temples and bahals in this northern area of Patan. Returning from the Kumbeshwar Temple to Durbar Square the small and inconspicuous double-roofed Uma Maheshwar Temple is set back from the road on its eastern side. Peer inside the temple where you will see (a light will help) a very beautiful black-stone relief of Shiva and Parvati in the pose known as Uma Maheshwar – the god sitting cross-legged with his shakti leaning against him rather seductively.

BISHWAKARMA TEMPLE

Walk south from Durbar Square through the Hauga area with its many brassware shops and workshops. There is a small bahal almost immediately on your right (west) and then a laneway also leading west. A short distance down this lane is the brick Bishwakarma Temple, with its entire facade covered in sheets of embossed copper. Directly above the doorway is what looks like a Star of David. The temple is dedicated to carpenters and craftworkers and, as if in proof, you can hear the steady clump and clang from metalworkers' hammers in nearby workshops.

Returning to the main road running south from Durbar Square you soon come to a chaitya shrine of Lakshmi Narayan on the eastern side of the road and the **I Baha Bahil monastery** on the western side. The monastery dates from 1427 but is now rather run-down and decrepit; part of it is being used as a school. A little further south is the old but recently restored **Chakba Lunhiti tank** with three waterspouts.

Bishwakarma Temple

RATO MACHHENDRANATH TEMPLE
Continue south from Durbar Square for a few more minutes' walk to the Rato (Red) Machhendranath Temple, on the western side of the road. Rato Machhendranath, the god of rain and plenty, comes in a variety of incarnations. To Buddhists he is the Tantric edition of Avalokitesvara while to Hindus he is another version of Shiva.

Standing in a large, spacious courtyard the three-storey temple dates from 1673 although an earlier temple may have existed on the site since 1408. The temple's four elaborately carved doorways are each

guarded by lion figures and at ground level on the four corners of the temple plinth are reliefs of a curious yeti-like creature. A diverse collection of animals (including peacocks, horses, bulls, lions, elephants and fish) top the pillars facing the northern side of the temple; they are the Tibetan symbols for the months of the year. The metal roof is supported by struts each showing Avalokitesvara standing above figures being tortured in hell. Prayer wheels are set into the base of the temple.

The Machhendranath image is just a crudely carved piece of red-painted wood, but each year during the Red Machhendranath celebrations it is paraded around the town on a temple chariot. The complex celebration moves the image from place to place over a period of several weeks in the month of Baisakh (April-May), finally ending at Jawlakhel where the chariot is disassembled.

Occurring on a 12-year cycle (the next time will be in 2003) the procession continues out of Patan to the village of Bungamati, five km to the south. Dragging the heavy chariot along this bumpy and often uphill track is no easy feat. In the village the god

Rato Machhendranath Temple

has another temple where, since 1593 it has been the custom for the image to spend six months of each year. The chariot is returned to Patan (usually on a palanquin) for the other six months.

MINANATH TEMPLE

To the eastern side of the main road from Durbar Square is a two-storey temple dedicated to a Buddhist Bodhisattva who is considered to be the brother of Rato Machhendranath. The Minanath image is also towed around town during the Rato Machhendranath chariot festival, but in a much smaller chariot. The temple originally dates from the Licchavi period but has undergone several recent restorations and 'improvements' and has roof struts carved with figures of multiarmed goddesses, all extraordinarily brightly painted. A large prayer wheel stands in a cage beside the temple.

Minanath Temple

MAHABOUDDHA TEMPLE

Despite its height, the Temple of the Thousand Buddhas, or Mahabouddha Temple, is not immediately visible because it is tightly surrounded by other buildings. It is a shikhara-style temple, modelled after the original Mahabouddha Temple at Bodhgaya

in India, where the Buddha gained enlightenment. At Pagan in Myanmar (Burma) there's another Mahabouddha Temple, which is also a copy of the Bodhgaya original.

Mahabouddha Temple

The temple takes its name from the terracotta tiles with which it is covered, each bearing an image of the Buddha. The temple is believed to have originally been built in 1585 although some sources suggest an earlier date. Whatever its first construction, it suffered severe damage in the 1934 earthquake and was completely rebuilt. Unfortunately, without plans to work from, the rebuilders ended up with a rather different-looking Mahabouddha Temple and there were enough bricks left over to construct a smaller shikhara-style shrine to Maya Devi, the Buddha's mother. It stands to the southwest of the Mahabouddha.

The Mahabouddha Temple is about 10 minutes' walk south-west of Durbar Square.

An arrow signpost points down a lane full of curio shops leading to the temple, but if you have trouble finding it simply ask directions. The roof terrace of the shops at the back of the courtyard gives you a good view of the temple.

RUDRA VARNA MAHAVIHARA

Also known as Uku Bahal, this Buddhist monastery near the Mahabouddha Temple is one of the best known in Patan. A large rectangular structure with two-storey gilded roofs encloses a courtyard absolutely packed with interesting bits and pieces. There are dorjes, bells, banners, peacocks, elephants, Garudas, rampant goats, kneeling devotees and a regal-looking statue of a Rana general. The lions are particularly curious – apart from regular Nepalese ones, seated on pillars with one paw raised in salute, there are also a couple with a decidedly British appearance, looking as if they should be guarding a statue of Queen Victoria in her 'not amused' incarnation rather than a colourful Nepalese monastery.

As you enter the courtyard look for the exceptionally finely carved wooden struts on the right. They are said to be amongst the oldest of this type in the valley and prior to a recent restoration they were actually behind the monastery but were moved to this safer location inside the courtyard. The monastery in its present form probably dates from the 19th century, but certain features and the actual site are much older.

HAKA BAHAL

Take the road west from the southern end of the Durbar Square, past the Cafe de Patan, and you soon come to the Haka Bahal, a typical rectangular building with an internal courtyard. Traditionally, Patan's Kumari (living goddess), is a daughter of one of the priests of this monastery.

ASHOKAN STUPAS

The four stupas marking the boundaries of Patan are said to have been built when the great Buddhist emperor Ashoka visited the valley 2500 years ago. Although remains of all four can still be seen today they probably bear little similarity to the original stupas. The Northern Stupa is just beyond the Kumbeshwar Temple, not far from the Durbar Square. It's well preserved and whitewashed. The other three are all grassed over. The Southern, or Lagan, Stupa is just south of the bus stand and is the largest of the four. The smaller Western, or Pulchok, Stupa is beside the main road from Kathmandu through to Jawlakhel and directly opposite the Narayani Hotel. Finally, and most remote, the small Eastern, or Teta, Stupa is well to the east of centre, across the Ring Rd and just beyond a small river.

ZOO

Nepal's only zoo is in the southern part of Patan, just north of Jawlakhel. It includes a reasonably extensive collection of Nepalese wildlife, including rhinos, tigers, leopards, monkeys and birds. It is yet another depressing and miserable animal prison, but the saddest thing you can say is that there are many others that are considerably worse.

Keen naturalists and students of the grotesque may still enjoy a visit – admission is only Rs 10. Palm readers and their clients gather in the dusty park in front of the zoo entrance and, amongst other things, may well be able to tell you which animal you will be when you are reincarnated.

JAWLAKHEL

The 'Tibetan Refugee Camp' is no longer really a camp at all, but a large centre for carpet production. It was established in 1960 with help from the International Red Cross and the Swiss government and employs 1000 refugees in the production of Tibetan carpets. This is where the enormous carpet industry of today got its start, and it is still the best place to begin if you want to buy a carpet yourself.

You may well be able to buy cheaper outside the camp, but the carpets in the shops by the entrance have marked prices so you can get a good idea of values (other Tibetan crafts are also on sale). You can also go inside to the workshop area and see the carpets being made. The road outside the centre is lined with carpet shops, and further up the hill, back towards Patan, is Khukuri House, a shop front for the official supplier of khukuri knives to the British Gurkha regiments.

KOTESHWAR MAHADEV TEMPLE
Actually outside the Patan city limits, the important temple of Koteshwar Mahadev is just north of the confluence of the Manohara and Hanumante rivers, which in turn joins the Bagmati River. Mahadev means 'great god', the usual term for Shiva, but Koteshwar can also be translated as 'millions of gods' so this is a temple of Shiva with many faces, a particularly powerful form of Lord Shiva. The shrine's Shiva lingam is said to date from the 8th century.

A little south of the temple is the **Kuti Bahal** where travellers bound for Tibet were customarily farewelled. The monastery has a 15th-century chaitya.

PLACES TO STAY
Apart from Nepal's only youth hostel, Patan's accommodation consists of middle-range and top-end places. Some overseas aid agencies are in Patan, particularly around Jawlakhel, and many long-term foreign residents of Nepal live here.

Places to Stay – bottom end
In the Jawlakhel area of Patan, the *Mahendra Youth Hostel* (☎ 01-521003) is the only youth hostel in Nepal, with 72 dorm beds at Rs 25. The dorms are clean and it's a peaceful area, but the hostel is a long way from the bright lights and big-city atmosphere of Thamel. It's open from 7 am to 10 pm in winter, 6 am to 10.30 pm in summer.

Right in the centre of Patan, a short walk from Durbar Square, the popular *Cafe de Patan* has added rooms to its menu. The position is excellent, and the rooms are pleasant, although a little overpriced. Clean singles/doubles with shared bathroom are Rs 250/300 ($5/6).

Places to Stay – middle
Patan has a popular mid-range hotel if you'd like a complete break from Kathmandu, although none of Patan's accommodation is that close to the centre of the old town. The *Aloha Inn* (☎ 01-522796) is in the Jawlakhel area, not too far from the southern edge of the old city. Rooms here are $20/28 plus 12% tax. The name is certainly a strange one for Nepal but it's a friendly place, clean, well kept and quiet, and is popular with people working at the aid agencies in the area. There's a very pleasant garden.

Places to Stay – top end
Patan now has a number of top-end hotels although none of them are close enough to the interesting centre of the old city to be really convenient. Two hotels are found very close to the UN office in Kopundol.

The *Summit Hotel* (☎ 01-521810; fax 523737) tops a hillock in the Kopundol area and has great views across the river to Kathmandu and the distant mountains. There's a very beautiful garden with a swimming pool – a real pleasure in hot weather. The Summit Hotel's inconvenient location is its only drawback; finding taxis can sometimes be difficult and taxi drivers can be reluctant to take you there without extra payment. Standard singles/doubles cost $60/75, while newer rooms are $70/80, all plus 12%. There's a pleasant bar and the Summit's Garden Restaurant turns out superb food, so the fact that you're a long way from the restaurants of Kathmandu is no hardship.

Also topping the Kopundol hill is the nearby *Hotel Greenwich Village* (☎ 01-521780, 522399) with singles at $40 and doubles from $50 to $60, which really puts it more in the middle price range. There's a top-floor restaurant to take advantage of the view.

Two other Patan hotels are more distinctly in the top-end price bracket. The *Hotel Narayani* (☎ 01-525015) has a garden, a swimming pool and singles/doubles at $70/85, plus 14% tax. The new *Hotel Himalaya* (☎ 01-523900) has terrific views, a swimming pool, tennis and badminton courts and is at the top of the Kathmandu price range with rooms from $85/100 plus 14%.

PLACES TO EAT

Just a few steps from the south-western corner of Patan's Durbar Square the small *Cafe de Patan* (☎ 01-525499) is a long-running favourite with two pleasant open-air dining areas – a small courtyard and a rooftop garden. It's a good place for a drink, snack or even a meal. It turns out a superb lassi and a number of good-value dishes from Rs 25 to Rs 50. See the following Things to Buy section about the music you hear with your meal. A little shop just across the alley sells delicious yoghurt in little clay cups for Rs 6.

Overlooking the square, the pleasant, nicely decorated *Third World Restaurant* has a brilliant rooftop area with views over Patan and on a clear day, pagodas with a Himalayan backdrop. Snacks are around Rs 40, burgers, pastas and sandwiches around Rs 60.

The *Cafe Pagode View* looks directly onto the square, but is tucked off the least interesting corner. Still, there's plenty to watch while you enjoy a drink or meal. The food is OK, and they have standard meals including pizza for Rs 60 and sandwiches for Rs 30.

Near the zoo roundabout at Jawlakhel the *German Bakery* does cakes, pastries, cold drinks and sandwiches. Across the road is the rather ordinary *Blue Fox Tiffin Room*. At the city gate, by the Patan bus stop, the *RM Momo Restaurant*, the *Cake & Coffee Corner*, the *Dorje Restaurant* and the *Yeti Restaurant* are other rather basic possibilities.

THINGS TO BUY

Patan has many small handcraft shops and for certain crafts it is the best place in the valley. The Tibetan Jawlakhel area in the south of Patan is the place for Tibetan crafts and carpets. There is a string of carpet shops as you enter Jawlakhel, and a shop front, Khukuri House, for the official supplier of khukuri knives to the British gurkha regiments.

Those interested in crafts should definitely visit the string of interesting shops at Kupandol, just to the south of the main Patan bridge. A number are run as part of nonprofit-making development organisations, so their prices are fair, and the money actually goes to the craftspeople, sometimes in the form of training and product development.

One of the best of these organisations is Mahaguthi, which was established with the help of Oxfam. It now has three shops and it sells a wide range of crafts produced by thousands of people. Amongst other things they sell beautiful handwoven cotton cloth *(dhaka)*, rice paper, pottery, block prints, woven bamboo, woodcrafts, jewellery, knitwear, embroidery and Mithila paintings. The Kupandol shop is on the right as you go up the hill, but there are also shops on Durbar Square, Patan, and on Durbar Marg, Kathmandu, towards the Royal Palace from the Hotel de l'Annapurna.

Further down the hill, nearer the bridge, Dhankuta Sisters is an outlet for women from the eastern hills. Their specialities are dhaka, and clothes. On the other side of the street to Mahaguthi is Dhukuti, a similar organisation, but working mainly with low-income women. Their specialities are textiles and paper products.

Actually in Patan, near the well-known Kumbeshwar Temple, the Kumbeshwar Technical School was established to help provide the untouchable community of Patan with skills. They now produce excellent carpets, jumpers and woodwork. You can buy direct, although they do not have a formal outlet.

Metalwork

Patan is the centre for bronze-casting and other metalwork. The statues you see on sale in Kathmandu will most probably have been made in Patan and there are a number of excellent metalwork shops just north of Durbar Square. They have fine images of Buddha, the Green and White Taras and other figures from the Tantric Buddhist pantheon. Good-quality gold plated and painted bronze figures will cost Rs 2000 ($40) to Rs 5000 ($100) for smaller ones, up to more than Rs 10,000 ($200) for large images.

Woodcarving
There are numerous shops around Bhaktapur, particularly around Tachupal Tole. Lee Berch (☎ 01-522627), PO Box 2633, Kathmandu, operates a woodcarving atelier in Jawlakhel, Patan, which could be of interest to serious aficionados.

Paintings
Immediately north of the square, just beyond the Bhimsen Temple, are a number of interesting shops selling paintings. The Arjun Art Gallery has Sherpa-style paintings rather like the naive art of the Balinese 'young artist'. It's clearly something developed for the tourist trade but never mind, they're nicely done and you can have all of the Kathmandu Valley, or even all of Nepal, in one painting. Prices range from around Rs 2000 ($40) to Rs 4000 ($80).

A couple of doors down is the Madhu Chandra Art Gallery which has excellent paintings of Nepalese birds by CB Singh. The prices range from Rs 300 ($6) or Rs 400 ($8) and up. The BB Thapa Gallery (☎ 01-270567) in Jawlakhel also has interesting artwork.

Carpets
Those interested in carpets must visit Jawlakhel, on the outskirts of Patan, and Bodhnath. The Tibetan 'Refugee Camp' at Jawlakhel is the best place to start, and there are numerous shops on the approach road where you can try your bargaining skills. The carpets at the Kumbeshwar Technical School (near the Kumbeshwar Temple) are fairly priced, and this is, as far as I know, the only place where you can buy carpets made from 100% pure Tibetan wool.

Toys
Just south of Patan's Durbar Square is Nepalese Wooden Kits, which sells wonderful wooden toys including authentic Nepalese trucks from Rs 475 to Rs 630 ($9.50 to $12.50), autorickshaws for Rs 380 ($7.50) and rickshaws for Rs 350 ($7). You can find these toys on sale in Kathmandu (including some of the craft shops), but they're cheaper here where they're made. The factory is only a stone's throw from the shop and it's fascinating to see the parts being cut out with pedal-operated jigsaws.

Music
A pleasant attraction at the popular Cafe de Patan near Durbar Square is the selection of Indian, Nepalese and Himalayan music played on cassette tapes while you eat. The tapes are sold by the adjoining shop and typically cost around $3 so if you like the music you hear with your meal you can take it away with you.

GETTING THERE & AWAY
You can easily get to Patan from Kathmandu whether it be by bicycle, taxi, bus or tempo. It's an easy five-km ride from Thamel to Patan's Durbar Square. The same trip will cost around Rs 80 by taxi, less if it uses its meter.

Before the Kathmandu Bus Terminal opened in 1992, buses left regularly from Ratna Park (Bus Stop 4) and dropped you at the Patan city gate, a short walk from the Durbar Square (Rs 2). Tempos also operate from the Kathmandu main post office as soon as they have six passengers.

Bhaktapur

Bhaktapur, also known as Bhadgaon (pronounced 'bat-gown') or the City of Devotees, is the third major town of the valley and in many ways the most mediaeval. Since the major West German-funded Bhaktapur Development Project in the 1970s, it has been a much cleaner and tidier town, but there's still a distinctly timeless air to the place. The project not only restored buildings and paved dirt streets but also brought sewerage facilities.

The oldest part of the town is around Tachupal Tole (Dattatraya Square), to the east of the town. Bhaktapur was the capital of the whole valley during the 14th to 16th centuries and during that time the focus of the town shifted west, to the Durbar Square area. Much of the town's great architecture dates from the end of the 17th century during the rule of King Bhupatindra Malla.

Malla Kings

As in Kathmandu and Patan, the town's important buildings date from the Malla period. Notable Malla kings of Bhaktapur include:

Yaksha Malla	1428-1482
Raya Malla	1482-1505
Eksha Mal Malla	1505-1568
Jagat Jyoti Malla	1613-1637
Jagat Prakash Malla	1644-1673
Jitamitra Malla	1673-1696
Bhupatindra Malla	1696-1722
Jaya Ranjit Malla	1722-1769

Ranjit Malla enjoyed a relationship with King Prithvi Narayan Shah which saved his city from destruction and also resulted in the deposed Malla kings of Kathmandu and Patan taking shelter here.

ORIENTATION & INFORMATION

Bhaktapur rises up on the northern bank of the Hanumante River. Although you can drive through Bhaktapur, thankfully most cars don't. It's basically a pedestrian's city and much better for it. Minibuses and taxis stop at the Navpokhu Pokhari on the western edge of town. If you come to Bhaktapur by trolley bus the stop is on the main road bypassing Bhaktapur, a 10 to 15-minute walk south of Taumadhi Tole.

For the visitor Bhaktapur is really a town of one curving road, punctuated by squares. From the bus and taxi halt you come first to the Durbar Square, then Taumadhi Tole with the famous five-storey Nyatapola Temple, then to Tachupal Tole, or Dattatraya Square. Keep walking in that direction and you'll eventually reach Nagarkot, high up on the edge of the valley.

Bhaktapur has several cheap guest houses around the centre of town and it's a fascinating place to stay overnight. There's a tourist information counter in Durbar Square.

NAVPOKHU POKHARI TO TOWN

Approaching Bhaktapur the road skirts an open field (also known as the Tundikhel) and the **Siddha Pokhari tank**. From the large Navpokhu Pokhari tank you simply follow the road a few hundred metres to Durbar Square. If you're staying overnight in Bhaktapur you'll want to get into town as quickly as possible to drop off your bags, but if you're not staying overnight, the southern route into town is much more interesting since it is the main road through Bhaktapur connecting Taumadhi Tole and Tachupal Tole.

Turn south from the corner of Navpokhu Pokhari and then left on the road, immediately before the town's Lion Gate. You pass a small tank on your right and then the much larger **Teka Pokhari**. Just before the next major road junction, to your left, is the constricted, tunnel-like entrance to the tiny **Ni Bahal**, dedicated to the Maitraya Buddha, the Buddha yet to come.

Cross the junction, where the road runs downhill to the **Mangal Tirtha Ghat**, and on your left is the red-brick **Jaya Varahi Temple**, jutting into the street. There are elaborately carved wooden toranas over the central door and the window above it. The

Jaya Varahi Temple

duits of which there are so many in Bhaktapur. A few more steps brings you to the turn-off to Potters' Square while a little further on you come to Taumadhi Tole.

DURBAR SQUARE

Bhaktapur's Durbar Square is much larger and more spacious than Kathmandu's and much less crowded with temples than Patan's. It wasn't planned that way: Victorian illustrations show the square packed with temples and buildings, but the disastrous earthquake of 1934 destroyed many of them and today empty plinths show where some of them once stood.

Erotic Elephants Temple (2)

Just before you enter the square, coming from the bus stop, pause for a little bit of Newari humour. On your left just before the entranceway to the square is a hiti. A few steps before that, but on the south side of the road, perhaps 100 metres before the entranceway, is a tiny double-roofed Shiva-Parvati temple with some erotic carvings on its temple struts. One of these shows a pair of copulating elephants, in the missionary position! It's a hathi (elephant) Kama Sutra.

Ugrachandi & Bhairab Statues

The square is entered from the western end, passing by an entry gate (5) with two large stone lions built by King Bhupatindra Malla. On the northern wall are statues (6) of the terrible Bhairab and the equally terrible Ugrachandi, or Durga, the fearsome manifestation of Shiva's consort Parvati. The statues date from 1701 and it's said that the unfortunate sculptor had his hands cut off afterwards, to prevent him from duplicating his masterpieces.

Ugrachandi has 18 arms holding various weapons and symbols and she is in the act of very casually killing a demon with a trident. Bhairab has to make do with just 12 arms but the god and goddess are both garlanded with necklaces of human heads! The gates and courtyard which these powerful figures guard are of no particular importance.

upper torana shows Vishnu in his boar incarnation, to whom the temple is dedicated. At the western end of the temple is the entrance to the upper floor, flanked by stone lions and banners. The ornate windows include two, on either side of the upper torana, which at one time were coloured gold and some traces remain.

A few more steps brings you to a small Ganesh shrine jutting out into the street. Continue to **Nasamana Square**, which is somewhat decrepit but has a Garuda statue without a temple. Almost immediately after this is a second square with the Jyotirlingeshwar, a shikhara-style temple which houses an important lingam. Behind the shrine is an attractive hiti, one of the sunken water con-

Bhaktapur

0   100   200 m

Navpokhu
Pokhari

Walking
Tour

Royal
Palace

Durbar
Square

See Durbar Square &
Taumadhi Tole Map

To Kathmandu
(13.5 km)

Tank

Teka
Pokhari

Taumadhi
Tole

Nasamana
Square

Potters'
Square

Mangal Tirtha
Ghat

Ram Ghat

Chuping
Ghat

Hanumante
River

To Kathmandu
(13 km)

To Surjya Binayak
Temple

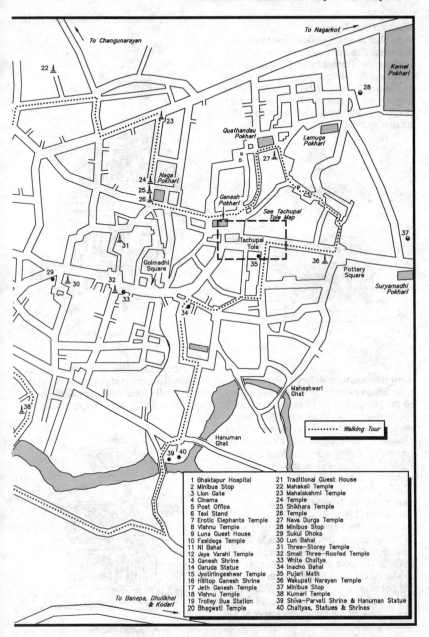

1 Bhaktapur Hospital	21 Traditional Guest House
2 Minibus Stop	22 Mahakali Temple
3 Lion Gate	23 Mahalakshmi Temple
4 Cinema	24 Temple
5 Post Office	25 Shikhara Temple
6 Taxi Stand	26 Temple
7 Erotic Elephants Temple	27 Nava Durga Temple
8 Vishnu Temple	28 Minibus Stop
9 Luna Guest House	29 Sukul Dhoka
10 Fasidega Temple	30 Lun Bahal
11 Ni Bahal	31 Three-Storey Temple
12 Jaya Varahi Temple	32 Small Three-Roofed Temple
13 Ganesh Shrine	33 White Chaitya
14 Garuda Statue	34 Inacho Bahal
15 Jyotirlingeshwar Temple	35 Pujari Math
16 Hilltop Ganesh Shrine	36 Wakupati Narayan Temple
17 Jeth Ganesh Temple	37 Minibus Stop
18 Vishnu Temple	38 Kumari Temple
19 Trolley Bus Station	39 Shiva-Parvati Shrine & Hanuman Statue
20 Bhagwati Temple	40 Chaityas, Statues & Shrines

Western End Temples

A number of less significant temples crowd the western end of the Durbar Square. They include the **Rameshwar Temple** (7) to Shiva and the **Bhadri Temple** (8) to Vishnu as Narayan. In front of them is an impressive larger **Krishna temple** (9) and just beyond that is a shikhara-style **Shiva temple** (10) erected by King Jitamitra Malla in 1674.

Vatsala Durga Temple

Krishna temple

King Bhupatindra Malla's Column (12)

King Bhupatindra Malla was the best known of the Malla kings of Bhaktapur and had a great influence on the art and architecture of the town. Like the similar column in Patan's Durbar Square this one was a copy of the original in Kathmandu. The king sits with folded arms, studying the magnificent entrance gate to his palace.

Vatsala Durga Temple (22) &
Taleju Bell (13)

Beside the king's statue and directly in front of the palace is the stone Vatsala Durga Temple, built by King Jagat Prakash Malla in 1672. The shikhara-style temple has some similarities to the Krishna Mandir in Patan. In front of the temple is the large Taleju Bell which was erected by King Jaya Ranjit Malla in 1737 to call the faithful to prayer at the Taleju Temple.

A second, smaller bell stands on the temple's plinth and is popularly known as the 'barking bell'. It was erected by King Bhupatindra Malla in 1721, supposedly to counteract

Chyasilin Mandapa

Durbar Square & Taumadhi Tole (Bhaktapur)

0   25   50 m

1 Shiva–Parvati Temple
2 Erotic Elephants Temple
3 Shiva Temple
4 House of a Malla Prince
5 Durbar Square Gate
6 Ugrachandi & Bhairab Statues
7 Rameshwar Temple
8 Bhadri Temple
9 Krishna Temple
10 Shiva Temple
11 Art Gallery
12 King Bhupatindra Malla's Column
13 Taleju Bell
14 Golden Gate (Sun Dhoka)
15 55 Window Palace
16 Vatsala Temple
17 Fasidega Temple
18 Stone Lions
19 Tadhunchen Bahal
20 Siddhi Lakshmi Temple
21 Chyasilin Mandapa
22 Vatsala Durga Temple
23 Water Tank
24 Pashupatinath Temple
25 Shiva Inn
26 Golden Gate Guest House
27 Marco Polo Restaurant
28 Nyatapola Temple
29 Bhairabnath Temple
30 Nyatapola Cafe
31 Dabu (Dance Platform)
32 Lun Hiti
33 Jagannath Temple
34 Shiva Shrine
35 Til Mahadev Narayan Temple

a vision he had in a dream, and to this day dogs are said to bark and whine if the bell is rung.

Chyasilin Mandapa (21)

Beside the Vatsala Durga Temple is an attractive water tank (23) and in front of that is the Chyasilin Mandapa. This octagonal temple was one of the finest in the square until it was destroyed by the 1934 earthquake. Using some of the temple's original components it has been totally rebuilt. There's a good view over the square from inside – not the metal construction inside this outwardly authentic building.

Siddhi Lakshmi Temple (20)

By the south-eastern corner of the palace stands the stone Siddhi Lakshmi Temple. The steps up to the temple are flanked by male and female attendants each leading a rather reluctant child and a rather eager-looking dog. On successive levels the stairs are flanked by horses, rhinos, man-lions and camels. The 17th-century temple marks the dividing line between the main Durbar Square and its secondary part, at the eastern end of the Royal Palace. Behind the temple is another **Vatsala temple** (16) while to one side of it are two rather lost-looking large

Siddhi Lakshmi Temple

stone lions (18), standing by themselves out in the middle of the square.

Pashupatinath Temple (24)
Behind the Vatsala Durga Temple is the Pashupatinath Temple, dedicated to Shiva as Pashupati. The temple dates from the 17th century and is a replica of the main shrine at Pashupatinath. It's notable for the erotic carvings on the roof struts which show some exhausting-looking positions.

Fasidega Temple (17)
The large, white, rather ugly Fasidega Temple is dedicated to Shiva and stands in the centre of the secondary part of the Durbar Square. There are various viewpoints around the valley – the Changu Narayan Temple is one of them – from where you can study Bhaktapur at a distance. In each case the white bulk of the Fasidega is always an easy landmark to pick out. The temple sits on a six-level plinth with elephant guardians at the bottom of the steps, lions and cows above them.

Fasidega Temple

Tadhunchen Bahal (19)
The southern and eastern side of the secondary part of the square is made up of double-storey *dharamsalas* (rest houses for pilgrims) now used as shops. As you enter the street leading east from the square, the Tadhunchen Bahal or Chatur Varna Mahavihara is an ancient-looking monastery on the southern side. In the inner courtyard the roof struts on the eastern side have some highly unusual carvings showing the tortures of the damned. In one a snake is wrapped around a man, another shows two rams butting an unfortunate's head from opposite sides while a third strut shows a nasty tooth extraction being performed with a large pair

Pashupatinath Temple

of pliers! The monastery dates from the 15th century.

ROYAL PALACE

Bhaktapur's Royal Palace was founded by Yaksha Malla and added to by successive kings, particularly Bhupatindra Malla. As with the old palaces of Kathmandu and Patan, visitors are restricted to certain areas, but only seven courtyards remain of the 99 the palace was once claimed to have. Unfortunately the palace suffered great damage in the 1934 earthquake and its subsequent reconstruction did not match its original artistry.

Art Gallery (11)

The western end of the palace has been made into an art gallery. The entrance to the gallery is flanked by figures of Hanuman the

Hanuman-Bhairab

monkey god and Vishnu as Narsingha, his man-lion incarnation. These guardian figures date from 1698 and Hanuman appears in Tantric form as the four-armed Hanuman-Bhairab. The gallery has a fine collection of Hindu and Buddhist paintings, palm-leaf manuscripts, thangkas and metal, stone and woodcrafts. This part of the palace was once known as the Malati Chowk. Admission to the gallery is Rs 5 and it is open from 10.30 am to 4 pm daily except Tuesdays.

Golden Gate (14) & 55 Window Palace (15)

Adjoining the gallery the magnificent Golden Gate, or Sun Dhoka, is the entrance to the 55 Window Palace. The Golden Gate is generally agreed to be the single most important piece of art in the whole valley. The gate and palace were built by King Bhupatindra Malla but not completed until 1754 during the reign of Jaya Ranjit Malla.

A Garuda, the vehicle of Vishnu, tops the gate and is shown disposing of a number of serpents, the Garuda's sworn enemies. The four-headed and 16-armed figure of the goddess Taleju Bhawani is below the Garuda and directly over the door. She is the family deity of the Malla dynasty and there are temples to her in the royal palaces in Kathmandu, Patan and Bhaktapur.

The Golden Gate opens to the inner courtyards of the palace. First you enter a small entrance courtyard then the larger **Mul Chowk** which leads round to the **Taleju Chowk** entrance. Unfortunately you cannot enter Taleju Chowk and a military guard ensures you don't try. The guard will, however, invite you to peer in from the doorway. Beyond Taleju Chowk is **Kumari Chowk** and **Sundari Chowk** with its bathing tank, the Kamal Pokhari.

TAUMADHI TOLE

A short street, lined with tourist shops, leads downhill from behind the Pashupatinath Temple in Durbar Square to the second great square of Bhaktapur, the Taumadhi Tole. Here you find the highest temple in the valley and also Cafe Nyatapola whose balconies provide a great view over the square. The building was renovated for its new purpose in 1977 and even has some finely carved roof struts with erotic themes.

Nyatapola Temple (28)

The five-storey, 30-metre-high Nyatapola Temple is not only the highest temple in the whole Kathmandu Valley, but also one of the best examples of traditional Nepalese temple architecture. The towering temple is visible from Durbar Square, but some of the finest views of the temple are from further away. If you take the road running out of the valley to Banepa and Dhulikhel or walk up towards the Surjya Binayak Temple south of Bhaktapur you can see the temple soaring up above the other buildings with the hills at the edge of the valley as a background behind.

The temple was built during the reign of King Bhupatindra Malla in 1702 and its design was so elegant and its construction so well done that the 1934 earthquake, which completely destroyed many buildings throughout the valley, only caused minor damage. The stairway leading up to the temple is flanked by guardian figures at each plinth level. The bottom plinth has the legendary wrestlers Jayamel and Phattu, said to have the strength of 10 normal men. On the plinths above are two elephants, then two lions, two griffins and finally two goddesses, Baghini in the form of a tiger and Singhini in the form of a lion. Each figure is said to be 10 times as strong as the figure on the level below and presiding over all of them, but hidden away inside the temple is the mysterious Tantric goddess Siddhi Lakshmi to whom the temple is dedicated.

Only the temple's priests can see the image of the goddess, but the temple's 108 carved and painted roof struts depict her in her various forms. Various legends and tales relate to the temple and its enigmatic inhabitant. One is that she maintains a balance with the powers of the terrifying Bhairab, comfortably ensconced in his own temple just across the square.

Bhairabnath Temple (29)

The triple-roofed Bhairabnath Temple (also known as the Kasi Vishwanath or Akash Bhairab) has an unusual rectangular plan and has had a somewhat chequered history. It was originally built as a one-storey temple in the early 17th century but rebuilt with two storeys by King Bhupatindra Malla in 1717. The 1934 earthquake caused great damage to the temple and it was completely rebuilt and the 3rd floor added.

Bhairabnath Temple

Casually stacked beside the temple you can see the enormous wheels and other parts of the temple chariot on which the image of Bhairab is conveyed around town during the Bisket festival. Curiously, despite Bhairab's fearsome powers and his massive temple, his image is only about 30 cm high! A small hole in the central door is used to push offerings into the temple's interior, but the actual entrance to the Bhairabnath Temple is through the small **Betal Temple**, behind the main temple. The temple is guarded by two brass lions and there's a host of interesting details on the front.

Til Mahadev Narayan Temple (35)

It's easy to miss the square's third interesting temple, the Til Mahadev Narayan, as it is hidden away behind the buildings on the southern side of the square. You can enter the temple's courtyard through a narrow entrance through those buildings or through an arched entrance facing west, just to the south of the square.

Til Mahadev Narayan Temple

This double-roofed Vishnu temple has a Garuda kneeling on a high pillar in front, flanked by pillars bearing Vishnu's conch and chakra symbols. Some of the temple's struts also have Garudas. A lingam in a yoni stands in a wooden cage in front and to one side of the temple. Despite the temple's neglected setting it is actually an important place of pilgrimage and one of the oldest temple sites in the town: an inscription indicates that the site has been in use since 1080. Another inscription states that the image of Til Mahadev installed inside the temple dates from 1170.

POTTERS' SQUARE

Potters' Square can be approached from Durbar Square, Taumadhi Tole or along the southern road into town from Siddha Pokhari and Navpokhu Pokhari. You also pass right by the square when walking into town from the trolley bus stop.

On the northern side of the square a small hillock is topped by a Ganesh shrine and a shady pipal tree. There are fine views from here over the river to the hills south of Bhaktapur. The square itself has two small temples, a solid-brick **Vishnu temple** and the double-roofed **Jeth Ganesh Temple.** The latter is an indicator how long the activity all around the square has been going on – the temple was donated by a wealthy potter in 1646 and to this day its priest is a potter. Pottery is very clearly what this square is all about. Under shady open verandahs or tin-roofed sheds all around the square, potters' wheels spin and clay is thrown. In the square itself, literally thousands of finished pots sit out in the sun to dry, and are sold in the stalls around the square and between the square and Taumadhi Tole.

TAUMADHI TOLE TO TACHUPAL TOLE

The curving main road through Bhaktapur runs from beside the Bhairabnath Temple in Taumadhi Tole to Tachupal Tole, the old centre of town. The first stretch of the street is a busy shopping thoroughfare with a constant hum of activity and everything from brass pots to video cassettes, from porters' tumplines (the leather or cloth strips across the forehead or chest used to support a load carried on the back) to tourists' mineral water, on sale.

As the road makes its first bend there are two interesting old buildings on the right-hand (southern) side. The **Sukul Dhoka** is a *math,* a priest's house, and has superb wood-carving both outside on its facade and inside in the courtyard. Almost next door is the **Lun Bahal,** originally a 16th-century Buddhist monastery, but which was converted into a Hindu shrine with the addition of a stone statue of Bhimsen. If you look into the sanctum, in the inner courtyard, you can see the statue, dating from 1592, complete with a ferocious-looking brass mask.

A little further along, the road opens into the **Golmadhi Square** with a deep hiti, the small, triple-roofed Golmadhi Ganesh Temple and adjacent to it a white chaitya. Another short stretch of road brings you to another small open area with a *path* or pilgrim's shelter on your right, behind it is a tank and the Inacho Bahal, described in the later Walking Tour section. A few more steps brings you to Tachupal Tole.

TACHUPAL TOLE

It's only about 10 minutes' walk from the temple of Nyatapola to the square containing the Dattatraya Temple and the Pujari Math monastery. Today you stroll down a well-paved street, a result of the major 'renovation' Bhaktapur underwent in the late '70s. These new-looking brick-paved streets are a real contrast to some of the muddy, potholed alleys which you can still find in the back blocks of town. South from this square a maze of narrow laneways, passageways and courtyards run down to the ghats on the river. Tachupal Tole, also called Dattatraya Square, was probably the original central square of Bhaktapur so this is the oldest part of the town.

Dattatraya Temple

This tall, square temple was originally built in 1427 but alterations were made in 1458. Like some other important structures in the valley it was said to have been built using the timber from a single tree. The temple is dedicated to Dattatraya although the Garuda-topped pillar and the traditional weapons of Vishnu indicate that Dattatraya is actually

another of Vishnu's many incarnations. He is also said to have been Shiva's teacher and is even claimed to have been a cousin of the Buddha so the temple is important to Shaivites, Vishnaivites and Buddhists.

The three-storey temple is raised well above the ground on its base, around which are carved some erotic scenes. The front section, which was a later addition to the temple, stands almost separate and the temple entrance is guarded by the same two Malla wrestlers who watch over the first plinth of the Nyatapola Temple.

Bhimsen Temple

At the other end of the square is the two-storey Bhimsen Temple, variously dated as 1605, 1645 or 1655. The temple is squat, rectangular and open on the ground floor. It's fronted by a platform with a small double-roofed Vishnu temple and a pillar topped by a brass lion. Behind it is the deeply sunken and rather pretty Bhimsen Pokhari.

Bhimsen Temple

Pujari Math & Museums

There are 10 buildings around the square which were originally used as *maths* or accommodation for monastic priests. The best known of these *maths* was the Pujari Math, which has been restored by the same West German aid project which has done so much work in Bhaktapur. The Pujari Math

Dattatraya Temple

Tachupal Tole (Bhaktapur)

was originally constructed in the 15th century during the reign of King Yaksha Malla, but restored in 1763. Until this century an annual caravan brought tributes to the monastery from Tibet.

The Pujari Math is principally famed for the superb peacock window, in the small alley alongside the monastery, on its left-hand side if you face it from the square. The window is reputed to be the finest carved window in the valley and is the subject of countless postcards and photographs. There are some extraordinarily rich woodcarvings inside the building's courtyard.

The building now houses a **Woodcarving Museum** which is open from 10 am to 5 pm daily except Friday, when it closes at 3 pm, and Tuesday, when it is closed all day. Admission is Rs 5 plus Rs 10 to use a camera. The museum has some fine examples of the woodcarving that Bhaktapur, and indeed the whole Kathmandu Valley, has long been famous for.

Directly across the square from the Pujari Math is the **Brass & Bronze Museum** with fine examples of metalwork from the valley. Its opening hours and admission price are the same as those for the Woodcarving Museum.

At the other end of the square, near the Bhimsen Temple, is a **Handicrafts Centre** selling woodcarvings and other examples of Bhaktapur crafts.

Salan Ganesh Temple
Just north of Tachupal Tole is another open area with the small Salan Ganesh Temple, dating from 1654. The open temple is ornately decorated, but the image is just a rock with only the vaguest elephant-head shape. To one side of the temple is the Ganesh Pokhari, a large tank.

WALKING TOUR
Bhaktapur is a fascinating town to wander in, and the lack of traffic makes walking a real pleasure, particularly in comparison to Kathmandu where walking would be so much more enjoyable without motor vehicles to dodge. This circular walk takes you by a number of interesting temples and shrines, but in Bhaktapur it's simply observing the timeless and seemingly unchanging rituals of life which is most interesting. Look for grains laid out to dry in the sun, people collecting water or washing under the communal taps, dyed yarns hung out to dry, children's games, fascinating shops, potters at work or women pounding grain, there's plenty to see. Perhaps most entrancing of all is Bhaktapur's mediaeval atmosphere.

North of Town
Starting from the north-eastern corner of Durbar Square (see main Bhaktapur map) walk to the east of the high Fasidega Temple, following the sign to the Luna Guest House, pass the guest house and a little further up the road, a walled-in Vishnu temple. Cross the junction and walk uphill past a large tank surrounded by fine old houses. Turn right towards Nagarkot and you soon come to the **Mahakali Temple** (22), where the shrine tops a small hill and is reached by a steep flight of steps.

Just beyond this temple turn right, walk downhill and then turn left and continue until you reach the tiny, open, double-roofed **Mahalakshmi Temple** (23). Turn right

(south) here and continue down to another large tank, the Naga (Snake) Pokhari. Bhaktapur has an amazing number of water tanks (known as *pokhari*), none of them looking particularly appetising! Here the green water contrasts nicely with the dyed yarns hung out to dry alongside the tank. On the western side of the tank two temples flank a central white shikhara while a cobra rears up from a small island in the middle of the tank.

Nava Durga Temple
Turn left around the tank, continue to a second tank and then to the Salan Ganesh Temple, described in the Tachupal Tole section. A little further on take a short detour north to the Nava Durga Temple (27). This Tantric temple is said to be the site for strange sacrificial rites. The golden door is surmounted by a golden window and is guarded by metal lions. It all contrasts nicely with the red-painted brick frontage. There's another large tank, the **Quathandau Pokhari**, just north of the temple.

Nava Durga Temple

Wakupati Narayan Temple
Back on the route you soon come back to the main east-west road which runs through

Left: Drying chillies, Bhaktapur (TW)
Right: Taumadhi Tole, Bhaktapur (TW)
Bottom: Durbar Square, Bhaktapur (SB)

Top: Pashupatinath, Kathmandu Valley (RE)
Middle: Sleeping Vishnu, Budhanilkantha (TW)
Bottom: Village scene, Kathmandu Valley (RI'A)

Taumadhi Tole and Tachupal Tole. Around this area there are more potters at work. Turn right (west) and immediately on your left is the entrance to the Wakupati Narayan Temple (36). The ornate, golden temple is double-roofed and is fronted by a line-up of no less than four Garudas!

Wakupati Narayan Temple

South of Town
Continue on to Tachupal Tole and turn left down the side of the Pujari Math (35); directions to its famous peacock window are well signposted. Jog right, left, right and left again then immediately on your left is the ornate little **Inacho Bahal** (34) with prayer wheels, Buddha figures and a strange miniature pagoda roof rising up on a pillar above the courtyard.

Riverside Ghats
From here the road drops down to the Hanumante River, leaving urban surroundings for rural ones and passing by a curious collection of shrines, chaityas, statues and lingams (40), including a bas-relief of a well-endowed nude Shiva. Just to the left of the bridge on the Hanuman Ghat is a shrine with a bas-relief of Rama and Sita, guarded by a statue of their faithful ally Hanuman. On the nearby building are four paintings including one showing Hanuman returning to Rama from his Himalayan medicinal herb foray, clutching a whole mountain in his hand. It's said that he paused here for a rest.

Cross the bridge and then take a hairpin turn back from the road onto a pleasant paved footpath. This rural stroll ends by another temple complex where you cross the river by the Chuping Ghat. Here, as at the Hanuman Ghat or the Ram Ghat by the bridge to the trolley bus stop, there are areas for ritual bathing and cremations.

Khalna Tole
Above the river is the open area of Khalna Tole, the centre for the spectacular activities during the annual mid-April Bisket Jatra. Bhairab's huge triple-roofed chariot is assembled from the parts scattered beside the Bhairabnath Temple and behind the Nyatapola Temple in Taumadhi Tole. The chariot is hauled here with Betal, his sidekick from the tiny temple behind the Bhairabnath Temple, riding out front like a ship's figurehead while Bhadrakali, his consort, accompanies them in her own chariot. The images of the gods shelter in the octagonal *path* during the festival and a towering 25-metre-high lingam is erected in the stone yoni base. Bisket ends and the Nepalese New Year starts when the lingam is taken down. Bhairab and Betal return to Taumadhi Tole while Bhadrakali goes back to her shrine by the river.

The circular walk ends with a gentle climb back into the town, emerging at the southern side of Taumadhi Tole.

SURJYA BINAYAK TEMPLE
About a km out of town this 17th-century Ganesh temple is said to be a good place to visit if you're worried about your children being late speakers! It's also popular with Nepalese marriage parties. To get there take the road down past the Potters' Square to Ram Ghat, cross the river and continue to the main road by the trolley bus stop. The road continues across the other side and rises

gently uphill with some fine views back over the rice paddies to Bhaktapur.

Where the road turns sharp right, a steep stairway climbs up to the temple on a forested hilltop. As you step inside the temple enclosure the very realistic-looking long-tailed rat, sitting on top of a tall pillar, immediately indicates that this temple belongs to Ganesh. The image of the god sits in an enclosure in the bottom of a shikhara and there's a second golden image on the shikhara spire. Statues of kneeling devotees face the image and the shikhara is flanked by large bells.

PLACES TO STAY

A growing number of visitors to Bhaktapur stay overnight. There's plenty to see and one of the pleasures is that once evening falls all the day-trippers from Kathmandu disappear, and don't return until after breakfast the next day. There are a number of small guest houses, all close to Durbar Square and all in the bottom-end category. If you want private bathrooms and other mod cons you'd better stay in Kathmandu.

The pick of the bunch is the new *Golden Gate Guest House* (☎ 01-610534), entered by a passageway from Durbar Square or from the laneway between Durbar Square and Taumadhi Tole. The owners are friendly, there are fine views from the roof and rooms cost Rs 150 ($3) for singles, Rs 200 ($4) for doubles or Rs 400/600 ($8/12) with private bath. Some of the rooms have balconies and there's also a restaurant downstairs.

Entered from behind the Pashupatinath Temple on Durbar Square, the *Shiva Inn* (☎ 01-610740, 610227) has singles/doubles at Rs 100/150 ($2/3). This is again simple and spartan with a restaurant on the top floor and rooftop.

Tigers & Goats
Nepal's national board game is *bagh chal*, which literally means 'move (chal) the tigers' (bagh). The game is played on a lined board with 25 intersecting points. One player has four tigers, the other has 20 goats and the aim is for the tiger player to 'eat' five goats by jumping over them before the goat player can encircle a single tiger and prevent it moving.

The game starts with the four tigers at the four corners of the board. Play alternates between the goats and the tigers and the goat player brings his goats on to the board one at a time. No goat can be moved from its initial position until every goat has been brought on to the board. By backing up one goat with another so that the tiger cannot jump them the goats can soon clutter up the board so effectively that the tigers cannot move. That is if the tigers haven't done a good job of eating goats!

All you need to play is a board scratched out on the dirt and 24 bottle caps or stones as markers, but you can also buy attractive brass bagh chal sets in Kathmandu, or in Patan where they are made. ∎

Just off Durbar Square, the *Traditional Guest House* (☎ 01-611057) has plain, but adequate rooms. The position is excellent and the views from the rooftop are simply stupendous. A dhal bhat dinner for guests only costs Rs 50, and singles/doubles are a reasonable Rs 100/150 ($2/3).

A few minutes' walk north of Durbar Square brings you to the basic but friendly *Luna Guest House* with rock-bottom accommodation for Rs 40/80.

PLACES TO EAT
Bhaktapur is certainly no competition for Kathmandu when it comes to restaurants, but you won't starve. Right in Taumadhi Tole the *Cafe Nyatapola* is in a building which was once a traditional pagoda temple, it even has erotic carvings on some of the roof struts! From upstairs there are good views over the square – but it is often dominated by large groups of tourists. Soft drinks are Rs 12, chips Rs 20, fried rice Rs 50.

On the corner of the square, beside the Nyatapola Temple, the *Marco Polo Restaurant* is a better bet than Cafe Nyatapola if you want a substantial meal. Pizzas are Rs 45, and there's a range of Chinese and Indian dishes for around Rs 30.

On Tachupal Tole – the most beautiful square in Bhaktapur – opposite the Dattatraya Temple, the *Cafe de Peacock & Soma Bar* is one of the best spots in the valley to while away an afternoon. The food is good and the views of the square mesmerising. The full international menu includes pizza and lasagne for around Rs 70, and there is also dhal bhat for Rs 60, and vegetable momo, Rs 28. The curd *(dahi)* is excellent. The cafe is open from 9 am to 9 pm.

Don't forget to try Bhaktapur's famous speciality *jujudhau*, the 'king of curds', while you are here. You can have it at the three main restaurants, and there are several places selling curd near the Navpokhu Pokhari bus stop.

THINGS TO BUY
As in Patan there are a number of crafts for which Bhaktapur is the centre. You'll find all the Kathmandu Valley crafts on sale in Kathmandu itself, but it's often fun to shop for them close to their point of origin and you may well find better examples or unusual pieces. There are plenty of shops and stalls catering to visitors around Durbar Square and Taumadhi Tole.

Pottery
Bhaktapur is the pottery centre of the valley and a visit to Potters' Square is a must. There are many stalls around the square or just below Taumadhi Tole selling pottery. Much of the work is traditional pots for use in Nepalese households (nice but not very transportable), but there are also items made to cater to tourist tastes such as attractive elephant or dragon planters.

Woodcarving & Puppets
Bhaktapur is renowned for its woodcarving and you'll see good examples in the Handicrafts Centre on Tachupal Tole. There are other shops around the squares and you will find unusual pieces in the alley beside the Pujari Math, right under the Peacock Window in fact. If you buy anything which looks like it might be old, make sure you get a descriptive receipt for it as it's likely to be checked on departure from Kathmandu. If it really is very old you will not be allowed to take it out of the country. Some of the best puppets, on sale in their thousands in all the valley towns, come from Bhaktapur.

Thangkas & Caps
Bhaktapur is reputed to be a centre for thangka paintings although these days you find them everywhere. Nepalese caps are another Bhaktapur speciality. There's a cap shop right beside the Bhairabnath Temple.

GETTING THERE & AWAY
Bus
Travelling by bus or minibus to Bhaktapur you disembark near the walled water tank called Navpokhu Pokhari, just beyond the even larger Siddha Pokhari and a short walk from Durbar Square. The minibuses from Kathmandu's Bagh Bazaar (Bus Stop 5) are

strictly for masochists and the poverty-stricken – they are nearly always crowded and can take over an hour, although they only cost Rs 2. If possible, try to get an express bus.

The Chinese-built trolley buses are preferable, although they can also get crowded (usually only around peak hour, though). At the Bhaktapur end, you have to walk 10 minutes to get to the town centre (by Ram Ghat and up into the town by Potters' Square).

The trolley buses leave Kathmandu from Tripureshwar Marg (Bus Stop 10), cost Rs 2, and will take around 35 minutes, unless you get caught in a traffic jam.

Bicycle

The main road to Bhaktapur runs through to Dhulikhel, Barabise and finally to Tibet, so it carries a lot of bellowing, belching buses and trucks. Avoid peak hours. A better alternative for cyclists is to ride via Thimi. Take the Thimi turn-off – left at a T-intersection after the Bhaktapur road crosses the Manohara River. The Herbs Production & Processing Co Ltd is reasonably prominently signposted at the corner.

Taxi

Taxis cost around Rs 200 ($4), one way. If you were to get the driver to wait for three or four hours and to return, the total bill would be around Rs 500 ($10).

Around the Kathmandu Valley

Apart from the three major cities of the valley – Kathmandu, Patan and Bhaktapur – there are countless villages, temples and stupas around the valley and on the surrounding hills. The crowds, traffic and modern trappings of Kathmandu can quickly be left behind for quiet villages and lush, terraced hills.

The valley beyond the cities has certainly changed over the years, and not always for the good, especially along the roads. Fortunately, however, aspects of customary life are maintained as the people of the valley coax their livelihood from the land, and temples continue to provide a focal point for their lives. The seasons roll on, and the timeless demands of the fields, the family and the gods are still major priorities.

You can even find good treks in the valley – ranging from day walks to more ambitious hikes. Some of the limitless possibilities are described in this chapter.

The ancient Buddhist stupa of Swayambhunath, a dramatic spot, within walking distance of central Kathmandu, is probably the best known site in Nepal and attracts a constant stream of worshippers. The hilltop site offers a fine view over the valley that is helpful for orienting yourself if you've just arrived.

The most important Hindu temple is Pashupatinath, on the eastern side of Kathmandu near the airport. It's a centre for pilgrims from all over the Indian subcontinent. A visit here can be combined with Bodhnath, another Buddhist stupa and the centre for a thriving Tibetan community.

If you will not have the opportunity to trek elsewhere, it is especially worth visiting one of the famous viewpoints on the rim of the valley, from where you can see the snow peaks of the Himalaya. There are numerous lodges and hotels at Nagarkot, Dhulikhel and Kakani.

If you have more time, there are less well known, although important, temples like Changu Narayan (north of Bhaktapur – a treasure house of Nepalese art), Dakshinkali (in the south-western corner of the valley – the site for animal sacrifices to Kali), or Budhanilkantha (north of Kathmandu – a massive 1400-year-old statue of Vishnu). There are many more.

The smaller towns and villages have tended to retain a more traditional Newari life style, and if you found Bhaktapur interesting consider visiting Kirtipur (south-west of Kathmandu), Sankhu (north-east of Bhaktapur) or Panauti (outside the valley near Banepa). Again, there are many more alternatives.

Daman, a viewpoint that overlooks the entire Himalaya from Dhaulagiri to Mt Everest is a day trip from Kathmandu not covered in this chapter which is worth considering (see the Terai chapter).

Some Cultural Considerations

You do not have to go far to escape the hordes of camera-clutching tourists, but you will nonetheless be unable to escape their legacy: suspicious people and the cries of 'One rupee...one rupee?' from the children. If you do venture off the beaten track, your responsibility as a visitor is greater than ever.

Whatever the temptation, do not give gifts to begging children. Do not intrude with a camera, unless it is clearly OK with the people you are photographing. Ask before entering a temple compound, although unless otherwise noted, it is permissible to enter and photograph the temples described in this chapter.

See the Avoiding Offence section in the Facts about the Country chapter for further details on cultural considerations.

GETTING AROUND

Swayambhunath and Pashupatinath can be reached on foot, but by far the easiest and most economical way of getting around the valley is by bicycle. If you are aiming for

Kathmandu Valley

0   2.5   5 km

somewhere on the rim of the valley, make sure you have a mountain bike! On a mountain bike it's possible for a reasonably fit person to go anywhere in the valley and return to Kathmandu within daylight.

Buses and minibuses service all of the roads, but although cheap, they are uncomfortable and limiting. If you are part of a group or if the budget allows, you could consider hiring a car or taxi for the day.

There are a number of companies that offer tours around the valley with prices ranging from Rs 175 ($3.50) to Rs 250 ($5) for half a day. If you have limited time or want a speedy introduction to the area, they're worth considering. On the other hand, taxis can be hired for Rs 450 ($9) per half day, Rs 750 ($15) per full day. With a taxi you aren't stuck to a schedule, and if you have this book who needs a guide?

Valley Walks

There are many interesting walks around the valley and many of them make pleasant alternatives to vehicles or bicycles. You can, for example, follow a trail from Kirtipur to Chobar and from there into Patan, or walk from the Gokarna Mahadev Temple to Bodhnath. These walks, and others, are detailed in the Getting There & Away information for the appropriate sections.

In addition, there are a number of interesting walks down from Nagarkot on the valley rim to various points in and outside the valley including a pleasant short stroll down to the beautiful temple of Changu Narayan.

For more details on walks on the edge of the Kathmandu Valley, look for Alton C Byers' *Treks on the Kathmandu Valley Rim*, or James Giamborone's *Kathmandu: Bikes & Hikes*, which are available in Kathmandu bookshops.

Routes

This chapter has been organised following the roads that radiate out from Kathmandu.

Distances quoted are from the centre of Kathmandu. Each route has been named for the most important sites along the route, which are given clockwise from the Swayambhunath route. In most cases there is no alternative to going and returning on the same route unless you walk cross-country.

Swayambhunath Route

SWAYAMBHUNATH (2 km)

The Buddhist temple of Swayambhunath, situated on the top of a hill west of the city, is one of the most popular and instantly recognisable symbols of Nepal. The temple is colloquially known as the 'monkey temple' after the large tribe of handsome monkeys which guard the hill and amuse visitors and devotees with their tricks including sliding gracefully down the double banisters of the main stairway to the temple. The roving band quickly snatch up any offerings of food made by devotees and will just as quickly grab anything you may be carrying.

Geologists believe that the Kathmandu Valley was once a lake and legends relate that the hill on which Swayambhunath stands was an island in that lake. It is said that Emperor Ashoka paid a visit to the site over 2000 years ago. An inscription indicates that King Manadeva ordered work done on the site in 460 CE and by the 1200s it was an important Buddhist centre. In 1346 Moghul invaders from Bengal broke open the stupa to search for gold. Under the Mallas various improvements were made and the great stairway to the stupa was constructed by King Pratap Malla in the 17th century.

Eastern Stairway

Although you can get to the temple by vehicle, and save yourself the long climb up the stairs, the eastern stairway is by far the best way of approaching Swayambhunath. Look for the yellow and red stone seated Buddha figures at the base of the hill. The bottom end of the steps is guarded by figures of Ganesh and Kumar on their animals. Near the start of the steps is a huge 'footprint' on a stone, said to be either that of the Buddha or of Manjushri. Halfway up the steps there's another small collection of stonework including a scene showing the birth of the Buddha, his mother holding a tree branch

and the Buddha taking seven miraculous steps immediately after his birth.

As you climb the final stretch look for the pairs of animals – Garudas, lions, elephants, horses and peacocks – the 'vehicles' of the Dhyani Buddhas. If you tire on the ascent, pause to watch the monkeys' antics and when you reach the top remember that you should always walk around a stupa in a clockwise direction.

Great Thunderbolt

As well as building the great stairway, Pratap Malla also added a pair of shikharas and the stone lions and dorje which visitors see immediately upon reaching the top of the stairs. Dorje is the Tibetan word for this thunderbolt symbol, in Sanskrit it is called a *vajra*. Dorjes are often accompanied by a bell, the thunderbolt symbolises male force and the bell symbolises female wisdom. Around the pedestal supporting Swayambhunath's mighty dorje are the animals of the Tibetan calendar.

Stupa

From the flattened top of the hill, the soaring central stupa is topped by a gold-coloured square block from which the watchful eyes of the Buddha gaze out across the valley in each direction. The question mark-like 'nose' is actually the Nepali number *ek* or one and is a symbol of unity. Between and above the two eyes is a third eye, symbolising the Buddha's clairvoyant powers.

Set around the base of the central stupa is a continuous series of prayer wheels which pilgrims, circumambulating the stupa, spin as they pass by. Each carries the sacred mantra *om mani padme hum*. The prayer flags fluttering from the lines leading to the stupa's spire also carry mantras and each wave in the breeze carries the words away. The stupa's white-painted base represents the four elements – earth, fire, air and water – while the 13 concentric rings on the spire symbolise the 13 degrees of knowledge and the 13 steps that must be taken towards nirvana, which in turn is represented by the umbrella at the top.

1 Shantipura Building
2 Avalokitesvara with four arms
3 Dhyani Buddha Aksobhya
4 Shantipura (Sky Symbol)
5 Agnipura (Fire Symbol)
6 Ancient Stone Inscription
7 Gompa Prayer Wheel
8 Buddha of Light
9 Hariti (Ajima) Temple
10 Nagpura (Water Symbol)
11 Path (Pilgrims' Shelter) & Gompa
12 Jamuna & Ganga Images
13 Swayambhunath Stupa
14 Pratapura Shikhara
15 Dorje (Thunderbolt Symbol)
16 Buddhist Museum
17 Vayupura (Air Symbol)
18 Vasupura (Earth Symbol)
19 Anantapura Shikhara

Dhyani Buddhas & Shaktis

A Amoghasiddhi
B Locana (Shakti of Aksobhya)
C Aksobhya
D Vairocana
E Mamki (Shakti of Ratnasambhava)
F Ratnasambhava
G Pandara (Shakti of Amitabha)
H Amitabha
I Tara (Shakti of Amoghasiddhi)

To other Stupas & Saraswati Shrine

To Kathmandu (on foot or by bicycle)

To Kathmandu (by car)

Swayambhunath

0   10   20 m

Stupa Platform

The great stupa is only one of many points of interest at Swayambhunath. Starting from the massive dorje at the top of the stairs turn right to the monastery or gompa where, with a great deal of crashing, chanting and trumpeting, a service takes place every day at around 4 pm. Inside the gompa there's a huge prayer wheel and a six-metre-high figure of Avalokitesvara. Behind the stupa, adjacent to the International Buddhist Library, is a *path* or rest house for pilgrims with an open ground floor and a gompa above it.

The dorje at the top of the stairs is flanked by two white temples in the Indian shikhara style, both dating from 1646. The one to the right, in front of the gompa, is the Pratapura shikhara while to the left is the identical Anantapura shikhara. Behind the stupa is the Hariti Temple, a pagoda-style temple with a beautiful image of Hariti, the goddess of smallpox. This Hindu goddess (to the Newaris she is Ajima), who is also responsible for fertility, indicates again the constant interweaving of Hinduism and Buddhism in Nepal.

Near the Hariti Temple there are pillars on which figures of various gods and goddesses are seated. Look for the figure of Tara making the gesture of charity. Actually, there

---

The Dhyani Buddhas

There are five Dhyani Buddhas or 'Buddhas in Meditation' who represent various aspects of Buddhahood, unlike the mortal flesh-and-blood Buddhas like Gautama Buddha. Around many stupas the figures of the five Dhyani Buddhas in different meditative postures face out from the stupa in niches, four of them facing the four cardinal directions. Once you know the hand positions you can use a stupa like a compass! The Swayambhunath stupa is a good place to study the Dhyani Buddhas, and the description that follows is from that stupa.

Amoghasiddhi faces north and raises his right hand, palm out to shoulder height in what is known as a protective position. His animal or 'vehicle' is the Garuda. You can see the animals in niches below the Buddhas' shrines. As you move round the stupa clockwise you'll come to Aksobhya, the lord of the east; one of his hands touches the earth. This is known as the position of subduing the devil Mara. The Buddha reaches down to touch the earth, in order that it witness his resistance to temptation. His vehicle is the elephant.

Facing south is Ratnasambhava who rides a horse and turns his palm outwards. Amitabha faces the west and his hands rest on his lap, palm up in a meditative position. His vehicle is the peacock. The fifth of the Buddhas is Vairocana who usually appears in the centre of the stupa and therefore is not so easily seen. If he is shown he normally faces the south-east, and at Swayambhunath you can see his figure standing beside Aksobhya in the eastern niche. His animal is the lion; his hands are held up to his chest and he makes two circles with his fingers, rather like a scuba diver's 'OK' sign!

Each Dhyani Buddha is identifiable by his colour, his hand positions, his direction and his vehicle but each also has a shakti or female companion and a Bodhisattva or spiritual follower. Their shaktis or consorts are shown at the subcardinal points around the stupa. Amitabha is the Dhyani Buddha of our era and his Bodhisattva is none other than Avalokitesvara or, as he is often known in the valley, Manjushri or Machhendranath. ■

A   Amoghasiddhi
B   Locana (shakti of Aksobhya)
C   Aksobhya
D   Vairocana
E   Mamki (shakti of Ratnasambhava)
F   Ratnasambhava
G   Pandara (shakti of Amitabha)
H   Amitabha
I   Tara (shakti of Amoghasiddhi)

are two Taras, Green Tara and White Tara, who are sometimes believed to be the two wives of King Songtsen Gompo, the first royal patron of Buddhism in Tibet. The Taras are two of the female consorts to the Dhyani Buddhas.

Behind the stupa, bronze images of the river goddesses Ganga and Jamuna guard an eternal flame in a cage.

The symbols for the four elements – earth, air, water and fire – can be found around the hilltop. Behind the Anantapura shikhara are Vasupura, the earth symbol, and Vayupura, the symbol for air. Nagpura, the symbol for water, is just north of the stupa while Agnipura, the symbol for fire, is at the north-western corner of the platform. Shantipura, the symbol for the sky, is at the extreme north of the platform, in front of the Shantipura building.

In this same northern area of the platform you will find an ancient stone inscription, dating from 1372, and a large image of the Buddha, next to the Agnipura symbol. There are numerous little shops and stalls around the stupa that sell jewellery and curios.

From its hilltop setting, Swayambhunath offers fine views over Kathmandu and the valley. It's particularly striking in the early evening when the city is illuminated, and the site is also very attractive under the soft glow of moonlight.

Around Swayambhunath

There are many small buildings and shrines down the hillside behind Swayambhunath. A smaller stupa stands on a hillock, with an adjacent gompa and an important shrine to Saraswati, the goddess of learning. At exam time, many scholars come here to improve their chances and schoolchildren come here during Basant Panchami, the Festival of Knowledge.

There are various Tibetan settlements and gompas around the base of the Swayambhunath hill. Just to the north of the long eastern stairway, on the road round the hill, is a **gompa** with an immense **prayer wheel** standing a good six metres high. The two or three-km walk beyond Swayambhunath will take you to Ichangu Narayan, an interesting Hindu temple (see the next section). The National Museum & Art Gallery, described in the Kathmandu, Patan & Bhaktapur chapter, is on the road from Kathmandu to the stupa.

The **Natural History Museum**, west of Swayambhunath, has a large collection of butterflies, fish, reptiles, birds and animals. It's open every day from 10 am to 5 pm except Saturdays and government holidays, and admission is free.

There are several routes to Swayambhunath from Kathmandu and if you take the route from Thamel, via the Chhetrapati Square and down to the Vishnumati River, there are three interesting temples to look at. The **Indrani Temple** is just beside the river on the Kathmandu side and is chiefly notable for the brightly coloured erotic scenes on its roof struts. There are cremation ghats beside the river; in 1989 the bridge here collapsed during the heavy monsoon. Across the river and just upstream is the **Shobabaghwati Temple**. A footpath runs from here up the steep hill to the **Bijeshwari Temple**, from where the road continues to the Swayambhunath hill.

Getting There & Away

You can approach Swayambhunath by taxi or under your own power – either on foot or by bicycle. The taxi will take you on the road via the National Museum & Art Gallery and deposit you at the southern entrance, from where it's just an easy climb to the top of the hill. Share-taxis also operate from Bangemudha, the junction a block south of Thahiti Tole going from Thamel towards New Rd. The other routes end with the long steep climb up the eastern stairway to the stupa, but this is a far more interesting way to approach Swayambhunath and the easy stroll from Kathmandu is a pleasure in itself.

There are two popular foot or bicycle routes to Swayambhunath, using both makes the trip into a pleasant circuit. Starting from Durbar Square take Maru Tole (Pie Alley) down to the river where a footbridge crosses to the western side. Flat, stone cremation

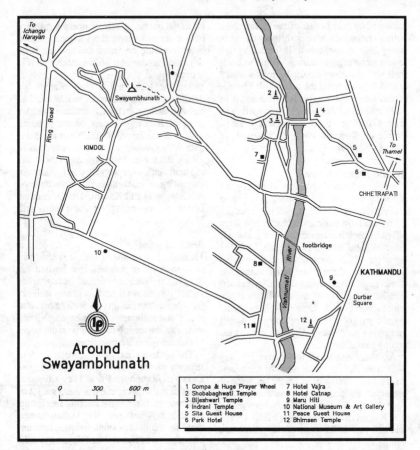

Around Swayambhunath

0   300   600 m

1 Gompa & Huge Prayer Wheel
2 Shobabaghwati Temple
3 Bijeshwari Temple
4 Indrani Temple
5 Sita Guest House
6 Park Hotel
7 Hotel Vajra
8 Hotel Catnap
9 Maru Hiti
10 National Museum & Art Gallery
11 Peace Guest House
12 Bhimsen Temple

ghats can be seen by the riverside. From there the path leads through houses and shops to the open green at the base of the hill. Along the way you'll see people working in vegetable gardens and preparing wool for Tibetan carpets. There's quite a Tibetan community in this area and also a small group of long-term Western visitors near the base of the hill.

If you go there by bicycle you are likely to find a number of small boys offering to 'look after' your bicycle. It's probably wise to pay a rupee or two of 'protection money',

otherwise you may find your tyres have gone mysteriously flat and a pump will then have to be rented from one of the nearby shops!

The alternative route starts from Chhetrapati, near Thamel. From the Chhetrapati Tole junction the road descends to the river, with the Swayambhunath stupa clearly visible in the distance, and passes the three riverside temples mentioned.

ICHANGU NARAYAN TEMPLE (5 km)

At the edge of the valley floor, two or three km beyond Swayambhunath, the shrine of

Ichangu Narayan is one of the Kathmandu Valley's important Vishnu shrines. The two-storey 18th-century temple is fronted by two square stone pillars bearing Vishnu's conch shell and chakra symbols. Various statuary can be found around the courtyard. The site of the temple was actually consecrated in 1200 and an earlier temple was built here after a famine in 1512. There's a small temple to Bhagwati on a hill overlooking Ichangu Narayan.

Getting There & Away

The road to Ichangu Narayan starts beyond the Ring Rd, on the western side of the Swayambhunath hill. It quickly changes from a road to a track and as it climbs a steep hill (look back for the views over the valley), the track soon becomes a footpath. From the top of the hill, marked by a small temple, the trail descends slightly and then continues to climb gradually, leaving the valley proper. Finally, at the end of a little village is the temple compound. Going back to Kathmandu by bicycle is one long downhill breeze but you'll certainly work up a sweat getting to the temple.

An alternative route to Ichangu is a day walk from Balaju, to the north of Kathmandu. The trail climbs from Balaju to the top of Nagarjun hill and skirts around the valley edge through the Jamacho forest reserve and the Nagarjun forest, descending to the Ichangu trail to the west of the village and temple.

Kakani & Trisuli Bazaar Route

Kakani is a viewpoint with spectacular views of the Ganesh Himal. A narrow, winding tarmac road, in reasonable, though not great condition, continues to Trisuli Bazaar. From Trisuli Bazaar to Dhunche the road deteriorates to very rough gravel, but the views are spectacular. Dhunche is the starting point for a number of treks in the Langtang region.

From Dhunche, a newly opened military road continues along the Langtang Valley before crossing the Trisuli and heading westwards to Samdang (at 3600 metres!) – 4WD is essential.

See the Mountain Biking chapter for details on a route that takes in Kakani. Just before Malekhu, on the Kathmandu-Pokhara (Prithvi) Highway, a new bridge is being built over the Trisuli River. When complete (late 93?) this will open up a new road to Trisuli Bazaar, and will supersede the existing road that leaves the valley at Kakani. An interesting circular bike ride will then be possible, taking in Kakani, Trisuli, perhaps Dhading (depending on the route), and Malekhu.

BALAJU (3 km)

The industrial centre of Balaju is less than two km north of Thamel, just beyond the Ring Rd, and the expansion of the capital has virtually swallowed up this nearby suburb. Despite this, the Balaju park is still a peaceful retreat and its image of the sleeping Vishnu makes an interesting contrast with the larger Vishnu image at Budhanilkantha.

The gardens at Balaju were originally constructed in the 18th century and are now known as **Mahendra Park**. They are something of a disappointment – there's a lot of concrete and litter, and numerous ineffectual gardeners. Apart from the Vishnu image, there are a couple of small temples, an interesting group of chortens and lingams (for the aficionado) and the 22 waterspouts from which the park takes its name, 'Bais Dhara Balaju'.

Officially, the Vishnu image at Balaju is said to be a copy of the older image at Budhanilkantha but there is no positive proof which one is actually older. Certainly the Balaju image is in more pleasant surroundings than its better known relation. Although the king of Nepal cannot visit Budhanilkantha (since he is an incarnation of Vishnu and to gaze on his own image could be disastrous) no such injunction applies to Balaju, where the Vishnu image is just a copy of the real thing!

Admission costs Rs 1, plus another Rs 1 if you take in a camera. The pool, which can often be very crowded, is open between March and September, and the admission fee is Rs 10.

Shitala Mai Temple

The double-roofed 19th-century Shitala Mai Temple stands in front of the Vishnu image and around it is a curious assembly of gods. They include a 16th-century image of Hari Shankar – the half-Shiva, half-Vishnu deity – and a 14th-century figure of the multi-armed goddess of smallpox, Shitala Mai. Others include Bhagwati, Ganesh and, in the usual clash of Hindu and Buddhist imagery, a statue of the Buddha protected by the hood of a snake.

Getting There & Away

You can get to Balaju by tempo from the National Theatre corner of the Rani Pokhari or walk there from Thamel. It's an interesting day walk from Balaju to Ichangu Narayan, west of Swayambhunath, skirting the edge of the valley.

NAGARJUN

On the hill behind Balaju is the walled Nagarjun forest reserve with pheasants, deer and other animals. This, along with the Gokarna Safari Park and Pulchowki, is one of the last significant areas of untouched forest in the valley. You can continue up the hill to Jamacho, a popular Buddhist pilgrimage site. There are excellent views to the north stretching, on a clear day, all the way from the Annapurnas to Langtang Lirung, while the whole of the Kathmandu Valley is laid at your feet to the south.

There's a steep, 37-km unpaved road to the top, or you can walk up a wide, easy-to-follow trail in about two hours. There are a number of picnic shelters around a stupa and a viewing tower.

Getting There & Away

The main entrance to the reserve is about a 20-minute bike ride from Thamel; entry is 25 paisa. The walking trail to the top begins just past the gate on the right. It's steep for the first hour, and there is no water along the way or at the top. There are several routes you can take on the way down. Don't take the road – it's 37 km long.

KAKANI (23 km)

Standing at 2073 metres on a ridge northwest of Kathmandu, Kakani is nowhere near as popular as Nagarkot but does offer magnificent views of Ganesh Himal and the central and western Himalaya.

Apart from looking at the view (one could argue this is enough) there's not much to do. There is a century-old summer villa used by the British Embassy and a large army camp, although this does not seriously impinge on the tranquillity of the surroundings.

The road to Kakani also offers beautiful views. Once you're through the pass and out of the valley Kathmandu seems light years away. Although the valley is terraced 1000 metres from top to bottom, many trees have been left behind and prosperous-looking houses dot the hillsides.

Place to Stay & Eat

The only accommodation in Kakani is the *Tara Gaon Kakani Hotel* (☎ 01-228222), an old-fashioned place with wonderful views. Although small, it's also quite comfortable. Singles/doubles cost $15/20 and the hotel serves reasonably priced meals. Payment must be in foreign exchange, or rupees backed up with a Foreign Exchange Encashment Receipt.

Although it's easy to get to Kakani on a day trip, it's worth staying overnight if you want to see the view (you stand a much better chance if you are there early in the morning before the clouds roll in).

Getting There & Away

Kakani is an hour by car from Kathmandu, so it would be a long, though rewarding, bike trip. The road is sealed almost all the way and it is a fairly gentle climb – although consistent. It is downhill all the way home! See the Mountain Biking chapter for details of a route that takes in Kakani.

Kakani is three km from the main Dhunche road. The dirt road is just before the Kaulithana police checkpoint (the first outside Kathmandu) and there is a signpost for a telecommunications tower.

Before the new Kathmandu Bus Terminal was opened, buses left Kathmandu from the intersection of Lekhnath Marg and the road to Balaju (Bus Stop 1 – Paknajol). Buses to Trisuli and Dhunche left at around 6.30 am, so you could catch one of them and get off at Kaulithana (about Rs 12).

TRISULI BAZAAR (68 km)

Trisuli Bazaar is a classically unattractive roadside town that owes its development to a large hydroelectric project on the Trisuli River, and the fact that it was once a trail head for treks into the Langtang region. These days trekkers head straight through to Dhunche, and there are very few persuasive reasons to stop. There's nothing to see, and the only oddity is the proliferation of hairdressers.

Nawakot, a small village a few km southeast of Trisuli, has the ruins of a fortress that was built by Prithvi Narayan Shah when he was planning his campaign to take the Kathmandu Valley. It can be reached by bike or foot and is an interesting spot.

Places to Stay

There are several thoroughly unimpressive places on the eastern side of the bridge, which you reach when you enter town, before the turn-off to Dhunche. If you continue over the bridge, there are a few dhal bhat restaurants and a couple of reasonable options. The *Trishuli Rest House* is the best of a bad lot, although the *Ranjit Hotel* is also OK. Doubles are expensive at Rs 100 ($2).

Getting There & Away

It is a spectacular drive from Kakani along a narrow, twisting road with great views, and would be an excellent long descent by bike. Buses to/from Kathmandu take five hours and cost Rs 29. Prior to the opening of the new Kathmandu Bus Terminal, buses left

from Paknajol (Bus Stop 1) between 6.30 am and 2.30 pm.

Dhunche (119 km)

By the time you reach Dhunche you have been inspected by countless redundant police and army checkposts, plus paid Rs 650 ($13) to enter the Langtang National Park. Irritation evaporates quickly however, because there are great views of the Langtang Valley, and although the modern section of Dhunche is pretty tacky, it's definitely a Tamang town, and the old section is virtually unchanged. Many people start trekking from Dhunche, although these days there is a bus to Syabru as well. (See the Trekking chapter.)

Places to Stay & Eat

There are a number of decent trekking-style hotel restaurants, although several of them are definitely at the up-market end of the spectrum. Prices are competitive. The *Hotel Namaste* is clean and decent, serves good food, and costs Rs 20 a double, Rs 10 for a dorm bed. The *Hotel Langtang View* has the same prices and is also OK.

Getting There & Away

The road to Dhunche is bad, but it deteriorates further if you continue to Syabru. The views on both stretches, are spectacular. Prior to the opening of the new Kathmandu Bus Terminal, buses left from Paknajol (Bus Stop 1) at 7 am, arriving in Dhunche at about 3.30 pm.

SAMDANG (153 km)

The road gets increasingly steep and spectacular after Dhunche. It drops down to cross the Trisuli, then climbs steeply up the other side, continuing to Samdang, at 3600 metres, where there is a pleasant lodge (☎ 01-227929, 271329; fax 471630), run by the same people who run the Gorkha Hill Resort at Gorkha near Pokhara. Advance bookings are essential. This would be a great base for day walks, and the views are stupendous.

Budhanilkantha Route

DHUM VARAHI (5 km)

Lying in an unprepossessing schoolyard just inside the Ring Rd to the north-east of the city proper, a huge pipal tree encloses a small shrine and a dramatic 5th-century sculpture of Vishnu. Vishnu is shown reincarnated as a wild boar with a stocky human body, holding Prithvi, the earth goddess, on his left elbow.

From a historical point of view, the statue is interesting because it is an original depiction of an animal-human, created before iconographic rules were established, which perhaps contributes to the unusual sense of movement and vitality that the statue possesses. The statue shows Vishnu rescuing Prithvi from the clutches of a demon.

Getting There & Away

A visit to Dhum Varahi could easily be combined with a visit to Budhanilkantha, especially if you are approaching the Budhanilkantha intersection on the Ring Rd from Chabahil and Pashupatinath. If you are coming from Chabahil take the third dirt road on your left after crossing the Dhobi River (see the map in the Pashupatinath section). The statue lies under a huge pipal tree in the grounds of the Shridhumrabarah Primary School.

If you are coming from the intersection of the Budhanilkantha road with the Ring Rd take the second dirt road after the Panchayat Silver Jubilee Garden, which features a square, black-marble column topped with a conch shell. Continue until you see the pipal tree after about a km.

BUDHANILKANTHA (9 km)

Vishnu has many incarnations and in Nepal he often appears as Narayan, the creator of all life, the god who reclines on the cosmic sea. From his navel grew a lotus and from the lotus came Brahma, who in turn created the world. So in the end everything comes from Vishnu and at Budhanilkantha the legend is made real. Here, a stone image of Vishnu lies serenely in a pond – the most impressive, if not the most important, Vishnu shrine in the kingdom.

The five-metre-long image of Vishnu as Narayan is believed to have been created in the 7th or 8th century. It was sculpted during the Licchavi period, probably somewhere outside the valley and laboriously dragged here. Two other similar figures of the reclining Vishnu were also carved out of stone and all three were subsequently lost for many centuries. The image here at Budhanilkantha was the first found and is also the largest, but whether it was also the original one (from which the others were copied) remains controversial.

Narayan lies back peacefully on a most unusual bed – the coils of the multiheaded snake, Ananta. The snake's 11 hooded heads rise protectively around Narayan's head. Narayan's four hands hold the four symbols of Vishnu – a chakra (representing the mind), a mace (primeval knowledge), a conch shell (the four elements) and a lotus seed (the moving universe). A legend relates that the lost image was discovered when a horrified farmer saw blood coming from the ground when his plough struck the huge buried image.

During the early Malla period, Vishnuism had gone into decline as Shiva became more popular. King Jayasthiti Malla is credited with reviving the popularity of Vishnu, in part by claiming to be an incarnation of the multi-incarnated god.

To this day, the kings of Nepal make the same claim and because of this they are forbidden, on pain of death, from seeing the image at Budhanilkantha. They are allowed to look at the valley's other two reclining Vishnu images, which are said to be simply copies of the Budhanilkantha figure. One of these 'replicas' is at Balaju, the other, not on view to tourists, is in the old Royal Palace in Kathmandu.

The sleeping Vishnu image attracts a constant stream of pilgrims, and prayers take place every morning at 9 am. Vishnu is supposed to sleep through the four monsoon months, waking at the end of the monsoon. A great festival takes place at Budhanilkantha each November, on the day Vishnu is supposed to awaken from his long annual slumber.

Getting There & Away

Before the completion of the Kathmandu Bus Terminal, buses and tempos left from the National Theatre building at the northwestern corner of Rani Pokhari (1½ hours, Rs 4). Buses run more regularly to Bansbari, site of a shoe factory about halfway from the centre of Kathmandu to Budhanilkantha. A taxi should cost around Rs 100 ($2). By bicycle it's a long uphill haul – hard, sweaty work rewarded with a very pleasant return trip. You could pause at Dhum Varahi on one leg of your trip.

Pashupatinath & Bodhnath Route

PASHUPATINATH (5 km)

Nepal's most important Hindu temple stands on the banks of the Bagmati River, between Kathmandu and the airport and slightly south-west of Bodhnath. You can visit Pashupatinath en route to Bodhnath – the two sites are an interesting short walk apart.

Festivals

Activities take place at Pashupatinath almost all the time but it is generally busiest (with genuine pilgrims, not tourists) from 6 am to 10 am in the morning and again from 6 to 7.30 pm in the evening. The best time to visit the temple is on Ekadashi – 11 days after the full and new moon each month. On those days there will be many pilgrims and in the evening the ringing of bells will indicate that the *arati* (light) ceremony is to take place.

In February-March each year, the festival of Shivaratri celebrates Shiva's birthday with a great fair at the temple. Another fair takes place in November.

Pashupatinath Temple

Not only is Pashupatinath the most important Hindu temple in Nepal, it's one of the most important Shiva temples on the subcontinent and draws numerous devotees from all over India each year, including many colourful sadhus, those wandering ascetic Hindu holy men.

Shiva is the destroyer and creator of the Hindu pantheon and appears in many forms. His 'terrible' forms are probably best known, particularly his appearances in Nepal as the cruel and destructive Bhairabs, but he also has peaceful incarnations including those of Mahadev and Pashupati, the lord of the beasts. As the shepherd of both animals and humans, Shiva as Pashupati shows his most pleasant and creative side.

Pashupati is considered to have a special concern for the kingdom of Nepal and accordingly he features in any message from the king. Before commencing any important journey the king will always pay a visit to Pashupatinath to seek the god's blessing. Although Shiva is often a bloodthirsty god he is not so in his incarnation as Pashupati so no animal sacrifices are made here although they are at the nearby Guhyeshwari Temple. Nor is leather (since it comes from cows) allowed inside the temple and you will see Hindus removing their shoes before entering.

Nandi

1 Pashupatinath Temple
2 Huge Trident
3 Hermits' Caves
4 11 Chaltyas
5 Lingam with Shiva face
6 Guhyeshwari Temple
7 Gorakhnath Temple
   Complex
8 Vishwarup Temple
9 Rajrajeshwari Temple
10 Cremation Ghats
11 Bachhareshwari Temple
12 Buddha Statue
13 Ram Temple

Bagmati River
To Bodhnath
dry weather only
To Ring Road
To Ring Road
To Ring Road

Pashupatinath

0   75   150 m

Near the entrance to the temple there are people selling flowers, incense and other offerings. Although non-Hindus are not allowed inside the temple you may catch a glimpse of the mighty figure of Nandi, Shiva's bull, inside the temple. It dates from the last century but the small bull in front of the temple is about 300 years old. The black, four-headed image of Pashupati inside the temple is said to be even older and an even earlier image was destroyed by Moghul invaders in the 14th century. Although Westerners are not allowed to enter the temple, there is plenty to be seen along the riverbanks and you can look down into the temple from the terraced hillside on the opposite bank.

The Riverbanks

The Bagmati is a holy river and, as at Varanasi on the Ganges, Pashupatinath is a popular place to be cremated. The burning ghats immediately in front of the temple, north of the footbridges, are reserved for the cremation of royalty although you will often see ritual bathing taking place in the river just here.

The four square burning ghats just south of the bridges are for the common people and there is almost always a cremation going on. The log fires are laid, the shrouded body lifted on top and the fire lit with remarkably little ceremony.

There's often a crowd of tourists – cameras and video cameras at the ready – watching like vultures from the opposite bank. Photography is currently permitted, but may not be for much longer if tourists continue to behave with such insensitive disregard for the funeral parties themselves. However extraordinary the sights might seem, this is a religious ceremony, often marking a family tragedy, and the participants should be accorded respect. Please be discreet, and behave as you would wish people to behave at a funeral in your home town.

Further south of these cremation ghats, but still on the western bank of the river, is the ancient 6th-century **Bachhareshwari Temple** with Tantric figures and erotic scenes. It is said that at one time the Shivaratri activities would include human sacrifices at this temple. Just outside the temple entrance, right at the end of the western embankment, is a half-buried, but quite beautiful, 7th-century standing Buddha image.

Two footbridges cross the Bagmati River, and facing the temple from across the river are 11 stone chaityas, each containing a lingam. From this embankment you can watch the activities on the other bank, in front of the temple. Offerings and flowers are on sale, devotees dip in the river and there's a constant coming and going. From the northern end of the embankment you can see the cave-like shelters which were used at one time by hermits and sadhus. These days the yogis and sadhus head for the **Ram Temple**, further down the river, especially during the great festival of Shivaratri.

The Terraces

Climb up the steps from the western riverbank to the terrace where you can look down into the Pashupatinath Temple. It's not a very inspiring sight: the golden roof of the central two-tiered pagoda, which dates from 1696, is surrounded by ugly corrugated iron roofs, just like some worn-out, inner-city Australian suburb. Look for the enormous golden trident rising up on the right (northern) side of the temple and the golden figure of the king kneeling in prayer on the left side. Behind the temple, you can see a brightly coloured illustration of Shiva and his shakti looking out over the temple.

At the northern end of this terrace is a Shiva lingam on a circular pedestal. A finely featured face of the god has been sculptured on one side of the lingam. It's an indication of the richness of Nepal's artistic heritage that this piece of sculpture, so casually standing here on the grassy terrace, is a masterpiece dating from the 5th or 6th century!

Gorakhnath & Vishwarup Temples

The steps continue up the hill and, as with the steps to Swayambhunath, are a popular playground for monkeys. The Gorakhnath complex is at the top of the hill. A shikhara fronted by a towering Shiva trident is the main structure but there's a positive jungle of temples, images, sculptures and chaityas with Shiva imagery everywhere. Images of the bull Nandi stand guard, tridents are dotted around and lingams rise up on every side.

You can turn right from the path to the Vishwarup Temple but there's no point since again Westerners are denied entry to the temple precinct and from outside there's nothing to see. Instead, continue beyond the Gorakhnath Temple where the pathway turns steeply downhill to the river.

Guhyeshwari Temple

The Guhyeshwari Temple is dedicated to Shiva's shakti in her terrible manifestation as Kali. Like the Pashupatinath Temple, entry is banned to all but Hindus and the high wall around the temple prevents you from seeing inside. Guhyeshwari was built by King Pratap Malla in the 17th century and the temple, standing in a paved courtyard surrounded by dharamsalas (rest houses), is topped by an open roof with four gilded snakes arching up to support the roof finial. You can see the snakes from outside. The temple's main entrance gate by the river is an imposing and colourful affair. To the west of the main temple building are a series of white, stupa-like temples.

The temple's curious name comes from *guhya* (vagina) and *ishwari* (goddess) – it's the temple of the goddess' vagina! When Shiva was insulted by his father-in-law, Parvati was so incensed that she burst into flames and it was this act of self-immolation which gave rise to the practice of *sati* or suttee, where a widow was consigned to the same funeral pyre as her deceased husband. The grieving Shiva carried off his shakti's corpse but as he wandered aimlessly, the body disintegrated and this is where her yoni fell.

Getting There & Away

Buses to Bodhnath go via Pashupatinath. Prior to the completion of the Kathmandu Bus Terminal, buses left from Rani Pokhari (Bus Stop 3) and the stop for Pashupatinath is called Gosala. Pashupatinath is an easy bicycle ride from Kathmandu: simply ride east from Thamel along Tridevi Marg, passing in front of the new Royal Palace. It gets a bit more complicated after that, but you can't really go wrong as long as you keep heading east. The airport is very close to Pashupatinath, so some of the roads carry a lot of traffic.

It's a pleasant short walk between Pashupatinath and Bodhnath. From the Guhyeshwari Temple, the dome of Bodhnath is clearly visible to the north but the foot-bridge shown on some maps right in front of Guhyeshwari does not exist! Walk west along the riverbank for a couple of hundred metres to the bridge by some ghats, cross the river and a footpath leads off north-east to Bodhnath. You eventually come out on the main road, right across from the main entrance to the stupa enclosure.

CHABAHIL (6 km)
The **Chabahil Stupa** is like a small replica of Bodhnath, about 1½ km west of Bodhnath, back towards Kathmandu. The small village of Chabahil has been virtually swallowed up by the expansion of Kathmandu but the site is very old and the original stupa was said to have been built by Ashoka's daughter Charumati. It certainly predates Bodhnath and around the main stupa are a number of small chaityas from the Licchavi period, dating back to between the 5th and 8th centuries. The site includes a metre-high 9th-century statue of a Bodhisattva which is claimed to be one of the finest pieces of sculpture in the valley.

Nearby is the small **Chandra Binayak Ganesh Temple** with a double roof in brass. Ganesh's shrew stands on a pillar in front of the shrine, waiting for the tiny image of the god inside. A short distance south, but still on the Kathmandu side of the main road, is the well-designed **Jayabageshwari Temple** dating from the late 17th century.

BODHNATH (6 km)
On the eastern side of Kathmandu, just north of the airport and an interesting walk from Pashupatinath, is the huge stupa of Bodh-nath, the largest stupa in Nepal and one of the largest in the world. It is the religious centre for Nepal's considerable population of Tibetans and there are a number of thriving monasteries and many small shops selling Tibetan artefacts (beware, prices are high and bargaining is essential).

Many of these Tibetans are refugees who fled their country following the unsuccessful uprising against the Chinese invaders in 1959. They have been energetic and successful in the intervening years, as the large houses surrounding Bodhnath testify. While the political and religious oppression continues in Tibet, this is one of the few places in the world where Tibetan culture is both accessible and unhindered.

Late afternoon is a good time to visit, when the group tours depart and the place once again becomes a Tibetan town. Prayer services are held in the surrounding gompas and as the sun sets the community turns out to circumambulate the stupa – a ritual that combines

Bodhnath Stupa

Bodhnath

0   25   50 m

To Kopan
Monastery

Nyingmapa
Gompa

Kargyupa/Nyingmapa
Gompa

Sakyapa
Gompa

Kargyupa
Gompa

Chinya–Lama
Gompa

To Lotus
Guest House

Stupa View
Restaurant

Entrance to
Upper Walkway

Ajima Shrine

Gelugpa
Gompa

Stupa

Sakyapa
Gompa

Dergey Tibetan
Restaurant

Bir
Restaurant

To Gokarna, Sundarijal,
Sankhu & Stupa Hotel

To Kathmandu

Hotel
Tashi
Delek

Walking Trail to
Pashupatinath

religious observance with a social event. Do not forget to walk around the stupa in a clockwise direction.

Bodhnath has always been associated with Lhasa and Tibetan Buddhism. One of the major trade routes from Lhasa came through Sankhu, and Bodhnath therefore lies at the Tibetan traders' entry to Kathmandu. One can easily imagine the traders giving thanks for their successful journey across the Himalaya, or praying for a safe return. People still come here to pray before undertaking a journey in the Himalaya.

Festivals

The Tibetan new year in February is celebrated by large crowds of pilgrims, who come to watch the lamas perform their rites. Long copper horns are blown, a portrait of the Dalai Lama is paraded around, and masked dances are performed.

Bodhnath Stupa

There does not seem to be any agreement on how old the site is, but it is likely that the first stupa was built some time after 600 CE, after the Tibetan king, Songtsen Gompo, was converted to Buddhism by his two wives: the Nepalese princess Bhrikuti (sometimes regarded as an incarnation of the Green Tara) and Wen Cheng Konjo from China (the White Tara). The current stupa was probably built after the depredations of the Moghul invaders in the 14th century.

Stupas were originally built to house holy relics, or to commemorate an event or place, with a structure that symbolises Buddhist beliefs. They are never hollow. It is not certain if there is anything interred at Bodhnath, but some believe that there is a piece of bone that once belonged to Gautama Buddha.

The base of the stupa takes the shape of a mandala (symbolising earth); on this four-tiered base sits the dome (symbolising water); then comes the spire (symbolising fire); the umbrella (symbolising air); and the pinnacle (symbolising ether). The Buddha's ever-watchful eyes glare out in four directions from the square base of the spire. There

is a third eye between and above the two normal eyes and the 'nose' is not a nose at all but the number one, signifying the oneness of all life. The spire is made up of 13 steps, representing the 13 stages on the journey to nirvana.

Around the base of the stupa's circular mound are 108 small images of the Dhyani Buddha Amitabha. A brick wall around the stupa has 147 niches, each with four or five prayer wheels bearing that immortal mantra *om mani padme hum*. On the northern side of the stupa is a small shrine dedicated to Ajima, the goddess of smallpox.

Gompas

There are a number of gompas surrounding Bodhnath that can be visited so long as you are respectful and discreet.

Do not forget to remove your shoes and hat before you enter one, and ask before taking photos. Smoking is not permitted anywhere in the main compounds. Do not step over or sit on the monks' cushions, even if no-one is sitting on them. During ceremonies enter quietly and stand by the wall near the main entrance; do not walk around in front of the altar, or between the monks, or cross the central area of the temple. Do not let loose with your flash in the middle of a service.

It is appropriate to make an offering to the lama, especially if you do take photographs. A khata (white scarf) is traditional, but these days rupees are also appreciated; monasteries depend for their existence on the donations of the faithful.

Decorations All the gompas are decorated with impressive mural paintings depicting mythological scenes, and sometimes thangkas (painted on cotton, framed in brocade and hung), although there is quite a range in quality. The subjects are usually gods, great lamas, ritual diagrams (mandalas which represent the forces of the universe and aid meditation) and the wheel of life. The wheel of life is represented in the porch of every gompa and represents Buddha's knowledge and the way humans can escape their conditioning and achieve nirvana. Extremely complex rules govern every detail of these traditional arts; all stress spirituality, order and symmetry, not originality.

You will also see huge statues of various Buddhas (the Tibetans believe Buddha has been reincarnated many times), prayer wheels, strategically arranged lamps filled with ghee (clarified butter), and sometimes offerings of rice. To the Western eye, the gompas are riots of colour, but awesome nonetheless. Most religious rites involve the recitation of sacred texts and chanting, often punctuated by musical instruments. The instruments dramatise and underline particular passages – usually in a quite unmusical way. Drums and cymbals crash, and trumpets and oboes moan repetitively. The result can be dramatic and moving.

Sects There are four major sects in Tibetan Buddhism and all of them are represented at Bodhnath: Nyingmapa, Kargyupa, Sakyapa (often, for obvious reasons, referred to as Red Hat sects), and Gelugpa (the Yellow Hat sect). The real differences are quite esoteric with their roots often in political rather than major theological disputes.

Sometimes the Nyingmapa sect is referred to as the Old One, because its teachings are based on Buddhist texts that were translated into Tibetan from the 7th to 11th centuries. The Kargyupa sect was founded by Marpa in the 11th century and has a strong Tantric influence. Marpa's most famous disciple was Milarepa, Tibet's most revered poet. The Sakyapa was also founded in the 11th century and it rose to a position where it ruled Tibet (with the support of the Mongols) until it ran into conflict with a strict 'reformed' sect, the Gelugpa which had been founded in the 14th century.

Unlike the Sakyapa, the Gelugpa (Yellow Hats) sect was celibate and disciplined. It introduced the system of reincarnated spiritual leaders and ultimately came to power – again with the support of the Mongols – in the late 17th century. It was a Mongol ruler who conferred the title Dalai Lama (which means 'ocean of wisdom') on its leader. The Gelugpa completely isolated Tibet and maintained a strict theocratic state.

Sakyapa Gompa This is the only gompa that opens directly onto the stupa (on the western side). There are some fine paintings and a magnificent Tara covered in beautiful embroideries. Don't miss the massive prayer wheel on the left of the entrance.

Chinya-Lama Gompa Named after a lama who had trained in China, this gompa is on

---

The Tibetan Calendar
Around the base of the great dorje at the top of the stairway to Swayambhunath are the symbols of the 12 animals of the Tibetan calendar. The animals are similar to those of the Chinese calendar and through this century they fall as follows:

Snake	1929	1941	1953	1965	1977	1989
Horse	1930	1942	1954	1966	1978	1990
Sheep	1931	1943	1955	1967	1979	1991
Monkey	1932	1944	1956	1968	1980	1992
Goose	1933	1945	1957	1969	1981	1993
Dog	1934	1946	1958	1970	1982	1994
Pig	1935	1947	1959	1971	1983	1995
Rat	1936	1948	1960	1972	1984	1996
Bull	1937	1949	1961	1973	1985	1997
Tiger	1938	1950	1962	1974	1986	1998
Hare	1939	1951	1963	1975	1987	1999
Dragon	1940	1952	1964	1976	1988	2000

the right of the path that leaves to the north of the stupa.

Nyingmapa Gompa This is one of the most recently completed (1984) and impressive gompas. It has a large and thriving community – there are lots of young novices. The gompa is a large, reddish-ochre building (designed after a monastery in Tibet) surrounded by lower, white buildings that form a large courtyard. There are some very fine interior decorations that are the work of artists from Bhutan.

Kargyupa/Nyingmapa Gompa Also known as the Ka-Nying Sheldrup Ling monastery, this large white gompa is equal to the Nyingmapa Gompa in size. It has a richly decorated interior with some fine paintings and large thangkas. The entrance is to the left of the main metal gates and Westerners are welcome; the lama speaks English. The gompa hosts an annual seminar on Vajrayana training, usually in October for two weeks. In 1992, the seminar cost Rs 1800 ($36), and accommodation was available for an additional payment.

Sakyapa Gompa This gompa, to the northeast of the stupa, does not have the imposing architectural unity of the previous two – it has obviously been built in stages over a number of years – but it is no less interesting. There are some high-quality frescoes (inside the vestibule) and the main room is richly gilded and atmospheric.

Gelugpa Gompa To the right of the lane that runs north-east from the stupa, the Gelugpa Gompa is the least imposing gompa in appearance, but it nonetheless attracts large crowds of worshippers and has many young monks.

Places to Stay

The *Hotel Tashi Delek* (☎ 01-471380) is right on the main road not far from the entrance to the stupa. The back rooms are reasonably quiet and look out across the fields to Pashupatinath. Doubles with shared bath are Rs 150.

The *Lotus Guest House* (☎ 01-472432) provides a very pleasant option if you want to escape the madness of Kathmandu for peace and quiet and if you want to be close to Bodhnath. Rooms are spotlessly clean and there is a nice garden. Singles/doubles with bath cost Rs 180/250 ($3.50/5), or Rs 150/220 ($3/4.50) without, plus 10% tax.

The *Bir Restaurant* on the main road has basic doubles for Rs 150 ($3).

The *Stupa Hotel* is on the main road to Sankhu, a 10-minute walk from the stupa. It's a new hotel with about 40 rooms at $12 a double.

Places to Eat

There are a number of small restaurants along the main road outside the stupa enclosure and a couple of restaurants around the stupa itself. On the main road, the best choice is the *Bir Restaurant*, which is a popular meeting place for the local Tibetans and Westerners living in the area. Most dishes are under Rs 20.

The newest and best choice near the stupa is the *Stupa View* which really does have a stupendous view, as well as excellent food (if a little overpriced). Main meals including a good range of vegetarian and Italian dishes are around Rs 90.

The *Stupa Hotel*, a 10-minute walk from the stupa, has an excellent garden restaurant with good food and reasonable prices.

Getting There & Away

Before the new Kathmandu Bus Terminal was completed, buses to Bodhnath ran from Rani Pokhari (Bus Stop 3), took one hour and cost Rs 2. Bicycles or taxis are better options. It's an interesting short walk between Bodhnath and Pashupatinath (see the Pashupatinath section for details).

Most tour operators include Bodhnath on their itineraries, usually in combination with Pashupatinath, and sometimes with Swayambhunath.

KOPAN (9 km)

The Kopan monastery (☎ 01-226717), a popular centre for courses on Buddhism and other Tibetan-related subjects, stands on a hilltop to the north of Bodhnath. You can visit Kopan on a walk between Bodhnath and the Gokarna Mahadev Temple, locals will point the way.

The centre has short courses on Tibetan medicine, thangka painting and other subjects but the major attraction for Westerners is the 10-day residential course introducing Buddhist psychology and philosophy. The cost is about $240 including accommodation and food, but the participants must observe strict disciplinary rules.

In Maharajganj in Kathmandu, the Himalayan Yogic Institute (☎ 01-413094) is associated with the monastery and also operates courses; they can provide information on Kopan. Call the monastery direct or write to the Nepal Mahayana Centre, PO Box 817, Kathmandu, Nepal for more information on Kopan.

GOKARNA MAHADEV TEMPLE (10 km)

Only a short distance beyond Bodhnath the Sundarijal road turns off from the Sankhu road and a couple of km of twists and turns takes you to the old Newari village of Gokarna, just north of the Gokarna Safari Park. The village is surrounded on three sides by the reserve and is notable for its fine riverside Shiva temple.

Built in 1582 the triple-roofed Mahadev (Great God) or Gokarneshwar (Lord of Gokarna) Temple stands on the banks of the Bagmati River and its inner sanctum enshrines a particularly revered Shiva lingam. Over the temple entrance is a golden torana with Shiva and Parvati making an appearance in the centre in the Uma Maheshwar position (Parvati's hand resting on Shiva's knee) with a figure of the Garuda above them.

For visitors, the temple's great interest is the surprisingly varied collection of sculptures and reliefs all around the site. They even line the pathway down from the road to the temple courtyard, starting with a Buddha figure at the top, and feature a varied collection of gods and goddesses, some dating back over a thousand years.

The sculptures include figures from Hindu mythology including Narad, Surya (sun god), Chandra (moon god) and Kamadeva (god of love). There's a bearded image of Brahma, Ganesh makes his usual cheerful appearance and Vishnu appears as Narsingha, making a particularly thorough job of disembowelling a nasty demon. Shiva's bull Nandi stands beside the temple and apart from the inevitable lingams dotted around there's even a nude figure of Shiva, complete with erect lingam. Durga makes three appearances, one of them as Ajima, the goddess of smallpox. The finest of the Gokarna statuary is housed in the small shrine house in the north-western corner of the courtyard. This 8th-century sculpture of the beautiful goddess Parvati shows her at her radiant best, you can see why Shiva fancied her!

To one side of the main temple, just above the river, is the small, open, single-storey **Vishnu Paduka**. This relatively recent addition shelters a metal plate bearing Vishnu's footprint. Outside, and set into the steps above the river, is an image of Shiva, reclining on a bed of cobras, just like the reclining Vishnu images at Budhanilkantha and Balaju.

Durga

Bagmati

River

Gokarna
Mahadev

1 Trident with skeleton
  figure at base
2 Figure of woman with
  four arms & a pot
  on her head
3 Paduka (Vishnu's
  Footprint)
4 Well-Endowed Shiva
5 Shiva Image reclining
  on a bed of snakes
6 Nandi (Shiva's Bull)
7 Gokarna Mahadev
  Temple
8 Golden Torana
  with Uma-Maheshwar
  in centre
9 Ganesh
10 Hanuman
11 Bearded Brahma
12 Narsingha (Vishnu's
   man-lion incarnation)
13 Buddha
14 Cow

0   5   10 m

Getting There & Away

You can walk, cycle or take a taxi to Gokarna but there's also an interesting walking route between Gokarna and Bodhnath via the monastery at Kopan. The clear trail starts from just beyond the bridge, on the Kathmandu side of Gokarna. It starts off steeply north-west and runs through fields and bamboo groves past teahouses to Kopan on top of a small hill. There are regular courses on meditation and Buddhism at the Kopan monastery and many Westerners take part. From Kopan it's an easy walk south-west to Bodhnath.

SUNDARIJAL (15 km)

At the edge of the valley, the streams which eventually join the Bagmati River flow over the waterfalls at Sundarijal into a 100-year-old reservoir. This is also the starting point for the popular trek to Helambu, and the main reservoir which supplies drinking water to the valley is about a two-hour walk uphill from here. A smaller trail forks off before the reservoir to a small rock cave, where a 13th-century image of Mahadevi (the Great Goddess) can be found. See the Nagarkot section for details of the long valley-rim walk to Sundarijal from Nagarkot.

Getting There & Away

Buses leave from Tukuchapul (Bus Stop 7) near the Central Bus Station and cost Rs 9. It's a pleasant bicycle ride along the quiet roads past Gokarna.

Sankhu & Vajra Jogini Route

The route to Sankhu follows the old Tibetan trade route past Bodhnath. After Bodhnath the road to Sundarijal turns off to the north-east and the road to Sankhu continues to the east.

GOKARNA SAFARI PARK (10 km)

Continuing beyond Bodhnath from Kath-mandu, the entrance to the Royal Game Reserve or King's Forest is off the Sankhu road. A deer park was created here late in the last century and the walled reserve has spotted deer (chital), hog deer (laghuna), monkeys and birds.

This is one of the few woodlands left on the valley floor, and is a pleasant spot for a picnic. You can go wandering on foot, ride an elephant for Rs 350 ($7) an hour, or ride a horse for Rs 250 ($5) an hour. There's also a decent nine-hole golf course. You can't use the elephants as golf buggies, but you do get caddies; unfortunately, the cost is a steep $25.

Entrance to the park costs Rs 50 and the park is open from 8 am to 6 pm in summer; it can get very crowded on Saturdays and during festivals.

Getting There & Away

The reserve is about 2½ km from Bodhnath, so it can be easily reached by bicycle. Prior to the opening of the new Kathmandu Bus Terminal, buses ran quite frequently to Sun-darijal from Tukuchapul (Bus Stop 7) and you could get off at the entrance; less frequent buses to Sankhu left from near the Martyrs' Memorial Gate (Bus Stop 9).

SANKHU (20 km)

Sankhu was once an important post on the trading route between Kathmandu and Lhasa, and although the town's great days are over, you can still see many signs of its former prosperity. The town was first settled in the Licchavi era and there are many old homes decorated with fine woodcarving. Although many traditional aspects of Newari life continue in the town, the most persuasive reason to visit this place is the beautiful Vajra Jogini Temple, about two km north of town.

Getting There & Away

Prior to the opening of the new Kathmandu Bus Terminal, buses to Sankhu left from near Martyrs' Memorial Gate (Bus Stop 9) – not far from the Bhadrakali Temple (two hours, Rs 9). You may also find a bus at the Central Bus Station (Bus Stop 6).

It's easy to reach Sankhu by bike. The road is sealed and flat (with a few minor exceptions), and basically follows the Manohara River. It's an attractive and interesting ride taking about 1½ hours beyond Bodhnath. Rather than backtrack all the way, in the dry season at least it is possible to cross the Manohara River and climb to the fascinating Changu Narayan Temple (see the Changu Narayan section for details). See the Nagarkot section for details of the interesting walk down to Sankhu.

VAJRA JOGINI (22 km)

Perched high above the valley, in a grove of huge, old trees, this complex of temples is well worth visiting. The main temple was built in 1655 by Pratap Malla of Kathmandu, but it seems likely that the site has been used for much longer than that. The origins of the Tantric goddess who is worshipped in this bewitching spot are hard to determine.

The climb up the stone steps to the temple is steep and hot but there are a number of waterspouts where you can cool off. About halfway up there's a shelter and some carvings of Kali and Ganesh. A natural stone represents Than Bhairab and sacrifices are made at its foot.

As you enter the main temple compound you will see several fine bells (the Tantric female equivalent to the vajra or thunderbolt) on your right. There are two temples and the one nearest to the entrance is the Vajra Jogini Temple, a pagoda with a three-tiered roof of sheet copper. There is some beautiful repoussé work on the southern facade. The struts are carved with protective animals and gods from the Buddhist pantheon. The goddess' image cannot actually be seen through the door.

The two-tiered temple furthest from the entrance enshrines a chaitya and commemorates Ugra Tara, or Blue (Nilo) Tara, a Buddhist goddess. The woodcarving around the doors is very fine. There are various chaityas around the platform and a gilt lion on a pillar. In the north-western corner of the courtyard (the far left when you enter) is the entrance to a cave, which is used for Tantric practices, and a Tibetan inscription. Behind the temples and up some stairs are buildings which were once used as pilgrim rest houses and priests' houses.

Tantric Goddesses
The name Vajra Jogini suggests a close association with Tantric beliefs. A *vajra* (*dorje* in Tibetan) is the Buddhist thunderbolt symbol that looks a bit like a hollow dumb-bell and Vajrayana is the name for the Tantric form of Buddhism. Tantric beliefs developed as a synthesis of ancient pre-Hindu religions and new ideas that rejected many orthodox Hindu and Buddhist beliefs. Tantric believers hold that endless rebirths on the journey to nirvana can be avoided by incorporating magical rites with all the energies of existence – both good and bad – under the strict tutelage of a lama. Sex and sexual imagery play a central role.

Hinduism was initially a patriarchal religion introduced by the Aryan invaders of India, and overriding the existing earth goddesses. The development of *shaktis* or the female consorts of the new male gods allowed the resurgence of the female forces. These goddesses have enjoyed tremendous popularity in the Kathmandu Valley, sometimes completely overshadowing their male counterparts, especially in Tantric belief. A parallel development in Buddhism produced the female counterparts to the Dhyani Buddhas.

A Jogini is the female counterpart to a Bhairab, one of the wrathful forms of Shiva. In other words, a Jogini is the wrathful form of Shiva's partner Mahadevi (the Great Goddess) who is Parvati in a more peaceful manifestation. Amongst some of Mahadevi's fearsome manifestations are Kali, Durga, Annapurna and Taleju.

So who is Vajra Jogini you ask? A Tantric goddess is the simple answer – a unique Nepalese goddess possibly combining elements from Hinduism, Buddhism and perhaps even earlier religions. ■

Getting There & Away

At Sankhu, turn left at the bus stop and walk north through the village (there is some beautiful woodcarving). Just after the road turns to the right take the road on the left which runs out of the village (under an ugly concrete archway). There are some fine stone carvings of Vishnu and Ganesh after the arch. The road then forks: the left fork is the traditional approach for pedestrians on foot and follows the small river; the right fork is drivable (though rough) and is OK for bikes.

There's a car park at the foot of the steps to the temple. If you get there by bicycle, it will be necessary to pay a few rupees to someone to look after it for you. It's quite a stiff climb to the temple.

Changu Narayan Route

THIMI (10 km)

Thimi is the fourth-largest town in the valley, outranked only by Kathmandu, Patan and Bhaktapur. It's a typical Newari town and its 'capable people' (the name of the town is derived from this Newari expression) operate thriving cottage industries producing pottery and papier-mâché masks. They also grow vegetables for the markets of Kathmandu.

The town's main road runs north-south between the old and new Bhaktapur roads which form the northern and southern boundaries of the town. In the centre of the southern square is the 16th-century **Balkumari Temple**. Balkumari was one of Bhairab's shaktis (a jogini) and a much less magnificent Bhairab Temple is found nearby (see the Vajra Jogini section for a brief discussion of Tantric goddesses). Thimi also has a 16th-century **Narayan temple** and a 15th-century **Mahadev temple**.

Just to the north of Thimi is **Nade** and from here a stone pathway leads up through an archway to the **Ganesh Dyochen**. Nearby is a locally popular triple-roofed **Ganesh temple**. Further north is Bode with

the interesting 17th-century **Mahalakshmi Temple**.

Festivals

In a Nepalese new year's day ceremony, 32 deities are carried to the Balkumari Temple in Thimi in palanquins. The arrival of the Ganesh image from Nade is the high point of the colourful (a great deal of bright red powder gets chucked around) festivities. A similar but smaller ceremony also takes place at the Mahalakshmi Temple in Bode.

CHANGU NARAYAN TEMPLE (22km)

The beautiful and historic temple of Changu Narayan stands on a hilltop at the eastern end of the valley, about four km north of Bhaktapur. Although the temple dates from 1702, when it was rebuilt after a fire, its origins go right back to the 4th century and there are many important stone images and sculptures dating from the Licchavi period.

Despite the temple's beauty and interest it attracts relatively few visitors because of its comparative inaccessibility, although these days you can drive right to the temple via Bhaktapur. Alternatively, it makes a pleasant walk from that town or an interesting destination on the walk down from Nagarkot.

The double-roofed temple is dedicated to Vishnu in his incarnation as Narayan and is exceptionally beautiful with quite amazingly intricate roof struts depicting multiarmed goddesses. The temple is fronted by a figure of Garuda said to date from the 5th century. The man-bird mount of Vishnu has a snake around his neck and kneels with folded hands facing the temple. Stone lions guard the wonderfully gilded door, flanked by equally detailed gilded windows. Two pillars at the front corners carry two of the traditional symbols of Vishnu, the conch shell and the chakra.

Despite the beauty of the temple itself it is, in Nepalese terms, relatively recent and the much older images found in the temple courtyard are of equal interest. Various images of Vishnu can be found around the courtyard, carrying the symbols associated with the god in his four hands. In the north-

Changu Narayan

0   5   10 m

To Manohara River

To Village & Bhaktapur

To the River

1   Vishnu & Garuda Image
    (from Rs 10 Note)
2   Krishna Shrine
3   Nriteshwar Shrine
4   Winged Lions
5   Vishnu Image
6   Mahavishnu
7   Mahadev Shiva Lingam
8   Images of Avalokitesvara & Vishnu
9   Pillar with Chakra Symbol
10 Garuda Image
11 Statue of King Bhupatindra Malla &
    His Queen
12 Stone Lions
13 Changu Narayan Temple
14 Griffins
15 Pillar with Conch Shell Symbol
16 Pashupatinath Shrine
17 Bhairab Shrine
18 Relief of Vishnu as Narsingha
19 Relief of Vishnu as Vikrantha
20 Lakshmi Narayan Temple
21 Reliefs of Narayan on
    the Serpent Ananta &
    Uma Maheshwar
22 Elephants
23 Mahadev Shiva Shrine
24 Ganesh Shrine

western corner of the courtyard there is an image of Vishnu astride the Garuda which is illustrated on the Nepalese Rs 10 note. Beside the Garuda figure which faces the front of the temple is one of the oldest Licchavi stone inscriptions in the valley.

Other images include one of Vishnu as Narsingha, his man-lion incarnation, in the act of disembowelling a demon. Another shows him as Vikrantha, the six-armed dwarf who transformed into a giant capable of covering the universe in three gigantic steps. Behind these two images is a small black slab showing Narayan reclining on the serpent Ananta at the bottom and Vishnu with 10 heads and 10 arms in the centre. This beautifully carved image dates from the 5th or 6th century.

Other points of interest include the statues of King Bhupatindra Malla and his queen, kneeling in a gilded cage in front of the temple. Look at the brick paving of the courtyard. In the centre, triangular bricks are used while out towards the edge there are older rounded-corner bricks. The village of Changu stands below the temple hill and has some Licchavi remains.

Changu Narayan

Places to Stay & Eat
The small *Restaurant Champak* is right inside the temple complex. On the road back to Bhaktapur, the *Changu Narayan Hill Resort* offers basic trekking-style accommodation.

Getting There & Away
There is no public transport to Changu Narayan. A taxi from Kathmandu will cost around Rs 300 ($6), and from Bhaktapur around Rs 100 ($2).

It takes about two hours on foot or about an hour by mountain bike to get to Changu Narayan from Bhaktapur. It's a wonderful downhill run on the way back but quite a steep climb on the way there. A long spur runs down from the eastern edge of the valley and the temple tops the final bump of this lengthy ridge. There is now a sealed road from Bhaktapur right to the village of Changu, which is only a short stroll from the temple, and you can easily get a taxi to Changu Narayan from Bhaktapur. A number of walking trails, clearly signposted, lead to Changu Narayan from Bhaktapur and once you get out of the town the hill is clearly visible.

If you're on foot or bicycle it's possible to continue to Bodhnath, Sankhu, the Royal Game Reserve at Gokarna or other attractions in the north-east of the valley. From the northern and western entranceways to the temple a short, steep path descends to the Manohara River, which can easily be waded

---

Narsingha

The image of Vishnu as Narsingha or Narsimha is a common one in the valley. In his man-lion incarnation the god is traditionally seen with a demon stretched across his legs, in the act of killing the creature by disembowelling it. You can find Narsingha at work at Changu Narayan, in front of the palace in Patan, just inside the Hanuman Dhoka palace entrance in Kathmandu and at the Gokarna Mahadev Temple.

The demon was supposedly undefeatable as it could not be killed by man or beast, by day or night or by any weapon. Vishnu's appearance as Narsingha neatly overcame the first obstacle for a man-lion is neither a man or a beast. He then waited until evening to attack the demon, for evening is neither day or night. And instead of a weapon Narsingha used his own nails to tear the demon apart. ∎

across or crossed by a temporary bridge during the dry season (it won't be possible in the monsoon). This brings you out to the Sankhu road at the village of Bramhakhel about 3½ km east of the Gokarna Safari Park.

If you approach Changu Narayan from the Sankhu road you'll see a small sign for Changu Narayan on a building wall on the south side at the entry to Bramhakhel. It's a five-minute walk across the fields to the river and the temporary bridge. It's quite a steep and difficult scramble up the hill that will take at least 45 minutes (especially if you're carrying a bike). You might like to go slower as there are a couple of small Newari hamlets along the way, and great views.

There's quite a labyrinth of paths up the hill and it's not a bad idea to have a guide (and bicycle carrier). You will probably find small boys offering their services – establish a price in advance. If not, just keep going up! From Changu Narayan it's an exhilarating half-hour bike ride to Bhaktapur, which is another 45 minutes from Kathmandu.

A third way of reaching Changu Narayan is by the pleasant downhill stroll from Nagarkot (see the following Nagarkot section). Walking down from Nagarkot to Changu Narayan and then on to Bhaktapur is a much more interesting walk than the straightforward walk down to Bhaktapur.

Nagarkot Route

The route to Nagarkot goes by Thimi and Bhaktapur before climbing steeply up to the village on the valley rim.

NAGARKOT (30 km)
There are various places around the edge of the Kathmandu Valley which offer great mountain views, but the resort village of Nagarkot is generally held to be the best. Every day mountain watchers make their way up to the village, stay overnight in one of Nagarkot's lodges, then rise at dawn to see the sun appear over the Himalaya.

Nagarkot is on a ridge on the north-eastern rim of the valley and the view extends all the way from Dhaulagiri in the west past Mt Everest (little more than a dot on the horizon) to Kanchenjunga in the east. An easy hour's walk north from the village will give an even better 360° view from a lookout tower on a ridge. You have to cross an army checkpost and they will only let you walk through in the morning.

A pilgrimage to Nagarkot will nearly always be rewarded with a view between October and March, but you will be very lucky to catch more than a glimpse through the clouds of some snow-capped mountain in the June to September monsoon period. It can get very cold at Nagarkot in autumn or winter so if you're staying overnight come prepared with warm clothing.

The main centre of Nagarkot, in reality a small cluster of guest houses, is a 10-minute walk north of the main road that runs through to the army camp. Nagarkot originally owes its existence to the camp, which lies to the south, but more lately to tourism. It was never a traditional village, so while the views can be stunning, and the surrounding countryside is great for walking, the unplanned scatter of lodges is not itself attractive.

There are a number of walks to and from Nagarkot, including fine walks down to Sundarijal, Sankhu, Changu Narayan or Bhaktapur in the valley or south to Banepa (beyond the valley). There is a cheese factory where you can buy some food to eat on your way down.

Places to Stay & Eat
Nagarkot has a small selection of lodges and guest houses, most offering a range of facilities at a range of prices. Most are expensive for the facilities you get – but what price the view? Most people eat at their lodge, and most are unimpressed with the cuisine.

Nagarkot accommodation is basically grouped around the small Mahakali Shrine, a 10-minute walk north of the bus stop on the main road that runs through to the army camp and continues to the lookout tower. Nagarkot is very much a one-night stand,

Nagarkot

0   400   800 m

To Sankhu &
The Farmhouse

1 Niva Home
2 Peaceful Cottage &
  Cafe du Mont
3 View Point Hotel
4 Mahakali Shrine
5 New Pheasant Lodge &
  Restaurant at the End
  of the Universe
6 Galaxy Hotel
7 Cheese Factory
8 Bus Stop
9 Tea House Restaurant
10 Nagarkot Sunrise &
   Moonbeam Guest House
11 Tara Gaon Lodge

To Changu
Narayan

Army Checkpost

Army Camp

To Bhaktapur &
Hotel Flora Hill

To Lookout
Tower

few visitors stay longer although you can make some pleasant strolls in the surrounding country.

Late in the afternoon each day there's a mass arrival and after breakfast each morning there's a mass departure. This means that every lodge can simultaneously run out of rooms, so when you reach Nagarkot make sure you find a room first. The best rooms go first, and late arrivals may find the accommodation standards dropping precipitously. In the off season there are fewer visitors and prices are highly negotiable.

In late '92, electricity was about to arrive,

so lighting, and hot water, currently a rare luxury, should be more reliably available. A torch is useful (for an early-morning start to the lookout tower) and warm clothing (even a sleeping bag) can be worthwhile. Most people are in bed pretty early, so bring a book.

Before you reach the main ridge, you'll pass the comfortable *Hotel Flora Hill* (☎ 01-226893). The location is quite pleasant, but you're a long walk (about three km) from the Himalayan views, which are really the main reason for visiting. Singles/doubles are $38/44.

The winding road takes a sharp turn at the cluster of shops which mark the Nagarkot bus stop. From here a dirt track veers left and after a couple of hundred metres comes to a hilltop group of hotels which are the most popular and best situated at Nagarkot. They cluster around the Mahakali Shrine, and many have rooms that offer Himalayan views straight from your bed. At the worst you'll just have to take a few steps outside to bring the whole panorama into view.

Above the intersection, a new restaurant aimed at day-trippers has been opened. The *Tea House* is an attractive building with good views, and it's open from 6 am to 8 pm. Main meals are around Rs 100 ($2), and a Coke is a steep Rs 30.

The *New Pheasant Lodge* has some standard rooms from Rs 150 ($3), including a few pleasant bamboo-walled cottages with attached toilet for Rs 200 ($4). None of the rooms have views. The lodge's wonderfully named *Restaurant at the End of the Universe* does have great views, however. With a carpeted bench around low tables it's a popular gathering place in the evening. The food is pretty good.

The *Galaxy Hotel*, just below the Pheasant Lodge, has singles/doubles with bath for $6/8, and some new luxury rooms for $15. Most rooms are reasonably pleasant, and have at least partial views, so you may consider the cost is worthwhile.

Continue beyond the Mahakali Shrine, skirting the bank official's house, and you reach the *Peaceful Cottage* (☎ 01-290877) which, like the Galaxy, has rooms of varying standards. The staff are helpful and the good rooms have fine views and are clean and well kept. The prices start from Rs 200 ($4), and there are also luxury rooms with private bath for $20. Topping the rise is the *Cafe du Mont* with magnificent views, and average food (you can't have everything!).

The newish *Hotel View Point* (☎ 01-417424) is the most luxurious option, with rooms starting at $10 and rising to $20 for a combination of comfort and views. All rooms have private bath with hot water. The restaurant has a fireplace.

Separated from this group of lodges by a couple of hundred metres is the *Niva Home* with simple, spartan rooms downstairs at Rs 150 ($3) and Rs 100 ($2) upstairs.

The best place is about four km away on the Sankhu road, past Niva Home. *The Farmhouse* is in an old, beautifully renovated Newari house and has been highly recommended. It's run by the Hotel Vajra, and rates are reasonably high, although meals are included. Singles/doubles are $20/40.

Getting There & Away

There's a road right to Nagarkot from Bhaktapur so you can take a bus or taxi all the way there. You don't even have to stay overnight as Kathmandu tour operators run dawn trips to Nagarkot to catch the sunrise. Walking to or, preferably, from Nagarkot is, however, an interesting alternative and there are several possible routes, all detailed in the Treks from Nagarkot section.

Buses operate to a somewhat unreliable schedule from Bhaktapur, departing every few hours and costing Rs 10. The bus can be very slow (taking up two hours) and extremely crowded. The roof is not only less crowded but also offers fine views. A taxi from Bhaktapur costs about Rs 400 ($8) one way or Rs 700 ($14) return.

From Kathmandu, most people catch the tourist bus which leaves from Thamel at 1.30 pm and arrives about 4 pm. Tickets are available from most tour agencies and tourist information centres. A one-way fare costs Rs 85, return Rs 165 ($1.50). Pre-dawn tours to Nagarkot from Kathmandu cost about Rs 200 ($4).

TREKS FROM NAGARKOT

There are a number of trekking routes to or from Nagarkot. As always with trekking it's easier to go down than up so if you only want to walk one way it's a good idea to take the bus to Nagarkot and walk back down. The following walks are all written heading downhill from Nagarkot.

Nagarkot to Bhaktapur

Until the road from Nagarkot to Bhaktapur was built, this walking trail was the only way to go. Now with buses running back and forth it's neither necessary nor all that enjoyable. You would be better off taking one of the alternative routes but if you do want to walk back down it's relatively easy to take the wide, easy trail which shortcuts across the road turns. The trail eventually joins the road on its final gradual ascent to Bhaktapur; you can follow this and turn off at the eastern end of the town or simply catch a bus, should one come by. It takes about two hours to walk down, and perhaps twice that walking up.

Going down you leave the main road to descend steeply through a pine forest, then follow a stream to a cluster of bamboo trees near the city reservoir where you rejoin the main road. From here you enter the town at the eastern end and continue to Tachupal Tole. If you want to walk up from Bhaktapur there are signs to Nagarkot in the town.

Nagarkot to Changu Narayan Temple

Walking down to Changu Narayan is a much more interesting alternative to the walk down to Bhaktapur. From Nagarkot it is very easy to see the long spur which extends into the Kathmandu Valley. At the very end of the spur the ridge line gives one final hiccup and then drops down to the valley floor. The beautiful temple of Changu Narayan is on the top of this final bump on the ridge line.

The walking trail from Nagarkot follows the road to Bhaktapur along a ridge, branching off at a sharp hairpin bend. It's easier to

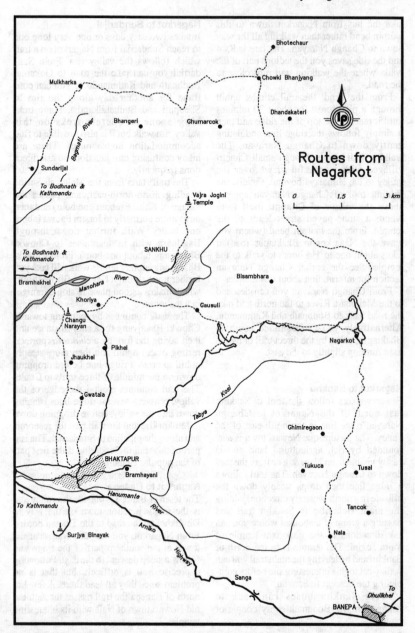

Routes from Nagarkot

take the bus from Nagarkot down to this hairpin bend rather than walking all the way down to Changu Narayan. The fare is Rs 4 and the ride saves you the tedious part of the walk, where the walking trail runs close to the road.

From the bend, the trail climbs uphill through a pine forest for about 20 minutes until it reaches the top of the ridge and then it simply follows the ridge line undulating gently down to Changu Narayan. The walking trail passes through small Chhetri villages with wonderful views over the valley to the Himalaya beyond. Finally, the shining roof of Changu Narayan appears above the village of **Changu** itself from where a stone-paved street leads to the temple. From the hairpin bend (where you leave the Nagarkot to Bhaktapur road) it takes about one to 1½ hours to walk to the temple. See the earlier Changu Narayan section for information about this temple.

From Changu Narayan you can descend to the Manohara River to the north and take the road back to Bodhnath and Kathmandu. Alternatively you can continue south to Bhaktapur, either by the direct trail or by the road running slightly to the east.

Nagarkot to Sankhu

Fewer walkers follow the trail to Sankhu, just north of the Nagarkot to Changu Narayan ridge line in the north-east of the valley. The picturesque Newari town is surrounded by rich agricultural land and is easily visible from Nagarkot or from the trail down to Changu Narayan. The trail follows a ridge line then drops steeply down the hillside in a north-westerly direction, joining the main Helambu to Sankhu trail and passing a group of teahouses where you can ask directions to the important temple of Vajra Jogini. The temple is to the north of Sankhu and by leaving the main trail you can walk west to this interesting site before completing the descent to Sankhu.

From Sankhu buses run back to Kathmandu via Bodhnath every couple of hours.

Nagarkot to Sundarijal

It takes two easy days or one very long one to reach Sundarijal from Nagarkot on a trail which follows the valley rim. From Sundarijal you can take the road to Gokarna, Bodhnath and Kathmandu or you can continue for another day along the rim to Sheopuri and Budhanilkantha. Some trekking agencies operate treks on this valley-rim walk but it is also possible to find accommodation in teahouses. There are many confusing trail junctions so ask directions frequently.

The trail starts from the Mahakali Shrine heading north-north-east, and passes the village of Kattike (about one hour) and then turns more northerly to Jorsim Pauwa (about one hour). Walk further down through Bagdhara with its teahouses to Chowki Bhanjyang (about one hour). From Chowki Bhanjyang another hour's walk will take you further north through Nagle to **Bhotechaur**, which makes a good place to stop overnight in a teahouse.

The walk continues by returning towards Chowki Bhanjyang for a short distance and then taking the fork by a *chautara* (porters' resting place) uphill and then more steeply uphill to cross a ridge line before dropping down on the middle of three trails to Chule. The trail contours around the edge of the valley, crossing several ridge lines running down into the valley, before dropping down to **Mulkarkha** and the trail past the reservoir and along the pipeline to Sundarijal. The last part of this trail to Sundarijal is the first part of the popular Helambu Trek.

Nagarkot to Banepa

The town of Banepa is outside the valley and is the major junction town on the way to Dhulikhel on the road to the Tibetan border. From Nagarkot, you start this walk near the tower at the southern part of the ridge and follow a steep descent to the east. Following a precise trail is difficult, but that is no problem since they all lead there. A few km north of Banepa the trail passes through the old Newari town of Nala with its interesting temples.

From Banepa, you can take a bus back to Kathmandu or continue to Dhulikhel where many travellers stay in the delightful Dhulikhel Lodge. See Dhulikhel in the next section.

Dhulikhel & Arniko Highway Route

The Arniko Highway to Dhulikhel passes by Thimi, skirts the southern side of Bhaktapur and then climbs out of the valley before dropping down to Banepa, continuing to Dhulikhel, the Tibetan border and on to Lhasa. This route is also covered in the Mountain Biking chapter.

BANEPA (26 km)

Just outside the valley, the small town of Banepa is a busy crossroads with a statue of King Tribhuvan marking the centre of town. The popular village of Dhulikhel is five km beyond Banepa; the temple town of Panauti is about five km south; the interesting village of Nala is just to the north-west; and Chandeshwari, with it's legendary old temple, is only a km or so north-east – yet Banepa itself is of very limited interest. Indeed the main road through town, all that most visitors see, is a dusty, noisy affair and waiting for a change of bus at that busy crossroads is often decidedly unpleasant.

Around Town

Banepa has few buildings of interest although there are some pleasant squares and quieter laneways in the older part of town to the north-west. The old town square has two Narayan temples with virtually back-to-back worshipful Garuda statues. Right beside the turn-off to Chandeshwari is an attractive tank with bas reliefs of gods at one end.

Chandeshwari Temple

Only a km or so north-east of Banepa the temple to the goddess Chandeshwari perches on the edge of a gorge. The road out of Banepa runs gently uphill then just as gently downhill through open fields and then a short village street, past an old tank right to the arched entrance gate to the temple.

The people of this valley were once terrorised by a demon known as Chand and when Parvati, in her demon-slaying mode, got rid of the nuisance she took the name Chandeshwari, 'slayer of Chand', and this temple was built in her honour. The temple is entered through a doorway topped by a brilliantly coloured relief of Parvati disposing of the demon. The triple-roofed temple has roof struts showing the eight Ashta Matrikas and eight Bhairabs but the temple's most notable feature is on the west wall which is painted with a huge and colourful fresco of Bhairab at his destructive worst.

The temple also has a Shiva shrine complete with lingam, and Nandi and Ganesh also make an appearance. The ghats below the temple, beside the stream, are an auspicious place to die and people come here when their end is nigh.

Getting There & Away

Regular buses leave from the Central Bus Station (Bus Stop 6) and the trip to Banepa takes about two hours and costs Rs 9. Buses continue on from Banepa to Dhulikhel and further towards Kodari on the Chinese border. There are also regular services south from Banepa to Panauti.

NALA

The interesting small town of Nala is about four km north-west of Banepa. Nala's **Bhagwati Temple** dominates the central square of the town and is one of the very few four-tiered temples in the valley area. On the edge of the settlement is the Buddhist pagoda temple of **Karunamaya**, dedicated to Avalokitesvara.

PANAUTI

Standing in a valley about six km south of Banepa, the small town of Panauti is at the junction of the rivers Roshi Khola and Pungamati Khola. Like Allahabad in India a third 'invisible' river is said to join the other two at the confluence. The town is relatively untouched and has a number of interesting temples, one of which may be the oldest in Nepal. Panauti once stood at the junction of important trading routes and had a royal palace in its main square. Today it's just a quiet backwater, but all the more interesting for that.

Festivals

Panauti celebrates a chariot festival at the end of the monsoon each year when images of the gods from the town's various temples are drawn around the streets in temple carts. The festival starts from the town's old Durbar Square.

There are a number of important religious sites across the subcontinent that play host to huge *melas* (religious fairs that attract enormous crowds of pilgrims, worshippers and sadhus). Every 12 years (next in 1998), the Magh Sankrati festival around mid-January (the Nepalese month of Magh), is celebrated with a great mela in Panauti.

Indreshwar Mahadev Temple

The three-storey Indreshwar Mahadev Temple in the village centre is a Shiva temple. The temple was originally built in 1294 over a Shiva lingam and was subsequently rebuilt in the 15th century. In 1988 an earthquake caused serious damage and there are plans to renovate it. In its original form it may well have been the oldest temple in Nepal – Kathmandu's Kasthamandap may predate it but Kasthamandap was originally built as a dharamsala, not as a temple.

Around the temple are many shrines including one dedicated to Ahilya, the beautiful wife of a Vedic sage.

Legends relate that she was seduced by the god Indra who tricked her by assuming the shape of her husband. When the sage returned and discovered what had happened he took a bizarre revenge upon Indra by causing his body to become covered in yonis, female sexual organs! Naturally Indra was somewhat put out by this and for many years he and his wife Indrayani repented at this auspicious confluence of rivers. Eventually Parvati, Shiva's consort, took pity upon Indrayani and turned her into the invisible river which joins the two visible ones in Panauti. More years passed and eventually Shiva decided to release Indra from his strange problem. Shiva appeared in Panauti as a great lingam and when Indra bathed in the river the yonis disappeared. The lingam is the one which stands in the temple.

The temple, run-down though it may be, is certainly a fine one and the roof struts depicting the various incarnations of Shiva and some discreetly amorous couples are said to be masterpieces of Newari woodcarving. The courtyard has numerous smaller shrines apart from the stone pillar to Ahilya. To one side of the main temple is a rectangular **Bhairab temple** with faces peering out of the three upstairs windows, rather like the Shiva-Parvati Temple in Kathmandu's Durbar Square. A small double-roofed Shiva temple stands by the north-western corner while a Vishnu shrine with a two-metre-high image of the god faces the temple from the west. Look for the pots and pans hanging under the roof eaves of the main temple. They're donated to the temple by newlyweds to ensure a happy married life.

Other Temples

Across the Pungamati Khola is the 17th-century Brahmayani Temple; a suspension bridge crosses the river at this point. Brahmayani is the chief goddess of the village and her image is drawn around the town each year in the chariot festival. This temple was restored with French assistance in 1982-83.

On the town side of the river, actually at the junction where the two rivers meet, is a Krishna Narayan temple with some woodcarvings of similar age and style to the Indreshwar Mahadev Temple. The riverbank stone sculptures are also of interest but unfortunately the late '80s were cruel to Panauti: apart from the earthquake there were also severe floods which swept away the cremation ghats at the river junction.

Getting There & Away

Buses between Dhulikhel and Banepa cost Rs 2. Buses run regularly to Panauti and

Dhulikhel

Krishna Temple

Bhagwati Shiva Temple

Vishnu Temple

Harisiddhi Temple

Tank

Ganesh Temple

To Banepa & Kathmandu

To Kodari

To Post Office, Mountain Viewpoint, Nawa Rangu Guest House, Shiva Temple & Namobuddha

To Panauti

Dhulikhel Lodge

Tank

leave from the junction by the king's statue in the middle of Banepa (Rs 2). See the Dhulikhel section for information on walking to Panauti.

DHULIKHEL (32 km)

Only five km beyond Banepa is the interesting small town of Dhulikhel. It's popular as a Himalayan viewpoint, in part because the road to Dhulikhel is easier than the steep and winding road to Nagarkot, but also because Dhulikhel is real, not just a tourist resort. It's also a good centre for short day treks – many visitors come here to stretch their legs before setting off on longer treks.

Dhulikhel is a district headquarters and has a number of government offices, a high school and even a small jail. Its population is Newari although there are people of many other groups in the surrounding villages. The prime Himalayan viewpoint is the parade ground, on the ridge just east of the centre. In the late '60s Dhulikhel was a gathering point for hippies who even planned to build their own temple here! An even better view can be found from the hill topped by a Kali temple, about 30 minutes' walk along the Namobuddha trail.

Temples

The old part of the town, west of the bus stop and the Dhulikhel Lodge, is an interesting area to wander around with some fine old Newari buildings and several interesting temples. The town's main square has a tank, the small triple-roofed **Harisiddhi Temple** and a **Vishnu temple** fronted by two worshipful Garudas in quite different styles. One is a kneeling stone Garuda topping a low pillar while the second Garuda is in bright metal, flanked by two kneeling devotees, and is more like the bird-faced Garudas of Indonesia than the conventional Nepalese Garudas. The triple-roofed temple has been decorated with brightly coloured ceramic tiles. Beyond the square, the western end of the town is marked by a hill topped by a modern **Krishna temple** and the **Bhagwati Shiva Temple**.

Walking in the other direction you pass the post office, the mountain viewpoint and reach the junction where the road turns south to Namobuddha. Continue straight on from the junction and dip down to a picturesque little **Shiva temple** at the bottom of a gorge. Water flows through the site where the main sanctum is a squat, square block decorated with coloured tiles and topped with a metal dome with four nagas arching down from the pinnacle. The temple is fronted by figures of Nandi on pillars and kneeling devotees. To one side is a fine image of Ganesh, while in a second small shrine only the feet remain of three images, the result of art thieves' work. Below that is a tank but this is a temple with everything – if you look around you can find images of Hanuman, Saraswati, Shiva and Parvati, lingams, tridents and much more.

Dhulikhel's final temple attraction is the **Kali Temple** high up the hill towards Namobuddha. Climb up here for the excellent view, not the temple which is of little interest.

Namobuddha Trek

The trek from Dhulikhel to Namobuddha or Namura is a fine walk in itself and also a good leg-stretcher for longer treks. It takes about three hours each way, so it makes a good day walk; the Dhulikhel Lodge has a sketch map of the route. The walk can be made either as a return trip or as a loop to avoid backtracking. If you start early enough you can even continue on from Namobuddha to Panauti and return from there via Banepa by bus.

Namobuddha is a relatively easy trek which can even be made during the monsoon. From Dhulikhel the trail first climbs up to the Kali temple lookout then drops down through the village of **Kavre** and past a number of teahouses. It then climbs again through pine woods past **Phulbari** and up and down a couple more hills before reaching the Namobuddha hill. Asking directions is no problem, any Westerner heading in this direction is assumed to be going to Namobuddha!

Surprisingly little is known about the stupa at Namobuddha although it is an important destination for Buddhist pilgrims. A legend relates that a Buddha came across a tigress close to death from starvation and unable to feed her cubs. The sorrowful Buddha allowed the hungry tigress to consume him, and if you climb to the top of the hill from the stupa, you will reach the site

where this is supposed to have taken place – a stone tablet on the hill here depicts the event.

There is an important festival at this site on Namobuddha hill in November.

In 1992 village-style accommodation was being constructed at Namobuddha, particularly for use by groups. For more details write to PO Box 5779, Kathmandu.

From Namobuddha the circuit walk continues downhill through **Sankhu** and past a couple of water mills then climbs for about one hour to **Batase**. Next it passes through another pine wood and drops down to cross a stream before climbing up again to Dhulikhel.

Panauti Trek

Another interesting walk leads from Dhulikhel to the small village of Panauti. The pleasant two-hour stroll starts off south from Dhulikhel then turns west, crosses rice fields and runs along the course of a small stream. It eventually meets the Banepa to Panauti road a little north of the town. Panauti is a beautiful little town with numerous temples and magnificent woodcarvings – see the earlier Panauti section.

From Panauti you can take a bus to Banepa, just six km north, and from there back to Dhulikhel or to Kathmandu. Alternatively you can keep on walking west to Godavari in the south of the Kathmandu Valley. There are several alternative routes to Godavari. One runs west through Bhaleswar and along the Roshi Khola Valley, taking about six hours direct to Godavari.

An alternative to this route runs south-west and climbs up the back of Pulchowki then takes the road down from Pulchowki to Godavari. A third route runs further south through Kalar but also climbs the back of Pulchowki before taking the road down to Godavari. Either route via Pulchowki entails a long day's walk from Panauti.

Places to Stay & Eat

Dhulikhel has a small number of places to stay – two in the town (although, sadly the best was planning to move), several before the town and a couple after the town towards the Chinese border. If you plan to stay in Dhulikhel itself, it would be worth ringing ahead to check whether the accommodation options still exist. Both the Himalayan Horizon and the Dhulikhel Mountain Resort, outside town, are deservedly popular meal stops for day-trippers from Kathmandu.

The *Dhulikhel Lodge* (☎ 011-61114) in Dhulikhel, is/was a very popular place for shoestring travellers. It's in a fine old building, and has an atmospheric restaurant and a pleasant open courtyard. Unfortunately, the growing family who run the lodge have decided to reconvert it into a family home, and they are building a new place on the way into town, near the Woodlands Mt Tower Resort, which is also under construction. The new lodge is planned to open by the end of '93 and will offer a range of traditional-style rooms, some aimed at backpackers, some aimed at more up-market travellers.

For the time being at least, singles/doubles cost Rs 70/110 ($1.50/2) and are very simple but quite comfortable. If you've got a room in the front you don't even need to climb out of bed to enjoy the Himalayan view, although Dhulikhel can be a surprisingly noisy town and front-room occupants can find the street activity a little disturbing. The lodge is a wonderful place to just laze around and talk to people. The food can be quite good and over the years a veritable library of guest books with lots of interesting information interspersed with the usual dreamy raves have accumulated. The showers and wash-room facilities beside the garden have hot water and there is electricity.

The closure of the old lodge will leave one very small and basic place in town, on the way towards the post office and Shiva temple. The *Nawa Rangu Guest House & Restaurant* (☎ 011-61226) is a curious place with a restaurant hung with interesting naive-style paintings, and basic trekking lodge-style rooms and bathroom facilities. The food is good, especially the custard pies and wheat porridge! While the Dhulikhel Lodge was operating it didn't get much business, but if it can hang on until the lodge

moves, its luck will change. Rooms are Rs 100 ($2).

A km back towards Banepa is the attractive *Himalayan Horizon Sun-n-Snow Hotel* (☎ 011-61296; 01-225092 in Kathmandu). Singles/doubles in this comfortable hotel are $40/50. The buildings feature traditional woodcarving and all the rooms face straight out on to the Himalayan peaks. There's a restaurant/terrace area in front of the hotel with equally good views plus a beautiful garden running down the hill. The restaurant is relatively expensive but has excellent food, including a variety of Nepalese dishes. It's better value to opt for the room-only accommodation prices, rather than all-inclusive rates.

The *Dhulikhel Mountain Resort* (☎ 011-61466; 01-220031 in Kathmandu), is another up-market place, four km beyond the village towards Barabise and the Chinese border. The Himalayan views from here are equally superb and singles/doubles cost $58/60. Accommodation is in luxurious, thatched cottages. There's no electricity at the attractive resort, but the bathrooms have solar-heated hot water.

Just past the Mountain Resort, there's an interesting budget alternative. The *Gauri Shankar Tara Bhancha Ghar* is fairly basic, and a bit overpriced for what it offers. On the other hand it's an atmospheric and friendly place based around a traditional family farmhouse. There's a decent restaurant, serving Newari food. Singles/doubles are Rs 250/400 ($5/8). To get there, catch a Barabise bus from Kathmandu (Rs 12).

Getting There & Away

Regular buses to Dhulikhel leave from Kathmandu's Central Bus Station (Bus Stop 6). The journey takes about two hours and costs Rs 10. The buses skirt Bhaktapur at the eastern end of the valley and then climb over the Sanga Pass out of the valley, before dropping down to Banepa then climbing again to Dhulikhel, 32 km from Kathmandu. The fare is Rs 2 for the short ride from Banepa to Dhulikhel. A taxi from Kathmandu will cost

Around Dhulikhel

0   1   2 km

To Nagarkot

Nala

To Kathmandu

Narayan Temples

Pretty Tank

BANEPA

King's Statue

Chandeshwari Temple

Himalayan Horizon Hotel

Gaurī Shanker Tara Bancha Ghar

Dhulikhel Mountain Resort

Arniko Highway

To Kodari & Tibet

DHULIKHEL

Shiva Temple

Kali Temple

Kavre

Pungamati Khola

Phulbari

Panauti

Brahmayani Temple

Batase

Bus Stop

Indreshwar Mahadev Temple

Krishna Narayan Temple

Rosi Khola

Sankhu

Namobuddha

about Rs 400 ($8), or from Bhaktapur about Rs 300 ($6).

The walk to Dhulikhel from Nagarkot is an interesting alternative. After watching the sunrise at Nagarkot you can walk down through Nala to Banepa, from where you can take a bus the last few km to Dhulikhel. See the Treks from Nagarkot section for more information.

ARNIKO HIGHWAY BEYOND DHULIKHEL

The Arniko Highway provides Nepal's overland link with Tibet and China. Many people who make the trek into the Solo Khumbu region and the Everest Base Camp travel out along the highway, taking the turn-off to Jiri, which is the last stop before you have to start walking. Buses to Jiri leave from Kathmandu between 5.30 and 6.30 am (10 hours, Rs 98).

Past Barabise the road is particularly vulnerable to landslides and during the monsoon large sections are swept away; it's very unlikely to be open between May and August. Even when the highway is passable it is of limited use in breaking India's stranglehold on Nepal. It is an enormous distance from Lhasa to the industrial centres of China, so it is, in most cases, still cheaper to ship Chinese goods via Calcutta than to truck them over the mountains.

When roadworkers first tackled the Himalaya, they decided to follow the rivers, which had already done the hard work of cutting through the mountains. They have now realised that the zone just above the rivers is particularly vulnerable to erosion from below and landslides from above – which is why Nepalese houses and traditional trails are often built along the top of ridges. As a result, many of the roads that have been developed by foreign countries' agencies have turned out to be serious liabilities for the Nepalese government, who must fund their ongoing maintenance.

After Dhulikhel the road descends into the beautiful **Panchkhal Valley**, reaching the town of Panchkhal after about 20 minutes' drive. About five minutes beyond Panchkhal a dirt road takes off to the left, giving road access to the Helambu region.

Eight km later you arrive at **Dolalghat**, a thriving town at the confluence of the Indrawati River and Sun Kosi (the departure point for many rafting trips). The turn-off to Jiri is another 14 km away, on the right.

Lamosangu

Lamosangu is a few km after the intersection, and is an interesting Sherpa town with some decent trade stores (compared with Barabise, Tatopani and Kodari). There are some standard dhal bhat shops, but nothing to do. The *Silu Lodge* is in the middle of town. It's a five-storey building with a shop on the ground floor. The first two floors house the owners of the shop and the top two floors are the lodge. Three rooms on the top floor have a terrace which is a good spot to sit outside and have a beer after a hard bike ride. Fairly clean doubles cost Rs 50.

Next you pass a magnesite mine (one of the few mines in the country) which only developed because of its placement beside a sealed road.

Barabise

Barabise is the next bustling bazaar town, the final stop for buses from Kathmandu, and the largest settlement along the road. ('Hell Hole!' is one way it has been described.) Barabise marks the end of the sealed section of the Arniko Highway, which continues in the form of an unsurfaced track. In the dry season, passing trucks kick up the top layer of dust causing choking dust storms. In the wet, the dust transforms into mud. Landslides are more frequent as the side of the gorge steepens, especially during or after heavy rain.

The *Himalaya Hotel* has doubles for Rs 40 (no toilet) and serves good dhal bhat below the rooms. The *Barabise Guest House* has doubles for Rs 50, some of which are at the rear of the building, so take one of these if you want to avoid being woken at the crack of dawn by noisy bus drivers. It has toilets and more than a few bed bugs. Both places are in the middle of town on the left side heading towards Tibet. There's nothing to do but sit and watch street life go past, or perhaps curse the bus drivers for your lack of sleep!

Tatopani

The next point of interest is Tatopani, a small village with a string of small guest houses which survive by housing visitors to the hot springs. It is in a more picturesque setting and is much quieter than Barabise. The *Sonam Lodge* has doubles for Rs 50, and dhal bhat is available. It's reasonably clean, and the owner is friendly. The *Sherpa Lodge* has doubles for Rs 40, and once again, dhal bhat is available. Both places are very similar, and both are at the southern end of town, two shops apart.

The thing to do here is go to the hot springs. Five minutes' walk north of the bazaar, look for a sign (with a direction arrow) on a building on the right-hand side. You then descend some steps to the springs which come out as a set of showers. (Great after a hard bike ride from Dhulikhel.) There is also a small gompa above the town, marked by the usual prayer flags, which has a fine view.

Kodari

Kodari is nothing more than a collection of shabby wooden shanties perched perilously on the edge of the gorge on the Nepalese side of the Friendship Bridge. There's one lodge, the *Laxmi Lodge & Bhojanalaya* which is very basic, serves dhal bhat, and has beds for Rs 20 per person.

It is possible to continue past the Nepalese checkpoint and across the **Friendship Bridge**. Stop in the middle to pose for photos on the red line drawn across the road. You can then continue straight past the Chinese guards and under the barrier into Tibet, which looks just like Nepal. With a bike, you can continue for eight steep km until you reach Chinese customs, on the edge of Khasa (Zhangmu), the first settlement. A visa is needed to progress further, but some people have managed to leave their bikes at the barrier and check the town out for a couple of hours. There's not much to see.

CHARIKOT

If you take the turn-off to Jiri, the first town you come to is Charikot, a pleasant place situated on a ridge with a stunning view. Just before the town sign, the *Sagun Guest House*, in a new building, has friendly staff and good food. A double costs Rs 50. Because of its position on the edge of town, it's quiet, but misses the view. The *Laxi Lodge & Restaurant* is in the main square and offers excellent views. It's a charming traditional building with spiral staircases leading to wooden balconies. Rooms at the front cost Rs 60; back rooms, with no view, are Rs 30.

JIRI

Jiri, also quite a pleasant place, has many lodges to choose from. The bus stops at the far end of town so you walk back up to find somewhere to stay. The *Sagarmatha Lodge & Restaurant* is pretty good with doubles for Rs 20. On the far side of town – furthest from the bus stop – *Sherpa Guide Lodge* has doubles for Rs 10. This is the cheapest and best place in town. The rooms are clean, the staff friendly, and the food good.

Godavari & Pulchowki Route

The road to Godavari is sealed and there's quite a bit of traffic, so this is not one of the best bike rides around the valley. There are quite a number of things to see, however.

If you have access to a car it is worth considering a trip to the top of nearby Pulchowki, especially in spring (March, April and May) when the rhododendrons are in bloom.

HARISIDDHI (10 km)

This is a small Newari village with a four-tiered pagoda temple to Harisiddhi Bhawani.

BISHANKHU NARAYAN (15 km)

If you're looking for an excuse to get off the beaten track, the shrine of Bishankhu Narayan will do nicely. The shrine itself is something of a disappointment, despite the fact that it is one of the most important Vishnu shrines in the Kathmandu Valley. A steep stairway leads to a tiny cave – more a fissure in the rock – and there's nothing much to see. On the way, however, you pass through an attractive village, and there are some good views from the shrine itself.

Getting There & Away

The unsealed road to Bishankhu Narayan takes off to the north from the undistinguished village of Bandegaon then veers to the south-east and crosses a small stream. After one km you come to a small village. The road forks at the 'village green'; take the left fork and continue for another km to reach the shrine.

GODAVARI (22 km)

Godavari is not really a proper town, although there are a number of points of interest in the vicinity. This is home to the Royal Botanical Gardens, St Xavier's College, Godavari Kunda, Pulchowki Mai as well as a controversial marble quarry. The sealed road from Kathmandu continues to the foot of the hills, and to St Xavier's College – the awful scars from the quarry are also clearly visible. At this point an unsealed road continues to the south and the sealed road veers left (north-east) to the botanical gardens.

Royal Botanical Gardens

The main entrance to the gardens is flanked by white-painted walls. Though a quiet and peaceful spot, few of the trees and plants are labelled, so unless you already know what you're looking at you won't end up any the wiser. There really aren't many persuasive reasons for visiting unless you're a keen botanist. The gardens are open from 10 am to 4 pm and entry is Rs 1.

Godavari Kunda

A dirt road continues past the entrance to the botanical gardens and after 100 metres or so you come to the Godavari Kunda – a sacred spring – on your right. It's a curious spot, and although none of the architecture or sculpture is particularly inspiring it is revered by Hindus. Every 12 years – next in 2003 – thousands of pilgrims come here to bathe and gain merit. Clear mountain water collects in a pool in an inner courtyard, then flows through carved stone spouts into a larger pool in the outer courtyard.

Pulchowki Mai

If you return towards the marble quarry and take the dirt road to the south, Pulchowki Mai is a couple of hundred metres past St Xavier's College and virtually opposite the main gates to the quarry. The site is dilapidated and somewhat overshadowed by the quarry. There's a three-tiered pagoda to a Tantric mother goddess flanked by a temple to Ganesh. There are two large pools before the temple compound fed by nine spouts that represent the nine streams that flow off Pulchowki.

Getting There & Away

There are local minibuses and several Sajha Yatayat buses. They leave from Lagankhel in Patan and the one-hour journey costs Rs

3.50. It would be quite feasible to ride a mountain bike – the road is good – but if you're going to make the effort, there are more interesting rides in the valley.

PULCHOWKI

This 2762-metre mountain is the highest point around the valley and not surprisingly there are absolutely magnificent views from the summit. This is also home to one of the last surviving cloud forests in central Nepal. The mountain is famous for its spring flowers, in particular its magnificent red and white rhododendrons.

Unfortunately, there's a telecommunications tower on the summit and an army camp. The open shrine to Pulchowki Mai may once have been a pretty spot, but it's now covered in rubbish. The views and the superb forest, however, make the journey worthwhile.

Getting There & Away

The unsealed road is rough in places but quite OK for a normal car if you take it slowly. It takes about 45 minutes from the bottom. You would need to be very keen to undertake the climb on a mountain bike, although it could certainly be done.

Chapagaon & Lele Route

The road to Lele is an ideal mountain-bike trip. It's sealed to Chapagaon and there are great views and some attractive villages along the way. Take the turn-off from the Ring Rd signposted to the Leprosy Mission. By bicycle it's quite a stiff climb in places – which is all the better for the return trip. Allow the best part of a day, although it's only an hour from the Ring Rd to Chapagaon.

SUNAKOTHI & THECHO

The small village of Sunakothi (10 km from Kathmandu) is strung out along the road.

There are two temples – one to Jagannath and the other to Bringarshwar Mahadev.

Two km further south, Thecho also has two temples, the brightly coloured Balkumari Temple and a two-tiered pagoda to Brahmayani.

CHAPAGAON (13 km)
Chapagaon is a prosperous village with a number of shops and temples and shrines strung along the road. Near the entrance to the village is a Ganesh shrine. There are two dilapidated two-tiered temples (one looks as if it has been hit by a truck) dedicated to Narayan and Krishna, and there's also a Bhairab shrine with erotic carvings on its struts.

Vajra Varahi
A small temple complex – an important Tantric site – lies about 500 metres east of the main road. When you enter Chapagaon take the path on your left after the two-tiered temples. Notice the disused irrigation system, with stone channels and bridges, behind the village. The temple lies in a grove of trees and was built in 1665, but is now surrounded by less-distinguished shelters and an unfortunate amount of litter. Nonetheless, it's an interesting and atmospheric place that has probably been a centre for worship for millennia. Photography is banned.

Getting There & Away
Local minibuses and a Sajha Yatayat bus leave from Lagankhel in Patan and the one to 1½ hour journey costs Rs 5. By mountain bike, Chapagaon is about an hour from the Ring Rd (note the comparison with the bus time!). About 10 minutes after Chapagaon the road starts to climb into the foothills. The sealed road continues to the Leprosy Mission and Tika Bhairab in the Lele Valley. If you are running out of enthusiasm an unsealed road takes off to the left – there's a pipal tree and chautara (stone resting platform). The road is in poor condition but you are rewarded with fantastic views across the valley to the Ganesh Himal. If you keep going you cross a saddle and enter the tranquil Lele Valley.

Bhairab

LELE (19 km)
The Lele Valley seems a million miles from the hustle and bustle of Kathmandu, and there are few visitors. It's a peaceful, beautiful valley that in many ways seems untouched by the 20th century.

Tika Bhairab
The Tika Bhairab is a huge, multicoloured painting on a brick wall. The shrine lies at the confluence of two rivers and is marked by a huge sal tree.

Bungamati Route

The road to Bungamati, one of the most picturesque small towns in the valley, provides yet another ideal mountain-biking expedition. The road to Bungamati is the continuation of the main road that runs through Jawlakhel (the Tibetan refugee camp on the outskirts of Patan), on the other side of the Ring Rd.

BUNGAMATI (10 km)

Bungamati is a classic Newari village dating from the 16th century. It is perched on a spur of land overlooking the Bagmati River and is shaded by large trees and stands of bamboo. Fortunately, the village's streets are too small and hazardous for cars. Visitors are rare, so tread gently.

Rato Machhendranath Temple

Bungamati is the birthplace of Rato Machhendranath, regarded as the patron of the valley, and the large shikhara-style temple in the centre of the village square is his home for six months of the year. He spends the rest of his time in Patan. The process of moving him around Patan and backwards and forwards to Bungamati is central to one of the most important annual festivals in the valley. See the Rato Machhendranath section in the Kathmandu, Patan & Bhaktapur chapter, and the Cultural Events section in the Facts for the Visitor chapter for details.

The *chowk* around the temple is one of the most beautiful in the valley – here one can see the heart of a functioning Newari town. There are many chortens, and a huge prayer wheel, clearly pointing to the syncretic nature of the Newari religion.

Karya Binayak Temple

Between Bungamati and Khokna, the Karya Binayak Temple is dedicated to Ganesh. The temple is not particularly interesting and Ganesh is simply represented by a natural stone but the view is spectacular. From this point, surrounded by trees, you can look over the Bagmati Valley to the foothills, or back to Bungamati, tumbling down the opposite hill.

Getting There & Away

Continue over the Ring Rd from the main road through Jawlakhel. After you cross the Niche River, veer left. The right fork takes you through to the Chobar Gorge where you can cross the river and return to Kathmandu by a different route. It's a pleasant ride along a gradually climbing ridge to get to Bungamati.

Approximately an hour after leaving the Ring Rd you'll come out at a viewpoint marked by a single, large tree. It's worth pausing here to take in the lie of the land. To the left lies Bungamati, then swinging to the right comes Karya Binayak then about one km away, Khokna. Follow the road down to Bungamati and take the right fork which passes to the left of a large pond. The footpath then veers to the left and climbs up to the distinctive, white shikhara temple and the town square.

Buses to Bungamati leave from Jawlakhel in Patan, take 1½ hours and cost Rs 5.

To get to Karya Binayak, retrace your steps to the first pond you came to, follow the path around it and take the right fork. It's a five-minute walk across the rice paddies to the temple.

KHOKNA

Khokna is not as appealing as Bungamati, partly because it was seriously damaged in the 1934 earthquake, but it has retained many traditional aspects of Newari life. It is famous for producing mustard oil. There is no central square, as in Bungamati, but there's plenty of action in the main street, including women spinning wool. The village's main temple is a two-tiered construction of little interest, dedicated to Shekali Mai a mother goddess.

Getting There & Away

From Karya Binayak Temple, Khokna is a 10-minute walk across the paddy fields. Take note of the water tank surrounded by a low brick wall on the outskirts of the village, because if you don't want to retrace your steps to Bungamati, the track that returns to the main road takes off from here.

Kirtipur, Chobar & Dakshinkali Route

KIRTIPUR (5 km)

Strung out along a ridge south-west of Kathmandu the small town of Kirtipur is a relatively neglected and timeless backwater despite its proximity to the capital. At one time it was associated with Patan and then became a mini-kingdom in its own right. During the 1768 conquest of the valley by Gorkha's King Prithvi Narayan Shah it was clear that Kirtipur, with its superbly defensible hilltop position, would be the key to defeating the Malla kingdoms so it was here the Gorkha king struck first and hardest.

Kirtipur's resistance was strong but eventually, after a bitter siege, the town was taken and the unfortunate inhabitants paid a terrible price for their courageous resistance. The king, incensed by the long struggle his forces had endured, ordered the nose and lips cut off every male inhabitant in the town. Fortunately, for a small minority, he was practical as well as cruel and those who could play wind instruments were spared. It is said that the news of this barbaric act considerably dampened plans for resistance amongst the inhabitants of the other valley towns, and Patan, Bhaktapur and Kathmandu quickly fell.

At one time there were 12 gates into the city and traces of the old city wall can still be seen. Today the Kirtipur Cottage Industry Centre is a major industry for the town. As you wander through Kirtipur, you can see dyed yarn hanging from upstairs windows and hear the background clatter of the town's handlooms. Many of the town's 9000 inhabitants are weavers or farmers; the lower caste people generally live outside the old city wall, lower down the hill. Kirtipur's hilltop position offers fine views over Kathmandu with the Himalaya rising behind.

Tribhuvan University

The campus of Nepal's university, named after King Tribhuvan, stands below the Kirtipur hill. The university library has the best facilities to be found in Nepal, but many Kirtipur farmers lost their land to the university site and have had to turn to other employment.

Temples

Kirtipur's ridge is actually two hills, with a lower saddle between them. The **Chilanchu Vihara** tops the southern hill and has a central stupa with four smaller stupas, numerous statues and bells and Buddhist monastery buildings around it.

At the bottom of the saddle where the hills meet is the **Bagh Bhairab Temple**, sacred to both Hindus and Buddhists. This famous triple-roofed temple is decorated with swords and shields from the Newari troops defeated by King Prithvi Narayan Shah. They can be seen attached to the walls of the temple, sheltered by the upper roof. The temple's principal image is of Bhairab in his tiger form. Look for the temple's torana to the left of the entrance door with an image of Vishnu astride the Garuda and, below him, Bhairab between Ganesh and Kumar. Sacrifices are made early on Tuesday and Saturday mornings.

From the saddle, a long stone stairway, flanked by stone elephants, leads to the triple-roofed **Uma Maheshwar Temple**, or Hindu Kvat. The elephants wear spiked saddles to keep children from riding them! Curiously, the main image of Shiva and Parvati is a standing one, not in the standard Uma Maheshwar pose. To the left of the central image of the god and his consort is a smaller image in the standard pose. The temple was originally built in 1673 and had four roofs until it was badly damaged by the great earthquake of 1934. Following its recent restoration the temple itself is not of great interest – the stairway and the fine views from the top are better. From this hilltop you can see the nearby villages of **Panga** and **Nagaon**.

Getting There & Away

Numerous buses and minibuses depart from Ratna Park (Bus Stop 4) and take around 45 minutes (Rs 3). They terminate at the university from where you can stroll up the hill to the town itself. Alternatively, and much more comfortably, it's a short trip by taxi (around Rs 100, or $2).

It takes around 1½ hours to reach Kirtipur by mountain bike, and it's quite a long steep hill from the Dakshinkali road (first left after the Ring Rd bridge over the Bagmati River). After about a km from the bridge, turn right at the road flanked by two low, brick gatehouses. Continue up the hill for a km or so and take the left fork where the minibuses park (right to the university). You'll notice a new Thai-designed Buddhist temple to the left of Kirtipur's Naya Bajaar (New Bazaar), which has grown up at the foot of the Kirtipur hill.

Instead of simply returning the same way you can continue from Kirtipur to Chobar and the Chobar Gorge then back through Patan, which is mostly rideable, but also an interesting walk. From the Chilanchu Vihara at the south-eastern end of Kirtipur, go down the hill by the mound known as the Mazadega (built with the intention of being the foundations of a stupa). At the base of the hill follow the Ring Rd around and take the trail leading towards Chobar, just past the Thai temple. You can't go wrong, since Chobar tops the prominent hill to the south-east.

A diversion further south will take you through the small village of Panga which has a number of temples, none of great age or interest. A path continues from Panga to Nagaon, an even smaller village. The trail to Chobar meets a wider road just before the base of the hill, but you can turn off this and follow a narrow footpath straight up the hill until you come into the centre of the interesting small village of Chobar, right on the top of the hill.

After you've visited Chobar's Adinath Lokeshwar Temple continue down the other side of the hill towards the river. Aim for the large cement works, clearly visible beside the river. The Chobar Gorge and the Jal Binayak Temple are immediately to the north of the cement works. See the Chobar Gorge section for the walk from there to Patan.

CHOBAR (6 km)

The picturesque little village of Chobar tops a hill overlooking the Bagmati River where it flows through the Chobar Gorge. Although the gorge is a regularly visited attraction, far fewer people come to Chobar itself. Perhaps they're put off by the steep hill.

Adinath Lokeshwar Temple

Chobar's main attraction is the Buddhist temple of Adinath Lokeshwar. The temple was originally built in the 15th century and reconstructed in 1640. Inside the main sanctuary the face of Rato Machhendranath can be seen peering out, the temple is dedicated to this popular valley deity and is sacred to both Hindus and Buddhists. Six Buddha faces are lined up beneath the temple's golden torana but the most interesting feature is the many metal pots, pans and water containers which are fixed to boards hanging all around the temple roofs. These kitchen utensils are donated to the temple by newlyweds in order to ensure a happy married life.

Getting There & Away

Transport to Pharping and Dakshinkali runs by Chobar, but see the Kirtipur and Chobar Gorge sections for details of walking between Kirtipur and Patan via Chobar and the Chobar Gorge.

CHOBAR GORGE (6 km)

Eons ago the Kathmandu Valley was the Kathmandu Lake. In that long-ago time the hill of Swayambhunath was an island; gradually the lake dried up to leave the valley we see today. Legends relate that the change from lake to valley was a much more dramatic one, for Manjushri is said to have taken his mighty sword and with one blow cut open the valley edge to release the pent-up waters.

The place where his sword struck rock was Chobar on the southern edge of the valley and the result was the Chobar Gorge.

Countless snakes were washed out of the valley with the departing waters but Kartotak, 'king of the snakes', is said to still live near the gorge in the Taudaha pond. Whether or not the great serpent is still there, the pond is certainly a place where ducks pause on their long annual migration from Siberia to India. A hill known as Dinacho (which means 'meditation point') or Champa Devi rises beyond the pond.

The Chobar Gorge is south of Patan and the Bagmati River cuts through the edge of the Chobar hill, the highest hill along this side of the valley. The pretty village of Chobar tops the hill and a stone-paved track runs from the river's edge right to the top of the hill where the Adinath Lokeshwar Temple forms the centre of the settlement. Down by the river, just south of the gorge, is another important temple, the Jal Binayak. The valley's first cement factory is a more recent and less pleasing addition to the scenery. A neat little suspension bridge spans the river; it was manufactured in Aberdeen in Scotland in 1903. From the bridge there are fine views of the gorge on one side and the Jal Binayak Temple on the other.

Jal Binayak Temple

Just below the gorge on the riverbank stands one of the valley's most important Ganesh shrines. The triple-roofed temple dates from 1602 although there was probably a temple here even earlier. On the temple's platform there is an aged and worn image of Shiva and Parvati in the Uma Maheshwar pose which predates the temple itself by 500 years.

The temple's Ganesh image is simply a huge rock, projecting out the back and bearing very little likeness to an elephant-headed god. The temple's roof struts depict eight Bhairabs and the eight mother goddesses or Ashta Matrikas with whom Ganesh always appears. On the lower roof Ganesh himself appears on some of the struts, with beautiful female figures standing beside him and tiny, brightly painted erotic depictions below. A bronze figure of Ganesh's 'vehicle', in this case a shrew rather than a mouse, stands respectfully in the temple courtyard, facing the shrine.

Getting There & Away

The Chobar Gorge is usually visited en route to Pharping and Dakshinkali by road. A more interesting way to reach the gorge is to walk there from Kirtipur via the village of Chobar. See the earlier Kirtipur section for more details.

From the gorge you can cross the bridge and walk up the hill turning north towards Patan. A road suitable for cars ends at a small village at the top of the hill and you can follow this road, past the Nakhu jail and across the Nakhu River, finally crossing the Ring Rd and entering Patan at Jawlakhel.

SEKH NARAYAN TEMPLE (18 km)

The small Sekh Narayan Temple is the centrepiece of an interesting collection of temples, pools and carvings. The pools are beside the road to Pharping, at a point where it makes a sharp left-hand turn (coming from Kathmandu) and they are often used by local women for washing clothes. The main temple is above the pools and is sheltered under a multicoloured, overhanging cliff. It forms an interesting juxtaposition between the work of man and god. In true Nepalese style, a Buddhist monastery has been built next door.

The temples and carvings have suitably diverse ages. The Sekh Narayan Temple, one of the most important Vishnu temples in the valley, was built in the 17th century, but it is believed the cave has been a place of pilgrimage for much longer than this. Beside the shrine is a bas relief of Vishnu Vikrantha, also known as the dwarf Vamana. This possibly dates from the Licchavi period, or the 5th or 6th century. Vamana was a dwarf who miraculously changed into a giant, the 'long strider', and crossed the world in three gigantic steps.

Half-submerged in one of the crystal-clear ponds is a sculpture of Surya, the sun god, framed by a stone arch and with a lotus

flower at each shoulder. This dates from the 12th or 13th century. Finally, the Tibetan gompa is a recent 20th-century addition. Hindus believe that Gautama Buddha was Vishnu's 10th incarnation, but I don't know if this is the connection.

Getting There & Away

Sekh Narayan is close to Pharping and is probably best reached by foot from the village if you haven't got your own transport.

VAJRA JOGINI TEMPLE (18.5 km)

On a hillside overlooking Pharping is the 17th-century Vajra Jogini Temple, dedicated to the same goddess as the Vajra Jogini Temple near Sankhu and built at about the same time. See the earlier Vajra Jogini section for a discussion on the goddess' origins. The pagoda-style temple is in a courtyard surrounded by relatively modern two-storey, Newari-style living quarters. Vajra Jogini is featured in the temple's toranas.

Getting There & Away

The temple is just a short walk behind Pharping on the hill that overlooks the town. The main gompa at Gorakhnath (see next section) is only a few hundred metres to the west up a flight of steps. It is possible to walk an interesting circuit from Dakshinkali to Gorakhnath, Vajra Jogini, Pharping and back to Dakshinkali in less than two hours. See Getting There & Away in the later Dakshinkali section.

Coming from Kathmandu and after Sekh Narayan, you approach Pharping past a soccer field. The main road swings left around the field, but if you continue straight ahead you will come first to Vajra Jogini (on the side of the hill) then Gorakhnath.

GORAKHNATH (19 km)

Several gompas and temples have sprung up around the Gorakhnath cave behind Pharping. The white Tibetan gompa – perched high on the hill like an eagle's nest, at the centre of a web of prayer flags – is particularly interesting.

There are magnificent views overlooking Pharping, the Bagmati River and the valley. You can even see the Himalaya on a clear day. Somewhere in the complex is a cave which the Tibetans associate with Padmasambhava, the Bodhisattva sometimes credited with introducing Buddhism to Tibet.

Getting There & Away

Gorakhnath is an easy walk from Pharping and Vajra Jogini, and a bit of a scramble from Dakshinkali. It can be combined with an interesting walk that takes in all these places (see the Dakshinkali section) or reached by road.

Coming from Kathmandu and after Sekh Narayan, you approach Pharping past a soccer field. The main road swings left around the pitch, but if you continue straight ahead you will come first to Vajra Jogini (on the side of the hill) then Gorakhnath.

PHARPING (19 km)

Pharping is a thriving, traditional Newari town, surprisingly untouched by the swarm of tourists that visit Dakshinkali. The main road skirts the village so there are few vehicles in the village proper. Before King Prithvi Narayan Shah unified Nepal this was another tiny city-state.

Places to Stay & Eat

The *Hattiban Resort* (☎ 01-221181) is a small hotel, popular for weekend lunches. The buildings are pleasant and there are great views. There are 24 rooms as well as workshop and conference facilities. Singles/doubles cost $55/65; the food is fairly pricey at around $10 for a main meal.

Getting There & Away

Prior to the opening of the new Kathmandu Bus Terminal, buses left from Martyrs' Gate (Bus Stop 9), took two hours and cost Rs 7. On days when buses don't run to Dakshinkali you can catch buses to Pharping, and walk to Dakshinkali, one km away. If you're on a bike, you'll be pleased to know it's all downhill.

DAKSHINKALI

At the southern edge of the valley, in a dark, somewhat spooky location in the cleft between two hills and at the confluence of two rivers, stands the bloody temple of Dakshinkali. The temple is dedicated to the goddess Kali, Shiva's consort in her most bloodthirsty incarnation, and twice a week faithful Nepalese journey here to satisfy her blood lust. The six-armed main image of Kali in the temple is of black stone and she tramples upon a male figure.

Sacrifices are always made to goddesses, and the creatures to be sacrificed must be uncastrated males. Saturday is the major sacrificial day of the week when a steady parade of buffaloes, chickens, ducks, goats, sheep and pigs come here to have their throats cut or their heads lopped off. Tuesdays is also a sacrificial day but the blood does not flow quite so freely as on Saturdays. During the festival of Dasain in October the temple is literally awash with blood and the image of Kali is bathed in it.

After their rapid dispatch the animals are butchered in the stream beside the temple and their carcasses will later be brought home for a feast, or a picnic may be held on the hillside. Non-Hindus are not allowed into the compound where Kali's image resides, but it is OK to take photos from outside. The temple itself is not particularly interesting, although there are some fine brass nagas forming a canopy over the compound.

This is one of the most important sites in the valley so on the sacrificial days it is crowded with Nepalese families – and tourists. Most of the big hotels and the tour companies cart busloads of camera-laden visitors along. Tours to the 'exciting animal sacrifices' are big business for Kathmandu travel agencies. As a result, there are a number of teahouses, and a good number of hustlers selling souvenirs and goodness knows what else. Be prepared to pay picturesque sadhus for the privilege of taking their photograph.

Despite the carnival spirit, witnessing the sacrifices is a strange and, for some, a confronting experience. The slaughter is surprisingly matter-of-fact, but it creates a powerful atmosphere. Unfortunately, many tourists behave poorly, hanging from every available vantage point in order to get the most gory possible photos. They are reminiscent of that most unattractive creature – the vulture. However extraordinary the sights might seem, this is a religious ceremony, and the participants should be treated with respect, not turned into a sideshow.

Getting There & Away

Buses only operate on Tuesdays and Saturdays – the most important days for sacrifice – and though there are plenty of them, they are very crowded. After you pass the police checkpoint on the Ring Rd you can sit on the roof and enjoy the spectacular views. If you have a car, allow 45 minutes for the journey.

It is an enjoyable, but exhausting two-hour bike ride from Kathmandu. The views are exhilarating, but it is basically uphill all the way – so mountain bikes are the way to go. Tuesday is probably the best day to pick as the traffic is not too heavy. Make sure you get an early start, as the shrine is busiest early in the morning. You're advised to pay someone a couple of rupees to mind your bike in the car park.

It's possible to make an interesting two-hour circuit walk from Dakshinkali to Gorakhnath, Vajra Jogini, Pharping and back to Dakshinkali. Take the path that runs above the left (southern) side of the sacrificial compound. This will bring you out into a cleared part of the gorge where there are several picnic shelters. There's a steep scramble up a goat track that follows a ridge on the right (north-western) side of the gorge. When you get to the top you come out on a plateau and you'll immediately see the white monastery surrounded by prayer flags on the nearby hill. Make your way through the paddy fields, on the narrow paths between the rice. It will take you about 40 minutes to get to Gorakhnath. Vajra Jogini is a few hundred metres down some steps to the east of the gompa, and a short walk to Pharping. From Pharping follow the main road about one km downhill to Dakshinkali.

The Terai

When people think of Nepal they think of soaring snow-clad mountains, not hot sub-tropical plains. Despite this, nearly half the country's population lives on a narrow strip of flat and fertile land that lies wedged between the Indian border and the mountains. This is known as the Terai (sometimes spelt Tarai).

With the Kathmandu Valley and the world's highest mountains a few hours away by bus, it is not surprising that the Terai is often just a transit zone for those travelling overland to and from India. Nonetheless, although there is nothing quite as startling as 8000-metre mountains, the region has a beauty of its own and some fascinating possibilities for travellers. The most well known are the magnificent Royal Chitwan National Park, famous for its elephant safaris and wildlife; Lumbini, the birthplace of Buddha; and Janakpur, the birthplace of Sita (Rama's wife, from the *Ramayana*).

Nobody could forget a dawn ride on an elephant through forests where you might come across tigers, rhinos, crocodiles and peacocks. Nor could anyone forget the neat mud-walled huts and brilliant saris amidst the vivid-green rice paddies that stretch the length of the Terai, nor the strange water-logged world of the Sapt Kosi's flood plain, with its birds, thatched villages, hyacinths and lilies.

Large sections of the Terai are still forested, and the land is cut by numerous rivers, often grey and turbulent with snow-melt and silt. These rivers burst from the hills onto the plains, a mere 100 metres above sea level yet over 1000 km from the Bay of Bengal. In most parts of the Terai Western visitors are rare and in the farmland outside the towns there is little to disturb the ancient routines of ploughing, planting and harvesting.

While many hill people have settled the region (every ethnic group in Nepal is represented) there are also indigenous peoples and large groups that are culturally a part of the great Indian civilisations of the Gangetic plain. Yet, despite this extraordinary diversity, the people of the Terai remain distinctively Nepalese – unhurried, good-humoured, courteous and friendly.

Unfortunately, most of the border towns are new, dirty and unattractive, with Dickensian-looking industries on their outskirts, streets choked with buses and trucks, and little in the way of history or culture. The exceptions are the pilgrim centres of ancient Janakpur, with its sadhus and temples, and Lumbini, which remains more significant for what it was than what it is.

The Chitwan should not be missed, and in the cool season (November to February) it is definitely worth travelling during the day and seeing the country, even if you have to suffer a crowded bus and stay in a grubby border town overnight. The western area of the Terai (west of Sunauli/Bhairawa) is one of the least visited, least developed and most interesting parts of the country. The completion of the Mahendra Highway, which will run the entire length of the Terai from Mahendranagar to Kakarbhitta, will link the region with the rest of Nepal and with India, so rapid change is likely.

HISTORY

Over the centuries, parts of the Terai have come under the sway of both Nepalese and Indian empires. Some regions were inhabited by sophisticated agricultural and urban communities as early as 800 BCE, but the empires have come and gone, and at times the countryside has been completely reclaimed by forest. The stories of decline and fall are largely unknown, but disease, and war certainly played a role – some areas were most recently depopulated as a result of the Muslim invasions from the 14th century, and malaria was a major problem until the 1960s.

Without doubt the Terai's most famous son is Siddhartha Gautama – Buddha – who was born in 563 BCE at Lumbini. Siddhartha was the son of Suddhodana who ruled a small state from Kapilavastu. The ruins near Taulihawa to the west of Lumbini are believed to be his capital, and archaeologists have identified 13 successive levels of human habitation at the site. (See the Taulihawa section later in this chapter.)

The Terai's most famous daughter is Sita, who is believed to have been born where present-day Janakpur now stands. The daughter of Janak, the king of Mithila (also known as Videha), Sita is famous for her faithful marriage to Rama, the hero of the Hindu epic the *Ramayana*, which was first written in the 1st or 2nd century BCE. The kingdom of Mithila lives on in the rich culture and language of Nepal's eastern Terai and India's northern Bihar region.

By 321 BCE the Mauryan empire based at Patna, India was on the rise, swallowing the small principalities around it. Under the great Ashoka, the empire controlled more of the subcontinent than any subsequent ruler until the British. Ashoka was one of Buddhism's greatest followers and missionaries, so it was perhaps inevitable that he would visit nearby Lumbini, then a thriving religious centre. In 245 BCE he erected a stone pillar at Lumbini that can still be seen today. Some believe he travelled as far as Kathmandu.

The next great empire to rise in the region was the Gupta empire, again originally based in Patna, which flourished between 300 and 600 CE. The empire extended its influence to Kathmandu and beyond. In the early 13th century invading Moghuls occupied large parts of northern India, driving many Hindu refugees towards Nepal and the Kathmandu Valley. It is believed that one of these groups founded the Malla dynasty, which by the 15th century under King Yaksha Malla had extended its power from Kathmandu south to the Ganges River.

The next (and current) Kathmandu-based dynasty, the Shah, won power in 1768 and continued to expand Nepalese borders until the kingdom was twice the size it is now – extending south into the Gangetic plain and

east and west along the Himalaya. Eventually the Shahs and their famous Gurkha soldiers ran up against the British East India Company. In 1816, after two years of relatively inconclusive war, the Nepalese were forced to sign a treaty that considerably reduced their territory. Some land (including the city of Nepalganj) was actually returned to Nepal as a reward for its support for the British during the 1857 Indian Mutiny (or War of Independence as it is known in India today).

Most of the Terai was heavily forested until the 1960s, although limited areas were settled, and indigenous Tharu groups were widely dispersed through the region. However, the drainage and spraying programmes begun in 1954 markedly reduced the incidence of malaria and this allowed mass migration both south from the hills and north from India. Fertile soils and easy accessibility led to rapid development. The Terai is now the most important region for agricultural and industrial production in Nepal, and the fastest growing.

GEOGRAPHY

The Nepalese Terai lies at the northern rim of the great Gangetic plain, ranges from 60 to 300 metres above sea level and never exceeds more than 40 km in width. The Gangetic plain runs table-flat from deep in India to the foothills of the Himalaya, the Chure Hills, (known as the Siwalik Hills in India) which abruptly jump 1000 metres.

Several flat, wide 'valleys' known as the Inner Terai lie behind the first range of hills. These include the valley along the Narayani and Rapti rivers (including part of the Chitwan National Park) and the Rapti River (east of Nepalganj).

The border with India is a political creation and does not conform to any particular geographic barrier. To further blur the demarcation, the inhabitants on both sides come and go as they please.

The Terai accounts for only 17% of Nepal's total area, but it is, in effect, the country's granary. In general, the soils are highly fertile and this, in addition to abundant water resources, permits the intensive cultivation of a wide variety of crops.

Unfortunately, outside the national parks the native forests are rapidly disappearing and suitable land is heavily exploited. Crop yields are already declining in some areas. The consequences of rapid population increase, deforestation and overworking the land are likely to be disastrous.

During the monsoon, parts of the Terai are subject to serious flooding. The relationship between deforestation in the hills and increased siltation and flooding on the plains is controversial, but there is no doubt that population growth in the hills and industrial development in the Kathmandu Valley is beginning to have a serious impact on downstream water quality. This is most critical in the dry season when many streams become mere trickles or dry up completely. Water flows are much reduced on even the major rivers.

Flora

The Terai is subtropical, and the flora and fauna reflect this. Rapid development has led to large-scale deforestation but fortunately, a surprising amount of forest remains.

Substantial areas are still cloaked in sal *(Shorea robusta)* forests. These forests characteristically grow on well-drained soils and form relatively homogeneous communities. Sal is a magnificent, highly valued hardwood. It grows straight and true (averaging 30 metres when mature), and has long been used by builders and woodcarvers. The longevity of the buildings and the carvings in the Kathmandu Valley is due to the strength and durability of this wood.

On swampier ground there are scrubby forests of khair *(Acacia catechu)* and shisham *(Dalbergia sissoo).* Simal trees *(Bombax ceiba)* stand out above the others. They are notable for their spring display of large red flowers and when they are old they develop huge buttresses at their base.

There are also grasslands that form a diverse and complex community of over 50 species. Elephant grasses (the saccharum family) can grow up to eight metres high, but there are also shorter species like khar that are vital for thatching. ■

Fauna

The fauna of the Terai is striking although, as always, shy. From the road, the most obvious species are the handsome black-faced, grey langur monkeys *(bandar)* and the common, brownish-red rhesus monkeys. You may also catch a glimpse of some of the many species of deer – including the spotted (chital), barking *(mirga)*, sambar *(jarayo)*, hog *(laghuna)* and swamp deer. The blue cow *(nilgai)*, Asia's largest antelope, is also quite common, but you won't see this unless you make an effort.

The largest mammal is the Asian elephant, although it is likely there are now only a few individuals surviving in the wild at the Royal Bardia National Park and Sukla Phanta Wildlife Reserve. Not far behind in scale and impressiveness is the great Indian one-horned rhinoceros, which can be seen at the Chitwan.

There are a number of carnivores, the most magnificent being the royal Bengal tiger *(bagh)* that, thanks to the Terai's national parks, seems to have escaped extinction. There are also leopards *(chituwa)*, wild dogs, jackals, civets, various species of mongoose and cats.

You might also find sloth bears *(bhalu)*, wild boars, porcupines, hares, bats, squirrels and snakes *(sarpa)* – some of which are poisonous (cobra, krait and viper).

The rivers and lakes are home to small numbers of mugger and gharial crocodiles, and the extraordinary Gangetic dolphin.

The Terai is also a bird-watcher's delight with more than 400 migrant and local species recorded. There are cormorants, herons, egrets, storks, cranes, ibis, ducks, kites, goshawks, hawks, eagles, osprey, falcons, kestrel, quail curlews, sandpipers, snipe, gulls, terns, pigeons, parakeets, cuckoos, owls, kingfishers, woodpeckers, swallows, orioles, drongos, babblers, flycatchers, warblers... ■

Little egret

CLIMATE

The Terai has a humid, subtropical climate with well over 1500 mm of rainfall in most places. The most pleasant time to visit is November to February when you can expect daytime temperatures to average in the mid to high 20°Cs, and cool nights. From March to September temperatures in the 40°Cs are common and this combines with the additional discomfort of the monsoon from June to September.

ECONOMY

Agriculture, as elsewhere in Nepal, is the major contributor to the economy, although the Terai is also home to most of the country's manufacturing industries (with the exception of the carpet industry). More than half the gross domestic product is produced in the Terai.

Many of the Terai's advantages come back to a single fact: it's flat! Development has been assisted by the relative ease with which roads and services can be established. Roads are crucial for industry, but they also enable health and education services, as well as fertilisers and improved seeds to be delivered more efficiently.

Cash crops like sugar cane, jute, tobacco and tea are grown alongside staples like rice, wheat and maize. Land-holdings are much larger than in the hills, but the average size is still under two hectares – hardly a Texan cattle ranch – and they are shrinking as the population grows. Many families work on a share-cropping basis for large landowners and moneylenders (zamindars) who take at least 50% of the crop and charge usurious rates of interest. Surplus food is sold to markets in the Kathmandu Valley, although a considerable amount is also given directly to less fortunate relatives in the hills.

Mechanised transport, proximity to Indian raw materials and the Indian market, and the availability of hydroelectric power has allowed the development of some industry. This is largely concentrated between Birganj and Hetauda, and around Biratnagar. Amongst other things there are jute mills, a sugar refinery, tanneries and leather factories, biscuit and cigarette factories, and drug manufacturers.

POPULATION

The population has increased rapidly since the 1950s. In 1991, 46.6% of the population, or over 8.6 million people, lived in the Terai. Due to migration from the mountains and hills plus a high birth rate, the population is increasing rapidly and will probably overtake that of the hills. Unfortunately, it is now clear that the Terai will not be able to absorb excess population from the hills indefinitely, yet the hill population has continued to grow. Population pressures are mounting at an alarming rate.

PEOPLE

Internal migration has meant that the indigenous people of the Terai have been joined by representatives of every ethnic group in the country. However, and not surprisingly, many people are closely related to Indian groups in Bihar and Uttar Pradesh: Indo-Aryan subsistence farmers with dark skin, and Hindu beliefs that are sometimes combined with forms of animism. Although the common language throughout Nepal is usually Nepali, in the Terai, people are just as likely to use Maithili, Bhojpuri or Hindi.

Maithili

The most widely spoken language of the Terai (excluding Nepali) is Maithili, a language and culture shared with people on the Bihar side of the border. It is spoken by around two million Nepalese, especially around Janakpur and Biratnagar. Maithili is the language of old Mithila and has its own script, Tirhuta, and a celebrated literature. Most of its speakers are farmers and orthodox Hindus.

Bhojpuri & Abadhi

The next most common language, Bhojpuri, is also used on both sides of the border and is spoken by around 1.5 million people in Nepal, especially around Birganj, though it mingles with Maithili.

Abadhi is another Indian-based language, spoken by around 250,000 Nepalese especially around Bhairawa and Nepalganj.

Tharu

One of the most visible groups in the Terai is the Tharu, a race who are believed to be the earliest inhabitants of the Terai (and immune to malaria!). Approximately 700,000 Tharu speakers inhabit the length of the Terai, including the Inner Terai around the Chitwan, although they primarily live in the west. There are caste-like distinctions between different Tharu groups or tribes. Most have mongoloid physical features, and their animist religion is increasingly influenced by Hinduism.

Nobody is sure where they came from, although some believe they are the descendants of the Rajputs (from Rajasthan) who sent their women and children away to escape Moghul invaders in the 16th century. The women later married into local tribes. Another belief is that they are descended from the royal Sakya clan, Buddha's family, although they cannot be described as Buddhist.

Customarily the women were heavily tattooed, although these days this is unusual and tattoos are rarely seen on young women. Some groups wear simple white saris, others colourful calf-length dresses and a short blouse or bodice that exposes their belly. Tharu houses have mud-rendered walls and thatched roofs; they are high, dark and cool, with few if any windows. Reliefs of domestic animals are often moulded on the mud walls.

Apart from farming, the Tharu are enthusiastic hunting and fishing people. In particular, groups of young women and children will often be seen heading off on fishing expeditions. Their beliefs are largely animistic, although increasingly influenced by Hinduism, and they live a life that is cleverly adapted to their environment.

Many Tharu are heavily exploited by newly arrived hill people, or zamindars (moneylenders). Large numbers have fallen into debt and have, as a result entered into a form of bonded labour (known as the kamaiya system), little different to slavery.

Other Peoples

There are quite a number of smaller ethnic groups, none exceeding 40,000 people. They include the Danuwar, Darai, Djanghar, Koche, Majhi, Rajbansi, Satar and Tajpuri.

INFORMATION

There are tourist information centres at the borders at Kakarbhitta, Birganj (☎ 051-22083), Bhairawa (☎ 071-20304) and Janakpur (☎ 041-20755).

Most services, including post, telephone and electricity are more widely and efficiently available in the Terai than in the rest of the country.

Malaria is the main worry. Make sure you take preventative medication. If you're coming from Westernised Kathmandu you may have been lulled into a false sense of security. Don't drink water or use ice unless you know it has been boiled or properly treated. Skip the dairy products (with the exception of curd) and salads, and peel the fruit. Wash your hands before eating. (See the Health section in the Facts for the Visitor chapter for more details.)

ACCOMMODATION

The main towns all have accommodation ranging from hotels of reasonable standard (where rooms with fans and mosquito nets are around Rs 150 ($3), or Rs 250 ($5) with air-con), to grimy, basic places catering to local demand for around Rs 30. Some of the cheap places will only have tattered mosquito nets, if any at all, so if you're on a tight budget and want to sleep at night, bring one with you.

With the exception of the main border towns and Sauraha on the edge of the Royal Chitwan National Park, tourists are basically unknown so there are no lodges specially designed for the discriminating backpacker. Small towns and villages rarely have formal places to stay as there is little or no demand. If you do want to stay off the beaten track it will be necessary to make an arrangement with a restaurant owner or family.

FOOD

Although dhal bhat tarkari (rice, lentil soup and curried vegetables) is the rule, in the small roadside teahouses (chiyaa pasal), the quality is high and the prices are low – say around Rs 20 per person. A reasonable variety of vegetables is available in the Terai and in general the dhal bhat tarkari is good, just a trifle repetitive if you eat it at every meal.

Most roadside stalls will be able to find a spoon with a dubious past if you insist, but

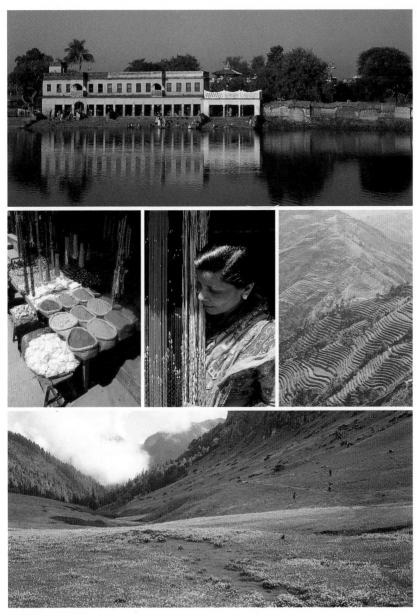

Top: Janakpur (RE)
Middle: Colourful offerings at Pashupatinath (RE); braid vendor,
Kathmandu (PS); terraced landscape, Helambu (TW)
Bottom: Danphe Lagna near Rana Lake (SA)

Top: Terai village on the Sapt Kosi flood plain (RE)
Left: Fields near Lalbiti, Terai (RE)
Right: Typical Terai house (RE)

animals of the park. An often heavy-handed army presence, which involves over 1000 men, has kept poaching and woodcutting to a minimum. This no doubt contributes to local resentment, but the two most significant problems are that the park ties up potential farming land and timber resources, and surrounding crops are frequently damaged by the park's animals.

The animals do not respect the park's boundaries. Rhinos wander out in November to wreak havoc on rice crops, and then again in February and March when they attack mustard, lentils and wheat. Deer, monkeys and wild pigs also cause a great deal of damage. The little lookout towers *(machan)* you see in many fields outside the park are used by watchmen who spend their nights in the fields waiting to scare off encroaching animals. Fortunately, tiger and crocodile attacks are rare, but they have caused fatalities.

On the positive side, in February each year neighbouring villagers are allowed into the park to harvest a number of grass species. They have numerous traditional uses, including roof thatching, and provide a valuable cash crop. Working for the park lodges also provides local employment though the many budget lodges in Sauraha, outside the park, arguably generate more money for the local economy. In contrast to the expensive lodges inside the park, where much of the money goes to owners in Kathmandu or overseas, many of the budget Sauraha lodges funnel money straight into the pockets of local families (although canny Kathmandu entrepreneurs are rapidly taking over).

The park is easily accessible from Kathmandu or Pokhara and is actually en route for those heading to/from the Indian border at Birganj and points east. There is something for every budget: at one extreme you can spend $250 a night to stay at the famous Tiger Tops Lodge, while at the other a simple double room in one of the many small lodges in Sauraha, right on the edge of the park in a prime game-viewing area, costs less than $2 a night.

Numerous travel agents in the West, as well as in Pokhara and Kathmandu, offer package tours to the park. This is the best approach if you plan to stay in one of the expensive lodges inside the park as you can book directly with the lodges' Kathmandu head offices and the package deals usually work out to better value than the nightly rack rate.

However, packages are both unnecessary and relatively expensive if you plan to stay in the budget lodges at Sauraha. The booking agent obviously has to make money on the deal (which adds to the cost), and although you save a little effort, you pay for this by committing yourself to a particular lodge (which you may or may not like) and to a limited time frame.

Many people find the two-night, three-day packages are too short, because by the time you subtract travelling time (between six and seven hours by bus from Kathmandu or Pokhara) you only have one full day to explore. For most, a visit of two full days is sufficient, although the peaceful atmosphere, good-value accommodation in Sauraha, and the range of potential activities can easily seduce you into staying longer.

GEOGRAPHY

Along most of the Terai the Gangetic plain runs to the foot of the Chure Hills (which then merge with the higher Mahabharat Range), but here the Someshwar Hills form the Chitwan Valley, also described as the Inner Terai, between the two.

To the north the park comprises a narrow strip of flood plain along the Narayani and Rapti rivers, a part of the Chitwan Valley, and the most visited section of the park. South of this the bulk of the park encompasses the Someshwars, which reach a maximum height of 738 metres, and are largely inaccessible to visitors. In the east the national park is adjoined by the Parsa Wildlife Reserve, which is not developed for visitors, but provides important additional territory for wildlife.

The park includes a number of small lakes or *tal*. The most interesting, particularly for viewing water birds, are Devi Tal near Tiger Tops, Lami Tal near Kasara, and Bis Hajaar

Tal (literally, '20,000 lakes') north-west of Sauraha.

The park, plus the adjoining Parsa Wildlife Reserve, covers 1431 sq km.

FLORA & FAUNA
Flora

The park has three basic vegetation types – open grasslands, riverine vegetation and hardwood forests, dominated by sal trees. The forests also have *shisham*, kapok, *palash* (or flame-of-the-forest), pipal, strangler fig and the scarlet-flowered *kusum* trees.

Fauna

The Chitwan has over 50 different species of mammals; bird-watchers can search for 400 different bird types; and in 1987-88 butterfly-spotters identified 67 different types of butterflies at the Machan Resort. Some of the most interesting creatures to be seen in the Chitwan include elephants, rhinos and tigers.

Elephants Although you're likely to see more elephants *(hathi)* than any other Chitwan animal, there are no wild elephants

Royal Chitwan National Park

in the park. The Chitwan's elephants are all trained Asian, or Indian, elephants.

Training an elephant takes about two years and the Chitwan elephants are usually acquired when they're eight to 20 years old, and can be expected to work until they are 40 or 50. Even elephants born in Nepal (not that there are many) have to go to India to be trained. A trained elephant is not cheap to purchase or to maintain. Typically they cost $3000 to buy and then have to be provided with 270 to 300 kg (over 600 pounds) of food a day.

When you're out on an elephant safari you'll see how even that isn't enough; they're constantly pulling up clumps of grass or other tasty vegetation, and shaking it around to dislodge any insects or dirt before stuffing it thoughtfully into their mouths. Their drinking capacity is just as impressive – an elephant needs more than 200 litres a day.

Keeping each elephant happy requires a support team of two or three people. The elephant's rider or master, commonly known as a mahout, is a *pahit* in Nepali. A pahit comes from India with the elephant and stays for three years while a local pahit is trained. The local pahit then stays with the elephant for life. He is backed up by one or two assistants *(patchouas)* whose main task is gathering the fodder to cater for an elephant's healthy appetite. They also assist the pahit when he saddles up the elephant with its howdah, the riding platform for passengers.

Notice the different ways elephants are ridden. At some lodges the howdah will be a square railed-in platform carrying one passenger at each corner, while at Sauraha the elephants carry the pahit and two passengers, all three sitting astride the elephant's back.

If you have aspirations of becoming a pahit you'll first have to learn some elephant commands, although each pahit will have his own particular words and ways of saying them:

sit	*baith*
lie down	*sut*
stand up	*maile*
hold your trunk out	
for me to climb up	*utha*
stop	*rhaa*
go	*agat*
shower me	*chhop*

The elephant has one of nature's most versatile appendages, a combination of nose and upper lip. The trunk has 100,000 muscles and can hold over nine litres of water.

It is not simply the size of the ears that distinguishes Indian (Asian) and African elephants; scientifically speaking, the two species are not closely related.

	Asian	African
toes	five front	four front
	four rear	three rear
ears	fold forward	fold back
tails		bristly
trunk	one finger	two fingers
ear	India shaped	
trunk	white patches	white stripes

The Indian elephant is noticeably smaller (males reach an average height of 2.75 metres and females grow to 2.45 metres), has smaller ears, a bulbous head and convex back. Only the males, but not all of them, have tusks. The African elephant has enormous ears, a sloping head, concave back and both the male and female have tusks. The Indian elephant has four nails on each hind foot where the African has only three.

Another major difference, as far as humans are concerned, is the domestication of these huge creatures. Indian elephants are easily trained, African elephants are not; though some people say that any elephant can be trained, and it is simply that in Africa, training elephants has not been widely attempted.

Elephants have a gestation period of 22 months and the mother is always assisted by another female in looking after the young calf. The calf is fed for three years and there is usually about seven years between pregnancies, although the elephants are on musth once a year. In the wild, the elephants live in a basically matriarchal society; the bulls do not travel with the herd. Elephants have four teeth and grow six sets during their life. Once the sixth set is worn out the elephant dies of starvation.

The numerous rivers in the parks have some fine swimming holes and if you're staying at one of the park lodges don't pass up the opportunity to lend a hand at elephant bath time. On a hot day in the Terai there's no better way of cooling off than to sit on an elephant's back in a river and shout *chhop*. If your accent is right you'll be rewarded with a cold shower!

Rhinoceros While elephants are the creatures you see most often in the Chitwan, it's the rhinoceros *(gaida)* you spend most time looking for, and with most hope of success. There are two types of rhino in Africa and three in Asia. The great Indian one-horned rhino, found in the Chitwan, is larger than the African black rhino although smaller than the African white. A fully grown Indian rhino can reach 180 cm at the shoulder and weigh more than two tonnes.

Rhinos are generally solitary creatures although several may occupy the same area. Their diet is chiefly grass and they have very poor eyesight although their sense of smell and hearing is good. It's their poor sight which leads to the rhino's reputation for bad temper. Since they cannot see very well rhinos are prone to assume almost any shape might be dangerous, so they charge it just in case.

Fortunately for the Indian rhino, its horn is not as large as the African variety and therefore not so valuable to poachers. Nevertheless, there are many superstitions about rhinos and almost every part of the creature is of value – the urine is considered a charm against diseases and ghosts, a rhino-skin bracelet wards off evil spirits, rhino blood cures menstrual problems, and the horn is used for medicinal purposes, and is famed as a sexual stimulant. Its value for Arab dagger handles has led to the disastrous decline in rhino numbers in Africa. Along the riverbanks in the Chitwan a rhino would mark its territories by dropping excreta in mounds. Since they walked backwards to approach these mounds a waiting poacher had easy prey.

Tiger The Chitwan's tigers are probably the most elusive of the park's wildlife. Without artificial assistance, such as staking a young buffalo calf out as live bait, you would have to be very lucky to see a tiger *(bagh)* in the Chitwan. Though their numbers have increased considerably since the park was opened, tigers are solitary creatures and they mainly hunt by night.

Tigers require an enormous amount of space. A male commands a territory of about 60 sq km, and a female about 16 or 17 sq km. Both sexes occupy an exclusive territory although a male's territory may overlap with several females. The Chitwan is simply not big enough to support the 50 breeding adults which is felt to be the minimum number to prevent interbreeding. This is part of the reason the adjoining Parsa Wildlife Reserve has been proclaimed.

Other Mammals The Chitwan is also known for more than 50 other mammals. Leopards *(chituwa)* are as elusive as tigers and the night prowling sloth bears *(bhalu)* are also rarely seen.

The Chitwan has four types of deer and you will often catch a fleeting glimpse of them as they dash through the undergrowth. There's the tiny barking deer *(mirga)*, the attractive spotted deer *(chital)*, the hog deer *(laghuna)* and the big sambar deer *(jarayo)*. Gaur, the world's largest wild cattle, are also found in the park.

Langur monkeys *(bandar)* are a common sight, chattering noisily in the tree tops or scattering vegetation down below. The spotted deer often follow the langurs around, taking advantage of their profligate feeding habits. The smaller macaque monkeys are the monkeys commonly found at temples in Nepal and all over the subcontinent. Freshwater or Gangetic dolphins are found in some river stretches in the park but they are rarely seen.

Reptiles The Chitwan has snakes *(sarpa)* of course, including some impressive pythons, plus turtles and two types of crocodiles. The marsh muggers are found in marshes, lakes and occasionally in rivers while the rarer gharial crocodile is exclusively found in rivers. The gharial, which grows to seven metres in length and is a harmless fish eater, was in danger of extinction and is still very rare. The Gharial Breeding Centre near Kasara, the park headquarters, has had considerable success, hatching eggs and raising the youngsters to a reasonable size before releasing them into Terai rivers.

WHEN TO GO

Many of the park lodges are closed during the May to August monsoon months when visibility is poor, the ground muddy and the flooding rivers make large parts of the park inaccessible. In September the lodges start to reopen, although at first the rivers are too high for 4WDs and transfers to the lodges have to be made by elephant.

The best time to visit the Chitwan is from October to February when the average daily temperature is 25°C. There are still cold, misty mornings, however, so a warm jacket is recommended. The Terai can be extremely hot and sticky, and even in October the humidity leaves everything feeling permanently damp.

From mid-January to the end of February the local villagers are allowed into the park to cut grass, which is an important part of the local economy. The grasslands are then burnt. While the villagers are crashing about, game is understandably scarce, but February through May is a prime time for game-viewing, thanks to the fact that the grass cover has been removed. Sporadic thunderstorms begin in April and the weather becomes unpleasantly hot.

WHAT TO BRING

Park visitors should come prepared for every eventuality. At times the Terai can be stiflingly hot so cool clothes are essential, however, because the sun can be fierce and there's little shade when you're sitting on an elephant's back, long sleeves, a shady hat and a good sunscreen are necessary. At the other extreme, the winter months can be surprisingly chilly, particularly if you're out on foot or on elephant back at dawn, so from November to February you should come prepared for the cold with sweaters and a jacket. Good walking shoes (that you don't mind getting wet) are essential at any time of year and you'll want a swimsuit for the rivers.

Neutral colours are best to ensure you blend into the background and are less likely to alert the wildlife. Reds, yellows and whites are particularly conspicuous.

Insect repellent is another Terai necessity. Malaria may have been wiped out but there are still plenty of mosquitoes and a wide variety of other voracious and crafty insects. Even people who are normally immune to insect attack may discover later that while they were propping up the bar in the evening a full-scale attack was being mounted on their ankles.

In addition to camera gear, preferably with a telephoto lens, binoculars are invaluable.

Warning

Come prepared for Nepal's famous jukha (leeches). These operate in force during the monsoon and will still be waiting for unwary jungle walkers during the first month or two of the dry season. See the Health section of the Facts for the Visitor chapter for tips on how to deal with these pests.

We have also received a letter from someone who contracted typhus fever after being bitten by a tick. Check with your guide whether they are a problem, and inspect exposed skin after walking.

INFORMATION

The park entry fee is Rs 650 ($13) and is valid for two days. If you're staying at a lodge in the park this will usually be included in your overall charge, but if you stay outside the park in Sauraha you have to pay the fee yourself. This can be arranged by most Sauraha guest houses, or you can easily get it yourself from the ranger's office next to the park visitors' centre, where you also book rides on government-owned elephants.

The visitors' centre in Sauraha is open from 6.30 am to 5 pm daily and has an interesting small museum with exhibits about the park, its creation, the problems it faces and its wildlife. The park headquarters is further west at Kasara where there is a small museum of skulls and a gharial crocodile breeding project.

There's no bank in Sauraha and the black market is surprisingly subdued, so you are best off changing money elsewhere. There is a bank at Tadi Bazaar, a few hundred metres east of the Sauraha turn-off.

See the Books section in the Facts for the Visitor chapter for books on wildlife and the park.

THINGS TO SEE & DO
Elephant Rides

The greatest thrill at Chitwan is the traditional elephant safari in search of wildlife – seeing a rhino from atop an elephant is an experience not to be missed. You won't want to spend your entire visit aboard an elephant, however. It is not a comfortable mode of travel and your first ride is likely to leave you with aches in muscles you didn't know you had, not to mention an interesting selection of bruises!

The lodges inside the park all have their own elephants and safaris are a standard activity; three, sometimes four, passengers ride on wooden railed howdah (seat).

At Sauraha, government-owned elephants are available for one to 1½-hour excursions into the park costing Rs 650 ($13). Howdahs are not used and two or three passengers sit astride the elephants' back. At peak times the number of visitors exceeds the supply of elephants so it's wise to book your elephant ahead of time; the lodges will generally offer to do this for you. It's easy to make a booking yourself at the ranger's office near the visitors' centre (open from 6.30 to 8.30 am and 1.30 to 3.30 pm), although there can be a queue. Elephant safaris usually start in the early morning or late afternoon, prime game-viewing times; the government elephants leave at 8 am and 4 pm.

Several Sauraha lodges now have elephants of their own. The going rate for a two-hour safari varied from Rs 400 ($8) to Rs 550 ($11), but in 1992 they were restricted to the Tikoli Forest, a buffer zone a few km to the west of the village and the elephant-breeding centre. This wildlife reserve is supposed to provide animals with a corridor they can use when moving between the park and the Chure Hills.

While there are still plenty of trees, the zone is heavily utilised by local villagers grazing animals and collecting fodder and firewood, so it is by no means a wilderness. Some people have seen rhinos and leopards here, and the operators (naturally) claim that game-watching here is as good as in the park. This is extremely unlikely, however, given the proximity of villages and the presence of so many people. If you only have time and money for one trip into the park you are much better off going into the park proper.

When booking a package tour in Kathmandu, or an elephant ride through a lodge, make sure you check whether your ride will take you inside or outside the park. People have been charged Rs 650 (instead of Rs 400) for a ride on one of the private elephants and have been mislead into thinking that the buffer zone is actually part of the park proper.

Jungle Walks

Visitors are allowed to enter the park on foot, but in order to get the most out of the experience, and for reasons of safety, it is best to go with a guide. Most lodges (including some in Sauraha) have their own naturalists, but there are also a number of independent guides. These young locals may not have much formal training, but they're often very knowledgeable about the park's wildlife and where to find it.

Walking is the ideal way to see the park's prolific butterflies and birds, and to see the flora close up. Walks are sometimes nothing more than a pleasant stroll through the jungle, but they can be exhilarating if you meet a rhino. Meeting a rhino when you're on foot is much scarier than seeing one from the lofty safety of an elephant's back. Caution is justified – tourists have been fatally injured by rhinos, and tigers and sloth bears can also be dangerous. Guides should brief you on safety procedures at the beginning of the walk.

Jungle walks from Sauraha usually cost around Rs 50 per person for two hours, Rs 100 ($2) for half a day, and Rs 200 ($4) for a full day. Short walks will generally cover grassland and riverine forest; you need a day to get into the jungle. Walks can also be combined with canoe trips (see following section). Some lodges and guides organise longer overnight treks into remote parts of the park.

Canoeing

A canoe trip along the Rapti or Narayani rivers is the most restful way of seeing the wildlife, particularly water birds, and with a bit of luck you may also see mugger and gharial crocodiles. With a great deal of luck you might catch a glimpse of a freshwater Gangetic dolphin, although they are as rare a sight as tigers.

Canoe trips from Sauraha cost Rs 100 per person, but trips are normally combined with a walk. The standard programme is a one-hour float down river, followed by a three-hour guided walk back to the village (costing around Rs 250, or $5, in total).

Jeep Safaris

Animals are surprisingly unconcerned by vehicles, so a jeep safari can be more productive than you might expect. It also gives you a chance to get beyond the immediate Sauraha area. Most jeep rides take three or four hours and include a visit to the park headquarters at Kasara, about 20 km west of Sauraha, and the nearby Gharial Breeding Centre. The cost is around Rs 650 ($13). Bear in mind that jeeps may not be able to get across the river into the park until the water levels drop sufficiently (maybe from January to April).

Terai Culture

Staying in Sauraha gives you an excellent opportunity to explore the surrounding countryside, either on foot or bicycle. Originally the surrounding area was dominated by Tharu, the indigenous tribespeople of the Terai, but over the last decade increasing numbers of hill people have bought up the land. Many villages are now a multicultural mixture. They're full of life (and hordes of children) and give a vivid insight into the rigours and pleasures of subsistence farming. The nearest Tharu village is **Bachauli**, east of Sauraha towards the Gaida Wildlife Camp.

Some lodges arrange visits to nearby villages and a number organise displays of traditional Tharu dances. The stick dance, with a great circle of men whacking their sticks together, is quite a sight. In Sauraha it's usually easy enough to find a lodge where there will be a performance; normally outside visitors are charged around Rs 50.

Wildlife Breeding

There are two important breeding projects associated with the national park: the elephant breeding camp four km west of Sauraha is worth visiting, as is the Gharial Breeding Centre near Kasara.

Cycling

Unfortunately bicycles are not allowed into the park proper – apparently nothing infuriates a rhino more than a bike – but the surrounding countryside is ideal for touring. You can hire standard Indian-made single-speed cycles in both Tadi Bazaar and Sauraha for around Rs 50 or Rs 60 per day, and these are adequate for negotiating the dusty tracks as long as you are not too ambitious about the distance you want to cover.

Just wandering along the tracks east and west of Sauraha is good fun, but if you like to have a specific destination, consider a trip to Bis Hajaar Tal ('20,000 lakes') about

1½ hours north-west of Sauraha. The lake is famous for its prolific bird life. To get there, ride to Tadi via the road at the eastern end of Sauraha (past the entrance to the Jungle Shangrila Camp). Turn left (west) onto the Mahendra Highway at Tadi and continue for about three km until you reach a signposted bridge over the Khageri Khola. Cross the bridge and take the dirt road on the left (south). After another small bridge the road forks; take the right fork and continue for about five km. The lake is on the right.

PLACES TO STAY & EAT

Basically you can stay inside the park, or at Sauraha, and the division between cheap and expensive places to stay is almost equally straightforward – most of the expensive places are inside, and the cheap ones are at Sauraha.

For those who can afford it, the lodges inside the park offer considerable luxury, well-organised game-watching activities, and an all-encompassing safari atmosphere. Although they can be pretty basic, the Sauraha lodges often have an interesting clientele, are scattered around an attractive, partly traditional village, and the full range of game-watching activities can be easily organised. When it comes to seeing the wildlife there's little difference between the two options. You've got just as much chance of seeing a rhino whether your room costs $2 or $200 a night.

Places to Stay – inside the park

Most visitors to the park lodges will arrive on package tours from Kathmandu, often as part of a larger tour of Nepal or the region. Advance bookings are necessary. Most of the lodges have attractive individual cottages dotted around a central dining room and bar area. Some have 'tented camps' with luxurious, semipermanent tents – you won't have a private bathroom, but you certainly won't be uncomfortable.

The lodges usually quote either an all-inclusive daily charge, which covers park entry fees, activities (including rides on their privately owned elephants) and all meals; or a two or three-day package that includes transport from Kathmandu. The only additional expenses will be for drinks and tips. Costs quoted here are per person on a double occupancy basis. There's usually a big price jump for single occupancy.

Tiger Tops (☎ 01-222706; fax 414075) PO Box 242, Durbar Marg, Kathmandu, is the best known and easily the most expensive of the lodges. This pioneer Chitwan jungle lodge is operated under the umbrella of Tiger Mountain, a very professional organisation, and enjoys a deservedly high reputation, particularly for its excellent guides and environmentally conscious approach. Whether you think it is worth the money probably depends on how much money you have.

Although the accommodation is comfortable and the food good, those expecting to be pandered to with extravagant five-star luxury can be disappointed. Tiger Tops has chosen neither to expand, nor to compromise the safari experience with unnecessary technological and consumerist trappings.

There are actually three Tiger Tops operations in the park. The well-known *Jungle Lodge* ($270 a night), is the original tree-top hotel. The buildings are on stilts and are constructed from local materials. Rooms are comfortable, the water is solar-heated, but there is no electricity. The *Tented Camp* ($191 a night) is three km east of the lodge in the beautiful Surung Valley. There are 12 safari tents with twin beds and modern toilet and shower amenities.

The *Tharu Village* ($133 a night) is the newest addition, and is built in traditional Tharu style: the long houses are constructed from timber, grass reeds and mud, and decorated with wall paintings. The rooms are attractive and comfortable; each has a queen-size and single bed, and a private bathroom. There's a swimming pool. The village is actually just outside the park on the northern bank of the Narayani River.

The Jungle Lodge and Tharu Village are open all year around, but the Tented Camp is closed from October to May. There are sometimes special offers outside peak

season, and permanent residents are also eligible for substantial discounts.

Temple Tiger (☎ 01-221585; fax 220178), PO Box 3968, Kantipath, Kathmandu, is at the western end of the park. Accommodation is in safari tents (complete with dressing room!) and costs $160 per night.

Island Jungle Resort (☎ 01-226022), PO Box 2154, Durbar Marg, Kathmandu, is also at the western end of the park on a large island in the middle of the Narayani River. The site is superb, one of the best in the park, but the resort can be crowded and noisy with package-tour groups from India. The original tents have been joined by cottages which, although comfortable, are not particularly attractive. Costs are around $125 a day, although packages can be considerably cheaper, and very good value.

Further east is *Gaida Wildlife Camp* (☎ 01-220186), PO Box 2056, Durbar Marg, Kathmandu, which is not far from Sauraha in the only section of park north of the Narayani River. The *Gaida Wildlife Jungle Camp* is eight km south at the base of the Someshwar Hills. The main camp has comfortable thatched huts, and the jungle camp has safari tents. The wildlife is not particularly prolific immediately around the main camp, but is meant to be excellent around the jungle camp. Packages from Kathmandu to Gaida including transport cost from $300 for two nights.

At the eastern end of the park the *Chitwan Jungle Lodge* (☎ 01-228918; fax 228349), PO Box 1281, Durbar Marg, Kathmandu, has rooms constructed in traditional Tharu style with mud walls and thatched roofs. There's no electricity but otherwise the rustic lodge has all mod cons including a restaurant, private bathrooms, and a very pleasant open-air bar. The forest is relatively undisturbed in this part of the park and a river with a terrific swimming (and elephant-bathing) hole runs close by. A package is $250 for a stay of two nights and includes land transport from Kathmandu. If you want to get there by raft then the cost increases to $300.

Finally, at the eastern end of the park, close to the boundary of the adjoining Parsa

Wildlife Reserve, is *Machan Wildlife Resort* (☎ 01-225001; fax 419749), PO Box 3140, Durbar Marg, Kathmandu. This is a particularly attractive resort, but the wildlife is said to be scarcer at this end of the park. Machan compensates by offering excellent facilities including an attractive swimming pool and a video library of wildlife films. In 1992, the owners were also caring for an orphaned, and very tame, rhino calf. The accommodation is in well-designed timber-frame bungalows with private bathrooms, and is decorated with superb Mithila murals.

There's also a Machan Tented Camp with safari-style tent accommodation deeper in the forest. A two-night stay costs $310 travelling overland from Kathmandu, $350 including a rafting trip. The resort and tent camp cost $188 and $233 respectively. Additional nights are $102 in the resort, $55 in the camp.

Places to Stay – Sauraha

Sauraha is just outside the park on the northern bank of the Rapti River, which forms the park's boundary. It lies six dusty km south of Tadi Bazaar (on the Mahendra Highway), where buses deliver you to a pack of waiting touts.

Sauraha is a simple, quiet little village – the sort of place nobody would usually visit – so it provides a good opportunity to observe rural life. There are glowing rice fields, neat mud-walled houses, barns, and a village well in the 'centre' of town. Ox carts rumble by and there's a constant background scene of ducks, chickens and children.

Progress is, however, making its inexorable mark and although it is still a very pleasant place to spend a few days, it is showing signs that it could degenerate into a Terai Thamel. There is still no electricity (although its arrival is imminent) and only a couple of two-storey monstrosities. Unfortunately there appears to be a complete absence of planning and no control over new developments.

The welcome given by the Tadi touts is the worst part of a visit to the Sauraha – with few exceptions they're slick, pushy and obnoxious. Treat all their claims with scepticism and definitely do not pay them for any tickets or tours until you have shopped around.

Normally jeeps from Tadi to Sauraha cost Rs 30 ($0.60) so the touts' first gambit is to offer you a cheap, or even free, ride to a lodge. In theory this places you under no obligation, but in practice it's not easy to avoid staying. You are much better off to pay the Rs 30 (hardly a king's ransom) and make it absolutely clear that you intend to check a few different places before you commit yourself.

There are so many lodges and competition is so intense that prices are ridiculously low. Many lodges have therefore come to depend on 'invisible' add-on charges (commissions or service charges for organising bus tickets and game-watching activities) to make a profit. While there is nothing wrong with a charge for services rendered, they can get completely out of hand in Sauraha. Prices are sometimes inflated by ridiculous amounts – particularly since in almost all cases it's easy and straightforward to organise tickets and activities yourself.

With literally dozens of places, it is impossible to mention them all here. The most important variable is the quality of the staff and your fellow travellers, both of which change, so ask other travellers for recommendations and check places for yourself. The main north-south road is busier and more developed than the roads that run east and west.

Bottom End The budget lodges at Sauraha are all very much out of the same mould: clean and simple mud-and-thatch cottages which sleep two and cost Rs 30/60 for singles/ doubles. Most have a small verandah, and those with a nice garden can be very pleasant places to stay. The mud-wall architecture keeps things surprisingly cool, and the rooms have insect screens on the windows and mosquito nets on the beds. Toilet and bathroom facilities are shared; hot water is unlikely, but this is not a major problem given the climate.

The *Chitwan Safari Camp* (☎ 056-20760)

has a nice garden and a quiet, but central position. It's old-fashioned and simple, and although it is a fraction more expensive than some of the other budget places (Rs 100/120, or $1/1.50 for singles/doubles) you really can't quibble at the price. In the same vein, the *Jungle Sunset Camp* and *Sauraha Jungle Lodge* are also recommended old-style places, although they have standard prices.

The *Annapurna View Lodge* is another classic budget place with a nice atmosphere. Next door, the *Crocodile Safari Camp* is busy and friendly with standard rooms for Rs

30/60 and rooms with private bath for Rs 300 ($6). The restaurant is good, but the garden is only ordinary.

The *Nature Safari Camp* is a new concrete construction lacking shade, but the rooms and bathroom facilities are good. Standard rooms are Rs 30/60 and there are also a couple with nice outlooks and private bathrooms for the bargain rate of Rs 100/150 ($2/3).

The *Jungle Shangrila Camp* (☎ 01-417986), an up-market package place, is very comfortable and pleasant. All rooms

■ PLACES TO STAY

1 Paradise Lodge
2 Tharu Lodge
3 Jungle Rapti Lodge
4 Hotel Jungle Camp
5 Hotel Holiday Safari
6 Rainforest Guest House
7 Chitwan Rest House
8 Jungle Express Camp
9 Hotel Shiva's Dream
10 Park Villa
11 Chitwan Resort Camp
12 Hotel Wildlife Camp
13 Rhino Lodge
14 Jungle Tourist Camp
19 Wendy's Lodge
20 Hotel Elephant Camp
21 Chitwan Tiger Camp
25 Chitwan Safari Camp
26 Jungle Sunset Camp
27 Sauraha Jungle Lodge
28 Jungle Safari Camp
29 Annapurna View Lodge
30 Crocodile Safari Camp
32 Eden Guest House
33 Travellers' Jungle Camp
34 Nature Safari Camp

▼ PLACES TO EAT

16 Sunset View Restaurant & Bar
17 Hungry Eye Restaurant & Bar
22 Jungle View Restaurant & Bar

OTHER

15 Rhino Book Shop
18 Bike Rental
23 Ticket Office
24 Visitor's Centre
31 Chitwan Tiger Guide
35 Smithsonian Nepal Terai Ecology Project
36 Elephant Stables (Hattisar)

have private bathrooms and cost $20 per night.

The *Chitwan Tiger Camp* (☎ 01-522641) has an excellent position overlooking the river. There are two bamboo machans on stilts with the best views in Sauraha, although they could be a bit exciting in a high wind. Singles/doubles are from $10/15 to $15/25 depending on the season.

Wendy's Lodge, one of the original Sauraha lodges, is an unchanged old-style budget place with rooms for Rs 30/60. The *Rainforest Guest House*, at the northern end of town, is a quiet and shady budget place with rooms for Rs 30/60. Recommended.

Middle-Range An increasing number of lodges are moving up-market, or at the very least adding some concrete and thatch cottages with private bathrooms, more-or-less guaranteed hot water and, sometimes, electricity, at present courtesy of noisy generators. These new constructions are generally ugly additions to the scene, but someone must want them. They range in price from around $6.50/8 to $10/13 for singles/doubles.

There are also a number of mid-range places dependent on the package trade which are happy to take on individuals if there are vacancies. Some are pretty good value with slightly more comfortable rooms and private bath, again from $6.50/8 a single/double.

Many of these places (the Rhino Lodge, Hotel Wildlife Camp, Chitwan Resort Camp, Jungle Express Camp amongst others) have offices in Kathmandu and Pokhara. The standard tour offered is three days and two nights, including transport, food, accommodation, entry fees, jungle walks, a canoe trip, an elephant ride, a performance of Tharu folk dancing, and a tour of a Tharu village.

Typically, the packages cost around $85 if you travel to the park by bus, or around $140 if you travel by private car – it is possible to spend considerably less by yourself. They also have combined rafting/Chitwan trips. These are competitively priced and can be as low as $150 for two nights and three days

rafting on the Trisuli followed by two nights at the Chitwan.

Rhino Lodge (☎ 01-413366), a reputable mid-range package-oriented place, has a range of rooms starting at Rs 250 ($5) and going up to Rs 300 ($6) and Rs 400 ($8). The food is pretty ordinary. The lodge is well geared for safari activities, however, and even has its own elephant. At present this can only operate outside of the park in the buffer zone to the west of Sauraha, but you do get a full two hours for Rs 400 ($8).

The *River View Jungle Camp* is a decent place, and although central, is not in any way spoilt. It's worth a look, with rooms for Rs 55/100, or Rs 400/600 ($8/12) with private bath.

The *Chitwan Resort Camp* (☎ 01-227711) has clean and decent rooms with private bath for Rs 300 ($6). The restaurant is particularly good. If you're looking for mid-range facilities this is recommended.

Hotel Wildlife Camp has a range of rooms starting at Rs 100 for a basic room with shared bath. Rooms with private bath are Rs 200 ($4), or $10 with hot water.

The *Jungle Express Camp* is aimed at the package trade and has good facilities, though is a bit overpriced for individuals at Rs 500 ($10).

Top-End At the top end, Sauraha also has some very comfortable 'resorts' charging around $20/30; in all but position and price they are equivalent to the luxury lodges inside the park.

Safari Adventure Lodge (☎ 01-223763; fax 226912) is an up-market camp to the west of Sauraha in the Badreni area. All inclusive prices (transport, accommodation, food and activities) start at $216 for three nights.

Places to Eat – Sauraha

Although there are a handful of small restaurants most people eat at their lodge. Some of the package-tour lodges have set menus, but most have a standard tourist-oriented menu that features dishes like dhal bhat, chop suey, curry, pasta and steak. Quality (average) and price (reasonable) don't seem to vary much.

GETTING THERE & AWAY

Air

Royal Nepal Airlines has daily flights to Meghauli, near the Tiger Tops, Temple Tiger and Island Jungle Resort lodges, for $72 each way. There are also daily flights to Bharatpur (Narayanghat) for $50 each way. The flights only take about half an hour.

Bus

Travellers intending to stay at Sauraha, the budget accommodation centre for the Chitwan, first have to get to Tadi Bazaar (sometimes spelt Tandi Bazaar), on the Mahendra Highway, about 15 km east of Narayanghat.

Ordinary Sajha Yatayat buses to Tadi cost Rs 55 from Kathmandu or Pokhara. Alternatively, tourist buses cost from Rs 120 ($2.50) and the trip typically takes six or seven hours. From September to April there are also minibuses, which take around five hours and cost Rs 200 ($4). Any travel agent in Kathmandu or Pokhara can make a booking. In Sauraha, lodges will book tickets (but beware of inflated prices) or you can book yourself in Tadi at booking stalls near the main intersection. Baba Travels (☎ 01-417111) have been recommended on the Kathmandu to Tadi route.

To Sunauli on the Indian border, buses take about five hours and cost Rs 90; to Birganj buses take about three hours and cost Rs 50. Minibuses run from Tadi to Narayanghat, take 30 minutes and cost Rs 5.

There are a number of possible methods of covering the six km from Tadi to Sauraha. You can walk in a couple of hours – which is pleasant and interesting if it's not too warm. You can take an ox cart (Rs 15), which is only marginally more comfortable and certainly no quicker than walking, although if you're not in a hurry it's an interesting ride. If your baggage allows, you could rent a bicycle (Rs 50 per day); there are a couple of rental shops near the junction. The easiest and quickest method, however, is by jeep (Rs 30); jeeps and touts meet all incoming buses.

On the way, you have to cross a small river at the village of Chitrasali (also known as Gauthali). If the river is high and you're cycling or walking, you'll have to cross in one of the dugout canoes that shuttle back and forth (Rs 5).

Car

Visitors to the park lodges usually get there by car from Kathmandu or Pokhara and this is usually arranged by the lodge operators. A car typically costs around $70 and the 160 to 180 km trip (depending where you're going) takes four to five hours. The driver hangs around for the two or three days his passengers are in the park.

If you're looking for transport from the park to Kathmandu or Pokhara it's often possible to negotiate a deal with these drivers, who will take you there and then return to pick up their round-trippers.

If you are coming or going from Kathmandu, you should try to convince your driver to take you one way via the Tribhuvan Highway passing through Daman and Hetauda. This route will cost extra as the narrow, winding road will add at least an hour to your travel time.

The road itself, an engineering feat courtesy of the Indian government, is sealed the whole way and is in good condition. The views along the way are stupendous. From Daman (80 winding km from Kathmandu) you can see the Himalaya stretching almost 180° from Dhaulagiri to Everest, weather-permitting.

The cars usually drop you at the turn-offs from the main road, from where your lodge vehicle will pick you up for the final trip into the park and across the river. This short trip is usually made by 4WD, although in the first month or two after the monsoon ends, September and October, the river may still be too high for vehicles and the transfer may be made by elephant. It's quite a surprise to arrive at the Chitwan Jungle Lodge turn-off, for example, and find an elephant waiting for the final seven km amble to the lodge!

Raft

The third way of getting to the Chitwan is by river and numerous Kathmandu rafting operators offer trips down the Trisuli River to the Chitwan. Most park lodges will organise a rafting trip in conjunction with your stay in the park.

The rafting trips start from Mugling, where the road to Narayanghat and the Chitwan turns off from the Kathmandu-Pokhara (Prithvi) Highway, or from further up the Trisuli. It takes two or three days to raft down to the Chitwan. Don't expect white-water thrills; this section of the river is more a gentle drift, although there are some fine views and the sandy beaches along the riverside offer great camping spots.

Prices range from around $30 to $75 per day for rafting only, while combination rafting/Chitwan trips (four nights, five days) can be priced as low as $140. Shop around and establish details before you hand over your money: where does the rafting trip begin? What size are the groups? What activities are included at the Chitwan? What transport is there from the river to your accommodation at the Chitwan? See the Rafting & Kayaking chapter for more information.

The Terai from East to West

There are a number of choices that travellers can make travelling to and from India and Kathmandu, so it is not possible to present the information in this chapter in an order that will suit everyone. Places are described from east to west, from Kakarbhitta to Mahendranagar. See the Getting There & Away chapter for more details on individual routes between India and Nepal.

The main east-west link is the Mahendra Highway, which varies in quality from good to abominable. The last incomplete link in the highway is the bridge over the Karnali River (between Nepalganj and Mahendranagar), but June 1993 was the planned completion date. Once this bridge is completed, the highway should be open all year,

although it is quite possible for sections to be temporarily cut by monsoon floods.

There are a number of attractive hill towns accessible from the Mahendra Highway and for the sake of convenience they have been included in this chapter. They are Ilam (accessible from Birtamod); Hile, Dharan Bazaar and Dhankuta (accessible from Itahari); Daman, which is between Hetauda and Naubise; and Tansen, which is between Bhairawa and Pokhara.

KAKARBHITTA

The sole reason for the existence of Kakarbhitta is its proximity to India. This is the border post for road traffic going to or from Siliguri and Darjeeling. In fact, it's not much more than a glorified bus stop and it's difficult to imagine that anyone would want to stay longer than to make a bus connection.

The surrounding countryside is attractive, however, and you can tell you're not far from Darjeeling when you see the tea plantations on the outskirts of town.

Orientation & Information

There's a tourist office just inside Nepal, past customs on the northern side of the road (on the right if you're coming from India). The Nepal Rastra Bank isn't signposted, but it's the unmistakable pink monstrosity on the left (south) side of the road.

The border is open to tourists from 7 am to 7 pm. There are two banks on the Nepalese side, but only the Nepal Rastra Bank changes money; it's also open from 7 am to 7 pm every day.

As you continue away from the border the main bus parking area is a dusty (or muddy, as the case may be) quadrangle on your right, followed by the bazaar and village.

Places to Stay & Eat

There are plenty of cheap but basic places to stay around the bazaar, but most are dreadful flophouses.

If you want to give yourself an even chance of getting a decent night's sleep there are a few places scattered around in slightly quieter locales.

The *Shere Punjab Hotel* just past the tourist office has grubby cells for Rs 40/80, but has a decent Indian restaurant.

There are several places in the village behind the bazaar – a two-minute walk from the bus station. The best is the *Upsara Lodge*, which is basic but clean and reasonably cheerful; singles/doubles are Rs 40/80. The *ABC Christian Lodge* was, in a previous incarnation, far and away the best place to stay. In fact it still is, but it is used for conferences and worship by local Christians and is no longer really functioning as a hotel. However, if you're a Christian and the lodge isn't full, clean and comfortable doubles cost Rs 80.

Getting There & Away

There are plenty of land connections to destinations both in Nepal and India. Many people buy through tickets between Kathmandu and Darjeeling, but this is relatively expensive, and unnecessary. With a through ticket you travel the Kakarbhitta to Kathmandu section at night and miss the sights.

Many travellers are ripped off buying through tickets between India and Nepal – bookings fail to materialise or are for lower quality services than were paid for. Admittedly, these problems are not nearly as common on this route as they are for some others. See the Getting There & Away chapter for more information.

To/From India It's a 10-minute walk from Kakarbhitta to the Indian border post of Raniganj; rickshaws cost Rs 5 (Indian Rs 3). From Raniganj you take a minibus 36 km to Siliguri; this takes around one hour and costs Indian Rs 5. From Siliguri you take a bus 78 km to Darjeeling; buses leave between 6 am and 6 pm, take around 3½ hours (make sure you catch an express) and cost Indian Rs 41. Depending on how quickly you made connections the total trip would not take more than six hours. It's possible to speed the process by an hour or two by catching a taxi from Raniganj to Siliguri (Indian Rs 30), or even from Raniganj to Darjeeling (Indian Rs

100). The overnight buses from Kathmandu all arrive in Kakarbhitta before 10 am; they leave from Kakarbhitta for Kathmandu between 3 and 5 pm.

To/From Pokhara or Kathmandu There is plenty of competition for your business if you plan to buy a bus ticket, so it's worth shopping around. The prices won't vary, but the departure times and the quality of the buses can.

Night buses for Kathmandu and Pokhara generally leave between 3 and 5 pm, take 17 or 18 hours, and cost Rs 232 ($4.50). Not only would this be an epic and unpleasant experience, but you'd miss the views. If time and weather allow, consider catching a day bus to Janakpur and stopping over there; they leave at 6.30, 7.30 and 9 am, can take up to 10 gruelling hours and cost Rs 93. The road is particularly interesting between Itahari and Janakpur; it runs across the flood plain of the massive Sapt Kosi. See the Getting There & Away chapter for more details.

There is one day bus (leaving 8.30 am) for Birganj that takes 12 hours and costs Rs 125 ($2.50).

Prior to the opening of the new Kathmandu Bus Terminal, buses for Kakarbhitta left from Ratna Park (to the left as you entered). The night express buses leave between 4 and 5.30 pm, but are often full, so book a day or two early.

ILAM

Ilam is an attractive small town at the centre of Nepal's tea industry; the climate of the surrounding hills is similar to Darjeeling's. Few Westerners visit but there is some basic accommodation available, and there are good walks, and tea plantations to see. The road from the Terai is very steep and the views are spectacular. In late 1992 it was in poor condition, but was being improved with a view to it being sealed. It already extends to Phidim and is being pushed further into the hills. Buses leave from Birtamod on the Mahendra Highway 13 km west of Kakarbhitta. They depart from 7 am to 1 pm, take seven hours and cost Rs 70. Buses to Phidim cost Rs 150 ($3).

BIRATNAGAR

The observation that Biratnagar is the second-largest city in Nepal, and an industrial centre, actually makes it sound worse than it is. It's an energetic bustling place with the crowds and shops you would expect of a city with several hundred thousand inhabitants. However, there's just nothing much to attract the visitor unless you are particularly interested in Nepal's somewhat shaky industrial development, or the strongest, most politicised unions in the country. The border is not open to tourists.

The countryside and surrounding villages are interesting, but difficult to explore without private transport. One possibility is to continue north along Main Rd (with the Hotel Namaskar and Nepal Bank Ltd); this veers left when you leave town; continue westwards until you reach a T-intersection; turn right (north) along a dirt road that parallels the sealed road and continue through Sigraha and Haraincha until you reach the Mahendra Highway to the west of Itahari.

Jute used to be grown in large quantities, and can still be seen, but the industry has been in decline for years. There are numerous groups of people in the region, but the most distinctive are the local Tharus and Danuwars. The Danuwars are very similar in culture and appearance to the Tharus, but the women wear a distinctive embroidered sari worn wrapped around the waist and with one end thrown over the shoulder, a bit like a toga.

Places to Stay & Eat

There's quite a range of places at varying prices. Bear in mind, however, that anywhere on Main Rd or near the bus station will be pretty noisy.

Dhankuta Lodge, opposite the bus station, is clean and decent with singles/doubles at Rs 40/50, or Rs 60/80 with bathroom. The *Padma Hotel & Lodge* is basic, but clean, and has rooms with/without bath for Rs 70/40.

The best value up-market place is *Hotel Namaskar* (☎ 021-21199) on Main Rd, a 15-minute walk from the bus station, which has a range of rooms from Rs 150 to 450 ($3 to $9). At the top price you get air-con and a private sitting room, but the cheaper rooms are clean and quite adequate. There's a good, reasonably priced restaurant frequented by the local notables.

A little less formal, but still comfortable, the *Hotel Geetanjali* is also across from the bus station on Main Rd. Set in a pleasant garden, the hotel charges Rs 185/125

1 Rastriya Banijya Bank
2 Statue
3 Everest Air
4 Police
5 Padma Hotel & Lodge
6 Hotel Namaskar
7 Nilgiri Cafe
8 Milan Hotel & Restaurant
9 RNAC
10 Hotel Geetanjali
11 Post Office
12 Bus Station
13 Dhankuta Lodge
14 Shanti Sital Lodge

($3.50/2.50) for doubles with/without bath. There's no restaurant, but decent Indian food is available.

Getting There & Away
There are daily RNAC (☎ 021-25576) flights to Kathmandu for $77. There are plenty of buses to Kathmandu, Kakarbhitta and Janakpur. Night buses to Kathmandu leave from 3.30 pm, take 14 hours and cost Rs 205 ($4). There are many day buses to Kakarbhitta (Rs 35), Janakpur (Rs 60), Rajbiraj (Rs 30) and Dharan Bazaar (Rs 15).

ITAHARI
Itahari is an undistinguished town at the intersection of the Mahendra Highway and the Biratnagar to Dhankuta road. There is an interesting market held along the dusty lanes south-east of the main intersection.

Places to Stay
There's one passable hotel in Itahari, which also has a decent restaurant. The *Jaya Nepal Hotel* has singles/doubles with shared bath for Rs 40/70.

Getting There & Away
All the long-distance, east-west buses stop in Itahari. There are also plenty of local buses which go to Biratnagar (one hour, Rs 8) and Dharan (½ hour, Rs 5). One bus a day leaves at 6 am for Dhankuta (five hours, Rs 33). It's best to make an advance reservation if you want to get a seat on a Kathmandu bus; they leave from 3 to 5.30 pm and cost Rs 197 ($4).

DHARAN BAZAAR
Dharan lies right at the foot of the Chure Hills, but the transformation from the Terai is dramatic. It's a bustling bazaar town catering to the hill people of eastern Nepal. It has grown rapidly despite suffering a major earthquake in 1988.

There are no sights of note, but if you're heading into the mountains this will be your best chance for final purchases. A small number of trekkers bound for Hile and Basantpur do come through town, and **Chatara**, the finishing point for raft trips on

the Sun Kosi, is only 15 km to the west. Baraha Chhetra, five km north of Chatara, is the site for an annual religious festival in late October/early November.

Places to Stay & Eat
There are two possibilities, but they'll only look good if you've been trekking for at least two weeks! Coming from Itahari, turn right at the statue of the king. The *Hotel Gurans & Bamboo Lodge* is labyrinthine, gloomy and not terribly clean. Singles/doubles with private bath are Rs 80/90. The *Hotel Evergreen* is a notch above in cleanliness and price, but nothing to write home about. Singles/doubles are Rs 100/150 ($2/3). Both hotels have reasonable restaurants.

Getting There & Away
Dharan Bazaar is 50 km from the attractive hill town of Dhankuta. Hile, the starting point for a number of treks in eastern Nepal is 12 km past Dhankuta. The spectacular road is sealed as far as Hile, but continues on to Basantpur, and will soon continue even further. Buses to Dhankuta take three hours and cost Rs 33; buses to Basantpur (via Hile) leave from 5 am to 2 pm, take five hours and cost Rs 74. There's also a direct link with Kakarbhitta, departing daily at 3 pm (Rs 204, or $4).

DHANKUTA
Although Dhankuta is only 50 km by excellent road from the Terai, it seems more like a million miles. The largest, flattest spot in the nearby vicinity is the bus station – it soon becomes very hard to remember that expanses of water-logged plains exist.

The town is strung along a ridge that basically runs north-south; the bus station is below the ridge. The sad remnants of the forest that once covered the hill are at the northern end of town. There is a collection of small, but decent, lodges which cater to a largely Nepalese clientele, but there's no real reason to stay here, unless you want to catch the colourful *haat bajar* (weekly bazaar) on Thursdays. Hile is more interesting and has better walking possibilities.

As you walk downhill (south) along the main street the road forks: the right fork goes down to the bus station; the left fork to a spur where there are fine views of the Himalaya. The latter is a pleasant 45-minute walk. After about 15 minutes the main track veers to the left and there is a stile over a barbed wire fence. Climb the stile and follow the ridge line up to the left. Eventually you'll come to a small shrine. There are plenty of flowers and birds along the way and, of course, good views.

Places to Stay

There are a number of small, clean, basic lodges on the main street. The *Najulo Lodge* and the pleasant *Nauke Lodge* cost Rs 25/40 with shared facilities.

The best of them all – and it would be a pleasant place to stay while you explored the surrounding hills – is the *Hotel Parichaya*. It's clean and sunny and there are superb views. To find it, walk north up the ridge until you get to a large pipal tree in the middle of an intersection. The hotel is on the right; singles/doubles are also Rs 25/40. According to one reader 'the toilet out back is like a safari park at night'.

Getting There & Away

Plenty of buses travel the spectacular road from Dhankuta to Dharan Bazaar (three hours, Rs 33). From Dhankuta the sealed road continues to Hile, then continues unsealed to Basantpur. Buses for Basantpur depart from 7.30 am to 2.30 pm, take three hours and cost Rs 41. The road is being pushed further into the hills, but there are no buses beyond Basantpur.

HILE

Hile, a bustling bazaar town, is the starting point for Arun Valley treks (possible for individuals) and for treks to Makalu (groups only). Kanchenjunga trekkers (also groups only) usually start at Basantpur. Hile would be a good base for day walks in the region.

Nepal's ethnic map is always complicated, but the mix at Hile is about as complicated as it gets, with Tibetans, Bahuns, Chhetris, Magars, Tamangs, Rais, Limbus and Indians.

There are fantastic views of the Himalaya, especially the Makalu massif, from the ridge above the town. Walk along the Basantpur road past the army base and a few hundred metres past the army checkpost (there's a boom across the road) you can cut up to the left onto a grassy ridge.

Places to Stay & Eat

There are a number of decent, but basic trekkers' lodges with not much to separate them. The *Hotel Gajur* has a recommended restaurant and the *Dama Hotel* is run by a friendly family. Singles/doubles in both hotels go for Rs 25/50.

KOSHI TAPPU WILDLIFE RESERVE

The Koshi Tappu Wildlife Reserve protects a section of the Sapt Kosi's flood plain that lies behind the Kosi Barrage. The Sapt Kosi is one of the Ganges' largest tributaries, and the Kosi Barrage is designed to minimise destructive annual floods. Most of the reserve is surrounded by eight-metre-high embankments that control the spread of the river and funnel it towards the barrage.

The main highway skirts the reserve and crosses the river at the barrage. It's a beautiful, fascinating water world. Small thatched villages perch on what little high ground there is and wherever you look there are water birds, and ponds full of flowering plants, all overwhelmed by fields of rice stretching to the horizon.

Behind the embankments the river continuously changes course, and regularly floods during the monsoon, although only to shallow depths. The vegetation is mainly tall grass, with some scrub and riverine forest. Local villagers are allowed to collect grass for thatching every January.

The reserve is home to the last surviving population of wild water buffalo (*arna*), various deer, blue cow (*nilgai*), gharial crocodiles and Gangetic dolphins. It is also either a permanent or temporary home to 280 different species of water birds (migratory and otherwise). These include 20 species of ducks, ibises, storks, egrets, cranes and herons. The migratory species, including the sarus crane from Siberia, and the ruddy shel-duck from Tibet, take up residence from November to February.

The reserve occasionally hosts bird-watchers between November and February, but very few people visit. The arrival of a tourist out of the blue gives everyone quite a shock. There's no accommodation, but there is an area where you could camp, and the helpful staff are happy to give visitors the use of a kitchen. The reserve has two elephants,

which can be ridden for Rs 650 ($13) for one hour. Canoes can also be arranged.

Orientation & Information

The reserve headquarters is at Kusaha, where all visitors must pay a Rs 650 ($13) entrance fee. Kusaha is a three-km walk from the highway, just outside the eastern embank-ment, on the eastern side of the barrage.

The turn-off to the reserve is about 11 km north-east of the Kosi Barrage, and about two km before the village of Laukhi. Coming from Itahari, it's about 46 km to Laukhi and

---

Ramayana

The *Ramayana*, or romance of Rama, is amongst the best loved and most influential stories in Hindu literature. Handsome Rama embodies chivalry and virtue, and his wife, the beautiful Sita, exemplifies devotion and chastity. Together with Rama's ally, the faithful monkey-god Hanuman, they are heroes and exemplars of immense popularity and like all great mythical archetypes they have somehow found an enduring place in the human psyche.

It's likely the legend has at least a basis in fact, and was first retold around village hearths. The *Ramayana* was first permanently recorded in Sanskrit, possibly as long as 2400 years ago by a sage and poet, Valmiki. Since then it has become a part of people's lives and imaginations throughout the subcontinent and, in various forms, as far as Bali, where to this day it features in puppetry and dance.

Rama was a reincarnation of Vishnu, born at the request of the gods to do battle with the ghastly demon king Ravana the King of Lanka (possibly Sri Lanka). He was reincarnated at Ayodhya (350 km west of Janakpur) as the eldest son of a wealthy king. Handsome, virtuous and strong, he grew up the idol of the people and especially one of his half-brothers, Lakshman.

In the kingdom of Mithila, good King Janak discovered baby Sita, the reincarnation of Lakshmi, lying in a furrow of a ploughed field. She too grew up to be wise and beautiful and so many men wanted to marry her that Janak set a test – a successful suitor had to bend the divine bow of Shiva. Rama, of course, drew the bow and he and Sita looked into each other's eyes and knew divine love.

Rama and his three half-brothers were married in a single ceremony – the brothers to neighbouring princesses – and there was much feasting, flowers falling from heaven, gorgeous processions across the plains, and so on. But this is where things took a turn for the worse.

After returning to Ayodhya, Rama and Sita were forced to leave the palace because of the intrigues of the detestable hunchback Manthara. While they wandered in exile, Rama and Lakshman were distracted by a golden deer, and Sita was kidnapped and carried off to Lanka by the demon king. Imprisoned, Sita was forced to defend herself from the disgusting advances of Ravana.

Meanwhile, Rama and Lakshman formed an alliance with a monkey kingdom. In particular they were served by the indomitable monkey god Hanuman. With Hanuman's loyal assistance Sita was finally rescued and the demon king Ravana destroyed.

Unfortunately, life didn't improve much for Sita who was forced to undergo an ordeal by fire to prove her chastity. Although Rama, now king of Ayodhya, believed her innocence, his people didn't and Sita was forced to go into exile again. Sita gave birth to Rama's twin sons and the family was later reunited, but Sita decided she had had enough of this mortal coil and was swallowed up by the earth.

There are many versions of the story recorded in many art forms and many different languages, including English. Trying to imagine the power and subtlety of the complete story by reading this condensation is a bit like trying to imagine a tree by looking at a match. ■

a further two km to the turn-off. There was no signpost in late 1992.

If you do plan a visit, and especially if you want to stay, ring ahead to get the latest information on access and the availability of facilities. You can contact Kusaha through the neighbouring army camp (☎ 025-20881), or try the Department of National Parks & Wildlife Conservation (☎ 01-220912; fax 227675), Babar Mahal, Kathmandu.

RAJBIRAJ

Rajbiraj is a dusty uninteresting little town, but it lies on the edge of the Sapt Kosi flood plain, so the countryside and wickerwork villages to the east are fascinating. Rajbiraj lies to the south of the main highway, but if you have private transport it's definitely worth the detour. You'd have to be pretty keen to build it into your itinerary if you are using local buses, but it could be done.

Place to Stay

There's only one place to stay – the *Sinha Lodge* – on the main road. It's very, very basic and singles/doubles are Rs 35/50.

Getting There & Away

Local buses from Janakpur and Biratnagar are frequent and cost Rs 35. The road starts to fall apart east of Rajbiraj and there are some very slow sections before the Kosi Barrage.

JANAKPUR

Janakpur is an interesting, attractive city of temples, pools, sadhus, rickshaws and rainbow-coloured saris. It's a tourist town, but the tourists are devout Indian pilgrims, not Western backpackers.

Janakpur's religious significance is due to its role in the famous Hindu epic, the *Ramayana*. It is the legendary birthplace of Sita, an incarnation of Lakshmi, and the place of her marriage to Rama, one of Vishnu's most popular incarnations. At times, especially during festivals, when strangely resonant vignettes from the *Ramayana* are played out

in the streets, it can feel as if the ancient myth has come to life.

Janakpur is situated in what was once the kingdom of Mithila, a region now divided between Nepal and India. The Maithili language, which also has its own unique script, is spoken by approximately two million Nepalese; only Nepali is spoken by a greater number of people.

Janakpur is at least the third city to be built on this site, and most buildings are less than a century old. The city that was mythologised in the *Ramayana* existed around 700 BCE, but it apparently sank back into the forest, perhaps destroyed by disease. Simaraungarh grew up in its place, but it was destroyed by Muslims in the 14th century, and once again the region was reforested.

Theologically, Janakpur is paired with Ayodhya, near Faizabad in Uttar Pradesh, where Rama is believed to have been born. In December 1992 Hindu zealots provoked widespread bloodshed across the subcontinent by destroying a Muslim mosque they claimed to have been built over a shrine marking Rama's birthplace. Fortunately, none of this fanatical intolerance is apparent in Janakpur.

Modern Janakpur is a Terai city that works: it's green and clean and the narrow lanes are interspersed with temples, pilgrim hostels *(kutis)* and both large and small sacred ponds (respectively *sagar* and *kunda)*. Legend says the ponds were created by King Janak for the use of the gods who came to the wedding of Rama and Sita. They take the place of a river for ritual bathing and are also used by the local dhobi caste who are clothes washers. Thanks to a successful development project, many are also stocked with fish that provide an important supplement to the local diet.

The city authorities have managed to keep most traffic out of the centre of town, which makes it pleasant to wander around. Sometimes the city feels like a big village, but when you stand in the broad square before the Janaki Mandir, it can also have a definite grandeur. If, at dusk or dawn, you take a slow rickshaw ride to one of the many temples or

Janakpur

0   300   600 m

To Mahendra
Highway

To Jaynagar &
Indian Border

Purare Chowk

Ratan Saga
Kunda

Sita
Kunda

Bihar
Kunda

Ramanand
Chowk

Kopal
Mauchami
Sagar

Ford
Sagar

To
Bijalpur

Bhanu Chowk

Ganga
Sagar

Danush
Sagar

Murali
Chowk

To Jaleshwar &
Indian Border

Campus Chowk

KUWA
VILLAGE

To Airport

1 Raj Yoga Ashram
2 Sajha Yatayat Bus Station
3 Cigarette Factory
4 Train Station
5 Hotel Rama
6 Big Monkey Temple
7 Hospital
8 Ram Sita Bibaha Mandir
9 Janaki Mandir
10 Ram Mandir
11 Hotel Welcome
12 King's Statue
13 RNAC Office
14 Tourist Information Centre
15 Telecommunications Tower
16 Bus Station
17 Police Station
18 Nepal Rastra Bank
19 Hospital
20 Gopal Dharamsala
21 Post Office
22 Macha Palan Fisheries Project
23 Janakpur Women's Development Centre

ponds on the outskirts of town you'll discover a peaceful beauty.

If you do have the time and the inclination to experience something of the Terai, Janakpur should be at the top of your list. It's possible to visit on the way to/from Kakarbhitta. Unfortunately, although the only steam railway in Nepal (in fact the only railway) connects Janakpur to the Indian town of Jaynagar, tourists are not allowed to cross the border (see the Around Janakpur section).

Orientation & Information

Janakpur is a hopeless tangle of mostly narrow streets, so the best way to get your bearings is from the telecommunications tower and the large concrete water tank on stilts. The town itself lies to the east of the main road that runs through to Jaleshwar at the border.

The Janaki Mandir is just to the south of the water tank, and the bus station is to the south-west of the temple near the telecommunications tower. The train station is about a 20-minute walk to the north-east of the large concrete water tank.

There is a helpful tourist information centre (☎ 041-20755) at Bhanu Chowk; there were plans for it to be relocated to the forecourt in front of the Janaki Mandir. Consider ringing to check the dates for major festivals. The office is open from 10 am to 5 pm, Monday to Friday, but closes an hour earlier from November to January. The RNAC office is opposite the tourist centre.

Janaki Mandir

The temple to Sita (who is also known as Janaki) is believed to be built over the spot where her father, King Janak, found her lying in the furrow of a ploughed field. It's impressively large yet surprisingly, you come across it from the winding Janakpur streets almost without warning.

Although it has no great architectural or historical merit – it was built in 1912 and might be described as baroque Moghul – it is nonetheless a fascinating place. There are instances of fine work, especially in some of the carved stone screens, and in the beautiful silver doors to the inner sanctum.

The inner sanctum is opened from 5 to 7 am and 6 to 8 pm, to reveal a flower-bedecked statue of Sita that was apparently miraculously found in the Saryu River near Ayodhya. She is accompanied by Rama and his half-brothers Lakshman, Bharat and Satrughna.

During the day, there are few people in the temple – some priests, sadhus and, if you're lucky, perhaps some musicians playing in the cloisters – but it comes alive in the evenings when Sita is displayed.

Ram Sita Bibaha Mandir

Virtually next door to the Janaki Mandir, but built with the traditional Nepalese pagoda roof, this rather bizarre temple is built over the spot where Rama and Sita were married. There's a bit of a scam at the gate – you pay to take in a camera, or to have it looked after. Entry is Rs 5. The temple itself has glass walls so you can peer in at the kitsch life-sized models of Sita and Rama, his half-brothers and sisters-in-law.

Ram Mandir & Danush Sagar

Located in the city's oldest quarter, to the south-east of the Janaki Mandir, Ram Mandir is another Nepalese-style temple that is the centrepoint for the Rama Navami celebrations. Immediately to its east is the Dhanush Sagar, which is considered to be one of the holiest ponds and is popular with pilgrims.

Other Temples & Ponds

There are numerous temples and ponds scattered around the outskirts of town. It is worth hiring a bicycle rickshaw to see them, although you could track them down on foot if you were energetic. They're reached by brick paved roads that wander off into the paddy fields. If you do hire a rickshaw, allow a couple of hours and expect to pay around Rs 50.

Start at the bizarre temple that is widely known as the **Big Monkey Temple**. Hanuman, the monkey god, is worshipped in

Mithila Painting

Mithila culture is essentially a culture of the Gangetic plain, and Hindu caste structure is strictly upheld. Most people are subsistence farmers, but landholdings are usually very small, and many families live on the edge of starvation. Many are in the grip of moneylenders, or *zamindars*.

Zamindars, usually from the Brahman (priest) or Kayastha (warrior, also Kshatriya) castes, occupy an almost feudal role as major landowners and through their traditional role as money-lenders. Their tenant farmers and debtors are effectively serfs trapped in a system of bonded labour.

Most Mithila people live in small villages, usually with no more than around 100 households. House walls are made from bamboo or thatch plastered with a mixture of cow dung and mud. The roofs are thatched, sometimes tiled. Most houses have a fenced courtyard which is also sealed with mud and cow dung.

Mithila women are raised with the expectation that they will be workers in their husband's home, and are frequently married as children. After puberty they are veiled so that they cannot be seen by males outside their family. As a part of their cultural and religious tradition, the women paint striking murals on the external walls of their homes. Inside, pottery storage containers and internal pillars also carry designs.

Different castes and different regions have developed distinctive styles and symbols, which are passed down from mother to daughter. Traditionally, painting and decoration is not undertaken purely to create an aesthetic result, nor is it purely cathartic or expressive. Painting largely springs from cultural and religious motives. The act of painting, as a part of some ritual, can be more important than the finished result itself, and completed paintings can act as charms, prayers and meditation aids.

Paintings often derive from Hindu mythology and can use complex symbols (sometimes with a distinct mandala-like quality), simple apparently abstract figures (including hand stencils, peacocks, pregnant elephants and fish), or can take on a narrative quality (representing religious stories). High castes, including the Kayastha, have developed extremely elaborate, abstract forms. Lower caste paintings are often simpler and more realistic, but they have an energetic expressionistic style, and retain a strong sense of formal design.

Mithila paintings from Madubani in Bihar, India, have been discovered by the international art world. The most well known are the elaborate Kayastha wedding paintings that are presented to the groom as part of the build-up to an arranged marriage. Until recently, little interest has been taken in the art produced on Nepal's side of the border.

This changed with the foundation of the Janakpur Women's Art Project in 1989 which had the dual aim of promoting traditional Mithila painting skills and empowering the women painters. The project will soon be housed in the Janakpur Women's Development Centre and it will be possible to visit the centre to see the women working, and to buy what they produce. (See the separate section under Janakpur.)

The project includes women of diverse castes and backgrounds and the art that is created reflects this variety: wedding paintings, pregnant elephants, gods, and abstract tattoo designs are just some of the subjects. Increasingly the paintings are changing to include scenes from the womens' lives, including childbirth and marriage. In addition to paintings (acrylic on daphne paper) the women are also producing ceramics (plates and figures), papier-mâché, patchwork tapestry, silk-screen prints and woven wall hangings.

All these creations can be bought at Janakpur Women's Development Centre. In Kathmandu, the project's goods are sold at Sana Hastakala, Mahaguthi, and a number of other reputable craft shops. See the Things to Buy sections in the Kathmandu, Patan & Bhaktapur chapter for more information. It's also possible to see examples of the women's work at the Kantipath branch of the Nepal Grindlays Bank, and at the United Nations building in Pulchowk. ■

the form of a rhesus monkey kept in a depressing cage. Despite this, it could well be monkey heaven since the attendants and pilgrims press food on their mascot. The constant supply of delicacies no longer arouses much interest or excitement, but temptation (or boredom) triumphs and the monkey keeps munching on. It is now so enormously overweight it can hardly move.

Two of the most interesting and attractive ponds can be reached by following the brick-paved roads to the west. They are **Bihar Kunda** and **Ratan Saga Kunda**. The countryside is lush and tropical with coconut palms and huge trees framing the temples and ponds that are scattered across the fertile plains.

Janakpur Women's Development Centre

The Janakpur Women's Art Project was started to promote traditional Mithila painting skills and to empower the local women who live in a highly restrictive patriarchal society (see later Mithila Painting section). In early 1993 plans to house the project in a specially built centre were well advanced.

The centre will incorporate aspects of traditional architecture and the beautiful site is on the edge of an interesting village, a short rickshaw ride and walk from the centre of town. It will be possible for visitors to see the women at work, and to purchase some of their striking creations at extremely reasonable prices; paintings start at Rs 200 ($4), ceramics at Rs 175 ($3.50). A visit is a must.

Take a rickshaw from town to Macha Palan (Fisheries Project). To get there, look for a sign for the National Agriculture Research Programme. The rickshaw should cost around Rs 10. Coming from town, a brick road on the left forms a T-intersection opposite the project. Follow it east to Kuwa village. Turn right at Kuwa village and continue until you reach a large, but unprepossessing temple. Turn left immediately before the temple and right immediately after it. Continue to the south; the road bends to the left, past a tank on the right. The route sounds complicated, but ask directions if in doubt and you shouldn't have

a problem. It's about a 10-minute walk from Macha Palan to the centre.

Festivals

On the fifth day of the waxing moon in late November or early December, thousands of pilgrims arrive to celebrate a re-enactment of Sita's marriage to Rama (Vivaha Panchami). This is also the occasion for an important fair and market that lasts a week. Rama's birthday (Rama Navami) in late March or early April is also accompanied by a huge procession.

Most Hindu festivals are major events in Janakpur. Deepavali is an interesting time to be in town, as this is when the Mithila women repaint the murals on their houses. On the day before Holi, Parikrama involves a ritual walk around the town's ring road. Holi itself can get very boisterous and wild; women should take care.

Places to Stay & Eat

Janakpur is desperately in need of a couple of decent hotels.

Despite the fact that it is disgracefully run-down, the best currently on offer is the *Hotel Welcome* (☎ 041-20224) on Station Rd. It does a thriving trade, so until there is some stronger competition there won't be much incentive to improve things. Although the rooms are bad, the staff are friendly and helpful, and the restaurant is good. At the bottom end they have a dormitory for Rs 35 per person and doubles with shared bath for Rs 75. Singles/doubles with private bath are Rs 150/200 ($3/4), with air-con Rs 450/600 ($9/12). Ask to see several rooms before you pick one, and check the plumbing, the mosquito nets and the cleanliness of the sheets.

The *Rama Hotel* (☎ 041-20059) is a gloomy alternative on the outskirts of town (not far from the cigarette factory). It doesn't have any particular advantages over the Hotel Welcome. Singles/doubles with private bath are Rs 100/200 ($2/4).

Getting There & Away

RNAC (☎ 041-20185) has three flights a week to Kathmandu for $77.

In Janakpur, private buses for Kathmandu leave from the main bus station between 5.30 and 6.30 pm. There are half a dozen express buses to/from Kathmandu that cost around Rs 142 ($3) and take about 12 hours. The government-operated Sajha Yatayat buses leave from a stop to the east of town on the main highway; they have day buses to Kathmandu leaving at 6.45 and 7.45 am and costing Rs 114 ($2). Prior to the opening of the new Kathmandu Bus Terminal, Sajha Yatayat buses left from Bhimsen Tower and private buses left from the Central Bus Station. Sajha buses left at 7 and 9 am and, 6.30 and 7.30 pm.

Private buses leave Janakpur for Kakarbhitta every half hour from 4.30 to 10 am, and cost Rs 107 ($2); the journey takes seven hours. There are also day and night buses for Narayanghat for around Rs 90.

AROUND JANAKPUR

The fields and villages around Janakpur form a lush and magical mosaic. It's worth exploring on foot or bicycle, or by rickshaw or train. Unfortunately there are no formal bicycle-hire places, but if you ask around something may turn up. Western visitors are rare, so tread gently, and always ask before taking photos.

It doesn't really matter which direction you choose to go. Jaleshwar on the Nepalese side of the border is a completely uninspiring town, but there are some interesting villages on the way. Other possibilities include the road that runs south to the airport, which turns to dirt and continues through a number of attractive villages, the road that runs north of the cigarette factory, and the road that runs west of Purare Chowk. **Dhanusa**, 15 km to the north, marks the spot where Rama allegedly drew Shiva's magic bow.

Janakpur is the terminus for two railway lines, one of which runs east to **Jaynagar** over the Indian border, and the other which runs north-west to Bijalpur. They're narrow-gauge trains and very slow, so they offer an ideal method of seeing the countryside.

The most interesting possibility is the Jaynagar train, because two daily services run in each direction and it is easy to put together a day trip. It's about 30 km (four hours!) to Jaynagar, but tourists are no longer allowed to cross the border into India, so you have to get off in one of the villages along the way. Trains leave both Janakpur and Jaynagar at 7.30 am and 3.30 pm. Tickets are Rs 13 in 1st class and Rs 9 in 2nd class.

The first stop after Janakpur is **Parbaha**, and there are interesting villages on either side of the tracks – you could walk back to town. Another interesting stop is **Baidehi**, about an hour (10 km) from Janakpur, where you could alight and catch the Janakpur-bound train that comes through an hour later. Alternatively, you could continue all the way to **Khajuri**, about three km from Jaynagar on the Nepalese side of the border and catch the afternoon Janakpur-bound train.

BIRGANJ

Birganj is one of the main border crossings between Nepal and India, and one of Nepal's most important industrial cities. This is an unfortunate combination. It has been one of the most unattractive places on the planet for some time, but it is not resting on its laurels. It is growing rapidly and the pollution and squalor are getting worse.

The congested main highway runs right through the centre of town so the overwhelming impression of the city is one of dust (or mud in season), diesel fumes, heat, trucks, and poverty. There were plans to open a bypass road to the east of town (perhaps in 1993?) so there is a chance things might improve. This would be a shame, because as it stands, the city provides a gruesome object lesson on what might well happen to other Terai cities – a vision of the apocalypse.

Birganj seems to stretch northwards for miles, strung along the impossibly congested main road. There are a large number of depressingly run-down factories, as the 'corridor' between Birganj and Hetauda is probably the most important centre for industrial development in Nepal. Amongst tanneries and other unattractive places there's a sugar factory and an agricultural implements factory.

There are immigrants from around Nepal and many from India; bear in mind that the only reason they come to Birganj is that the alternative of remaining in their place of birth is worse. The local language is Bhojpuri, which is spoken on both sides of the border.

Birganj is probably the most important entry point for Indian imports, but most travellers (especially those coming from Varanasi) now enter through Sunauli to the west. Birganj remains the most convenient entry point, however, for those coming from Patna or Calcutta.

Fortunately, there are plenty of day and night buses to and from Kathmandu and Pokhara and points south (in India) so there should be no necessity to stay more than a night – hopefully not even that.

Orientation & Information

Birganj and Raxaul Bazaar (on the Indian side of the border) virtually run together, although it's a 30-minute rickshaw ride from one bus station to the other. Basically, Birganj is strung along the north-south highway, although a bypass road one km to the east may open in 1993.

The old Birganj bus station was one block west of the main road, but in late 1992 a new bus station was opened beside the bypass road that was being built to the east. Needless to say, this created maximum confusion. In the long term it is likely the old bus station will continue to be used by local buses, while long-distance buses use the new one.

The various official offices on either side of the border all have different opening hours, but are all open between 7 am and 7 pm, as is the bank on the Nepalese side.

Things to See

If you do find yourself with a couple of hours to kill in Birganj you could hire a rickshaw

To Hotel
Samjhana (1 km)
& Kathmandu

Tank

Main Road

To Customs &
Immigration (3 km)
& Indian Border (4 km)

1 Clocktower
2 New Bus Station
3 Gita Temple
4 Maystan Temple
5 Bal Mandir
6 Nepal Rastra Bank
7 Government Offices
8 Hotel Kailas
9 Hotel Diyalo
10 Bus Station

Birganj

0   250   500 m

Bureaucratic Blackmail in Birganj – Warning

In November 1992, the Nepalese immigration officers at Birganj ran a particularly infuriating scam. They insisted they could only accept the $20 visa fee in cash dollars. Although the bank at the border would happily change foreign currency and give an official Foreign Exchange Encashment Receipt, the immigration officials would under no circumstances accept rupees, or any other currency. This was definitely not official policy, but they had the magic stamp and they stuck to their guns.

When I visited, two travellers had actually proffered a $100 note, but the immigration officials had no change in either rupees or dollars. The nearby bank would not change the note to low-denomination US notes, but it would change the note to rupees. As noted, however, the immigration officials would not accept rupees. This meant the travellers had to wait until the officials had collected $60 in change from other people coming through. This potentially meant sitting in no-man's land for many hours. Quiet persuasion which soon escalated to angry abuse left the officials unmoved.

Sitting in the immigration office while people screamed at each other seemed to be above and beyond the call of an LP researcher's duty, so I'm not sure how the story ended. To give credit where credit is due, it is possible that the officials were simply stupid – but it is much more likely that they were dishonest. No doubt after an hour or three of softening up, the travellers would have been prepared to accept any deal they were offered – getting their $60 change in rupees (at a rate determined by the immigration people), or maybe even abandoning their $60 change altogether. What price freedom? ∎

for an hour or two (at around Rs 30 an hour) and have a bit of a wander. The town has a certain gruesome fascination and there are a couple of modern temples and muddy ponds. The most interesting is the **Bal Mandir**, a modern Buddhist temple about a km west from the main road.

Places to Stay & Eat

The places to stay are clustered around the old bus station. The really cheap places are a pretty disgusting lot, and can't be recommended. If you can afford it, especially if you're travelling in the hot season, go for something a bit more comfortable.

The *Hotel Kailas* is a short block from the bus station, beside the Hotel Diyalo. It has a range of decent rooms and a good tandoori restaurant. Rooms with shared bath start at Rs 50/70, rise to Rs 170/240 ($3.50/5) with private bath and to Rs 410/580 ($8/11.50) with air-con.

The *Hotel Diyalo* (☎ 051-22370) directly overlooks the old bus station, but with the opening of the new bus station this is no longer a problem. It's a well-run hotel with immaculate rooms that are very reasonably priced for what you get. It also has a good restaurant. Singles/doubles with bath range from Rs 200/250 ($4/5) to Rs 575/625 ($11.50/12.50) with air-con.

The *Hotel Samjhana* (☎ 051-22122) is quite a distance from the bus station, but it has parking and decent food. This is the Birganj Ritz. A room in their new wing, with all mod cons except air-con cost Rs 600 ($12), or Rs 1200 ($24) with air-con. The old section of the hotel is not particularly appealing, but rooms vary from Rs 336 ($7) to Rs 800 ($16).

Getting There & Away

To/From India It's a 30-minute, Rs 10 rickshaw between the Birganj bus station and the border, and another 30 minutes and Indian Rs 12 between the border and the Raxaul Bazaar bus station. Expect to pay Rs 38 for the five-hour journey to Patna from Raxaul Bazaar. It's possible to make a single all-inclusive booking for the trip between Patna and Kathmandu (which includes overnighting at Birganj) for Rs 250. See the Getting There & Away chapter for a discussion of some of the problems with through tickets.

To/From Nepal There are plenty of day and night buses to and from Kathmandu. The

Sajha Yatayat buses, with an office at the new bus station, are recommended.

Despite the fact that the Tribhuvan Highway from Hetauda to Naubise looks like the best route to Kathmandu, all buses travel west to Narayanghat before they climb into the hills. The night buses leave Birganj between 6 and 8 pm, cost Rs 102 ($2) and take 11 hours. Day buses leave early and take an hour or two longer, but the views make this worthwhile.

It is possible to catch a bus from Hetauda (Rs 17 from Birganj) to Kathmandu that traverses the Tribhuvan Highway – it's slow, but there are superb views. See the Hetauda section later in this chapter, and the Getting There & Away chapter.

Prior to the opening of the new Kathmandu Bus Terminal, Sajha Yatayat buses left from Bhimsen Tower and private buses left from the Central Bus Station. Sajha buses left at 7 and 9 am, and 6.30 and 7.30 pm.

There are day/night buses from Birganj to Pokhara for Rs 97; one day bus to Janakpur leaving at 5.30 am (Rs 55); and buses to Tadi Bazaar (for Sauraha and the Chitwan National Park) leaving at 4.30 am, 2 and 3 pm (Rs 50).

Getting Around
Rickshaws cost around Rs 30 per hour, and this will be the charge if you get one to take you all the way through to Raxaul Bazaar (recommended).

HETAUDA
Hetauda is the starting point for a cableway that carries bulk goods (especially bulky items like cement, fertiliser, etc) from the Terai to Kathmandu. It's quite an amazing construction, similar in concept to a ski lift. The current cableway dates from 1958 and can carry 25 tonnes per hour. Unless you want to catch a bus over the superb Tribhuvan Highway, there's no need to stop. Normally, buses turn west to Narayanghat.

Places to Stay & Eat
The *Motel Avocado* (☎ 20429, 20235), on the way out of town on the Tribhuvan

Highway to Daman, has accommodation in a quiet, pleasant garden (with avocado trees). 'Luxury' rooms are in an old Nissan hut and are spacious, comfortable and rather idiosyncratic. They come with fans and air-con (don't expect too much of the air-con) and are a bit expensive at Rs 450/550 ($9/11) for singles/doubles. There are some cheaper rooms – a lot smaller and a bit shabbier – for Rs 350/250 ($7/5).

The *Neelam Lodge*, also on the Daman road, but nearer the main intersection in the centre of town and beside a big pipal tree, has clean, good-value doubles for Rs 60.

Getting There & Away
One Sajha Yatayat bus a day runs over the magnificent Tribhuvan Highway via Daman. There are spectacular views and this route is well worth considering. Before the new Kathmandu Bus Terminal opened, the Sajha bus left from near the Bhimsen Tower in Kathmandu at 7 am (eight hours, Rs 48). The bus station in Hetauda is to the south-east of the main intersection and the Daman/ Kathmandu bus also left at 7 am.

A number of companies go to Kathmandu and Pokhara via Narayanghat and Tadi Bazaar. Buses to Tadi take around three hours and cost Rs 50. There are numerous buses to Birganj for Rs 17.

DAMAN
Daman is 2322 metres above sea level, midway between Kathmandu and Hetauda. Its claim to fame is that it has, arguably, *the* most spectacular outlook on the Himalaya – there are unimpeded views of the entire range from Dhaulagiri to Mt Everest. If you have the opportunity it should not be missed.

There is a viewing tower, with a telescope, a restaurant and not much else. On the Hetauda side of Daman there is a magnificent rhododendron forest – which would be particularly worth seeing in spring – then great views over the Terai to India.

Place to Stay
It is possible to stay in the viewing tower – the *Everest View Tower & Lodge*. Unfortunately

it is now pretty run-down – though reasonably clean – and there are only four beds. You certainly could not find a better view, especially for only Rs 50!

Getting There & Away
Daman is about three hours by car and four hours by bus from both Kathmandu and Hetauda. Unless you're on your way to/from Birganj hiring a car and making a day trip from Kathmandu is the ideal way to get to Daman – but it won't be cheap. Think in terms of $60. If you had a group and it was clear weather, it would be worth it. Alternatively, this is one of the most spectacular (and gruelling) mountain-bike routes in the world. See the Mountain Biking chapter for details.

From Daman there's one northbound (Kathmandu) and one southbound (Hetauda) Sajha Yatayat bus a day. In the other direction, buses leave Kathmandu and Hetauda at 7 am and cost Rs 25.

TADI BAZAAR
In the Chitwan Valley between Hetauda and Narayanghat, the small town of Tadi Bazaar (sometimes spelt Tandi Bazaar) is nothing more than a junction town for Sauraha, the budget accommodation centre for the Royal Chitwan National Park. For more details see the earlier section on the park.

Getting There & Away
See Getting There & Away in the Royal Chitwan National Park section for details on transport to/from Tadi and the nearby village of Sauraha.

NARAYANGHAT & BHARATPUR
Narayanghat is a fast-growing new town on the banks of the massive Narayani River, just downstream from the junction of the Kali Gandaki and Trisuli rivers. It has developed because it lies at the intersection of the Mahendra Highway, which runs the length of the Terai, and the main road into the hills to Kathmandu and Pokhara. It is the administrative and trading centre for the district.

Bharatpur is contiguous with Narayanghat, and has an airport.

Although on the map the most direct route from eastern Nepal to Kathmandu is the road from Hetauda to Naubise, almost all traffic takes the better road from Narayanghat to Mugling. The so-called Rajpath (Tribhuvan Highway) from Hetauda to Naubise is a magnificent drive, but its endless narrow corners mean it is not appropriate for trucks and buses.

Narayanghat will, for most people, simply be a chai stop en route to the Chitwan or India, and apart from the river there's not much of interest in the town. However, it's not a bad spot to stop if you are exploring the Terai, and there's an interesting excursion to Devghat, a holy site north-west of town at the confluence of the Kali Gandaki and Trisuli rivers.

Places to Stay & Eat
The *Rooftop Restaurant & Bar* is a Western-style restaurant overlooking the main intersection just to the east of the bridge. There's a fine view over the chaos, and the food is OK. Breakfast is Rs 40, and continental main dishes are around Rs 60.

Far and away the nicest place to stay, is the *Gainda Lodge* (☎ 056-20590) on the western bank of the Narayani (across the bridge and first right). It's not exactly luxurious, and mosquito repellent is a good idea, but the welcome is warm, the rooms are clean, and there's a courtyard garden area. It's a quiet spot, and beautiful, especially at dawn and dusk when you can watch the activities along the river bank. Rooms are Rs 100 per person per night. Simple food is available, including the best dhal bhat tarkari (Rs 30) you are likely to sample.

There are some cheaper places around the northern bus station. The *Hotel River View* has been recommended and has singles/doubles for Rs 60/80.

The up-market *Hotel Narayani Safari* (☎ 056-20130, 20634) is primarily used as a base for trips to the Chitwan; it is part of a small chain of hotels that includes the Hotel Narayani in Kathmandu. It is well run, and has air-con, a swimming pool, a tennis court and an excellent restaurant. Singles/doubles cost $30/40. The hotel has eight cottages near the Rapti River about 15 km east of Sauraha which they utilise in their safari packages. (A three-night, four-day Chitwan package includes an elephant ride, a visit to a Tharu village, an excursion to Devghat, and so on, for a very reasonable $330.)

Getting There & Away

RNAC (☎ 056-20326) has three flights a week from Kathmandu to Bharatpur for $50.

Buses from Narayanghat to Pokhara and Kathmandu leave from a bus park at the northern end of town on the road to Mugling.

Buses to/from most Terai destinations stop over at the main T-intersection just to the east of the bridge. From Kathmandu the Sajha Yatayat buses leave early in the morning from near the Bhimsen Tower and private buses leave from Ratna Park, both costing Rs 65.

Minibuses for Tadi Bazaar (Chitwan) leave from the side of the Mahendra Highway just before the second intersection

Narayanghat & Bharatpur

To Mugling & Devghat
To Butwal
Narayani River
NARAYANGHAT
To Hetauda & Tadi Bazaar
BHARATPUR
Mahendra Highway
Canal

1 Hotel River View
2 Mahendra Bus Station (for Pokhara & Kathmandu)
3 Gainda Lodge
4 Temples
5 Nepal Bank
6 Rooftop Restaurant & Bar
7 Minibuses for Tadi Bazaar
8 Bus Station (for Terai destinations)
9 Hotel Narayani Safari

Left: Suspension bridge across the Tamba Kosi, near Sun Kosi (RE)
Right: Small bridge on Annapurna Circuit Trek (JL)
Bottom: The road to Lhasa and the Friendship Bridge between Nepal & Tibet (RE)

Top: Rhinoceros (RI'A)
Left: Snow leopard (JS)
Right: Elephants, Royal Chitwan National Park (RI'A)

east of the main T-intersection; they cost Rs 5 and take 30 minutes.

DEVGHAT

Devghat (also known as Deoghat and Harihara Chhetra) is an ancient holy site that was first mentioned in the Skanda Purana. It's a suitably beautiful spot, with forest-clad hills, a large sandy beach, and a number of shady shrines and temples overlooking the swirling waters where the Kali Gandaki and Trisuli meet. The confluence of rivers – particularly when they are major tributaries of the Ganges – is always regarded as religiously significant by Hindus, as it is believed a third spiritual river also joins.

Many elderly high-caste Hindus come here to quietly live out their last days, and finally to be cremated on the river banks, thus gaining religious merit and hopefully avoiding a stay in hell while they wait for reincarnation. In fact, all sorts of religious rites, including marriages, are performed at Devghat and they often involve large family groups. The atmosphere is peaceful and tranquil, not at all gloomy.

Devghat is one of the main sites for the festival of Magh Sankranti, and pilgrims come from around Nepal and India to immerse themselves in the river (see the later Ridi Bazaar section). This festival takes place on the first day of the Nepalese month of Magh, in mid-January, and celebrates the gradually lengthening days and the onset of warmer weather.

Western visitors (untouchables) are rare, and should bear in mind that caste-related ideas of ritual pollution may mean that some of the orthodox pilgrims and inhabitants could be offended by any contact. Do not enter homes or temples without invitation and do not touch anything that could be holy (which means almost anything!). There is nowhere to stay, and not even a chai stall, so bring drinks and food.

Getting There & Away

There are frequent minibuses to/from Narayanghat. By road, you head north from town on the Mugling road for three km, turn left on a signposted dirt road just before a police checkpost and continue for two km, then take the right fork and continue for another three km. It is possible to walk along the eastern bank of the river, although the track there is a bit overgrown and it's easiest to pick up and follow it from the Devghat end.

SUNAULI & BHAIRAWA

Sunauli is a small, grubby collection of offices and hotels right on the Indian border. Bhairawa is somewhat more substantial, a dusty, bustling town nearly four km inside Nepal; officially Bhairawa's name has been changed to Siddharthanaga, but this is rarely used.

There are three points in favour of visiting this part of the world. Firstly, Sunauli is the most convenient border crossing for those coming and going between Nepal and northern and western India (including Varanasi, Agra and Delhi). Secondly, Bhairawa is the closest town to Lumbini, the birthplace of Buddha. And thirdly, although Sunauli and Bhairawa are hot and featureless, they're still relaxed and pleasant by comparison to Birganj, the next major crossing point to the east.

There is some small-scale industry, a couple of banks and government offices and plenty of shops. Most pre-arranged bookings to/from India involve a night's stop in Sunauli, and most individual travellers do the same.

Orientation & Information

The Indian customs and immigration departments are apparently open 24 hours, but Nepal's officials only do business from 6 am to 7 pm.

Indian rupees are accepted in Sunauli, but not beyond, so most people will have to change money. There are two options, neither very good, so change a minimum amount. The Nepal Rastra Bank in Sunauli, which is open from 7.30 am to 6 pm, changes at the official government rate, which is slightly less than the legal commercial rate offered by private banks (see the Facts for

1 Hotel Himalayan Inn
2 Nepal Rastra Bank
3 Sajha Yatayat Office & Bus Stop
4 Hotel Yeti
5 Sayapati Guest House
6 Kasturi Restaurant
7 Shree Pashupati Lodge & Hotel
8 Agriculture Bank
9 Hotel Mamta
10 Nepal Rastra Bank
11 Nepalese Customs
12 Nepal Guest House
13 Buses
14 Nepalese Immigration &
   Tourist Information
15 Indian Customs
16 Indian Immigration

the Visitor chapter). The bank does not re-exchange Nepalese rupees. There are black-market operators, but they don't offer very good rates either. The bank on the Indian side of the border doesn't open until 10 am – after the buses have left.

There is a tourist information centre (☎ 071-20304) at the border. The Department of Tourism's *Visitors' Guide* (free) is worth picking up, but don't expect much more.

Bhairawa is a 20-minute rickshaw ride to the north. Most shops and businesses in Bhairawa are strung along Narayan Path or

Bank Rd. The Siddhartha Highway runs along the eastern edge of town to the border. Lumbini is 22 km to the south-west, but there are frequent buses, and most people stay in Bhairawa if they plan to visit the site.

Places to Stay & Eat

It doesn't really matter whether you stay in Bhairawa or Sunauli since it's easy and cheap to go between the two (see the Getting Around section).

Budget travellers in transit to or from India will find a couple of accommodation options in Sunauli, but there really is *nothing* to do so consider staying in Bhairawa where there's a bit of life.

Sunauli There are a couple of options in Sunauli, with not much between them. First choice is the *Nepal Guest House*, which has a reasonable restaurant, is reasonably priced, and reasonably clean. It's hooked up to an artesian bore so you can have warmish showers anytime. The place is something of a labyrinth and the rooms vary – ask to see several before you settle in. There are four-bed dorms with beds for Rs 15, doubles with fan and bath for Rs 80, and singles for Rs 50.

The *Hotel Mamta* (☎ 20512) across the road is not very inspiring, but it would do. This is almost certainly where you'll find yourself if you've bought pre-arranged tickets through an agent. A single bed in a six-bed dorm costs Rs 15 and a double with private bath is Rs 80.

Apart from the restaurants attached to hotels, there are only a couple of small restaurants; the *New Shambala* is OK.

Bhairawa The highest quality hotel in the area is the *Hotel Yeti* (☎ 071-20551) on the corner of Bank Rd and Siddhartha Highway. This is where the tour groups that occasionally pass through stay. It's spotlessly clean, there's a decent restaurant and, for what it delivers, the prices are reasonable – $12/16 for a single/double. The only problem is that the hotel overlooks a main intersection (where the buses stop) so it can be a bit noisy.

The *Hotel Himalayan Inn* (☎ 20347) is a bit out of town to the north on the Siddhartha Highway. Although it has been left behind by the Hotel Yeti and is struggling a bit, it's still just OK. There is off-road parking. The restaurant is cavernous, and empty, and the food distinctly average. Singles/doubles with bath are Rs 350/450 ($7/9).

The *Sayapati Guest House*, which is close to the Sajha Yatayat bus stop on Bank Rd, is a cheap place to stay, but is very basic and the rooms are dark and cell-like. Singles/doubles are Rs 40/80.

The *Shree Pashupati Lodge & Hotel* on Narayan Path is a good 10-minute walk from the bus stop, but it's acceptably clean and wins hands down on character. It's definitely the best budget option. A double with bath is Rs 94, and a single with shared bath costs Rs 39.

The nearby *Kasturi Restaurant* is a pleasant high-ceilinged place with uniformed waiters and excellent vegetarian Indian food. Dishes like pulau and korma cost around Rs 20.

Getting There & Away
There are plenty of bus connections to destinations in both Nepal and India. Whether you have booked a 'through' ticket or not, everyone changes buses at the border, and most people spend the night in Sunauli. There are no 'tourist' buses.

To/From India You catch buses to Indian cities on the Indian side of the border. There are direct buses to Varanasi for Indian Rs 56 to Rs 100, depending on the degree of luxury, and the journey takes about nine hours.

There are also buses to Gorakhpur where you can connect with the Indian broad-gauge railway (three hours, Indian Rs 17). From Gorakhpur, buses leave every half hour from 5 am to 7 pm; you'll need to catch the first bus if you want to connect directly with the day buses from Sunauli to Kathmandu, which leave from 4.30 to 9.30 am. See the Getting There & Away chapter for more information.

To/From Nepal RNAC (☎ 071-20175) operates four flights a week between Kathmandu and Bhairawa for $72.

Travelling north, most buses start their journey in Sunauli, stopping in Bhairawa. It's best to join the bus in Sunauli. In Bhairawa the bus companies' offices are around the intersection of Bank Rd and the Siddhartha Highway. The Sajha Yatayat booking office is opposite the Yeti Hotel and these buses are recommended, although they only operate to Kathmandu.

There are several night and day buses to Pokhara and Kathmandu. The day buses are a bit quicker and cheaper, plus you see the views. The road to Pokhara (nine hours, Rs 66) is particularly beautiful (for great views of Machhapuchhare if you're heading north, get a seat on the left-hand side), but the journey to Kathmandu is also rewarding.

From Kathmandu, buses leave at around 7 am (nine hours, Rs 86), and 6 and 7 pm (10 hours, Rs 107 or $2). See the Getting There & Away chapter for more details.

If you want to go to the Royal Chitwan National Park from Sunauli, there are buses for Birganj (seven hours, Rs 82) that leave at 5.30 and 7.30 am. Get off at Tadi Bazaar if you're heading to Sauraha (four hours, Rs 40). There's a night bus to Kakarbhitta at 2 pm (Rs 223, or $4.50, 17 hours). There are plenty of local buses to Butwal for Rs 8.

For transport to Lumbini see the Lumbini Getting There & Away section.

Getting Around

The only time you'll need transport will be to go between Sunauli and Bhairawa – it's four hot, flat km. A rickshaw will cost around Rs 10 and take 20 minutes. The other alternatives are quicker and cheaper, but considerably less pleasant. A tempo (three-wheeled minibus) will cost Rs 2 and a bus, Rs 1.

LUMBINI

Lumbini is believed to be the birthplace of Siddhartha Gautama – the founder of Buddhism, known as Buddha, or the enlightened one. This is confirmed by the existence of an inscribed pillar erected 318 years after the event by the great Buddhist emperor Ashoka, and the presence of a number of ancient ruins.

Fittingly, Lumbini is an example of how ephemeral the results of human effort are. There's not much to see and it requires a serious effort of the imagination to conjure up the ghosts of the past. Lumbini is not a

To Lumbini Mehalbar (2 km) & Bhairawa (22 km)

Car park

Lumbini

0   150   300 m

Approximate scale

1 Sacred Flame
2 VIP Plantation
3 Ashokan Pillar
4 Maya Devi Temple
5 Bodhi Tree
6 Archaeological Office
7 Tibetan Gompa
8 Canteen Lumbini
9 Dharamsala
  (Pilgrims' Accommodation)
10 Lumbini Restaurant
11 Therevada Temple
12 Bodhi Tree
13 Police Station
14 Mahendra Pillar
15 Old School
16 Lumbini Development Corporation
17 Restaurant
18 Information Office

Mound
Tank
Mound

To Lumbini Guest House (3 km)

Car park

Bethlehem or Mecca – there is no city, no impressive architecture, no pilgrim-jammed car park, no heavily armed soldiers, no hustlers, not even a postcard stand.

In the end, it is the absence of all these things, and the peacefulness of Lumbini that make a visit worthwhile. In some ways, Tilaurakot (see later section), the site of Kapilavastu, the fortress-palace where Buddha was raised as a prince of the royal family is more evocative.

It's curious that the Buddha should have been born and raised on a fertile tropical plain, a place of such contrast to the deserts of the Middle East where so many religions originated; strange that he should have been born a wealthy prince; and almost bizarre that this privileged life and rich countryside should have inspired a belief that suffering is synonymous with existence.

Allow yourself an hour or two to wander around and soak in the atmosphere. The important sights don't take long to cover – the Maya Devi Temple, the Ashokan Pillar, the Sacred Pond and the Tibetan and Theravada viharas. Then find a shady spot where you can watch the parrots squabbling in the branches of the massive *bo* trees.

There are grandiose plans for the development of Lumbini, with the aim of creating a place of pilgrimage and a tourist attraction. It will be interesting to see whether this can be achieved by government decree. A plan by the Japanese architect Kenzo Tange was adopted in 1978 – it involves canals, gardens, a library and museum, monastic zones, a pilgrim lodge and a hotel. There has been some slow progress. The major earthworks are complete, there are a couple of buildings quite a distance from the site proper, which are forlornly empty, and a luxury hotel, which is actually operating.

History

The great Indian emperor Ashoka visited Lumbini in 245 BCE, and left a number of his famous inscribed pillars in the region. In 403 CE the region was visited by Fa Hsien a Chinese pilgrim who described a ruined Kapilavastu and a deserted countryside.

In 636 Hsuan Tang, another pilgrim, described 1000 derelict monasteries and Ashoka's pillar at Lumbini, shattered by lightning and lying on the ground. Derelict it may have been, but the site was still known in 1312 CE when Ripu Malla visited, possibly leaving the nativity statue which is still worshipped in the Maya Devi Temple.

Moghul invaders arrived in the region at the end of the 15th century, and in common with their zealous actions elsewhere on the subcontinent, it is likely that the remaining 'pagan' monuments at Kapilavastu and Lumbini were destroyed. The whole region returned to wilderness and the sites were lost to the jungle, until the governor of Palpa (Tansen), Khadga Shumsher Rana, who had a keen interest in archaeology, began the excavation of a pillar – which turned out to be Ashoka's Lumbini pillar – in late 1896.

Today, no trace of the Lumbini forest remains, but the pond where Maya Devi is believed to have bathed, can still be seen, although in much restored form. The brick foundations of stupas and viharas dating from the 2nd century BCE can be seen around the pond. The Maya Devi Temple is built on ancient foundations, but the functional part of the temple is a modern structure built after 1899.

After the discovery of Lumbini, the ruins near Tilaurakot were identified as Kapilavastu. There has been some archaeological work, which has revealed the remains of moated city walls, impressive gates, and the foundations for a palace complex.

Most of the surrounding countryside is now dominated by extremely poor Muslim peasant farmers. There are no Buddhists.

Ashokan Pillar

Emperor Ashoka is one of the greatest figures in Indian history. Throughout his massive empire he left pillars and rock-carved edicts, which even to this day delineate the extent of his power. They can be seen in Delhi, Gujarat, Orissa, Uttar Pradesh, Madhya Pradesh – and Nepal.

The pillar at Lumbini commemorates Ashoka's pilgrimage to the birthplace of

Buddha. It is six metres high, although half of it is underground, and it is inscribed with the following:

King Ashoka, the beloved of Gods, in the 20th year of the coronation, made a royal visit. A stone railing and a stone pillar were erected in honour of Buddha who was born here. Because Buddha was born here the village of Lumbini was freed from paying tax.

Maya Devi Temple

Parts of the Maya Devi Temple are believed to be over 2000 years old, and it is possible that it is built over a stupa that was erected by the emperor Ashoka. It is not, however, architecturally or artistically interesting in any way, and the functional part of the temple was probably built around the turn of the century. A huge pipal tree is gradually tearing the temple apart – some believe this is the tree that Maya Devi held while giving birth to Siddhartha.

The temple itself is attended by a Hindu priest, and Hindu women in particular revere a stone carving showing the birth of Buddha. Possibly dating from the Malla dynasty (approximately 14th century CE) the sculpture was the centre of a fertility rite, and it has almost been reduced to formlessness by the wear of constant puja. One can still make out Maya Devi, with her right hand raised to hold the pipal tree branch, as she gives birth. There is also a modern marble interpretation, along with a number of small sculptures left by devotees.

A major Hindu festival is held on the full moon of the Nepalese month of Baisakh (April-May), when thousands of local Hindus come to worship Maya Devi as Rupa Devi, the mother goddess of Lumbini, and to celebrate Buddha as the 9th incarnation of Vishnu. The Buddhist celebration of Buddha's birthday, or Buddha Jayanti, is celebrated around the same time, but is lower key. During winter, when it's not too hot, Buddhist pilgrims from the Kathmandu Valley often come to worship on Purnima (the night of the full moon) and Astemi (the eighth night after the full moon).

Other Attractions

The square pool beside the temple is believed to be the spot where Maya Devi bathed before giving birth to Buddha; needless to say, it has been heavily restored. The foundations for a number of stupas and viharas (monasteries) dating from the 2nd century BCE to the 9th century CE lie in the vicinity.

There are also two modern temples although, unfortunately, neither are particularly interesting or well maintained – both are slated for demolition under the Lumbini Development Plan. One was built by the Nepalese government in 1956, and one was built in traditional Tibetan style in 1968.

The two large mounds on either side of the site are not impressive stupas, as you might suspect, but simply the spoils from modern archaeological digs.

Places to Stay & Eat

Most people simply make a day trip from Bhairawa, but there are a couple of places to stay and eat.

There are two very basic restaurants either side of the Nepalese temple that serve chai and simple meals to pilgrims.

The *Lumbini Guest House*, south-west of the main site, was closed in late 1992, but was, at least in theory, due to be reincarnated in March '93. It used to have clean and comfortable rooms with singles/doubles at $14/20. Food was limited and expensive.

The ex-manager of the guest house has opened the *Lumbini Village Lodge*, a simple place in Lumbini Mehalbar, the small market town about two km east of the main site. The village is an undistinguished little place, but there is a lively market on Mondays, and the rest of the time it is simply a peaceful corner of the Terai. For what you get the prices are a bit steep, with dorm beds for Rs 100, and singles/doubles for Rs 150/250 ($3/5). There is reasonable food at around Rs 30 for a main course.

Despite the prices and the basic standards, this is a pleasant and interesting place to stay. It is possible to contact the owners (to check

Siddhartha Gautama

Two and a half thousand years ago the region at the foot of the Himalaya was broken up into a number of small republics and principalities who were vassal states to larger empires based on the Gangetic plain. Siddhartha Gautama was the son of Suddhodana (of the Sakya clan) who ruled the republic of Kapilavastu, and Maya Devi (of the Koliya clan) the daughter of the ruler of the neighbouring state of Dewadaha. The ruins of Kapilavastu lie at Tilaurakot, 27 km west of Lumbini, but Dewadaha has not been conclusively identified.

It is believed that Maya Devi was 10 months pregnant when she decided to visit her parents' house in Dewadaha. On the way from Kapilavastu, her entourage had to pass through the grove of Lumbini, which was a famous beauty spot with a pond surrounded by sal trees. On the day she reached Lumbini, in May 563 BCE the sal trees were in full bloom, so Maya Devi stopped to enjoy the scene and to bathe in the pond. Leaving the water, she suddenly felt labour pains. She raised her right hand and caught hold of the drooping branch of a pipal tree, and the baby was born.

Maya Devi returned to Kapilavastu where her son Siddhartha was given a sheltered, privileged upbringing. At the age of 29, while wandering in the town outside the palace walls, he came across an old man, a sick man, a corpse and a hermit. This confrontation with suffering and death impelled Siddhartha to renounce his luxurious life and to leave Kapilavastu.

He spent the next five years seeking to understand the nature of existence. Mostly he wandered as an itinerant ascetic – no doubt much like the Hindu sadhus of today – but he found that extreme self-denial did not provide him with any answers. Finally, after 49 days meditating under a bodhi tree at Bodhgaya he attained enlightenment. From Bodhgaya he travelled to Sarnath, near Varanasi, where he preached his first sermon.

The Buddha spent the next 46 years teaching his 'middle way'. Suffering, he taught, is a natural part of life, but suffering is caused by attachment, desire and delusion, and if these negative forces are controlled (by following the noble 'eightfold path'), it is possible to reach nirvana.

Although some people believe Buddha visited the Kathmandu Valley, there is no firm evidence for this. Most of his preaching was undertaken in northern India and across the Gangetic plain. He died at the age of 80 at Kushinagar, near Gorakhpur, about 100 km south-east of Lumbini.

Despite his disavowal of divinity, the main sites associated with Buddha's life (Lumbini, Kapilavastu, Bodhgaya, Sarnath and Kushinagar) soon became centres for pilgrimage, and monasteries and temples sprang up. There are only sparse records of Lumbini's and Kapilavastu's history, however. ∎

the lodge is still operating) through a Kathmandu office (☎ 01-271061).

There's very, *very* basic pilgrim accommodation in the dharamsala between the two temples at the main site. Literally, all you get is a roof over your head and a bed (no mattress), and the toilets are vile. If you've got food and camping equipment and you do stay, pay a donation.

At the other extreme, the *Lumbini Hokke Hotel* (☎ 071-20236) is one of the best hotels in Nepal. It lies several km north of the main site, just off the dirt road to Tilaurakot. It has been built with Japanese pilgrims in mind, and most of the rooms have been furnished in traditional Japanese style with tatami floors, paper partitions, and Japanese furniture. There are also a number of European-style rooms.

All rooms are air-conditioned, and all have attached bathrooms. Considering the luxury, prices are not unreasonable, with singles/doubles at $77/114. Meals are expensive – lunch is $12 for non-guests. Mountain bikes are available for guests to use, but most people visit with their own transport, or as part of a tour.

Getting There & Away

There are regular minibuses that make the 22-km journey from Bhairawa to Lumbini for Rs 10, but they are agonizingly slow (1½ hours) and drop you off on the main road a km from the main site. The roof is the place to be. The last bus back passes the turn-off at about 5 pm (but check). They leave Bhairawa near the main intersection, across the road from the Hotel Yeti.

If you are in a group or have the funds it would be immensely preferable to hire an autorickshaw (from Rs 150, or $3, to Rs 250, or $5) or a taxi-jeep (from Rs 300, or $6, to Rs 500, or $10). These prices include two hours' waiting time, which should be sufficient for most people.

The best method of transport for budget travellers would be bicycle, but there are no formal rental places in Bhairawa. If you ask around (start at your hotel, then try bicycle repair shops) you might turn something up.

TAULIHAWA & TILAURAKOT

Tilaurakot is nothing more than a tiny hamlet three km north of Taulihawa, which is a bustling Terai centre. Tilaurakot was once, however, the capital of the republic of Kapilavastu, where Buddha spent the first 29 years of his life.

Taulihawa is a vibrant town with the usual multicultural mix of peoples found in Terai cities. There is a temple complex known as **Tauleshwar**, now used by Shaivites, in the centre of town.

Although even less visited than Lumbini, Tilaurakot is in many ways the more atmospheric of the two spots. There is a small group of farming households outside the ruins of the city walls, which along with their moat, can be clearly discerned. The whole complex is shaded by large trees and has the peaceful atmosphere of a park.

The scattered foundations that can be seen within the walls give only the most minimal indication that there was once a palace, but archaeologists have found 13 successive layers of human habitation, dating back to the 8th century BCE. Today the only sign of life is a small run-down shrine to a Hindu goddess, Somaya Mai.

The scene outside the walls could be unchanged from that which Siddhartha himself might have seen. Timeless patterns of subsistence farming unfold along the banks of the Banganga River, and on the north side of the river there is an expanse of untouched sal forest. It is not hard to imagine Siddhartha walking out through the imposing gateway of the palace and as he

wandered, seeing an old man, a sick man, a corpse and a hermit...

About 400 metres from the ruins, a small **museum** (closed on Tuesday and Saturday) displays some of the artefacts that were found at the site – including coins and pottery.

Places to Stay & Eat

There are plenty of food stalls in Taulihawa. The *Lumbini Hotel*, on the road to Tilaurakot, is very basic, but acceptably clean; singles/doubles cost Rs 25/40. There are no facilities at Tilaurakot.

Getting There & Away

A reasonable (though badly corrugated) dirt road links Taulihawa with Lumbini, 27 km to the east. The road passes the Lumbini Hokke Hotel, and a number of Muslim villages. Slow and crowded local buses link Taulihawa with Bhairawa, but once again bicycle is the best method of transport.

Tilaurakot is three km north of Taulihawa. At the end of the bitumen the museum is on the left and the ruins are 400 metres away down a dirt track on the right. In winter it is possible to cross a ford over the Banganga River, and to continue 14 km due north along a dirt road through the Sagar Forest, finally joining the Mahendra Highway about 35 km west of Butwal and 80 km east of Lumihi (also spelt Lamahi).

BUTWAL

Lying at the very foot of the Chure Hills, Butwal is an unattractive, dirty town. The approach from Tansen, to the north, is dramatic: one moment you're in a narrow mountain gorge, the next you are surrounded by people, dust, rickshaws and Hindi film posters. There's no apparent reason to stop.

Places to Stay

The *Hotel Sindoor* (☎ 073-20381) is an up-market and expensive hotel catering to visiting bigwigs. Though overpriced and a bit gloomy, it is clean, quiet and unquestionably the best place in town. Singles/doubles are $18/27; it wouldn't hurt to ask for a discount.

The nearby *Butwal Guest House* is much cheaper but is pretty basic and noisy. It overlooks the T-intersection between the roads to Pokhara and Nepalganj. Dorm beds are Rs 30, rooms with shared bath are Rs 45, and rooms with attached bathrooms (well nearly) are Rs 165 ($3).

Getting There & Away

The bus station is at the western end of town near the bridge over the Tinau River, but buses passing through stop at a bazaar area at the eastern end of town. Buses to/from Kathmandu leave early in the morning or in the evening. They travel via Mugling, take about nine hours and cost Rs 82. There are frequent buses to Sunauli for Rs 8.

TANSEN

Tansen is just off the Siddhartha Highway, between Pokhara and Sunauli/Bhairawa. Historically, it has enjoyed a strategic position on the trade and pilgrim route between the hills and the plains.

Prior to the unification of Nepal under the Shahs, it was the capital of the Palpa kingdom, which was ruled by the Sen dynasty. Prithvi Narayan Shah, the Gorkha king who founded modern Nepal, was the product of an arranged marriage between the Shah and Sen families.

For many years Palpa fought in alliance with Gorkha, and together the two states defeated the independent kingdoms of western Nepal. Finally in 1806, the last king of Palpa, Prithivipal Sen, was lured to Kathmandu and beheaded. Palpa was annexed, but Tansen remained the administrative centre for the region. A number of its subsequent governors were high-ranking members of the ruling Shah and, later, Rana families who were exiled from Kathmandu for plotting against the king of the day.

Tansen is still the administrative centre for a large region but it sees few visitors, and as it is increasingly sidelined by the development on the Terai and at Pokhara, it is gently falling apart.

The town sprawls over a steep ridge and quite a few of the main streets are too steep for cars, which helps to keep some of the less pleasant aspects of the 20th century at bay. In the older sections of the town, attractive Newari buildings line cobbled streets that are reminiscent of parts of Kathmandu.

Most of the surrounding countryside is dominated by Magars, but there are also Bahuns and Chhetris. Newaris form the majority in Tansen itself. They migrated from the Kathmandu Valley to take advantage of the new opportunities for trade between the hills and India that opened up in the 19th century – traditional crafts and agricultural surpluses were traded for the products of the British Industrial Revolution (especially cotton fabrics) that were flooding into India from Britain. Tansen is still famous for metalware, and for dhaka, the woven material that is made into topis (Nepalese hats).

There are great views over the bowl-shaped **Madi Valley** from the town itself and a spectacular view of the Himalaya from the nearby hill, Srinagar Danda. There are some interesting walks in the surrounding countryside, including a two-hour trek to the banks of the Kali Gandaki River and the vast, deserted Ranighat Palace. Tansen is a pleasant place to break the journey between Pokhara (3½ hours) and Bhairawa (two hours).

Amar Narayan Temple

The Amar Narayan is a classic three-tiered pagoda-style temple, considered to be one of the most beautiful outside the Kathmandu Valley. There is some fine woodwork, with erotic figures on the roof struts, and beautifully carved doors. The temple was built in 1806 CE by Amar Singh Thapa, the general who annexed Tansen to Nepal. Sadhus often stay in the rest houses around the temple on their way to Muktinath, north-west of Pokhara on the popular Annapurna Circuit. There's a large bat colony in the surrounding trees, and several tanks where local women do their washing.

```
To Ridi           To Ranighat
Bazaar (28 km)    Durbar                    Srinagar   Danda

Tansen

        0      0.5        1 km

      Approximate scale

┌─────────────────────────────────────────────┐
│ 1  Hotel Srinagar      10  Sajha Yatayat     │
│ 2  Ganesh Temple           Bus Booking Office│
│ 3  Mission Hospital    11  Santosh Cinema    │
│ 4  Sitalpati (Public Square) 12 Tribhuvan Campus │
│ 5  Amar Narayan Temple 13  Hotel Janpriya    │
│ 6  Bhagwati Temple     14  Hotel Siddhartha  │
│ 7  Tansen Durbar       15  Tundlkhel         │
│ 8  Nepal Bank              (Parade Ground)   │
│ 9  Gautam Siddartha Hotel 16 Bus Station     │
└─────────────────────────────────────────────┘
```

Tansen Durbar

The palace of the provincial governor was built in the heavy-handed Rana style in 1927 and is now home to the local bureaucrats. The imposing, though dilapidated, entrance gate on the eastern side of the compound is called Baggi Dhoka. It is meant to be the biggest and tallest gate in Nepal, and its dimensions allowed the governor to make his suitably impressive entrance on an elephant.

A public square called Sitalpati lies just outside the gate; it's named after the building in the centre, which was, before renovation, an unusual octagonal shape.

Bhagwati Temple

The Bhagwati Temple, near the durbar, is a rather garish construction that was unsympathetically renovated after an earthquake in 1935, and again in 1974. It was originally built in 1815 to commemorate a Nepalese victory over the British at Butwal.

There are a number of smaller temples in the vicinity, to Shiva, Ganesh and Saraswati.

Places to Stay

There are some hotels around the bus station with singles/doubles for around Rs 60/80, but they're all pretty awful. The best cheapie is a 15-minute walk away and worth the effort. The *Hotel Gautam Siddartha* (075-20280) is basic, but clean, decent and quiet. Rooms with twin beds are Rs 80.

The most luxurious option is about three km away on the ridge above town. The *Hotel Srinagar* (☎ 075-20045) is rather isolated, but it's comfortable and the views are sensational. It would be worth ringing in advance because the hotel deals mainly with groups and isn't all that used to people arriving unannounced. Singles/doubles with private bath are $20/28.

Getting There & Away

There are two buses a day from Pokhara for

Rs 46; buses leave for Pokhara at 6 and 9 am. There are numerous buses to Butwal for Rs 15, and five per day to Sunauli/Bhairawa for Rs 25.

The north-south highway is magnificent, so if you can, find a place on the roof to appreciate the views. If you're inside and coming from Pokhara try to get a seat on the right side of the bus.

AROUND TANSEN
Srinagar Danda
Srinagar Danda is a 1600-metre hill directly north of town, and a steep half-hour walk from Sitalpati. From the pine-forested top there's a spectacular view over the gorge of the Kali Gandaki River to the Himalaya – the panorama stretches from Kanjiroba in the west, to Dhaulagiri, the Annapurnas, and Langtang in the east.

The *Hotel Srinagar* is 20 minutes' walk west of the summit on the main ridge.

Ridi Bazaar
Ridi is a holy town, mainly populated by Newaris, at the confluence of the Kali Gandaki and Ridi rivers. The confluence of tributaries to the Ganges are always regarded as holy, and Ridi has been further sanctified by the presence of saligrams, black ammonite fossils that have a spiral shape and are regarded as emblems of Vishnu. Saligrams are found in a number of places along the Kali Gandaki, most notably north of Jomsom around Muktinath.

Although Ridi's religious popularity has declined, cremations are still relatively frequent, and pilgrims come for ritual bathing, marriage ceremonies and other rites and rituals. Pilgrims believe that if they fast and worship for three days, then take a ritual bath in the Kali Gandaki, all their sins will be forgiven.

The most important festival is Magh Sankranti, when many pilgrims come to immerse themselves in the river (see the earlier Devghat section). This festival takes place on the first day of the Nepalese month of Magh, in mid-January, and celebrates the

gradually lengthening days and the onset of warmer weather.

Worshippers also gather every Ekadashi (the 11th day after the full moon). The festival of Ridi is held in November.

The commercial end of town is across the Ridi River, and the Rishikesh (a manifestation of Vishnu) Temple is near the bus station. It is believed the temple was founded by Mukund Sen in the early 16th century, but the current temple dates from the 19th century. It is also believed that the statue of Rishikesh was discovered in the river, and that the figure of the god has gradually aged from boyhood to adulthood.

It is a 13-km trek from Tansen to Ridi. You can leave the road just to the west of the Hotel Srinagar, and pick it up again about seven km from Ridi. Alternatively, it is 28 km by road. Buses leave Tansen at 6, 9 and 11 am, take two hours and cost Rs 34.

Ranighat Durbar
Sometimes fancifully referred to as Nepal's Taj Mahal, Ranighat Durbar was built by Khadga Shamsher Rana in 1896. Khadga was exiled to Tansen and made governor for plotting to become prime minister. While he was in exile, he consoled himself by building a spectacular palace, supposedly in memory of his wife, Tej Kumari.

The palace is now a huge, white baroque ruin dramatically perched on a rocky crag above the Kali Gandaki River. It was used for 25 years as a luxurious dharamsala (pilgrims' rest house) by aristocrats who ostensibly came to bathe in the Kali Gandaki, and no doubt to party and plot with Khadga. Khadga was an ambitious man and in 1921 he made another abortive attempt to seize power. As a result he was exiled further away – this time in India. On his departure the building was stripped of its valuable furnishings, and has been gradually collapsing ever since.

The trail to Ranighat begins a short distance to the east of the Hotel Srinagar, at the edge of the pine forest. It's an attractive seven-km hike down to the river and takes about two hours each way.

NEPALGANJ

The most important town in western Nepal,
Nepalganj at times feels more Indian than
Nepalese. It's a border town that owes as
much to trade (read smuggling) as it does to
its position as a major administrative centre.
It has more of an air of permanence than
some other border towns and planners have
had the good sense to run the highway to the
west of the main town.

The old part of town has a garish temple,
the **Bageshwari Mandir**, honouring Kali.
There's also a vibrant bazaar selling everything except kitchen sinks (although I'm sure
one of the metalworkers could knock one up
if you needed it). It is well worth wandering
around the centre of town. The crush of
people, the smells, the food, the shops, the
film posters, and the rickshaws give a vivid
taste of the subcontinent.

Nepalganj is a densely crowded city, and
every possible Nepalese ethnic group is represented. There is an unusually large Muslim
community, many of whom settled here to
escape the violence of the 1857 Indian
Mutiny. The Muslim men are distinctive,
with their long beards and skull caps, as are
the women, some of whom dress in black and
are completely veiled. The colourful throngs
in the streets, however, include Shaivite
sadhus, Tharu women (with tight bodices,
bare midriffs and bright skirts), turbanned
Sikhs, Bajis (Abadhi speakers from India),
Bahuns, Chhetris, Newaris, Magars,
Gurungs, Thakuris, and even Tibetans (who
look a bit hot in their traditional gear).

A steady trickle of travellers come through
Nepalganj on their way to the Royal Bardia
National Park (see later in this chapter), or to
Jumla. It can also be a useful back-door entry
into Nepal from central Uttar Pradesh;
Lucknow is about four hours away.

Orientation

The airport is six km north of Birendra
Chowk (with the statue), to the east of the
main road. The long-distance bus station is
also north of town. One km north of Birendra
Chowk there's an accumulation of local
buses (including buses for Mahendranagar)

around a T-intersection. Turn right and continue for another km down an incredibly
rough road and you come to the long-distance bus station (for Kathmandu and points
east). Book your return ticket before you go
into town to save yourself a trip.

The town is about six km north of the
border. The old, interesting part lies to the
east of the main road around Tribhuvan
Chowk, although virtually all the hotels are
on the highway.

The various customs and immigration
offices at the border all have different closing
hours, but they are all open from 8 to 11 am
and from 1 to 5 pm. There is no bank on the
Nepalese side of the border.

Places to Stay & Eat

There are two reasonable hotels, both on the
way to the Indian border on the highway.
They're set back from the road so noise and
parking aren't problems.

The most popular, and the best, is the
Hotel Sneha (☎ 081-20119) which has a
range of large, clean rooms, and helpful staff.
A new wing of high-standard rooms has
recently been built around a courtyard
behind the original hotel. Standard singles/
doubles are $10/15, and deluxe rooms with
air-con are $15/20, plus 12% tax. There's a
good restaurant, but lunch and dinner will set
you back $7 per person. The hotel can
arrange transport to/from the airport.

Virtually next door, the *Hotel Batika*
(☎ 081-21360) is newer, and even has a
swimming pool and tennis court. Despite
this, it's not in the same league as the Sneha.
Singles/doubles are $7/10. The owners of the
Batika have recently opened the second
lodge to operate in the Royal Bardia National
Park; see that section for more details.

The cheapies are around Birendra Chowk,
the main intersection with the inevitable
statue. The best is the *Punjabi Hotel & Restaurant* which has large comfortable rooms
and is acceptably clean. Doubles with private
bath cost Rs 250 ($5); singles/doubles with
shared bath are Rs 80/120. The restaurant's
Indian dishes are particularly good. The

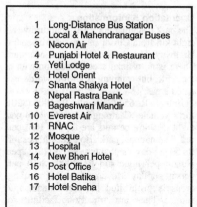

1	Long-Distance Bus Station
2	Local & Mahendranagar Buses
3	Necon Air
4	Punjabi Hotel & Restaurant
5	Yeti Lodge
6	Hotel Orient
7	Shanta Shakya Hotel
8	Nepal Rastra Bank
9	Bageshwari Mandir
10	Everest Air
11	RNAC
12	Mosque
13	Hospital
14	New Bheri Hotel
15	Post Office
16	Hotel Batika
17	Hotel Sneha

Hotel Orient is also decent. Singles/doubles with private bath are Rs 165 ($3).

Getting There & Away
This is Royal Nepal Airlines' western headquarters (☎ 081-20239) so there's a modern airport, now very run-down, plus housing for pilots and their families. Unfortunately this doesn't mean that you are any more certain to arrive or depart on the promised hour or day than you are anywhere else in Nepal. The usual possible disasters apply – weather, VIPs, or a group booking for Karnali or Jumla. There are daily flights to Jumla for $44 and to Kathmandu for $99.

It is possible to hire private cars for the journey to Kathmandu. This would take around 12 hours and cost $200. If all else fails, there's always the bus. The Sajha Yatayat buses are the best option; one leaves at 5.30 am and there are several between 4.30 and 6.30 pm. They take about 16 hours and cost Rs 162 ($3). There are only night buses to Pokhara; they leave from 4.15 to 5.30 pm and cost Rs 172 ($3.50). You can get to Narayanghat for Rs 115 ($2).

Buses for Mahendranagar leave from the T-intersection on the highway at 7 am (nine to 12 hours, Rs 140 or $3). It's advisable to book at least one day in advance, although you can be lucky.

Prior to the opening of the new Kathmandu Bus Terminal, Sajha Yatayat buses left from Bhimsen Tower at 7 am and 4 pm.

Getting Around
It costs from Rs 20 to Rs 30 to take a rickshaw from the airport to town, or the border to town. To get to the long-distance bus station costs Rs 10.

ROYAL BARDIA NATIONAL PARK
The Royal Bardia National Park is the largest untouched wilderness area in the Terai. It's

bordered to the north by the crest of the Chure Hills and to the west by the Geruwa River, a branch of the mighty Karnali, one of the major tributaries of the Ganges.

You stand a better chance of seeing a tiger here than anywhere else in Nepal (including the Chitwan). It's a stunning place that seems a very long way from the 20th century – watching the sun rise over the forest from the back of an elephant is like having a box seat ·at the dawn of time.

Most of the reserve is covered with open sal forest, with the balance a mixture of grassland, savannah and riverine forest. The grassed areas (phanta) are excellent for game-viewing. Most people will visit in the hope of seeing a royal Bengal tiger, but there are also leopards, jungle cats, mongoose, sloth bears, blue cow (nilgai), langur and rhesus monkeys, and sambar, spotted, hog, and barking deer. The Asian one-horned rhinoceros was reintroduced from the Chitwan in 1986, and though breeding successfully the numbers are still small. There's at least one wild male elephant.

The Geruwa River rushes pell-mell through a gap in the hills at Chisopani, grey with silt and snow-melt. It's home to the famous mahseer game fish, gharial and mugger crocodiles, and the strange Gangetic dolphin.

More than 30 different mammals and 250 species of birds have been recorded in the park. Birds include numerous species of heron, stork, geese, duck and parakeet as well as endangered birds like the Bengal florican and sarus crane.

In some ways Bardia is like the Chitwan; the major difference is the degree of isolation and the limited number of visitors. The main disadvantage of Bardia is that it takes a day of travelling to get to or from Kathmandu, although it also takes a minimum of five hours to get to the Chitwan. This means you need a minimum of four days: day one – Kathmandu to Bardia; days two and three – exploring the park, the river and the surrounding villages; day four – Bardia to Kathmandu.

Orientation & Information

The park headquarters are at Tharkurdwara, eight km from Chisopani, on the Mahendra Highway. The park entrance is at Motipur. There is no official accommodation within the park, but camping is allowed in designated areas.

Entry is Rs 650 ($13), plus Rs 1000 ($20) for a vehicle. Camping is Rs 300 ($6) per night. Fishing permits are Rs 300 ($6) per rod. The national park also offers guides for Rs 50 per day, elephants at Rs 650 ($13) per person per hour and Rs 3000 ($60) per person per day. Movement outside camping areas is prohibited between sunset and sunrise. There are virtually no facilities so make sure you stock up before you arrive.

Places to Stay

Tiger Mountain (☎ 01-222706; fax 414075), PO Box 242, Durbar Marg, Kathmandu, the same company that runs the famous Tiger Tops Lodge in the Chitwan, runs all-inclusive tours. The Tiger Tops Karnali Lodge and Tented Camp are simply outstanding. Although they aren't cheap, at $150 and $120 a night respectively, they do offer an extraordinary experience. Those that have been to both the Chitwan and Karnali almost unanimously vote Karnali superior. The lodge closes from the middle of May to the end of September during the monsoon.

The lodge is on the edge of the park, a short walk from an interesting Tharu village. It's built from traditional materials – thatch and mud – and is extremely comfortable. The staff is knowledgeable and helpful, without being intrusive. It's a place where you can abdicate all responsibility, relax and just enjoy. The principle activity is exploring the forest from elephant back (Tiger Tops has its own elephants) but the staff will also organise walks to the nearby village or through the bush.

The Tented Camp is beautifully sited on a bluff overlooking the Churia River, in the shadow of the Chure Hills – the peace and quiet is almost overwhelming. A camp it might be, rough it is not. The beds are comfortable, the food is good and the water is hot.

Again activities revolve around the elephants, but another highlight is a float down the river – a bird-watcher's delight.

A number of other organisations are poised to start operations in the Bardia National Park. The first cab off the rank is the Hotel Batika in Nepalganj, which will open the *Karnali Safari Lodge* in 1993. The lodge is close to the park headquarters at Thakurdwara, and was built using traditional materials. Singles/doubles cost $115/150 plus a one-off charge of $16 to cover park fees. The tariff covers all activities, meals and activities. The lodge does not have its own elephants, but uses government-owned elephants kept by the national park authorities.

Getting There & Away

Although the park is accessible from the Mahendra Highway, most people fly to Nepalganj ($99) where they are then picked up by the Tiger Tops people. The main highway is now in excellent condition and the drive from Nepalganj should take less than 2½ hours. It's an interesting drive past thriving villages.

ROYAL SUKLA PHANTA WILDLIFE RESERVE

Sukla Phanta is smaller and more isolated than Bardia, yet similar in some respects. In the extreme south-west of the country, it covers 155 sq km of riverine flood plain, which includes open grass plains (phanta), forest (primarily sal), a lake and a river.

It is home to tigers, leopards, various species of deer (including an important colony of swamp deer), gharial and mugger crocodiles, otters and a wide variety of bird life.

Information

The ranger's office is three km past the airport (which is accessible by rickshaw from Mahendranagar). Entry is Rs 650 ($13), and it is possible to organise elephant rides for Rs 650 ($13).

Places to Stay

Silent Safari (☎ 01-227236; fax 225524) is currently the only company operating in the park, but it has been recommended by several visitors. There are a number of fascinating tours, an average of five days long, leaving from Mahendranagar, or Dhangadhi. Itineraries normally incorporate time in a couple of Tharu villages (accessed by bullock cart), safaris by jeep and elephant, and guided walks. Accommodation is in comfortable tents, a lodge at the entrance to the wildlife reserve, and, if requested, in Tharu houses.

It is possible for individuals to stay at the lodge if there's room; the rate is $20 per person per night. Food is available, but costs extra.

Silent Safari has an office at Jyatha, Kathmandu, behind the Tibet Rest House (GPO Box 1679). Tours operate from November to April and cost $125 per person per night for an individual or couple, $88 per person in a group of three to five, and $82 in a group of six to 10. This includes accommodation and all activities, plus pick-up from the Mahendranagar airstrip. Park entrance fees ($16), airfares, bar bills, and transfers to Dhangadhi ($40) are extra.

Apparently it is possible to stay near the park entrance for Rs 100, although there are no cooking facilities or restaurants (bring food).

Getting There & Away

Silent Safari picks up guests from the airport at Mahendranagar or Dhangadhi. Royal Nepal Airlines flies to Mahendranagar every Sunday via Nepalganj ($160) and to Dhangadhi on Thursdays ($149). Silent Safari can also arrange road transport through to New Delhi, which is about nine hours away by bus.

MAHENDRANAGAR

Mahendranagar is an uninspired village that owes its existence to the nearby border crossing. There's absolutely nothing to see, and the locals are quite unused to dealing with tourists. A few words of Nepali are very useful. The surrounding countryside is inhabited by traditional Tharu communities, although here, as elsewhere, there is an increasing number of hill people.

Orientation
The town is laid out to the south of the main highway with the bus park at the north-western end. The main landmark is the King Mahendra Square with streets one to five leading off from one side. At the end of Fifth St there's a well-kept park.

Mahendranagar is about six km from the Indian border. Banbassa is the first town on the Indian side. Unfortunately the border is not open all the time and follows no known pattern; you will just have to take your chances, though your chances will be best in the morning.

Places to Stay
Most signs around town are in Nepali so it can be a bit difficult finding a hotel. In general, the standard is spartan and not exactly clean. Some hotels don't have bathrooms, let alone private ones. Singles/doubles are around Rs 60/80.

The *Hotel Sunrise* off King Mahendra Square is very run-down, and the bathroom is the water pump out the back, but there's a good view of life on the square. Just across the road is the *Hotel Moonlight* which has fans and reasonably clean bathrooms.

Getting There & Away
The road from Nepalganj is nearing completion. The only remaining challenges are the bridges over the Karnali and three small rivers further to the west, but in late '92 the authorities were optimistic all would be complete by mid-93. Once this section is complete, the highway will be open all year (barring the occasional short-term monsoon flood). Until that time however, it is strictly a dry-season route.

Two direct buses a day left Kathmandu for Mahendranagar at 4.30 pm (around 24 hours, Rs 260 or $5).

In late '92 buses were taking at least nine hours to journey to/from Nepalganj, but this frequently became much longer thanks to delays getting over the Karnali by pontoon. The only direct bus from Mahendranagar to Nepalganj left at 4 am and cost Rs 140 ($3).

Buses leave Mahendranagar every half hour for the border. It's easiest to take a rickshaw between the Nepalese and Indian checkpoints (10 minutes), and on to Banbassa, the nearest Indian town (20 minutes). Banbassa is on the Indian narrow-gauge rail, and there are buses to Almora and New Delhi. There are at least three direct buses a day to the New Delhi Interstate Bus Station (12, 2.30 and 5 pm); they take around 11 hours and cost Indian Rs 56.

There is an RNAC (☎ 099-21196) flight every Sunday to Kathmandu ($160), via Nepalganj ($77).

DHANGADHI
Dhangadhi is rarely visited by Westerners, but it is apparently possible to cross the border here and to hook up with the Indian narrow-gauge railway for places like Lucknow. The locals are friendly, but there's really nothing to see. The RNAC's telephone number is ☎ 091-21205. There are a few basic places to stay; the *Hotel Taruan* has been recommended.

Pokhara

Pokhara is the most popular destination in Nepal after Kathmandu. Its fame rests on the natural beauty of its lakeside location and its proximity to the mountains however, not on a great historical or cultural endowment. It's the starting point for some of the most famous treks in Nepal, and there are also plenty of short walks and day trips that can be made around the valley.

Pokhara has an enormous number of good-value hotels and restaurants, and although it is undoubtedly a tourist town, it has a relaxed and peaceful atmosphere, completely removed from the hectic bustle of Kathmandu and even further removed from the outright chaos of many Indian cities. It's an oasis where leisurely meals, good books, and short walks can easily fill several days – ideal if you are recovering from (or gearing up for) a trek, or for travel in India.

The roads linking Pokhara with Kathmandu and the Indian border are comparatively recent innovations and as a result the region is changing rapidly. The road from Naubise to Pokhara, the Prithvi Highway, was originally built with Chinese assistance in the early '70s. The Tribhuvan Highway (or Tribhuvan Rajpath, sometimes simply referred to as the Rajpath) was the first road link with Kathmandu and was completed by the Indian government in 1956; it joins the Kathmandu-Pokhara (Prithvi) Highway at Naubise, 29 km from Kathmandu. The most direct route between Pokhara and Sunauli on the Indian border is the attractive Siddhartha Highway, also built by the Indian government.

Most of the heavy traffic from the Terai and India to Kathmandu and Pokhara now uses the road between Narayanghat and Mugling, then either turns east to Kathmandu or west to Pokhara. The sections between Narayanghat and Mugling, and Mugling and Kathmandu are particularly busy. Mountain biking is a great way to get around Nepal, but it would be worth catching a bus over both these sections.

Kathmandu to Pokhara

For many people, the 206-km Kathmandu-Pokhara (Prithvi) Highway will be the first taste of Nepal's Middle Hills and although for most of the way the road follows rivers at the bottom of deep valleys there are still some magical views – rock gorges and river rapids, precipitous hills, tiered rice terraces and glimpses of the Himalaya.

Between Kathmandu and Mugling the road parallels the Trisuli River, the most popular rafting river in the country. It then follows the Marsyandi (which joins the Trisuli at Mugling) as far as Dumre, and from Damauli to Pokhara it follows the Seti Gandaki.

Migrants from around the country (but especially the Kathmandu Valley) have been attracted by the minimal economic opportunities offered in the roadside towns that have sprung up. Most towns are the usual unattractive collection of shanties and two-storey concrete boxes. There are, however, some interesting places (west of Mugling and off the main road) that are worth visiting: Gorkha, which was the original capital for the Shah dynasty; and Bandipur, an old Newari trading settlement.

The countryside is inhabited by Bahuns, Chhetris, Magars and Gurungs. The large multistoreyed houses, especially before Mugling, are most likely owned by Bahuns and Chhetris, but around Mugling the region is dominated by Magars, and to a lesser extent, Gurungs. Historically, the Magars had their own independent kingdoms in western Nepal, and both Magars and Gurungs played a major role in Prithvi Narayan Shah's armies (which unified Nepal), and have since been recruited in large numbers by the British and Indian armies to serve in so-called Gurkha regiments.

Partly thanks to the money that these Gurkhas earn, much of the region seems relatively prosperous, although some Magar families are desperately poor. Land-holdings are small, but the region seems to have avoided major problems with overpopulation, deforestation and land degradation. The intensive, traditional forms of agriculture – based on rice cultivation and a small number of domestic animals – are sophisticated and appear to be sustainable.

KATHMANDU TO NAUBISE
The road leaves from the western end of Tripureshwar Marg and runs through straggling roadside bazaars. Ten km from town, all heavy traffic stops at a police checkpost to pay a toll, and four km later the road crosses the rim of the valley. In clear weather there are views (from east to west) of Ganesh Himal, Himal Chuli, and the twin peaks of Manaslu Himal. You also look down over incredible terracing rising from the Trisuli and Mahesh Kola.

In late 1992 the road from the rim of the valley to Naubise was in extremely poor condition. It snakes down the hill in a series of switchbacks and is further enlivened by Tata trucks overtaking on blind corners. At Naubise, the Tribhuvan Rajpath joins the highway after its epic journey from Hetauda.

NAUBISE TO MUGLING
From Naubise, the road follows the small Mahesh Khola to the point where it joins the Trisuli River just past Baireni (52 km from Kathmandu). It then continues along the Trisuli Valley through the small town of Gajuritar.

Around Malekhu the gorge is still attractively forested. Just before Malekhu, a new bridge is being built over the river. When complete (late 93?) this will open up a new road to Trisuli Bazaar, superseding the existing winding one-track road that leaves the valley at Kakani.

Just after Malekhu there are a number of small restaurants which are good places to break the journey, and which also cater to intrepid rafters. The *Hill Top Restaurant* has a great view over the beach where most rafting trips start, and has good, reasonably priced food and clean toilets. The *Blue*

Heaven Restaurant is virtually on the beach, which is about 70 km from Kathmandu, and four km before Benighat.

At Benighat, the large Buri Gandaki River flows into the Trisuli from the north, giving the rafters the volume of water required for plenty of excitement. The road continues to follow the westward flowing Trisuli to Mugling where it meets the equally large eastward flowing Marsyandi.

The road from Naubise to Mugling was upgraded in the early '90s, and is, without doubt, the best bit of road in the country – beautifully engineered, smoothly surfaced – and as dangerous as hell. It seems ironic that accidents have increased since the road has been improved from the cratered, axle-busting slalom course that challenged drivers in the late '80s. The truth is that it's so good that every driver worth his dhal bhat, goes as fast as his Tata will carry him. In absolute terms this is not very fast, but it is nonetheless about 30 km/h faster than is safe.

MUGLING
Mugling is at the junction between the most important road from the plains (from Nar-

ayanghat) and the Kathmandu-Pokhara (Prithvi) Highway, so it is a popular stop for buses and trucks. It's 110 km from Kathmandu and 96 km from Pokhara, and it lies at an elevation of just 208 metres, making it the lowest town between Kathmandu and Pokhara.

The town is also at the junction of the eastward flowing Trisuli and the westward flowing Marsyandi rivers, which together form the Narayani, a major tributary of the Ganges. This is the finishing point for most of the serious white-water rafting trips on the Trisuli, and the launching place for the more sedate trips down the Narayani to Narayanghat and the Royal Chitwan National Park.

Mugling is not an attractive place. Poverty-stricken Magars from the surrounding hills scavenge a living alongside poverty-stricken refugees from the plains. The town is notorious for prostitution, although this will not be obvious to Westerners stopping over for dhal bhat during the day. The girls are sold by Magar families and the clientele are the long-distance truck drivers.

Places to Stay & Eat

There are literally dozens of restaurants that serve good dhal bhat for around Rs 25. Most are owned by Thakalis, and there is little to distinguish one restaurant from another.

Mugling would not be a pleasant place to spend a night. There are dozens of hotels, but few are interested in having a Westerner stay, since their main business is prostitution. One that does accommodate the occasional stranded backpacker is the *Hotel Laligurans & Lodge*, at the western end of town, near the suspension bridge over the river and the intersection with the Narayanghat road. The hotel has the advantage of being set back from the road, but it's very basic and not very clean. Singles/doubles are Rs 50/60.

For those with more cash, there is an attractive, slightly incongruous motel on the Pokhara side of town just over the bridge. The *Motel du Mugling* (☎ 01-225242; fax 225236) is operated by the Hotel de l'Annapurna (see Kathmandu) and is comfortable, and expensive. Singles/doubles are $25/35 plus 10% tax; meals are $8.

MUGLING TO ABU KHAIRENI

Leaving Mugling, a long suspension bridge crosses the Narayani River just below the junction of the Trisuli and Marsyandi. Two km further on you reach the **Marsyandi Hyroelectric Powerhouse**, which generates more than a quarter of the country's electricity. Water is diverted to the building you see beside the road from a dam 12 km away. Its completion in 1990 has failed to avert power shortages throughout the country. The road deteriorates after Mugling, and there are some very rough, very dusty sections until you get past Dumre.

Eight km from Mugling you reach Abu Khaireni, another roadside bazaar town, which is at the intersection of the road to Gorkha, and is the starting point for the climb to **Manakamana**, one of the most popular temples in Nepal. It is believed that the goddess Bhagwati will grant wishes in exchange for prayer and animal sacrifices, and she is particularly popular with newlyweds seeking sons. The hereditary role of temple priest is filled by a Magar (not a Brahman as is usually the case with Hindu temples), suggesting that the goddess is a survivor from the pre-Hindu, shamanistic religion of the Magars.

To get to the temple, turn right off the highway on the road to Gorkha; continue for a km until you see the Manakamana Hotel on the right; turn right and cross the river on a suspension bridge; then climb for three or four hours!

GORKHA

The ninth Shah king, King Prithvi Narayan Shah, was born in the family's palace that perches over Gorkha. Prithvi Narayan was crowned King of Gorkha in 1743, and proved to be an extraordinary man.

At the time he came to power, Nepal was broken up into numerous small principalities, but by the time he died he had created a unified state that was sufficiently strong to successfully resist the colonial forces that engulfed virtually every other country in Asia.

Although he was a great fighter, he was also an accomplished tactician and administrator. His reputation for religious and cultural tolerance, and for the justice and effectiveness of his administration, was a significant element in his success. He was able to maintain the commitment of his subjects through a process that continued for nearly 30 years – the Kathmandu Valley was not completely conquered until the early 1670s – and he succeeded in convincing a number of states to accept his rule without resorting to direct violence. He had the guile to exploit existing rivalries between states, and where necessary utilised expedient alliances, notably with Palpa (see the later Tansen section).

Gorkha was the name given to the fearsome soldiers (mostly Bahuns, Thakuris, Chhetris, Magars and Gurungs) under his command. The term Gurkha was later applied to all Nepalese soldiers, irrespective of where they were recruited and what group they belonged to. Many have served, and still serve, in the British and Indian armies.

Gorkha, 18 km north of the Kathmandu-Pokhara (Prithvi) Highway, is accessible by a good sealed road that intersects with the highway at Abu Khaireni, eight km west of Mugling. The countryside is spectacular and Gorkha itself is well worth visiting.

Gorkha Durbar

Gorkha Durbar, a fort, palace and temple complex, is the centrepoint and highlight of a visit to Gorkha. Some of the building is believed to date from the reign of King Ram Shah (1606-36), but successive generations have made alterations and additions, often utilising Newari craftspeople. The complex is a triumph of Nepalese architecture – perched like an eagle's nest high above the town in a perfect defensive position – with superb views of plunging valleys and the soaring Himalaya. You can easily imagine an ambitious prince looking out over this dramatic landscape and dreaming of ruling all he could see – and more.

To get to Gorkha Durbar, walk north from the bus station until you come to several small temples (to Vishnu, Krishna and

1 Ganesh Temple
2 Sobrakhutte Pati
3 Krishna Temple
4 Column with Prithvipati Shah Statue
5 Vishnu Temple
6 Prison
7 Tallo Durbar
8 Bus Station
9 New Hotel Thakali & Lodge
10 Hotel Gorkha Bisauni

Ganesh) surrounding a tank. Head to your right until you come to a square, to the right of which is **Tallo Durbar**, a large, square Newari-style building that was built in 1835 to house a Rana who had been banished from Kathmandu for playing a role in one of the never-ending palace intrigues. The building is slowly being renovated and will eventually house a museum.

You pay for the impressive view from the Gorkha Durbar with a steep one-hour walk from Tallo Durbar. Return to the square from Tallo Durbar and continue to the east. The town itself is inaccessible to cars, so it's quite pleasant to wander the cobbled, shop-lined streets.

On your left after about 100 metres you'll see some well-made steps heading directly up to Gorkha Durbar. If you get to the gully where village women wash clothes you've gone too far.

The hillside has a network of paths and retaining walls that must have cost a fortune to build. When you get to the big pipal tree, the path forks and though you can take either path, the gentlest ascent is to the left. After about 200 metres there is another junction; again head to your left. When you get to the ridge you are greeted with stupendous views of the Ganesh and Annapurna himal.

From the ridge, you obviously turn right to the palace, but if you turn left you soon come to **Tallokot**, a small, old fort now used as a sacrificial site.

Photography is not permitted once you are inside the Gorkha Durbar complex, and this is strictly enforced by soldiers, so you may want to try to capture something on film from here. You are not allowed to wear leather inside the complex, so wear sandshoes or a thick old pair of socks if you are going to do some serious exploration. (This rule seemed to have been relaxed in 1992.)

If you enter from the west, the first building on your left is the Kalika Temple (note the 'Star of David' window), which has some superb woodcarving. Only a special caste of Brahman priests and the king can enter, but sacrifices are made outside.

The main palace, or Dhuni Pati, has lat-ticed windows all around the top floor, but unfortunately you are not allowed to enter, so you can only imagine the breezy rooms that lie behind. This was Prithvi Narayan's birthplace and an eternal flame has been kept burning inside ever since his rule.

Next, go up a few steps. There is a priests' house on the left and two bells on the right. Between the latter are stairs descending to a cave where a reclusive saint named Gorkhanath once lived.

Beyond the priests' house is a four-faced shiva lingam. You can descend to servants' quarters and a temple on the next level, then down again to a crude but dramatic repainted carving of Hanuman and six carved stele.

From here it's another half-hour walk east to **Upkallot**, the highest point on the ridge, with the ruins of a fort, and a telecommunications tower. The views over the palace and across to the Himalaya are stupendous.

Places to Stay

There are some cheap, basic places to stay near the Gorkha bus station, but the best budget place to stay is down the hill at the entrance to town. The *Hotel Gorkha Bisauni* (☎ 064-20107) is quite a decent place and also has a reasonable restaurant. There are dorm beds for Rs 25, rooms for Rs 75, doubles with private bath for Rs 150 ($3), and deluxe rooms for Rs 200 ($4) and Rs 300 ($6).

The up-market *Gorkha Hill Resort* (☎ 01-227929, 271329; fax 471630) has a superb site four km before town (800 metres down a dirt road to the east of the main road). The buildings have been thoughtfully designed and most rooms have spectacular views. Though not cheap, the resort is worth the $30/40 for singles/doubles. Main meals are $8.

Getting There & Away

There are several buses a day to and from Pokhara for Rs 40, and six buses to and from Kathmandu for Rs 35. Buses from Gorkha all leave early in the morning. There are also direct buses from Gorkha to Birganj for Rs 62 and to Sunauli for Rs 68.

If you were dropped off at Abu Khaireni, eight km from Mugling on the Kathmandu-Pokhara (Prithvi) Highway, you would find local minibuses to Gorkha (Rs 8). It's an enjoyable drive on a good road, but there's a steep climb for cyclists.

DUMRE

Dumre, 18 km past Abu Khaireni, a new town which only came into existence after the construction of the road, is a typical, dirty roadside bazaar. Apart from being the turn-off to Besisahar, the starting point for the Annapurna Circuit trek, it has nothing at all to recommend it. For circuit trekkers it's the last place where there is a decent range of supplies at reasonable prices.

Places to Stay & Eat

Trekkers may have to spend the night at Dumre if they arrive late. Try the basic *Hotel Mustang*, opposite the roadside temple in the middle of town, which has singles/doubles for Rs 50/60; beware the steep 50-metre climb to the outside toilet, and keep a torch handy! Another reasonable alternative is the *Manang Guest House* just off the main road.

Getting There & Away

By bus, Dumre is about five hours from Kathmandu and 2½ hours from Pokhara. A public bus from Kathmandu (which left from Bhimsen Tower before the Kathmandu Bus Terminal opened) costs Rs 67 and could take longer; from Pokhara it costs Rs 35. The tourist buses that travel between Pokhara and Kathmandu cost around Rs 150 ($3).

Many people start their trek by catching shared jeeps or trucks to Besisahar. Expect to pay around Rs 250 ($5), although porters will pay Rs 150 ($3). The road is very rough and the journey can take up to five hours.

BANDIPUR

Overlooking Dumre from its hilltop position, Bandipur is a beautiful Newari town just south of the Kathmandu-Pokhara (Prithvi) Highway. Before the construction of the road, Bandipur was a major Newari

trading centre, and its bazaars still hint of those days. Stone-paved roads pass between temples and multistoreyed houses, and along the way there are excellent views of the Annapurnas and Machhapuchhare. It takes about two hours to walk up to Bandipur from Dumre, 45 minutes to drive.

DAMAULI

From Dumre it's just 16 km to the district headquarters of Damauli which has a bustling bazaar. The main road in the town leads to the panchayat building, while a path to the left drops down to the junction of the Madi Khola and Seti Gandaki rivers. If you walk upstream about 100 metres you will find a beach which is good for swimming.

DAMAULI TO POKHARA

Soon after Damauli the road crosses the Madi Khola, via a large bridge, and follows the Seti Gandaki River for the remaining 54 km to Pokhara. The next town is Khaireni, where a West German-assisted agricultural project is based.

After Khaireni, the road passes the turn-off to Rupa Tal and Begnas Tal, which are the second and third-largest lakes of the Pokhara Valley. Sisuwa, only 12 km from Pokhara, is the last place before you arrive at the Pokhara bus station which is immediately north of the airport and some distance south of the busy bazaar area of the town.

Pokhara

After travelling elsewhere in Nepal or in India, Pokhara has an almost Disneyland unreality about it. The climate is mild; incredible snowcapped mountains are reflected in a sheltered lake; cool Western music drifts from every restaurant; menus offer everything in the world except dhal bhat; hotel rooms are clean, and open onto sunny gardens; there's very little traffic; village life persists, but everyone speaks English; and it's very relaxed.

To Siklis
To Kahun Danda
Bhalam Khola
Phulbari
Seti Gandaki River
Kali Khola
River
Patan
Gandaki
Seti
Nadipur
Bazaar
Bhim Bazaar
Bazaar
Bag Bazaar
Bazaar
1
Park
2
Bharab Tole
3
To Mahendra Cave
Pokhara–Baglung Highway
To Baglung
Yamdi Khola
GYARJATI
To Sarangkot
To Sarangkot

1 Natural History Museum
2 Binde Basini Temple
3 Bhimsen Temple
4 Post Office
5 Telecommunications Building
6 Hospital
7 Tibetan Buddhist Monastery
8 Bhadrakali Temple
9 Pokhara Museum
10 Bus Station
11 Stadium
12 Hotel New Crystal
13 Tourist Office
14 Hotel Mt Annapurne
15 Immigration Office &
   Annapurna Conservation
   Area Project (ACAP) Office
16 Foreign Exchange Counter
17 Hotel Tragopan
18 Fish Tail Lodge
19 Royal Palace
20 Varahi Temple

Pokhara

To Kathmandu,
Rupa Tal &
Begnas Tal

Mahendrapul Bridge

Ranipauwa

Ram Ghat

New Bazaar

Dobo Tole

Chipledhunga

Shreejana Chowk

Nadipur

Seti Gandaki River

Airport

Siddhartha Chowk

Manwara

Rastrabank

See Pokhara
Damside Map

PARDI

Pardi Dam

See Pokhara Lakeside Map

BAIDAM

Pardi Khola

Pardi Bazaar

Devi Falls

Phewa Tal

Tashiling
Tibetan
Village

To Bhairawa
& Tansen

Siddhartha Highway

The first tourists to discover Pokhara were the hippie travellers of the early seventies. In Pokhara many discovered the perfect venue for doing the things they were best at – getting stoned, eating, growing their hair, talking, and staring into the middle distance while looking cool. They came for a week and stayed for months. The world has changed since then (and so have the drug laws and visa regulations), but Pokhara retains something of the laid-back, hedonistic style of the '70s.

Viewed from Pokhara, the Himalaya is indeed a mighty mountain range, looming over the horizon much closer than it does in Kathmandu. Only foothills separate the town from the full height of the mountains, and the magnificent 8000-metre peaks of the Annapurna Range utterly dominate the view to the north. In the Kathmandu Valley the high temples are all around you, in the Pokhara Valley it is the mountains.

The valley has three large lakes. Two of them, Rupa Tal and Begnas Tal, are slightly to the east of town while the third and largest, Phewa Tal, is the focal point for Pokhara's tourist industry.

Pokhara stands at 884 metres above sea level, about 700 metres lower than Kathmandu. The autumn and winter temperatures in Pokhara are generally much more comfortable than in often-chilly Kathmandu but the monsoon rains are twice as heavy.

Although the Pokhara Valley is chiefly inhabited by Bahuns and Chhetris, the hills around Pokhara are predominantly inhabited by Gurungs. These sturdy tribal people continue to play an important part in the Gurkha regiments in India and overseas and their earnings have a major impact on the local economy.

Pokhara's development has been recent and rapid. Only with the eradication of malaria in the 1950s did it become safe to live here. The construction of the airstrip in the '50s, the hydroelectric power dam (with Indian aid) in 1968 and the building of the roads to Kathmandu and the Indian border in the early '70s, catapulted Pokhara into the 20th century.

ORIENTATION

Pokhara is a surprisingly sprawling town, stretching in a north-south direction for about five km. Starting from the north there's the busy bazaar area which also contains the oldest part of Pokhara – the town as it was before electricity, roads, and the airport totally transformed it. South of the bazaar is the bus station and south again is the airport.

West of the bus station and airport is Phewa Tal, the lakeside tourist centre where Pokhara's great and growing number of hotels and restaurants are predominantly located. It's a long walk from place to place in Pokhara and if you go from south to north it's uphill all the way.

Most of Pokhara's local shops and the post office are around the Mahendrapul (or Mahendra Pool) Bridge in the bazaar area. The bazaar is a long, strung-out affair and the campus of the Pokhara University is also found in that area.

The tourist office and two of the town's larger hotels are beside the airport while a number of government buildings, including the immigration office, are between the airport and Phewa Tal.

Starting at the south-eastern end of the lake, near the airport, there's a hydroelectric station. This area is often rather confusingly called Damside (although the dam and the lake are continuous) or Pardi. There are quite a number of hotels in the Damside area although the lakeside has even more.

Finally there's the lakeside area itself, also known as Baidam, where the majority of foreign visitors to Pokhara stay. Along the lakeside road there's a continuous tawdry stretch of small hotels, restaurants and shops. In this book, Lakeside has rather arbitrarily been divided into three sections: Lakeside East (or Ammat) ending at the Royal Palace; Lakeside West (or Pallo Patan) ending just before the main road that returns eastward to town; and Lakeside North (or Khaharey).

INFORMATION
Tourist Office

Pokhara's tourist office is right across the road from the airport terminal. Depending on the Nepalese calendar the office is open approximately mid-February to mid-November from 10 am to 5 pm, and mid-November to mid-February from 9 am to 4 pm. On Fridays, however, it closes at 3 pm and is closed completely on Saturdays and public holidays. The office has some limited information, but is not very helpful.

Money

There's an exchange counter, opposite the Nepal Rastra Bank and not far from the immigration office, that is open daily from 11 am to 3.30 pm. For those staying at Lakeside the Nepal Grindlays Bank may be more convenient. Although it is only open standard banking hours, you can make cash and travellers' cheque advances against Visa and MasterCard.

Post & Telecommunications

The post office is a long way from the Lakeside and Damside hotels in the bazaar area near Mahendrapul Bridge. If you want to make overseas phone calls or calls to Kathmandu, there's a telecommunications building east of the post office along the bridge.

Immigration Office

The office is convenient to the Lakeside and Damside area hotels. It can only extend visas for a maximum of six weeks (within the 90-day tourist visa period), and issue trekking permits to the Annapurna region. It's open from 10.30 am to 1 pm for applications and from 3 pm for passport pick-ups.

Bookshops

There are numerous bookshops along the lakeside road offering both new and second-hand books and maps. Good shops include the Pokhara Bookshop, the As You Like It Bookshop, the Kiwi Book Shop, the Collectors Bookshop and the Holy Bookshop. The Bongsor Valley in Han Suyin's *The Mountain is Young* is based on the Pokhara Valley.

PHEWA TAL

Phewa Tal, or Phewa Lake, is the tourist centre of Pokhara and the second-largest lake in Nepal. Only Rara Lake in the far west of the country is larger.

From Phewa Tal you can set off on walks or bicycle rides, or take to the lake in one of the numerous boats *(doongas)* available for rent from the lakeside canoe operators. The boats cost from Rs 20 or Rs 50 ($0.40 to $1) an hour, and are most expensive opposite the Varahi Temple but get cheaper as you head south to Damside. You can simply paddle yourself lazily around or jump overboard for a swim in the pleasant waters. If rowing yourself is too strenuous, a boat plus boatman will cost from around Rs 80 to Rs 100 ($1.70 to $2) per hour. Sail boats are hired near the Hotel Fewa for Rs 200 ($4) per hour, less for half a day.

The lakeside villages are mainly inhabited by Chhetris although these days there is a great deal of outside influence as well. Although there have been recent efforts to clean out Pokhara's drug pushers, this area still has a bit of the old hippie-scene feel about it.

Along the lakeside are a number of banyan and pipal trees with chautaras built around them. These stone platforms were designed to provide a resting place and shade for walkers, and building them was one good way of improving one's karma for future existences.

MOUNTAIN VIEWS

The wonderful Annapurna panorama forms a superb backdrop to Pokhara. You can see the mountains clearly from the lake, while from the other side of Phewa Tal, by the Fish Tail Lodge, you can actually see them twice if you count their reflection in the often placid waters.

Alternatively you can climb to Sarangkot or one of the other lookout points around the valley and enjoy a closer uninterrupted view.

The incredible Annapurna massif includes mountains like Lamjung Himal, Hiunchuli, Varahashikhar, Khangsar Kang, Tarke Kang and Gangapurna; but it's the five Annapurna peaks, Annapurna I to IV plus

View of Himalayan Ranges from Pokhara

Annapurna South 7273 m

Annapurna I 8091 m

Machhapuchhare 6997 m

Annapurna South, and the magnificent Machhapuchhare which are best known.

Machhapuchhare means 'fish tail' and if you walk several days west along the Jomsom Trek route you will find that the mountain actually has a second peak, and from that side it does indeed look like a fish tail. From Pokhara, however, it's simply a superb pyramid; a Himalayan Matterhorn, only much higher.

Machhapuchhare stands out not only because of its prominent shape and lonely position, but because it is closer to Pokhara than the other peaks. In actual fact, at 6997 metres, it is lower than the five Annapurnas. Remarkably, it has never been successfully climbed.

An attempt in 1957, led by the legendary Mountain Travel founder JOM Roberts (who, incidentally, settled in Pokhara after his retirement), got to within 50 metres of the top but turned back when the Sherpas refused to conquer such a holy summit.

Climbing is now not allowed on this mountain. Robert Rieffel in *Nepal Namaste* questions how Machhapuchhare acquired its holy image: if it's so significant, why on earth is it called 'fish tail' when so many other unholy Nepalese peaks are named after gods and goddesses?

The other peak with a mountaineering tale to tell is Annapurna I which, at 8091 metres, is the highest in the range. It's also part of a long ridge line and because it's further north appears less conspicuous.

Annapurna I's claim to fame is that when a small French expedition, led by Maurice Herzog, reached the summit in 1950 it was the first time an 8000-metre peak had been climbed.

Herzog's book *Annapurna*, a mountaineering classic, traces the hardships of organising a climb in what was then a remote, inaccessible and little-known area. The harrowing aftermath of the climb, when a severe storm caught the retreating mountaineers, resulted in Herzog losing most of his fingers and toes from frostbite.

To the west of the Annapurnas is Dhaulagiri, at 8167 metres. The Kali Gandaki River, which cuts the deepest gorge in the world, flows between Dhaulagiri and the Annapurnas and actually predates the rise of the Himalaya. For a while, before more precise measuring methods were available, it was thought that Dhaulagiri was the world's highest mountain.

TEMPLES

Pokhara, unlike the towns of the Kathmandu Valley, is not noted for its temples. In fact there are very few of even the most minor note.

In the lake there's a small island with the double-roofed **Varahi Temple** dedicated to Varahi, who is Vishnu in his boar incarnation.

In the northern part of the bazaar area, is the small, double-roofed **Bhimsen Temple** with some small and not very notable erotic carvings on the roof struts. The streets of the bazaar area become steadily more attractive and traditional as you move north from the newer area around the bus station to what

Annapurna III
7555 m

Annapurna IV
7525 m

Annapurna II
7937 m

was the centre of the original settlement of Pokhara. Bhimsen Temple, very much in the Newari style of the Kathmandu Valley, is right on the main road in the oldest part of town.

Slightly further north, atop a small hill with a park at its base, is Pokhara's best known temple, the **Binde Basini Temple**. Its pleasant and shady setting is actually more impressive than the white shikhara-style temple itself. The temple is dedicated to Durga (Parvati) in her Binde Basini Bhagwati manifestation, and interestingly the image of the goddess is a saligram. These black ammonite fossils of marine animals date from the Jurassic period over 100 million years ago and are found in the Himalaya, north of Pokhara, and at several points along the Kali Gandaki. Saligrams provide clear proof that this region was once under the sea.

MUSEUMS

Pokhara has two museums. The **Pokhara Museum** is north of the bus station on the main road and has exhibits on local history. Entry is Rs 5, except on Tuesdays when it's closed.

At the northern end of town, on the Pokhara University campus, is the **Natural History Museum**, also known as the Annapurna Regional Museum. The Annapurna Conservation Area Project (ACAP) has some interesting exhibits on the environmental problems of the area. The natural history section has cement models of Nepalese wildlife (you don't have to feed

them) and a large butterfly, moth and insect collection. The museum is open from 9 am to 1 pm and from 2 to 5 pm; there's no entry charge, but make a donation.

SETI GANDAKI RIVER

The Seti Gandaki River flows right through Pokhara but in places it runs completely underground, sometimes dropping to 50 metres below ground level. *Seti* means 'white' and the water's milky colour comes from limestone in the soil.

There's a good view of this elusive river from the bridge near the old Mission Hospital at the northern end of the bazaar; though an even more dramatic view can be found just over the airport runway. Cross the runway by the terminal (it's a busy thoroughfare and a warning is sounded when an aircraft approaches) and follow the trail to the river where a footbridge crosses the canyon. The bridge is only about 10 metres wide but the river flows past a good 30 metres below.

Another good view of the river can be found at Mahendrapul Bridge in the main bazaar area.

DEVI FALLS

Also known as Patale Chango, Devin's or David's Falls, this waterfall is about two km south-west of the airport on the main Siddhartha Highway and just before the Tashiling Tibetan village.

The Pardi Khola is the outflow from Phewa Tal and at Devi Falls it suddenly drops down into a hole in the ground and disappears.

One of its alternate names comes from a tale that a tourist named David disappeared down the hole as well, taking his girlfriend with him! There's a Rs 3 admission charge to the falls – if there's anyone there to collect it.

The river emerges from its subterranean hideaway 200 metres away and then joins the Phusre Khola before flowing into the Seti Gandaki River.

TIBETAN SETTLEMENTS

There are a number of Tibetan settlements around Pokhara and you see many Tibetans around the lake selling their crafts and artefacts. The Tashiling Tibetan village, where they weave Tibetan carpets, is only a couple of km south-west of the airport.

There's a larger settlement known as Tashipalkhel at Hyangja, a short drive or an hour or two's walk north-west of Pokhara on the start of the Jomsom Trek route.

TIBETAN BUDDHIST MONASTERY

Cross Mahendrapul Bridge from the bazaar area and follow the road, at first paved, to this hilltop monastery. It's a comparatively recent construction with a large Buddha statue and colourful wall paintings.

WALKS

The Pokhara area offers some fine walking possibilities ranging from day walks like the climb up to Sarangkot to short three or four-day treks. See the Around Pokhara section for full details.

PLACES TO STAY

There are four accommodation areas in Pokhara: around the bus station and bazaar, by the airport, Damside (Pardi), and Lakeside (Baidam).

There's really no reason to stay in the bazaar area; it's crowded, dirty and noisy. Several of Pokhara's larger and more expensive hotels are near the airport, but the advantages of comfortable hotels have to be weighed against the disadvantage of being a long walk from Lakeside.

Damside (Pardi) at the south-eastern end of the lake is more popular, and many of the aggressive touts at the Pokhara bus station will insist that this is the place to go. They will be at pains to point out that the distinction between Damside and Lakeside is meaningless. In one sense they're right (it is a continuous body of water we're talking about), but in several others they're wrong. Damside has a completely different atmosphere to Lakeside.

Firstly, there is quite a difference between being able to look out across the lake proper, as you can at Lakeside, and looking out on the narrow neck of water by the dam. Damside is a new, rather desolate area, and there are fewer farmhouses, fields and trees interspersed between the hotels. Many of the buildings are the bleak concrete three-storey variety and there is a limited range of restaurants – most people eat in their hotels. Finally, you're a 15-minute walk from the action at Lakeside.

On the other hand, there are a couple of pleasant middle-range hotels, and some people prefer to escape the Lakeside scene. They are further rewarded by the best mountain views – the further south you go, the less the mountains are obscured by the intervening foothills.

The major accommodation site is Lakeside, where you'll find an enormous number of budget to middle-range lodges and guest houses. The lakeside road is a continuous strip of excellent restaurants that spill out into the open air, and little shops selling everything a traveller could want – tickets, trekking gear, books, fruit juice, clothes, souvenirs. However, if you take any of the eastward-running roads, you quickly escape to land where the buffalo roam. Within two minutes you can be in a cheap and comfortable guest house amongst rice fields, vegetable gardens and Chhetri farmhouses.

Sadly, the traditional village culture is disappearing – for it is the combination of the magnificent location, good-value accommodation and food, and (not least) the proximity of local village life that accounts for much of Pokhara's appeal.

There are so many places and they change so quickly, that making individual recommendations (especially among bottom and middle-range places) is a chancy game. Listen to other travellers' recommendations, and if you arrive by bus avoid the clutches of the bus station touts. The best thing you can do is grab a taxi to somewhere central on Lakeside, have a drink and a bite to eat at one of the restaurants and then ask to leave your bag somewhere safe (most restaurants will happily do this) while you check out some hotels for yourself.

When looking for somewhere to stay – at any price range – the important variables are the quality of the room, the views and the garden; and the availability of hot water; and the position. If you're staying in one of the really rock-bottom Lakeside places take care of your valuables, as theft is not unknown.

Bazaar Area

There are numerous cheaper hotels around the bus station and near the Mahendrapul Bridge in the bazaar area. It's a much less pleasant place to stay than the lakeside and there's no real reason to do so.

By staying in the bazaar area you may be a little closer to the start of the Jomsom and Annapurna trekking trails, but these days you can travel some distance out of Pokhara by road before you start walking, so being a km or two closer will make no difference at all.

Airport Area

Two of Pokhara's large hotels are directly opposite the airport terminal, as is Pokhara's tourist office.

The *Hotel Mt Annapurna* (☎ 061-20027/37) is decorated in Tibetan style; the murals in the restaurant showing Tibetan traders and other scenes are particularly impressive. There's also a fine view of the Annapurna skyline from the roof, and a pleasant garden area. All rooms have private bathrooms and cost $24/33 a single/double,

plus 12% government tax, which is good value.

The *Hotel New Crystal* (☎ 061-20035; fax 01-228028) has singles/doubles with air-con for $38/55 as well as some rooms in an annexe without air-con for $21/28. All rooms have private bathrooms and there's a 13% government tax. The facilities are good, but it's a big soulless place that could be pretty much anywhere.

Damside (Pardi) Area

South-west of the airport, at the south-eastern end of Phewa Tal, is the Damside or Pardi area. There are a number of lodges and hotels, many of which are run by Thakalis from the Kali Gandaki Valley.

Hotel Tragopan (☎ 061-21708) is in an intermediate position between Damside and Lakeside, overlooking a busy road. There's a nice garden and the rooms have good views; they're pleasant and well equipped though rather expensive at $35/45.

The *Hotel Pokhara View* (☎ 061-20189) is a small two-storey place with clean rooms, some of which have excellent mountain views. Singles/double with shared bath cost from Rs 200/300 ($4/6), rooms with bath are Rs 400/500 ($8/10). The *Annapurna Hotel* is also very clean, but a bit more expensive at $15 for a double with bath.

There is a group of decent mid-range places right by the dam – there's not much to separate them, and the most crucial variable is probably which direction your room happens to face, because the views can be impressive. The *Ashok Guest House* (☎ 061-20374) is well kept and has singles/doubles with private bath for $10/15, $15/20 if you want the view. There are a few cheaper rooms for $5. The *Mona Lisa* is similar.

The *Dragon Hotel* (☎ 061-20391, 20052) is quite luxurious. Singles/doubles with air-con and private bath are $25/35, plus 12% government tax. There's a restaurant, bar and roof garden.

The *New Hotel Pagoda* (☎ 061-21802) is excellent value – a definite Pardi star. There are views, and the rooms are very clean.

Singles/doubles are $2/3 with shared bath, $7/10 with private bath.

The *Hotel Green View* is a friendly place with some very basic rooms for $2.50/3. There's also a comfortable new building where singles/doubles with good views and private bath go for $10/15.

Hotel Garden (☎ 061-20870) and *Hotel Peaceful* (☎ 061-20861) are both decent places with a range of comfortable rooms. Singles/doubles are $2/3 with shared bath, $5/8 with private bathrooms. The Hotel Garden also has deluxe rooms for $20/30, some with excellent views.

Lakeside (Baidam) Area

The road running alongside Phewa Tal is the real visitors' centre for Pokhara. Not only does it have the largest number of hotels, guest houses and lodges it also has the widest selection of shops, bookshops, restaurants, travel agencies, bicycle-rental and so on.

Although the majority of the lakeside places are firmly in the budget range, an increasing number are aiming for the middle range with en-suite bathrooms, carpets, and comfortable beds.

Many of the budget lodges and guest houses along the lake have similar facilities and prices. Prices tend to vary with demand, rising and falling with the season and the number of travellers passing through. There's usually hot water available in the bathrooms and many places offer very pleasant garden areas, often right in front of your room. The rooms are usually quite simply furnished, but good Pokhara guest houses are clean and well kept.

Standard doubles cost around Rs 100 ($2) for a room with shared bath, or from Rs 250 ($5) with private bath. There are increasing numbers of new concrete hotels with totally uninspiring architecture, but comfortable rooms. They're relatively expensive with

1 Hotel Pokhara View	16 Hotel Try Star
2 Annapurna Hotel	17 Dragon Hotel
3 Osho World Travel	18 Hotel Garland
4 Rodee Restaurant	19 Poonam Guest House
5 Hotel Florida	20 Hotel Sakura
6 Hotel Yad	21 Sherpa Guest House
7 KC's Restaurant	22 Hotel Mary Ward
8 Mona Lisa Guest House	23 New Hotel Pagoda
9 Ashok Guest House	24 Hotel Holiday
10 Yeti Restaurant	25 Friendly Guest House
11 Hotel Peaceful	26 Super Lodge
12 Hotel Garden	27 Hotel Anzuk
13 Hotel Mount View	28 Hotel Green View
14 German Bakery	29 Purna Guest House
15 Hotel Nascent	30 Hotel Twin Peak

Pokhara
Damside

Top: Phewa Tal from Sarangkot (TW)
Left: Boy on swing, Pokhara (RE)
Right: Boats on Phewa Tal, Pokhara (TW)

Top: Mt Everest from Kala Pattar (SA)
Middle: Machhapuchhare and the Annapurnas (DA)
Bottom: Annapurna South (SB)

rates starting at about $10, and while there's little room for bargaining for the cheapest rooms, there certainly is for the more expensive ones, especially if you plan to stay more than a couple of days.

You can stay close to the centre of things, on or near the main lakeside road, or opt for a quieter location either back from the main road or way down at the northern end of the lake. The price for peace and quiet is a slightly longer walk to get to the restaurants and other activities by the water. The further north you go (towards the foothills), the more restricted are the views of the mountains.

The following suggestions are just a handful of standard places, plus some of the pricier alternatives (fewer in number). Lakeside has rather arbitrarily been divided into three sections: Lakeside East (or Ammat) ending at the Royal Palace, Lakeside West (or Pallo Patan) ending just before the main road that returns eastward to town, and Lakeside North (or Khaharey).

Lakeside East (Ammat) Pokhara's most expensive hotel is the beautifully positioned *Fish Tail Lodge* (☎ 061-20071, 20984). It's across the lake from the lakeside development and guests are shuttled over to the hotel by a rope-drawn pontoon.

The hotel takes its name from Machhapuchhare, the fish-tail mountain that dominates the skyline of Pokhara. From the hotel there are superb views of the mountains particularly at dawn when they are reflected in the still waters of the lake. The buildings have been imaginatively designed with references to the local architecture, and sit in attractive gardens.

The rooms have all the usual luxury mod cons and cost $60/72 a single/double, plus 12% tax. The hotel is extremely popular, so it is worth booking well in advance if you want to stay. Book through Annapurna International (☎ 061-221711; fax 225236), PO Box 140, Durbar Marg, Kathmandu. There's a pleasant bar and restaurant although the food is only average.

Lakeside's other places are all on the northern side of the lake, and one of the first you come to is the comfortable, mid-range *New Pokhara Lodge* (☎ 061-20875). It looks a little garish, but is well run. Singles/doubles with private bath are reasonable value from $10/15.

Take the first right after Baba Lodge & Restaurant and you come to the *Base Camp Resort* (☎ 061-21226; fax 20903), one of the best of the new breed of expensive up-market offerings. A number of two-storey bungalows are grouped around an attractive garden. There's satellite TV, international direct dial telephones and gas heating. This is a good option if the Fish Tail is booked out – which it often is. Singles/doubles are $46/52.

Heading away from the lake's edge you end up in a pleasant village-like area. The first place you come to is the *New Nanohana Lodge* a new, fairly undistinguished place which has a range of rooms with private bath from Rs 150 ($3) to $10. Nearby is the *New Star Lodge* which has basic rooms for Rs 80/100 a single/double, and rooms with bath for Rs 250 ($5).

Keep going to find the excellent *Gurkha Lodge* a small, immaculate place with a lovely garden. There are only five double rooms, all with private bath, and there has been a real effort to build in sympathy with the local architecture. It's definitely worth the price – $11 per room. A bit further on, the *Garden Rest House* is a real find. It's clean, there's a nice atmosphere and prices are good. Rooms are Rs 100 with shared bath, Rs 250 ($5) with private bath. The nearby *Garden Guest House* is run by the same family, but is not in the same league.

The next road leading inland from the lake is lined with places to stay, and though they're convenient, and the mountain views are good, there's not much atmosphere. The *Kiwi Guest House* (☎ 061-21587) is a decent place with a helpful family. The garden is a bit cramped, but there are good views from the hotel roof. The Kiwi advertises Kiwi management, which is more literally true than some such claims, since Lal, the owner, did study management in New Zealand.

There are a range of rooms, all of them fair value for what you get. Singles/doubles are $2.50/4 with shared bath, $5/9 with private bath, and $15/19 for deluxe.

The new *Stay Well Guest House* is a small place with clean and comfortable singles/doubles for $10/20. *Dharma House* and *View Corner Lodge* are both decent cheapies with doubles for Rs 100. The *Hotel Bedrock* (☎ 061-21876) is a large new multistoreyed place with comfortable, but expensive rooms from $25/45.

The *Hotel Kantipur* (☎ 061-20886), on the main road, was once very pleasant, but had declined to a point where it was overpriced and scruffy when I visited. The position is good, however, so hopefully it will be restored. Standard rooms (with bath) are $10/15; deluxe rooms are $40/50.

There are a number of cheap places down the first eastward road past the small temple shrine on the lake's edge. These include the *Gauri Shanker* and *Gautama*. The *Shanti Guest House* has OK singles/doubles for Rs 80/100, or Rs 150/250 ($3/5) with private bath. The *New Tourist Guest House* (☎ 061-21479) is a nice place with a decent garden and a range of prices depending on the quality of the room and the time of year. Prices start at Rs 100 for a double, but go up to $8 for a luxury double room.

The next laneway heading inland has a few twists and turns, and a couple of cheap and decent places, in pleasant surroundings. *Villa Papillon* has singles/doubles for Rs 80/100 rising to Rs 325 ($6.50) if you want a private bathroom. *Heaven's Gate* is a family-run hotel with big clean rooms and similar prices.

Lakeside West (Pallo Patan) The real centre of Lakeside activity is beyond the Royal Palace at the point where the road forks around three chautaras and several enormous pipal trees. The *Hotel Hungry-Eye* (☎ 061-20908) is a popular survivor behind the restaurant of the same name, but it's a bit overpriced and lacks a nice garden. Singles/doubles are $20/30. The nearby *Snowland Hotel* (☎ 061-20384) is another long-time favourite, with decent-value rooms.

The road running eastward from the next chautara (beside the incongruous Cape Cod-style Hotel Meera) has a number of options, but the laneway itself is not as pleasant as some. First there are a couple of very simple, very basic, but cheap places – *Noble House* and *Island Cottage*. Further on there are a couple of well-run mid-range places – the *Iceland Guest House* and *Hotel Osho*. They're both pleasant and comfortable with prices starting at $6/10 for singles/doubles.

The next eastward lane (just before the next chautara) is very pleasant and retains some of the old Pokhara atmosphere, with a number of surviving traditional round thatched cottages plastered in red clay. There are a number of cheapies (around Rs 100) including the *Namaste Lodge*, *Quiet View Lodge*, *Nepali Cottage* and *Swiss Cottage*. The *French Cottage* is particularly pleasant for the price range.

Right on the main road, the *Hotel Mountain Top* (☎ 061-20779) is an unmissable four-storey monstrosity – the shape of things to come? I'm loathe to say it, but the comfortable rooms have superb views and they're not bad value. Singles/doubles with private bath are $20/29, and deluxe rooms are $30/40.

The only hotel on the western side of the road is the superbly situated *Hotel Fewa*, right on the edge of the lake. Unfortunately, the rooms are pretty run-down and expensive at $10/15 a single/double. There's also a cheap and basic annexe, which is definitely worth considering at Rs 75/100.

Back on the eastern side, the *Tranquillity Lodge* (☎ 061-21030) is a pleasant modern hotel set in a sunny garden. Rooms are large and comfortable, but a bit overpriced at $15/25 – there's certainly room for bargaining, especially out of season. The nearby *Temple Villa* (☎ 061-21203) is a small and pleasant lodge also in a quiet location. The operation, despite the claim of its Nepalese-German management, is considerably more Nepalese than German. Especially the plumbing. It is clean, however, and the

■ PLACES TO STAY

1 Shiva Guest House
2 Pinky Lodge
3 Hotel Lake View
5 Silver Mount Guest House
6 Camping Ground
7 Prince Guest House
8 Hong Kong Hotel & Restaurant
9 Hotel Woodland
12 Mountain Villa
17 Tranquillity Lodge
18 Butterfly Lodge
19 Temple Villa
20 Hotel Skyland
21 Hotel Monal
22 Yeti Guest House
23 Hotel Fewa
26 Future Way Guest House
27 Lovely Guest House
28 Hotel Mountain Top
29 Sunshine Hotel
30 Alka Guest House II
33 Alka Guest House I
36 Pushpa Lodge
37 Quiet View Lodge
38 Nepali Cottage
39 Moonland Guest House
40 Swiss Cottage
41 French Cottage
42 Namaste Lodge
46 Hotel Meera
47 Island Cottage
48 Noble House
49 Iceland Guest House
50 Osho Hotel
51 Hotel Sarowar
53 Snowland Hotel & Restaurant
57 Hungry–Eye Hotel & Restaurant
58 Dhaulagiri View Guest House
59 Tourist Bungalow
60 Villa Papillon
63 Lonely Guest House
64 New Hotel Angel
65 Heaven's Gate Guest House
66 Gauri Shanker Guest House
67 Gautama Guest House
68 Shanti Guest House
69 New Tourist Guest House
72 Hotel Kantipur & Restaurant

73 New Lake View Guest House
74 Everest Guest House
75 Hotel Lakeside & Restaurant
77 Dharma House
78 Stay Well Guest House
79 Kiwi Guest House
80 View Corner Lodge
81 Gurkha Lodge
82 Hotel Bedrock
83 Pilgrim Inn
84 Nightingale Lodge
86 Pumori Hotel
89 New Star Lodge
90 New Nanohana Lodge
91 Base Camp Resort
92 New Pokhara Lodge

▼ PLACES TO EAT

4 Al Pollo Restaurant
10 Little Tibetan Tea Garden
11 Marco Polo Restaurant
16 Moti Mahal Restaurant
25 Tea Time Restaurant
32 Beam Beam
34 Pokhara Maya
35 Chung Fa
43 Boomerang Restaurant
   & German Bakery
54 Cuckoo Restaurant
55 Café du Corner
56 Moondance Restaurant
61 Annapurna Restaurant
62 Laxman Restaurant
76 Lhasa Tibetan Restaurant
85 Le Bistro

OTHER

13 Supermarket
14 Nepal Grindlays Bank
15 Old Blues Night
24 Yeti Reservation Service
31 Okinawa Bookshop
44 Swiss Reservation Service
45 Memoire Tours & Travel
52 Student Travel & Tours
70 Boat Hire
71 Holy Bookshop
87 Collector's Bookshop
88 Kiwi Bookshop

To Sarangkot &
Banana Garden Lodge

LAKESIDE NORTH
(KHAHAREY)

To Bus
Station

LAKESIDE WEST
(PALLO PATAN)

Boat
Landing

LAKESIDE EAST
(AMMAT)

To Garden
Rest House

Royal
Palace

Small Temple

Phewa Tal

Pokhara
Lakeside

0   100   200 m

To Damside
& Airport

Pontoon to
Fish Tail Lodge

rooms are large and comfortable. They're a bit overpriced at $10/15, or $15/25 with private bath.

The *Tourist Bungalow*, at the end of the lane running east from the Hungry-Eye, is a reasonable basic hotel, but prices are high, unless bargaining is allowed. Singles/doubles are $5/8 with shared bath, or $10/15 with private bath.

Lakeside North (Khaharey) There are more places to stay beyond the intersection between the lakeside and main roads, both on the lakeside and on the main road itself. Once you get this far north you are tucked in under the foothills and don't get great views of the mountains.

The places along the main road don't appeal very much. Not surprisingly, the road lacks the peaceful rural atmosphere that the best parts of Pokhara have, and although the traffic is not particularly heavy, there are regular buses and taxis. Most of the hotels are new and are two or three-storey monstrosities with mid-range prices. Some of the possibilities include the *Hotel Woodland*, *Prince Guest House* and *Hong Kong Hotel*. One of the nicest is the *Mountain Villa* (☎ 061-21954) which has fairly typical prices at $16/20 for singles/doubles. The garden is pleasant and rooms have private bathrooms.

There are some peaceful good-value alternatives along the road that continues around the lake, including the *Silver Mount Guest House*, *Hotel Lake View*, *Pinky Lodge* and *Shiva Guest House*. One of the best is the *Banana Garden Lodge*, right on the outskirts, which is a bit of a walk from the restaurants, but has great views over the lake. Doubles are a bargain Rs 70.

PLACES TO EAT

Pokhara may not match the variety of food offered in Kathmandu but you can certainly eat well although, as usual in Nepal, a little caution is always wise. Upset stomachs are as common in Pokhara as anywhere else in the country.

The bazaar area has local restaurants, and other eating possibilities are found in the big hotels or amongst the numerous cheaper hotels particularly along Lakeside. At most of these travellers' restaurants you'll find the standard 'try anything' menu – which currently means lots of Italian dishes backed up by Indian, Nepalese, Mexican, 'Continental' and whatever other possibilities present themselves. The range is certainly an improvement over endless dhal bhats or thalis, but despite the apparent variation everything very quickly tastes the same! Most main meals cost from Rs 50 to Rs 100, and a bottle of beer is usually Rs 70.

There is not a great range of restaurants in the Damside area, as most people eat at their hotels. *KC's Restaurant* (no relation to KC's in Thamel) has a pleasant outdoor area and the classic range of Indonesian, Mexican, Indian and Italian dishes. Most are a reasonable Rs 80. In the same area, the *Rodee Restaurant* is also popular.

Most dining possibilities are along the main road skirting Lakeside. Starting at Lakeside East, the first possibility is the *Baba Restaurant* with its fine terrace overlooking the lake. The food is good and the service is snappy.

Continuing on you come to more places, all with the standard Nepalese travellers' menu and with open eating areas overlooking the lake. *Le Bistro* has everything from Mexican, Italian, Chinese and Indian to Nepalese and they seem to do a pretty good job of all of it. The apple pies are not bad either!

The *Lhasa Tibetan Restaurant* is a big outdoors place with a standard 'try-anything' menu, in addition to a number of Tibetan specialities. The food is very good and the service is fairly fast. *Sha bhakley*, a Tibetan meat pie, is Rs 70, and momo (meat/vegetable-filled pasta) is Rs 40. Chicken tikka kebabs with nan (bread) and salad for Rs 80 is good value, as are the pizzas and vegetable curries.

The *Annapurna Restaurant* has a nice garden and a 4 to 7 pm happy hour when a beer and chips costs Rs 55. A substantial curry costs from Rs 45.

The *Hungry-Eye* is a long-standing survivor and one of the biggest restaurants on Lakeside. The food is still good (the cakes for Rs 30 are excellent), but the service is chaotic and prices are a bit steep. Pizza ranges from Rs 74 to Rs 103 ($2) and a steak will set you back Rs 124 ($2.50).

Next door, the *Moondance Restaurant* has average prices and food, but a good atmosphere. There's a fireplace inside. The *Snowland* has an enormous menu featuring all the standard Indian, Chinese, Mexican and European dishes you can think of. They are all done remarkably well, but the Indian food is excellent.

The *Boomerang* is one of a new generation of places that have sprung up right on the edge of the lake. Given that this space should never have been developed, it must also be said that the opportunity has not been wasted. There's a nice garden dotted with chairs, tables and thatched shelters – and great views. It's a great place for breakfast (around Rs 50) or lunch, but dinner is less impressive – for a start you'll be inside, so you're less likely to be tolerant of the friendly but haphazard service. They have the normal eclectic menu and prices.

The *Chung Fa* has the best Chinese food in Pokhara, and its prices are very reasonable. Most main dishes are from Rs 50 to Rs 75. The 'drumstix of heaven' (Rs 75) are so good they have to be the work of the devil!

Beam Beam also fronts onto the lake, and although the garden is much smaller than the Boomerang's it is still very pleasant – in some ways cosier. The entire restaurant – inside and out – has a pleasant atmosphere, and the decor and layout is considerably more imaginative than most of the clone-like offerings along the lake. The service is excellent, and although the menu is pretty standard, the food is good.

At the top end of the spectrum, the bar and restaurant at the *Fish Tail Lodge* could be a fine place for a more expensive night out but the food is only average, the service, once you depart from the fixed meals, is appallingly slow and the clientele uninspiring. The fixed breakfast costs Rs 420 ($8.50), and an à la carte dinner for two will probably come to at least Rs 1000 ($20). The lakeside restaurants can turn out good food in half the time for a fraction of the cost.

ENTERTAINMENT

The Fish Tail Lodge puts on an excellent nightly cultural programme featuring Nepalese dancing by the Danfe Dance Club. It runs from 6 to 7 pm in winter, 6.30 to 7.30 pm in summer and the admission charge is Rs 75. Pokhara is not the place to go if you're in search of evening entertainment.

THINGS TO BUY

Pokhara's large Tibetan population sells many crafts and artefacts. Carpet-weaving is a major local industry for these people.

Saligrams, the fossilised sea creatures found north up the Kali Gandaki Valley, are a popular souvenir, but they are often radically overpriced. You shouldn't pay more than Rs 100 ($2).

Devotee spinning a prayer-wheel

Trekking Equipment

There are a number of rental shops in Pokhara, and prices are similar to those in Kathmandu – for example down sleeping bags and jackets are around Rs 10 to Rs 15 per day. The range of equipment is not so large however, so if you want anything out of the ordinary you are best off to bring it from Kathmandu.

GETTING THERE & AWAY

A number of travel agencies in Pokhara offer 'through' tickets or package-deal tickets to cities in India. These are dubious value at the best of times and a number of travellers have written to us complaining of various rip-offs perpetrated by unscrupulous Pokhara agents. These range from promises of tourist buses (in 1992 there were no tourist buses running to/from any of the border cities), to reserved seats that were definitely not reserved, and air-con train sleepers that turn out to be 2nd class.

See the Getting There & Away chapter for more information, but if you do decide to buy a package, make sure you get everything spelled out in a receipt, and hang on to the receipt. Buses through to Varanasi cost from Rs 500 ($10), and to Darjeeling Rs 700 ($14). Bus/train packages to Agra cost Rs 1850 ($37) with an air-con sleeper, Rs 850 ($17) 2nd class; and to Delhi Rs 1950 ($39) with air-con, Rs 1000 ($20) 2nd class.

Air

There are a number of daily services between Kathmandu and Pokhara. As the route is something of a cash cow all the private companies have jumped on the bandwagon; Everest Air is recommended. The flight takes less than an hour and costs $61. RNAC (☎ 061-71021) has a booking office at the airport; Everest Air and Nepal Airways are just across the road.

There are great Himalayan views if you sit on the right-hand side of the plane from Kathmandu to Pokhara, and on the left side from Pokhara to Kathmandu.

Bus

To/From Kathmandu The bus trip between Kathmandu and Pokhara takes seven or eight hours and most departures are early in the morning. The first stretch of road from Kathmandu to Naubise is in appalling condition, it's excellent from Naubise to Mugling, appalling from Mugling to Dumre, and fair from Dumre to Pokhara.

Public buses (from the bus station) cost Rs 70, the large tourist buses cost from Rs 120 ($1.50) and tourist minibuses cost from Rs 200 ($4). It's a bit dubious whether the extra expense of tourist buses is worthwhile. The minibuses are certainly quicker (often considerably scarier as a result), but the full-sized tourist buses aren't significantly different to the public express buses in terms of either time or comfort.

The tourist buses are, however, more convenient when you consider where they pick you up and drop you off. In Kathmandu they pick up and drop off at the Thamel end of Kantipath – although this could well change with the opening of the new Kathmandu Bus Terminal. In Pokhara, the tourist buses pick up Kathmandu-bound passengers outside their hotels, although all buses coming from Kathmandu terminate at the appalling main Pokhara bus station. Public buses all start and finish at the Pokhara bus station. Whichever bus you take it's wise to book at least a day ahead.

Apparently the tourist-bus operators were forced to unload at the bus station by the Damside area hotel owners who observed that most tourists chose to be dropped off at Lakeside. Now everyone is deposited in the squalid bus station where, tired and bewildered, they are fair game for a horde of extremely pushy touts – and the touts representing the Damside hotels are on an equal footing with everyone else.

There is absolutely no reason to get sucked in by these characters who will, apart from anything else, get a 50% commission from the hotel they take you to. The best thing you can do is grab a taxi to somewhere central on Lakeside, have a drink and a bite to eat at one of the restaurants and then ask to leave your bag somewhere safe while you check out some hotels for yourself.

To/From the Chitwan Public buses between Pokhara and Tadi Bazaar cost Rs 55, large tourist buses cost Rs 120 and minibuses cost from Rs 200 ($4). See the Royal Chitwan National Park section of the Terai chapter for more details.

To/From the Indian Border Buses to Sunauli/Bhairawa near the Indian border depart from the main Pokhara bus station, cost Rs 66 and take nine hours; buses for Birganj cost Rs 97; and buses for Nepalganj leave at 3.30 pm, take 15 hours and cost Rs 172 ($3.50). We have received a number of letters complaining that Pokhara agents sell overpriced tickets for alleged tourist buses to the border. There are no tourist buses; so while you do get picked up outside your hotel, you go from there to the bus station where everyone else gets on!

The road to India is called the Siddhartha Highway because it ends close to Lumbini where the Buddha, Siddhartha Gautama, was born. See the Getting There & Away chapter for more details on transport to India.

To/From Trekking Routes Pokhara is the base for popular treks such as the Annapurna Sanctuary Trek, Jomsom Trek, and the Annapurna Circuit, plus a number of other lesser known alternatives. A road is now being pushed through the hills from Pokhara to Baglung. In 1992 the road was finished to Kusma, and the whole road to Baglung was expected to be finished by the end of 1993. As it extends, the options for trekkers will obviously change, so get up-to-date advice. In 1992, those starting out for the Sanctuary or for Jomsom were catching buses (Rs 15), or taxis (Rs 250 to Rs 350, or $5 to $7) to Phedi and walking from there, or catching trucks that went as far as Chandrakot near Birethanti (Rs 40). The buses left from Bag Bazaar at the northern end of town.

GETTING AROUND

It's a long way between the bazaar and Lake-

side; a taxi will cost around Rs 80 ($1.75). It's a battle to extract fair prices when catching a taxi from Lakeside to the airport or bus station. Expect to pay at least Rs 50, possibly as much as Rs 100. Buses shuttle between the lake, airport and bazaar with per-person fares at around Rs 5.

There are lots of bicycle-rental places along the lake, by the dam or by the airport. Ordinary bikes typically cost from Rs 20 to Rs 30 per day, mountain bikes from Rs 80 to Rs 100. You can also rent children's bicycles. Pokhara looks deceptively flat but actually slopes steadily uphill as you move north. If you ride a bicycle from the lake to the Binde Basini Temple at the northern end of the bazaar area you'll find it's a wonderfully long freewheel on the way back.

Renting a motorbike costs from Rs 400 ($8) to Rs 500 ($10) per day – a bit more than in Kathmandu. Pokhara and the surrounding roads will not be improved by the growing number of motorbikes.

Around Pokhara

Pokhara is the starting or finishing point for some of Nepal's most popular treks like the Annapurna Circuit, the Jomsom Trek and the Annapurna Sanctuary Trek.

For those with limited time, less enthusiasm for walking or with small children in tow, the Pokhara area also has some fine short treks ranging from half-day and day walks to longer treks lasting anything from two or three days to a week.

DAY WALKS

The following walks can all be made in a day or less.

Sarangkot

This very pleasant walk up to Sarangkot, at an elevation of 1592 metres, is probably the most popular short excursion from Pokhara. It can be a good, pre-breakfast stroll to admire the mountain views, a leg-stretcher before you start out on a longer trek or a place you pass through on the first or last hours of one of the longer treks from Pokhara.

There are a number of places to stay or eat at Sarangkot – like the *Didi Lodge, Restaurant Sarangkot, Trekking Lodge* or *New Tourist Lodge* – so you can climb up to Sarangkot in the evening, stay overnight there and catch the view at dawn, or simply walk up for breakfast. The *View Top Restaurant & Lodge* has the prime views over the lake and pretty good food and it's extensively advertised on the steps up from the lake.

There are a number of routes to Sarangkot but the easiest way is to walk up from the Binde Basini Temple in Pokhara Bazaar and then head straight down from the top to the lake.

As you approach the temple from the bazaar, ignore the sign to Sarangkot just south of the temple and continue a little further to look at the temple before you start the walk.

From the temple head directly east and follow the vehicle track which runs most of the way up. You can short-cut many of the sharp corners and from where the vehicle track ends there is virtually a stairway to the top. On the way up you pass several places where women work at handlooms. It takes about 1½ to two hours to walk to Sarangkot from Binde Basini Temple, versus three or four hours from the lakeside area *if* you don't get seriously lost!

Sarangkot once had a fort or (kot) and its remains can be seen on the very top of the ridge above Sarangkot. There is a lookout point actually inside the old fort walls and the view of the Annapurnas to the north is superb.

The view back down over Phewa Tal is equally fine and from the top it only takes about two hours to walk down to the lake. It's easy to get lost on the way up from the lake but coming down from Sarangkot is straightforward: you make a very steep

Around Pokhara

0   2   4 km

descent, stone-staired all the way, down the hillside and through the forest. If you're exhausted when you reach the lake, there are often boatmen waiting to paddle you back to the lakeside lodge area.

An alternative to the Binde Basini Temple or Phewa Tal routes to the top is the walk from Bhairab Tole in Pokhara via the village of Gyarjati. Another hour's walk beyond Sarangkot will take you to Kaski or Kaskikot at 1788 metres. The hill is topped by an unprepossessing Bhagwati temple.

Kahun Danda

To the east of the bazaar area of Pokhara is Kahun Danda. *Danda* means ridge in Nepali. It takes about three hours to walk to this popular viewpoint at 1560 metres and there's a lookout tower on top of the ridge. The walk starts from the Mahendrapul Bridge and continues through Phulbari and up the gradual slope to the top. The remains of the 18th-century Kanhu Kot stands on the hilltop.

Mahendra Gufa

The limestone caves at Mahendra Gufa have stalactites and stalagmites and make a good destination for a two-hour walk north from Pokhara. The trail to the caves crosses the bridge just north of Bagar at the end of the bazaar and heads toward the village of **Batulechaur**. This village was once an important centre for growing citrus fruit until an epidemic killed all the citrus trees in the Pokhara Valley.

Rupa & Begnas Tals

These two lakes are the second and third largest in the valley, but few travellers visit them even though they're only 15 km east of the town.

Buses run regularly from Pokhara to Begnas Bazaar (Rs 6) the small market centre at the very end of the ridge which divides the two lakes. From there it's a pleasant stroll along the ridge to the other end of either lake.

SHORT TREKS
Annapurna Skyline Trek

The three or four-day Annapurna Skyline Trek has also been dubbed the 'Royal Trek' as Britain's Prince Charles walked it a few years ago. It's a fine trek to do with children, as it doesn't reach any great altitudes, doesn't entail any particularly long walking days and there's always plenty to see. (See the Trekking With Children section in the Trekking chapter for more information about this trek.) It's not a heavily trekked area, however, so there is no village inn accommodation along the route.

There are several variations on the route but basically the walk starts from the Kathmandu-Pokhara (Prithvi) Highway, a few km east of Pokhara, climbs up to a ridge and then for most of the walk follows ridges with fine views of the Annapurnas and back down into the Pokhara Valley.

The walk passes through small villages like Kalikathan, Shaklung and Chisopani before it drops down to the stream which feeds Rupa Tal. The final stretch is along the ridge separating Rupa Tal and Begnas Tal, emerging on the valley floor at Begnas Bazaar from where buses run to Pokhara.

Ghandrung to Ghorapani Trek

This week-long trek to the west of Pokhara also gives fine views of the Annapurnas. The walk essentially links the first few days of the Annapurna Sanctuary Trek as far as Ghandrung with the first few days of the Jomsom Trek as far as Ghorapani, then crosses between those two villages.

Near Ghorapani is Poon Hill, one of the finest lookout points in the region.

Ghachok Trek

An interesting two-day trek goes north from Pokhara to the interesting Gurung villages around Ghachok. The walk starts from Hyangja, with its Tibetan settlement, and crosses the Mardi Khola to Lhachok then Ghachok before turning south and returning to Pokhara through Batulechaur.

Naudanda Trek

This two-day walk, a shorter variation of the Ghandrung to Ghorapani Trek, takes you from Hyangja to Suikhet then to Naudanda and back to Pokhara through Kaski and Sarangkot. Naudanda has a variety of guest houses and shops.

The Himalaya & Mountaineering

The word *Himalaya* is Sanskrit for 'abode of snows' and Nepal's stretch of the Himalaya includes eight peaks over 8000 metres, including the highest of them all, mighty Mt Everest. Known to the Tibetans as Chomolongma and to the Nepalese as Sagarmatha the world's highest place was the overpowering attraction which drew in Nepal's first modern tourists – the mountaineers.

During the 1950s and 1960s most of the important Nepalese peaks were conquered, but just because it is no longer possible to be the first to set foot on top has certainly not diminished the attraction of Himalayan mountaineering. Climbing these giants today is often an adventurous sporting activity, whereas 30 years ago it required huge and well-sponsored expeditions.

There are 14 peaks over 8000 metres in the world, and of the 10 highest no less than eight are in Nepal, although some of the peaks actually straddle borders – Everest is in Nepal and China for example, Kanchenjunga is in Nepal and India. The heights of the 14 highest peaks, followed by the highest peaks in South America, North America, Africa, Russia, Antarctica, Europe, Australia and Britain can be seen in the World Mountain Heights diagram.

Nepal's magnificent mountains can be enjoyed in three distinctly different fashions. The easiest way is to simply look at them. This can be done by flying past them – either on regular flights or the daily tourist-season mountain flights. Or you can admire them from the various popular mountain viewpoints such as Nagarkot or Dhulikhel near Kathmandu or Sarangkot above Pokhara.

Getting to these viewpoints is covered in the appropriate chapters.

If simply looking at the mountains isn't enough you can get right in amongst them by trekking. Trekking is not mountain-climbing: apart from high passes on certain treks and the approach to the Everest Base Camp you are unlikely to go above 3500 metres. Trekking, however, does provide breathtaking views. Full details on trekking are given in the Trekking chapter.

Finally, there is real mountain-climbing and while getting to the top of an 8000-metre peak is strictly for the professionals, there are plenty of 'trekking peaks' which small-scale amateur expeditions can readily attempt. This is not to say that mountaineering in Nepal can be easy – climbing mountains this high always involves an element of risk – but getting to the top of a worthwhile Himalayan peak doesn't necessarily require millionaire status or big commercial backers.

Mountain Flights Every morning during the clear dry-season months, Royal Nepal Airlines' and Everest Air's mountain flights offer panoramic dawn views of the Himalaya. Passengers on the Everest Air flight are all guaranteed a window seat, and the hourlong flight from Kathmandu costs $95. If the weather is clear, the views are stunning.

MOUNTAINEERING

Mountaineering became a fashionable pursuit in Europe during the second half of the 1800s and, having knocked off the great Alpine peaks, the much greater heights of the Himalaya were an obvious new challenge.

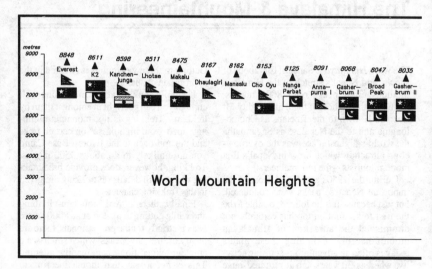

World Mountain Heights

An English gentleman named WW Graham made a mountaineering visit to Nepal in 1883 and managed to reach the top of a 6000-metre peak. Tom Longstaff, another Englishman, climbed 7215-metre Trisuli in 1907 and for the next 20 years this remained the highest summit reached anywhere in the world. An Italian attempt on K2 in Pakistan two years later was the first of the huge Himalayan expeditions with hundreds of porters.

First Attempts on Everest
During the 1920s and 1930s, reaching the top of Mt Everest came to be seen as the major goal, but apart from the difficulties inherent in reaching such heights there were also political constraints. Nepal continued to be a totally secluded country and attempts on Everest were all made from the Tibetan side of the range.

British assaults were made in 1921, 1922 and 1924. The 1922 expedition used oxygen to reach 8326 metres, while the 1924 expedition fell just 300 metres short of the top, reaching 8572 metres without the use of oxygen. Apart from numerous climbers and support staff, the 1924 expedition utilised no

less than 350 porters; such huge expeditions set a pattern which was to continue until recent years.

One of the enduring mysteries of mountaineering history has its origins in 1925 when the British climbers Mallory and Irvine disappeared within sight of the top. Did they reach it? We will never know. However, Mallory did leave behind that famous explanation for why mountaineers do what they do – he said he was climbing Everest 'because it's there'. Further expeditions followed through the remaining years of the '20s and '30s but no real progress was made, although the 8000-metre level was breached on a number of occasions. Maurice Wilson added his name to the Everest legends, and the Everest death roll, when he died during a bizarre solo attempt on the mountain in 1934.

Post WW II Attempts
The West's new-found affluence after its recovery from WW II, together with more modern equipment, vastly improved oxygen apparatus, new mountaineering skills and the reopening of Nepal led to a golden age of Himalayan mountaineering.

There hadn't been any Himalayan mountaineering in the 1940s, and through the '30s only two significant summits had been reached – Kamet at 7761 metres in 1931 and Nanda Devi at 7822 metres in 1936. Interestingly, the Kamet summit group included HW Tilman and the Nanda Devi group included Eric Shipton, whose descriptions of their trekking and mountaineering experiences helped to spark the current interest in trekking. Shipton was said to have planned his lightweight expeditions on the back of an envelope.

The prewar failures were abruptly reversed in the 1950s, beginning with Maurice Herzog's valiant French expedition on Annapurna in 1950. His team's horrific storm-plagued struggle down the mountain turned an extremely difficult climb into an epic of human endurance – but for the first time mountaineers had reached the top of an 8000-metre peak. After descending the mountain they then had a month-long struggle through the monsoon with the expedition doctor having to perform amputations of frostbitten fingers and toes as they went.

Herzog's book *Annapurna* (Jonathan Cape, London, 1952) remains a classic of mountaineering literature. It's indicative of how things have changed in Nepal that Herzog had trouble even finding his way to the mountain! Today thousands of trekkers pass by the Annapurnas every year and, where Herzog once had to search desperately for supplies for his hungry climbers, there are now comfortable lodges offering bed and breakfast to trekking parties.

Conquest of Everest
Everest was also getting its share of attention, and in 1951 a climber who would soon become very famous took part in an exploratory expedition to the mountain – he was New Zealand climber Edmund Hillary. Another name, soon to be equally famous, appeared on the list of climbers on the Swiss Everest expedition of 1952 when Sherpa climber Norgay Tensing reached 7500 metres. The conquest of Everest finally took place in 1953 when the British team led by John Hunt put those two climbers, Tensing and Hillary, on top of the world's highest peak.

Repeat performances came much easier than the first time and the second success came in 1956 when a Swiss party reached the

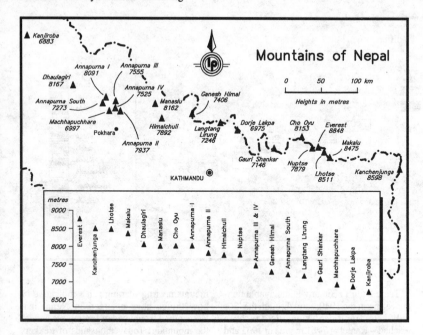

summit. In 1960 it was the People's Republic of China who managed the feat, this time from the Tibetan side. A huge US expedition with the climbers backed up by nearly 1000 porters got to the top in 1963 and in 1965 it was the turn of an Indian expedition. Another huge party, this time from Japan, was on top in 1970 and one utterly fearless climber ensured his place in the Everest history books by making an extremely rapid descent on skis! Further attempts included the massive Italian expedition which reached the summit in 1973 and the victorious Japanese women's party which celebrated International Women's Year by putting a woman climber on top.

The success of the 1953 British expedition to Everest had begun a trend for larger and larger expeditions. Proponents of this form of 'siege' mountaineering believed that this was the only way to conquer the great Himalayan peaks. A series of camps would be established higher and higher up the moun-

tain with constant 'carries' of supplies eventually resulting in climbers reaching the top. This theory of Himalayan climbing reached its ultimate expression with the '73 Italian Everest expedition when 64 climbers were backed up by 100 sherpas and nearly 2000 porters! Helicopters ferried supplies and, hardly surprisingly, this massive effort put nine people on the summit in two parties.

The few climbers who did reach the summit from these expeditions required a huge pyramid of supporters below them. The effect on the country could be devastating as forests fell to provide firewood for the expeditions and vast amounts of mountaineering equipment and garbage were left behind. The Everest Base Camp has been aptly titled the 'world's highest garbage dump'. Lightweight expeditions had been successful, but Helmut Bhul's solo climb to the summit of Nanga Parbat in Pakistan and his lightweight expedition to the top of Broad Peak were looked upon more as aberrations requiring superhuman effort than as pointers towards a different way of doing things.

New-Style Mountaineering

Inevitably, a reaction set in and, while the checklist of important summits was methodically knocked over by huge and expensive expeditions, young climbers were perfecting a wholly different style of climbing on the peaks of Europe and North America. Getting to the top was no longer the sole aim, you had to reach the top with style.

The 'easy' ridge routes to the top were ignored while climbers scaled the most difficult faces using a combination of athletic skills and high-tech equipment. British mountaineer Chris Bonnington was the chief protagonist for this style of climbing and his brilliant conquest of the southern face of Annapurna in 1970, followed by an expertly organised race up the hitherto unthinkable south-western face of Everest in 1975 were supreme examples of this trend.

Lightweight Expeditions

Attempting the difficult faces and routes was one trend but lightweight expeditions were another. In 1978 the Austrian expedition to Everest put Reinhold Messner and Peter Habler on top without the use of oxygen. Once this 'impossible' feat had been achieved other climbers also found they could reach the top without oxygen and, freed from the necessity of carting heavy oxygen cylinders up the mountains, much smaller parties could attempt the big mountains. Only two years later Reinhold Messner made a solo ascent of Everest, climbing the North Face on the Tibetan side in the fastest ascent ever made.

In early 1990 Tim McCartney-Snape, an Australian, went several steps further. He walked and climbed from sea level at the Bay of Bengal, to the top of Mt Everest, alone and without oxygen.

Mountaineering Today

Himalayan mountaineering today not only provides a great deal of free publicity for tourism to Nepal, it's also a very useful source of income for the government. If you want to attempt a Himalayan peak there's a fee to be paid to the government even before you get your climbing permit, and the higher and more famous the mountain the higher the fee that must be paid. Everest is currently $50,000 and is usually 'booked out' for years ahead. Annually, 600 to 900 climbers come to Nepal to try their luck, but there are still many sizable peaks which have not been successfully climbed, and some which haven't even been attempted.

Today mountaineering is a sport pure and simple – there's no noise made about its scientific value. In fact the successes and failures of the various expeditions are regularly reported on the sports pages of the *Rising Nepal*. Of course it's also a decidedly dangerous sport: over 200 climbers have reached the top of Everest (some of them three, four and even five times), but nearly 100 climbers have died in the attempt. Some other mountains in Nepal have an even worse record: almost as many climbers have lost their lives climbing Annapurna as have managed to reach the top.

Permits To climb any of the mountain peaks that are open to expeditions, a mountaineering team should obtain permission from the Ministry of Tourism's Mountaineering Section (☎ 01-211286), Tripureshwar, Kathmandu. Every team must be represented by a licensed trekking agency in Nepal.

TREKKING PEAKS

There are many smaller mountains in Nepal called 'trekking peaks' (ranging from 5587 to 6654 metres) which keen trekkers can climb. Most Everest Base Camp trekkers make the ascent of Kala Pattar for the view of Everest and at 5545 metres this would be a substantial peak anywhere else in the world. In his book *Many People Come, Looking, Looking* (The Mountaineers, Seattle, 1980) Galen Rowell tells of a little jaunt up a 6500-metre peak as a prelunch sidetrip while crossing the Thorong La pass on the Annapurna Circuit trek.

The trekking peaks are:

Peak	Height
Chulu East	6584 metres
Chulu West	6419 metres
Hiunchuli	6441 metres
Imja Tse	6183 metres
Kangja Chuli	5844 metres
Khongma Tse (or Mehra)	5849 metres
Kusum Kanguru	6367 metres
Kwangde	6011 metres
Lubuje	6119 metres
Mardi Himal	5587 metres
Mera Peak	6654 metres
Paldor Peak	5896 metres
Parchemuche	6187 metres
Pisang	6091 metres
Pokalde	5806 metres
Ramdung	5925 metres
Singu Chuli (or Fluted Peak)	6501 metres
Tharpu Chuli (or Tent Peak)	5663 metres

By Himalayan standards these are minor peaks, but some of them provide challenging snow and ice climbing. To climb trekking peaks, a permit is required from the Nepal Mountaineering Association, Kamaladi, PO Box 1435, Kathmandu.

Fees (or royalties, as they are often referred to) depend on the altitude of the peak, starting at $1000 for peaks below 6501 metres and rising $500 for every 500-metre increment to $3000 for peaks from 7501 to 8000 metres.

Climbing gear can be bought or rented in Kathmandu, and while tents, stoves, sleeping bags and down gear should pose no problems, socks, shoes, clothing and freeze-dried food are likely to be harder to find.

Bill O'Connor's book *The Trekking Peaks of Nepal* (Crowood Press, 1989) gives a detailed description of climbing each of the peaks plus the trek to the mountain. Equipment, applications, procedures, weather, health and other matters are also comprehensively covered.

Trekking

For the people in the hills of Nepal walking has always been the main method of getting from A to B. There were no roads into the hill country from the Terai and India until the Tribhuvan Highway to Kathmandu was constructed in the 1950s. Pokhara was not connected to the outside world by road until the 1970s. Even today the vast majority of villages can only be reached on foot, although every year the roads penetrate further into the hills and mountains.

The Nepalese people, making their way from village to village on the well-worn trails, were only joined by Western visitors when Himalayan mountaineering came into vogue. It was the accounts of those pioneering mountaineers, who had to make their way to the base of the great peaks on foot, which inspired the first trekkers. The word 'trekking' was first applied to Nepalese hiking trips in the 1960s and the enormous popularity of trekking today has developed since that time.

Trekking in Nepal means a walking trip following trails, many of which have been used for communication and trade for many years. Trekking is not mountaineering. Some of the popular trekking trails are used by mountaineering expeditions on their approach marches, but most are used by Nepalese for everyday travel and trade. A trekking trip can be any length you choose – there are popular short treks around the Kathmandu and Pokhara valleys which only take a day to complete, there are short treks of two or three days, or there are longer treks lasting from a week to a month. You could even string a series of popular treks together and walk for months on end.

Three major attractions account for trekking's enormous popularity – the scenery, the people, and the flora and fauna.

Scenery

There is no question that Nepal offers some of the most spectacular and beautiful scenery in the world. Of course it's the mountains that are best known, and the exploits of mountain photographers have made Everest, Machhapuchhare, Ama Dablam, and other mountains instantly recognisable to keen walkers all over the world. Nepal has a near monopoly on the world's highest peaks – eight of the 10 highest are found in Nepal and a number of the popular trekking routes offer you wonderful views or even visits to the base camps used by mountaineering expeditions. Mountain flights may give you superb views, but there is absolutely nothing like waking up on a crystal-clear Himalayan day and seeing an 8000-metre peak towering over you, seemingly just an arm's length away.

The mountains may be the most obvious scenic attraction, but trekkers soon find there are plenty of other treats for the eye. The hill country is often breathtakingly beautiful with pretty little villages, attractive houses, neat fields and interesting temples. As you climb higher the subtropical lowlands give way to meadows, stretches of forest, swift-flowing rivers and deep canyons before you reach the cold and often barren regions at the foot of the great peaks. The views change with the seasons, whether it is the cycle of planting and harvesting or the brilliant displays of wild flowers in spring and autumn.

People

Nepal is a country of contrasts and this extends to the people as well as the landscape. Trekking in Nepal is not like hiking through the often uninhabited countryside of a North American, Australian or European national park. People are constantly passing by on the trails, and along many routes there are regularly spaced villages to pause in. The villages and their people can be as interesting as the scenery, as you meet people from many of Nepal's wide diversity of ethnic groups. The outgoing nature, general friendliness and good humour of the Nepalese is often commented on by trekkers. Colourful festivals can make trekking at certain times of year even more enjoyable.

Of course, your trekking companions can be another important part of the trekking experience. A long trek can be a great opportunity to enjoy yourself with good friends. Despite stories you may have heard about the Himalaya being overrun with hordes of trekkers the reality is very different. Certainly there may be many trekkers on the most popular routes, particularly the Jomsom Trek, but compared to the crowds visiting national parks in the West the numbers are often minuscule. The trails of Nepal are a long way from being overcrowded.

About Trekking

Although Nepal offers plenty of opportunity for short treks lasting a day or less, most treks last considerably longer. From Pokhara or around the Kathmandu Valley you can make a variety of two, three or four-day walks, but Nepal's most popular treks take at least a week. For the very popular Everest Base Camp and Annapurna Circuit treks you have to allow three weeks. Don't take on one of these classic long treks too lightly: the end of the first week is not the ideal time to discover you're not keen on walking.

The combined Kathmandu Environment Education Project (KEEP) and Himalayan Rescue Association (HRA) Trekkers' Information Centre in the Hotel Tilicho, near the immigration office on Tridevi Marg, Kathmandu gives free, up-to-date information on trekking conditions, health risks and how to minimise your impact on the environment. They also have useful notebooks with up-to-date information from other trekkers, and an excellent notice board.

WHEN TO GO
Put very simply the best time to trek is from October to May (the dry season) and the worst time is from June to September (the monsoon). This generalisation does not allow for the peculiarities of individual treks, however. Some people even claim that the undeniable difficulties of trekking during the monsoon are outweighed by the virtual absence of Western trekkers.

The first two months of the dry season, October and November, are probably the ideal period for trekking in Nepal. The air, freshly washed by the monsoon rains, is crystal clear, the mountain scenery is superb and the weather is still comfortably warm. At low altitudes in October it can actually be quite balmy, and trekkers may find they complete a whole trek in T-shirt weather.

December, January and February are still good months for trekking, but the cold can be bitter at high altitudes. Getting up to the Everest Base Camp can be a real endurance test and the Thorung La pass on the Annapurna Circuit is sometimes blocked by snow.

March and April offer better weather but at the price of hazy visibility. By this time of year the weather has been dry for a long time and dust is starting to hang in the air. The poorer quality of the Himalayan views is compensated for by the superb wild flowers, particularly Nepal's wonderful rhododendrons.

By May it starts to get very hot, dusty and humid, and the monsoon is definitely just around the corner. From June to September the trails can be dangerously slippery due to the monsoon rains, and raging rivers often wash away bridges and stretches of trail. Nepal's famous jukha (leeches) are an unpleasant feature of the wet season, but with care, trekking can still be possible in the wet season and there are certainly fewer trekkers on the trail.

TRAIL CONDITIONS
Most trekkers want to get away from roads as quickly as possible, and although roads reach further into the hill country every year, it is still possible to leave them quickly behind. Nepalese trails are often steep and taxing. The old adage that the shortest path between two points is a straight line appears to have been firmly drummed into the Nepalese, irrespective of any mountains which

may get in the way! In compensation, the trails are often very well maintained. Busy trails up steep slopes are often flagged with stones every step of the way.

Walking the trails of Nepal often entails a great deal of altitude gain and loss, and it is as well to remember that even the base of the great mountains of the Himalaya can be very high. Most treks which go through populated areas stick to between 1000 metres and 3000 metres, although the Everest Base Camp Trek and the Annapurna Circuit trek both reach over 5000 metres. On high treks like these it is wise to ensure adequate acclimatisation, and the old maxim of 'walking high, sleeping low' is good advice: your night halt should be at a lower level than the highest point reached in the day.

A typical day's walk lasts from five to seven hours and involves a number of ascents and descents. It's rare to spend much time at the same level. On an organised camping trek the day is run to a remarkably tight schedule. A typical pattern would be: up at 6 am, start walking at 7 am, stop for lunch at 10 am, start after lunch at noon, stop walking at 3 pm. The Nepalese rise early, eat

very little for breakfast, eat a large lunch in the late morning and a second meal before dark, then retire early – you are best off following a similar schedule. Although a little rudimentary knowledge of Nepali will help to make your trek easier and more interesting, finding your way is rarely difficult on the major trekking routes and English is becoming more widely spoken.

ACCOMMODATION & FOOD

Organised treks camp each night and all you have to do is crawl into your tent. Even erecting the tent is handled by the trekking group who put it up for you at the site selected by your *sirdar* or group leader.

Independent trekkers usually stay in the small lodges, guest houses or village inns which have appeared along almost all the main trails. At first this sort of accommodation was simply a matter of local teahouses letting you unroll your sleeping bag on the floor. Today along some of the most popular trails the lodges are quite luxurious and offer private rooms, extensive menus and even showers. It's even possible to make quite long treks without bringing a sleeping bag with you.

On a typical organised trek your only concern with food is sitting down to eat it. The porters carry all the food along with them, and there will be a cook with well-drilled assistants who can turn out meals of often stunning complexity. Baking a cake on a campfire is just one of the tricks trekking party cooks like to perform to display their virtuosity. Hopefully, however, this trick is on the wane, because organised groups should always cook with kerosene to avoid putting further pressure on Nepal's shrinking forests.

Independent trekkers will usually find places to eat along the most popular trails, although it's often wise to carry some emergency food supplies like cheese, dried fruit or chocolate bars. Food may vary from dhal and rice at simple teahouses to surprisingly good meals on the more popular trails.

The standard of cuisine on the Jomsom Trek is so high that it has been dubbed 'the apple pie trail' as that dish features on so many village-inn menus. It's surprising how many places even have cold beer available as well; before you complain about the price contemplate the fact that somebody had to carry that bottle of beer all the way there and will probably have to carry the empty bottle back again!

If you're going right off the beaten track and exploring areas which have only recently been opened, like Makalu and Kanchenjunga in the east or Jumla and Dolpo in the west, you must be very self-sufficient. In these relatively untouched areas there is probably very little surplus food for sale and the practice of catering to Western trekkers has not yet developed.

HEALTH

See the Health section in the Facts for the Visitor chapter for more information on trekking health. Acute mountain sickness or altitude sickness is the major concern on high-altitude treks, but for the majority of trekkers health problems are likely to be minor ones, such as stomach upsets. While paranoia is not required, common-sense precautions are.

Basic rules for healthy trekking include taking care that water is always boiled, or adequately treated. The best method is to treat water with iodine, as this is safe and does not require the use of firewood or kerosene. Diarrhoea is one of the comparatively minor problems which can ruin a trek so take care in what you eat and make sure your medical kit has a medication such as Lomotil or Immodium. The food on an organised trekking expedition is unlikely to cause any problems, but village-inn trekkers are at risk.

At high altitudes the burning power of the sun is much stronger, so make sure you have a pair of good sunglasses, and a maximum-protection sunscreen for your skin. Blisters can take the fun out of trekking so make sure your shoes and socks are comfortable and come prepared with Band-aids and mole-skins just in case they aren't. Many people suffer from knee and ankle strains, particularly if they are carrying their own pack. If

you have a predisposition for these injuries, carry elastic supports or bandages.

Make sure you are in good health before departing as there is very little medical attention along the trails and rescue helicopters are not only very expensive but usually must be paid for in advance! See the individual treks for more information on possible medical assistance. In general, Himalayan hospitals can offer only very limited facilities and expertise.

The Himalayan Rescue Association (HRA) can offer valuable advice on trekking medical matters and has an excellent pamphlet on acute mountain sickness. It shares the Trekkers' Information Centre in the Hotel Tilicho, on Tridevi Marg, not far from Kathmandu's immigration office.

SAFETY

In the mid-70s it was possible to claim that Nepal was totally immune from theft, assaults and other assorted vices of contemporary Western 'civilisation'. Unfortunately that claim can no longer be made and in a number of places in Nepal it would not be wise to trek alone, and a sharp eye should be kept on your possessions.

If you're intending to trek independently and don't have a partner it's usually relatively easy to find one. Notice boards around Kathmandu or Pokhara often have signs up from people looking for partners. In Kathmandu, the Trekkers' Information Centre and the Kathmandu Guest House have particularly good boards.

Usually, the further you get from roads and population centres the fewer problems there will be, but several basic rules should be followed. Don't trek alone, don't make ostentatious displays of valuable possessions and don't leave lodge doors unlocked or valuables unattended. If you hire porters make sure they are reputable by hiring them through an agency or with good recommendations. A porter or guide found at a street corner can easily disappear along the trail with all your gear.

Walking at high altitudes on rough trails can be dangerous. Watch your footing on

Minimising Your Impact

Recently, the ecological impact of trekkers in the Himalaya has become a major concern. While trekkers certainly contribute to the problems of firewood use and the appearance of rubbish along the trails they are certainly not the only culprits. The depletion of forests is a severe problem throughout the Himalaya and, as modern non-biodegradable packaging becomes increasingly common in Nepal, garbage is starting to appear along village trails untravelled by Western trekkers.

On the positive side, trekking plays a vital role in the economy of many mountain areas. Without the influx of cash, many more people would be forced to abandon the villages for the cities, which are already suffering the negative results of rapid population increase. A number of impressive organisations are attempting to deal with the problems, including the Annapurna Conservation Area Project (ACAP), which has done a great deal to encourage sustainable development in the Annapurna region.

Trekkers can definitely do their part to aid Himalayan conservation, however. You can minimise the use of firewood by staying in lodges that use kerosene or fuel-efficient wood stoves and solar-heated hot water. Avoid using large open fires for warmth – wear additional clothing instead – and keep showers to a minimum if wood is burnt to produce the hot water.

Consolidate cooking time (and wood consumption) by ordering the same items at the same time. Dhal bhat is usually readily available for large numbers of people, does not require special lengthy cooking time, and is nutritious and inexpensive. Remember that local meals are prepared between 10 and 11 am, so eating then will not require an additional fire. Treat your water with iodine, rather than boiling it.

Those travelling with organised groups should ensure that kerosene is always used for cooking, that toilet tents are properly organised, and that rubbish is carried out. Check on the company's policies before you sign up.

Independent trekkers should always carry their garbage out or burn it, although you should remember that the fireplace in a Nepalese home is a sacred institution and throwing rubbish into it would be a grave insult.

Toilet paper is a particularly unpleasant sight along trails: if you must use it, carry it out in a plastic bag until you can burn it. Better yet, carry a small plastic trowel to bury the shit (well away from any streams) and a small plastic water container so that – like the vast majority of people in the world – you can clean yourself with water instead.

Before bargaining, try to establish a fair price by talking to guides and other travellers. Paying too much feeds inflation, while paying too little denies the locals a reasonable return for their efforts and investments. Not everything is subject to bargaining: respect standard food, bed and entry charges and follow the going rate for services.

Bargaining should never be treated as a matter of life and death importance – it's usually regarded as an integral part of a transaction and is, ideally, an enjoyable social exchange. Nepalese do not ever appreciate aggressive behaviour. A good deal is when both parties are happy. Try to remember that Rs 5 might quite a difference to the seller, but in hard currency amounts to $0.10.

Regrettably, some nationalities have established such a reputation for unpleasant, mean-minded bargaining that they are no longer welcome in many lodges or restaurants. Israelis will find that previous hard-core shoestring 'travellers' have created a negative impression that may well take a long time to erase.

Don't encourage begging children; tell them *Na raamro*, 'Not good', and remember that hand-outs can create dependence and other negative side effects. (See Begging in the Facts for the Visitor chapter.)

Trekkers should respect Nepalese culture and traditions. Dress modestly – women should not wear short or revealing clothes (loose pants or a calf-length dress are ideal) and men should not go shirtless. Don't put down what you may see as shortcomings in the Nepalese life style; remember life in the West has many problems and drawbacks as well. Every visitor's maxim should be: Nepal is here to change you, not for you to change it.

For more information on minimising your impact, visit the Trekkers' Information Centre run by KEEP and HRA. Most Thamel bookshops also stock *Trekking Gently in the Himalaya* by Wendy Brewer Lama (Rs 30) a small brochure that has essential tips for trekkers. ∎

slippery trails, and never underestimate the capacity of the weather to change extremely rapidly for the worse – at any time of the year. If you are crossing high passes where snow is a possibility, never walk with less than three people, carry a supply of emergency rations, have a map and compass (and know how to use them), and have sufficient equipment to deal with cold, wet, blizzard conditions.

All embassies and consulates strongly recommend that their citizens register with them before they head off into the boondocks. They have standard forms that record your name, rough itinerary, insurance details and next of kin, and can obviously speed up a search, or a medical evacuation. These are usually kept at the embassies' reception desks and take two minutes to complete. Several keep registration forms at the KEEP/HRA Trekkers' Information Centre in the Hotel Tilicho on Tridevi Marg.

Preparations in Nepal

PERMITS
Travel in Nepal is still highly restricted and your visa only allows you to visit the areas around the Kathmandu and Pokhara valleys, Royal Chitwan National Park and the routes covered by drivable roads. If you intend to strike out more than a days' walk from the main roads, you must first apply for a trekking permit.

If you are trekking with an organised group this will be arranged for you. If you're doing it yourself it is possible to obtain the permit the same day, although you must make your application as early as possible in the morning. Be prepared for a distinctly tiring battle with bureaucracy.

Trekking permits are issued in Kathmandu and Pokhara, and can only be extended in those cities.

Trekking permits can be obtained from Kathmandu's immigration office. It's open from 10.30 am to 2 pm Sunday to Thursday and 10.30 am to noon on Fridays for applications, although you have to go back later to retrieve your passport. It's wise to start the process early as it can be time-consuming.

There are regular trekking permit inspection points along most trails and you won't get far out of Kathmandu or Pokhara before being stopped and turned back if you don't have one. Trekking fees vary depending on the area you intend to explore. If you plan to trek in two different areas, two trekking permits are needed. Two passport photos are required with each application:

Area	Fee
• Annapurna, Everest, Langtang, Gorkha, Jumla & others	first four weeks – $5 per week; after four weeks – $10 per week
• Kanchenjunga & Dolpo	first four weeks – $10 per week; after four weeks – $20
• Mustang	$700 for 10 days
• Manaslu	$75 per week

Finally, if you plan to trek through a national park, wildlife reserve or conservation area – this will be necessary in the case of the Mt Everest, Langtang and Annapurna treks – you will need to pay a park entrance fee. Currently, there is a Rs 650 ($13) entry fee for the Sagarmatha and Langtang national parks and a Rs 200 entry fee to the Annapurna Conservation Area, which encompasses the main treks from Pokhara. An additional fee is levied for video cameras that are taken into the national parks. This is currently an outrageous Rs 10,000 ($200). The only alternative is to leave the camera at the entrance, and to collect it on your return.

MONEY
Except perhaps on the Jomsom Trek, changing foreign money is likely to be very difficult if not impossible. Bring enough money for the whole walk and carry it in small denominations.

EQUIPMENT

It's always best to have your own equipment since you will be familiar with it and know for certain that it works. If there is some equipment which you do not have, however, it can probably be bought or rented from one of Nepal's many trekking shops. The equipment available is usually of excellent quality and the rental charges are generally not excessive, but large deposits are often required (usually equal to a generous valuation of the equipment itself). Never leave your passport as a deposit.

In 1993 and depending on quality, rates were as follows:

Equipment	Rate
mattress	Rs 5 to Rs 6
sleeping bag	Rs 15 to Rs 25
down jacket	Rs 10 to Rs 15
pack	Rs 15 to Rs 20
tent	Rs 20 to Rs 70

Kathmandu is still the centre for trekking equipment and there are many outlets around Thamel. These days Pokhara also has some trekking equipment places and so do popular destinations like Namche Bazaar. The equipment available in Nepal used to be mainly expedition leftovers and at Namche Bazaar, the important 'last stop before Mt Everest', this will still be the case. In Kathmandu, however, there is now a great deal of new equipment obviously brought into the country purely for resale purposes.

Clothing

The clothing you require depends on where and when you trek. If you're going up to the Everest Base Camp in the middle of winter you must be prepared for very cold weather with down gear, mittens and the like. On the other hand, if you're doing a short, low-altitude trek early or late in the season the weather is likely to be fine for T-shirts and perhaps a sweater to pull on in the evenings. If you don't have your own down jacket and pants, these can be rented in Kathmandu; however, they may not be particularly clean.

Apart from ensuring you have adequate clothing to keep warm, the important considerations are that your feet are comfortable and that you can keep dry if it rains or snows. Uncomfortable shoes or blistered feet are the worst possible trekking discomfort. Make sure your shoes fit well and are comfortable for long periods. For most trekking, running shoes are quite adequate, but they're inadequate if you come to snow or wet weather.

Books & Maps

Books and maps are readily available in Kathmandu and Pokhara bookshops. See Lonely Planet's *Trekking in the Nepal Himalaya* by Stan Armington for the complete story on trekking. It has considerable advice on equipment selection, an excellent medical section oriented towards trekking and the mountains, and comprehensive route descriptions not only of the popular treks covered more briefly in this book, but also of a number of interesting but less heavily used treks.

The Schneider Maps, named after their cartographer, are the best available trekking maps but they're mainly for the Everest trek and are expensive. The locally produced Mandala series now has the colour maps *Helambu & Langtang* and *Round Annapurna*, as well as the older dyeline maps for other regions.

All the trekking maps, including the Schneider maps, suffer from a number of problems. For a start the trails change faster than the maps: you may well find a new trail in use or a route change necessitated by an avalanche or flood. Equally disorienting is the fact that Nepalese villages are often hard to pinpoint (they sprawl over hills and down valleys) and often have very different names depending on which map you look at or whom you ask. Treat any map with suspicion.

Other Gear

In winter or at high altitudes a high-quality sleeping bag may be necessary. However, if you are going on an organised trek check exactly what equipment is supplied: it's a waste of time bringing your own sleeping bag if the company supplies one. If you need to hire one, it may be grubby; check for fleas or worse.

Rain is unlikely during most of the trekking season, but waterproof gear or at least an umbrella is necessary if there is rain or snow. The rainy season also brings leeches and it's nice to have some salt or matches to deal with them.

Take a torch (flashlight) for those inevitable calls of nature on moonless nights.

Cigarettes and matches are popular small gifts to have with you on treks, but beware of encouraging children begging for 'one rupee' or a 'school pen' – see the earlier section on Minimising Your Impact.

INDEPENDENT TREKKING

At one extreme, independent trekking can mean simply trekking from lodge to lodge along the main trekking trails with one or more friends. All you need is your trekking permit and your walking gear and off you go. The popular trekking trails all have accommodation along their entire length. People have even walked the complete Annapurna Circuit without a sleeping bag, although this is not recommended.

For most moderately fit people, guides and porters are not necessary on the Annapurna or Mt Everest treks. A good guide/porter will enhance your experience, but a bad one will just make life more complicated.

There are many factors that influence how much you spend on an an independent trek. In most places, accommodation costs around Rs 15, a simple meal of rice and dhal around Rs 25 – note that on the Annapurna Circuit, prices can be twice as high. After a long day hiking, however, most people will weaken when confronted by a cold beer or an apple pie and these will start to add to your costs. Even with luxury items thrown in, however, it will be difficult to spend $10 a day. Between $5 and $7 would be a more usual average.

According to some studies, competition on the Annapurna Circuit is so intense, and the need for money so desperate, that lodges have been known to provide food and accommodation at below cost. Remember this – and the real value of the rupee – if you start to get carried away with bargaining.

Guides & Porters

If you can't (or don't want to) carry a decent-sized pack, if you have children or elderly people in your party, or if you plan to walk in regions where you have to carry in food and tents, help should be considered. It's fairly easy to find guides and porters, but it is hard to be certain of their honesty and ability.

Unless you have first-hand recommendations, you're best to hire someone through a guest house or agency. Arranging expeditions where guides, porters, tents and food are required can be very time-consuming and can quickly become extremely complicated. In such cases you're definitely best off putting this in the hands of a professional.

There is a distinct difference between a guide and a porter. A guide will speak English, know the terrain and the trails, and supervise porters, but will probably not be interested in carrying a load or doing menial tasks like cooking and putting up tents. Porters are generally hired for load-carrying, although an increasing number speak some English and know the trails well enough to act as guides.

If halfway through a trek you decide you do need some help (illness, problems with high altitude or ordinary old blisters might contribute) it will generally be possible to find someone. A large village or a hill-country airstrip would be a good place to look. At airstrips like the ones in Lukla or Jomsom there are often porters who have just been paid off from a trekking party and are looking for another load to carry. Large organised trekking parties carry most of their own food and as the food is used up, fewer porters are needed and the extra porters are paid off along the route – so you can find experienced porters in the most unlikely places.

Whether you're making the arrangements yourself or dealing with an agency, make sure you clearly establish where you will go, how long you will take, how much you are going to pay and what you will be obliged to supply along the way. Most agreements provide that guides and porters pay for their own food and accommodation out of their wages, but this means you will have to stay in villages that supply such services. Arrangements where you pay for the porter's accommodation and food can end up being surprisingly expensive. The amount of food a hungry Nepalese porter can get through, when you're footing the bill, can be simply stunning.

You may also be responsible for outfitting guides and porters to cope with cold and snow. If you are going above the snow line you must make absolutely certain that porters have goggles, shoes, shelter and appropriate clothing. There are still regular horror stories about ill-equipped porters tackling the Thorung La (the pass between Manang and Muktinath on the Annapurna Circuit). Frostbite, snow blindness and death have resulted.

If you make arrangements with one of the small trekking agencies in Kathmandu expect to pay $12 per day for a guide, $8 per day for a porter. If you find a porter yourself or through a guest house, the costs will be lower – say $5 per day. Local agencies are listed in the following section.

ORGANISED TREKKING
Organised treks can also vary greatly in standards and costs. At one extreme there are the big international adventure travel companies that market trips in the West. You book your trek through them and everything is organised and arranged before you leave home. Your cost will probably include flights to and from Nepal, accommodation in Kathmandu before and after the trek, tours and other activities as well as the trek itself. A fully organised trek will provide tents, sleeping bags, food, porters and an experienced

Trekking with Children
Taking children trekking in Nepal can be surprisingly enjoyable. Both of our children's treks were of the organised variety but I have met other trekkers who have successfully tackled village-inn treks with children. One New Zealand couple I met in Kathmandu had just done the complete Annapurna Circuit with a baby. They had taken along a porter/guide who apart from all the expected duties had found himself drying nappies (diapers) in front of the fire each night.

Tackling a long, high-altitude trek like the Annapurna Circuit with small children might be asking too much. With our children we planned on shorter treks (we didn't want them getting fed up) which avoided very high altitudes. We also opted for organised treks to make it easier for both sides – we didn't have to worry about finding food and shelter and the kids were likely to eat better.

Our first trek with children was the short Annapurna Skyline Trek (see the Pokhara chapter) when our daughter Tashi was eight and our son Kieran was six. Back home, like most kids, they seemed to think getting from the car to the video recorder a long walk but in fact they walked the whole way and still had energy for frantic games with the porters and local village kids after we set up camp each night.

Our enthusiasm must have been catching because three years later we found ourselves back in Nepal, this time with seven friends and neighbours and six children (two aged six, two aged eight, one 10-year-old and one 11-year-old). This time we opted for the Helambu Circuit as it was reasonably short, didn't go too high and is not too heavily trekked. Malla Treks in Kathmandu, who organised the trek for us, made it even more interesting by sending along a bunch of Nepalese children, who also happened to be on school vacation. Our resulting 'international trek' was a great learning experience, and once again our kids turned out to be hardier than we'd expected. Only on one day, when a misunderstanding with the porters resulted in us having to climb a 3500-metre pass late in the day, did the two six-year-olds require a little carrying. Apart from that, the whole noisy mob walked the entire eight days. We're already planning our next children's trek.
Tony Wheeler

English-speaking sirdar (trek leader). All you need to carry is your day pack and camera.

Companies organising trekking trips in Nepal include well-known names like Mountain Travel or Wilderness Travel in the USA, World Expeditions or Peregrine Adventures in Australia, and Sherpa Expeditions in the UK. Although the trek leaders may be experienced Western walkers from the international company the actual organisation in Nepal will probably be by a locally based trekking company.

Local Trekking Agencies

It's quite possible to join a fully organised trip when you get to Nepal (and save a lot of money), but unless you have a decent-sized group or have made arrangements in advance, you will be dependent on whether there is a vacancy on a trip with pre-established starting and finishing dates. With the best of these companies a trek may cost upwards of $60 or $70 a day and you'll trek in real comfort with tables, chairs, dining tents, toilet tents and other luxuries which seem quite incompatible with walking in the wilds! Some of the large Nepal-based trekking agencies that have been recommended include:

Ama Dablam Trekking
    Lazimpat (☎ 01-410219)
Himalayan Adventure
    Thamel (☎ 01-414344)
International Trekking
    Naxal (☎ 01-214159)
Lama Excursion
    Durbar Marg (☎ 01-410786)
Malla Treks
    Malla Hotel (☎ 01-418389; fax 418382)
Tiger Mountain (the same organisation as Tiger Tops)
    PO Box 170, Durbar Marg (☎ 01-414508; fax 414075)
Yangrima Trekking & Mountaineering
    Kantipath (☎ 01-227627; fax 227628)

There are more than 80 trekking agencies in Nepal, ranging from the big ones tied up with international adventure travel companies, down to small agencies who specialise in handling independent trekkers. These small agencies will often be able to fix you up with individual porters or guides. A group trek organised through one of these smaller trekking agencies might cost $30 to $50 a day. Group treks staying at village lodges along the route can be cheaper still (around $25 a day).

Trekking agencies that have been recommended in this category include:

Above the Clouds Trekking
    Durbar Marg (☎ 01-312921)
Asian Trekking
    Thamel (☎ 01-212821)
Greenhill Tours
    Thamel (☎ 01-414803; fax 411933)
Himalayan Hilltreks
    Namche Arcade, Thamel (☎ 01-411764; fax 417367)
Lamjung Treks & Expeditions
    Deo Building, Kopundol (☎ 01-522964; fax 226820)
Lucky Trekking Service
    Thahiti Tole (☎ 01-223690)
Machhapuchhare Trekking
    Jyatha, Thamel (☎ 01-414873)
Mandala Trekking
    Kantipath (☎ 01-214700)
Nepal Tashi Taki Trekking
    Jyatha, Thamel (☎ 01-211045)

TREKS

There are countless long treks in Nepal, many of which still see only a handful of Western walkers each year. Two new routes have been opened up, but only for trekkers in organised groups: in the Dolpo region west of the Kali Gandaki Valley and to the Kanchenjunga Base Camp in the north-east of the country.

The six very popular longer treks, described in detail in this chapter, are the Everest Base Camp Trek, Helambu, Langtang and Jomsom treks, the Annapurna Circuit and the Annapurna Sanctuary Trek.

The Everest Base Camp Trek takes about three weeks and reaches a maximum height of 5545 metres at Kala Pattar, the small peak offering fine views of Mt Everest. Although the final part of the trek is through essentially uninhabited areas, these days small lodges operate in the trekking season so it's quite suitable for independent trekkers. The flights in or out of Lukla at the start and/or finish of the trek can be a real problem.

The Helambu Trek, a one-week trek that can start from and finish in the Kathmandu Valley, does not offer superb mountain scenery but is culturally interesting. The maximum height reached is only 2800 metres and there is plenty of accommodation along the route.

The Langtang Trek lasts 10 to 12 days if you walk in and out, but it can be varied by flying out or by crossing a high pass down to the Helambu region. There are fine views, interesting villages, and although there are some relatively uninhabited stretches, accommodation is available. The maximum height reached is 3800 metres.

The Jomsom Trek, from Pokhara up the Kali Gandaki Valley, is the most popular in Nepal with superb scenery, interesting people and the best trailside accommodation in the country. It takes a week to reach Muktinath, the end point of the trek. Walking back takes another week or you can fly from Jomsom. Muktinath, the high point of the trek, is at 3700 metres.

It takes nearly three weeks to walk the entire Annapurna Circuit, but for scenery and cultural diversity this is the best trek in Nepal. It crosses to the north of the main Himalayan range, on to the Tibetan Plateau, and crosses a 5400-metre pass. The last week of the trek is the Jomsom Trek in reverse.

The Annapurna Sanctuary Trek into the centre of the Annapurna Range also starts from Pokhara, and offers unparalleled mountain scenery. The trek takes 10 to 14 days and reaches a maximum height of 3000 metres. Finding shelter in the uninhabited sanctuary area was a real problem at one time, but recently numerous lodges have sprung up along the route.

Everest Base Camp Trek

Everybody knows of Mt Everest and that's the simple reason why the Everest Base Camp Trek is so popular. The trek has a number of stunning attractions, but it also has some distinct drawbacks which might well deter potential trekkers were it not for the undeniable plus point of being able to say

The Yeti
Like Big Foot in North America, the Loch Ness monster in Scotland or even the elusive bunyip in Australia, the yeti or abominable snowman is much hunted but little seen. The yeti is a shy humanoid creature which lives high in the most remote regions of the Himalaya. There are countless yeti legends told by the Sherpas and other hill peoples. They tell of its legendary strength, its ability to carry off yaks and even abduct people.

Nobody has ever managed to get a clear photograph of the yeti: footprints in the snow are generally the only indication that a yeti has been by, although hastily gnawed yak bones also add to the yeti legend.

Of course there are plenty of scientific explanations for yetis. The footprints may have been a human print or some other natural footprint which has appeared to grow larger as the snow melts. Rigorous studies have been made of the yeti scalps found in various monasteries, in particular the one at the Pangboche monastery, and they have all turned out to be fakes. Keep your camera loaded though, a good photo of a yeti (even a small yeti) will probably be worth a fortune. ■

you've been to the base of the highest mountain in the world.

The attractions include spectacular scenery and the outgoing Sherpa people of the Solu Khumbu, the region where Mt Everest and its attendant lesser peaks are located. The drawbacks include the long, hard slog to get there and the acclimatisation problems caused by the region's considerable altitude.

It's not until you get right into the Solu Khumbu region that the Everest trek really gets interesting. The first part of the trek is not only a hard slog, but is also pretty sparse in the breathtaking views department. The hard slog comes about because the trek doesn't follow valleys – like the Annapurna treks – instead the Everest trek cuts across the valleys. So for day after day it's a tiring process of dropping down one side of a steep valley and climbing up again on the other. By the time you reach the base camp your ascents will total almost 9000 metres, the full height of Everest from sea level!

The Everest trek starts in the Nepali-speaking Hindu lowlands and ends in the Tibetan-Buddhist highlands where the Sherpas are renowned for their enterprise, hard work, civic responsibility and devotion to the practice of Buddhism. In their often inhospitable land, the potato, a relatively recent introduction, is the main crop, but these days trekking and mountaineering is the backbone of the Sherpa economy. More than half the population in the region is now involved with tourism and Namche Bazaar looks more like an alpine resort than a Sherpa village.

Most Everest trekkers opt to fly one way to avoid having to repeat all those ups and downs. This introduces its own problems as the Lukla to Kathmandu flights are notorious for cancellations, waiting lists and short-tempered trekkers. Kathmandu to Lukla flights are less heavily used (more people fly out than fly in) but it's preferable to walk up and fly back in order to aid the acclimatisation that is necessary for the extreme altitudes encountered.

The Everest trek may not be quite as good as the Pokhara area for village-inn treks, but these days accommodation is available during the trekking season even in the normally uninhabited areas around the high peaks.

Medical Services There are small hospitals in Jiri, Phaplu and Khunde, while the Himalayan Rescue Association has a medical facility in Pheriche, and the Edmund Hillary Hospital is at Khumjung.

EVEREST BASE CAMP TREK
Day 1: Kathmandu via Lamosangu to Jiri
The Everest trek has been getting steadily shorter over the years. The members of the 1953 British expedition which put Hillary and Tensing on the top started their walk to Everest at Bhaktapur in the Kathmandu Valley. Today you can take the Kodari road to Lamosangu, 78 km from Kathmandu, and turn off there to Jiri, a further 110 km. Buses to Jiri leave from Kathmandu's Central Bus Station (or did, before the opening of the Kathmandu Bus Terminal) between 5.30 and 6.30 am, cost Rs 98 and take around 10 hours (keep a close eye on your luggage).

Jiri at 1860 metres is a relatively new town which has developed since the road was completed. There's a short take-off and landing (STOL) airstrip and a hospital and you can fly here to save the long bus trip. Jiri has a weekly market on Saturdays and there are several hotels in town. The bus stops at the far end of town so you walk back up to find somewhere to stay. The *Sagarmatha Lodge & Restaurant* is pretty good with doubles for Rs 20. On the far side of town – furthest from the bus stop – is *Sherpa Guide Lodge* with doubles for Rs 10. This is the cheapest and best place in town. The rooms are clean, the staff friendly and the food good.

Day 2: Jiri to Bhandar
The walk starts with a climb to the ridge top at 2400 metres then drops down to Shivalaya at 1800 metres. Before the Jiri road was opened the trek used to go through Those,

which at that time was the busiest market town between Lamosangu and Namche Bazaar. It's still possible to walk from Jiri to Those and Shivalaya.

From Shivalaya you climb again to Sangbadanda at 2150 metres and from here you start to see the mani stone walls which indicate you are entering a Buddhist region. Walk to the left side of these walls. You reach Kosaribas at 2500 metres, then a pass at 2705 metres before descending again to Bhandar at 2200 metres. This Sherpa settlement has a gompa and a number of hotels. It's possible to take a detour between Sangbadanda and Bhandar to visit Thodung at 3090 metres where there's a cheese factory, established with Swiss aid in the 1950s.

Day 3: Bhandar to Sagar/Sete
The trail drops down to the Likhu Khola and crosses the river at 1580 metres, climbs through Kenja and then rises steeply to a fork where you choose the route to Sagar at 2440 metres or Sete at 2575 metres. If you're in a group Sagar is preferable (the camping site is better), but if you're not camping then Sete offers a better choice of hotels. From here on the villages are almost all inhabited by Sherpas (alternative village names are given in brackets).

Day 4: Sagar/Sete to Junbesi
It's a long but gradual climb to the Lamjura pass at 3530 metres. You're rewarded with frost and often snow along the trail in winter or with flowering rhododendrons in the spring. Goyem at 3300 metres on your way to the pass is a good lunch stop. The pass is the highest point between Jiri and Namche Bazaar and from the top you descend to Tragdobuk at 2860 metres, then to the pretty Sherpa village of Junbesi at 2675 metres. It has a monastery, some good hotels and is a good place for a rest day with some interesting walks in the vicinity.

Day 5: Junbesi to Nuntala
The trail drops to Phaplu where there is an airstrip, then climbs to a ridge at 3080 metres where for the first time you can see Everest.

The route then descends to Salung at 2980 metres and the Ringmo Khola at 2650 metres. This is the last chance to wash in a river, as the Dudh Kosi is much too cold! Then it's up to Ringmo where apples and other fruit are grown. The new trail from here to Namche Bazaar was built in the '80s and avoids many of the steep descents and ascents of the old route.

A short climb from Ringmo Khola takes you to the 3071-metre Trakshindo pass, then the trail drops down past the monastery of the same name, and on to Nuntala (Manidingma) at 2320 metres where there are a variety of hotels offering a variety of standards.

Day 6: Nuntala to Khari Khola
The trail descends to the Dudh Kosi at 1500 metres and crosses it to follow the other bank. The trail climbs to Jubing (Dorakbuk) at 1680 metres and continues up to Khari Khola at 2070 metres. The old trail along the Dudh Kosi to Namche Bazaar usually required a stop here, and if you're walking with porters this may still be the traditional stopping place. If not you can push on to Bupsa (Bumshing) on Day 6 and then reach Ghat (Lhawa) on Day 7 and Namche Bazaar on Day 8, saving a day's walk.

Day 7: Khari Khola to Puiyan
The trail first drops to 2010 metres then climbs to Bupsa at 2300 metres. From here the trail climbs gradually, offering views of the Dudh Kosi 1000 metres below at the bottom of the steep-sided valley, until it reaches a ridge at 2900 metres overlooking Puiyan. Puiyan is at 2730 metres in a side canyon off the Dudh Kosi Valley.

Day 8: Puiyan to Phakding
The trail climbs to a ridge at 2800 metres then drops down to Surkhe (Buwa) at 2293 metres. Shortly beyond Surkhe is the turn-off to Lukla with its airstrip. It continues to climb through Mushe and Chaunrikarka at 2680 metres to Chablung, then drops to Ghat at 2550 metres. Another climb takes you to

Phakding at 2650 metres and from here on the trek is pretty much up, up, up.

Day 9: Phakding to Namche Bazaar

The trail climbs to Benkar at 2700 metres, then Chomoa, with the curious *Hatago Lodge* run by a resident Japanese gentleman, and Monjo before dropping down to cross the Dudh Kosi. On the other side it's up to Jorsale at 2850 metres where there are a number of good places to stay and eat. Here you enter the Sagarmatha National Park and must pay the entry fee.

It's a steady climb from here to Namche Bazaar at 3440 metres. This is the main centre in the Solu Khumbu region and has shops, restaurants, a bakery, hotels with hot showers, a national park office, a police checkpost (where your trekking permit will be inspected) and even a bank. Namche Bazaar even has hydroelectricity, mainly used for lighting. There is a colourful market each Saturday.

Day 10: Namche Bazaar

There is plenty to do around Namche Bazaar and a day should be spent here acclimatising.

Remember that the victims of altitude sickness are often the fittest and healthiest people who foolishly overextend themselves.

Day 11: Namche Bazaar to Thyangboche

The slightly longer route from Namche Bazaar to Thyangboche via Khumjung and Khunde is more interesting than the direct one. It starts by climbing up to the Shyangboche airstrip at 3720 metres. Above it is the Everest View Hotel, a Japanese scheme to build a deluxe hotel with great views of the highest mountains on earth. The idea fell flat on its face, since flying straight up to nearly 4000 metres is not good for people's health, especially for the elderly folk who were generally the ones who could afford it.

From the hotel or the airstrip you continue to Khumjung and then rejoin the direct trail to Thyangboche. The trail descends to the Dudh Kosi at 3250 metres where there is a small teashop and a series of picturesque water-driven prayer wheels. A steep ascent brings you to Thyangboche (Tengpoche) at 3870 metres. The famous monastery, a

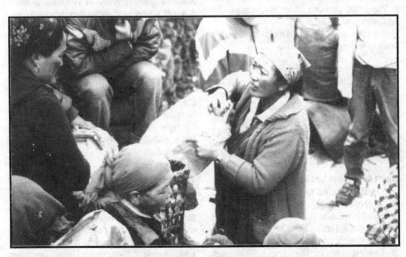

Selling produce at the Saturday weekly market, Namche Bazaar

photographer's favourite with its background of Ama Dablam, Everest and other peaks, was burnt down in 1988; although it's being rebuilt, 1989 was not an auspicious year for building things so a start wasn't made until 1990. There's a camping area, a number of places to stay, and during the November-December full moon the colourful Mani Rimdu festival is held here with much singing and dancing.

Day 12: Thyangboche to Pheriche
Beyond Thyangboche the altitude really starts to tell. The trail drops down to Devuche, crosses the Imja Khola on a frightening bridge and climbs past superb mani stones to Pangboche at 3860 metres. The monastery here has a 'yeti scalp' and the village is a good lunch stop.

The trail then climbs to Pheriche at 4240 metres where there is a trekkers' aid post and possible medical assistance. Pheriche has a number of hotels and restaurants which usually feature exotic dishes left over from international mountaineering expeditions.

Day 13: Pheriche
Another acclimatisation day should be spent at Pheriche. You can either laze around the settlement or make a day trip to Nangkartshang Gompa or up past Dingboche. Either walk offers good views.

Day 14: Pheriche to Lobuje
The trail climbs to Phalang Karpa at 4340 metres then Duglha at 4620 metres before reaching Lobuje at 4930 metres. The lodge accommodation here is all dormitory-style and the altitude, the cold and the crowding combine to ensure less than restful nights. The views, however, are superb!

Day 15: Lobuje to Gorak Shep
The trail continues to climb to Gorak Shep at 5160 metres. You reach there by lunch time and in the afternoon can rest or continue to Kala Pattar (Black Rock). At 5545 metres this small peak offers the best view you'll get of Everest without climbing it. Although there is usually accommodation at Gorak

Shep it's nothing to write home about. Making the Lobuje, Gorak Shep, Kala Pattar, Lobuje circuit in a single day is a better idea if you're not on an organised trek with camping equipment.

Day 16: Gorak Shep to Lobuje
After a sleepless night at Gorak Shep, the altitude hits nearly everybody; getting back down to Lobuje or even better to Pheriche makes a real difference. If you want to actually get to the base camp then it's about six hours round trip from Lobuje, and there's no view, so if you only have the energy for one sidetrip on day 16 or 17 then make it Kala Pattar. It's downhill, but tiring, back to Lobuje.

Day 17: Lobuje to Dingboche
Staying the night at Dingboche instead of Pheriche makes an interesting alternative. It's a 'summer village' at 4360 metres.

Days 18, 19 & 20: Dingboche to Lukla
The next three days retrace your steps down to Lukla via Thyangboche and Namche Bazaar. You have to arrive at Lukla the day before your scheduled departure in order to reconfirm your flight. Lukla has a number of places to stay including the relatively expensive *Sherpa Co-operative Hotel*, and life revolves around wondering whether flights

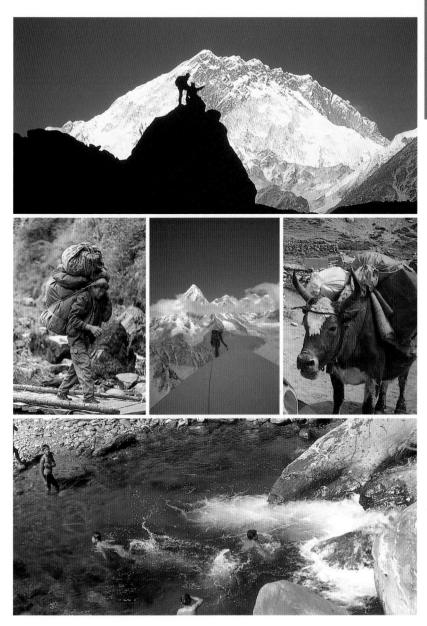

Top: Nuptse, near Mt Everest (PS)
Middle: Porters, Annapurna Circuit Trek (SR); Sherpa climber,
Solu Khumbu region (JW); yaks used to carry trekkers' gear (JW)
Right: Swimming hole near Keswa village (SA)

Top Left: White-water rafting (DA)
Top Right: Mountain bike, Ichangu Narayan (TW)
Bottom Left: Marpha, Jomsom Trek (JL)
Bottom Right: Narayani River, Royal Chitwan National Park (RE)

will come in and who will manage to get on them.

Day 21: Lukla to Kathmandu
If the gods are with you, your flight comes in and your reservation hasn't been cancelled. Then, after it took you so many days to get here by road and foot, your aircraft only takes 35 minutes to fly you back.

VARIATIONS & SIDETRIPS
See the Other Treks section later in this chapter for information on the long trek south from the Solu Khumbu region to Dhankuta, an interesting alternative to going straight back to Kathmandu. Alternatives to hanging around in Lukla waiting for flights or walking all the way back to Jiri are also possible but not very satisfactory. Going down to Phaplu, two or three days south of Lukla, is unlikely to get you out any faster. It's a four or five-day walk down to Lamidanda from where there are several flights a week to Biratnagar and Kathmandu.

Experienced trekkers could take the little-frequented Barabise to Shivalaya route in, avoiding the Jiri road completely. It's an interesting six-day round trip from Namche Bazaar to Gokyo and back. This trek ends at another Kala Pattar with fine, but different, views of Everest. You can even combine both Kala Pattars by crossing the 5420-metre Chola La pass, but you had better bring your ice axe and crampons and know how to use them.

A shorter sidetrip from Namche Bazaar is to Thami, the gateway to Tesi Laphcha and the Rolwaling Himal. You can do a round trip to Thami in a day, although it's better to stay overnight in order to catch the morning views.

Helambu & Langtang Treks

Although they are not as well known and popular as the Everest Base Camp Trek or the Annapurna Circuit these two treks offer a number of distinct advantages. The treks are north of the Kathmandu Valley, so both are easily accessible from Kathmandu. Indeed, you can leave your hotel in Kathmandu and set foot on the Helambu trail within an hour. The Helambu Trek only takes a week so it is ideal for people who do not have the time for one of the longer treks. Since it stays at relatively low altitudes it does not require fancy cold-weather equipment and clothing.

The Langtang Trek, on the other hand, gives you the opportunity to get right in amongst the Himalayan peaks and to walk through remote and relatively unpopulated areas. If you want real adventure then these two treks can be linked by high-altitude passes, either via the Gosainkund Lakes or across the 5000-metre Ganja La pass.

Medical Services The only medical facilities on the Helambu and Langtang treks is the Dhunche dispensary.

HELAMBU TREK
The Helambu Trek only takes seven days, starts from Sundarijal at the eastern end of the Kathmandu Valley and does not climb above 3500 metres. It makes a loop through the Sherpa-populated Helambu region to the north-east of Kathmandu and only the first day's walk is repeated on the return trip. The trek's main drawback is that it does not offer fine Himalayan views, like some other treks, but it can be trekked on a village-inn basis as there are guest houses and lodges in many of the villages along the trail.

The Sherpa people of the Helambu region are friendly and hospitable, just like their better known kinfolk of the Solu Khumbu region. In other ways, however, they are quite different from the Sherpas from around Mt Everest. The Sherpa women of Helambu are renowned for their beauty and during the Rana period many of them worked for aristocratic families in Kathmandu.

As in the Solu Khumbu the potato is a vitally important crop and not only forms a large part of the local diet but is also exported

Helambu & Langtang Treks

0   5   10 km

Heights in metres

LANGTANG   HIMAL

Langtang II
6541

Langtang Lirung
7246

Bhote Kosi

Langtang
Village

Kyanjin
Gompa   Yala

Ghora
Tabela

Langtang   Khola

Syabrubensi   Syapargaon   Chongong   Ngegang

Ganja La

Syabru

Dhunche   Bharku   Sing   Gosainkund
Gompa   Lake   Keldang

Thare   Saraswatikund Lake   Lauribina

Bhairabkund Lake   Dukpu

Ramche

Phatangu   Khola   Gopte   Malemchigaon

Tharepati   Gekye
Gompa

Trisuli   HELAMBU   Tarke Gyang

Kholа   Betrawati   Kakani

Malemchi   Thimbu   Sermathang

Trisuli Bazaar   Tadi   Khola   Khutumsang   Kiul

Mahenkal

Gul Bhanjyang   Indrawati

Likhu Khola   Chipling   Taramarang   Khola

Batache

Rani Pauwa   Pati Bhanjyang   Thakani

Kakani   Malemchi

Borlang Bhanjyang

Chaurabas   Bahunpati

Mulkharkha

Sundarijal

To Pokhara   Bodhnath   Sankhu

Nagarkot

KATHMANDU

Bhaktapur   Panchkhal

Dhulikhel

Banepa

to the Nepalese lowland in exchange for rice and other lowland produce.

Day 1: Kathmandu via Sundarijal to Pati Bhanjyang

Buses do not usually run all the way to Sundarijal, 15 km from Kathmandu, but you can get to the start of the trail by taxi, or get a bus at least as far as Bodhnath. From Sundarijal the trail starts off up concrete steps beside the pipeline which brings drinking water down to the valley. Eventually the trail leaves the pipeline from near the dam and reaches Mulkharkha, sprawling up the ridge around 1895 metres, 600 metres above Sundarijal. There are superb views back over the valley and some convenient tea shops for rest and refreshment.

The trail continues to climb, but less steeply, through Chisopani then drops down to Pati Bhanjyang at 1770 metres. Chisopani is rather like a grubby little truck stop without the trucks but the mountain views in the morning can be very fine. Take care of your possessions here, it's still rather close to the Kathmandu Valley. There are lodges at Chisopani and at Pati Bhanjyang which also has a police checkpost where your trekking permit may be inspected.

Day 2: Pati Bhanjyang to Khutumsang

The trail rises and falls through Chipling at 2170 metres then over a 2470-metre pass and down past a large chorten to the village of Gul Bhanjyang. The Rs 650 entry fee to the Langtang National Park is collected at the office here. From here the trail climbs again to reach a 2620-metre pass before descending along a rocky route to Khutumsang at 2470 metres. There are lodges at Gul Bhanjyang and Khutumsang or there's the *Dragon Lodge* beside a pleasant meadow about 45 minutes before Khutumsang.

Day 3: Khutumsang to Malemchigaon

The trail follows a ridge line with views of the Langtang and Gosainkund peaks through sparsely populated forests to Magen Goth with an army checkpost before finally reaching the Tharepati pass at 3490 metres. The

trail to Gosainkund branches off north-west from here. Tharepati has several lodges including the very nicely situated *Himaliya Lodge* on the Khutumsang side. It can get pretty chilly up here at night. From the pass the trail turns east and descends rapidly down a ravine to reach the pretty Sherpa village of Malemchigaon at 2530 metres. There are a number of lodges in the village and a very brightly painted gompa.

Day 4: Malemchigaon to Tarke Gyang

From Malemchigaon the trail continues to drop, crossing the Malemchi Khola by a bridge at 1890 metres and then making the long climb up the other side of the valley to Tarke Gyang at 2743 metres. This is the largest village in Helambu and the prosperous Sherpas who live here specialise, amongst other things, in turning out 'instant antiques' for gullible trekkers. There are a number of lodges including the pleasant *Mount View Hotel* on the Malemchigaon side of the village. Tarke Gyang makes a good place for a rest day or you can take a sidetrip up to the peak overlooking the village. This is the end of the route down from the Ganja La pass.

Day 5: Tarke Gyang to Kiul

From Tarke Gyang there is a very pleasant alternative route, described after the final day of this trek report. On the loop trek the wide and well-used trail descends through rhododendron forests and past Buddhist chortens and mani walls to Kakani at 2070 metres and Thimbu at 1580 metres. By the time you reach Kiul at 1280 metres you have left the Sherpa highlands and entered the warmer lowland areas where rice is grown. Kiul is at a lower altitude than Kathmandu.

Day 6: Kiul to Pati Bhanjyang

The trail descends along a river, crossing it on the second suspension bridge at just 1190 metres then joining a roadway at Mahenkal and following it to Taramarang at 940 metres. Here the trail leaves the road and climbs steeply to Batache and then Thakani, on the ridge top, at 1890 metres. From here the trail follows the ridge to Pati Bhanjyang where the Helambu circuit is completed.

Day 7: Pati Bhanjyang via Sundarijal to Kathmandu

The final day retraces the first day's walk.

Alternative Routes from Tarke Gyang

An alternative route can be followed from Tarke Gyang through Sermathang and then along a long ridge through Kakani and Dubhachaur to join the road at Malemchi, south of Taramarang. This route is very pleasant as far as Malemchi and attracts relatively few trekkers. There are numerous lodges at Sermathang and Malemchi but the choice is limited elsewhere.

From Malemchi the final stretch is along a dusty roadway which brings you out on the Kathmandu to Kodari road at Panchkhal, from where you will have to take a bus 55 km back to Kathmandu via Dhulikhel. You can usually get a ride on a bus or truck down the road from Malemchi and this route does avoid having to duplicate the final stretch from Pati Bhanjyang through Sundarijal.

Another Helambu alternative is to start and finish from Panchkhal on the main road, completing the shorter loop through Malemchi, Taramarang, Kiul, Tarke Gyang, Sermathang and Malemchi. It's also possible to walk on from Bahunpati to Sankhu or Nagarkot, completing a loop which starts and finishes in the Kathmandu Valley but does not retrace your steps at any point.

The alternative routes are as follows:

Day 5: Tarke Gyang to Sermathang

The easy trail descends gently through a beautiful forest to Sermathang, the centre of an important apple-growing area. Sermathang is more spread out than the closely spaced houses of Tarke Gyang and there are fine views of the valley of the Malemchi Khola to the south. Trekking permits are checked at Sermathang and if you do the trek in the reverse direction this is where you must pay the Rs 650 entry fee to the Langtang National Park.

Day 6: Sermathang via Malemchi to Panchkhal

From Sermathang the trail continues to descend to Kakani and Dubhachaur then steeply down to Malemchi where it meets the road. You should be able to get a ride from here down to Panchkhal on the Kathmandu to Kodari road. From there you can catch a bus to Dhulikhel or Kathmandu. If you can't find transport it's another day's walk down the roadway, following the Indrawati River, to Bahunpati and Panchkhal.

LANGTANG TREK

Langtang Lirung (7246 metres) is visible to the north of Kathmandu on clear days. The Langtang trek takes up to two weeks and leads to a glacier in the valley at the base of Langtang Lirung, close to the peak's base camp. The trail passes through Tibetan and Tamang villages and offers fine views of the Ganesh Himal. Though the trek passes through comparatively lightly populated and undeveloped areas, it is still possible to stay at village inns along the route. Ascending from just 541 metres at Trisuli Bazaar to 3800 metres at Kyanjin Gompa the trail passes through an ever-changing climate and offers trekkers an exceptional diversity of scenery and culture.

Day 1: Kathmandu via Trisuli to Dhunche

It's 72 km from Kathmandu to Trisuli Bazaar – about four hours by car or six by bus. The road is paved but very winding and offers some fine mountain views. Rani Pauwa is the only large village along the route. From here the 50-km road to Dhunche is steep, winding and rather hairy, passing through Betrawati and Thare. Transport can be problematic from Betrawati, only eight km beyond Trisuli. If you can't find transport for the four-hour drive you face a two-day walk. There is now a daily bus from Kathmandu to Dhunche, the 12-hour trip costs Rs 80.

Dhunche is a pretty village at 1950 metres and here you will have your trekking permit checked and must pay the entrance fee to the Langtang National Park. Eventually the road will continue beyond here towards the Ganesh Himal.

Day 2: Dhunche to Syabru

Soon after Dhunche the trail leaves the road and follows the Trisuli Khola, crossing it and climbing steeply then leaving the Gosainkund trail and following a ridge to Bharku at 1860 metres. Most of the Trisuli River's water comes from the Bhote Kosi River, from Tibet. (Bhote Kosi means 'river from Tibet'.) From Bharku there are alternative routes to Langtang but the newer southern route through Syabru is better than the longer northern route through Syabrubensi and Syapargaon.

From Bharku you climb to 2300 metres and enter the Langtang Valley with views of Himalayan peaks to the west, north and east. The trail descends rapidly to Syabru at 2130 metres where there are good hotels.

Day 3: Syabru to Chongong

The trail descends through forest to the Langtang Khola at 1890 metres then follows the river upstream, crossing from the southern to northern bank to reach Chongong at 2380 metres. Some maps show this as *Lama Hotel*, the name of one of the places to stay here.

Day 4: Chongong to Langtang Village

The trail continues to follow the Langtang Khola, climbing steeply, at times very steeply, to Ghora Tabela at 3000 metres where there are fine views of Langtang Lirung. Although there is no permanent settlement here, there is a good lodge, and your trekking permit and national park entry permit will be checked here.

From Ghora Tabela the trail climbs more gradually to Langtang village at 3500 metres. The national park headquarters is here and Langtang and the villages around are in Tibetan style with stone walls around the fields and herds of yaks.

Day 5: Langtang Village to Kyanjin Gompa

Passing through small villages it only takes the morning to climb to Kyanjin Gompa at 3800 metres where there is a monastery, a lodge and a cheese factory. There are a number of interesting walks from the gompa and if you are intending to continue over the Ganja La pass to Helambu you should spend some time here acclimatising. From the gompa you can climb to 4300 metres on the the glacial moraine to the north for superb views of Langtang Lirung. Day walks can also be made to Yala or further up the valley for more spectacular views.

Alternative Routes from Kyanjin Gompa

There are a number of alternative routes back to Kathmandu. Quickest is the flight by Pilatus Porter from the nearby STOL airstrip but a charter usually must be arranged in advance. Alternatively you can simply retrace your route back down the valley to Dhunche or, if the season and weather permits, attempt the high routes over the Ganja La pass or via the Gosainkund Lakes to Helambu.

Across the Ganja La Walking from the Kyanjin Gompa at the end of the Langtang route south to Tarke Gyang in Helambu involves crossing the 5106-metre Ganja La pass. The pass is usually blocked by snow from December to March and at any time a bad weather change can make crossing the pass decidedly dangerous. This is one of the more difficult passes in Nepal and should not be attempted without local advice, adequate acclimatisation, good equipment and some experience. The walk takes four days and between Kyanjin and Gekye Gompa (shortly before Tarke Gyang) there is no permanent settlement.

Some altitude acclimatisation around the Kyanjin Gompa is a very wise idea before commencing the crossing. Day 1 from the gompa is a short walk to Ngegang at 4000 metres, the last good place to camp before the pass. Staying here shortens the crossing over the pass and also increases your acclimatisation.

From Ngegang the trail climbs steeply and crosses a snow slope to the pass, marked by rock cairns and prayer flags and with a spectacular view of the peaks to the north and the hills to the south. A steep and dangerous descent follows to Keldang at 4270 metres. Coming the other way over the pass the long ascent from Keldang means you must spend an additional night on the southern side of the pass. From Keldang it's a long day's walk to Dukpu at 4080 metres and another day from there to Tarke Gyang at 2743 metres. The last day's walk offers tremendous views of the Himalaya as you cross a 4020-metre pass soon after leaving Dukpu.

Gosainkund Lakes The trek via the Gosainkund Lakes is another way of crossing between Langtang and Helambu. Again, adequate preparation is necessary and finding food and accommodation along the way is not always possible. It takes four days to walk from Dhunche, at the start of the Langtang Trek, to Tharepati in Helambu. The trek can also be made from Helambu or by turning off the Langtang route from Syabru.

Gosainkund is the site for a great pilgrimage in August each year – this is the height of the monsoon, not a pleasant time for trekking. The large rock in the centre of the lake is said to be the remains of a Shiva shrine and it is also claimed that a channel carries water from the lake directly to the tank at the Kumbeshwar Temple in Patan, 60 km to the south.

Day 1 takes you from Dhunche at 1950 metres to the Sing Gompa at 3350 metres. The route from Syabru to the gompa can be confusing. The second day's walk climbs steeply with fine mountain views then drops down to Saraswatikund at 4100 metres, the first of the Gosainkund lakes. The second lake is Bhairabkund, the third is Gosainkund itself at 4380 metres. There are stone shelters at Gosainkund, used by pilgrims during the festival at the August full moon.

From the lake the trail climbs still higher to the four lakes near the Lauribina pass at 4610 metres, then drops down to Gopte at 3430 metres where you can shelter in a cave.

It was here that an Australian trekker got lost in 1991 and was not found for 43 days. The final day's walk descends to a stream and then climbs to Tharepati at 3490 metres.

Jomsom, Annapurna Circuit & Other Pokhara Treks

Pokhara is the starting or finishing point for some of the best trekking in Nepal and the long Annapurna Circuit trek is the most popular trek in the country.

The reasons for the area's popularity are numerous. You can start your trek from Pokhara itself: no long, uncomfortable bus rides or problematic flights are required to get to the starting point. You are in the mountains immediately: the Annapurna Range is very close to Pokhara.

The treks in this part of the country offer a great deal of cultural and geographic diversity; indeed the Jomsom and Annapurna Circuit treks both go to the north of the Himalayan watershed, into the dry desert area which is properly part of the Tibetan Plateau. Finally, these treks are the best in Nepal for independent trekkers and a network of lodges and guest houses can be found along all the main trails. The Annapurna Circuit has even been dubbed 'the apple pie trail'.

The Pokhara area also offers a number of one-day treks or short three or four-day treks. These are covered in the Around Pokhara section of the Pokhara chapter. There are three popular longer treks from Pokhara, all of which follow the same route at some point.

The Annapurna Sanctuary Trek takes you right in amongst the mountains of the Annapurna Range to the Machhapuchhare Base Camp. This trek takes about eight days. The Jomsom Trek takes about seven days in each direction, but it is possible to fly back to Pokhara from Jomsom. Most trekkers continue a day further to the holy temple of Muktinath. Finally, the Annapurna Circuit takes a full three weeks and completely encircles the Annapurna Range. The last seven days of the circuit walk from Muktinath to Pokhara are the same as the Jomsom Trek, but in reverse.

The Annapurna Range is the centre for all these Pokhara treks. For most of Nepal's length, the Himalaya form the border between Nepal and China. The Annapurna mountains are different in that the border is well to the north so the Jomsom and Annapurna Circuit treks both go north of the Himalayan watershed, into the high-altitude desert which is characteristic of the Tibetan Plateau.

Medical Services Around the Annapurna Circuit the only facilities are the small hospitals at Jomsom, Besisahar and Baglung. There are two small government dispensaries on the Manang side of the Thorung La pass.

JOMSOM TREK
The Jomsom Trek is essentially the final third of the Annapurna Circuit. It follows the Kali Gandaki Valley between the soaring peaks of Annapurna and Dhaulagiri and finally emerges to the north of the main Himalayan range, on the dry, desert-like Tibetan Plateau. The final destination is the holy temple of Muktinath, a further day's walk beyond Jomsom. The return to Pokhara can either be made by retracing your steps down the Kali Gandaki Valley or by flying from Jomsom to Pokhara or Kathmandu.

Day 1: Pokhara to Naudanda
Like many other treks in Nepal this one is getting shorter as the road gradually extends further into the mountains. Eventually it will probably be possible to drive all the way to Jomsom. A road is now being pushed through the hills from Pokhara to Baglung. In late 1992 the road was finished to Kusma, and the whole road to Baglung was expected to be finished by the end of 1993. As it

---

Saligrams
The black fossils of marine animals known as saligrams are found at several points along the Kali Gandaki, most notably in the area north of Jomsom around Muktinath, but also at Ridi Bazaar and Devghat. These ammonite fossils date back to the Jurassic period over 100 million years ago and provide dramatic evidence that the mighty Himalaya were indeed once under water.

Saligrams are considered holy emblems. They are sometimes believed to represent Vishnu, and are often held during worship and when making a vow. In Pokhara, the image of the goddess Durga (Parvati) in her Binde Basini Bhagwati form is a saligram.

You will see many on sale in Pokhara or along the Jomsom trail. Think twice before buying them: firstly, it is actually illegal to collect them, because the government is concerned at the potential damage that is done to Nepal's fossil record, secondly, they're overpriced, and thirdly, adding rocks to your backpack is never a good idea! ∎

extends, the options for trekkers will obviously change, so get up-to-date advice. In 1992, those starting out for the Sanctuary or for Jomsom were catching buses (Rs 15), or taxis (Rs 250 to Rs 350, or $5 to $7) to Phedi and walking from there, or catching trucks that went as far as Chandrakot near Birethanti (Rs 40). The buses left from Bag Bazaar at the northern end of town.

It's still possible to walk of course. The route goes from Pokhara through Hyangja at 1070 metres, Suikhet at 1125 metres and on to Phedi. From there the trail climbs relatively gradually to Naudanda's ridge-top position at 1430 metres. There are fine views of the whole Annapurna Range and back over Pokhara and Phewa Tal from this large village. Naudanda has a choice of hotels and a trekking permit checkpost, so for day-trekkers without a permit this is the end of the line.

It's also possible to reach Naudanda by walking through Sarangkot (see the Pokhara chapter for details) and along the ridge to Kaski, which has the ruins of a small palace, and on to Naudanda.

Day 2: Naudanda to Tirkedungha

From Naudanda the trail climbs to Khare at the top of the Yamdi Khola Valley at 1710 metres. The trail then drops down to Lumle at 1585 metres, where there are a number of hotels and a British-aided agricultural project. Don't take the wrong turning here and get on the Dhorpatan, Baglung and Beni trail. The next village is Chandrakot at 1550 metres where there are more fine Annapurna views and again more hotels and good places to eat.

From Chandrakot the trail drops steeply to the Modi Khola and crosses it at 1065 metres to the large village of Birethanti where you can really see how civilised this trek is. Birethanti even has sidewalk cafes! Trails to Ghandrung turn off from Chandrakot or Birethanti. Birethanti has excellent hotels but you may want to continue further to shorten the next day's long climb. Sticking to the northern side of the Bhurungdi Khola, the trail climbs to Hille and nearby Tirke-

dungha at 1525 metres. Both Tirkedungha and Hille have places to stay.

Day 3: Tirkedungha to Ghorapani

From Tirkedungha the trail climbs very steeply to Ulleri, a large Magar village at 2070 metres. It continues to ascend, but more gently, through fine forests of oak and rhododendron to Bahunthanti at 2250 metres and then Nayathanti at 2460 metres. Another hour brings you to Ghorapani at 2775 metres.

Only a short walk beyond Ghorapani is the Deorali pass (deorali actually means 'pass') with spectacular views. An hour's climb from here will take you to Poon (or Pun) Hill, one of the best Himalayan viewpoints in Nepal. There are hotels at Ghorapani and at Poon Hill. Ghora means 'horse' and pani means 'water' and indeed long caravans of pack horses are regularly seen all along the Jomsom Trek. A trail also runs from Ghorapani to Ghandruk. This part of the trek is plagued by leeches during the monsoon and there may be snow on the trail in the winter.

Day 4: Ghorapani to Tatopani

The trail descends steeply to Chitre at 2390 metres where there are more lodges offering accommodation. From here the hills are extensively terraced as the trail drops down through Sikha, a large village with shops and hotels at 1980 metres, and then descends gently to Ghara at 1705 metres. A further steep descent of 500 metres takes you to the Ghar Khola where the trail crosses the river on a suspension bridge and then climbs up above the Kali Gandaki River before crossing that too.

Turning north the trail soon reaches Tatopani at 1189 metres. It's a busy population centre where you will find some of the best food along the whole trail, and you can even get a cold beer to go with it. Tato means 'hot' and pani is 'water', a name earned courtesy of the hot springs by the river. Tatopani is a popular destination for a shorter trek out of Pokhara.

Day 5: Tatopani to Kalopani

The trail follows the Kali Gandaki Valley all the rest of the way to Jomsom. The river cuts a channel between the peaks of Annapurna I and Dhaulagiri, thus qualifying the Kali Gandaki Valley for the title of the world's deepest gorge. The two 8000-metre mountaintops are only 38 metres apart and the river flows between them at a height of less than 2200 metres.

The Kali Gandaki Valley is also the home for the Thakalis, a group noted for their trading and business expertise, particularly in running hotels and lodges not only here in their homeland but also in Pokhara and elsewhere in Nepal. Thakali women are very liberated and many of the lodges are run by women, whose menfolk have been taken elsewhere by business.

From Tatopani the trail climbs gradually to Dana at 1400 metres. This is where the difficult track branches off to Maurice Herzog's base camp, used for his historic ascent of Annapurna in 1950.

The trail continues to climb to Rukse Chhara and at one stage takes a precarious route through a very steep and narrow section of the gorge. Another suspension bridge crosses the river at 1935 metres and the trail then goes through Ghasa at 2000 metres, the first Thakali village.

A steep climb through forest takes you to the Lete Khola, then to the village of Lete at 2470 metres with a superb view of the western flank of Dhaulagiri and finally to Kalopani at 2560 metres. Kalopani has great mountain views and some comfortable lodges to view them from.

Day 6: Kalopani to Jomsom

For a distance from Kalopani there are trails on both sides of the river to choose from. Larjung on the west bank at 2560 metres has interesting alleyways and tunnels between the houses, an attempt to avoid the fierce winds that often whistle down the Kali Gandaki Valley. Khobang is the next village, with a gompa above it, and the mountain views on this stretch are the best to be seen. Tukche at 2590 is one of the most import-

ant Thakali villages, once a meeting place for traders from Tibet. Despite the growth of tourism in this area Tukche is still a quieter, smaller place than it was during the era of trade with Tibet.

From here the landscape changes as you enter the drier and more desert-like country north of the Himalayan watershed. It also gets windier: gentle breezes from the north in the morning shift to a gale from the south every afternoon. Marpha, at 2665 metres, virtually huddles behind a ridge to keep out of the wind! The village also has some of the most luxurious accommodation to be found along the trail and is a good alternative to staying in Jomsom. A government-established project between Tukche and Marpha grows fruit and vegetables for the whole region.

At 2713 metres, Jomsom is the major centre in the region and has a hospital and the inevitable trekking-permit checkpoint. If you're heading in the opposite direction on the Annapurna Circuit you must get your permit stamped here as it will be checked further south. This is the last Thakali village – those further north are inhabited by people of Tibetan descent. Jomsom has regular flights to Kathmandu ($75) and Pokhara ($45), but the Kathmandu to Jomsom flights can be problematic since in winter Kathmandu is often closed by fog in the early morning while the wind stops flights into or out of Jomsom later in the morning. Pokhara to Jomsom flights are less likely to be affected.

Day 7: Jomsom to Muktinath

If you have time, it's worth making the side-trip to the mediaeval-looking village of Kagbeni at 2810 metres. This very Tibetan-influenced settlement is as close as you can get to Lo Monthang, the capital of the legendary kingdom of Mustang further to the north. From here the trail climbs steeply to rejoin the regular trail before Khingar is reached at 3200 metres. The trail climbs through a desert landscape then past meadows and streams to the interesting village of Jharkot at 3500 metres. A further climb brings you to Ranipowa, the accommodation area of Muktinath, at 3710 metres.

Muktinath is a pilgrimage centre for Buddhists and Hindus. You'll see Tibetan traders as well as sadhus from the far south of India. The shrines in a grove of trees include a Buddhist gompa and the Vishnu temple of Jiwala Mayi. An old temple nearby shelters a spring and natural gas jets which provide Muktinath's famous eternal flame. It's the earth-water-fire combination that accounts for Muktinath's great religious significance.

From Muktinath you can retrace your steps to Pokhara, or simply to Jomsom and hope to catch a flight from there. It is possible to continue beyond Muktinath and cross the Thorung La pass to walk the rest of the Annapurna Circuit but this long walk is better made in the opposite direction.

ANNAPURNA CIRCUIT

Since it opened to foreign trekkers in 1977, the three-week Annapurna Circuit has become the most popular trek in Nepal. It passes through country inhabited by a wide diversity of peoples, it offers spectacular

Annapurna Treks

mountain scenery and it goes to the north of the main Himalayan range on to the high and dry Tibetan Plateau. To many independent trekkers it also offers the considerable advantage of having accommodation available each night. Some trekkers even walk the circuit without a sleeping bag, although that is not wise since there is always the possibility of finding no beds available at some village or other.

The circuit is usually walked in a counter-clockwise direction because of the difficulties of crossing the Thorung La pass. Travelling clockwise the longer ascent and shorter descent from west to east is too much for many people to manage in one day. The Thorung La pass at 5416 metres is closed by snow from mid-December to mid-April and bad weather can move in at any time. Trekkers should be prepared to turn back due to the weather or if they suffer from altitude sickness. If you take porters over this pass you must make sure they are adequately equipped for the cold weather.

The circuit is usually started from Dumre, on the Kathmandu to Pokhara road. These days there are jeeps north from Dumre as far as Besisahar. Some treks now walk the circuit starting directly from Pokhara by walking from Begnas Bazaar, by Begnas Tal and Rupa Tal, through Karputar to Besisahar. Although this route avoids some tedious road travel it does cross country where you will have to camp since village inns are not (yet) available. Another variation at the beginning of the trek is to start from Gorkha and walk across to intersect the route up from Dumre, again avoiding that tedious initial stretch of road.

After you cross the Thorung La pass from Manang to Muktinath the final seven days of the circuit trek are the same as the Jomsom Trek from Pokhara, but in reverse.

Day 1: Kathmandu via Dumre to Besisahar

It's a long and somewhat tedious drive from Kathmandu to the turn-off at Dumre. Starting from Pokhara is much easier since Dumre is 137 km from Kathmandu but only 70 km from Pokhara and, more importantly, the first stretch out of Kathmandu is in very bad condition. From Dumre, at 440 metres, 4WDs run regularly to Bhote Odar, which is about three hours' walk from Besisahar at 790 metres. If you can't get a 4WD up the road then an extra day must be added.

Day 2: Besisahar to Bahundanda

The trail drops, then climbs to Khudi at 790 metres. This is the first Gurung village that you reach (many of Nepal's Gurkha soldiers are Gurungs). From Khudi the trail offers fine views of Himalchuli and Peak 29 (Ngadi Chuli) as it climbs to Bhulbhule at 825 metres; it then goes to Ngadi before reaching Lampata at 1135 metres and nearby Bahundanda at 1310 metres. Both Lampata and Bahundanda have hotels although Lampata probably offers a better choice.

Day 3: Bahundanda to Chyanje

From Bahundanda the trail drops steeply to Syange at 1070 metres. The trail crosses the Marsyandi River on a suspension bridge and then follows the river to the stone village of Jagat before climbing through forest to Chyanje at 1400 metres.

Day 4: Chyanje to Bagarchhap

The rocky trail follows the Marsyandi River steadily uphill to Tal at 1675 metres, the first village in the Manang district. The trail crosses a wide, flat valley then climbs a stone stairway to 1860 metres before dropping down to another stairway. The trail continues up and down to Dharapani at 1890 metres, which is marked by a stone entrance chorten typical of the Tibetan-influenced villages from here northwards. Bagarchhap at 2160 metres has flat-roofed stone houses of typical Tibetan design although the village is still in the transition zone before the dry highlands.

Day 5: Bagarchhap to Chame

The trail, often rough and rocky, climbs to Tyanja at 2360 metres and then continues through forest, but near the river, to Kopar at 2590 metres. Chame at 2685 metres is the headquarters of the Manang district and its buildings include a bank. There are fine views of Annapurna II as you approach Chame and two small hot springs by the town.

Day 6: Chame to Pisang

The trail runs through deep forest in a steep and narrow valley, crosses a river on a long bridge at 2910 metres and then another bridge at 3040 metres. Views include the first sight of the soaring Paungda Danda rock face. The trail continues to climb to Pisang which sprawls between 3200 and 3300 metres and has many hotels.

Day 7: Pisang to Manang

The walk is now through the drier upper part of the Manang district, cut off from the full effect of the monsoon by the Annapurna Range. The people of this area herd yaks and raise crops for part of the year, but they also continue to enjoy special trading rights gained way back in 1784. Today they exploit these rights with shopping trips to Singapore and Hong Kong where they buy electronic goods and other modern equipment to resell in Nepal. Not surprisingly they are shrewd traders and hard bargainers.

From Pisang there are alternate trails north and south of the Marsyandi River which meet up again at Mungji. The southern route by Ongre, with its airstrip, at 3325 metres involves less climbing than the northern route via Ghyaru. The trail continues from Mungji past the picturesque but partially hidden village of Bryaga at 3475 metres to nearby Manang at 3535 metres where there are a number of hotels.

Day 8: Manang

It's a good idea to spend a day acclimatising in Manang before pushing on to the Thorung La pass. There are some fine day walks and magnificent views around the village. The Manangbhot people's legendary trading skills are seen at their keenest here – buy with caution!

Day 9: Manang to Phedi

From Manang it's an ascent of nearly 2000 metres to the Thorung La pass. The trail climbs steadily through Tengi, leaving the Marsyandi Valley and continuing along the Jarsang Khola Valley. The vegetation becomes steadily more sparse as you reach Ledar (or Lathar) at 4250 metres. Finally, you descend to cross the river at 4310 metres and then climb up to Phedi at 4420 metres. There are hotels here and the range of accommodation is being expanded. At the height of the season as many as 100 trekkers a day may cross over the Thorung La pass and beds can be in short supply. Some trekkers find themselves suffering from altitude sickness symptoms at Phedi. If you find yourself in a similar condition you must retreat downhill; even the descent to Ledar can make a difference.

Day 10: Phedi to Muktinath

Phedi means 'foot of the hill' and that's where it is, at the foot of the 5415-metre Thorung La pass. The trail climbs steeply but is regularly used and easy to follow. The altitude and snow can be problems: when the pass is snow-covered it is often impossible to cross. It takes about four hours to climb up to the pass, marked by chortens and prayer flags. The effort is worthwhile as the view from the top is magnificent. From the pass you have a tough 1600-metre descent to Muktinath.

Days 11-17: Muktinath to Pokhara

The remaining seven days of the trek simply follow the Pokhara, Jomsom, Muktinath route but in the opposite direction. Completing the Annapurna Circuit in 17 days allows for only one rest and acclimatisation day at Manang. It's very easy to slot a few additional days into the schedule.

ANNAPURNA SANCTUARY TREK

The walk up to the Annapurna Base Camp is a classic walk right into the heart of the mountains. The walk ends at a point where you are virtually surrounded by soaring Himalayan peaks. At one time this trek was a real expedition into an uninhabited wilderness area, but now there are a string of temporary lodges set up during the trekking season. The return trip takes 10 to 14 days and the walk to the base camp can be tacked on as a sidetrip from the Jomsom or Annapurna Circuit treks.

There are several routes to the sanctuary, all meeting at Ghandrung. The diversion from the Jomsom and Annapurna Circuit treks is made from Ghorapani to Ghandrung.

Day 1: Pokhara to Dhampus
The walk from Pokhara leaves the Jomsom and Annapurna Circuit routes at Phedi – buses now run to Phedi. From Phedi the trail climbs to Dhampus which stretches for several km from 1580 to 1700 metres and has a number of widely spaced hotels. Theft is a real problem in Dhampus, so take care.

Day 2: Dhampus to Ghandrung
The trail climbs to Pothana, descends steeply through a forest to Bichok and finally emerges in the Modi Khola Valley. It continues to drop to Tolka and then the Gurung village of Landrung (or Landruk) at 1650 metres. The trail continues to descend to a

suspension bridge at 1370 metres, then climbs steeply to join the trail from Birethanti and finally follows a long, long stone stairway to Ghandrung. There are many hotels in this large and confusing village; the biggest ones are near the top. From here Machhapuchhare really does begin to appear to have a fish tail.

Day 3: Ghandrung to Chhomro
The trail climbs to a pass at 2220 metres, then descends steeply to the Khumnu Khola at 1770 metres before climbing up again to Khumnu (or Kimrong). The trail continues to climb higher before dropping down to Chhomro at 1950 metres, the last permanent settlement in the valley. There are a number of places to stay and to stock up on supplies.

Day 4: Chhomro to Khuldi
The trail drops down to the Chhomro Khola, then climbs to Khuldi at 2380 metres. There are many leeches around here early and late in the trekking season.

Day 5: Khuldi to Hinko
The trail climbs through bamboo, then rhododendron, forests to Hinko at 3020 metres and on past the Machhapuchhare Base Camp (which isn't really a base camp since climbing the mountain is not permitted) to the Annapurna Base Camp. This area is called the Annapurna Sanctuary since it is totally surrounded by mountains.

Back to Pokhara
On the return trip you can retrace your steps, or divert from Ghandrung to Ghorapani to visit Poon Hill and follow the Annapurna Circuit or Jomsom route back to Pokhara.

The Ghorapani to Ghandrung walk is becoming increasing popular as a way of linking the Annapurna Sanctuary Trek with treks up the Kali Gandaki Valley. It's also used for shorter loop walks out of Pokhara (see the Around Pokhara section of the Pokhara chapter for details of these walks).

There's an alternative route between Pokhara and Tatopani, via Kusma and Beni, that comes out on the Bhairawa road south of Pokhara.

Other Treks

The Everest Base Camp Trek in the east, the Langtang and Helambu treks to the north of Kathmandu and the three Pokhara area treks in central Nepal between them are used by the vast majority of all trekkers. Yet there are other alternatives taking you to areas still relatively unvisited.

KANCHENJUNGA BASE CAMP

The trekking route up to the Kanchenjunga Base Camp in the extreme north-eastern corner of the country has recently been opened to trekkers, but you have to go with a recognised agency. The starting point can be Ilam or Basantpur by road, or Tumlingtar or Taplejung by air.

MAKALU BASE CAMP

It's a long but fine trek from Hile or Tumlingtar up the Arun River to the Makalu Base Camp in eastern Nepal.

SOLU KHUMBU TO DHANKUTA

As an alternative to flying back to Kathmandu from Lukla, or walking back to Jiri, the Everest Base Camp Trek can be extended by walking for 11 days south to Hile. From

Hile you can travel by road through Dhankuta and Dharan to Biratnagar from where there are buses and flights to Kathmandu.

DOLPO

Trekking to the Dolpo region has only been permitted since mid-1989. The region lies to the west of the Kali Gandaki Valley. Permits are still not easy to get and from Pokhara it's a tough 14-day trek to Phoksundo Lake and beyond. You can only trek there with a recognised agency.

RARA LAKE

The eight-day round trip trek from Jumla to the Rara Lake and back still gets less than 50 trekkers a year. Trekking here requires real planning since flights are difficult to get on, porters are hard to find and little food is available.

MUSTANG

Mustang has lured trekkers for many years, and has only recently been opened. It was closed, both because of guerrilla war that was waged along the border with Tibet, and because of the ecological sensitivity of the region. The area is part of the Tibetan plateau, and is high dry and beautiful. It lies to the north-west of the Kali Gandaki, beyond Kagbeni, which is as far west as you can go on the Jomsom Trek. It is only possible to enter with an organised group, and permits are a steep $700 for 10 days.

Panchkhal Valley to join the Bhote Kosi River which you follow for the rest of the journey. The road is a mixture of surfaced and unsurfaced, due mainly to landslide damage. Traffic can be quite heavy along this section as it is also the road to Jiri, a popular starting point for the Everest Base Camp Trek. The road climbs at a gentle gradient as it follows the river.

A couple of km past the turn-off to Jiri is Lamosangu, 23 km from Dolalghat. Lamosangu provides a far more pleasant place to spend the night than Barabise thanks to the fact that fewer buses stop. See the Arniko Highway section in the Around the Kathmandu Valley chapter for information on accommodation.

The next day's ride continues past Barabise where the road changes into a compacted track with a top layer of dust. This dust cover is transformed into choking clouds when buses pass, or mud in wet weather. Care should be taken during heavy rain as this section of the road is particularly vulnerable to landslides. The valley's sides begin to steepen and it gradually changes into a beautiful gorge with spectacular waterfalls. The track climbs practically the entire 34 km to Tatopani to complete the second day. (See the Arniko Highway section for information on accommodation.)

Tatopani is five km from the border post of Kodari. This section, as it climbs towards the Friendship Bridge, is probably the most beautiful section of the ride. It is now possible to cycle beyond the bridge and climb a rough track to the Chinese customs checkpost (11 km) just outside Khasa, which is visible from the bridge. It should be possible to return as far as Lamosangu the same day, taking advantage of a mainly downhill ride.

The ride back to Dhulikhel is 43 km and includes the long climb out of Dolalghat which you should allow time for. Depending on how you feel after the climb, you can stay in Dhulikhel or complete the trip by returning to Kathmandu.

THE RAJPATH

The Tribhuvan Highway (or Rajpath as it is popularly known) was the first highway to connect Kathmandu with the rest of the world. The road switchbacks 150 spectacular km from Kathmandu to Hetauda. Most traffic from the Terai and India now uses the highway between Narayanghat and Mugling which, although longer, is actually quicker. The Rajpath has light traffic and magnificent scenery, culminating at Daman with an incomparable Himalayan view. It's a classic ride.

The ride begins on the Kathmandu-Pokhara (Prithvi) Highway, which gives the only access to the valley. After leaving the valley, the highway descends to Naubise, at the bottom of the Mahesh Khola Valley, 27 km from Kathmandu, where the Rajpath intersects with the Prithvi Highway. Take the Rajpath, which forks to the left, and start a 35-km climb to Tistung at a height of 2030 metres. You climb through terraced fields, carved into steep hillsides. On reaching the pass you descend for seven km into the beautiful Palung Valley before the final steep nine-km climb to Daman, at a height of 2322 metres.

This day's ride, almost all climbing, will take between six and nine hours in the saddle. It is possible to stay in an observation tower at Daman, which will give you the thrill of waking up to the broadest Himalayan panorama Nepal has to offer. On a clear morning you can see from Dhaulagiri to Everest, a view worth the peddle. The following day the road climbs a further three km to the top of the pass, at 2488 metres. At this point, you can savour the prospect of an exhilarating 2300-metre descent in 60 km!

As you descend towards the Indian plains you will notice a contrast with the side you climbed – the south side is lush and semitropical. The road eventually flattens out when you reach a series of electricity transformers. The rest of the journey is a gently undulating route alongside a river – a further 10 km brings you to Hetauda. See the Hetauda section in the Terai chapter for details on accommodation. After a night's rest you can continue along the Rajpath towards India or turn right at the statue of the king in the centre of town and head towards the Royal Chitwan National Park.

HETAUDA TO NARAYANGHAT

Hetauda is just to the east of the Royal Chitwan National Park, which has a wide selection of accommodation, both in the park and in the town of Sauraha, as well as a great range of activities. (See the Royal Chitwan National Park section in the Terai chapter for more details.) You are prohibited from riding inside the park, but are allowed to ride directly to your resort.

As you cycle along the flat, smooth road towards Narayanghat enjoying the lush subtropical scenery watch out for resort signposts on your left-hand side. Machan Jungle Resort's turn-off is 40 km from Hetauda, and the resort can be reached after a further four km of beautiful trail riding with three river crossings. Alternatively, a further 23 km from the Machan turn-off brings you to the Chitwan Jungle Resort turn-off. A further 14 km brings you to Tadi Bazaar and the turn-off for Sauraha, the park's main budget accommodation centre. Sauraha is reached by an interesting six-km jeep track.

Narayanghat, 20 km from Sauraha on the banks of the Narayani River, gives a choice of further routes. From here you can return to Kathmandu or Pokhara via Mugling, though the section from Narayanghat to Mugling is probably best avoided by catching a bus. If you're heading to Pokhara it's also a good idea to miss the busy highway between Mugling and Pokhara by catching a bus in Mugling.

POKHARA

Pokhara is famous for its beauty, and the spectacular views of the Annapurnas and Manaslu Himal. The surrounding area provides excellent opportunities for trail riding around lakes and rivers and towards the mountains. The area is less populated than the Kathmandu Valley, so although there are less trails, villages and temples to explore, the rides are more tranquil.

Sarangkot

The ride to Sarangkot provides an excellent, challenging day trip.

Leave early and ride along Lakeside (towards the mountains) to the intersection with the Manswara road (which returns to the bazaar area). Continue straight on (north) and after two km the road becomes a track which heads to Sarangkot. This turns into a single track which closely hugs the edge of Phewa Tal. Continue until you join the trail heading up an extremely steep spiral to

Sarangkot. From this point it is far easier to continue straight ahead, riding narrow trails before descending to the valley of the winding Harpan Khola.

You will need to make a number of river crossings (impassable during monsoon) before rejoining the trail, which travels along narrow rice paddy fields – a good test of nerve and balance. The trail soon begins to climb to Kaski, towards the hill immediately in front of you. This section will take approximately one hour, and you will need to carry your bike on the steeper section near the crown of the hill. Once you have reached the top, you join a trail which connects Naudanda with Sarangkot, at approximately 1590 metres. The trail is narrow and rocky so you'll need to carry your bike for about 20% of the time.

The view from this ridge is spectacularly beautiful. Dhaulagiri, Manaslu, the Annapurnas and Machhapuchhare create a classic Himalayan panorama, especially on a cool clear morning. To the south you can look down over Pokhara and Phewa Tal.

Naudanda

From Sarangkot point you have the choice of continuing left or right. Heading left towards Naudanda the trail continues along the spine of the ridge before joining the recently surfaced Pokhara-Baglung Highway which connects Pokhara with Lumle (a popular starting point for trekking in the Annapurnas). Naudanda is 32 km from Pokhara, above a twisting six-km descent into the Madi Khola Valley. The highway has an excellent asphalt surface and descends gently as it follows the river, allowing an enjoyable coast almost all the way back to Pokhara.

An alternative is to turn right and head along the ridge for eight km to Sarangkot. After stopping to admire the view and have refreshments head steeply down stone steps, carrying the bike for half an hour, until you reach a jeep track. The track descends quickly in an exhilarating spiral pattern for eight km until it connects with the Pokhara-Baglung Highway, only four km north of Lakeside.

Rafting & Kayaking

Nepal has plenty of dramatic mountain rivers so it's hardly surprising that rafting has become so popular. The bulk of this chapter was written by David Allardice, the operations manager for Ultimate Descents, a company which organises rafting and kayaking tours throughout Nepal. The Information section was written by Richard Everist.

About Rafting

Nepal is earning the reputation for being one of the best places in the world for whitewater rafting and kayaking. Mountain scenery has drawn trekkers and climbers for many years, but these same mountains also feed some of the world's most challenging and beautiful rivers. The combination of spectacular rivers, mountain scenery and a rich cultural heritage make Nepal an obvious river runner's destination.

No other country has such a choice of trips on wild rivers with warm water, a subtropical climate, and huge white-sand beaches that are ideal for camping.

Rivers are graded for difficulty on an international scale from Class 1 to 6, with Class 1 defined as easy-moving water with few obstacles, and Class 6 being considered nearly impossible to negotiate and a hazard to life.

As long as people are in reasonable physical shape and aren't afraid of water they can safely go rafting on rivers with gradings from Class 1 to 3. For more difficult and exciting Class 4 and 5 rivers, people should be active, confident in water, and preferably have some rafting experience.

Rafting in Nepal has an image of extremely difficult white water, which is well justified at times of high-water flow (during the monsoon), but at most flows the more difficult rivers are Class 3 to 4. There are also many easier Class 1 and Class 2 rivers where you can float along admiring the scenery and running a few small rapids.

WHEN TO GO

The best times for rafting are late September to early December, and March to May. From late September to early October the rivers can be extremely high with monsoon run-off. Any expeditions attempted at this time require a very experienced rafting company and strong teams. From mid-October onwards the weather is settled and this is one of the most popular times. In December many of the rivers become too cold to enjoy, and the days are short with the start of winter. The spring season from March to May has lower water flows to begin with, which generally means the rapids aren't as powerful. The rivers rise again in May with pre-monsoon storms and some snow-melt.

From June to August the monsoon rains arrive and the rivers carry 10 times their low-water flows, and can flood with 60 to 80 times as much. High flows can obviously make rivers much more difficult.

TYPES OF RAFTING TRIPS

For many people a rafting trip in Nepal will be their first white-water experience. There are many different kinds of rafting trips, and it's important to choose the right one. The style of trip, difficulty of the river and length of time you have are all factors that will shape your decision.

Any raft can be paddled, or rigged with an oar frame and rowed. With an oar frame the guide normally sits in the middle and rows, while the other passengers enjoy the scenery – and hold on through the rapids. With a paddle raft the guide normally sits at the back calling instructions and steering, while the crew provides the power. Most active people prefer the teamwork and group participation of paddle rafting, but it can also be quite strenuous work. With a strong team a paddle raft can probably run harder rapids than an oar raft, and the sense of achievement cannot be compared.

Rafting trips vary from quite luxurious trips where you are rowed down the river and staff do everything for you (pitch camp, cook and so on) to trips where you participate in the running of the expedition, pitching tents, helping with the cooking and camp chores. The quality of the rafting equipment is another variable, and can make a huge difference to the comfort and safety of participants.

SAFETY

Safety is the most important part of any river trip. Unfortunately, at the moment there are no minimum safety conditions enforced by any official body in Nepal. This makes it very important to choose a professional rafting company.

If a group has recently returned from a trip, speak to its members. This will give you reliable information about the quality of equipment, the guides, the food, and the transportation. Question the company about how you get to and from the river, how many hours are spent paddling or rowing, where the camps are set up (near to villages?), what food is available, who does the cooking and work around the camp, what cooking fuel is used (wood?), what happens to rubbish, what hygiene precautions are taken, and what activities are there at night? Many companies have a photo file in their office. Have a look through this as it will give an impression of the equipment and safety.

The following check list is based on the experience of many international guides and should help in the process of selecting a company.

Raft Numbers

There should be a minimum of two rafts per trip. If anyone does fall out of a raft (known as a swimmer in the trade!) the second raft can help with any rescue. In higher water three rafts are safer than two. Many experts also agree that one or two safety kayakers can replace the second raft.

Check how many people have booked and paid for a trip, and the maximum number that will be taken. Obviously if the trip is leaving in two days and you are the only person booked, you are not going to have enough people to run a safe trip.

Safety Kayakers

Having good kayakers along will not only add to the safety of the trip, but on the easier river sections, they will often teach people to kayak. For more adventurous people, some of the inflatable kayaks and catamarans that are just turning up in Nepal are an excellent way to get the feel of controlling your own craft. These are a lot of fun, but it's important if you have these craft on a trip that the guides have the experience to know which rapids are safe to run. If you are interested in kayaking, a few companies have kayaks and kayaking gear for hire.

Raft Guides

The person leading the trip must be a qualified, trained guide with a minimum of 50 days rafting experience. They should also have done at least five previous trips on the river. All raft guides should have done the river before.

If possible, speak with the guide who will lead the trip. This will give you a chance to form an impression of the people you will be spending time with and the type of trip they run. Ask them about their previous experience. Overseas experience or training allows the guides to keep up with the latest advances and safety training.

All guides should have a current first aid certificate and be trained in resuscitation.

Equipment

Quality equipment is important, both for safety and comfort. Relatively new self-bailing rafts are better for more difficult trips. Good life jackets are essential and helmets are obligatory on any white-water trip. Modern plastic and alloy paddles are preferable to locally made wooden ones. New roll-top dry bags will keep your gear dry even if the raft flips. Waterproof camera containers will allow you to take photos all the way down the river. The companies should also supply tents. Ask how old the equipment is.

Ask what spare and repair equipment is carried, and what first-aid equipment is carried. On a long wilderness trip it's important that the guides are capable of dealing with any situation that occurs.

On the River

At the river your guide should give you a safety talk and paddling demonstration before you launch off downstream.

- Always wear your life jacket in rapids. Wear your helmet whenever your guide tells you, and make sure that both the helmet and jacket are properly adjusted and fitted.
- Keep your feet and arms inside the raft. If the raft hits a rock or wall and you are in the way, the best you'll escape with is a laceration.
- If you do swim in a rapid, get into the 'white-water swimming position' – on your back, with your feet downstream and up where you can see them. Hold on to your paddle as this will make you more visible. Relax and breathe when you aren't going through waves. Turn over and swim at the end of the rapid when the water becomes calmer.

Information

Anyone who is seriously interested in rafting and kayaking, and especially anyone contemplating a private expedition, should get hold of *White Water Nepal* (Rivers Publishing, UK; Menasha Ridge Press, USA) an excellent guidebook by Peter Knowles & David Allardice. It should be possible to get copies of the book in Kathmandu. It has incredibly detailed information on river trips, with 60 maps, river profiles and hydrographs, plus advice on equipment and health – in short all the information a prospective river runner could want.

INDEPENDENT RAFTING & KAYAKING

Anyone who plans to raft or kayak privately should also contact local rafting companies to get up-to-date information. Himalayan rivers are dynamic, and rivers and their rapids change every monsoon.

Getting Your Gear to Nepal

Most airlines will carry short kayaks on the same basis as surfboards or bicycles – there's no excess baggage charge, so long as you are within the weight limits. If you are a group, negotiate a deal at the time of booking. If there are just one or two of you, just turn up, put all your bulky light gear in the kayak, heavy items in your carry-on luggage, and smile sweetly! (Phone them in advance and they have to quote the rule book and start talking air cargo.)

Permits

Rafters and kayakers are required to have rafting permits, which are obtained from the Ministry of Tourism, Tripureshwar (near the football stadium) and cost $5. There's a list of rivers where rafting is permitted (including all the rivers in the previous section), but this is constantly being expanded, so it's best to check the situation when you arrive. Of course, if you have to walk in to the river, you'll also need a trekking permit.

ORGANISED RAFTING & KAYAKING

If you go on an organised rafting trip the necessary permits will be arranged for you. No special equipment is required. Usually you will only need light cotton clothing, with a slightly warmer change for nights. A swimsuit, sun hat, sunscreen, and light tennis shoes or sandals are all necessary, but can also be bought in Kathmandu. For overnight trips a sleeping bag is necessary, but this can easily be hired.

There are about 50 companies in Kathmandu claiming to be rafting operators. A few are well-established older companies with good reputations, and the rest are newer companies, often formed by guides breaking away and starting their own operations. Although these new companies can be

Minimising Your Impact

With no regulatory body, it's up to the people who raft to help shape the sport in Nepal.

Show respect for the environment and make sure that your group and company does the same. Camp sites should be kept scrupulously clean. Burn all burnable waste. Bury organic waste away from camp and below the high-water level. Toilet pits should also be away from camp and below the high-water level. Toilet paper should be burnt. Leave only footprints.

Use only as much driftwood as you need, and do not use wood that would otherwise be used by villagers. If there is no driftwood use an alternative fuel like gas or kerosene.

Show your respect for the people and their culture by acting and dressing appropriately. If you visit a village or temple dress modestly.

Rural villagers are extremely honest, but it's still worthwhile making sure you know where your valuables are at all times. Don't leave gear lying around at camp sites – put it inside your tent. Don't take any valuables you don't need on the river, instead store them in Kathmandu. Many of the rafting operators will store them for you. On rivers with road access you should be even more careful about possible theft.

If you have any suggestions or complaints, write to the Nepal Association of Rafting Agents (NARA) PO Box 2586, Kathmandu.

David Allardice

enthusiastic and good, they can also be shoe-string operations that may not have adequate resources in terms of equipment and staff.

Most of the small travel agencies simply sell trips on commission; often they have no real idea about the details of what they are selling and are really only interested in getting bums on seats. To further confuse the situation, there are also sometimes complicated subcontracting arrangements between companies. It is immensely preferable to deal directly with the company you will be rafting with.

If time is limited you may choose to book a trip before you leave home, however all the operators accept bookings in Kathmandu. In many ways it's preferable to book in Kathmandu, because you have the opportunity to meet the people you will be rafting with before you make a commitment. Trips depart on a regular basis (at least one long trip a week during the season), and the best companies will refer you to a friendly competitor if they don't have any suitable dates.

Trips range in price from $15 to $70 a day, and generally you get what you pay for. At $15 you don't get much at all. It is better to pay a bit more and have a good, safe trip, than to save $100 and have a lousy, dangerous trip. Bear in mind that trips in Nepal are generally less than half the cost of similar

trips in the USA, so in relative terms all the prices are extremely reasonable. Particularly if you plan to do a longer trip on a remote and difficult river like the Sun Kosi or Karnali, it's important to choose a company that has the experience, skills and equipment to run a safe and exciting trip.

With the constant change in rafting companies it's difficult to make individual recommendations; the fact that a company is not recommended here does not necessarily mean they will not deliver an excellent trip. Nonetheless, the following companies have been recommended for their professionalism. Their prices range from $50 to $70 a day.

Equator Rafting
Tukche Peak Guest House compound, Thamel, Kathmandu. This is a new company with experienced staff, and specialises in long participatory rafting and kayaking trips (☎ 01-414803; fax 411933).

Himalayan Encounters
Kathmandu Guest House compound, Thamel, Kathmandu. This company is associated with Encounter Overland and has earned a solid reputation through many trips on the Trisuli and Sun Kosi (☎ 01-432632).

Himalayan River Exploration (HRE)
Lazimpat, Kathmandu. This group is part of the the Tiger Tops organisation (one of Nepal's original companies) and is an up-market operation,

running a lot of catered trips with rowing rigs
(☎ 01-418491; fax 414075)).

Raging River Runner
Jyatha, Thamel. This group is at the budget end
of rafting (☎ 01-214712; fax 229983).

Ultimate Descents
Yeti Cottage compound, Thamel, Kathmandu.
This group has been in operation for five years
and specialises in long, participatory rafting and
kayaking trips (☎ 01-412818; fax 411933).

West Himalayan Outdoors
(☎ 01-416968; fax 415346).

White Magic
Jyatha, Thamel (☎ 01-226885; fax 226885).

Selecting a River

The longer river trips offer the best range of
scenery and rapids and allow participants
enough time to develop skills and friend-
ships. Most long trips take from eight to 12
days, with a lot of time rafting in wilderness.
If you have the time the choice is between
the Karnali, the Sun Kosi and the Tamur.
They are all classic rivers with exciting white
water and excellent beaches.

If you don't have time to do a long trip,
but still want to experience a multiday trip
there are several medium-length options.
The rivers that lend themselves to medium-
length trips are the Trisuli, the Kali Gandaki,
the Seti and the Marsyandi.

Short day trips are mainly run on the
Trisuli, close to Kathmandu, but the Upper
Sun Kosi and Bhote Kosi are also possibili-
ties.

The following section only describes
some of the major rivers in Nepal. There are
many other rivers that offer good trips suited
to specialised expeditions.

KARNALI

The Karnali combines a two-day trek
through the Chure Hills with one of the best
big-volume river trips in the world. The
rapids are more challenging than the Sun
Kosi, and the river flows through pristine
wilderness. The Karnali is the longest and
largest river in Nepal, draining most of
Nepal's 'wild west'. There is a lot of wildlife.

If you stay a couple of days in the Royal
Bardia National Park at the end of the river
trip, you will have put together one of the
world's best combined rafting and trekking
trips.

It's a one-day drive from Kathmandu to
Surkhet and the start of the trek. After sorting
all the expedition equipment and supplies for
the porters you trek for two days through
lowland forest and small villages. The
rafting starts at Sauli and finishes 180 km
later at Chisopani. The river section takes
about seven days, which gives you plenty of
time to explore some of the Karnali's side
valleys and villages, and includes a rest day.
The return to Kathmandu takes another day.

Most of the rapids are in the first 90 km
from Sauli down to the confluence with the
Seti River. This is not a river to take lightly.
For a lot of the trip you are in an isolated
wilderness area, at least three days' walk
from any roads. The river flows through
steep-walled canyons with rapids coming
close together. This makes the potential consequences of accidents serious.

Getting to and from the river is not easy
and is one of the reasons why it is seldom
rafted, although anyone who has done the
trip will agree that it is worth the time and
effort. It is a full day's travel from Kathmandu by road, but it is also possible to fly to
Nepalganj, and then drive for four or five
hours to Surkhet where the trek starts.

SUN KOSI

The Sun Kosi is one of the easiest of the long
trips to organise since there is road access at
the start and finish. This also makes it the
cheapest. It is an excellent trip at all water
levels, with rapids all the way down the
270-km section from Dolalghat, past Dhulikhel, to the finishing point at Chatara, near
Dhankuta.

Many people consider this river to be one
of the 10 classic rivers in the world. It has
many large-volume rapids similar in nature
to the Grand Canyon in Colorado. The
beaches are huge, and ideal for camping.

The starting point at Dolalghat is two to
three hours' drive from Kathmandu along the

Rivers of Nepal

Arniko Highway (which runs through to the Tibetan border). The natural progression of rapids makes the river an excellent choice for someone doing their first river trip in Nepal.

The first couple of days are not difficult, although there are plenty of Class 2 to 3 rapids, which give you a good chance to learn the skills and teamwork that are necessary for the more difficult rapids lower down. From the third day onwards you raft Class 3 to 5 rapids each day, as well as many smaller ones. It's unusual for the lower sections of a large river to have many rapids, but the last few days on the Sun Kosi have some of the best.

The Sun Kosi winds its way through the beautiful Mahabharat Range, collecting all the rivers in eastern Nepal – its tributaries drain the highest mountains in the world. One of the most dramatic moments of the trip is when you finally emerge from the hills at Chatara to see the vast Gangetic plain stretching endlessly before you.

You need eight to 10 days to raft the Sun Kosi. This will give time to explore villages, jungle and some of the small Hindu temples along the way.

TAMUR RIVER

The Tamur drains the Kanchenjunga area, and this trip combines one of the most spectacular short treks in Nepal with a river that is world class. There are 120 rapids in the 120 km from the starting point at Dobhan. During high-water flows this would probably be more difficult than the Karnali and Sun Kosi.

The trip normally takes 11 or 12 days, with one full day spent driving to Basantpur, three days' trekking to Dobhan, six or seven days on the river, and one day returning to Kathmandu.

The long drive from Kathmandu to Basantpur is a fairly brutal start to a trip, but once the road climbs up to Hile the views are spectacular. The trek follows a ridge through forests of rhododendrons to Gupha Pokhari at 3000 metres, then drops down to the river at Dobhan. On clear days the views are incredible, with Makalu and Kanchenjunga to the north and Everest in the distance.

At Dobhan three tributaries of the Tamur join forces. The rafting in the top section is intense with perhaps 40 rapids in the first 16 km. Below this the number of rapids eases slightly, but there are still plenty of challenges. The best section is when the river finally turns back to the west (in the last few days). Here the river is steep and powerful, with 40 to 50 rapids in the last canyons before the Tamur cascades out into the Sun Kosi.

TRISULI RIVER

The Trisuli is a popular choice because it is close to Kathmandu and has easy access. There are a lot of companies running a range of trips on the Trisuli, and the trips they run are among the cheapest you can tackle.

The reason the river is so cheap and accessible is also one of the main drawbacks – the Kathmandu-Pokhara (Prithvi) Highway runs right beside the river. This, and the number of companies using the river, detracts from the experience. Many companies misuse the beaches, leaving trash and toilet paper behind. They also burn a lot of firewood that the local villagers gather for them.

Depending on water flows, the best trip on the Trisuli starts at Baireni and finishes three or four days later at Narayanghat. It is possible for shorter trips to be combined with a stay in Chitwan or Pokhara. The best section for white water is from Baireni to Mugling. At high-water levels the Trisuli is a very challenging and exciting river to run.

KALI GANDAKI RIVER

The Kali Gandaki is an excellent medium-length wilderness trip. This is a better trip than the Trisuli as there is no road along the river, the scenery is impressive and the camp sites good. This is also one of the holiest rivers in Nepal, and the junctions of every major tributary are marked by the fires of many cremations.

When the new road from Pokhara to the starting point at Kusma is finished (mid-93?), this will become one of the most popular trips in Nepal and will offer a great alternative to the Trisuli.

The upper section from Kusma to Ramdhighat is 90 km of Class 3 to 4 white water and takes about four days to complete. At Ranighat, below Tansen, there's an incredible derelict palace that is worth visiting.

It is possible to finish at Ramdhighat (on the Siddhartha Highway between Pokhara and Sunauli) or to continue to the confluence with the Trisuli at Devghat (just north of Narayanghat). This adds another 130 km and three or four more days. The lower section doesn't have many rapids, but it is a very isolated area with lots of wildlife.

Combining the upper and lower sections of the Kali Gandaki would create an excellent long trip for people wanting to do an easier river than the Sun Kosi.

SETI RIVER

The Seti is an excellent two-day trip in an isolated area, with beautiful jungle and plenty of easy rapids. The logical starting point is Damauli on the Kathmandu-Pokhara (Prithvi) Highway between Mugling and Pokhara. This would give you 32 km of rafting to the confluence with the Trisuli River. It is possible to raft a higher section, starting at Dule Gouda, which would add another 30 km, but considering the quality of the rapids it probably isn't worth it. Beware if you decide to try the upper section of the river as it disappears underground above Dule Gouda!

MARSYANDI RIVER

The Marsyandi is one of the most beautiful mountain rivers in Nepal. It has magnificent mountain views and continuous Class 4 rapids. Since the building of the hydroelectric dam near Mugling, however, the possible trip has been shortened to two days.

The section from Bhote Odar to Bimalnagar is 28 km – a great short run for an expert group that would combine well with a Seti trip.

UPPER SUN KOSI

The Upper Sun Kosi from Khadichour to Dolalghat is a beautiful 20-km introduction to rafting with lots of rapids and clear blue water.

BHOTE KOSI

The Bhote Kosi, which roughly translates as 'river from Tibet' is a tributary that joins the Upper Sun Kosi. It has been rafted from 10 km above Barabise down to the dam at Lamosangu. This is one of the most challenging short rafting trips in Nepal. The 16-km section takes a full day and is extreme rafting all the way.

OTHER RIVERS

The **Bheri**, which is in the west, is a great float trip with incredible jungle scenery and lots of wildlife. This is one of the great fishing rivers and can be combined with a visit to the Royal Bardia National Park. The **Arun River** from Tumlingtar makes an excellent three-day wilderness trip, and the final two days on the Tamur make an exhilarating trip.

Glossary

Beware of the different methods of transliterating Nepali and the other languages spoken in Nepal. There are many and varied ways of spelling Nepali words. In particular the letter 'b' and letter 'v' are often interchanged. The god Bhairab becomes Bhairav or the thunderbolt symbol changes from Vajra to Bajra.

Adi Buddha – the original self-generated Buddha of Tantric Buddhism who created the Dhyani Buddhas.
Aditya – ancient Vedic sun god.
Agni – ancient Vedic god of the hearth and fire. He rides a chariot drawn by parrots and his four arms hold flames, a ball of fire, a trident and a rosary.
Agnipura – Buddhist symbol for fire.
Aksobhya – the Dhyani Buddha of the east; his vehicle is an elephant and he is often seen with one hand touching the ground in the gesture known as subduing Mara.
Amitabha – the Dhyani Buddha of the west; his animal is the peacock.
Amoghasiddhi – the Dhyani Buddha of the north, his consort is Green Tara and in Nepalese stupas he sits under a seven-hooded snake canopy.
Ananda – the Buddha's chief disciple
Ananta – the cosmic serpent upon which Vishnu reclines.
Annapurna – the goddess of abundance and an incarnation of Mahadevi.
arak – a fermented drink made from potatoes or grain.
Ashoka – Indian Buddhist emperor who spread the religion throughout the subcontinent.
Ashta Matrikas – the eight mother goddesses.
asla – river trout.

Avalokitesvara

Asuras – demons ruled by Rawana, king of Lanka in the *Ramayana*. The name can be a suffix as in Mahishasura.
Avalokitesvara – as Gautama Buddha is the Buddha of our era, so is Avalokitesvara the Bodhisattva of our era. In Nepal he has become a Hindu/Buddhist god of mercy whose incarnation is Machhendranath or Manjushri.
avatar – an incarnation of a deity living on earth.

bahal – a Buddhist monastery, usually two storeys high and built around a courtyard. There are a great number of bahals in the towns of the Kathmandu Valley but few of them continue to function as monasteries. Many are used as schools.
bahil – a simpler version of a bahal.
bakba – Tibetan clay mask.
bajra – see vajra.
Balarama – Krishna's brother.
Balkumari – one of Bhairab's consorts.
Banrhas – Buddhist hereditary priesthood.
bazaar – market area; a market town is called a bazaar or bazar.
bell – see ghanta.
bel tree – it is a Newari custom to 'marry' young girls to a bel tree so that they can never be widowed.
betel – mildly intoxicating concoction of areca nut and lime which is wrapped in betel leaf and chewed. The red splashes you see on the ground throughout South Asia are spat out by betel chewers. Regular betel chewing leads to dark-red stained teeth.
Bhairab – the 'terrific' or fearsome Tantric form of Shiva in Nepal. Bhairab has 64 manifestations.
Bhadrakali – a Tantric goddess who is also a consort of Bhairab.
Bhagavadgita – Krishna's lessons to Arjuna, part of the *Mahabharata*.
bhati – term for a teahouse in western Nepal.
Bhimsen – a deity noted for his strength and bravery.
Bhot – high-altitude desert valleys north of the Himalaya bordering Tibet. In Nepal Tibetans are known as Bhots.
Bhote – Nepali for Tibet.
bodhi tree – or bo tree, a pipal tree under which the Buddha was sitting when he attained enlightenment.
Bodhisattva – a near-Buddha who renounces the opportunity to attain nirvana in order to aid humankind.
Bon – the animist religion of Tibet prior to Buddhism.
Brahman – the highest Hindu caste, said to originate from Brahma's head. Priests are drawn from this caste although Brahmans may have many other occupations.

chaitya

chaitya – small stupa which usually contains a mantra rather than a Buddhist relic.
chakra – Vishnu's disc-like weapon, one of the four symbols he holds.
chang – Tibetan rice beer.
chapatti – unleavened Indian bread.
Chaturmukha – Shiva lingam with four images of the god's face.
chautara – stone platforms around trees which serve as shady places for porters to rest.
Chenrezig – Tibetan name for Avalokitesvara.
Chhetris – the second caste of Nepalese Hindus and the prince and warrior caste to which the Ranas and the Shah kings belonged. Chhetris are said to originate from Brahma's arms.
chirag – ceremonial oil lamp.
Chitrakar – special caste of Newari painters.
Chomolongma – the Tibetan name for Mt Everest; literally, 'Mother Goddess of the World'.
chortens – Tibetan Buddhist stupas.
chowk – a courtyard or marketplace such as Indra Chowk, the old market area of Kathmandu.
chuba – long woollen Sherpa coat.
chura – beaten rice.
curd – yoghurt.

Dalai Lama – incarnation of a Bodhisattva who is the spiritual leader of Tibetan Buddhists.
Damais – a caste of tailors who perform music at weddings.
danda – hill.
Dattatraya – deity who is thought of as an incarnation of Vishnu, Shiva's teacher, or the Buddha's cousin.
deval – Nepali word for temple.
Devanagari – Sanskrit Nepali script.
Devi – the short form of Mahadevi, the shakti to Shiva.
dhaki – handwoven cotton cloth.

dhal – lentil soup; the main source of protein in the Nepalese diet.
dhami – priest claiming occult powers, a sorcerer.
dharma – Buddhist teachings.
dharamsala – rest house for pilgrims.
dhoka – door or gate.
dhwaja – metal ribbon streaming out from the roof of a temple and acting as a pathway for the gods.
dhyana – meditation.
Dhyani Buddhas – the original Adi Buddha created five Dhyani Buddhas who in turn create the universe of each human era. Amitabha is the Dhyani Buddha of our era. See Swayambhunath in the Around the Kathmandu Valley chapter for more information.
dighur – Thakali cooperative economic system where members of a group pool their money to support one person's plans.
doko – basket carried by porters.
doonga – boat.
dorje – Tibetan word for *bajra* or *vajra*.
durbar – palace.
Durga – fearsome manifestation of Parvati, Shiva's consort.
Dwarapala – door guardian figure.
dyochhen – a form of temple enshrining Tantric deities.
dzopkyo – male cross between a yak and a cow; also zopkiok.
dzum – female offspring of a yak and a cow; also zhum.
dzu-tch – large yeti that eats cattle.

ek – Nepalese number one, a symbol of the unity of all life.
Ekamukha – Shiva lingam with one image of the god's face.

gajur

freaks – '60s term from the overland era for the young Westerners who wandered the East and could be found congregating in Bali, Kabul, Goa and Kathmandu.

gaines – beggar musicians.
gajur – bell-shaped top to a bahal.
ganas – Shiva's 'companions'.
Ganesh – Shiva and Parvati's son, instantly recognisable by his elephant head.
Ganga – goddess of the River Ganges.
ganja – hashish.
Garuda – the man-bird vehicle of Vishnu.
Gautama Buddha – the Buddha of our era.
Gelugpa – Yellow Hat sect of Tibetan Buddhism. This is the reformed sect headed by the Dalai Lama.
gada – club-like weapon of Vishnu.
ghanta – Tantric bell which is the female equivalent of the dorje.
ghat – steps beside a river. A 'burning ghat' is used for cremations.
ghee – clarified butter.
gompa – Tibetan Buddhist monastery.
gopis – cowherd girls. (Krishna had a lot of fun with his gopis.)
Gorakhnath – 11th-century yogi now said to be an incarnation of Shiva.
gurkha – Nepalese mercenaries who have long formed a part of the British army. The name comes from the region of Gorkha.
Gurkhali – British army name for the Nepali language.
gurr – traditional Sherpa potato dish.
Gurungs – western hill people, predominantly from around Gorkha and Pokhara.
Guthi – Newari community group offering mutual support to its members.

Hanuman – monkey god.
Harisiddhi – a fearsome Tantric goddess.
harmika – eyes on a stupa which face the four cardinal directions, or the 13 steps of a stupa steeple, symbolising the 13 stages to enlightenment.
hashish – dried marijuana plant resin.
hiti – water conduit or tank with waterspouts.
hookah – water pipe for smoking.

impeyan pheasant – Nepal's national bird.
incarnation – a particular life form; in the case of mortals, determined by karma. Vishnu has 10 different incarnations.
Indra – king of the Vedic gods, god of rain.

Jagannath – Krishna as 'Lord of the World'.
Jambhala – god of wealth; look for his money bag and his attendant mongoose.
Jamuna – goddess of the River Jamuna.
janai – sacred thread which high-caste Hindu men wear looped over their left shoulder and replace once each year; also Munja.
jatra – festival, as in Indra Jatra.
Jaya Varahi – Vishnu's consort when the god takes on his boar incarnation.
jhankri – sorcerer.
Jogini – mystical goddesses, counterparts to the 64 manifestations of Bhairab.
jukha – Nepali word for leech.

Kala – see Mara.
kalakuta – the poison which Shiva swallowed when he was in the form of Nilakantha.
kalasa – a pot, or a pot-shaped top to a temple.
Kali – most terrifying manifestation of Parvati.
Kalki – Vishnu's 10th, and as yet unseen, incarnation when he will come riding a white horse and wielding a sword to destroy the world.
Kalpa – a day in the age of Brahma.
Kam Dev – Shiva's 'companion'.
Karkotak – chief naga of the Kathmandu Valley.
karma – Buddhist and Hindu law of cause and effect which continues from one life to another.
Kartikkaya – god of war and son of Shiva, his animal is the cock or peacock and he carries a variety of weapons. Also known as Skanda or Kumar.
kata – the Tibetan prayer shawl which should be presented to an important Buddhist personage when introduced.
Kaukala – a form of Shiva in his fearsome aspect; he carries a trident with the skeleton of Vishnu's gate-keeper impaled upon it: a result of banning Shiva from Vishnu's palace!
Khas – Hindu hill people.
khola – stream or tributary.
khukuri – traditional curved knife of the Gurkhas.

khukuri

kinkinimali – temple wind bells.
kosi – river.
Krishna – the fun-loving eighth incarnation of Vishnu.
Kshatriyas – Indian equivalent of the Chhetri caste.
Kshepu – snake-eating figure often seen on toranas.

Kubera – see Jambhala.
kundalini – female energy principle.
Kumar – see Kartikkaya.
Kumari – the living goddess, a peaceful incarnation of Kali.
kunda – water tank fed by springs.

la – mountain pass.
Lakshmi – goddess of prosperity and Vishnu's consort.
laliguras – Nepalese word for rhododendron, the national flower.
lama – Tibetan Buddhist monk or priest.
lingam – phallic symbol of Shiva's creative powers.
Locana – consort of the Dhyani Buddha, Aksobhya.
Lokesvara – Lord of the World, an aspect of Avalokitesvara but often mingled with the Hindu gods in Nepal. He appears as Nilakantha, an aspect of Shiva, and as Natesvara, much like Natraj, the dancing Shiva whose cosmic dance created the world.

Machhendranath – patron god of the Kathmandu Valley and an incarnation of Avalokitesvara or Lokesvara.
Mahabharata – one of the major Hindu epics.
Mahadeva (Mahadeo) – another name for Shiva; *maha* translates as 'great', *deva* as 'god'.
Mahadevi – Great Goddess, sometimes known simply as Devi, the shakti to Shiva.
Mahakala – protector of the mandala and a Tantric equivalent of Shiva; literally, 'great black one'.
maharishi – great teacher.
Mahayana – form of Buddhism (the 'greater vehicle') prevalent through East Asia, Tibet and Nepal.
Mahayuga – each day of Brahma (see Kalpa) is divided into 1000 Mahayugas or Great Ages.
Mahishasura – buffalo demon killed by Durga.
mahseer – game fish of the Terai rivers.
Maitreya – a Buddha who will come in a future era.
Makara – mythical water monster, often appears as a waterspout on buildings.
Mali – Newari gardener caste.
Malla – royal dynasty of the Kathmandu Valley responsible for most of the important temples and palaces of the valley towns.
mandala – geometrical and astrological representation of the world.
mandap – roofless Tantric shrine.
mandir – Nepali word for temple.
Manjushri – god who cut open the Chobar Gorge so that the Kathmandu Lake could become the Kathmandu Valley.
mani – stone carved with the Tibetan Buddhist chant *om mani padme hum.*
mantra – prayer formula or chant.
Mara – Buddhist god of death, has three eyes and holds the Wheel of Life.

math – Hindu priest's house.
mela – a country fair.
mithuna – Sanskrit term usually referring to a depiction of gods engaged in intercourse in erotic art; *yab-yum* in Tibetan.
moksha – spiritual release, Hindu equivalent of nirvana.
mudra – symbolic hand gesture of the gods.
Munja – see Janai.

naga – serpent deity. The eight nagas have control over water, and are often seen over house entrances to keep evil spirits away.
nagini – female naga.
Nagpura – Buddhist symbol for water.
nak – female yak.
namaste – Nepalese greeting.
Nandi – the bull, vehicle of Shiva.
Narayan – Vishnu as the sleeping figure on the cosmic ocean. From his navel Brahma appears and goes on to create the universe. Narayan is Vishnu's most important appearance in Nepal but it is simply another name for Vishnu, not another incarnation.
Narsingha (Narsimha) – man-lion incarnation of Vishnu.
Newaris – people of the Kathmandu Valley.
Nilakantha – blue-throated form of Shiva, a result of swallowing poison that would have destroyed the world.
nirvana – final escape from the cycles of existence.
Nriteshwar – god of dance.
Nyingmapa – one of the three Red Hat sects of Tibetan Buddhism.

om mani padme hum – sacred Buddhist mantra which translates as 'hail to the jewel in the lotus'.
oriflammes – prayer flags; the wind carries off the prayers written on them.

padma – lotus flower.
Padmapani – literally 'lotus in hand'; a manifestation of Avalokitesvara as he appears in many Nepalese viharas, holding a tall lotus stalk.
Padmasambhava – Bodhisattva who founded the Nyingmapa Tibetab Buddhist sect.
pagoda – multistoreyed Nepalese temple. This style was later exported from Nepal to China and Japan.
panchayat – the non-party parliament of Nepal until 1990.
Panduravasini – consort of the Dhyani Buddha Amitabha.
Parvati – Shiva's consort.
pashmina – goat's wool blanket or shawl.
Pashupati – Shiva as Lord of the Animals.
patakas – see dhwaja.
path (pati) – small raised platform to shelter pilgrims.
patuka – waistcoat to carry things.

pith – open shrine for a Tantric goddess.
prajna – female counterparts of male Buddhist deities.
pokhari – large water tank.
Prajnaparamita – consort of the Dhyani Buddhas Vairocana and Aksobhya.
prasad – food offering.
prayer flags – each carries a sacred mantra which is 'said' when the flag flutters.
prayer wheels – cylindrical wheel inscribed with a Buddhist prayer or mantra which is 'said' when the wheel spins. There are even water-driven prayer wheels.

prayer wheel

Prithvi – Vedic earth goddess.
puja (pooja) – religious offering or prayer.
Puranas – Hindu holy books of around 400 BC which heralded the shift from the Vedic gods to the Hindu trinity of Brahma, Vishnu and Shiva.
puri – town.

Radha – Krishna's wife.
rajpath – road or highway, literally 'king's road'.
rakshi – rice spirit.
Rama – Vishnu's seventh incarnation, and hero of the *Ramayana*.
Ramayana – Hindu epic which recounts the adventures of Rama, Sita, Hanuman and the demon king Rawana.
Rana – hereditary prime ministers who ruled Nepal from 1841 to 1951.
rath – the temple chariot in which the idol is conveyed in processions.
Ratnasambhava – Dhyani Buddha of the south.
Rawana (Ravana) – the demon king of Lanka in the *Ramayana*.

rikhi doro – golden thread worn around the waist by Shiva devotees.
rimpoche – abbot of a gompa.
Rudra – Vedic god of lightning, an early version of Shiva.

sadhus – wandering Hindu holy men, generally Shaivites who have given up everything to follow the trail to religious salvation. Many sadhus come from India to visit Pashupatinath, the great Shiva temple of Nepal
Sagarmatha – Nepalese name for Mt Everest.
Sakyamuni – another name for Gautama Buddha.
sal – tree of the lower Himalayan foothills.
saligrams – black ammonite fossils of Jurassic period sea creatures, proof that the Himalaya was once under water.
sankha – conch shell symbol of Vishnu.
sanyasin – religious ascetic who has cut all ties with normal society.
saranghi – small violin played by the Gaines.
Saraswati – goddess of learning and the creative arts, and consort of Brahma. She can often be identified by the flute-like instrument which she plays called a *vina*.
satal – pilgrim's house.
Shaivites – followers of Shiva who cover their faces in ashes, paint three horizontal lines on their forehead and carry a begging bowl and Shiva's symbolic trident.
Shakti – dynamic female element in male-female relationships; a goddess.
Shantipura – Buddhist symbol for the sky.
Sherpas – literally 'people from the east', the Sherpas are Buddhist hill people famed for their stalwart work with mountaineering expeditions. With a small 's' sherpa means trek leader.
Sherpanis – female Sherpas.
Sheshnag – some believe that this snake, not Ananta, is the one which Vishnu reclines on.
shikhara – Indian-style temple with a tall corncob-like spire.
Shitala Mai – ogress who became a protector of children.
Shiva – most powerful Hindu god, the creator and destroyer.
Shivaratri – birthday of Shiva.
Simhanada – a form of Avalokitesvara who rides a lion.
sindur – red dust and mustard oil mixture used for offerings.
sirdar – leader/organiser of a trekking party.
Sita – Rama's wife in the *Ramayana*.
Skanda – see Kartikkaya.
Solu Khumbu – Everest region of eastern Nepal where the majority of the Sherpas live.
sonam – the karma acquired through successive incarnations.

STOL – short-take-off-and-landing aircraft used on mountain airstrips.
stupa – hemispherical Buddhist religious structure; always walk around stupas clockwise.

stupa

Sudras – the lowest Nepalese caste, said to originate from Brahma's feet.
sundhara – fountain with golden spout.
Surya – see Aditya.
suttee (sati) – practice of throwing widows on their husband's funeral pyre.

tabla – hand drum.
tahr – wild mountain goat.
Taleju Bhawani – Nepalese goddess, an aspect of Mahadevi and the family deity of the Malla kings of the Kathmandu Valley. There are Taleju temples in the old royal palaces of Kathmandu, Patan and Bhaktapur.
Tantric Buddhism – form of Buddhism which evolved in Tibet during the 10th to 15th centuries.
Tara – as White Tara she is the consort of the Dhyani Buddha Vairocana, as Green Tara she is associated with Amoghasiddhi. Either way she is a very popular figure in the Buddhist pantheon and may also be adopted by the Hindus as Shiva's wife in her peaceful mood.
tempos – small Indian three-wheeled transports commonly used in Kathmandu (similar to the Thai *samlor*).
Terai – flat land south of the Himalaya in Nepal.
Thakalis – people of the Kali Gandaki Valley who specialise in running hotels.
thangka – rectangular Tibetan painting on cotton, usually of mandalas or Tantric deities.

third eye – symbolic eye on Buddha figures, used to indicate the Buddha's clairvoyant powers.
tika – red sandalwood paste spot marked on the forehead, particularly for religious occasions.
thukba – thick Tibetan soup.
tole – street or quarter of a town, sometimes used to refer to a square such as Kel Tole in Kathmandu or Tachupal Tole in Bhaktapur.
topi – traditional Nepalese cap.
torana – portico above temple doors which can indicate the god to whom the temple is dedicated.
Tribhuvan – king who ended the Rana period and Nepal's long seclusion in 1951.
trisul – trident weapon symbol of Shiva.
tsampa – barley-flour porridge of the Sherpas.
Tulku – Tibetan Buddhist reincarnation of a great lama.
tulsi – sacred basil plant.
tunal – carved temple strut.

Uma – one of the peaceful incarnations of Shiva's consort Parvati.
Uma Maheshwar – Shiva and Parvati in a pose where Shiva sits cross-legged and Parvati sits on his thigh and leans against him.
Upanishads – ancient Vedic scripts, the last part of the Vedas.
urna – the bump on the forehead of a Buddha or Bodhisattva.
Usha – Vedic goddess of the dawn.

vahana – a god's animal mount or vehicle.
Vairocana – the central Dhyani Buddha and the 'embodiment of perfection'.
Vaisya – caste of merchants and farmers, said to originate from Brahma's thighs.
Vaishnavites – followers of Vishnu.
vajra – the 'thunderbolt' symbol of Buddhist power in Nepal; (*dorje* in Tibetan).

vajra

Vajra Jogini – a Tantric goddess, shakti to a Bhairab.
Vajrapani – literally 'thunderbolt in hand', a manifestation of Avalokitesvara holding a thunderbolt.
Vajrayana – literally 'vehicle of the thunderbolts'; this is a variety of Buddhism which involves magical spells.
Vamana – see Vikrantha.
Varahi – Vishnu's boar incarnation.
Varuna – ancient Vedic god of wisdom and morality.
Vasudhara – wife of Jambhala the god of wealth; she rides a chariot drawn by a pig.
Vasupura – Buddhist symbol for the earth.
Vayupura – Buddhist symbol for the air.
Vedas – ancient spiritual texts, the orthodox Hindu scriptures.
Vedic gods – ancient Hindu gods of the Vedas.
vehicle – the animal which a Hindu god is associated with. Shiva's vehicle is a bull, Ganesh's is a mouse while Vishnu's is the man-bird Garuda.
vihara – Buddhist religious buildings and pilgrim accommodation.
Vikrantha – Vishnu's fifth incarnation when he appeared as a dwarf, then grew so large that he could cross the universe in three strides.
Vishnu – the preserver, one of the three main Hindu gods.

Vishnu Chaturmurti – four-faced Vishnu with faces of a lion, boar, human and demon.

Wheel of Life – held by Mara, the god of death. The wheel's concentric circles show a stage of existence, those who are chained to the cycles of existence, the forces which keep the wheel turning or the desires which keep humankind chained to the cycle.

yab-yum – Tantric erotica.
yak – main beast of burden and form of cattle above 3000 metres.
yakshas – attendant deities.
Yama – Vedic god of death, son of Aditya or Surya; his messenger is the crow.
yeti – the abominable snowman.
yi-dam – protective deities of the Buddhas; they have a fierce form in contrast to the peacefulness of the Buddhas.
yoni – female sexual symbol, equivalent of a lingam.
Yuga – each Mahayuga is divided into four Yugas.

zamindar – absentee landlord and/or moneylender.
zhum – see dzum.
zopkiok – see dzopkyo.

Index

Dear traveller

Prices go up, good places go bad, bad places go bankrupt...and every guidebook is inevitably outdated in places. Fortunately, many travellers write to us about their experiences, telling us when things have changed. If we reprint a book between editions, we try to include as much of this information as possible in a Stop Press section. Most of this information has not been verified by our own writers.

We really enjoy hearing from people out on the road, and apart from guaranteeing that others will benefit from your good and bad experiences, we're prepared to bribe you with the offer of a free book for sending us substantial useful information.

Thank you to everyone who has written and, to those who haven't, I hope you do find this book useful – and that you let us know when it isn't.

Tony Wheeler

There were devastating floods throughout the country in late July 1993. The Terai was the worst affected region with thousands made homeless and many killed.

The Prithvi (or Pokhara) Highway between Kathmandu and Mugling was washed away in three places (now replaced with Bailey bridges), and landslides left a number of one-way sections. Until repairs are completed this will mean a major increase in the number of trucks using the old Tribhuvan Highway (or Rajpath).

The heavy rains and floods throughout the country have made good roads bad, and bad roads indescribable.

Money & Costs
The currency exchange rate is Rs 46.5 to US$1.

Getting There & Away
The border between Nepal and Tibet in the far west has been opened to allow groups to visit Mt Kailash and Lake Mansarovar. The trip involves flying to Simikot, crossing a 5800-metre pass and the Tibet border in a seven-day walk, travelling by road to Mt Kailash, then circumnavigating Mt Kailash. The round trip to/from Kathmandu will take about 21 days, and will only be available to

organised groups. Several companies are planning trips in 1994.

According to one letter we have received, individuals can fly to Tibet from Nepal if they already have a Chinese visa on arrival in Nepal. You simply book a flight from Kathmandu to Lhasa in the office of China South West Airlines. There are no problems with individual travel once you have landed in Lhasa.

There are now flights between Kathmandu and Paro (Bhutan) on Monday and Thursday all year round.

Those travelling to Kathmandu via Bangkok who wish to stay near Bangkok's Don Muang Airport now have a cheaper option than the Airport Hotel. The *Don Muang Mansion Hotel* (fax 566 3514) is just behind the Airport Hotel, but charges only US$44 for a double with air-con and TV. For detailed directions, contact the Thai Hotel Association desk in the airport arrival area.

Kathmandu
The *Thamel House Restaurant* (☎ 410388), past the now defunct Hotel Dreamland shown on the Greater Thamel map, has opened in a beautifully restored Newari house – one of the few left in Thamel. There is a traditional Nepalese menu, as well as

Chinese and Western ones. It's expensive at around Rs 300 per person, but worth it.

The long-running *Utse Restaurant* has moved to the Utse Hotel in Jyatha.

Ultimate Descents (☎ 01-226277; fax 01-411933) has moved to Him Thai Plaza, Thamel, near the Him Thai Restaurant.

Himalayan River Exploration (☎ 01-418491; fax 414075) now has an office in Namche Arcade, Thamel, near the Nepal Grindlays bank.

Himalayan Hilltreks and River Tours (☎ 01-410740; fax 01-471630), PO Box 1066, has moved to a new office in Baluwatar near the Russian Embassy.

The new Kathmandu Bus Terminal (Gongbu Bus Park) was still not in operation in late 1993. Don't hold your breath.

Thanks

Thanks also to those travellers who took the time and trouble to write to us about their experiences in Nepal. Writers (apologies if we've misspelt your name) to whom thanks must go include:

Mark Agnew (UK), Madeleine Allsop (Aus), Fred Ameling (NL), Ronnie Asbell (USA), Aryun Bahadur (Nep), John & Carolyn Barr (UK), Dr Buddha Basnyat (Nep), Omar E Beretta (Arg), O W Biddington (NZ), V Bjorn (DK), Brian Boland (USA), Andrew Bowdler, Jeff Brauer (USA), Pieter Brethouwer (NL), Arian C Brouwer (NL), Alison Bryan, E Butler (C), Ian Buttenshaw, Cas Bylhott (NL), Doug Callaghan (Aus), Patrik Christensson (S), Pierre-Michel Clesse (B), Sue Connor (Aus), Miss R Dalipe (Nep), A Damasceno, Wilson Danny (Aus), Carol Darby (IRL), Tom Davis (USA), James Davis (USA), Harry Dawson (Aus), M de Vries, Luc & Kristel De-Noyette (B), Tashi Delak, Alan Deverell (UK), LLoyd Donaldson (NZ), Ms S A Downs (UK), Graham Dutfield (UK), Gokarna Duwadi (Nep), Ms J Early (UK), Kenneth Eichel (USA), Alan Fischl (USA), Brent Fishlock (C), Nicole Fitton, Adam Friedensohn, Steve Fuller (UK), Sarah Geiger (UK), Mrs S Goddard (UK), Ernst Goslinga (NL), Stephanie Grover (Aus), Esther Gyssel (NL), Lisa Haas (USA), Robyn Hall (Aus), Reijo Harkonen (Fin), Chris Harries (Aus), Leonard Harrison (USA), Sue Hartshorne (Aus), Sarah Haspel (UK), Mitch Haspel (Isr), Charley Haynes (USA), Hans Holsmann (NL), Cath & Chris Howell (UK), Paul Hunter (Aus), Adrian Illingworth (UK), Tim Ingles (Aus), Darren Izzard (Aus), Karen Jackson (UK), Lisa Jackson (UK), Vassilis Kassimatis (G), Judith Kooleshevich (USA), Ruth Kunkel (D), John Lampert (USA), Erik Langen (NL), Sean Lawson (C), John Litchfield (UK), Brad Little (C), Kate Lodge (UK), Steve Lowe (Aus), Eugene Margulis (CH), Joyce McCallum (UK), Eric McClusky (USA), Nell McCombs (USA), N K McKinnon (Aus), Marie Mills (NZ), John Monaghan (UK), David Morey (Aus), Susanna Morey (UK), David Murdoch, Michael Murphy (UK), Eva Neerup (DK), Rob Nelson (Aus), RH Newton (Aus), Kelly O'Neill (C), David Olive (Aus), Andrew Olson, Peter Owen (UK), Carolyn Owens (UK), Viji Padmanabhan (USA), Neena Pallipamu (USA), Rita Parker (USA), Wendy Paterson (Aus), Tim Penney (NZ), Maureen Peters, Edward Peters (Aus), Cies Pierrot (NL), Paul Joseph Platinelli (USA), K A Prentice, Soren Prins (DK), Derek Purcell (UK), Miriam B Rosenthal (USA), Jens Roth (D), Thea Rottier (NL), Nigel Sawyer (UK), Karin Schon (CH), Irene Sclavounos (G), Matoula Serefa (G), Surendra Shahi, David Sheard (Aus), A Sheppard (UK), Shlomo Shmueli (Isr), Huta Raj Shrestha (Nep), Bruce Smith (Aus), F J Smouter (NL), Huub Sporck (NL), Katy Starr (UK), P G Stokes (UK), Jack Switzer (C), Suzanne Sziranyi (UK), B K Tamot (Nep), Philippe Terrenoire (F), Jocelyne Thapa Chhetri (Nep), Blake Thompson (C), Dave Thompson (UK), Roger & Jacki Tilbrook (UK), David Trimble (UK), Keith Tully (Aus), Pete Turner (USA), Douglas & Nancy Umbach (C), Steve van den Neucker (B), George Varveris (G), Bradley Wenman (Aus), Jesper Wichmann (DK), Tim Wild (UK), Graham Williams, Glen & Denise Wills (C), Chantal Wood (F), Eric Young (UK), and Werner Zwick (D).

Arg – Argentina, Aus – Australia, B – Belgium, C – Canada, CH – Switzerland, D – Germany, DK – Denmark, F – France, Fin – Finland, G – Greece, Irl – Ireland, Isr – Israel, Nep – Nepal, NL – Netherlands, NZ – New Zealand, S – Sweden, UK – United Kingdom, USA – United States of America.

Guides to the Indian Subcontinent

Bangladesh – a travel survival kit
This practical guide – the only English-language guide to Bangladesh – encourages travellers to take another look at this often-neglected but beautiful land.

India – a travel survival kit
Widely regarded as *the* guide to India, this award-winning book has all the information to help you make the most of the unforgettable experience that is India.

Karakoram Highway the high road to China – a travel survival kit
Travel in the footsteps of Alexander the Great and Marco Polo on the Karakoram Highway, following the ancient and fabled Silk Road. This comprehensive guide also covers villages and treks away from the highway.

Kashmir, Ladakh & Zanskar – a travel survival kit
Detailed information on three contrasting Himalayan regions in the Indian state of Jammu & Kashmir – the narrow valley of Zanskar, the isolated 'little Tibet' of Ladakh, and the stunningly beautiful Vale of Kashmir.

Pakistan – a travel survival kit
Discover 'the unknown land of the Indus' with this informative guidebook – from bustling Karachi to ancient cities and tranquil mountain valleys.

Sri Lanka – a travel survival kit
Some parts of Sri Lanka are off limits to visitors, but this guidebook uses the restriction as an incentive to explore other areas more closely – making the most of friendly people, good food and pleasant places to stay – all at reasonable cost.

Tibet – a travel survival kit
The fabled mountain-land of Tibet was one of the last areas of the world to become accessible to travellers. This guide has full details on this remote and fascinating region, including the border crossing to Nepal.

Trekking in the Indian Himalaya
All the advice you'll need for planning and equipping a trek, including detailed route descriptions for some of the world's most exciting treks.

Trekking in the Nepal Himalaya
Complete trekking information for Nepal, including day-by-day route descriptions and detailed maps – a wealth of advice for both independent and group trekkers.

Also available:
Hindi/Urdu phrasebook, *Nepal* phrasebook and *Sri Lanka* phrasebook.

Lonely Planet Guidebooks

Lonely Planet guidebooks cover every accessible part of Asia as well as Australia, the Pacific, South America, Africa, the Middle East, Europe and parts of North America. There are six series: *travel survival kits*, covering a country for a range of budgets; *shoestring guides* with compact information for low-budget travel in a major region; *walking guides*; city guides, travel atlases and *phrasebooks*.

Australia & the Pacific
Australia
Australian phrasebook
Bushwalking in Australia
Islands of Australia's Great Barrier Reef
Outback Australia
Fiji
Fijian phrasebook
Melbourne city guide
Micronesia
New Caledonia
New South Wales & the ACT
New Zealand
Tramping in New Zealand
Papua New Guinea
Bushwalking in Papua New Guinea
Papua New Guinea phrasebook
Queensland
Rarotonga & the Cook Islands
Samoa
Solomon Islands
Sydney city guide
Tahiti & French Polynesia
Tonga
Vanuatu
Victoria
Western Australia

North-East Asia
Beijing city guide
China
Cantonese phrasebook
Mandarin Chinese phrasebook
Hong Kong, Macau & Canton
Japan
Japanese phrasebook
Korea
Korean phrasebook
Mongolia
Mongolian phrasebook
North-East Asia on a shoestring
Seoul city guide
Taiwan
Tibet
Tibet phrasebook
Tokyo city guide

South-East Asia
Bali & Lombok
Bangkok city guide
Cambodia
Indonesia
Indonesian phrasebook
Ho Chi Minh City city guide
Jakarta city guide
Java
Laos
Lao phrasebook
Malaysia, Singapore & Brunei
Myanmar (Burma)
Burmese phrasebook
Philippines
Pilipino phrasebook
Singapore city guide
South-East Asia on a shoestring
Thailand
Thailand travel atlas
Thai phrasebook
Thai Hill Tribes phrasebook
Vietnam
Vietnam travel atlas
Vietnamese phrasebook

Middle East
Arab Gulf States
Egypt & the Sudan
Arabic (Egyptian) phrasebook
Iran
Israel
Jordan & Syria
Middle East
Turkey
Turkish phrasebook
Trekking in Turkey
Yemen

Africa
Africa on a shoestring
Central Africa
East Africa
Trekking in East Africa
Kenya
Swahili phrasebook
Morocco
Arabic (Moroccan) phrasebook
North Africa
South Africa, Lesotho & Swaziland
West Africa
Zimbabwe, Botswana & Namibia
Zimbabwe, Botswana & Namibia travel atlas

Mail Order

Lonely Planet guidebooks are distributed worldwide. They are also available by mail order from Lonely Planet, so if you have difficulty finding a title please write to us. US and Canadian residents should write to Embarcadero West, 155 Filbert St, Suite 251, Oakland CA 94607, USA ; European residents should write to 10 Barley Mow Passage, Chiswick, London W4 4PH; and residents of other countries to PO Box 617, Hawthorn, Victoria 3122, Australia.

Indian Subcontinent
Bangladesh
India
India travel atlas
Hindi/Urdu phrasebook
Trekking in the Indian Himalaya
Karakoram Highway
Kashmir, Ladakh & Zanskar
Nepal
Trekking in the Nepal Himalaya
Nepali phrasebook
Pakistan
Sri Lanka
Sri Lanka phrasebook

Central America & the Caribbean
Baja California
Central America on a shoestring
Costa Rica
Eastern Caribbean
Guatemala, Belize & Yucatán: La Ruta Maya
Mexico

North America
Alaska
Backpacking in Alaska
Canada
Hawaii
Honolulu city guide
Pacific Northwest USA
Rocky Mountain States
Southwest USA
USA phrasebook

Europe
Baltic States & Kaliningrad
Baltics States phrasebook
Britain
Central Europe on a shoestring
Central Europe phrasebook
Czech & Slovak Republics
Dublin city guide
Eastern Europe on a shoestring
Eastern Europe phrasebook
Finland
France
Greece
Greek phrasebook
Hungary
Iceland, Greenland & the Faroe Islands
Ireland
Italy
Mediterranean Europe on a shoestring
Mediterranean Europe phrasebook
Poland
Prague city guide
Russia, Ukraine & Belarus
Russian phrasebook
Scandinavian & Baltic Europe on a shoestring
Scandinavian Europe phrasebook
Slovenia
Switzerland
Trekking in Greece
Trekking in Spain
Vienna city guide
Western Europe on a shoestring
Western Europe phrasebook

South America
Argentina, Uruguay & Paraguay
Bolivia
Brazil
Brazilian phrasebook
Chile & Easter Island
Colombia
Ecuador & the Galápagos Islands
Latin American Spanish phrasebook
Peru
Quechua phrasebook
Rio de Janeiro city guide
South America on a shoestring
Trekking in the Patagonian Andes
Venezuela

Indian Ocean
Madagascar & Comoros
Maldives & Islands of the East Indian Ocean
Mauritius, Réunion & Seychelles

The Lonely Planet Story

Lonely Planet published its first book in 1973 in response to the numerous 'How did you do it?' questions Maureen and Tony Wheeler were asked after driving, bussing, hitching, sailing and railing their way from England to Australia.

Written at a kitchen table and hand collated, trimmed and stapled, *Across Asia on the Cheap* became an instant local bestseller, inspiring thoughts of another book.

Eighteen months in South-East Asia resulted in their second guide, *South-East Asia on a shoestring*, which they put together in a backstreet Chinese hotel in Singapore in 1975. The 'yellow bible' as it quickly became known to backpackers around the world, soon became *the* guide to the region. It has sold well over half a million copies and is now in its 8th edition, still retaining its familiar yellow cover.

Today there are over 140 Lonely Planet titles in print – books that have that same adventurous approach to travel as those early guides; books that 'assume you know how to get your luggage off the carousel' as one reviewer put it.

Although Lonely Planet initially specialised in guides to Asia, they now cover most regions of the world, including the Pacific, South America, Africa, the Middle East and Europe. The list of *walking guides* and *phrasebooks* (for 'unusual' languages such as Quechua, Swahili, Nepali and Egyptian Arabic) is also growing rapidly.

The emphasis continues to be on travel for independent travellers. Tony and Maureen still travel for several months of each year and play an active part in the writing, updating and quality control of Lonely Planet's guides.

They have been joined by over 50 authors, 110 staff – mainly editors, cartographers & designers – at our office in Melbourne, Australia, at our US office in Oakland, California and at our European office in Paris; another five at our office in London handle sales for Britain, Europe and Africa. Travellers themselves also make a valuable contribution to the guides through the feedback we receive in thousands of letters each year.

The people at Lonely Planet strongly believe that travellers can make a positive contribution to the countries they visit, both through their appreciation of the countries' culture, wildlife and natural features, and through the money they spend. In addition, the company makes a direct contribution to the countries and regions it covers. Since 1986 a percentage of the income from each book has been donated to ventures such as famine relief in Africa; aid projects in India; agricultural projects in Central America; Greenpeace's efforts to halt French nuclear testing in the Pacific; and Amnesty International.

Lonely Planet's basic travel philosophy is summed up in Tony Wheeler's comment, 'Don't worry about whether your trip will work out. Just go!'

Mountain Biking

Nepal's tremendously diverse terrain and its many tracks and trails create an ideal venue for mountain biking. This section was written by John Prosser, a keen cyclist who has explored many Nepalese biking routes. In 1992 he started Equator Mountain Bikes, which operates cycling tours around Nepal.

People everywhere are discovering that the versatile mountain bike is perfect for commuting to work as well as for weekend rides and cycle touring. With its strong wheels, knobbly tyres, wide selection of gears, and overall strength, the mountain bike is an ideal machine for exploring Nepal. These attributes make it possible to escape paved roads, and to ride tracks and trails to remote, rarely visited areas of the country. Most importantly, they allow independent travel – you can stop whenever you like – and they liberate you from crowded buses.

Nepal offers challenging mountain roads that climb thousands of metres to reach spectacular viewpoints and reward with exhilarating descents. The Terai has flat, smooth roads, and mountain biking is an excellent way of getting to the Royal Chitwan National Park. For the adventurous there are still large areas of the country, particularly in the west and the Terai, still to be explored by mountain bike.

The Kathmandu Valley has a vast network of tracks, trails and back roads and some of which are the most rugged in the country. Mountain biking is the perfect means of transport to visit the valley's wealth of temples, stupas and mediaeval towns. Where a mountain bike really comes into its own, however, is when you get off the beaten track and discover idyllic Newari villages that have preserved their traditional, rural lifestyle. To ride a network of trails alongside paddy fields to areas rarely visited by tourists allows you to experience the tranquillity of rural Nepal.

Many trails are narrow walkways and are not shown on maps, so you need a good sense of direction when venturing out without a guide. It is important to know the name of the next village you wish to reach so locals can point you in the right direction. The most detailed Kathmandu Valley map is commonly referred to as the 'German map' (also Schneider and Nelles Verlag), and is widely available in Kathmandu.

TRAIL CONDITIONS

Traffic travels on the left-hand side with smaller vehicles giving way to larger ones. Bikes are at the bottom of the list, and definitely come off second best if they mess with Tata trucks! Nepalese roads carry a vast array of vehicles: autorickshaws, tempos, buses, motorbikes, cars, trucks, tractors...Throw in a few holy cows, wheelbarrows, dogs, people, chickens, and rickshaws all moving at different speeds under a barrage of blowing horns, and you have a typical Nepalese street scene!

The centre of Kathmandu, unfortunately, is becoming a very unpleasant place to ride due to pollution and heavy traffic – if you are sensitive to traffic fumes, consider bringing some sort of mask.

Extreme care should be taken near villages as young children play on the trails and roads (I've come across toddlers sitting right in the middle of a main highway!) All animals should be approached with caution – chickens and buffaloes are particularly unpredictable.

A few intrepid mountain bikers have taken bikes into trekking areas hoping to find great riding. What they discovered is that these areas are not suitable for mountain biking. The tracks and trails through Nepal's hills and mountains usually have considerable sections of stone steps that are impossible to ride. In addition, there are always trekkers, porters and local people clogging up the trails. Bikers just add one more problem to these heavy-traffic areas.

Riders who have taken bikes to such places as the Everest Base Camp or around the Annapurnas have found that they carry their bikes for between 70% and 90% of the time! If you do insist on carrying something on your trek, try a bath tub. (I don't think anyone has done so yet, and the tub is potentially useful.)

Local buses are useful if you wish to avoid some of the routes that carry heavy traffic. You can place your bike on the roof for an additional charge, which varies between Rs 20 and Rs 60, depending on the length of the journey and the bus company.

The bus driver will normally provide rope and the luggage boy will assist you. It is important to make sure the bike is held securely to cope with the rough roads and that it is lying as flat as possible to prevent it catching low wires or tree branches. Unless you travel with foam padding it is hard to avoid the frame receiving a few scratches.

It is not possible to carry bikes on internal flights.

EQUIPMENT

If you plan to do more than use roads it is a good idea to bring your own bike. At present the only bikes you can hire in Nepal are of low quality and are not suitable for the rigours of trail riding. In addition, rental shops do not supply pannier bags, luggage racks, or tools for on-road repairs. See the Kathmandu and Pokhara Getting Around sections for information on bike hire.

Your bike can be carried as part of your baggage allowance on international flights. You are required to deflate the tyres and turn the handle bars parallel with the frame. Nepalese customs will sign the bike into your passport to make sure you take it with you when you leave the country.

If you bring your bike it is essential to bring tools and spare parts, as these are not available in Nepal. Unfortunately, carrying a complete tool kit and spares for everything that might fail is impractical, so it is quite likely you will have to improvise. Specialised tools, such as bottom-bracket wrenches, will not be available, but it might be possible to use a hammer and screw driver, or even to get tools made locally. If you put a hole in your tyre beyond repair, a local tyre will enable you to complete the journey.

Fortunately, what local bike repair shops lack in spare parts and knowledge of the latest fads, they make up in their ability to improvise. Their standard of workmanship is usually high.

ORGANISED BIKE TOURS

There are a small number of companies offering guided trips on mountain bikes. They provide high-quality bikes, local and Western guides, pannier bags and helmets. There is normally a trip minimum of four clients per trip. Vehicle support is available for longer tours at extra cost.

Equator Mountain Bikes (☎ 01-416717; fax 419858) operates through West Himalayan Outdoor, which has an office in Thamel next to the Kathmandu Guest House. West Himalayan also has a London office (☎ 081-749 2265; fax 746 2415) at 42 Loftus Rd, Shepherd's Bush, London W12 7EN. Equator specialises in custom-designed mountain-bike expeditions throughout the Himalaya. There are also day trips ($25), two-day trips ($80), as well as longer trips to the Tibetan border and Chitwan National Park which cost $40 per day; prices include food and accommodation.

Himalayan Mountain Bikes or HMB (☎ 01-417036; fax 416870) operates through Sagarmatha Trekking, PO Box 2236, Kathmandu. HMB offers a range of tours from day trips ($30), to overnight trips ($80) to longer, fully supported tours of Nepal at $45 a day.

Nepal By Bicycle, which operates through Surendra's Trekking (☎ 01-228033; fax 524750), PO Box 2078 Jyatha, Thamel, Kathmandu, was the first company to introduce cycling tours to Nepal in 1983. The company is more oriented towards standard cycle tours on paved roads but it also uses mountain bikes. All-inclusive prices are $25 for a day trip, $90 for an overnight trip, and $350 for tours to the Tibetan border.

Touring Routes

THE SCAR ROAD

The Scar Rd is considered to be the Kathmandu Valley's classic off-road adventure. It's a 70-km round trip.

Leaving Kathmandu, head towards Balaju only two km north of Thamel, and onto the Trisuli road. At this point you start to climb out of the valley towards Kakani, 23 km away at an altitude of 2073 metres. The road twists and turns at an even gradient past the Nagarjun forest reserve, which provides the road with a leaf canopy.

Once you're through the initial pass and out of the valley, the road continues in a north-westerly direction and offers a view of terraced fields on your left. On reaching the summit of the ridge turn right instead of continuing down to Trisuli Bazaar. From this

point magnificent views of Ganesh Himal give the required inspiration to complete the remaining four km of steep, narrow blacktop to the Tara Gaon Kakani Hotel at the crown, for a well-deserved rest.

It is possible to spend the night at the hotel to take advantage of sunrise and sunset. See the Kakani section of the Around the Kathmandu Valley chapter for details.

After admiring the view from the hotel's garden terrace, descend for just 30 metres and take the first left onto a jeep track. This track takes you in an easterly direction towards Shivapuri. The track ends abruptly, after a few km, at a metal gate. After passing through the gate, you are faced with a 10-minute walk up to an army checkpost with the Scar Rd clearly visible in front of you. Once you pass through the checkpost, you are at the day's high point – approximately 2200 metres.

Taking the right-hand side track you start to descend dramatically along an extremely steep, rutted single trail. The trail is literally cut into the side of the hill, with sharp drops on the right which challenge a rider's skill and nerve. As you hurtle along, take time to admire the sprawling Kathmandu Valley below.

The trail widens, and after one long climb before the saddle it is relatively flat as it travels through the protected Shivapuri watershed area. This beautiful mountain-biking section lasts for nearly 25 km before the trail descends into the valley down a seven-km spiral. The track joins a paved road, to the relief of jarred wrists and buttocks, at Budhanilkantha, where you can buy refreshments. The road descends gently for the remaining eight km back to Kathmandu.

DHULIKHEL

This two or three-day circular tour takes you through a classic cross section of valley sights. The first day to Dhulikhel is 32 km; the second day is 58 km. Dhulikhel is an interesting hilltop town at 1500 metres.

From Thamel, head out of town in the direction of Pashupatinath and once onto the Ring Rd proceed towards Tribhuvan Airport.

Shortly after the descent past the airport, branch left and climb up to join the beginning of the Arniko Highway (which runs through to the Tibetan border).

The Arniko Highway was built by the Chinese and carries an enormous amount of traffic, including Chinese-donated electric trolley buses. It is a far nicer ride along the old road via the village of Thimi, which is famous for its handcrafts. Take the first left off the main highway and onto the narrow road that heads back towards the airport before continuing on to complete the 16 km to the mediaeval town of Bhaktapur.

Mountain bikes are a great way to explore Bhaktapur's narrow streets. After time in this magical city, continue east. Facing Bhaktapur's 30-metre-high Nyatapola Temple, take the exit from the square on your right-hand side. This narrow street twists and turns on its way out of the city. After leaving the brick-paved streets, join a tarmac road and continue straight on.

The tarmac road ends and continues in the form of a compacted track towards the rural village of Nala. This route is an excellent alternative to the Arniko Highway and takes you through a beautiful corner of the valley. The track climbs gradually, and progressively steepens near the top. Three km of gentle downhill gradients bring you to Nala with its rural lifestyle and pretty temples.

Turn right upon joining the tarmac road and continue for a couple of km to Banepa. Turn left and continue along the paved road for a further five km to Dhulikhel, which is visible on your right-hand side as you approach, thus completing the first day. See the Dhulikhel section in the Around the Kathmandu Valley chapter for more information on accommodation, food, and things to see.

Namobuddha is a popular day trek starting and finishing in Dhulikhel and offers superb trail riding with spectacular views of the Himalaya. From Dhulikhel's main square, which has a small pond set, head along a paved road in the direction of a Kali temple set on a hillside above the town. The paved road ends and starts to climb the hill in the

form of a rough jeep track. The track twists its way up a testing three km to reach the temple, which is a spectacular viewpoint. From the temple you can see the track snake its way across the terraced landscape.

Continue along the track, which provides exhilarating downhill runs before it starts a five-km climb towards Namobuddha. After completing the climb, descend for a short while until you reach a T-junction. Turn right and Namobuddha will appear shortly after on the left, so completing a 12-km journey from Dhulikhel. Refreshments are available in the small shops near the stupa, which provides an interesting place to rest before continuing to Panauti.

Leaving Namobuddha you continue down the track, which takes you through a series of turns – a great mountain-bike descent. The track finally drops to the bottom of the valley and travels in undulating fashion to complete a 14-km ride to the historic city of Panauti. This ancient Newari town has some of the oldest temples in Nepal – cross the footbridge if you want to explore further. See the Around the Kathmandu Valley chapter for information about Panauti.

Leaving Panauti you join a paved road that runs flat along the valley to Banepa. From this point you can either return to Kathmandu which is 26 km via the Arniko Highway or complete a 33-km circuit by returning to Dhulikhel.

KODARI & TIBETAN BORDER

It is possible to continue 82 km along the Arniko Highway from Dhulikhel to the Friendship Bridge at Kodari (1500 metres) that marks the Tibetan border. This is a four-day return trip from Dhulikhel.

From Dhulikhel you immediately begin a descent into the Panchkhal Valley, with majestic views of the Himalaya adding to a thrilling ride – you descend almost 900 metres. A couple of short climbs interrupt the descent as you cycle to Dolalghat, a popular starting point for Sun Kosi River rafting trips.

After 20 km you cross the bridge over the Indrawati River and climb out of the